FOUNDATION ACCOUNTING

A. H. Millichamp
M.Soc.Sc., F.C.A., A.T.I.I.

Alan Millichamp is a former senior lecturer in accounting at The Polytechnic, Wolverhampton

SECOND EDITION

DP Publications Limited
Aldine Place, 142/144 Uxbridge Road,
Shepherds Bush Green,
London W12 8AA
1989

ACKNOWLEDGEMENTS

The Author wishes to express his thanks to the following for permission to reproduce past examination questions:

Chartered Association of Certified Accountants (ACCA)

Chartered Institute of Management Accountants (CIMA)

Association of Accounting Technicians (AAT)

Royal Society of Arts (RSA)

London Chamber of Commerce and Industry (LCCI)

Note that all answers to the questions given in this book were devised by the author and are his sole responsibility.

A CIP catalogue record for this book is available from the British Library.

First Edition   1984
Second Edition 1989

ISBN 1 870941 38 1

Copyright A.H. Millichamp © 1989.

Printed by The Guernsey Press Company Ltd
Braye Road, Vale,
Guernsey, Channel Islands

PREFACE

Aims of the manual

1. This manual provides a thorough understanding of the **theory** and **practice** of accounting at foundation level. it aims to present all the information necessary for students to approach with confidence the foundation examinations of the professional and other examining bodies.

2. The manual is intended for use on the foundation financial syllabuses of:

    Chartered Association of Certified Accountants (Level 1)
    Association of Accounting Technicians (Preliminary and Intermediate)
    Institute of Chartered Secretaries and Administrators (pre-professional programme)
    Chartered Institute of Management Accountants (Stage 1 and Stage 1 Exemption)
    London Chamber of Commerce
    Royal Society of Arts
    BTEC National and Higher national Diplomas in Business Studies
    Foundation Courses in Accountancy
    Degree courses in Accounting and Business Studies
    GCSE
    GCE 'A' Level

3. **Note to second edition**

    In preparing the **second edition**, account has been taken of constructive criticism from lecturers and students. In particular this edition contains:

    *   graded exercises after each chapter. These are designed for class use but can equally be used for private study. Brief answers are provided in an appendix to some of these. Answers to the remainder are in the Lecturer's supplement.

    *   carefully selected examination questions after most chapters. These give students the experience of actual examination questions. Like the exercises they can be used in class, for private study and for homework.

    *   sufficient material on costing to enable the underpinnings of stock and work in progress valuation to be fully understood.

    *   a chapter on computers in accounting.

Approach

4. Accounting deals with the real world of business. The manual reflects this by relating each topic to real situations in a lively and occasionally humorous way.

5. The basic structure of each of the topics dealt with is:

    (a) The general background is given to put the topic in context.

    (b) The financial accounting methods and procedures are explained in detail with examples.

    (c) A theoretical justification and criticism is given.

    (d) Exceptions, alternatives and practical problems are discussed.

6. The accounting conventions are introduced as they become relevant (for example the realisation convention is first discussed in the chapter on the trading account) and the whole subject of the conventions is summarised in Chapter 56.

7. There are six chapters on interpretation and the author has attempted to inculcate the idea of Financial Statements giving useful if limited information with ratio analysis being an aid to interpretation but not an infallible guide.

8. At the end of each chapter are to be found:

   (a) A summary of the points made in the chapter.

   (b) Points to note. These cover difficulties, exceptions and points that need special emphasis.

   (c) Comprehensive self testing questions. These are useful in ensuring that the student has fully grasped the points made and are also essential in revision.

   (d) Graded exercises.

Appendices

9. There are three appendices:

   1. Answers to exercises

   2. A set of five case studies. These are designed to enable students to integrate the ideas from several chapters and to give scope for imagination. They could also be used as assignments. Outline answers to the cases are included in a supplement which is available to lecturers.

   3. A Glossary of accounting terms.

10. **Lecturers supplement.** Lecturers supplement is available free of charge to those lecturers using the book as a main course text. Please request a copy from the publishers on departmental headed notepaper.

Suggestions and criticisms

11. In the preparation of this manual, I have drawn on my long experience of preparing students for examinations and of marking their examination scripts. I have received many helpful suggestions for the second edition from colleagues and students. I would welcome many more.

CONTENTS

Some Accounting Complexities

Putting it all together

Final Accounts

Accounting Systems and EDP

Manufacturing and Accounting

Other Types of Enterprise

Partnerships

Companies

Interpretation of Accounts

Accounting Theory

Accounting and Planning

More Advanced Matters

Introduction to Accounting

The first four chapters of this manual give a general introduction to accounting and to the context in which it is carried on. The first chapter defines and explains what accounting is. The second gives a general understanding of the business environment in which accounting operates. Within this environment, Chapter 3 explains how accounting fits in with the need for information in business generally and Chapter 4 explains how accounting fits in with kindred activities such as tax and auditing.

In this way before accounting is examined in detail you will have a broad picture of how the subject fits into the business world as a whole.

1. What is Accounting?

INTRODUCTION
1. This chapter begins with two definitions of accounting. The definitions are then considered in detail and three sub-divisions of accounting are introduced with examples.

DEFINITIONS
2. Here are two definitions of accounting:

(a) Accounting is the art of recording, classifying and summarising in a significant manner and in terms of money, transactions and events which are, in part at least, of a financial character, and interpreting the results thereof.

(b) Accounting is the process of identifying, measuring, and communicating economic information to permit informed judgements and decisions by the users of the information.

3. These definitions suggest that accounting has the following stages:

(a) Transactions of a business that have, at least in part, a financial character are identified and recorded. Transactions mean business activities such as sales of goods, purchases of goods, payment and receipt of money, the incurring of an expense etc.

(b) The recording is done in a way which identifies the different classes and types of transaction. For example sales of goods are recorded separately from purchases of goods.

(c) The resulting records are summarised in such a way that the owners or others who have an interest in the business can see the overall effect of all the transactions. The statements produced by the summarising process will show the *profit* (or loss) made by the business over a period of time and the total *capital* employed in the business.

(d) The statements showing profit and capital are used by management and others to make business decisions.

SUB-DIVISIONS OF ACCOUNTING
4. Accounting is *one* subject although a very complex one. However it is customary to divide it up into three separate sub-divisions which continuously interconnect:

(a) Bookkeeping.
(b) Profit or loss and capital measurement and reporting.
(c) Management Accounting.

I will introduce each in turn.

BOOKKEEPING
5. Bookkeeping is the making of records of business transactions. The need to record business transactions is as old as civilisation itself and the great majority of writings excavated from the Middle East are business records. One 4,000-year-old writing listing expenditure on sheep and cattle is notable as containing an error of calculation.

6. Modern bookkeeping was developed in Italy in the period 1300–1500 AD. Merchants of the time would join together to organise expeditions to the east to trade Italian products for the spices and silks of the east. Careful recording of all the goods bought and sold and the expenses incurred had to be made. A merchant would make the recording on any scrap of paper, but would then run the risk of losing it! He would do better to record all transactions in a formal, logical way. Until recently the recording of transactions or bookkeeping as it is called was done by hand in leather bound volumes. This is still done today to some extent but modern bookkeepers are making increasing use of computers.

PROFIT OR LOSS AND CAPITAL
MEASUREMENT AND REPORTING

7. Consider two situations:

(a) John buys a house with ten acres of ground on 1 April 19-2. In the year to 31st March 19-3 he buys 30 goats and grazes them on the land. The goats breed and ten kids are born. The goats produce milk, some of which he sells, and some of which he turns into cheese and then sells the cheese.

Six goats and four kids are sold. Two goats are killed for meat and eaten by John and his family.

Various expenses are incurred including some (*e.g.* goat food and vet's fees) which relate solely to goat-keeping, and some (*e.g.* local rates) which relate to the house and the pasture land.

After 31st March 19-3 John wonders whether it was all worth while financially. The Tax Inspector sees that John has a business and thinks John should pay tax on the profit arising from it.

The way the profit is measured has to be done in a way which is acceptable to both John and the Tax Inspector.

Accounting is about *measuring* the *profit* or *loss* made by a *business* over a period of time. This is not a simple matter as you will have gathered from the example. When you have studied all of this book, you should know how accountants might measure the profit or loss made by John's business.

(b) Enoch, a poor but energetic music teacher, dreams of opening a music shop in the centre of his home town. £20,000 is needed to start the venture off and although he has no money of his own, he is able to persuade three of his friends to buy shares in the business. After the shop has been open for one year, his backers want to know what has happened to the money (= capital) they have invested in the business. They expect Enoch to tell them in the form of a report.

8. Bookkeeping is about making a record in a formal manner, of each business transaction. It is necessary for day-to-day business control as a businessman will need to be continuously aware of, for example, who owes him money and how much; or who he owes money to and how much. These records also form the raw data from which the *summary* statements of profit and loss and capital can be extracted. These reports can then be used by owners and investors (backers) alike to judge how the business has progressed.

MANAGEMENT ACCOUNTING

9. The definition of management accounting is the application of professional knowledge and skill in the preparation and presentation of accounting information in such a way as to assist management in the formation of policies in the planning and control of the undertaking.

Thus management accounting (and its subsidiary subject - costing) is concerned with information which is used by *management* in planning and controlling the business and in making decisions. Management accounting is covered in a companion volume.

However, financial accounting is also used in decision making and some costing ideas are used in financial accounting. Consequently the basic elements of costing are included in this manual.

SUMMARY

10. (a) Accounting is the art of recording and classifying business transactions, summarising the records into statements showing profit or loss and capital and reporting these summary facts to interested parties so that they can make informed business decisions.

(b) Three sub-divisions of accounting are:

Bookkeeping.
The measurement and reporting of profit or loss and of capital.
Management Accounting.

POINTS TO NOTE

11. (a) Bookkeeping serves two purposes:

     (i) A record of business transactions is useful in itself - most people keep a note of the amount in their bank accounts by notes in the cheque book.

     (ii) It forms the information from which the formal accounting statements of profit or loss and capital can be extracted.

  (b) The "books" and the formal accounting summary statements are themselves useful to the management. However, management have information needs which are not satisfied from the traditional bookkeeping records and management accounting has developed to meet these needs.

  (c) Accounting is always in terms of money. This does not mean that accountants think of nothing else but money. It means that money forms a common standard with which business activity can be measured.

  (d) Accounting is concerned to record and summarise transactions and events which have already occurred. It is largely a historical process. However accountants are also interested in the future and the accounting record of recent past events is very useful in considering future activities.

  (e) Accounting is an *art* rather than a science. This manual will instruct you in numerous formal rules but the business world is so diverse and so complex that formal rules often have to be bent or modified to fit special situations and to make accounting information useful and meaningful.

  (f) Two small points:

     (i) Accounting and Accountancy are two separate words and students wonder what are the differences in meaning. They mean the same thing. Modern accountants tend to prefer the word Accounting.

     (ii) Bookkeeping has various spellings - Book keeping, bookkeeping, book-keeping. It does not matter which you use.

SELF TESTING QUESTIONS

1. *Give two definitions of accounting (paragraph 2).*
2. *Give three sub-divisions of accounting (4).*
3. *How do bookkeeping and profit reporting relate? (8 and 11a).*
4. *When was modern bookkeeping developed? (6).*
5. *Why is it desirable to measure the profit made by a business? (7).*
6. *In what way does accounting use money? (11c).*
7. *In what way is accounting a historiographical process? (11d).*
8. *In what way is accounting an art? (11e).*

Exercises (Answers begin on page 445)

1. *Penny is in business as a builder. She erects garages and other small extensions to the houses of customers. She also effects domestic building repairs. She has a small yard at the back of her house to store materials and her van and pick up truck. She employs three people and also uses sub-contractors.*

Required:
(a) In what way will accounting as an art affect Penny and her business?
(b) Will accounting affect Penny in her private life?

2. *Evelyn is in business as a steel stockholder. The business accountant does many things including:*

(a) Recording all cheques drawn.
(b) Summarising the sales made so that Evelyn can know the monthly and annual volume of business done.
(c) Monitoring continuously the prices for steel charged by suppliers and by Evelyn's competitors so that sales price adjustments can be made as necessary.
(d) Recording continuously the tonnage in stock of each type of steel.
(e) Calculating, paying and recording the wages due to the employees.
(f) Sending quarterly profit statements to Evelyn's banker who has lent the business money.

Which of these items are "accounting" and to which branch of accounting, if any, does each belong?

Exercises without answers
3. Consider Bookkeeping, Profit measurement and Management Accounting from the point of view of:

(a) Money.
(b) History.
(c) Art/Science.

4. Keep a record of your receipts and payments in cash and of your transactions with the bank for a period of one week. Consider how the record relates to the three main branches of accounting.

5. Obtain the annual accounts of some social, sporting or charitable organisation with which you are connected. See how much of the information given in them is understandable to you.

2. The Business Environment

INTRODUCTION

1.   It is not possible to understand accounting without an understanding of the business environment in which it is carried on. This chapter introduces you to four aspects of the business world:

    (a)   Types of business activity.
    (b)   Modes of ownership.
    (c)   Trading on credit.
    (d)   Documents.

TYPES OF BUSINESS ACTIVITY

2.   Different types of businesses and organisations have different accounting requirements. It is always necessary to bear in mind the *type* of business when preparing financial statements.

3.   For accounting purposes we can divide businesses into the following different types:

    (a)   **Retailing.** This is the most familiar. The retailer is a *trader*, that is, he buys goods at one price and sells the goods unchanged at a higher price.

    (b)   **Wholesaling.** The wholesaler is also a trader. He buys goods from others (*e.g.* manufacturers and importers) and sells the goods to retailers. The goods are essentially unchanged but an important role of the wholesaler is the breaking of bulk.

Wholesaling and retailing involve the activities of marketing of products, the breaking of bulk and the holding of stock.

    (c)   **Manufacturing.** The manufacturer makes *things* (products) from materials and components and sells them to the public, retailers, wholesalers, exporters, etc.

    (d)   **Service industries.** Service enterprises supply not a product but a service to their customers. Such enterprises include professional people (*e.g.* accountants, doctors), transport undertakings (*e.g.* bus companies, hauliers), banks, insurance companies, teaching institutions, etc.

    (e)   **Non-profit making organisations.** Not all undertakings exist to make profits. Some exist to supply services with no intention of making a profit, although income is generally required to match expenditure. Examples of non-profit making organisations include clubs, societies and professional bodies.

MODES OF OWNERSHIP

4.   Ownership of business enterprises can be in any of the following modes:

    (a)   Sole trader.
    (b)   Partnership.
    (c)   Limited Company.
    (d)   Unincorporated Associations.
    (e)   Public Ownership.

Again, the accounting requirements of a business will vary with the mode of ownership and it is important to understand how the Financial State-ments of businesses are designed to reflect the differing modes of ownership.

5.   We will look briefly at each in turn.

    (a)   **Sole trader.** This is the simplest form of ownership. It means that the business has just one *proprietor* who both owns and manages the business personally. The business and its owner are one and the same.

    (b)   **Partnership.** The business is *owned* and *managed* by two or more people who are called partners. In general the law restricts the number of partners to twenty.

    (c)   **Limited Company.** The business is owned by shareholders. The number of shareholders can be as few as two (for example, a man and his wife) or as many as required. Large companies can have over 100,000 shareholders. With a company its owners (shareholders) *may* be different from its management (directors). Clearly all 100,000 shareholders of a company cannot concern themselves with day-to-day management.

(d) **Associations.** These are clubs, societies and groups of people who join together for sporting, educational, social or charitable purposes. Some clubs trade, for example, by having a bar.

(d) **Public ownership.** The nationalised industries, local and central government. The accounting requirements of public sector enterprises are outside the scope of this book, although the financial statements of nationalised industries are prepared on similar lines to the accounts you will learn to prepare.

6.   There are a few other modes of ownership such as trusts, or incorporation by Royal Charter or special Act of Parliament but we need not concern ourselves with them.

TRADING ON CREDIT

7.   Before studying the measurement of business profit, we have to understand the basic notions of how business is done. If I want to buy a magazine, I walk into the local newsagents and buy it. Simple, but in fact a number of things have occurred:

(a) The *possession* and *ownership* of the magazine has passed from the newsagent to me.
(b) I have paid by passing *cash* to the news-agent.

The sale and the payment are *simultaneous*. This is called a *cash sale*.

It may be that I have forgotten my wallet but remembered my cheque book, so that instead of paying cash I give the newsagent a cheque. This is still called a cash sale because sale and payment are simultaneous.

If I like the magazine, I may arrange for future editions to be delivered together with my morning newspaper. I then pay for it at the end of each month, for the obvious reason that it would be inconvenient for all concerned for the newsboy to collect payment every morning.

In this case, the *sale* and the *payment* are not simultaneous. The sale comes first and the payment comes later. This is called *trading on credit*. In practice, most retail sales are cash sales and most sales by manufacturers and wholesalers are on credit. You will appreciate that selling on credit means the seller parting with ownership and possession of the goods without any certainty about when, if at all, payment will be made.

CREDIT CARDS

8.   In addition to cash sales and credit sales, another form of trading is now very common. That is the use of credit cards - Access, Visa, American Express etc.

The procedures that are applied are:

(a) Members of the public have a small plastic credit card.

(b) This is used to pay for goods. The retailer fills in a form with details of the goods and uses the embossed nature of the credit card to print the data on the customer on the form. The customer retains a copy of the form.

(c) Each day the retailer sums the amounts on the forms and pays them into the bank. The amounts are credited to his account and debited in the bank account of the credit card company.

(d) Each month the credit card company charges the retailer with commission on the deals and extracts it from the retailers bank account by direct debit. The rate of commission varies between 1% and 4%.

(e) The credit card company send a monthly account to their card holders who pay or, if they do not pay, suffer an interest charge until they do.

From the point of view of the retailer, credit card selling is equivalent to cash sales except that there is a cost - a monthly commission charge.

DOCUMENTS

9.   There are a large number of common business documents. Examples are invoices, clock cards showing the number of hours worked by a worker, personnel records and stock record cards. Try to examine any business document you come across!

At this stage we need to consider three only of the main documents.

(a) **The Invoice.** (See Fig. 2.1).

The purpose of the invoice is to evidence a sale by the seller (vendor) to the buyer (purchaser). It is sent by the seller to the buyer. Try to think of the purpose of each field (= item of information). Note that the *terms of trade*, in this case net thirty days, means that the seller *hopes* that the buyer will pay within thirty days. In practice, few keep to the terms!

INVOICE				No. 11747	

NUTCASE HARDWARE LIMITED

To: Smith Hardware
187 The Croft
Northtown NO6 8JQ

Unit 8, Foley Industrial Estate
Tettenhall, Wolverhampton WV6 8LT
Telephone 758095
VAT No. 900 27734 321

Your Order Number	Despatch Date	Delivery Note Number	Invoice Date	Remarks
432689A	24.6.-6	B76543	25.6.86	

Product Description	Quantity	Price	Per	VAT Rate	Amount
Small Widget sets	36	£2.40	each	15	86.40
Nylon Collars	500	£18.98	100	15	94.90

Terms and Conditions: Nett thirty days

Total Goods	181.30
Total VAT	27.19
Amount Due	£208.49

Nutcase Hardware Ltd: Company number 2786542   Directors: J. Jones, D. Jones.   Secretary: F. Jones

Fig. 2.1

(b) **The Credit Note.** (See Fig. 2.2).

CREDIT NOTE			No. 345	

NUTCASE HARDWARE LIMITED

To: Smith Hardware
187 The Croft
Northtown NO6 8JQ

Unit 8, Foley Industrial Estate
Tettenhall, Wolverhampton WV6 8LT
Telephone 758095
VAT No. 900 27734 321

Your Debit Note No.	Our Invoice No.	Date of Receipt	Credit Note Date
43	11747	n/a	29.6.-6

Product Description	VAT Rate	Amount
Incorrect Price – 36 small widgets charged at £2.40 – should be at £2.30	15	3.60
Nylon Collars short delivery by ten items		1.90
Total Goods		5.50
Total VAT		.82
Total Credit		£6.32

Fig. 2.2

The functions of a credit note are:

(i)   To evidence the acceptance of the return of goods by the seller from the buyer. Usual reasons for the return of goods are that they were faulty or otherwise unsatisfactory or they were damaged.

(ii) To evidence to a buyer that he need not pay for goods invoiced to him because the goods have been lost in transit.

(iii) To correct errors on invoices. Such errors may be over pricing or inclusion of goods not actually sent.

(c) **The Statement of Account** (See Fig. 2.3).

This document is sent by the seller to a customer who is buying goods on credit. Usually it is sent monthly. It summarises the transactions between the seller and the buyer since the previous statement. Note that brief details of the invoice and credit note illustrated earlier appear on this statement.

STATEMENT		No. 11747	

NUTCASE HARDWARE LIMITED

To: Smith Hardware
187 The Croft
Northtown NO6 8JQ

Unit 8, Foley Industrial Estate
Tettenhall, Wolverhampton WV6 8LT
Telephone 758095
VAT No. 900 27734 321

Date 30/6/-6

Date	Reference	Description	Value
16.4.-6	9032	Invoice	240.68
27.4.-6	9039	Invoice	387.95
18.5.-6	10054	Invoice	132.99
25.6.-6	11747	Invoice	208.49
29.6.-6	345	Credit Note	6.32*
		Statement Total	£963.79

Accounts overdue for payment:

3 months and over	2 months	1 month	current month	
nil	628.63	132.99	202.17	

Fig. 2.3

SUMMARY

10. (a) Business activities are of several different types. They can be listed as:

Retailing
Wholesaling
Manufacturing

Service Industries
Non-profit activities

(b) Ownership of businesses can be one of several different modes: sole trading, partnership, limited companies, unincorporated associations and public ownership. In some, ownership and management can be by different persons.

(c) Trading or the sale of goods and services can be for cash or on credit.

POINTS TO NOTE

11. (a) We have talked about the business. Accountants distinguish the business from the owner. A businessman may have more than one business; for example, he may have an engineering business, a farm *and* a supermarket. Each year the profit made by each activity is separately measured.

(b) Try to realise that selling involves two separate but related activities. The sale with transfer of ownership and possession of the goods, and the payment. **There** may be a time lag between the two happenings.

(c) We have distinguished different types of business. Some businesses are mixed. For example, the local pharmacist supplies both goods and a service, and many manufacturers also import finished goods and wholesale them.

SELF TESTING QUESTIONS

1. *List the different types of business activity. (2).*
2. *List the different modes of ownership. (4).*
3. *Distinguish cash sales from credit sales. (7).*
4. *Design an invoice for a limited company engaged in manufacturing. (9).*
5. *Outline the procedures involved in credit card trading. Who are the parties involved and to what extent are they taking or receiving credit and at what cost? (8).*
6. *What fields would be different on an invoice compared with a credit note? (9). (a "field" is an item of information on a document.)*
7. *What is the purpose of a statement of account? How does it differ from an invoice? (9).*
8. *What is a trader? (3).*

Exercises (Answers begin on page 445)

1. *Dave and Marge intend to set up a business as dealers in light fittings. They intend to import goods from the Far East and also to buy from British firms. Some goods will come as components and they will assemble and pack them. They intend to sell the goods to retailers around the country and also to the public in their own shop in North Bromwich. They also intend to use their knowledge of import documentation to advise other importers.*

Required:
(a) What types of business activity will Dave and Marge be carrying on?
(b) What mode of ownership will be used?
(c) In what ways will their sales of goods and resulting cash inflows differ in time?
(d) What trading documents will they receive? and send out?

2. *What type of business activity is carried on and what mode of ownership is used by the following:*

(a) Fred, a chiropodist.
(b) Sam and his son who have a fish shop.
(c) The Society of Accounting Authors.
(d) British Gas plc.
(e) British Coal.
(f) Akhbar Khan Ltd, makers of ladies' dresses.

Which of them are likely to trade on credit?

Exercises without answers

3. *Obtain an invoice, a credit note and a statement of account. How do they differ from the examples given in this chapter?*

4. *Consider the following businesses:*

(a) William Nutcase Limited who buy chocolates from specialist manufacturers on the continent and sell them to retailers in the UK.
(b) Hogwash, Rott & Co, Certified Accountants.
(c) Tring who repairs motor bicycles for motor cyclists and local garages.
(d) The Tettenhall Sporting Club which supplies squash and tennis facilities to its members.

What type of business activity fo they carry on?
What mode of ownership is concerned?
Will they sell for cash or on credit?

5. *What are the purposes of a credit note? Draw up a series of credit notes to illustrate each purpose.*

3. Accounting in Context

INTRODUCTION

1. Bookkeeping is the systematic recording of each relevant business transaction as it occurs. From the books maintained by the bookkeeper, summary accounts (called financial statements) measuring the profit or loss made by the business and the capital employed in the business are prepared at intervals of a year or more frequently. The financial statements give *information* to the people for whom they are prepared.

Each business has a number of categories of people who have *contact* with the business and each category has specific information needs. In this chapter we are going to discuss what categories of people have contact with a business, what their information needs are; and finally, to what extent the books and financial statements meet those needs.

BUSINESS CONTACT GROUPS

2. The main contact groups for a business are:

(a) **Owners.** Owners of businesses may be sole proprietors, partners, or shareholders of limited companies. Sole proprietors, partners and, shareholders who are also directors of their companies, will also manage the business. Shareholders, who are not also directors of their companies, will not normally have day-to-day contact with the business.

(b) **Managers.** Managers of businesses may also be the owners (sole proprietors, directors, shareholders) but may be salaried directors or simply employees.

(c) **Lenders to the business.** Businesses often borrow money from individuals or more commonly from their bankers.

(d) **Customers.**

(e) **Suppliers.**

(f) **Employees.**

(g) **The Government.** Businesses today are subject to a wide range of government regulations (for example, on health and safety at work, planning, pollution, redundancy). The principal government office with contact with a business is the Inland Revenue who are concerned to extract taxation from the business. It is difficult to answer the contention that with Corporation Tax at 35% of taxable profits, the government have nearly as great an interest in a company as its shareholders.

INFORMATION NEEDS

3. Each of the contact groups we have noted, require information about the business in order that they can take rational decisions in their dealings with the business. It is not possible to summarise all the information that each group might want but we will consider some of their more important information needs and how accounting meets their requirements.

(a) **Managers and Owners who also manage.** Managers of enterprises need day-to-day information on all aspects of the business and of the outside world in which the business operates. They will also need an understanding of the probable outcome of present uncompleted matters and of the future generally. Accounting cannot possibly provide for more than a fraction of management's information needs. However it does provide information on:

    (i) Up-to-date information on how much and to whom money is owed; how much and by whom money is owed to the business; and the cash balance at bank and in hand.

    (ii) A summary of how much profit or loss the business has made in each year (or more frequently) and the capital employed in the business.

(b) **Owners who are not concerned with day-to-day management.** Owners are concerned to receive information about the progress of their business and the competence of those who manage it. The financial statements go some way towards meeting this need.

(c) **Lenders.** Bankers and others who lend money to a business are primarily concerned with the ability of the business to make payments of interest and repayments of capital in the future and of the possibility and the consequences of a default. Bankers regard the financial statements as meeting a small part of their information needs.

(d) **Customers.** Customers also have information requirements (*e.g.* about product, prices, quality, reliability, delivery dates) about the business which are not met by accounting. Customers may also like to know whether a business is financially sound so that they know that guarantees are worthwhile, or spare parts etc. may be obtained in the future.

(e) **Suppliers.** The primary information needed by suppliers of goods on credit to a business is whether or not the business is able to pay for the goods and the probability of delay in payment. Financial statements can be of assistance to suppliers in assessing the credit worthiness of potential customers but in practice the financial statements are not always available to them.

(f) **Employees.** Employees clearly have need of information about their employer's business in connection with their personal dealings with the company (*e.g.* work requirements, hours, pay, holidays). They do not, in general, have an interest in the profitability or capital employed in their employer's business. Union negotiators however, do take account of such information.

(g) **The Government.** Government agencies have a wide range of information needs about a business including statistical data about employment and production. These needs are frequently met from the data found in bookkeeping records. More directly, the financial statements provide data from which taxes (*e.g.* VAT, national insurance, PAYE, income tax, corporation tax) can be assessed and collected.

INFORMATION NEEDS AND ACCOUNTING

4. Contact groups have widely different information needs about a business. Accounting provides information of a very limited kind. Accounting information has two particular characteristics which limit its usefulness:

(a) It is *historical*. Accounting is concerned to record events as they happen or within a short time of occurrence but always after the event.

Financial statements summarise profit or loss and capital employed in the recent past. Historical information is useful in predicting the future but accounting is not concerned with the systematic collection of probable future happenings.

(b) It is in terms of *money*. Accounting provides information on events and transactions that are of a financial nature or can be expressed in financial terms. It does not give information in quantity or size terms or in qualitative matters like usefulness.

SUMMARY

5. (a) Contact groups who are interested in a business include:

(i) owners	(v) suppliers
(ii) managers	(vi) employees
(iii) lenders	(vii) government.
(iv) customers	

(b) Each contact group has particular needs for information about the business to enable it to make rational decisions.

(c) Accounting provides a very limited range of information.

(d) The principal limitations of accounting information are that accounting information is:

(i) historical
(ii) of a financial nature.

POINTS TO NOTE

6. (a) In considering contact groups, those currently dealing with the business have information needs but also those who are considering contact also have information needs. For example, potential suppliers may need information to help them decide whether or not to supply goods on credit.

(b) The historical nature of accounting is fundamental to accounting. However management accounting which is outside the scope of this book is largely concerned with forecasting the future.

(c)   Accountants have in recent years come to hold important positions in industry and commerce, frequently as chairman or managing directors or chief executives of companies. This has led to some criticism that in executive decision making, too much weight is given to financial considerations.

(d)   The different information needs of contact groups has led to the legend that businesses keep three sets of books. By this means the annual profit can be measured as:

(i)   high – so that the bank manager will regard the business as one to which he will wish to lend money.
(ii)   accurate – to enable the proprietor to make rational decisions.
(iii) low – so as to pay little tax.

Businesses do not really do this!

SELF TESTING QUESTIONS

1.   *Summarise the groups who have contact with a company. (2).*
2.   *What are the main limitations of accounting as a source of information about business? (4).*

Exercises (Answers begin on page 445)

1.   *Chump Garages plc is a public company whose shares are traded on the Stock Exchange. The company has 3,500 shareholders, none of whom own more than 5% of the share capital. The company is managed by its board of directors – seven people, none of whom own more than a tiny fraction of the share capital. The principal business of the company is operation of a chain of garages selling new and second hand cars and trucks, petrol and diesel oil and spares and accessories. They also do repairs. The company have in recent years moved into property development as a consequence of developing some of their own properties and are heavily indebted to the bank.*

Required:
(a)   What actual or potential contact groups will have need of information about the company?
(b)   What information will actually be available to them?

2.   *Consider the following businesses:*

(a)   Janet and Bill, who run a hairdressing salon.
(b)   Fred Ltd an engineering company whose directors AND shareholders are both Mr and Mrs Fred.
(c)   Ginger a student who owns "Mr Generous" a large do-it-yourself warehouse which is managed by Mr Macbeth who previously managed it for Roger who left it to his nephew Ginger.
(d)   Bosk Investments Ltd owned by Mr Smart who takes the savings of his customers and invests them in various enterprises found by him.
(e)   The Foley Design Partnership Ltd which remunerates its highly qualified and talented employees almost entirely by a share in the profits.
(f)   Titanic plc a shipyard on the Tyne.

How would the information required by contact groups be limited by the limitations of accounting information.

3.   *"The profits made by my business and the capital I have employed in it is no concern of anybody but myself" – a quotation by Jim, an Insurance broker. How true is this statement?*

Exercises without answers

4.   *You are a branch manager of Folio Books plc which has some 20 bookshops. What information about the financial affairs and performance would you require from the company? Consider why you might need the information.*

5.   *You are contemplating the purchase of Jenny's hairdressing business. She has supplied you with the annual accounts for the most recent past years. What are the limitations of these accounts in helping you make up your mind on whether to buy and at what price? What specific information will not be supplied by these accounts?*

6.   *Ted trades as Ted Limited, suppliers of widgets to local manufacturers. What groups would have contact with the business?*

4. The Accounting Scene

INTRODUCTION

1. Accounting is carried out by accountants. Most accountants are members of professional bodies. In this chapter some statistics are given about the accountants' professional bodies. Some accountants are employed by a particular business and spend their whole time in that business. Some accountants are self-employed and offer their services as accountants to business firms and to private individuals. These accountants are said to be in practice. Some accountants practice as sole practitioners. Some form firms which can be very large, employing thousands of people and operating world wide. Accountants in practice are said to be in the profession. Accountants who are employees of business firms are said to be in industry or commerce.

2. The second part of this chapter considers related activities which are performed by accountants in addition to accounting functions.

PROFESSIONAL BODIES

3. The major professional bodies of accountants in the British Isles are shown in Fig. 4.1.

4. The first three all require training to be with professional firms in private practice.

5. The last body is sometimes known as the "second tier". Its entry requirements and examinations are of a lower standard than the other bodies.

AUDITING

6. Accounting is about the preparation of Financial Statements which can take many forms. The best known are the profit and loss accounts and balance sheets of businesses. In the specific case of limited companies, financial statements are produced annually and take the form of an "Annual Report and Accounts" which include a profit and loss account and balance sheet. The Annual Reports of companies are produced by directors of companies (the work is usually delegated to accountants) who send them to the shareholders. The difficulty which arises is that the Annual Report may be misleading, fraudulent, or full of errors. To prevent Financial Statements from showing other than a *true and fair* view, the law provides for an *audit*. An audit is a detailed examination of the financial statements with a search for *evidence* to *substantiate* all the figures in the statements and of the records from which they were prepared. The audit is followed by an expression of opinion by the auditor who says whether or not the statements give a true and fair view.

7. Audits can be carried out on any set of financial statements not only those of limited companies.

8. Audits are carried out by professional accounting firms whose reputation for independence, integrity and competence give the Financial Statements *credibility*.

	Membership	Student Numbers	Designating Letters
Institute of Chartered Accountants in England and Wales	89,000	21,500	FCA, ACA
Institute of Chartered Accountants in Ireland	6,500	2,000	FCA, ACA
Institute of Chartered Accountants of Scotland	12,000	1,500	CA
Association of Certified Accountants	33,000	75,000	FCCA, ACCA
Institute of Cost and Management Accountants	28,000	43,000	FCMA, ACMA
Chartered Institute of Public Finance and Accountancy	10,000	2,800	CIPFA
Association of Accounting Technicians	13,000	30,000	MAAT

Fig. 4.1

TAXATION

9. The amount of income tax paid by private businesses and firms and corporation tax paid by limited companies is dependent on the amount of profit made. As accountants are concerned with the preparation and audit of financial statements it follows that they should also be concerned with the computation of tax payable. This work is usually carried out for their clients by professional accounting firms. The work involves agreement of the amount of profit assessable and of the amount of tax payable, with H.M. Inspectors of Taxes. In practice accountants also have expertise in other taxes and they also give advice to clients on how to arrange their affairs to minimise the tax payable.

INSOLVENCY

10. Not all businesses are successful and failure is followed by legal consequences. The law is concerned to ensure that the business assets are realised (turned into cash) and the resulting cash is properly distributed to those entitled. The consequences of failure by individuals and partnerships may include bankruptcy when the Court appoints a *trustee* to look after the affairs of the bankrupt. The consequences of failure by a limited company may be the appointment of a receiver or of a liquidator or both. Persons appointed as trustees in bankruptcy and as receivers or liquidators of companies are usually accountants, specially licensed for these duties.

COMPUTING

11. Most of this book describes accounting as if it were carried out manually on books and paper. Bookkeeping is a tedious process involving entry into the books of large numbers of similar transactions. In consequence, bookkeeping is an ideal subject for computerisation and the rapid development of cheap computer systems has led to many businesses maintaining their books by computer. The one-off nature of the preparation of financial statements has meant that these are still manually produced in most cases.

The development of computerised bookkeeping has deeply involved most accountants in computing and many accountants have become recognised as experts in this field.

SUMMARY

12. (a) Accounting is carried out by accountants who combine into professional bodies.
    (b) There are six major accounting bodies in the UK and one fast growing body of accounting technicians.
    (c) Accountants in practice also engage in related activities including auditing, taxation, insolvency and computer work.

POINTS TO NOTE

13. (a) Accountants regard accounting as a profession. It is not easy to define the word profession. However the following attributes characterise most professions including accounting:

      (i)   A recognisable, discrete body of knowledge.
      (ii)   An educational process.
      (iii)   A system of examinations.
      (iv)   A system for licensing practitioners.
      (v)   A professional association.
      (vi)   A sense of responsibility to society.
      (vii) A code of ethics.
      (viii) A set of technical standards.

SELF EXAMINATION QUESTIONS

1. List the professional accounting bodies in the UK. (3).
2. What services are provided by professional accounting firms? (12c).
3. What are the characteristics of a profession? (13a).

Exercises (Answers begin on page 446)

1. Solange is the proprietor of a shop which sells small and large electrical appliances in a suburban shopping precinct. She is considering converting the business into a limited company with herself and her daughter as shareholders and directors. She is also considering taking a lease on a city centre shop which will be very risky but potentially very profitable. This will involve borrowing from the bank. The books of her business are kept by her nephew Tony who finds the manual bookkeeping system very tedious.

Required:
(a) In what ways may her accountants Little and Co, Certified Accountants, assist her and her business?
(b) Tony who has two A levels is considering qualifying as an accountant while remaining with the business. Which body should he attempt to join and how can he go about it?

2. In what ways is the Chartered Association of Certified Accountants a professional body as defined in paragraph 13(a)?

Exercises without answers

3. Find some advertisements from accountants operating in your area. What services do they offer?

4. Obtain the "Annual Report and Accounts" of some public companies. What is the role of the auditor in regard to these documents?

5. (a) *Distinguish between accounting and auditing.*
    (b) *Consider the suggestion that computers have made accountants obsolete.*
    (c) *Consider the statement that the sole objective of an accountant is to save tax for his clients.*

The Balance Sheet

The next two chapters introduce one of the most important financial statements, the Balance Sheet. Chapter Five gives the form of a balance sheet and explains its structure and gives some theoretical principles. The balance sheet is a static picture of a business at a particular moment and Chapter Six shows how the picture changes with time.

5. The Balance Sheet of the Sole Trader

INTRODUCTION

1. A balance sheet is a document which lists:

    (a) the assets of the business;
    (b) the liabilities of the business;
    (c) how the business is financed - its capital.

and gives values to each item.

All businesses produce a balance sheet at least once a year.

2. In this chapter we will describe the balance sheet of a sole trader. Balance sheets of other organisations are much the same and differ primarily in the financing section.

FORMAT

3. At Fig. 5.1 is the general format of the balance sheet of a sole trader.

I will discuss each line separately.

(a) **The name of the business is given first.** The objective is to identify the business. In many cases, as here, just the name of the *proprietor* is given. The name of the business (*e.g.* The Foley Fish Company) may also be given.

(b) **Balance sheet** - it is clearly necessary to identify the document as a balance sheet.

			line
James Brown			a
Balance Sheet as at 31st December 19-8			b
Fixed Assets		£	c
Premises		20,000	d
Plant and equipment		11,500	e
Vehicles		16,200	f
		47,700	g
Current Assets	£		h
Stock	65,200		i
Debtors	31,000		j
Prepayments	400		k
Cash in hand	800		l
		97,400	m
		145,100	o
Current Liabilities			n
Creditors	27,000		p
Accruals	1,000		q
Bank overdraft	34,000		r
		62,000	s
		83,100	t
Capital		83,100	u

Fig. 5.1
Balance Sheet Vertical Format

At at 31st December 19-8. A Balance Sheet describes the situation at a particular specified moment in time; in this case as at 31st December 19-8.

(c) **Fixed Assets** - assets are things which the business owns or possesses and which have value to the business. Fixed assets are those assets which were acquired for continuous use in the business and which have useful lives extending over a number of years.

(d) **Premises** - or land and buildings. All the items in a balance sheet are shown as having monetary values. The values quoted are often not the values that a layman would expect. Accounting is very much about deriving appropriate methods of valuation for balance sheets. In most sole trader balance sheets, premises will be valued at what they cost the business when they were acquired.

(e) **Plant and Equipment and Vehicles.** The valuation of these fixed assets is more complicated and is dealt with under the heading of depreciation in Chapter 13. At this stage, it is enough to know that they are valued by reference to the original cost of acquisition.

(g) **The balance sheet is divided into sections** - fixed assets, current assets, current liabilities, capital and it is necessary to show the total value of *each* section.

(h) **Current assets** consist of goods which were acquired for the purpose of sale (stock), sums due to the business by others (debtors), benefits of paid expenditure which are still be come, *e.g.* rent paid in advance (prepayments), and cash at bank and in hand. The distinguishing characteristic of current assets is that they exist for a short time only before being converted into assets of other kinds. For example, stock is sold on credit and thus converted into debtors. Debtors pay and thus the sum due is converted into cash.

(i) **Stock** (sometimes known as inventory)
Consists of:

> Goods held for resale.
> Raw materials held for conversion into a saleable product.
> Work in progress - partly finished goods which on completion will be held for sale.

Stock may also include consumable stores (heating oil, cleaning materials, lubricants, stationery etc.) and spare parts for machinery.

Counting and valuing stock is the most difficult and time consuming part of preparing the data for inclusion in a balance sheet.

(j) **Amounts due by debtors.** Debtors are people or firms who have bought goods before the balance sheet date (in our case 19-8) but who had not paid by that date but will pay after the balance sheet date (in our case in 19-9).

(k) **Prepayments;** they arise out of payments which were made before the balance sheet date but which will give the business benefits after the balance sheet date. Examples are rent, rates or insurance paid in advance.

(l) This business has no cash at bank (it has an overdraft) but many businesses will have cash at the bank as well as cash in hand.

(m) As in line g, the total of each section must be shown.

(n) The total value of all the assets is shown.

(o) **Current liabilities** - liabilities are amounts owing by the business. Current liabilities are usually defined as amounts falling due within one year. In this case, the current liabilities are payable by 31st December 19-9. In practice most of them will be paid early in 19-9.

(p) **Creditors** - this item includes mainly sums due for goods which were supplied to the business in 19-8 but which had not been paid for in 19-8. Clearly, most goods bought in 19-8 are paid for in 19-8 but as Brown buys on credit, some goods bought in 19-8 will be paid for in 19-9.

(q) **Accruals** - this will be an unfamiliar word to you. In this context it means sums due for those services supplied in 19-8 which had *not* been paid for by the end of 19-8. Examples are electricity used but not paid for, or interest on loans which has become due by the passage of time but which has not been paid.

(r) **Overdraft** – many businesses have money in the bank but many others, like James Brown's, have with the bank's approval drawn more from the bank than they have put in. The excess is known as an overdraft and is a liability of the business. It is a current liability because it is technically repayable on demand.

(s) Similar to g and m.

(t) It is useful to measure and show the total value of the assets employed in the business less the liabilities to other people.

(u) **Capital** – so far the idea of listing and valuing the assets and liabilities of the business is one which is not difficult to grasp. The financing section of the balance sheet is slightly more difficult to understand. In this case, the financing section consists of one item only – capital. It means:

   (i)   that all the resources needed to acquire the net assets (assets minus liabilities) came from the proprietor, James Brown.

   (ii) the value of the resources invested by James Brown in the business amounts to £83,100.

   (iii) the business can be said to owe £83,100 to its proprietor, James Brown.

METHODS AND PROCEDURES

4.   The best approach to the preparation of a balance sheet is:

(a) *Memorise* the format and write down the words.

(b) Complete the balance sheet by filling in the appropriate amounts. In examinations, the required data is often given in the form of a *trial balance* and notes or in the form of notes only.

Once the format has been memorised, the preparation is usually relatively simple as all balance sheets are basically similar in content.

THEORY AND CRITICISM

5.   The form and content of balance sheets were not originally given to mankind in the way that the law was given by God to Moses and Moses to the people. Instead the present form and content developed over the centuries by the experiment and experience of businessmen by trial and error methods. In recent times academic accountants have developed a body of theory to describe the actual *practice* of accountants in producing balance sheets.

6.   The theory consist of a series of ideas variously known as postulates, principles, concepts, conventions or other words. In this work, I shall use the word *convention* but you will find other words meaning the same thing.

7.   In this chapter, we will look at four conventions: periodicity, business entity, money measurement and historical cost.

8.   **Periodicity.** Balance sheets can be prepared as often as is desired but there is some considerable labour involved and in consequence, the *convention* has grown up by preparing them at yearly intervals. The life of a business is divided into individual accounting years. Each business proprietor needs to determine at the business commencement what date his accounting year will end on. There are *no rules* on this but many businesses choose from:

   (i)   The month end nearest the anniversary of commencement.
   (ii) The calendar year end *i.e.* 31st December.
   (iii) The government's year end *i.e.* 31st March.
   (iv) A month end when business is usually slack so that the year end things can receive reasonable attention.

9.   **Business entity.** In drawing up his balance sheet, a business proprietor is concerned only with the assets and liabilities of the *business*. He excludes other assets and liabilities which are private or domestic or are assets of another, completely separate, business. The convention has therefore developed of looking upon the business as a separate entity from its proprietor. By so doing, it is possible to see the business entity as *owing* the amount of its capital to the proprietor. The business entity convention is a fiction (the assets and liabilities of the business are still legally the assets and liabilities of the proprietor) but a convenient one.

10. In practice, it is not always easy to decide if some assets are private assets or business assets. For example a car may be used for business *and* private purposes. Where duality of purpose or use is found, the asset is commonly regarded as a business asset.

11. **Money measurement.** If I have three oranges and buy four more, I have seven in total. Similarly if I have a home, a car and six tins of soup, I have eight things altogether. But the number eight here, is hardly useful information. The problem is to find some common unit in which to convert assets and liabilities so that the *total* number of units becomes meaningful. The convention in accounting is to use pounds ste-ling (or in Nigeria, Naira; in India, Rupees; etc).

Money has several uses including:

(a) It is a store of value.
(b) It is a means of exchange.
(c) It is a *measure* of value.

This use by accountants of money as a measure of value has two difficulties:

(i) Accountants have acquired a reputation (undeserved) of being obsessed with money to the exclusion of other, more human factors.

(ii) Those unversed in accounting may confuse the uses of money with money itself. For example "capital" measures the total value of assets less liabilities, it is not itself money.

12. **Historical Cost.** In a balance sheet, assets such as premises have values placed upon them. There are several possible ways of finding a basis for valuing business premises (imagine a shop). Here are three:

(a) What the shop could be sold for, if sold as a shop.
(b) What the shop could be sold for, if sold for some other use.
(c) What the business originally paid for it when the business acquired it.

Methods (a) and (b) seem useful at first sight but the figure can only be obtained by forming opinions, making an estimate or simply guessing. Such methods are *subjective* and accountants prefer to be *objective,* and so prefer method (c).

It is possible to argue that showing the shop on the balance sheet at historical cost £20,000 because it cost that amount twenty years ago, gives information of no possible relevance. This argument is in fact accepted and company balance sheets usually have the estimated resale value shown also, as a note.

13. In times of high inflation, the historical cost convention used by accountants, has been much criticised and the profession has developed a method of adjusting accounts to reflect the effects of inflation without abandoning the basic preference for cost as a measure of value.

ALTERNATIVE FORMATS

14. The format shown at Fig 5.1 is a common one. It is known as the vertical format. Other formats are acceptable and include the horizontal format. Fig. 5.2 is the same balance sheet drawn up in horizontal format.

The horizontal format is the more traditional one and the vertical format is considered to be more modern.

Students are often confused by differences in format. Think of a balance sheet as having sections (fixed assets, current assets, current liabilities, capital) which can be arranged in different ways. A slight rearrangement of the vertical format is often found as:

		£
Fixed Assets		47,700
Current Assets	97,400	
less Current liabilities	62,000	35,400
		83,100
Capital		83,100

This changes the effect on a reader produced by the balance sheet in that emphasis is placed on the relative totals of current assets and current liabilities (this net total is called the *working capital*).

JAMES BROWN
BALANCE SHEET AS AT 31st DECEMBER 19-8

	£		£
Capital	83,100	**Fixed Assets**	
		Premises	20,000
		Plant and Equipment	11,500
Current Liabilities		Vehicles	16,200
Creditors	27,000		47,700
Accruals	1,000		
Bank Overdraft	34,000 62,000	**Current Assets**	
		Stock	65,200
		Debtors	31,000
		Prepayments	400
		Cash in hand	800 97,400
	145,100		145,100

Fig. 5.2
Balance Sheet – Horizontal Format

CATEGORIES

15. You will have realised that a balance sheet is not a long list of individual assets. (Adam owes us £60, Alfred owes us £75 . . .). Such lists may be useful but the aim of a balance sheet is to show the overall position. Assets and liabilities are summarised into categories. The categories selected are a matter of choice on appropriateness and convenience. Fixed assets in a shop business may be best categorised as:

Fixtures and Fitting (to include shelving, counters, display cabinets, etc.).
Equipment (to include cash registers, cold cabinets, etc.).

Other types of businesses may use different categories.

COMMON ERRORS

16. Here is a list of errors made by students in preparing balance sheets which you should try to avoid:

(a) Failure to state the name of the proprietor and/or the business.
(b) Incorrect heading. "Balance Sheet as at . . . " is always correct.
(c) Failure to use the general headings: fixed assets, current assets, current liabilities etc.
(d) Untidiness; for example, failing to write down words and figures directly underneath each other.
(e) Failure to show sub-totals of the general categories; fixed assets, current assets, etc.
(f) Writing down the current assets in the wrong order. This may seem a petty sin but in practice, the order shown is always used.
(g) Failing to use more than one column.
(h) Putting the lines ____ or ____ in the wrong places. Note where I have put them.
(i) Abbreviating - do not be impatient.
(j) Failure to realise that other people will have to make sense of your work.
(k) Errors in addition.

SUMMARY

17. (a) The balance sheet of a business is a classified list with values of the assets employed in, and the liabilities of, the business at a particular date.

(b) Capital is defined as assets less liabilities.

(c) The vertical format for a sole trader balance sheet should be memorised.

(d) The periodicity convention recognises the fact that businessmen can draw up balance sheets for their businesses at intervals, usually of one year. Any date can be selected but is usually adhered to in successive years.

(e) The business entity convention requires a focus of attention on the business as a separate entity from its proprietor.

(f) Balance Sheets are drawn up with values in terms of money. Money is used as a *measure* of value.

(g) Accountants value assets by reference to historical cost.

POINTS TO NOTE

18. (a) A balance sheet shows the assets and liabilities and capital at a particular moment in time. It is a static snapshot picture of what in reality is an ever changing thing. Students initially tend to confuse *movements* or *flows* of assets and liabilities with assets and liabilities at a particular moment. There are other financial statements to measure movements and flows over time.

(b) The words assets and liabilities are difficult to define with precision because of the diversity of assets and liabilities which can be found in the complex business world. Students should familiarise themselves with what is meant by a business asset or liability which should appear on a balance sheet by constant observation of actual balance sheets.

Liabilities must in general involve:
(i)   a sum of money owing by the business at the balance sheet date.
(ii) for some goods supplied or services supplied or other happening before the balance sheet date.

(c) The balance sheet is a summary. In practice:

Fixed Assets   £6,432,000

is too much of a summary and some break-down into sub-categories is usually made. Perhaps as:

Fixed Assets	£
Land	1,000,000
Buildings	2,342,000
Plant and Machinery	1,190,000
Motor Vehicles	1,900,000
	6,432,000

It is difficult to generalise as to how much sub-categorisation is appropriate. You should try to see as many balance sheets as you can. Clubs, societies, students' unions and public companies all publish their balance sheets.

(d) Businesses can have many different types of assets and liabilities but all balance sheets are basically similar. Once you have learned the basic form and content, you will find that more complex balance sheets (for example, those of partnerships, limited companies and groups of companies) still follow the basic design and only the detail has to be understood and learned.

(e) Note carefully that assets and liabilities and capital are *measured* in money terms, they are not themselves money.

(f) The idea of a Fixed asset is that it is some asset which has *cost* more than some trivial amount and will *last* and give *future benefits* over several years. Thus buildings and machinery are both expensive and long lasting and are thus Fixed assets.

(g) Current assets are also things of value which will give future benefits. But they are of a transitory nature such that the benefits will be received entirely in the *near* future.

(h) The four categories of current asset are the common ones and you should commit them to memory. They are always found in the same order and you should design your balance sheets that way also.

(i) The capital of the business is simply equal to the total of assets minus the total of the liabilities. Commonly, the word capital is used but other words can be found including:

- proprietorship.
- net worth.
- owners equity.

James Brown owns his business. The business is not an abstract idea, it is composed of a set of specific assets and it also has liabilities. It is useful to determine the *net* amount of the assets less liabilities because:

(i)   It tells the owner/proprietor what resources he has tied up in his business. If he sold the assets and paid off the liabilities he would have money which he could use in other ways.

(ii) Any change in the capital since the previous balance sheet was drawn up needs to be explained.

(j)   The notion that Capital = Assets - Liabilities is often known as the Accounting Equation. The equation can be manipulated so that, for example, Assets = Capital + Liabilities.

SELF TESTING QUESTIONS

1.   (a) *Draft a balance sheet for a sole trader:*

   (i)   *Showing the assets total (vertical format).*
   (ii)   *Showing working capital (vertical format).*
   (iii) *In horizontal format.*

   (b) *Explain:*

   (i)   *Fixed assets.*
   (ii)   *Current assets.*
   (iii) *Stock.*
   (iv)   *Debtors.*
   (v)   *Current liabilities.*
   (vi)   *Accruals.*
   (vii) *Capital.*

   (c) *What is the periodicity convention? (8).*
   (d) *What is the entity convention? (9).*
   (e) *What is the money measurement conven-tion? (11).*
   (f) *What is the historical cost convention? (12).*
   (g) *What are the uses for money in an economy? (11).*
   (h) *What formats are possible for a balance sheet and why might the format be changed? (14).*
   (i) *Why are assets grouped into categories and only the total of each category shown? (15).*
   (j) *List the common errors in balance sheets made by students. (16).*
   (k) *What exactly is Capital? (18).*
   (l) *What is the Accounting Equation?*

Exercises (Answers begin on page 447)

1.   Draw up a balance sheet of Bill's business as at 31.12.-8 in (a) vertical form including total assets; (b) a vertical form showing working capital; (c) horizontal form, from the following:

	£
Premises	50,000
Stock	16,440
Trade creditors	13,920
Vehicle	11,600
Fixtures and Fittings	5,300
Accrued rent	200
Prepaid insurance	361
Cash at Bank	320
Prepaid rates	890
Cash in hand	35
Trade debtors	12,610
14% Loan repayable 4.3.-9 from James	1,000
Accrued interest on the loan	70

2.   Which of the following would appear in the balance sheet as at 30.6.-9 of William, a greengrocer with a lock-up shop. In each case state whether the item is (a) a fixed asset, (b) a current asset, (c) a current liability, and, if none of these, state why:

A contract for 2 years to 19-0 to supply a local restaurant.

A caravan at Brighton for holidays.

A pair of scales.

A life assurance policy paid in advance.

Overdue rent on the shop.

A bank loan.

Amounts owing to wholesalers.

An Austin estate car.

A fur cost for Mrs William paid for from the shop bank account.

Stock of tinned goods.

Costs of redecorating the shop.

A cash register bought in June 19-8.

The amount owing for the cash register. This was paid in August 19-8.

A contract signed in June 19-8 for the erection of a chill room in the shop for £2,000, work to commence in July 19-8. This will enable William to sell fish.

A lease of the shop for seven years signed on 31.12.-6 at an annual rent of £1,500.

A personal computer which Williams uses for business and which William Jr. is using for his studies at the local college.

A refrigerator in the shop owned by A.H.M. Icecream Ltd.

3. "My capital appears on the liabilities side of the balance sheet. I thought that the capital of the business was my main asset." Explain.

4. Draw up a balance sheet for Terry's business as at 30.6.-8 in (a) vertical form including total assets and (b) a vertical form showing working capital and (c) in horizontal form from the following:

	£
Prepaid rent	500
Fixtures and Equipment	6,400
Stock of goods for resale	9,250
Loan at 10% repayable on 1st December 19-8	10,000
Trade Creditors	3,800
Cash in hand	140
Bank Overdraft	2,600
Bank Loan repayable in May 19-9	3,000
Motor Vehicles	11,200
Prepaid insurance	680
Trade Debtors	13,190
Accrued interest on bank loan	400
Estimated cost of repairing in 19-8/-9 faulty goods sold in 19-7/-8	2,100
Leasehold premises	15,000
Prepaid subscriptions	630
Stock of heating oil	350
Accrued Accountancy charges	500

5. A local newspaper reports that Mr John Rich, an accountant aged 45, had died of overwork leaving £260,000. Do you think this means £260,000 in the bank? If not, what might it mean?

Exercises without answers

6. Which of the following would appear as liabilities in a balance sheet at 31st December 19-8, of George, a manufacturer?

(a) A sum owing to Fred, a supplier, for goods supplied in October 19-8.

(b) A sum owing to Sam, a mechanic, for work done on George's car in December 19-8.

(c) Interest on a loan of £10,000 to the business by Dare, lent on 1st November 19-8. The loan carries interest at 12% per annum.

(d) An agreement signed on 5th October 19-8 with Jim to supply a machine for £1,000. The machine was partly constructed at 31.12.-8 and was supplied and invoiced in February 19-9.

(e) An overdraft facility of £2,000 agreed by the bank on 14th December 19-8. At 31.12.-8 George's account was in credit.

7.   Draw up balance sheets for the following businesses.

	Alan	Betty	Ceri	Donald
	£	£	£	£
Creditors	7,430	23,260	7,200	31,400
Vehicles	8,300	40,100	31,000	–
Prepayments	1,420	2,300	1,640	2,300
Accruals	860	1,700	800	900
Capitals	?	89,100	?	150
Bank balance (overdraft)	(2,460)	?	1,240	?
Premises	10,000	25,000	–	15,000
Plant	7,240	1,200	12,600	12,600
Stock	16,300	34,295	15,200	2,000
Debtors	11,200	16,800	9,600	–
Cash in hand	830	–	400	–

Identify the mistakes you have made using the list of common errors in paragraph 16 of the chapter.

8.   Lou owns a grocery and general goods shop in the high street of a small town and he and his family live in rooms at the back of the shop. What accounting conventions would be applied to the balance sheets of his business? What specific problems would exist in applying these conventions?

9.   Consider the following matters in connection with Gail's restaurant business:

(a) She sold her van for £2,000 in December 19-7 and paid the cheque into the bank on 16 December 19-7.
(b) She negotiated an overdraft facility with her bank for £10,000. At 31 December 19-7, the actual overdraft was £2,760.
(c) She paid the rates for the restaurant on 14 November 19-7 for the half year to 31 March 19-8 £2,100.
(d) She ordered a consignment of frozen foods on 18 December 19-7 costing £4,200. These were delivered and invoiced to her on 4 January 19-8.

State precisely how these items would appear (if they do) in the business balance sheet at 31 December 19-7.

10. Ken dies on 1 January 19-8 leaving his car sales business to his cousin Griselda. The accountant provided a balance sheet at 31 December 19-7 for the business showing a capital of £31,200. Griselda's husband Graham was sorry about Ken's death but could not help thinking about how he would spend the £31,000.

Explain Graham's misconception.

11. The accruals of Sid's business at 31 August 19-7 are Rent £200, Rates £521, Electricity £240, Wages £240.

Explain how these items would appear in the balance sheet at 31 August 19-7. Also explain why they appear in the way you have suggested.

12. On 31st October 1979 the financial position of J. Frost was as follows:

Cash at Bank £900, Trade Creditors £1,750, Motor Vehicles (Cost £1,000) £750, Sundry Debtors £1,200, Cash in Hand £50, Stock-in-trade £2,000, Drawings £2,000, Capital at 1st November 1978 £2,600.

During the year ended 31st October 1979 Frost earned a Net Profit of £2,550.

Required:
Prepare J. Frost's Balance Sheet as at 31st October 1979 in vertical form, showing clearly all the totals and sub-totals normally found in a Balance Sheet including "Working Capital".   (RSA)

13. Complete the following table:

	A £	B £	C £	D £	E £	F £
Assets	4,000	6,000			4,000	6,200
Liabilities	1,000		60	8,200	950	8,300
Capital		2,000	450	3,500		

14. Draft balance sheets for Harold, a retailer, from the following figures:

	at 31.12.-7 £	at 31.12.-8 £	at 31.12.-9 £
Land and Buildings	10,000	10,000	10,000
Prepayments	1,200	600	432
Cash in hand	18	142	60
Equipment	6,100	6,200	4,300
Creditors	3,200	7,000	16,000
Loan repayable in 5 yrs	1,000	4,000	10,000
Debtors	4,800	5,100	1,300
Bank overdraft	1,200	–	3,250
Stock	6,300	4,200	3,005
Vehicles	4,820	2,000	1,005
Cash at Bank	–	1,320	–

15. Ted has just started to study for the level 1 examinations of the ACCA. He has been asked by his employers (a firm of accountants) to produce a balance sheet as at 30.11.87 for a client, Silas, a wholesaler of Gubbins. This is his first draft:

BALANCE SHEET 1987

Land and Buildings		60 000
Plant and Equipment		49,888
Motor Vehicles		26235
Current Assets		
Cash in hand	2 537	
Debtors	59 769	
Rates in advance	900	
Insurance in advance	765	
Prepaid vehicle tax	544	——
		64515
		200538
C. Liabs		
Creditors		46 980
Bank Overdraft		23 550
Accruals		165
		987
		240
		128616
		——
Cap		128 716

Required:
Identify the TYPES of error in this presentation. Redraft the balance sheet correctly. Consider if Silas is likely to be aware of the four accounting conventions mentioned in this chapter. Would it be possible to prepare balance sheets without using these conventions? Would such balance sheets be at all useful? What use is the conventional balance sheet you have now prepared?

6. Transactions and their effect on the Balance Sheet

INTRODUCTION

1. A balance sheet is a classified summary of the assets and liabilities of a business at a specific moment in time. It has been likened to a snapshot or a "still" from a moving picture. If successive balance sheets were prepared with only a short time interval between them, each succeeding balance sheet would show small differences in the assets and liabilities.

2. The events which cause changes in the constituent parts of a balance sheet are known as *transactions*. In this chapter we will look at a range of possible transactions and examine their effect on successive balance sheets.

3. In practice, balance sheets are not prepared after each transaction, but in preparing balance sheets at intervals of a year the *accountant* is *summarising* for the *proprietor* (or other user) the *cumulative* effect of all the transactions in that year.

TRANSACTIONS

4. At Fig. 6.1 is the balance sheet of Alfred Harbridge at 31st July followed by a table of some possible transactions (Fig. 6.2) with their effect on the constituent parts of the balance sheet.

Alfred Harbridge . . . costume jewellery wholesaler
Balance Sheet as at 31st July, 19-8

	£	£
Fixed Assets		
Fixtures and Fittings		15,200
Vehicles		17,100
		32,300
Current Assets		
Stock	18,920	
Debtors	21,300	
Cash at Bank	1,250	
Cash in hand	85	41,555
		73,855
Less **Current Liabilities**		
Creditors		16,800
		57,055
Capital		57,055

Remember that capital simply measures the total amount of assets less liabilities.

Fig. 6.1

---

5. TABLE OF TRANSACTIONS

Category		Amount £	Effect on: Assets		Creditors	Capital
(a)	Purchase of a new storage rack, on credit	800	Fixtures	+	Creditors +	0
(b)	Purchase of stock for resale, on credit	1,050	Stock	+	Creditors +	0
(c)	Purchase of second-hand van by cheque	500	Vehicles	+	0	0
			Cash at Bank	−		
(d)	Debtor pays by cheque	720	Debtors	−	0	0
			Cash at Bank	+		
(e)	Payment of a creditor in cash	40	Cash in hand	−	Creditors −	0
(f)	Purchase of stock by cheque	200	Stock	+	0	0
			Cash at Bank	−		

Key: + = increase in an asset or a liability.
     − = decrease in an asset or a liability.
     0 = no effect.

Fig. 6.2

6.   You should make sure that you can follow the effect of each transaction on the balance sheet items.

Note:

(a)   Each transaction changed *two* of the items composing the balance sheet. This is known as the *dual aspect principle.*

(b)   None of these transactions changed the net sum of assets and liabilities; that is, none of them changed the capital. While the detailed components of the balance sheet changed, the total remained the same.

7.   The cumulative effect of the transactions is summarised in a balance sheet after the transactions have been effected (Fig. 6.3).

Alfred Harbridge
Balance Sheet at conclusion of transactions a–f

	£	£
Fixed Assets		
Fixtures and Fittings		16,000
Vehicles		17,600
		33,600
Current Assets		
Stock	20,170	
Debtors	20,580	
Cash at Bank	1,270	
Cash in hand	45	42,065
		75,665
Less **Current Liabilities**		
Creditors		18,610
		57,055
Capital		57,055

Note that the capital has remained unchanged after all these transactions.

Fig. 6.3

---

8.   **Transactions which change the assets and capital of a sole trader.** Fig. 6.4 is a table of some categories of transactions which change individual assets and also the *capital.*

Category		Amount £	Effect on: Assets	Liabilities	Capital
(g)	Cash taken by proprietor for his own private use (drawings).	20	Cash in hand −20	0	−20
(h)	Sale on credit of stock which had cost £30.	55	Debtors +55 Stock −30	0	+25
(i)	Sale for cash of stock which had cost £7.	9	Cash in hand + 9 Stock − 7	0	+2
(j)	Proprietor took a brooch from stock to give to his daughter (= drawings) Brooch had cost £15.	15	Stock −15	0	−15
(k)	Proprietor won a lottery prize and paid the cheque into his business account.	1,000	Cash at Bank +1,000	0	+1,000
(l)	Proprietor inherited a bicycle valued at £50 which he put into the business.	50	Vehicles +50		+50
(m)	Paid by cheque rent for the quarter year to 31st October 1984.	270	Prepayment +270 Cash at Bank −270	0	0

Fig. 6.4

9.   These transactions are more difficult to follow, so we will examine them in detail.

(Item g) The *entity* convention points out that we regard the assets and liabilities in the business as the subject of the balance sheet and disregard all private assets of the proprietor. Consequently when a business asset (part of the cash in hand) ceases to be a business asset and becomes a private asset, the balance sheet must reflect the smaller quantity of cash held as a business asset. Cash or other assets taken from the business by the proprietor are known as *drawings*.

The effect on Capital may be seen in two possible ways:

   (i)   The *net total* of *assets less liabilities* (which = capital) has been reduced by £20.

   (ii) The capital can be seen as a liability of the business to the proprietor. By paying £20 to the proprietor, this liability has been reduced.

Note that the purpose to which the £20 is put is irrelevant to our purposes as we are concerned only with the *business*.

(Item h) As we have seen, assets are usually recorded in the balance sheet at their cost of acquisition. Thus when stock which had cost £30 leaves the business, the asset stock must be reduced by this amount in order to *leave* the rest of the stock at its cost. However, the sale is at a selling price of £55 and the debtors (sums due by customers for goods supplied but not paid for) must go up by £55 as this is the amount due. The effect on the *net total* of *assets less liabilities* is an increase of £25 and hence capital is increased by £25.

You may have noticed that three items in the balance sheet have been affected despite the *dual aspect* principle. We could say that the sale is really *two* transactions viz:

   (i)   The transfer of stock to the customer.
   (ii) The taking of a *profit* of £25.

Each of these transactions has a dual aspect.

(Item i) This is similar to (h).

(Item j) This transaction is similar to (g) but stock is reduced instead of cash. *Drawings* of this type are called *drawings in kind*.

Again, the ultimate use of the brooch is irrelevant to our purposes.

(Item k) This transaction is called *capital introduced*. A *private* asset has been introduced into the business, thus increasing the asset Cash at bank. From the *capital* point of view this can be viewed in two possible ways:

   An increase in assets less liabilities (net assets) which equals capital by definition.
   An increase in the amount owed by the business to the proprietor.

(Item l) This is similar to (k).

(Item m) This anticipates later Chapters when we consider profit computation. Clearly the asset Cash at bank has been reduced by £270, and if we assume that all these transactions occurred very shortly after 31st July 19-8 then the benefit of the rent (the right to occupy the premises) is a future benefit. Hence we regard the payment as bringing into existence an asset "prepayment".

As time goes on the prepayment will cease to be an asset and become an *expense*.

10. *The effect of all these transactions on the business can be summarised as:*

Alfred Harbridge
Balance Sheet at conclusion of transactions a–f

	£	£
Fixed Assets		
Fixtures and Fittings		16,000
Vehicles		17,650
		33,650
Current Assets		
Stock	20,118	
Debtors	20,635	
Prepayment	270	
Cash at Bank	2,000	
Cash in hand	34	43,057
		76,707
Less **Current Liabilities**		
Creditors		18,610
		58,097
Capital		
as at conclusion of transactions a – f		57,055
Add net profit from transactions g – m		27
assets introduced to business		1,050
		58,132
Less Drawings		35
as at date of balance sheet		58,097

You should follow the transactions to see that this balance sheet is correct.

11. You will notice that the Capital section of the balance sheet is an expansion of the previous simple statement of capital £57,055. What we are showing is:

(i)   The capital as it was at the date of the previous balance sheet.
(ii) Changes in the capital since the last balance sheet.

These are usually:
     Introductions of capital
     Profit
     Drawings
and are shown *in this order* with a sub-total £58,132.

This expansion is normally given in balance sheets of sole traders.

THEORY

12. The dual aspect principle means that:

(a) Every transaction will affect *two* items in a balance sheet.
(b) Each item will be affected by the same amount.
(c) The balance sheet will always balance. (Because capital = assets - liabilities).
(d) Total assets will always equal total liabilities plus capital.

13. The points to grasp are:

(a) The balance sheet must always balance because capital is the difference between assets and liabilities. It is helpful to view the balance sheet as firstly, a list of assets and secondly, as a list of claims against those assets. The creditors have the first claims against the assets and the proprietor has *residual* claim against all the rest of the assets.

(b)   By thinking clearly about the effect of a transaction and recognising that two balance sheet items change (two assets, two liabilities, or an asset and a liability), it should be possible to ensure that the balance sheet always balances.

(c)   The capital will only be changed by:

(i)   Profit, for example, stock at cost being changed into debtors at selling price.
(ii)   The proprietor putting private assets (*e.g.* goods or cash) into the business - capital introduced.
(iii) The proprietor taking assets out of the business (goods or cash) for private use - drawings.

PROBLEMS IN IMPLEMENTATION

14.   So far, we have included as liabilities only *current liabilities*. Current liabilities are defined as liabilities which are due and payable within one year of the balance sheet date. In practice most current liabilities are paid within a short time of the balance sheet date. For example, if Leo, a trader pays his suppliers three months after he receives the goods and his balance sheet date is 31st December, 19-8, then the creditors figure at 31st December 19-8 will be the total of goods supplied in October, November and December 19-8. Payment will be made in January, February and March 19-9 respectively.

15.   One particular current liability which is not obviously payable within one year is "bank overdraft". The reason is that the normal agreement with the bank is for the overdraft to be repayable on demand. In practice, banks do not usually demand repayment, and overdraft *facilities* are renewed on a regular basis, sometimes for many years.

Long term liabilities

16.   Some liabilities are payable more than one year after the balance sheet date. These liabilities are called *long term liabilities*. Examples are loans.

The position for long term liabilities in a balance sheet is as in the attached example (Fig. 6.5). The business has assets and current liabi-lities which come to £78,620. The finance to acquire this quantity of net assets came from:

the proprietor	£50,980
long term lenders	£27,640

SUMMARY

17.   (a)   A balance sheet is a view of the assets, liabilities and capital of a business at a *single instant of time*.
(b)   A business will engage in *transactions* which will affect the individual assets and liabilities in a balance sheet.
(c)   The *dual aspect* principle describes the fact that each transaction affects *two* items in a balance sheet.
(d)   Some transactions affect the net total of assets less liabilities. Since capital is defined as assets less liabilities, such transactions affect the capital.
(e)   The capital in a balance sheet usually shows the *balance* as in the previous balance sheet, a summary of changes and the *balance* at the balance sheet date.

These changes are:

introductions of assets into the business by the proprietor
withdrawals of assets (drawings) from the business by the proprietor
profits

(f)   Long term liabilities appear below the capital in the balance sheet of a sole trader (See Fig. 6.5).

POINTS TO NOTE

18.   (a)   Be careful to distinguish the capital of the proprietor from the long term liabilities.

(b)   Interest is usually payable on loans at a percentage rate. Interest accrues (grows) on a time basis. Thus a loan of £10,000 at 20% made on 1st July 19-4 would begin to earn interest from that date at £2,000 a year. In the balance sheet of the borrower at 31st December 19-4, the loan would appear in long term liabilities at £10,000. If the interest had been paid for the half year to 31st December, no liability would appear for interest. However, if the interest for the half year had not been paid, then the interest outstanding £1,000 would appear in *accruals* in current liabilities.

DAVID WATKINS – COMPUTER RETAILER
BALANCE SHEET AS AT 29th FEBRUARY 19-8

Fixed Assets		£
Premises		36,200
Equipment		5,763
Vehicles		20,879
		62,842
Current Assets		
Stock	15,472	
Debtors	31,987	
Prepayments	870	
Cash in hand	715	49,044
		111,886
Less Current Liabilities		
Creditors	23,500	
Accruals	2,131	
Bank Overdraft	7,635	33,266
		78,620
Financed by:		
Capital as at 28th February 19-7	46,589	
Net Profit for the Year	23,541	
	70,130	
Less Drawings	19,150	50,980
Long term liabilities		
Bank Loan repayable 19-1	17,640	
Loan, Aunt Mary at 10% repayable 19-2	10,000	27,640
		78,620

Fig. 6.5

SELF TESTING QUESTIONS
Explain the following words:

(a) *transactions*
(b) *capital*
(c) *dual aspect principle*
(d) *drawings*

(e) *in kind*
(f) *prepayment*
(g) *long term liabilities*

Exercises (Answers begin on page 448)
1. *George started in business as a retailer of office machinery on 1st January 19-7 by transferring £1,000 to his business bank account. On 1st January he completed the following transactions:*

(a) *Regarded his car, valued at £3,000, as a business asset.*
(b) *Purchased on credit from Bill, office machinery for resale - £1,000.*
(c) *Paid the insurance premium for the car for the year ending 31st December 19-7, £220, by cheque.*
(d) *Sold an office machine for £300. He was paid immediately by cheque. The machine had cost £210.*
(e) *Drew £10 from the bank for a petty cash float.*
(f) *Borrowed, interest free, £3,000 by cheque from his aunt with repayment due by half-yearly instalments of £500 beginning on 30th September 19-8.*
(g) *Took £3 from the petty cash to buy himself a theatre ticket.*
(h) *A cheque for £620 was received for redundancy money from his previous employment. He paid this into the business bank account.*
(i) *Sold an office machine which had cost £85 to Ted for £105 on credit.*
(j) *He decided to use a typewriter, which had cost £100, as his office typewriter. It had been included in trading stock.*

Draw up a table to show the effect of these transactions on the assets, liabilities and capital of the business and prepare a balance sheet at the conclusion of the transactions.

2.   Phil's balance sheet as at 31st July 19-8 was:

	£		£	£
Capital	29,800	**Fixed Assets**		
		Premises at cost		10,000
		Vehicles at cost		6,000
				16,000
Current Liabilities		**Current Assets**		
Creditors	6,000	Stock at cost	15,000	
		Debtors	4,000	
		Prepayment	-	
		Cash at bank	800	19,800
	35,800			35,800

Shortly afterwards, the position had become:

	£		£	£
Capital	36,000	**Fixed Assets**		
		Premises at cost		15,000
		Vehicles at cost		9,000
				24,000
Current Liabilities			**Current Assets**	
Creditors	6,600		Stock at cost	14,900	
Overdraft	1,550	8,150	Debtors	4,900	
			Prepayment	350	20,150
		44,150			44,150

Given that there were no drawings, explain the transactions that had probably occurred.

3.   The following is a balance sheet drawn up by Nickleby who is a trainee accountant:

	£		£
Capital	23,407	**Fixed Assets**	
Drawings	(7,100)	Premises	10,000
Profit	6,000	Plant	4,820
Cash introduced	2,000	**Current Assets**	
Current Liabilities		Debtors	4,000
Creditors	3,700	Cash in hand	120
Electricity owing	210	Stock	15,630
Telephone owing	103	Cash at bank	(1,300)
Audit fee due	450	Rent in advance	200
15% loan due 31.12.-8	5,000	Rates in advance	300
	33,770		33,770

Assuming that the figures are all correct, redraft the balance sheet in vertical form to accord with the layout recommended in this book.

4.   Here is the balance sheet of Jon at 31st December 19-8.

		£	£
Fixed Assets			
Land and Buildings at cost		12,000	
Plant and Machinery at cost		23,100	
Vehicles as valued by the proprietor		1,800	
Current Assets			
Debtors	13,100		
Stock	14,300		
Prepayments	850		
Cash in hand	130	28,280	
	c/fwd	65,180	

	b/fwd	65,180
Current Liabilities		
Loan at 15% repayable 19-9	5,000	
Creditors	11,720	
Bank Overdraft	1,690	18,410
		46,770
Capital		43,200

Identify the errors in this balance sheet (there are 7).

Exercises without answers

5. *Gordon's balance sheet at 31st January 19-8 was as follows:*

	£	£
Fixed Assets		
Plant and Machinery		14,900
Vehicles		30,200
		45,100
Current Assets		
Stock	23,000	
Debtors	19,000	
Cash at bank	1,400	43,400
		88,500
Current Liabilities		
Creditors		16,180
		72,320
Capital		57,320
Loan 16%		15,000
		72,320

On 1st February 19-8 the following transactions took place:

(i)   Sold on credit stock which had cost £100 for £180.
(ii)   Received a cheque for £280 from Alf, a debtor.
(iii) Bought a car for £4,200, paying by cheque.
(iv)   Drew a cheque for cash for private purposes £50.
(v)   Bought goods on credit from Jim £346.
(vi)   Gordon drew goods for his own private use which had cost £30.
(vii) A loan from Bert of £5,000 repayable in December 19-8 was received.
(viii) Sold a vehicle which was valued on the balance sheet at £500 for £800. The purchaser agreed to make payment in March.
(ix)   Bought a piece of land for £4,000 paying by cheque.
(x)   Paid rent on his premises £800 being for the three months to 30th April.

Make a list showing the effect of each of these transactions on the assets, liabilities and capital and draft the balance sheet at the end.

6. *The balance sheet of Gill at 31 December 19-7 showed:*

	£		£
Capital	2,095	Fixed Assets	500
Creditors	429	Stock	760
Accruals – rent	80	Debtors	1,020
		Bank	324
	2,604		2,604

During January 19-8, the following transactions occurred:

(a) Gill introduced his car valued at £2,000 into the business.
(b) Rent paid for the 3 months ending 28th February 19-8 - £240.
(c) A debtor paid £200.
(d) Paid a creditor £129.
(e) Gill withdrew £100 for her own use.

(f) Bought goods on credit for £700.
(g) Sold on credit goods that had cost £205 for £348.
(h) Borrowed £100 interest free from Dan, the sum is repayable in August 19-8.
(i) Bought by cheque a red van for £1,500.
(j) Drew a cheque for cash £20 for a petty cash float.
(k) Bought goods for £150 paying by cheque.

Required:
    (a) Draw up a table showing the effect of each transaction on individual assets and liabilities and on capital.
    (b) Draw up a balance sheet in good form as at 31 January 19-8.

7.   Here are the balance sheets of Joan on two dates, a week apart.

June 1st

	£		£
Capital	8,240	Plant	3,200
Creditors	1,830	Vehicles	4,350
Overdraft	-	Stock	1,700
		Debtors	-
		Cash at bank	820
	10,070		10,070

June 8th

	£		£
Capital	11,550	Plant	5,600
Creditors	2,030	Vehicles	6,350
Overdraft	420	Stock	1,650
		Debtors	400
		Cash at bank	-
	14,000		14,000

Required:
    (a) Explain the transactions that seem to have occurred.
    (b) Redraft the June 8th Balance Sheet in *good form*.

8.   The following table shows the cumulative effects of a succession of separate transactions on the assets and liabilities of a business.

Transaction: *Assets*	£000	A £000	B £000	C £000	D £000	E £000	F £000	G £000	H £000	I £000
Land and buildings	500	500	535	535	535	535	535	535	535	535
Equipment	230	230	230	230	230	230	230	200	200	200
Stocks	113	140	140	120	120	120	120	120	119	119
Trade debtors	143	143	143	173	160	158	158	158	158	158
Prepaid expenses	27	27	27	27	27	27	27	27	27	27
Cash at bank	37	37	37	37	50	50	42	63	63	63
Cash on hand	9	9	9	9	9	9	9	9	9	3
	1,059	1,086	1,121	1,131	1,131	1,129	1,121	1,112	1,111	1,105
Liabilities										
Capital	730	730	730	740	740	738	733	724	723	717
Loan	120	120	155	155	155	155	155	155	155	155
Trade creditors	168	195	195	195	195	195	195	195	195	195
Accrued expenses	41	41	41	41	41	41	38	38	38	38
	1,059	1,086	1,121	1,131	1,131	1,129	1,121	1,112	1,111	1,105

Required:
Identify clearly and as fully as you can what transaction has taken place in each case. Give TWO possible explanations for transaction I. Do not copy out the table but use the reference letter for each transaction.
    (AAT)

Bookkeeping

The next two chapters introduce the subject of bookkeeping. All the transactions of a business are recorded using a bookkeeping system and summarised into financial statements at least annually. The process is as follows:

(a) Transactions take place (*e.g.* sales, purchases, receipts, payments).

(b) Documents evidencing the transactions are created (invoices, cheque stubs, etc).

(c) Entries are made in the books of account.

(d) Production of financial statements.

The process of entering the details of transactions in the books of account is known as bookkeeping. Bookkeeping is done in a formal manner using the method known as double entry bookkeeping. Chapter 7 outlines the objectives and includes an historical note. Chapter 8 introduces the entries for assets and liabilities including cash at bank.

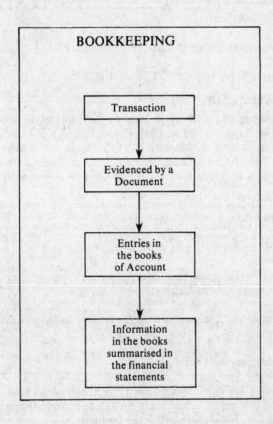

7. Objectives and Origins of Double Entry Bookkeeping

INTRODUCTION

1. The method of bookkeeping known as double entry bookkeeping is practised worldwide and has a long history. This chapter outlines the purposes served by bookkeeping, explores its origins, begins your study of how it is done and concludes with a note on the involvement of computers in bookkeeping.

BOOKKEEPING FULFILS NEEDS

2. The following are the objectives of keeping books of accounts:

(a) A permanent record is made of all transactions.

(b) Management have a continuous record of debtors (who owe the business money) and creditors (who the business owes money to).

(c) Management can control and safeguard the business assets (fixed assets, cash at bank, etc.).

(d) Managers have *information*, without which management would be impossible.

(e) The law requires certain records - PAYE, VAT, Statutory sick pay, for all businesses. Companies are required to maintain certain specified records.

(f) Failure to maintain records can be an offence in bankruptcy.

(g) Records are essential for the production of financial statements.

LUCA PACIOLI AND THE ITALIAN METHOD

3. Double entry bookkeeping developed gradually in Italy in the years after about 1200 AD. By the end of the fifteenth century the method was well established and in 1494 an Italian monk and mathematician Fra Luca Pacioli published a great work on mathematics. One of the sections of this book was a treatise on double entry bookkeeping which is the oldest surviving text book on accounting. It is available in English translation in several versions and I commend it to you. There have been developments since 1494 but in essence the method is still used today.

4. Pacioli is especially good at disciplining his readers in making entries so that they can avoid errors. He includes a chapter summarising the rules. Among them are:

(a) All entries must be double, that is if you make one creditor you must make one debtor.

(b) Each entry in the debit or in the credit must contain three things; viz. the day of the payment, the amount of the payment and the reason for the entry.

These are examples of his very simple instructions. Bookkeepers have failed to keep them for nearly five centuries.

DEBIT AND CREDIT

5. The essence of the double entry method is:

(a) The keeping of a book or a series of books called the books of account or simply "the books".
(b) The division of each book into separate "accounts". Account is another word for *story*. A separate account is required for each subject on which a record is to be kept.
(c) Each account is divided into two halves, a left-hand side called the debit (abbreviated to Dr) and a right-hand side called the credit (Cr). It is advisable to memorise, now, which side is which.
(d) All transactions are entered on *two* accounts (hence double entry); on the debit side of one account and the credit side of another.

COMPUTERISED RECORDS

6. Bookkeeping has traditionally been carried out by bookkeepers in bound books of good quality paper. However bookkeeping is a tedious process and the costs of the skilled labour required for a complete set of records has become very high in the 1980's. Various devices were developed to mechanise the process including accounting machines and punched card machines.

7.   The invention of the computer and especially the cheap micro computer has brought automated bookkeeping within the financial means of almost all businesses. It has been suggested that the existence of cheap hardware (the actual machines) and software packages (the computer programs) will make the accountant and the bookkeeper redundant. This is unlikely to be so because:

(a)   The computer has not changed the fundamentals of bookkeeping, only the method of processing and the media on which the information is stored. A ledger account recorded on a floppy disc is still a ledger account.

(b)   Using and interpreting the information recorded in the "books" requires a technical knowledge of the processes and organisation of bookkeeping information. This knowledge is not usually held by computer people.

(c)   Bookkeeping is not an end in itself but a means to an end (or several ends). The bookkeeper and accountant use the information in their work. For example, the chasing of slow payers is still required whatever medium is used for bookkeeping.

SUMMARY

8.   (a)   Bookkeeping fulfills several business needs. It is also a statutory requirement in many cases.

(b)   Double Entry bookkeeping developed in renaissance Italy. The earliest surviving text book is that of Luca Pacioli published in 1494.

(c)   The essence of bookkeeping is the entering of the details of transactions in separate accounts. Each account is in effect a story about some relevant subject - an asset, a liability, an expense, a revenue etc.

(d)   Accounts have two sides - a debit on the left and credit on the right.

(e)   "Books" are now frequently kept by computers with the information stored on magnetic discs. This changes the processes and storage media but has left bookkeeping unchanged in its essence.

POINTS TO NOTE

9.   (a)   A book in which double entry accounts are kept is called a *ledger*. The accounts themselves are sometimes called ledger accounts.

(b)   If double entry accounts are maintained on a computer, the expressions, accounts, ledgers, books are still used.

SELF TESTING QUESTIONS

(a)   List the objectives of bookkeeping. (2).
(b)   What may be the effect of computers on bookkeepers and accountants? (7).
(c)   What is:

(i)   An account.
(ii)   A ledger.
(iii) The debit side.

(d)   Why will computerisation not make accountants obsolete? (7).
(e)   What are the "books"? (5).

Exercises (Answers begin on page 449)

1.   Ognir Ltd trades as a music publisher. The company buy from printers and other suppliers on credit and sell to retailers also on credit. Payment of royalties is made to each composer on a quarterly basis based on sales of that composer's music in that quarter. The company trades on an overdraft and needs to monitor the amount closely. The company are registered for VAT and employ 5 staff. The company monitor the sales of each composer's work and have to continuously make decisions on whether or not to publish new and existing composers.

The books are kept by a part-qualified trainee certified accountant. The directors are considering making him redundant, buying a computer and appointing a computer operator with no knowledge of bookkeeping or account-ing to maintain the computerised records.

Why is it necessary for the company to maintain good double entry records? How can the current bookkeeper argue to keep his job if a computer is installed?

Exercises without answers

2.   Dave is setting up a business wholesaling widgets. He will employ 5 workers and have a bank overdraft facility of £5,000.

Explain to Dave why he will need comprehensive double entry records.

3.   Dave, a manufacturer, is considering using a computer with some accounting packages to do his bookkeeping. He reckons that by using a computer, he can use a person who has only office skills and some moderate typing ability and thus not employ a more expensive person with a knowledge of bookkeeping and accounting. Is he right?

4.   Locate a copy of Luca Pacioli's great work and read some or all of it.

8. Asset and Liability Accounts

INTRODUCTION

1. One of the major functions of bookkeeping is the keeping of records of assets and liabilities. It is important that a businessman should know what assets and liabilities his business has, including how much and *from* whom money is owed and how much and *to* whom money is owed.

ASSET ACCOUNTS AND LIABILITY ACCOUNTS

2. Every account has two sides and students have to learn which side entries should go. Remember that:

   (a) Entries on *asset* accounts are made on the *debit* side if the entry records an increase in the asset.
   (b) Entries on the *liability* accounts are made on the *credit* side if the entry is an increase in the liability.

3. Here are some transactions carried out by Steven, a trader in 19-8.

Jan 1	Purchased a Ford delivery van on credit from Adam	£2,400
Jan 10	Purchased a display cabinet from Brian on credit	£130
Jan 12	Purchased a small warehouse from Charles for £10,000 with the help of a loan from David of £8,000. He will pay Charles the balance later.	
Jan 19	Purchased an Austin Delivery van from Eric on credit	£4,000
Jan 20	He sold the first van on credit to Fred. He was able to obtain the same price that he had paid.	

These would be entered in the books as:

DEBITS   **CREDITS**

Dr.   Delivery Vans Account   Cr.
                                      £   £

1.1.-8	Adam – Ford	2,400	20.1.-8	Fred – Ford	2,400
19.1.-8	Eric – Austin	4,000	20.1.-8	Balance c/d	4,000
		6,400			6,400
20.1.-8	Balance b/d	4,000			

Fixtures and Equipment Account

| 10.1.-8 | Brian – Display Cabinet | 130 | | | |

Warehouse Account

| 12.1.-8 | Charles | 10,000 | | | |

Adam Account

| | | | 1.1.-8 | Delivery Van | 2,400 |

Brian Account

| | | | 10.1.-8 | Display Cabinet | 130 |

Charles Account

| 12.1.-8 | David – Loan | 8,000 | 19.1.-8 | Warehouse | 10,000 |

Eric Account

| | | | 19.1.-8 | Van | 4,000 |

David Account

| | | | 12.1.-8 | Loan for Warehouse | 8,000 |

Fred Account

20.1.-8   Delivery Van   2,400

Note:

    (a) Each entry consists of a date, an amount, and a description of the transaction. The description may consist of the opposite account name (e.g. the Display cabinet was bought from Brian) and/or a description of the transaction. There are no rules on this.

    (b) A separate account is opened for each asset or for each class of asset.

    (c) A separate account is opened for each debtor and each creditor.

    (d) The sale of the van to Fred goes on the credit side of the delivery van as it reduces the asset.

Having entered the three transactions in the delivery vans account, it is desirable to compute the overall effect, and so a balance is struck, by entering the difference between the two sides on the lesser amount side and giving the description-balance carried down (c/d). The double entry is completed by entering the same amount lower down and describing the entry as balance brought down (b/d).

4. Steven could review his books so far and would see that:

    (a) **Accounts with entries on the debit side (assets)**
        He has a delivery van which had cost £4,000.
        He has fixtures and equipment which had cost £130.
        He has a warehouse which had cost £10,000.
        He is owed £2,400 by Fred.

    (b) **Accounts with entries on the credit side (liabilities)**
        He has liabilities in that he owes

£2,400 to Adam	£8,000 to David
£130 to Brian	£4,000 to Eric
£2,000 to Charles	

THE CASH BOOK

5. (a) One of the more important assets of a business is cash. In practice businesses keep very little cash on the premises and cash is kept in the bank. Consequently, the account which records cash transactions normally records the transactions going through the bank account.

    (b) In practice, a business has so many transactions in the bank account that a separate book is required to record them. The account is thus usually called the *cash book*.

6. Steven's business had the following transactions which *at the time* involved the bank account:

Jan 1	Paid into the business bank account from private sources	£6,000
Jan 3	Lent to Henry	£500
Jan 9	Purchased a typewriter paying by cheque	£400
Jan 24	Paid Brian	£130
Jan 27	Paid Charles	£500 on account
Jan 30	Received from Fred	£2,400

These would be entered in the cash book like this.

Dr.		£			Cr. £
1.1.-8	Capital – Steven	6,000	3.1.-8	Henry	500
30.1.-8	Fred	2,400	9.1.-8	Typewriter	400
			24.1.-8	Brian	130
			27.1.-8	Charles	500
			31.1.-8	Balance c/d	6,870
		8,400			8,400
31.1.-8	Balance b/d	6,870			

Note:

(a) *Money going into the bank goes into the debit side - it increases the asset, cash at bank.*

(b) *Money going out of the bank (cheques etc) goes on the credit side (it reduces the asset, cash at bank).*

(c) *By summing both sides and inserting the balance c/d on the side with the smallest money total of entries, we determine how much money is in the bank at the conclusion of the series of transactions.*

7. Let us now complete the double entry of the bank transactions.

DEBITS			CREDITS	

Brian Account

		£			£
24.1.-8	Cash	130	10.1.-8	Display Cabinet	130

Capital Account

			1.1.-8	Cash	6,000

Fred Account

20.1.-8	Delivery van	2,400	30.1.-8	Cash	2,400

Henry Account

30.1.-8	Cash	500			

Office Equipment Account

9.1.-8	Cash - Typewriter	400			

Charles Account

27.1.-8	Cash	500	19.1.-8	Warehouse	2,000
31.1.-8	Balance c/d	1,500			
		2,000			2,000
			31.1.-8	Balance b/d	1,500

Note:

(a) *I have not included the account for the vans, the fixtures, Adam, Eric, the warehouse or David as no cash entries were required.*

(b) *Fred's account and Brian's account now have the same monetary amount on each side. The accounts are said to have nil balances and as you will realise, Fred no longer owes anything to the business and the business owes nothing to Brian.*

(c) *The capital account represents the amount owed (it is a credit balance) to the owner of the business, Steve.*

8. Reviewing the accounts we now have:

(a) Debit balances - accounts with more money amounts on the debit than on the credit side:

	£
Delivery vans	4,000
Fixtures and equipment	130
Warehouse	10,000
Cash at bank	6,870
Henry	500
Office equipment	400
Total	21,900

(b) Credit balances - accounts with more money amounts on the credit side than the debit side:

	£
Adam	2,400
Charles	1,500
Eric	4,000
David	8,000
Capital	6,000
	21,900

9. **You will notice:**

(a) The total of the debit balances equals the total of the credit balances. This is a very useful verification of the accuracy of entries.

(b) A balance sheet could be drawn up very easily as:

Steven

Balance Sheet as at 31st January 19–8

Fixed Assets	£	£
Warehouse at cost		10,000
Delivery van at cost		4,000
Fixtures and Equipment at cost		130
Office Equipment at cost		400
		14,530
Current Assets		
Debtors	500	
Cash at bank	6,870	7,370
		21,900
Less **Current Liabilities**		
Creditors		15,900
		6,000
Capital		6,000

Note:

I have assumed that David's loan to the business is repayable before 31.1.-9 and so I have totalled the creditors and not shown them individually.

SUMMARY

10. (a) Separate accounts are kept for each class of fixed asset, each debtor, each creditor and the cash at bank.

(b) Increases in asset accounts are entered on the Dr side.

(c) Decreases in asset accounts are entered on the Cr side.

(d) Increases in liability accounts are entered on the Cr side.

(e) Decreases in liability accounts are entered on the Dr side.

(f) When it is desired to sum up the entries in an account, both sides are summed and "balance c/d" is entered on the side with the smallest money total. The balance b/d is entered below, on the opposite side to balance c/d.

(g) The cash at bank account is often entered in a special book, the cash book. Money deposited at the bank is entered on the debit side, cheques and other withdrawals on the credit.

(h) Every debit is matched with an equal credit and vice versa.

(i) An account with a larger debit money total than credit money total is called a debit balance. The converse accounts are credit balances.

(j) The total of all debit balances should equal the total of all the credit balances. The list of all the balances, made up to see if the debit total equals the credit total is called a *trial balance*.

(k) A balance sheet can be extracted very easily from a set of books kept on double entry lines or from the trial balance.

POINTS TO NOTE

11. (a) There are few difficulties in this chapter. However the rules must be *learnt by heart* and applied rigidly.

(b) Common errors include:

Failing to complete the double entry.
Entering the balance c/d and balance b/d on the wrong sides.
Omission of dates.
Failing to open a separate account for *each* debtor and creditor.
Inadequate descriptions.
Untidiness.

(c) There is no need to balance off an account if the balance is obvious. For example:

Mitchell Account

14.6.-8   Invoice   £136

Nothing is gained by adding balance c/d to the credit and balance b/d to the debit.

or

Vehicles Account

		£
15.6.-8	Ford	2,564
	Austin	3,210
	Triumph	6,935
		12,709

It is obvious the balance is £12,709 and balance c/d, balance b/d are superfluous.

SELF TESTING QUESTIONS

(a) *An increase in an asset is recorded on which side of an asset account? (3).*
(b) *On which side of the cash book are receipts entered? (6).*
(c) *What is a debit balance? (10).*
(d) *What is a trial balance? (10).*
(e) *When should an account be balanced off? (11).*

Exercises (Answers begin on page 449)

1. *The following are transactions completed by Bennett in his first week's trading:*

Jan 2   Paid £4,000 into a business bank account.
Jan 3   Borrowed £2,000 from Vokes.
Jan 4   Bought on credit, office equipment from Fellows £600, a typewriter from Rowes £300, a copier from Robertson £300.
         Lent £4,000 to Pinkney, and £600 to Richards.
Jan 5   Bought on credit a property for £5,000 from Rackman.
Jan 6   Paid £600 to Fellows and £150 to Rowes. Drew from the bank for private purposes £100.
Jan 7   Bought a car, paying by cheque £700. Paid £50 to Rowes.

Enter all these transactions in double entry accounts; bring down balances where needed (i.e. when balance is not obvious); extract a trial balance; draw up a balance sheet in good form.

2. *The following are transactions of Wood in the week beginning 10th June:*

June 10   Paid £4,500 into his business bank account. Introduced his Jaguar car valued at £2,000 into the business. Bought on credit a machine from Elm £1,200. Paid out a cheque for another machine £600.

June 11 *Borrowed £14,000 from Beech and purchased a property for £12,000 from Gray paying by cheque.*

June 12 *Sold the Jaguar car on credit to Elder for £1,600. Bought a Daimler car from Larch for £3,000 paying £1,500 immediately and agreeing to pay the rest in July.*

June 13 *Paid Elm £100.*

June 14 *Received £400 from Elder.*

June 15 *Lent Tree £100 and Bush £500.*

June 16 *Drew £1,000 from the bank for private purposes. Paid £200 to Douglas for goods to be delivered as soon as they were completed.*

Enter all these transactions in double entry accounts; bring down balances where needed; extract a trial balance and draw up a balance sheet in good form.

Exercises without answers

3.   *The following transactions occurred in Phil's business in his first week's trading in 19-7.*

Mar 23   *Paid £3,000 into his business bank account*

Mar 23   *Brought his van valued at £1,500 into the business*

Mar 23   *Borrowed £600 from Janice*

Mar 24   *Bought on credit a machine from Lawton £700*

Mar 25   *Bought on credit a property from Will £4,000*

Mar 26   *Lent Joe £500*

Mar 26   *Paid Lawton £100 on account*

Mar 26   *Bought a car from Ralph paying by cheque £2,000*

Mar 26   *Joe repaid £150*

Mar 26   *Received a credit note from Ralph of £200 as the car was faulty and the price was reduced*

Mar 27   *Paid Janice £300 on account.*

Required:

Enter all these transactions in double entry accounts; bring down the balances where needed (i.e. where the balance is not obvious); extract a trial balance; check the trial balance to ensure all the Dr balances are assets and all Cr balances are liabilities; (draw up a balance sheet in good form).

9. The Trial Balance

INTRODUCTION

1. This chapter considers the structure and role of the trial balance in bookkeeping and points out that some errors can be detected by a difference on a trial balance and some cannot.

TAKING OUT A TRIAL BALANCE

2. In a double entry *system*, entries are made such that:
    (a) every debit entry has a corresponding credit entry; and
    (b) every credit entry has a corresponding debit entry.

Thus the total of debits should equal the total credits. In order to discover if this is so, a trial balance can be *extracted*. This is not done by summarising the debits and credits on each account but by taking out the balances on each.

Example: here is a double entry asset account recording the amount in the bank account of Fiona, a trader:

Cash book

		£			£
January 5	Capital introduced	750	January 7	Equipment	500
January 8	Loan from Godfrey	200	January 9	Loan to Henry	375

In order to extract a trial balance it is first necessary to balance off all the accounts. Thus:

Cash book

		£			£
January 5	Capital introduced	750	January 7	Equipment	500
January 8	Loan from Godfrey	200	January 9	Loan to Henry	375
			January 9	Balance c/d	75
		950			950

January 10	Balance b/d	75	

The usual form of a trial balance is:

Fiona
Trial balance as at 9 January

	Dr	Cr
Capital		750
Loan to Henry	375	
Cash at bank	75	
Equipment	500	
Loan from Godfrey		200
	950	950

Note that a *debit balance* is the balance on an account where the money total on the debit is greater than the money total on the credit side and a *credit* balance is the converse. Debit balances go in the debit column of the trial balance.

ERRORS IN TRIAL BALANCES

3. Some errors are revealed by a trial balance. These include:

   (a) a debit entry has no corresponding credit;
   (b) a credit has no corresponding debit;
   (c) the debit and credit sides of a double entry are of different amounts;
   (d) a debit (or credit) entry which should have a corresponding credit has instead another debit (or credit) (this is a common error as students do not always know which side of an account to make an entry).

4. Some errors are not revealed by a trial balance:

   (a) complete omission of a required double entry for a transaction;

(b)   entries on the wrong account (eg a credit on T Jones account instead of G Jones account);

(c)   double entries are made but of the wrong amount (eg a payment of £23 was entered in both the required accounts as £32 - this is called *transposition* of figures and is a common error).

USES OF THE TRIAL BALANCE

5.   The trial balance has several uses:

(a)   as a check on the accuracy of bookkeeping - but note that not all errors are revealed by differences on trial balances;

(b)   as a list of balances which can be assembled into a Balance Sheet or, as we shall see soon, into a Profit and Loss Account and a Balance Sheet.

WHICH SIDE SHOULD A BALANCE APPEAR ON

6.   In a trial balance different types of balances appear always on a particular side. So far the types of account we have met should appear as:

Debit side	*Credit side*
All assets	All liabilities
Debtors	Creditors
Cash at bank	Capital
Cash in hand	Bank overdraft

Note that capital can appear on the debit side if the proprietor has drawn more from the business than he/she has put in.

If you are given a trial balance and see an entry: Jones £238 you can tell if Jones is a debtor or creditor by noting which side of the trial balance it is entered on. Examiners often enter 'bank balance £x' in a trial balance without specifying whether it is cash at bank or an overdraft. Once again the side of the balance gives you the clue needed.

SUMMARY

7.   (a)   A trial balance is a summary of the balances in a double entry system showing, in two columns, the debit balances and the credit balances. The two columns should have the same total.

(b)   Trial balances are designed to provide a check on the accuracy of double entry bookkeeping but not all errors are revealed by a difference in the trial balance.

(c)   Trial balances are used also to provide the raw material from which Financial Statements (balance sheets etc) can be prepared.

POINTS TO NOTE

8.   It is a useful check to go through trial balances to see what the accounts mean. If a balance is on a particular side it can only have a limited range of meanings. Assets are *always* debits and liabilities are *always* credits.

SELF TESTING QUESTIONS

(a)   What is a debit balance?
(b)   What errors are indicated by a difference in a trial balance?
(c)   What errors are not revealed by a difference on a trial balance?
(d)   What are the uses of a trial balance?
(e)   On what side of a trial balance would the following appear:

  (i)   assets;
  (ii)   cash at bank;
  (iii)   liabilities;
  (iv)   a bank overdraft;
  (v)   capital;
  (vi)   debtors;
  (vii)   creditors;
  (viii)   cash in hand.

Exercises (answers begin on page 449)

1. From the following list of transactions, enter the detail in double entry accounts and extract a trial balance and prepare a balance sheet as at 15 January for Henri's business:

January 1   Henri paid in to the bank £1,700 from his private resources.
January 2   Paid cheque for a motor car £500.
January 3   Bought a word processor for £1,200 on credit from William.
January 4   Borrowed £700 from Philip.
January 5   Bought a copying machine paying by cheque £800.
January 6   Lent James £100.
January 7   Repaid Philip £60.
January 8   Drew £70 from the bank for private use.
January 9   Introduced a desk valued at £200 into the business.
January 10   Paid William by cheque £90.
January 15   Bought a display counter for £920 paying by cheque.

Exercises without answers

2. From the following trial balance prepare a balance sheet in good order:

Wulfruna - trial balance as at 31 March 19-5

	Dr £	Cr £
Capital		12,500
Drawings	1,700	
Smith	2,000	
Office equipment	5,800	
Brown		720
Robinson	3,500	
Bank balance		620
Rowland	1,000	
Shelley	100	
Tromans	40	
Upton		300
	14,140	14,140

3. From the following list of transactions of Ellen enter the double entry accounts and extract a trial balance and a balance sheet as at 10 February 19-8.

19X8

February 1   Introduced a car into the business worth £3,000.
February 2   Bought equipment on credit from Archie £1,900.
February 3   Obtained an overdraft facility from Mercian Bank plc £10,000.
February 4   Paid by cheque for office equipment £300.
February 5   Borrowed £2,000 from Patel.
February 6   Sold some of the equipment to Harris on credit fro £100 making no profit or loss.
February 7   Drew £125 from the bank for private use.
February 8   Paid Patel £200 by cheque.
February 9   Drew cash from the bank £70 for business purposes.
February 10 Paid Washington £1,240 for rent for the three months ending 10 May 19-8.

The Trading Account

The next two chapters introduce the study of profit measurement. Chapter 10 deals with the measurement of the profit earned by trading, that is buying and selling. Chapter 11 deals with the bookkeeping entries required to supply the information necessary to prepare the trading account. Finally Chapter 12 deals with the asset of stock.

10. The Trading Account

INTRODUCTION

1. (a) This chapter begins a study of *profit* measurement by introducing the *trading account*.
    (b) Two more accounting conventions are discussed, the realisation convention and the matching convention.
    (c) The gross profit percentage and average mark-up are described and calculated.

THE FORMAT OF THE TRADING ACCOUNT

2. The format of the trading account is a matter of personal taste. A common format is this.

	£	£	Line
Henry – his business			1
Trading account for the year ending 30th June 19-8			2
	£	£	3
Sales		100,000	4
Less Cost of goods sold:			5
Opening stock	24,000		6
Purchases	71,000		7
Available for sale	95,000		8
Less Closing stock	27,000		9
		68,000	10
Gross Profit		32,000	11

3. We will deal with each line in turn.

Line 1
It is essential to identify the *business entity*. Remember that it is the business profit that is being measured. Henry's other interests are excluded.

Line 2
A precise title to the financial statement is required. The heading must also identify exactly the time period concerned.

Line 3
It may seem obvious that financial statements give information in terms of pounds sterling (or other currency). However, good practice requires an indication of the standard of measure used.

Line 4
Sales is a technical term. It means:

(a) Sales of *goods dealt in*. For example, a greengrocer sells fruit and vegetables, a garage sells cars and petrol. Businesses may occasionally sell other things, for example redundant fixed assets. Such items are not "sales" in the technical sense and should not be included in the "sales" figure in the trading account.

(b) Sales made in the period. This means the *inclusion* of goods *sold in the period* for which the cash was received in the period and also for which cash was received in the preceding period or the next period. It *excludes* sales made in other periods even if the cash was received in *this* period.

Note that this is *not what the layman would imagine.*

Line 5

Sales represents the sum of all the individual sales made in the period. Cost of goods sold represents the sum of all the cost prices of the items sold in the year. In practice this is difficult to measure. For example, a shopkeeper always records a sale (*e.g.* of an orange) but does not usually record at the same time what that orange cost him.

Instead, lines 6 to 10 are used to calculate the input cost of all the goods sold in the period.

Line 6

Opening stock is the value of the items in stock at the beginning of the year. The value was obtained by:

   (a) Identifying each category of stock.

   (b) Counting, weighing or measuring the quantity of each category of stock.
   (c) Determining the cost (*not* the selling price) of each category.
   (d) Valuing each category by multiplying quantity x cost price.
   (e) Sum the values of the individual categories to find the total cost of stock owned.

Line 7

"Purchases" is also a technical term. It means:

   (a) All purchases of *goods dealt in* (bicycles for bicycle shop, widgets for a widget wholesaler). Only goods intended for resale in the normal course of business should be included.

      Exclude
      (i)   purchases of fixed assets
      (ii)   purchases of goods which are intended for use but not for resale (*e.g.* cleaning materials or office stationery).

   (b) *All* purchases made in the period even if payment was made in preceding or following periods.

Note again that this is not what is intuitively expected.

Line 8

We now have all the goods that could be sold, namely:

   What was in stock at the beginning of the year.
   What was bought during the year.

Line 9

Closing stocks represents the cost price of all the stock owned at the end of the period. If the cost price of all the goods available for sale in the period was £95,000 and the cost price of the goods unsold at the end, was £27,000, then the cost price of the goods sold in the period must have been £68,000.

Line 10

Cost of goods sold. Note that this is at the *cost* to the enterprise.

Line 11

Gross profit. If a good is sold for £1.00 and it had cost the business 68p, then a profit of 32p is made. The gross profit of the period is the sum of the profits made on all the goods sold in the period.

The gross (= large or fat) profit is thus the difference between the selling price and the cost price of all the goods sold in the period.

All businesses incur overhead expenses (rent, rates, wages etc), and the net (= after necessary deductions) profit is the gross profit less the overhead expenses. This is dealt with in Chapter 11.

THEORY AND CRITICISM

4. The Realisation convention

This convention means that accountants only recognise a profit when the good is sold.

Consider the following sequence of events in Henry's business:

Jan 10   Ordered a widget from Joe.
Mar 4   The widget is delivered to Henry invoiced at £100 and placed in stock by Henry.
May 11   Henry paid Joe.
June 4   Order received by Henry for the widget from Keith.
June 7   The widget is delivered to Keith and invoiced at £140.
Aug 14   Keith pays

At what date has Henry earned a profit?

There are several possibilities, but the use of the realisation convention means that June 7th is the date selected.

Henry - Trading Account for year ending 30th June, 19–8

				Inclusion of the widget deal	
	£	£	£	£	
Sales		100,000		140	(June 7)
Less cost of goods sold:					
Opening stock	24,000		–		
Purchases	71,000		100		(March 4)
Available for sale	95,000		100		
Closing stock	27,000	68,000	–	100	
Gross Profit		32,000		40	

Criticism of the realisation convention

5. The realisation convention has been criticised for the following reasons:

(a) It is unduly pessimistic and conservative. Profit in a period is *restricted* to those gains which have been *realised* through a transaction which gives legal rights to receive an agreed sum of money.

(b) It is unduly optimistic as sales made in a period where the customer has not paid by the period end may not result in cash being received. In practice, the majority of sales on credit do result in cash.

(c) It distorts the process of measuring income in successive time periods. Accounting purports to measure profit by comparing "wealth" at the end of the period with wealth at the beginning and yet increases in value which have not been realised (turned into cash or a legally enforceable debt) are excluded from this wealth.

(d) It is inappropriate in businesses with a long trading cycle such as ship builders, civil engineers and building contractors. In practice, modifications to the convention are applied in such cases.

6. The matching convention

This is a more general convention than the realisation convention but is closely related. It implies that revenue (= income, especially from making a sale) should be matched with associated costs and expenses and both dealt with in the same period.

In a trading account, which measures the profit from the sale of goods, the matching convention is clearly demonstrated in that sales are matched with the cost of the goods sold.

In businesses, other than retail and wholesale, the matching convention is much more difficult to apply and we will deal with this more in a later chapter.

7. Problems in Implementation

Cut off

The matching convention is strictly applied in practice but a problem called *cut off* causes more errors in accounting than any other.

Consider the following sequence of events:

June 27 Alf despatches goods by rail to Henry and invoices them at £108.
June 30 Henry counts the stock in his warehouse.
July 3 The goods are delivered to Henry.

The trading account should include for this event:

	£	
Sales		-
Opening Stock		-
Purchases	108	
Available for sale	108	
Less closing stock	108	-
Gross profit		-

Because the goods were despatched to and invoiced to Henry in the year to June 30th, they should be included in purchases of that year and as they were owned by Henry at June 30th, they were part of this stock. However, as they were in *transit* at the year end, they were not counted at the stocktake and unless great care is taken to identify such matters, stock will be understated.

Any failure to apply cut off precisely will mean that the matching convention is not properly applied.

RETURNS

8. Sales are made and evidenced by invoices. However:

    (a) The invoice may have an error, resulting in overcharging.
    (b) the goods may be returned by the cus-tomer as damaged, unsuitable or not as ordered.
    (c) The goods may be lost in transit.

In such cases, the business will issue a *credit note*.

The effect of (a) to (c) is that the amount of the sale evidenced by the invoice is overstated. The true sales figure must be the sum of invoices less the sum of credit notes.

Example:	£
Total invoices in the year	100,000
Total credit notes in year	4,000
Entry in the Trading Account - Sales	96,000
or	
Sales	100,000
Less sales returns	4,000
	£96,000

9. Purchases evidenced by suppliers invoices may also be returned and evidenced by credit notes. Treatment in the trading account is similar to the treatment of sales returns.

CARRIAGE

10. Supplier may include the cost of transporting the goods from their premises to the buyer in the invoice price. Alternatively, they may not, in which case the buyer will need to arrange for and pay for such transport.

In the second case, the cost of transport is part of the cost of the goods supplied and "purchases" in the trading account should include such costs. Treatment will usually be:

	£	£
Purchases	46,000	
Carriage Inwards	1,800	47,800

or simply:

		£
Purchases		47,800

FINDING SALES AND PURCHASES

11. The procedures for finding the total sales and total purchases in an accounting period are dealt with in a later chapter, but in outline they are:

Sales are found by:

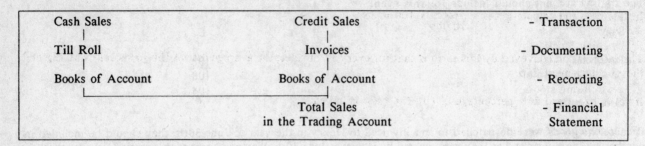

Purchases are found by:

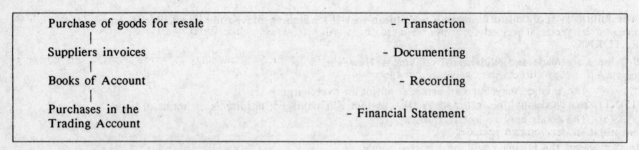

COST OF GOODS LOST OTHERWISE THAN BY SALE

12. In the explanation to line 9, I said that:

Line 8 gave the total goods available for sale in the year,
Line 9 gave the goods still in stock at the year end, and therefore, line 8 minus line 9 gave the cost of goods which left the business in the year. The presumption was that these goods had been sold. However, in practice goods are lost by other means, for example:

(a) Theft.
(b) Breakages.
(c) With liquids; evaporation.

(d) With perishables; natural detiorations.
(e) With some foodstuffs; eaten by mice.

It is not normally possible to measure the cost of losses occasioned by these causes and no mention of them is made in the trading account. You should note that gross profit is actually:

(a) The sum of gross profit of all sales made in the period
     less
(b) The cost of all goods lost in the period through theft, breakages, etc.

GROSS PROFIT RATIO

13. The trading account can be reduced to three elements:

	£	
Sales	20,000	(a)
Cost of goods sold	15,000	(b)
Gross Profit	5,000	(c)

Item (c) can be expressed as a percentage of (a) or (b).

If (c) is expressed as a percentage of (a), the ratio is called:

> *Gross Profit as a percentage of sales*

or gross profit percentage
or gross profit margin

In this case the calculation is $\dfrac{5,000}{20,000} \times 100 = 25\%$

The information conveyed by this ratio is that for every £1 of sales, the average cost of the goods sold was 75p and the profit element 25p.

If (c) is expressed as a percentage of (b), the ratio is called:

> *average mark up*

In this case the calculation is $\dfrac{5,000}{15,000} \times 100 = 33\tfrac{1}{3}\%$

The information conveyed by this ratio is that the business adds an average $33\tfrac{1}{3}\%$ on to the cost to fix the selling price of its goods. If a good costs the business £6, it will on average sell it for £6 + £2 = £8.

14. In practice, it is important to *specify* which ratio (gross profit percentage *or* average mark up) is being discussed. Each ratio can be derived from the other.

15. Traders calculate and derive much information from using these ratios.

Information derived can include:

(a) A check on the accuracy of the trading account.

(b) A check that *all* sales have been included. It would be possible for a shop manager to steal and not record some cash sales.

(c) A comparison of price levels, or profit-ability with those achieved in previous years; forecasts and other businesses.

As an example, consider a retailer of fruit and vegetables whose policy is to add 50% on to cost to fix his selling price.

If the trading account showed:

	£
Sales	120,000
Cost of sales	85,000
Gross Profit	35,000

Then his *achieved* mark up is only 41%. Possible causes will be considered:

(i)   Not all goods were priced at cost + 50%.
(ii)   Losses caused by natural deterioration.
(iii) Inaccurate weighing.
(iv)   Omission of sales.
(v)   Theft.
(vi)   Unsold goods having to be thrown away.
(vii) Errors in stocktaking.
(viii) Failing to record goods taken by the proprietor for his own use.
(ix)   Cut-off errors.
(x)   Accounting errors, *e.g.* inclusion of non-purchases in purchases.

SUMMARY

16. (a) Businesses which trade by buying goods and reselling them, measure their profit from buying and selling in the form of a trading account with the format

Sales	x
Less cost of goods sold	x
Gross Profit	x

(b) "Cost of goods sold" is derived from

Opening stock	x
Plus Purchases	x
Goods Available for sale	x
Less Closing stock	x
Cost of goods sold	x

(c) *"Sales"* and *"purchases"* are technical terms and include only sales and purchases of goods dealt in.

(d) The realisation convention implies that the accountant recognises a profit at the moment when a good is sold. The practical consequences in a trading account are that *sales* and *purchases* include all items sold and bought in the period *irrespective* of *cash* receipts and payments.

(e) The matching convention implies that revenues (*e.g.* from sales) should be *matched* with associated costs and expenses and dealt with in the same period. The consequences for the trading account are:

    (i)   That sales and the cost of the goods sold should be precisely matched. Cut-off is a technical term for the practical difficulties in doing so.

    (ii)   Losses (*e.g.* from theft) should appear in the trading account in the accounting period when they occur.

(f) Sales and purchases should be net of returns.

(g) Purchases should include associated costs such as carriage-in and import duties.

(h) The trading account includes "cost of goods sold". In practice this term includes also the cost of goods stolen or otherwise lost and destroyed. This fact is not usually stated as the cost of such losses is not measured.

(i) The gross profit percentage is $\dfrac{\text{Gross Profit}}{\text{Sales}} \times 100\%$

(j) The average mark up is $\dfrac{\text{Gross Profit}}{\text{Cost of goods sold}} \times 100\%$

POINTS TO NOTE

17. (a) Remember that sales and purchases are sales and purchases made in the period and *not* cash received and paid.

(b) It is normally too expensive to have a recording system such that would measure directly the cost of goods sold. Instead a global figure of *cost of goods sold* is obtained from:

Opening stock + purchases - closing stock

This item includes the cost of goods lost otherwise from sales but measurement of the cost of such losses is not normally obtained.

(c) The trading account heading must always indicate the precise period covered. Avoid:

Trading account for the period ending .... as the length of the period is not specified.

(d) Do not include in sales and purchases any sales and purchases of goods such as fixed assets which are not the goods dealt in.

(e) *Sales* is sometimes referred to as *turnover*.

(f) In this chapter, I have assumed stock is valued at *cost (not* selling price). In practice, some stock can be valued at *below* cost and this is dealt with in a later chapter.

(g) Be careful to deduct items when *less* occurs in the trading account. Arithmetic errors are very easy to make. After the preparation of a trading account, always calculate the gross profit percentage and ask yourself if it appears to be reasonable.

(h) The realisation convention and the matching convention may appear similar.

Remember that the realisation convention is concerned with the timing of profit recognition and that the matching convention is concerned with the relation of revenues with associated costs and expenses.

SELF TESTING QUESTIONS

(a) *Draft a trading account. (2).*
(b) *What is included in sales? (2-4).*
(c) *What is included in purchases. (2-7).*
(d) *What is meant by gross profit? (2-11).*
(e) *How does the gross profit relate to the net profit? (2-11).*
(f) *What is the realisation convention? (3).*
(g) *List the criticisms of the realisation convention. (5).*
(h) *What is the matching convention? (6).*
(i) *Define cut-off. (7).*
(j) *How are "returns" treated? (8).*
(k) *How is "carriage in" treated? (10).*
(l) *What losses cause reductions in gross profit? (12).*
(m) *How is the gross profit ratio calculated and what does it indicate? (13).*
(n) *How is the average mark up calculated and what does it mean? (14).*
(o) *What can cause the gross profit ratio to differ from expectation? (15).*

Exercises (Answers begin on page 449)

1. *From the following separate sets of data, draw up trading accounts:*

	£	£	£	£
	a	b	c	d
Purchases on credit	8,000	13,000	6,000	15,000
Cash purchases	3,000	–	8,000	800
Opening stock	700	800	3,700	1,200
Closing stock	850	1,250	4,800	900
Sales on credit	12,200	14,900	17,200	–
Cash sales	1,200	3,000	2,000	18,000

Calculate (a) the average mark up on cost, and (b) the gross profit to sales percentage in each case.

2. *Given that the average mark up on cost is (a) 20% and (b) 37%, calculate the gross profit to sales percentage.*

3. *Given that the gross profit to sales percentage is (a) 27% and (b) 34%, calculate the average mark up.*

4. *Should the following items be included in the "purchases" of (a) a motor car dealer and (b) a hardware shop and (c) a business equipment dealer.*

(i)   *a motor car.*
(ii) *a lawnmower.*
(iii) *a typewriter.*
(iv) *a jar of coffee.*
(v)   *a mousetrap.*

5. *Discuss why the "cost of goods sold" cannot usually be measured directly (think of a newsagent's business).*

6. *A veterinary surgeon has drawn up his trading account as follows: (I have omitted the heading but you should never do so!)*

	£	£
Charges to customers		16,820
Opening stock of drugs	700	
Purchases of drugs	4,100	
	4,800	
Closing stock of drugs	1,100	3,700
Gross profit		13,120

Is there a "match" between sales and cost of sales? How could this "match" be made?

7.   Hubert is a small builder. He has contracted to build an extension to Ian's house. Details are:

Contract signed June 15th at a price of £4,500.
Work commenced July 4th.
Work completed September 18th.
Ian paid: £1,000 on July 30th.
          £1,5000 on August 28th.
          £2,300 on September 30th (there were some extras).

When was the profit on this contract earned?

Why does determining a date when profit is considered to have been earned, matter to an accountant?

8.   Insert the missing figures in the following trading accounts:

	£		£		£	
Sales	1,400		2,700		?	
less cost of goods sold:						
opening stock	250		300		490	
purchases	1,200		?		2,670	
available for sale	1,450		1,760		3,160	
closing stock	?	1,000	800	960	?	2,900
Gross Profit		?		1,740		1,100

9.   Given that the average mark up is (a) 55% and (b) 34% what is the gross profit percentage on sales?

Exercises without answers
10.   Given that the gross profit percentage on sales is (a) 30% and (b) 23% what is the average mark up?

11.   Should the following be included in purchases of (a) an office stationer, (b) a greengrocer and (c) a sports outfitter?

(i)   envelopes.
(ii)   paper bags.
(iii)   a motor car.
(iv)   a pot of glue.
(v)   invoice from Graham for carriage of goods to the shop.

12.   Should the following be included in "sales" for the year ending 31.12.-8 of a fishmonger?

(i)   sales of fish for cash in the year.
(ii)   sale of a car no longer used by the business.
(iii)   sales of fish on credit to Hugh on 23.12.-8 (payment received on 2.1.-9).
(iv)   Sales of fish on credit to Evan on 30.12.-7 (payment received on 3.2.-8).
(v)   Returns of fish which were off - refund given 5.6.-8.
(vi)   Credit notes given to Martin on 30.12.-8 for fish short delivered.

13.   What is the stock of Nigel a dealer of widgets at 31.12.-7?

Category	Quantity/Weight	Cost per Item/Kilo
Large mark 2	39	£3.80
Large mark 3	120	£3.90
Medium grade 3	289	£1.60
Medium grade 6	217	£2.10
Small	46 kilos	£4.50

14. *What is the stock of Bruno at 31.12.-7. He is a dealer in building materials.*

Category	Quantity/Measure		Cost per Item/measure
Sand	4	tons	£40 a ton
Gravel	7.5	tons	£60 a ton
Slabs 2 x 3	46		£5.20 each
Bricks	864		£4.80 a dozen
Timber	68	metres	£2.00 a metre
Nails	13	pounds	10p an ounce

Why is stock valued at cost and not at selling price?

15. *Jill is in business making sailboats to order. The following transaction occurred with Ted in 19-7:*

1st January Ted made an enquiry about a boat; 10th January Jill sent a quotation to Ted at £800; 11th February Ted sent an official order; 14th February Jill commenced manufacture; 3rd March Ted paid £300 on account; 5th April boat completed and delivered to Ted and the amount due invoiced; 3rd June Ted paid; 5th October guarantee expired.

Jill's year end is 30th April.

    (a) When should Jill regard the profit on the deal as having been made?

    (b) In which financial year will the profit fall?
    (c) Why does this matter?
    (d) What accounting convention is involved?

16. *Mary is in business selling hand made jewellery. Her year end is 31st March. In the year 19-8 the following transaction occurred:*

1st January Mary ordered a special jewel from Alphonse; 3rd February the jewel arrived with invoice for £120; 5th March sold the jewel to Lady D on credit and invoiced it at £232; 7th April Paid Alphonse; 8th May Lady D paid.

    (a) When is the profit made by Mary on this transaction?
    (b) In which financial year is this profit made?
    (c) What accounting convention is involved.
    (d) Mary produces MONTHLY trading accounts. Show the entries for this transaction in each of her monthly trading accounts for January, February, March, April, May and June.
    (e) Show also the entries in her Balance Sheets at these month ends.

17. *Willie sent 40 widgets which had cost him £3 each to Tom on 28th December 19-7 and invoiced them at £5 each on the basis that Tom would sell them if he could at £7 each.*

One parcel of 20 widgets arrived at Toms on 30th December and Tom immediately sold 6 of them. The remainder arrived on 5th January. Tom sold 31 in January and returned 3 to Willie at the end of January as he could sell no more. Willie accepted them back.

What problems does this story pose for Willie's accountant who prepares the trading account for the year ending 31st December?

What problems are posed for Tom's accountant assuming Tom has the same year end?

How would these items be treated in their respective trading accounts and balance sheets?

18. *Samantha has a bookshop. She expects to make a gross profit on sales price of 30%. In fact her trading account showed a gross profit to sales ratio of only 28%. List all the possible causes of the difference.*

19. *Ludwig sells music and records. His trading account includes a figure of £36,782 as cost of goods sold. His accountant explains that that figure is not only the cost of the goods actually sold to customers. What else is included in it?*

20. *What documents might be the source of information about the sales in the year of (a) a football club, (b) a supermarket, (c) a kettle manufacturer and (d) a hotel?*

21. Samantha is setting up a business to buy pots and other ornaments from manufacturers and wholesale them to retailers and also retail them from her own shop. Outline systems for dealing with her sales and purchases.

22. From the following separate sets of data, draw up trading accounts:

	a	b	c	d	e Period 1	Period 2
	£	£	£	£	£	
Purchases on credit	4,700	19,000	17,000	6,000	11,750	12,030
Cash purchases	800	8,200	1,000	4,050	1,250	1,500
Opening stock	1,200	4,700	3,400	1,230	5,820	?
Closing stock	1,400	4,200	4,800	1,180	7,100	6,450
Sales on credit	8,700	36,100	21,200		16,200	17,100
Cash sales	100	4,200		14,000	3,500	6,403
Sales returns	350				1,400	1,800
Purchases returns	100		1,700	100	1,100	700

Also calculate mark up and gross profit to sales percentages. In the case of (e) suggest as many reasons as possible why the gross profit margins in the two periods are different. The business is a garden centre.

23. Danielle's retail furniture business suffered a disastrous fire in the night of 24 January 19-8 when all the stock was destroyed. In the year ending 30 September 19-7, her sales had been £64,640 and cost of goods sold calculated by opening stock £24,200, Purchases £46,800 and closing stock £32,600. In the period 1st October 19-7 to 24 January 19-8 sales had been £24,000 and purchases £12,400. Calculate a figure for the value of stock destroyed by fire. Is the value you have calculated the cost to Danielle or her selling price?

24. Ranjit ordered some goods for his widget wholesale business on 3 December. They arrived on 28 December 19-7 and an invoice dated 31 December 19-7 arrived on 5 January 19-8 in the sum of £800. Some of the goods were faulty and Ranjit returned them on 29 December 19-7, a credit note being received on 18 January 19-8 for £60. An invoice £40 for carriage of the goods from the manufacturer to Ranjit was received on 14 January 19-8 and paid the next day. Ranjit had a customer for exactly one quarter of the sound goods and these were despatched and invoiced on 31 December for £330. Ranjit paid in cash the carriage charge to British Rail £20 but did not recharge this cost to the customer. Ranjit paid his suppliers on 30 January 19-8 and his customer paid on 2 February 19-8.

How would these transactions appear in the trading account of Ranjit for the year ending 31 December 19-7?

25. Answer the following simple questions:

(a) Why is the profit from a sale of an item by Tom on 4 December 19-7 included in the profit of the year ending 31 December 19-7 when the bill was paid by the customer on 4 February 19-8?

(b) Why is the sale of Ted's old van in November 19-7 not included in the sales of his printing business at the year ending 31 December 19-7?

(c) Why is the invoice for advertising not included in the purchases of Ted's accounts?

(d) Wally has a business such that he has a van equipped with repair apparatus and he visits his customers in their homes repairing and fitting new parts to their cars. Is the calculation of a gross profit appropriate for his business?

(e) Sid commissioned Fred to write a computer program for £1,000 in 19-8. This was done and Sid paid Fred. Sid sold copies of the program to his customers in 19-9 and 19-0, after which the program became obsolete. Should the £1,000 appear in Sid's trading account in 19-8, 19-9 or 19-0? What convention is involved?

26. On 14 April 1985 the warehouse of Joseph Shipley caught fire and the whole of his stock in trade was destroyed apart from goods with a cost price value of £285.

Fortunately Shipley's books and records were kept in a fire proof safe and the following information is available.

(1) Stock in trade at 31 December 1984 was £1,344 at cost price.

(2) Purchases from 1 January 1985 to the date of the fire amounted to £1,960. Of these, goods to the cost price of £70 were still in transit at the time of the fire.

*(3) Sales from 1 January 1985 to the date of the fire amounted to £2,775 and all these goods had been despatched **before** the fire took place.*

(4) Shipley's Gross Profit is 20% of sales.

Required:
Calculate the value – at cost price – of the goods destroyed in the fire.

NOTE: Calculations must be shown. *(LCCI)*

11. Bookkeeping for Sales and Purchases

INTRODUCTION

1. In a double entry bookkeeping system it is not feasible to maintain an account called "stock" in which all inputs and outputs of stock are entered with a balance which shows the total stock on hand at cost. This is because the account would need to record outputs (sales) at *cost* price and too much labour would be required to determine this for each sale.

2. If it is necessary to record stock quantities for each category of stock this is done *outside* the bookkeeping system. This is known as *continuous* or *perpetual* inventory.

3. In order to prepare the trading account, totals of sales and purchases are required and these are accumulated in accounts called "sales account" and "purchases account".

DEBITS AND CREDITS

4. Sales, both cash *and* credit, are entered on the *credit* side of the sales account.

Purchases, both cash *and* credit, are entered on the debit side.

5. Some sales and purchases are returned, cancelled or amended and credit notes issued. These are called *sales returns* and *purchases returns*. There is a choice in the bookkeeping entries for these items. Some systems include separate accounts for these items and some systems enter returns in the sales and purchases accounts but on the opposite side.

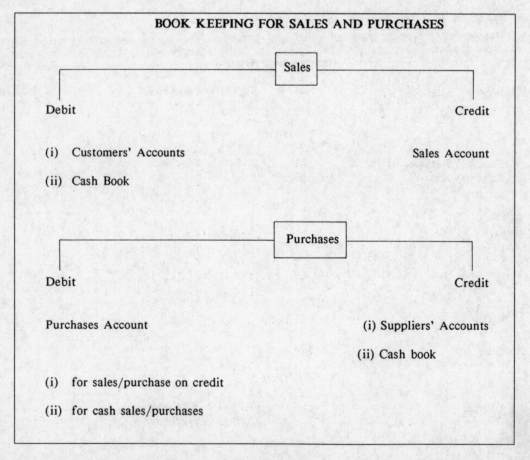

6. Here are some transactions of Fringe Ltd, dealers in widgets:

19-3		
October		£
1	Purchased widgets for cash	104
3	Purchased widgets by cheque	262
7	Purchased widgets on credit from Alan	311

10	Returned some faulty widgets to Alan - received credit note	62
11	Sold widgets for cash	210
15	Sold widgets to Brown who paid with a cheque	64
16	Sold widgets to Colin on credit	304
17	Purchased widgets from Dave on credit	299
18	Received a credit note from Alan who had overcharged	10
20	Sold widgets for cash	132
21	Sold widgets on credit to Eric	200
22	Purchased an office desk from Frank on credit	80
23	Purchased widgets on credit from Dave	206
24	Paid Dave the amount owing by cheque	

Enter these transactions in the appropriate accounts:

Dr.   **Cr.**

Cash Account

		£			£
11.10.-3	Sales	210	1.10-3	Purchases	104
20.10.-3	Sales	132			

Purchases

		£			£
1.10.-3	Cash	104	10.10-3	Alan	62
3.10.-3	Bank	262	18.10-3	Alan	10
7.10.-3	Alan	311			
17.10.-3	Dave	299			
23.10.-3	Dave	206			

Cash at Bank Account

		£			£
18.10.-3	Brown - Sales	64	3.10.-3	Purchases	262
			24.10.-3	Dave	505

Alan

		£			£
10.10.-3	Purchase Returns	62	7.10-3	Purchases	311
11.10.-3	Purchase Returns	10			

Sales

		£			£
			11.10.-3	Cash	210
			15.10.-3	Brown - cheque	64
			16.10.-3	Colin	304
			20.10.-3	Cash	132
			21.10.-3	Eric	200

Colin

		£			£
16.10.-3	Sales	304			

Dave

		£			£
24.10.-3	Cheque	505	17.10.-3	Purchases	299
			23.10.-3	Purchases	206

Eric

		£			£
21.10.-3	Sales	200			

Frank

		£			£
			22.10.-3	Office Desk	80

Office Furniture

		£		£
22.10.-3	Frank - office desk	80		

Note:

Each entry has a description or narration e.g. cheque or sales. Many bookkeepers use the words "goods" or "invoice" instead of "sales" or "purchases". The important thing is that the nature of the transaction should be clear.

7. Follow the entries for each transaction and note:

(a) For each debit there is a credit and vice versa.

(b) The Cash account and the Cash at Bank account would probably have other entries *e.g.* wages paid, proprietor's drawings etc.

(c) The purchase returns have been put on the purchase account. The alternative would be to have separate accounts for them as:

Purchase Returns

	£			£
		10.10.-3	Alan	62
		18.10.-3	Alan	10

(d) The purchase of office furniture is entered in the *fixed asset account* office furniture.

"Purchases" has a technical meaning. It means purchases of goods which are to be resold in the normal course of business. Thus the business of Fringe Ltd is dealing in widgets, then the purchases account is to record the purchase of widgets. Similarly sales account is to record sales of widgets.

In some businesses, care has to be taken to distinguish "purchases" from fixed asset acquisition. For example, a car dealer will acquire cars for resale (purchases) or to use as demonstration models (fixed assets).

MEANING OF EACH ACCOUNT

8. Now that these transactions have been entered into the double entry bookkeeping system, what do these accounts show?

(a) **Purchases.** In October 19-3, the company purchased widgets for resale at a total cost of £1,182 (check my addition!), reduced by credit notes (for faulty goods and pricing errors), totalling £72. This total includes goods bought for cash with immediate payment, and goods bought on credit with payment in a later month.

This *net* total £1,110 will form a necessary part of the trading account.

(b) **Alan.** This is a summary of Fringe Ltd's dealings with their supplier Alan. It will be seen that the business has bought goods to the value of £311 and has received credit notes totalling £72, so that at the end of the month the business owes Alan £239. This is a *liability* account.

(c) **Sales.** In October 19-3, the company sold goods to customers at a total sales value £910. Some of these sales were for cash and some on credit. The date of payment is irrelevant. What matters is that these were the sales made in this month.

This total will be required for the trading account.

(d) **Colin.** This account shows that Colin owes the business £304 for goods that he purchased on October 16th. This is a debtor account - an asset account.

(e) **Dave.** This account shows the dealings of the business with Dave. The company bought goods from him on credit and paid for them during the month. Thus, at the month end nothing was owing. The account is *closed*.

(f) **Eric.** This account shows that Eric bought goods on 21.10.-3 and at the month end still owed for them.

(g) **Frank.** This account shows that the company have bought an office desk on credit from Frank and had not paid for it by the end of the month.

(h) **Office furniture.** This account would probably have other entries. It records the cost of office furniture owned by the firm. It is an asset account.

NARRATIONS

9. In practice each side of an account will have these columns:

Date　　Narration　　Folio　　Amount

(a) The date and the amount are not usually problems!

(b) The narration has three purposes:

(i)　To describe the transaction.
(ii)　To name the *other* account affected by the transaction.
(iii)　To refer to a document (*e.g.* a numbered invoice) or a document file or book of prime entry.

Modern practice is to have only a very brief narration.

(c) The folio (= leaf or page) is a jargon word for the reference number of the account with the corresponding debit or credit, or of the book of prime entry from which the entry was *posted*.

STATEMENTS OF ACCOUNT

10. Harry is in business as a wholesaler. He sells goods on credit to Jim, a customer. At the end of June 19-8, Jim's account in HARRY'S ledger looks like this.

Jim

Dr.		£			Cr. £
June 1	Balance b/d	264	June 17	Cash	120
June 4	Invoice 238	189	June 23	Credit Note 12	56
June 9	Invoice 298	76			
June 21	Invoice 354	643			
June 27	Invoice 410	466	June 30	Balance c/d	1,462
		1,638			1,638

In early July, Harry will wish to inform Jim of the total amount owing and will send to Jim a *statement of account*. This could be a copy of Jim's account in Harry's ledger or may be in a different form but giving the same information. An example of a statement of account is in Chapter 2. On receipt of the statement of account Jim may make a payment or at least Harry hopes so.

At the same time Jim has been recording the same information in Harry's account in Jim's ledger but in Jim's ledger the account is a *liability account* and all the entries appear on the opposite side. In fact it appears like this.

Harry

Dr.		£			Cr. £
June 17	Cash	120	June 1	Balance b/f	264
June 23	Credit note	56	June 4	Goods	189
June 30	Cash	144	June 21	Goods	643
			June 27	Goods	466
June 30	Balance c/f	1,242			
		1,562			1,562

When Jim gets the statement of account from Harry, he will compare it with his record of the transactions (the account above) and discovers that there are two differences. You might identify what these are. You should find that:

(a) Jim has recorded a payment on June 30 which Harry has not recognised. This can easily be accounted for by the delay in sending the cheque through the post.

(b) Jim has not recorded invoice number 298. Perhaps it has been lost or Jim is querying it and will not enter it until the matter is resolved. In any event the sending of a statement of account, not only acts as a request for payment but is also a means of ensuring that the records in the books of both debtor and creditor are the same or can be reconciled one with the other.

SUMMARY

11. (a) Sales are entered on the credit side of the sales account. The objective of the sales account is to accumulate and so to determine the total sales made in a period.

(b) Purchases are entered on the debit side of the purchases account.

(c) Sales returns and purchases returns are entered on the debit and credit sides respectively of sales returns and purchases returns accounts. Or they may be entered on the debit and credit respectively of sales and purchases account.

POINTS TO NOTE

12. (a) Purchases are entered on the *debit* side and sales on the *credit* side in the *sales* and *purchases* accounts.

(b) Sales and purchases accounts have a totally different function from asset and liability accounts. Asset and liability accounts are used to show a businessman what assets (including debtors) and liabilities (including creditors) he has at each *moment of time*. The balances appear in the *balance sheet*.

Sales and purchase accounts are used to determine the total sales and total purchases *over a period* of time. The amounts appear in the *trading account*.

(c) *All* accounts are of course used as a permanent record of business transactions.

SELF TESTING QUESTIONS

(a) On which side of which accounts are (i) sales, (ii) purchases entered? (5).
(b) What are the functions of sales and purchases accounts? (13b).
(c) What is the function of a statement of account? (10).
(d) Why may the information on a statement of account differ from that shown in the creditor account in the recipient's books? (10).

Exercises (Answers being on page 450)

1. At 31st October 19-8 M, a dealer in antiques, head the following debtors and creditors in his ledger:

	Dr. £	Cr. £
Nutt	100	
Oliver		150
Preston	262	
Richard	300	

Enter the following transactions into the ledger accounts:

19-8		£
Nov 1	Bought antiques for cash at auction	500
Nov 2	Sold antiques to Preston on credit	320
Nov 4	Bought antiques on credit from Oliver	132
Nov 7	Returned faulty antique to Oliver	16
Nov 9	Sold antique for cash	100
Nov 11	Sold antique to Nutt	70
Nov 14	Preston paid, on account	100
Nov 15	Gave a credit note to Nutt for error in the invoice	3
Nov 16	Bought antiques for cash	120
Nov 17	Sold antiques on credit to Quint	135
Nov 18	Sold antiques for cash	30
Nov 24	Richard paid the amount due by him	
Nov 29	Sold for cash antique chest used by M for storage of documents	100

2. (a) If M had a stock of antiques which had cost £1,103 at 31st October 19-8, can you tell from your bookkeeping entries what the stock at cost was at 30th November 19-8?

(b) Do you think that M would need a detailed record of the antiques he has in stock and what each one cost?
(c) Who owed M money at 30th November 19-8 and how much?
(d) Who did M owe money to and how much?
(e) What was the total cost to M of antiques purchased in November 19-8 and the total turnover for that month.

3. At 31st July 19–8, Nick a retailer of office equipment had the following debtors and creditors in his ledger:

	Dr. £	Cr. £
Pinkerton	134	
Green	162	
Brown		342
Gray	101	
Scarlet	58	

His stock at the date was valued at cost at £2,319 and he had £180 in the bank.

In August 19–4, he had the following transactions:

19–4 August		£
1	Bought goods from Brown	600
3	Sold goods to Black	205
4	Bought goods from White	140
6	Sold goods to Gray	183
7	Paid Brown	100
9	Received cheque from Scarlet	58
10	Gave credit note to Pinkerton	44
15	Sold goods to Pinkerton	246
18	Pinkerton paid	134
21	Sold goods to Green	84
22	Gray paid	51
23	Bought goods, paying by cheque	50
24	Sold goods to Violet	341
26	Received credit note from Brown	35

Required:
(a) Enter all transactions in double entry accounts.
(b) Prepare a trading account for the month of August. Assume stock is valued at cost at £2,373.
(c) Who owed Nick money at 31.8.–4 and how much?
(d) Who did Nick owe money to at 31.8.–4 and how much?
(e) What was the bank balance at 31.8.–4?

Exercises without answers
4. Leonard is one of your SUPPLIERS. His account in your ledger appears as

		£			£
July 4	Credit note	55	July 1 Balance b/d		766
July 7	Cash	344	July 5 Invoice		244
July 15	Credit Note	98	July 23 Invoice		222
July 30	Cash	111	July 31 Invoice		887
July 31	Balance c/d	1,501			
		2,119			2,119

During the first week of August the following statement of account is received from Leonard:

		Dr	Cr	Balance
July 1	Balance b/f			766
July 4	Credit note		55	711
July 5	Invoice	244		955
July 7	Cash		344	611
July 9	Invoice	102		713
July 15	Credit note		98	615
July 23	Invoice	222		837
July 31	Invoice	887		1,724

(a) Explain why the entries which you have entered on the debit of the account in your ledger appear as credits in the statement of account.

(b) Prepare the reconciliation statement to explain the differences between the two closing balances. Suggest reasons why these differences may occur.

5. *Pat is a customer of yours. His account in your ledger appears as:*

		£			£
Sept 5	Balance b/d	35	Sept 9	Cash	35
Sept 14	Invoice	75	Sept 22	Credit Note	12
Sept 23	Invoice	89			
Sept 26	Invoice	90			
Sept 28	Invoice	32	Sept 30	Balance c/d	264
		311			311

Early in October you send him a copy of the account as a statement of account. He pays you a cheque in the amount of £242. Why did he not pay you £264?

6. *Williams is in business as a wholesaler.*

At 31.12.-7 customers owing him money were: Adam £444; Butler £98; Craig £3,990; Dalton £21; Eve £333.

At 31.12.-7 suppliers to whom he owed money were: Frank £887; Geoff £180; Harris £330; Ian £11.

Also at 31.12.-7 the balance of the cash book was £1,000.

In January 19-8:

Credit sales were to Adam £332 and £789; Craig £990; Dalton £100 and £580; Jenks £370.
Credit purchases were Geoff £760; Ian £43 and £780 and £21; King £213.
Credit notes were given to Adam £10 and Craig £105.
Credit notes were received from Geoff £5 and Ian £2.
Cash was received from Adam £444; Butler £39; Eve £100; Jenks £50.
Cash was paid to Frank £800; Geoff £180; Harris £330.

  (a) Enter all these transactions in ledger accounts.

  (b) Bring down the balances.

  (c) Prepare a trial balance (include a credit balance: capital £4,178).

  (d) Extract a list of amounts owing to suppliers showing total owing to each supplier and how much is for 19-7 and how much is for January 19-8.

  (e) Extract a list of amounts owing by debtors showing the amount owing by each debtor and how much is for 19-7 and how much for January 19-8.

7. *Francine has a business retailing microwave ovens to caterers. At 31 January 19-8, debtors and creditors were:*

Debtors

	£
Lester	2,400
Derby	800
Paisley	720
Roaster	2,319

Creditors

	£
Hull	860
Kingston	1,240
Wooster	6,280
Chester	1,725

The trial balance included cash £2,400, Capital £5,914 and stock, valued at £7,380. In February 19–8, transactions were:

	Sales on credit	£
Lester		1,400
Paisley		882
Winton		2,600
Paisley		1,725
Roaster		(200)

	Purchases on credit	£
Kempton		830
Kingston		1,700
Chester		1,325
Tipton		1,005
Hull (credit note)		(86)

Cash

		£
Receipts		
Lester		2,400
Roaster		500
Winton		700

		£
Payments		
Hull		600
Wooster		6,280
Drawings		500

Required:
(a) Enter all these transactions in double entry accounts.
(b) Extract a trial balance.
(c) Prepare a trading account (stock at 29.2.–8 was £8,140).
(d) Calculate the gross profit ratio.

Assume there are no other balances or transactions.

8. *Distinguish between accounts for sales and purchases and accounts for assets and liabilities.*

12. The Asset of Stock

INTRODUCTION

1.   The asset of stock is *not* recorded continuously and this chapter tells you how stock is dealt with in the bookkeeping system and in the trading account.

BOOKKEEPING FOR STOCK

2.   You will have noticed that purchases are recorded in a purchases account and that sales are recorded in a sales account. Both purchases and sales are movements or changes in the asset "stock". Note well that changes in the asset stock are *not* recorded continuously. Why is this?

In order to record the asset stock on a continuous basis common pricing must be used. Thus purchases are recorded at cost but also sales would have to be recorded at cost. However input cost is not known for each sale. Imagine a newspaper shop trying to record his stock continuously and having to determine the cost to him of each newspaper he sells.

For the preparation of the profit and loss account and balance sheet it is sufficient to record total sales and purchases. Of course opening and closing stocks must be known and these values are obtained by counting and valuing the stock at period ends. The only time the value of the asset stock is known then is at the period end when it is counted.

3.   The actual bookkeeping entries for stock are:

At the first period end:

Dr Stock Account   Cr Trading Account
With the stock at that date.

At each subsequent period end:

Dr Trading Account   Cr Stock Account
With the stock as it was at the previous period end

and

Dr Stock Account   Cr Trading Account
With the stock at the period end

Example

Georgina commenced in business on 1.1.-7. At 31.12.-7 her stock was valued at £2,300. At 31.12.-7 bookkeeping entries were:

Stock Account

31.12.-7 Trading Account	£2,300	

Trading Account

		31.12.-7 Stock Account	£2,300

At 31.12.-8 her stock was valued at £3,780 and entries were:

Stock Account

31.12.-7 Balance b/f	£2,300	31.12.-8 Trading Account	£2,300
31.12.-7 Trading Account	£3,780		

Trading Account

31.12.-7 Opening Stock	£2,300	31.12.-8 Closing Stock	£3,780

Remember that the trading account IS a double entry account like this:

31.12.-7	Opening Stock	2,300	31.12.-8	Sales	32,665
31.12.-8	Purchases	21,700	31.12.-8	Closing Stock	3,780
31.12.-8	Gross Profit c/f to				
	profit and loss account	12,445			
		36,445			36,445

In practice to present to interested people it is reformatted as in the example in chapter 9.

Note that the stock account contains a balance of £2,300 for the whole year 19-8. The balance is only changed once a year. Thus in trial balances you usually see the stock of **the previous year**. The value of the stock at the trial balance date is given not in the trial balance but in a note.

SUMMARY

4. (a) There is an account for stock in most double entry systems but this is *not* continuously updated.

   (b) The account for stock is updated once a year when stock is counted and valued. The double entries are to the trading account.

POINTS TO NOTE

5. Most beginning students want to debit purchases and sales to a stock account. This is not correct and purchases and sales are entered in the purchases and sales accounts. Stock is updated only when a trading account is prepared.

SELF TESTING QUESTIONS

(a) What is the double entry for:

   (i) sales of goods; and
   (ii) purchases of goods?

(b) What is the double entry for goods counted and valued at the end of a financial year? (3)

(c) At what date will the stock be in a trial balance? (3)

Exercise (answer being on page 451)

1. *The following items appear in the trial balance of Foster as at 31 July 19-3. The previous trading account was prepared for the year ending 31 July 19-2:*

	£	£
Stock	*23,005*	
Purchases	*145,800*	
Sales		*174,700*
Purchase returns		*1,745*
Carriage inwards	*6,700*	

The stock was counted on 31 July 19-3 and valued at £25,987.

Show the stock account and prepare a trading account for the year to 31 July 19-3.

Exercises without answer

2. *The following transactions occurred in the month of October 19-7 in Freda's business:*

Stock at 30.9.19-7	*7,300*	*at 31.10.19-7*	*8,200*
Debtor at 30.9.19-7 - Hugh	*3,500*		
Creditor at 30.9.19-7 - Walter	*200*		

Purchases (all on credit)		*Sales (all on credit)*	
Graham	*4,800*	*Hugh*	*8,000*
Walter	*3,000*	*Swallow*	*10,000*
Graham	*2,580*		
Walter	*2,600*		

Payments		Receipts	
Walter	3,190	Hugh	6,200

Enter these items in double entry accounts (note cash balance at 30.9.19-7 was £567) and prepare a trading account for the month. Show how all the balances would appear in the balance sheet at 31.10.19-7.

The Profit and Loss Account

The trading account of a retailer or wholesaler measures the gross profit. The next part of the manual deals with profit measurement by considering the *expenses* incurred in a year and any *revenues* additional to the gross profit. Chapter 13 is concerned with the profit measurement aspects and Chapter 14 with the bookkeeping entries.

13. The Profit and Loss Account and Accruals and Prepayments

INTRODUCTION

1. The trading account is an account which measures the gross profit earned by a business during the accounting (usually one year) period. Gross profit is the sales less the cost of the actual goods sold.

2. In addition to the cost of the goods actually sold, the business will also have overhead expenses. The *net* profit of the year is the gross profit less all the overhead expenses of the year.

3. The net profit is calculated and demonstrated in an account called the profit and loss account.

4. The precise *amount* to be included in the profit and loss account for each type of expense, is the subject of the *accruals* convention.

FORMAT

5. The modern format of a profit and loss account is:

		Henry	a
	Profit and Loss account for the year ending 30th June 19-8		b
		£	c
Gross Profit		32,000	d
Less Expenses:			e
Wages and Salaries	8,300		
Rent	1,000		
Rates	1,300		
Insurance	425		
Heating and Lighting	861		
Repairs	380		
Telephone	514		
Motor expenses	2,320		
Printing and Stationery	1,100		
Advertising	500		
Loan Interest	300		
Accountant's fee	500		
Sundries	1,103	18,603	f
Net Profit		13,397	g

(a) The name of the business must be given.

(b) The period must be precisely stated. In this account, we are measuring the profit earned in the year ending on 30th June, 19-8.

(c) The unit of account must be indicated.

(d) The account starts with the gross profit derived from the trading account.

(e) The expenses are listed under suitable categories. The precise categorisation of expenses depends on the type of business and the type of expense incurred.

(f) The individual expenses accounts are shown in an inset column and the total thrown out so that the total is below the figure of gross profit.

(g) The net profit is then calculated.

EXPENSES

6.   An inspection of the list of expense headings will give you some idea of the meaning of the term expense. Expenses are the *costs* of goods and services *consumed* by the enterprise *in the year*.

7.   Certain items are *excluded*. These include:

(a) **Capital expenditure.** Capital expenditure is the *acquisition* of an item which will give benefit to the business for more than one year. Examples are the acquisition of *fixed assets*. If Henry's business buys a delivery van, this is the acquisition of a *fixed asset* which will appear on the balance sheet. The van will give benefit to the business over several years. The *cost of acquisition* is *not* an expense of the year and is, therefore, excluded from the expenses in the profit and loss account.

Clearly the van wears out over the years and a *portion* of its acquisition cost can be regarded as an expense of each year that it is used. This portion is determined by the depreciation process which is described in the chapter on depreciation.

Trivial items of capital expenditure (*e.g.* a ruler for use in the office which may be in use for several years) *are* treated as expenses.

(b) **Purchases.** These are dealt with in the trading account.

(c) **Drawings.** Profit is earned so that drawings can be made. Profit is measured so that the proprietor can determine how much he can safely draw out of the business. You will remember (or revise) the treatment of drawings on the balance sheet.

(d) **Loan repayments.** You will remember from Chapter 7 that these do not affect the total of assets less liabilities.

Expenses do reduce net assets.

ACCRUALS

8.   Expenses are the costs of goods and services *consumed* by the enterprise in the year.

Consider the cycle:

(a) Business commences 1st Jan 19-8 and electricity supply is connected.

(b) Electricity is consumed continually during the year 19-8.

(c) The meter is read on 3.3.-8; 25.5.-8; 4.9.-8; 29.11.-8.

(d) Invoices are received from the electricity board following the meter readings. These invoices are dated 7.3.-8; 2.6.-8; 7.9.-8 and 3.12.-8. The amounts are £164; £132; £162 and £191 respectively.

(e) Payment is made following reminders by the electricity board on 3.4.-8; 3.7.-8; 8.10.-8 and 4.1.-9.

How much do we include as an expense in the profit and loss account under the heading elec-tricity?

Date of Reading	Date of Invoice	Date of Payment	Amount £
3.3.-8	7.3.-8	3.4.-8	164
25.5.-8	2.6.-8	3.7.-8	131
4.9.-8	7.9.-8	8.10-8	162
29.11.-8	3.12.-8	4.1.-9	191
			648

Clearly the answer is the amount *consumed*. The cost of this up to 29.11.-8 is £164 + £131 + £162 + £191 = £648. But this excludes the amount consumed from 30.11.-8 to 31.12.-8. This must be determined or estimated from:

(i)   Reading the meter and calculating the cost from the tariff charged by the electricity board.
(ii)   Apportioning the bill received in February 19-9.
(iii) Guessing intelligently.

Suppose the amount was £75, then the expense for the year in the profit and loss account would be £648 + £75 = £723. Thus £723 is the cost of electricity consumed in the whole year going right up to the end.

The £75 is described as an *accrual*.

As the £75 had been consumed before 31.12.-8 (the year end) but will not be paid for until 19-9 it will be included in the accruals item in current liabilities in the balance sheet.

Similarly the bill for £191 was for electricity consumed *and* invoiced before 31.12.-8 but paid for in 19-9 so it will be included in the *creditors* item in current liabilities in the balance sheet.

PREPAYMENTS

9. Expenses are the costs of goods and services *consumed* by the enterprise in the year. Accruals are required because invoicing and payment for an expense consumed in the year often occurs *after* the year end. Sometimes invoices are received and/or payments made *in the year* for expenses items which will give *benefit* (= be consumed) in the following year. These are called *prepayments*.

Motor and other insurances are normally paid in advance. Thus if a business has its year end on December 31st 19-8 and an insurance premium of £240 is paid in July 10-8 for insurance cover for the year ending on 31st July 19-9, then the amount to be included in the profit and loss account for 19-8 would be $\frac{5}{12}$ x £240 = £100. The remainder £140 will be an expense in 19-9 and in the balance sheet at 31st December 19-8 it will be included as a prepayment.

THE ACCRUALS CONVENTION

10. The accruals convention can be stated as requiring that costs and expenses are recognised and included in the profit and loss account as they are incurred and not as money is paid. This, like the cost convention and the realisation convention is contrary to the expectations of those untutored in accounting.

11. The accruals convention means that the cost of the resource consumed is included for each year. This means that comparisons of expenditure under each heading can be made from year to year. The alternatives to accrual accounting are:

(a) Including expenses only when invoiced in the year. This has the drawback that invoices may be sent at random intervals. For example, electricity bills are sent when the meter is read and this is not done at precisely regular intervals. In addition, some expenses, *e.g.* discounts, are not evidenced by incoming invoices.

(b) Including expenses in accordance with cash payments. This suffers the drawback, that payments are made randomly and no comparisons can be made. For example, three payments of quarterly rent might be made in 19-4 and five payments in 19-5. This may occur because it is almost a chance event whether the December 19-4 quarter is paid at the end of 19-4 or the beginning of 19-5.

PROBLEMS OF IMPLEMENTATION

12. The consumption of resource under most expense headings is relatively easy to find. There are certain expenses which are made for specific periods of time, *e.g.* rent, rates, insurance premiums, vehicle licences.

13. Some expense headings are more difficult:

(a) **Heat and light.** Precise measurement of the cost of consumption up to date of the balance sheet is difficult as meter readings are not usually taken at year ends. In the case of coal or oil, it is necessary to take stock of any fuel in stock at the year end.

(b) **Repairs.** Strictly speaking, the cost of property or equipment repairs should not fall in the period when the repairs took place but in the periods when the deterioration, that the repairs are making good, took place. In practice, however, repairs are usually, but not always, allowed to fall into the period when the repairs took place.

(c) **Advertising.** It is sometimes argued that the benefits of advertising are long term (especially with the launch of a new product) and that the cost of advertising should fall into the periods when the benefit is felt. However, in practice, the date of appearance of the advert is taken as the determining date.

(d) **Accountants fee.** The work of preparing (and/or auditing) the financial statements for the year ending 30th June 19-4 will mostly be done in the following year and the accountants' fee will be invoiced and paid in the year ending 30th June 19-5. None the less, the fee for preparing the Accounts to 30th June 19-4 is put back into the Accounts for that year.

(e)   **Depreciation, discounts, bad debts.** These items are discussed in separate chapters.

(f)   **Losses on stocks; sales and purchase returns.** These items appear in the trading account and are not profit and loss account items. However, if a measurable uninsured loss of stock due to fire or theft occurs, it may appear in the profit and loss account with a corresponding reduction in the figure of purchases.

(g)   **Carriage of goods.** Carriage of goods from suppliers to the business's shop, factory or warehouse (carriage *in*) is considered part of the cost of the goods and appears in the trading account. Carriage of goods to customers (carriage *out*) is a profit and loss account expense.

14. Some businesses also have additional *revenues* such as rents received and interest received from investments and financial deposits. These can be shown in the profit and loss in one of two places as:

		£	£'000
Gross Profit			643
Add Interest receivable		61	
Rents receivable		19	80
			723
Less Expenses:			
Rent and Rates		102	
Heat and Light		83	
Wages		237	
Sundries		61	483
Net Profit			240

or

		£	£'000
Gross Profit			643
Less Expenses:			
Rent and Rates		102	
Heat and Light		83	
Wages		237	
Sundries		61	483
			160
Add Interest receivable		61	
Rents receivable		19	80
			240

Revenues are subject to the accruals convention in the same way as expenses.

SUMMARY

15.   (a)   The net profit for an accounting period (usually one year) is calculated and demonstrated by showing gross profit, taken from the trading account, and deducting the itemised expenses.

(b)   Expenses are categorised according to custom or convenience to inform readers of the type of expense incurred.

(c)   The amount of an expense is not the amount invoiced or the amount paid but the cost of the *resource consumed* in the period.

(d)   The effect of taking precise consumption as the amounts of expenses in the profit and loss account is that at the year ends there are *accruals* and *prepayments*. Accruals are the cost of resources consumed by the year end but not invoiced or paid. Prepayments are the costs of resources paid for in the year but not consumed until the following year.

POINTS TO NOTE

16.   (a)   In practice a trading account and a separate profit and loss account are not usually produced. Instead they are combined as per Fig. 11.1.

(b)   The word "accrual" stems from a latin root meaning "to grow". Thus interest due on a loan accrues or grows with the passage of time.

Humphrey
Trading and Profit and Loss Account for the year ending 31st December 19-8

	£'000	£'000
Sales		163
Less Cost of goods sold:		
Opening stock	23	
Purchases	104	
	127	
Closing stock	28	99
Gross Profit		64
Less Expenses:		
Wages and Salaries	17	
Rent and Rates	6	
Heat and Light	4	
Telephone	2	
Motor expenses	7	
Sundries	3	
Discounts	5	
Bad debts	2	
Carriage outwards	6	52
Net Profit		12

Fig. 11.1

(c) In preparing a profit and loss account for presentation to the owners or managers of a business (or to examiners!), the calculation of the amounts to be included under an expense heading, should be done in *workings* which are *not* part of the profit and loss account. Thus:

Workings:	£
Rent and Rates - paid	2,000
Add accrued rent	400
	2,400
Less rates in advance	520
Expense of the year	1,880

The profit and loss account entry would simply be:

Rent and rates	£1,880

(d) The precise placing of an expense into the correct years is not always done in practice. For example, the expense, motor running expenses, would include the cost of petrol consumed. Strictly to place the cost in a particular year, the stock of petrol in the tanks of vans and cars should be determined. But as the difference made to the expense measurement of the year would be small and the organisational problems considerable, this would not be done. However, if the difference made was large (material is the accountant's word), then the stock would be taken. This might occur in shipping companies where the stock of fuel oil can be very significant and differ from year to year.

(e) The order in which expense headings are listed is not important. However, the largest amounts are often placed at the top of the list. Depreciation is usually placed at the bottom.

(f) If the number of expense headings are very large, then sub-divisions can be used. For example:

	£'000	£'000
Occupancy costs		
Rent	400	
Rates	280	
Fire Insurance	36	
Repairs	143	859
Selling costs		
Salesmen's salaries	361	
Motor expenses	110	
Advertising	292	763

SELF TESTING QUESTIONS

(a) What is the function of the trading account? (1).

(b) What is the function of the profit and loss account? (3).

(c) Draft a profit and loss account. (5).

(d) Explain the word "expense". (6).

(e) What items must be excluded from expenses? (7).

(f) What are accruals? (8).

(g) What are the alternatives to the accruals convention? (11).

(h) What treatments are possible for revenues in a profit and loss account? (14).

(i) How should the workings used to calculate the amount to be included under an expense heading be shown in a profit and loss account? (16c).

(j) When is sub-categorisation of expenses appropriate? (16f).

Exercises (Answers begin on page 451)

1. Cedric commenced in business on 1st January 19-4. His payments included:

Rent

		£
2. 2.-4	March 19-4 quarter	250
9. 6.-4	June 10-4 quarter	250
5.10.-4	September 19-4 quarter	250
2. 1.-5	December 19-4 quarter	250

Rates

6. 8.-4	March 19-4 quarter	310
	September 19-4 half year	662
24.12.-4	March 19-5 half year	662

Electricity

3. 5.-4	Meter read 24.4.-4	291
8. 8.-4	Meter read 26.7.-4	358
19.11.-4	Meter read 7.11.-4	401
3. 3.-5	Meter read 14.2.-5	461

Accountancy

15. 6.-5	Invoice dated 30.4.-5 for preparing accounts for the year 19-4	850

In each case, calculate the amount to be included in the profit and loss account for the year 19-4, under each expense heading.

2. Lana is in business as a florist. Her year end is 31 December 19-9 and around the year 19-9 she had the following transactions in van running expenses (in addition to petrol):

		£
October 1 19-8	Van licence paid	128
September 28 19-9	Van licence paid	160
July 1 19-8	Van insurance paid	388
July 1 19-9	Van insurance paid	452
December 7 19-8	Repair invoice received	230
January 8 19-9	Repair invoice paid	230
December 29 19-9	Repair completed	
January 3 19-0	Repair invoice received	140
February 18 19-0	Repair invoice paid	140
March 30 19-9	New sign on van paid for	100
November 19-9	New engine supplied and fitted and paid for	890

Calculate the profit and loss account figure for van running expenses in 19-9 if total petrol costs were £1.580.

3. *From the following figures prepare trading and profit and loss accounts and balance sheet for 19-8:*

	Henry Dr £	Henry Cr £	Lisa Dr £	Lisa Cr £
Sales			132,600	240,630
Stock 1st January 19-8	7,400		31,300	
Purchases	51,280		128,735	
Sales returns	1,043			
Vans	12,000		18,600	
Premises	124,000		101,000	
Rent	8,000		9,000	
Rates	6,500		5,800	
Carriage Inwards	2,120		1,240	
Carriage Outwards	830		1,600	
Capital 1 January 19-8		122,128		107,365
Drawings	13,000		12,800	
Repairs	6,200		17,100	
Loan to Fred at 15%	10,000			
Interest received		750		
Motor expenses	2,980		4,320	
Rent received				800
Insurance	4,260		1,260	
Debtors and Creditors	15,800	11,300	24,700	6,260
Bank balance	1,365			2,400
	266,778	266,778	357,455	357,455

For Henry
  (a) Stock at 31 December 19-8 is £8,200.
  (b) An invoice for £240, carriage inwards in December is not included in the above.
  (c) The above do not include rent for the half year to 31 March 19-9 £6,000.
  (d) The above figures do include insurance on Henry's life £1,200 and fire insurances of the business £900 for the twelve months to 30 April 19-9.
  (e) The interest £750 on the loan to Fred is for the half year to 30 June 19-8.
  (f) Repairs includes £4,500 for a new storage shed.
  (g) Ignore depreciation.

For Lisa
  (a) Stock at 31 December is £32,400.
  (b) Sales include £1,400 in December 19-8 to Smith. These goods were found to be broken and worthless on arrival and Smith was granted a credit note in January 19-9.
  (c) Rates do not include rates for the half year to 31 March 19-9 £5,200.
  (d) Accrue the accountant's fee £600.
  (e) Purchases includes £200 which was taken by Lisa for her own consumption.
  (f) Motor expenses includes tax on a van for the year to 31 July 19-9 £240.
  (g) Rent receivable for the half year to 31 December 19-8 has not been received or included in the above figures: £400.
  (h) Ignore depreciation.

4. *Wright rents a property in downtown Tipton. His year end is 31st December. Payments of rent and Receipts in respect of sublets are:*

30.12.-7	Paid Rent for quarter ending 31.3.-8	500
31.12.-7	Received rent for sublet for six months ending 31.5.-8	600
30. 4.-8	Paid rent for half year to 30.9.-8	1,400
30. 6.-8	Received rent for sublet for six months ending 31.11.-8	600
23.10.-8	Paid rent for quarter ending 31.12.-8	700

The sub tenant continued to rent into 19-9.

  (a) Calculate the rent payable charge to Profit and Loss account for the year 19-8 and the rent receivable credit to Profit and Loss Account for the same year.

(b) State the accruals and prepayments at 31.12.-7 and 31.12.-8.

(c) What assumptions have you made?

Exercises without answers

5.   *Karl commenced business on 1st June 19-4 and makes up his accounts to 31st May in each year. His payments included:*

Insurance	£	
3. 6.-4	*Fire Insurance year to 31.5.-5*	135
10. 8.-4	*Employers liability – provisional premium (a) year*	
	to 31.7.-5 530	
31.10.-4	*Consequential loss (b) year to 31.10.-5*	625
30.11.-4	*Public liability - year to 30.11.-5*	430
15. 8.-5	*Adjustment to E.L. (a) premium year to 31.7.-5*	68

Note:

(a) Employers liability insurance is compulsory for employers and insures against the risk of having to pay damages to employees who are injured at work. The premium is based on the wages paid in the year and if this is not known at the time of payment of the premium, an adjustment is required later.

(b) If a fire occurs, the loss of property is recovered under the fire policy but the loss of profits due to disruption of the fire is recovered under a consequential loss policy.

Telephone	£	
13. 6.-4	*Installation charge*	190
	Rent – quarter to 31.8.-4	80
18.10.-4	*Calls – quarter to 31.8.-4*	101
	Rent – quarter to 30.11.-4	80
19. 1.-5	*Calls – quarter to 30.11.-4*	124
	Rent – quarter to 28.2.-5	80
1. 5.-5	*Calls – quarter to 28.2.-5*	130
	Rent – quarter to 31.5.-5	80
2. 8.-5	*Calls – quarter to 31.5.-5*	146
	Rent – quarter to 31.8.-5	100

Printing and Stationery		
3. 8.-4	*Letterheads and sundries invoiced 2.6.-4*	440
3.11.-4	*Sundry stationery invoiced 1.10.-4*	260
14. 6.-5	*Letterheads delivered and invoiced 25.5.-5*	300

Interest		
30.11.-4	*Interest on loan of £40,000 bearing interest at 10%*	
	per annum for the half year to 30.11.-4	2,000
	Repayment of part of the loan	2,000

Calculate the accruals and the amounts to be included in his profit and loss account under each expense heading for the year 31st May, 19-5.

6.   *Which of the following items would not appear in the profit and loss account of Humbert whose business is a grocery shop in the high street:*

Repairs to the shop; his accountant's fee; van running expenses; a new deep freeze; insurance on the shop; a consignment of cheese; the rates on Humbert's house; a telephone bill; cash drawn from the shop for Humbert's own use; a new shop front; interest on a loan from Kay; a repayment of part of the loan from Kay; carriage of goods from a supplier to the shop; postage on sending some smoked salmon to a customer; rent received?

In each case explain why.

7. Gray is in business as a printer. His year end is 31st December. Among his expense payments are:

Advertising

21.12.-7	Advert in local paper to appear 12.1.-8	56
14. 1.-8	Advert in journal issue dated November 19-7	122
13. 6.-8	Advert in local paper to appear 4.7.-	845
11. 8.-8	Advert in local free paper June edition	66
5. 9.-8	Advert in journal to appear in October issue	127
13.12.-8	Advert in journal to appear in December, January and February editions	210
12. 1.-9	Advert in local paper of 23.12.-8	99

Subscriptions

22.12.-7	to "the new stationer" for 19-8	24
24. 1.-8	to the Chamber of Commerce for 19-8	60
12. 2.-8	to his Rotary Club	75
4. 5.-8	to "Stationery Now" for the 12 monthly issues beginning June 19-8	36
5.10.-8	to National Stationers Society for 19-8	71
7.12.-8	to "the new stationer" for 19-9	28
3. 1.-9	to the Midland Small Business Club for the year ending 31st October 19-9	108

(a) Calculate the amounts to be included in his profit and loss account for each of these expense headings for the year ending 31.12.-8.

(b) State the accruals and prepayments at 31.12.-7 and 31.12.-8.

(c) What accounting convention is involved here?

8. The following figures relate to (A) Paul's bicycle business (B) Clare's boutique and (C) Wayne's car spares business.

	A	B	C
Purchases	36,000	58,000	36,000
Sales	59,000	93,000	57,000
Stock 1.1.-7	10,800	9,820	4,700
Stock 31.12.-7	12,467	12,300	6,400
Sales returns	760		800
Purchase returns		1,500	1,300
Carriage inwards	254	318	210
Wages	6,877	8,933	7,540
Drawings	5,700	4,770	3,600
Interest receivable		1,232	
Rent	2,800	2,590	2,400
Rates	1,600	1,820	1,800
Repairs		1,622	2,600
New Van	2,677		
Extension to shop		4,500	
New racking system			3,500
Electricity	1,790	1,200	970
Accountants Fee	400	800	500
Carriage outwards	300	321	320
Van expenses	980	2,310	2,400
Stationery	543	780	590
Advertising	200	1,654	1,650

Notes:
for A: Rent includes rent for the quarter ending 28.2.-8 £600; electricity accrued is £432; the stock at 31.12.-7 did not include £300 from Black which was for goods in transit at 31.12.-7 which were invoiced in 19-7 and included in purchases.

for B: Rates includes rates for the half year ending 31.3.-8 £750; van expenses does not include a repair carried out in December 19-7 but not yet invoiced. It is expected to cost £258; stationery stocks at 31.12.-6 were £105 and at 31.12.-7 £143.

for C: Rent includes rent for the half year to 30.4.-8 £900; advertising includes a prepaid advertisement which will appear on 23.1.-8 £270; repairs includes £1,000 for a new shopfront.

(a) In each case, prepare trading and profit and loss account for the year.

(b) In each case, explain your treatment of drawings, carriage inwards, capital expenditure, carriage outwards and all accruals and prepayments.

9. *P.R. Match produces from his Trial Balance at 31st August, 1979 the following information.*

	£
Stock 1st September, 1978	2,000
Purchases	18,000

Match has a "Mark up" of 50% on "Cost of Sales". His average stock during the year was £4,000.

Required:
(a) Calculate the closing stock for P.R. Match at the 31st August, 1979.

(b) Prepare his Trading Account for the year ended 31st August, 1979 and

(c) Ascertain the total amount of Profit and Loss Expenditure that Match must not exceed if he is to maintain a Net Profit on Sales of 10%.   *(RSA)*

14. Bookkeeping for Expenses and Revenues

INTRODUCTION

1. At the end of each accounting period, a profit and loss account is prepared. This requires that details of the total expenditure on each category of expense will be available.

2. The information is obtained from the bookkeeping system which is designed so that the data is continuously available.

3. This chapter explains:

    (a) The day to day bookkeeping procedures for dealing with expenses.
    (b) The year end procedures.

BOOKKEEPING PROCEDURES – EXPENSES

4. Procedures are:

    (a) Determine what expense headings (rent, sales, heat and light etc.) are to be used.
    (b) Open accounts in the ledger under each expense heading in the form

Dr.		**Repairs to equipment**			Cr.
Date	Details	£	Date	Details	£

    (c) Enter details of incoming invoices for supplies and services into the appropriate account, *e.g.*

Dr.		*Printing and Stationery*	Cr.
19-5		£	
Jan 15	Philip – Letterheads	200	
Apr 19	Quintin – Posters	152	
July 24	Roger – Envelopes	181	
Nov 8	Steve – Sundry	63	
Dec 4	Cash*	102	
		698	

Note:

    (i) Entries on expense accounts are made on the debit side.

    (ii) The double entry is completed by crediting the accounts of the suppliers (Philip, Quintin etc), or if the supply was not on credit, the cash book (as item starred).

    (iii) The total expenditure in the year is determinable by totalling the account.

BOOKKEEPING PROCEDURES – REVENUES

5. Procedures are:

    (a) Determine what revenue headings are required. There are unlikely to be many - perhaps:

        Rent receivable
        Interest receivable
        Dividends from investments

    (b) Open accounts for each in the same manner as for expenses.

    (c) Enter details of revenues as they accrue or are received in the appropriate accounts as:

	Rent Receivable		
Dr.	19-5		Cr.
	Jan 19	Rent due from Tom	80
	Mar 14	Cash	20
	June 30	Rent due from Una	104
	Nov 8	Rent due from Tom	80
			284

Note:
(i)   Revenues are entered on the credit side.
(ii) Double entry is completed by debiting the cash book (e.g. the March 14th item) or the account of Tom or Una.
(iii) The total revenue in the year is determinable by totalling the account.

YEAR-END PROCEDURES
6. During the year 19-5, the following expenditures have occurred:

Dr. 19-5		**Insurance**	*Cr.*
		£	
Jan 15	Fire - year to 31.12.-5	620	
Mar 18	Burglary - year to 31.3.-6	428	
May 24	E.L. to 31.5.-6	710	
July 19	P.L. to 31.7.-6	464	
		2,222	

Note:
E.L.=   *Employers' liability.*
P.L.=   *Public liability (insuring against risk of paying damages for injury caused to a member of the public).*

7. Procedures are:

(a) Review the expenditures to see if any relate to 19-6.

The following do so:

Burglary	1.1.-6 – 31.3.-6	$\frac{3}{12}$ x 428 = 107
E.L.	1.1.-6 – 31.5.-6	$\frac{5}{12}$ x 710 = 296
P.L.	1.1.-6 – 31.7.-6	$\frac{7}{12}$ x 464 = 271
		674

This total is a prepayment and must be taken out of the account. This is accomplished by *crediting* as prepayment c/d and debiting the account in the next period as prepayment b/d.

(b) Consider if there are any unpaid insurances. Suppose that a special short period insurance cover for an explosion risk was negotiated for the Christmas 19-5 period. This was paid for in January 19-6 and cost £30. This is an *accrual* and should be *added* to the other expenditures by debiting the account as an accrual c/d. This is entered on the *credit* of the account in the next period – 19-6.

(c) The balance of the account now represents the total cost of insurance cover for the twelve months ending 31st December 19-5. Double entry is:

Credit: Insurance Account
Debit: Profit and Loss Account

		£
The total is:	Fire	620
	Burglary $\frac{9}{12}$ x 428	321
	E.L. $\frac{7}{12}$ x 710	414
	P.L. $\frac{5}{12}$ x 464	193
	Explosion	30
		1,578

(d) The account will appear as:

		£			£
	Balance as above (para 6)	2,222	31.12.-5	Prepayment c/d	674
31.12.-5	Accrual c/d	30	31.12.-5	Profit and Loss Account	1,578
		2,252			2,252
1.1.-6	Prepayment b/d	674	1.1.-6	Accrual b/d	30

Note:
The prepayment and the accrual will appear in the balance sheet at 31.12.-5 in current assets, and current liabilities respectively.

A TWO-YEAR EXAMPLE

Rent and Rates

19-4

		£			£
Jan 1	Rent – March ¼	500			
Apr 18	Rent – June ¼	500			
Sept 16	Rates – March ¼	475	Dec 31	Profit and Loss a/c	3,960
Sept 24	Rates – Sept ½	990			
Nov 16	Rent – Sept ¼	500	Dec 31	Prepayment c/d	495
Dec 30	Rates – Mar 85 ½	990			
Dec 31	Accrual	500			
		4,455			4,455

19-5

		£			£
Jan 1	Prepayment b/d	495	Jan 1	Accrual b/d	500
Jan 15	Rent – Dec 84 ¼	500	Dec 31	Profit and Loss Account	4,255
Mar 28	Rent – Mar ¼	550			
May 24	Rates – Sept ½	1,040	Dec 31	Prepayment c/d	610
June 19	Rent – June ¼	550			
July 8	Rent – Sept ¼	550			
Oct 3	Rent – Dec ¼	550			
Dec 28	Rent – Mar 85 ¼	610			
Dec 31	Accrual c/d	520			
		5,365			5,365

19-6

		£			£
Jan 1	Prepayment b/d	610	Jan 1	Accrual b/d	520

COMMENTARY

(a) The account is divided into separate periods, 19-4, 19-5 and 19-6.

(b) Expenditure is accumulated as it occurs, on the debit of the account. For 19-4 this is January 1st £500 to December 30th £990.

(c) At the year ends, accruals are computed. For 19-4 this is rent for the December Quarter and is entered on the debit *and* on the credit of the next year.

(d) At the year ends also, prepayments are computed. For 19-4 this is rates for the quarter to March 19-5 (half of £990) and it is entered on the credit of the account in 19-4 and on the debit in 19-5.

(e) The balance of the account is £3,960, representing rent and rates precisely for the year ending 31.12.-4. Double entry is:

Debit: Profit and Loss Account for 19-4
Credit: Rent and Rates Account

(f) Entries on the Rent and Rates Account are now £4,455 on *both* sides and the account is "empty".

(g) In 19-6, there appears £610 being rates for the first quarter of the year. This will be needed for the total of rent and rates for 19-6.

(h) In 19-5, on the debit, is some rent for 19-4, £500. This is not required for the 19-5 total and is taken out by the credit entry in 19-5 "Accrual b/d" £500.

SUMMARY

8. (a) Expense accounts in a double entry system are used to collect the data required of total analysed expenses for entry in the annual profit and loss account.

(b) Entries are made on the debit with double entry completed in the credits of accounts of suppliers or by a credit in the cash book.

(c) Revenue accounts are similar but are entered on the credit side.

(d)   At the year end, accruals are added on the debit and prepayments are deducted by entry on the credit. The double entry is completed by entries in the same account in the next period.

POINTS TO NOTE

9. (a)   In practice, individual expense invoices are first entered in a book called a daybook (or journal or invoice register) the entries therein are analysed under expense headings and the items under each heading are totalled and it is these totals which are entered on the debit of the appropriate accounts. This is discussed further in Chapter 15.

(b)   An account is filled up, say with the rent and rates, of 19-4. It must then be emptied so that the account is free to accept 19-5 items. If this was not done, then the total rent and rates would accumulate for ever. The emptying is done by crediting the account with "Profit and Loss account £x" and completing the double entry in the profit and loss account.

(c)   Wages accounts reflect the way wages are calculated and paid and the effect of income tax and national insurance.

The stages of wage payments are:

(i)   **Gross** pay is calculated. This may be 40 hours at £3.00 an hour = £120.

(ii)   Deductions are calculated. These might be Income tax - PAYE (Pay-as-you-earn) £20; National Insurance £11.

(iii)   The *net* pay which is actually paid to the worker is £120 - £20 - £11 = £89.

(iv)   At monthly intervals the amounts deducted (plus employer's contribution to national insurance), are paid to the Collector of Taxes.

Thus a wages account may look like this:

Wages Expense Account

19-4		£	19-4		£
Dec 31	Cash - weekly net wages	50,634	Dec 31	Profit and Loss Account (ii)	68,818
Dec 31	Payments to Collector of Taxes	16,104			
Dec 31	Accrual c/d (i)	2,080			
		68,818			68,818
			19-5		
			Jan 1	Accrual b/d (i)	2,080

(i)   The accrual represents deductions for PAYE and national insurance (plus employers' contributions), deducted from workers in 19-4 but not paid to the collector by 31st December 19-4.

(ii)   This represents the gross pay plus employer's contributions.

SELF TESTING QUESTIONS

(a) On which side of an expense account are the expenses incurred entered? (4).
(b) What is the function of an expense account? (1).
(c) Summarise the year end procedure re an expense account. (7).
(d) What is the purpose of the entry "transfer to profit and loss account" in an expense account? (9b).
(e) What revenue accounts may be required? (5a).

Exercises (Answers begin on page 452)

1. From the following data, write up the account:

"Heating Oil" in Adam's ledger for 19-5:

		£
1. 1.-5	Stock of heating oil at cost	420
4. 3.-5	Invoice received from Evan for oil	586
3. 7.-5	Invoice received from Frank for oil	269
5.10.-5	Cash paid to local church for surplus heating oil	100

| 28.12.-5 | Invoice received from Evan for oil | 1,390 |
| 31.12.-5 | Stock of oil at cost | 1,240 |

You should complete the account and show the transfer to profit and loss account and bring down any balance into the new period.

2.   *Jeff started in business on 6th April 19-4. He took on one employee, Marvin, and paid him monthly at an annual rate of £4,800. Each monthly cheque was £314.*

being	gross		400
less	PAYE	50	
	National Insurance	36	86
			314

Eleven cheques were paid. The cheque for the month ending 5.4.-5 was paid to Marvin on 10.4.-5. Ten cheques were sent to the Collector of Taxes being the PAYE, National Insurance deducted from Marvin and the employer's contribution to National Insurance up to 5.2.-5.

Each cheque was:

PAYE		50
National Insurance:	employee	36
	employer	42
		128

Write up the "salary" expense account for the year ending 5th April, 19-5.

3.   *Data concerning weekly salaries of Bert's business for 19-5 was:*

	£
Cheques paid to salaried employees during the year	87,643
Cheques paid to the Collector of Taxes in the year for PAYE and National Insurance	24,310

At the year end, the following were outstanding:

| Salary cheques for December 19-5 | 8,200 |
| PAYE and National Insurance | 2,919 |

Write up the account. Make the transfer to profit and loss account at the year end, bring down the balances.

4.   *Graham is a printer, but he also publishes a monthly newspaper which he started in October 19-4. Advertising revenues invoiced for the newspaper for the year ending 31st December, 19-4 were:*

		£
Invoiced in October:	for October Issue	2,105
	for November Issue	684
	for insertion in all Issues October 19-4 to March 19-5	540
Invoiced in November:	for November Issue	3,680
	for December Issue	2,086
	for insertion in all Issues November 19-4 to February 19-5	1,080
Invoiced in December:	for December Issue	5,200
	for January Issue	2,335

January 19-5 invoices included £400 for the December 19-4 issue.

Credit notes were issued in November 19-4 for £10 and in December 19-4 for £180 for cancelled advertisements.

Write up the advertising revenue account for the year ending 31st December 19-4, showing the transfer to profit and loss account and bringing down the year ending balances.

5.   *Enter the following transactions into the books of Walter, a trader, and balance the accounts.*

		£
at 30th June 19-3	Owing to P.M. Supplies Ltd	380
	Stock of packing materials	260
in 19-3/-4	Invoices from P.M. Supplies Ltd for packing materials	1,390

	Credit notes from P.M. Supplies Ltd	102
	Cash paid to P.M. Supplies Ltd	1,161
	Packing materials transferred by Walter to his private use	
	(for moving home)	120
	Damaged and scrapped packing materials (estimated cost)	100
at 30th June 19-4	Stock of packing materials	290

Exercises without answers

6.   Enter the following in the books of Oliver, an accountant who also acts as an insurance agent. He does not keep personal accounts for the insurance companies.

		£
at 30th Sept 19-4	Commission owed by insurance companies	390
in 19-4/-5	Received cheques from insurance companies for commission	1,480
	Received cheque for commission on policy taken out by Oliver on his own life	400
	Received cheque from Incredible Insurance Ltd for commission £190 less a premium due for a P.L. insurance policy of Oliver's £50	140
at 30.9.-5	Due from insurance companies for commission	530

7.   Williams commenced in business on 1.1.-7. In respect of rent and rates he made the following payments:

19-7		£
Jan 3	Rent for year to 30.6.-7	1,200
Jan 24	Rates for ¼ to 31.3.-7	380
May 19	Rates for ½ to 30.9.-7	840
Jun 23	Rent for ¼ to 30.9.-7	600
Nov 30	Rent for ½ to 31.3.-8	1,200
19-8		
Jan 4	Rates for ½ to 31.3.-8	840
March 19	Rent for ½ to 30.9.-8	1,300
Sept 16	Rates for ½ to 30.9.-8	910
Dec 7	Rates ½ to 31.3.-9	910
19-9		
Jan 14	Rent for ½ to 31.3.-9	1,400

Show the expense account Rent and Rates in Williams' ledger for the two years 19-7 and 19-8. Bring down the balances into 19-9. Explain the profit and loss charge to Williams who cannot see why the charge should not be the total payments made in each year. How would the balances of the account in each year appear in the balance sheet?

8.   The following balances and transactions are pertinent to the business of Shark, a manufacturer.

		£
31.12.-8	Heating Oil Stock	1,200
31.12.-8	Owing to HOS Ltd for Heating Oil supplied	630
21.1.-9	Invoice for Heating Oil from HOS	890
26.3.-9	Cheque to HOS	1,520
28.5.-9	Invoice for Heating Oil from HOS	2,300
14.7.-9	Transfer of Heating Oil to Shark's home	500
18.9.-9	Paid HOS	2,300
24.10-9	Invoice from HOS	1,130
24.11.-9	Credit note from HOS	240
30.12.-9	Paid HOS on account	300
31.12.-9	Heating Oil stock	820
13.1.-0	Paid HOS the amount owing	?
18.2.-0	Invoice from HOS	1,300
19.4.-0	Paid HOS on account	600
24.8.-0	Invoice from HOS	2,100
18.11.-0	Invoice from HOS	1,700
20.12.-0	Paid HOS	2,800
31.12.-0	Heating Oil stock	340

Write up the accounts "Heating Oil expense" and "HOS Limited" for 19-9 and 19-0.

9. Bill started in business on 1 January 19-9. He did not at first take out any insurance but gradually added policies as the year went on. These were:

Fire – year to 31 January 19-0	£600
E.L. – year to 28 February 19-0	£960
Household – year to 30 June 19-0	£132
P.L. – year to 30 September 19-0	£1,700

Write up his insurance expense account for 19-9.

10. The following is the expense account for Advertising for the year 19-9 for Lewis, a trader in carpets:

1.1.-9	Balance b/d	180	1.1.-9	Balance b/d	630
31.12.-9	Invoices	2,360	31.12.-9	Credit Notes	232
31.12.-9	Balance c/d	700	31.12.-9	Profit and Loss Account	2,138
			31.12.-9	Balance c/d	240
		3,240			3,240

Explain all the entries on the account.

11. (a) Mr A. Breviate has the following account in his ledger:

Rent and Rates

1983		£	1982		£
March 31 Cash – Rent		9,600	April 1 Balance b/f		2,200
Cash – Rates		2,400	1983		
			March 31 Cash from sub-tenant		800
Balance c/f		1,200	P & L A/c		10,200
		13,200			13,200

Upon enquiry you find that at the beginning of the year Breviate owed £2,400 rent in respect of the previous quarter, had prepaid rates to the extent of £600 and had received £400 in advance from a sub-tenant.

At the end of his financial year Breviate owed £2,400 for rent and had paid rates in advance amounting to £800. The sub-tenant owed £400 in respect of the previous quarter.

During the year Breviate paid £9,600 in respect of rent and £2,400 in respect of rates.

You are required to prepare separate accounts for rent payable, rent receivable and rates showing clearly the opening and closing balances and the transfers to Profit and Loss Account.

(b) At the beginning of his financial year Mr Breviate had a stock of stationery valued at £2,200, and at the end of the year £1,670. At the beginning of the year he owed £600 for stationery, paid £6,100 to suppliers of stationery during the year, and owed £520 at the end of the year.

You are required to prepare Mr Breviate's Stationery Account for the year.   (AAT)

12. The following are some of the balances which remain in the books of A. Small after compilation of a Trading Account for the year ended 31st December 1979.

	£
Proprietor's drawings	3,000
Rates	500
Staff salaries	3,000
Stationery	750
Insurance	400
Capital	20,000
Gross profit	9,000
Creditors	500

The following should be taken into consideration:

(a) £100 of the payment for rates is for the first quarter of 1980.

(b) Salaries due but unpaid on 31st December 1979 amount to £50.
(c) There is a stock of unused stationery valued at £150.
(d) £50 of the insurance payment is unexpired.

(i)   Prepare a profit and loss account for the year ended 31.12.79.

(ii)   Write up the proprietor's capital account for the year ended 31.12.79.

(iii) Write up the stationery account showing clearly the amount to be charged to the profit and loss account.   *(RSA)*

Depreciation

The next part of the manual is concerned with the *fixed assets* of a business and details the depreciation process whereby the cost of fixed assets is apportioned to the profit and loss accounts of successive periods.

Chapter 15 describes *capital expenditure* and the various depreciation methods and the treatment of disposals of fixed assets.

Chapter 16 is concerned with the bookkeeping aspects.

15. Depreciation

INTRODUCTION

1. This chapter is concerned with depreciation of fixed assets and is divided into six sections:

    (a) What depreciation is.
    (b) Depreciation methods.
    (c) Particular fixed assets.
    (d) Disposals of fixed assets.
    (e) Entries in Financial Statements.
    (f) Problems of implementation.

WHAT DEPRECIATION IS

2. Before describing depreciation, the definitions of fixed assets and capital and revenue expenditure must be considered.

3. Fixed assets are long lived resources which are used in the production of goods or services; examples are land, buildings, plant and machinery, office equipment, vehicles.

4. *Capital expenditure* is expenditure incurred in the *acquisition* of a fixed asset. *Revenue expenditure* is expenditure on a good or service which is consumed either immediately or within the space of the current or next accounting period.

5. It is the nature of a fixed asset that it gives benefit to the business for more than one accounting year. As an example, consider the purchase for £5,000 of a motor van to be used in the business for delivering goods to customers. The van will be used in the business for several years until it wears out or is otherwise disposed of.

The van will have a limited life, and if we assume that it will be used for five years and then be sold for scrap for £100 then it will give benefit to the business for five years and the net cost of that benefit is expected to be £4,900.

CAUSES OF AN ASSET HAVING LIMITED LIFE

6. Causes include:

    (a) **Wear and tear.** Physical assets inevitably decline with use, the effects of weather and other physical causes.

    (b) **Obsolescence.** Assets which are operationally effective may cease to be *economically* effective due to the effect of technological change or changes of fashion.

    (c) **Effluxion of time.** Some assets have intrinsically limited lives. For example, leasehold property and patent rights.

7. Profit for any given year is computed by summing the revenues of that year and deducting all the expenses incurred in earning those revenues. The van will be used in five separate accounting years and, therefore, its cost (or part of it) will be an expense of each of the years. The depreciation process is required to determine how much of the net cost of the van should be *allocated* to each year in which the van was in use.

DEPRECIATION METHODS

8. There are numerous *methods* of depreciating fixed assets. Three are considered here, two common methods:

    (a) The straight line method.
    (b) The reducing balance method.

    and one more rarely used
    (c) The Sum of the Digits method.

9.   In addition to the cost of acquisition of the fixed asset, there are two *estimates* required:

    (a) The *estimated* useful life.
    (b) The *estimated* residual, disposal or salvage value.

10. The Straight Line method

This is the simplest and commonest method. It *assumes* that the fixed asset net cost should be allocated in equal amounts to the years in which it is used.

    Example:
        Cost £5,000 on 1st Jan 19-3
        Estimated useful life 5 years.
        Estimated salvage value £100.
        Assume the accounting year ends on 31st December.

        Depreciation will be: $\dfrac{£5,000 - £100}{5} = £980$ a year.

Thus profit will not be reduced by £5,000 in 19-3, but by £980 in each of the years 19-3 to 19-7.

11. The Reducing Balance method

This method is used where it is assumed that more of the net cost of a fixed asset should be allocated to the earlier years of use than later years.

The computation takes place using the following stages:

    (a) Determine cost (c) and estimate useful life (n) and salvage value (s).
    (b) Insert in the formula:

$$r = 100\left(1 - \sqrt[n]{\frac{s}{c}}\right) \text{ to find } r, \text{ a percentage}$$

        In our example: $r = 100\left(1 - \sqrt[5]{\frac{100}{5,000}}\right) = 54.27\%$

    (c) Allocate as:

			£
	Cost		5,000
19-3	54.27% of 5,000		2,713
		(i)	2,287
19-4	54.27% of 2,287 (i)		1,241
			1,046
19-5	54.27% of 1,046		568
			478
19-6	54.27% of 478		259
			219
19-7	54.27% of 219		119
			100

    (i)   The £2,287 is described as the reducing or diminishing balance.

Thus profit will be reduced not by £5,000 in 19-3 but by different amounts in each of the five years of use, with the first year having the largest allocation and each succeeding year having a reducing or diminishing amount.

12. The Sum of Digits method

This method also assumes that more of the net cost of the fixed asset should be allocated in the earlier years, but it avoids extremes (£2,713 in 19-3 and only £119 in 19-7 in the reducing balance method).

The method is:

    (a) Determine cost and estimate useful life and salvage value.
    (b) Count down from number of years of useful life as follows:

$$5$$
$$4$$
$$3$$
$$2$$
$$\frac{1}{15}$$

and sum:

(c) Apply:

		£
19-3	5/15 of £4,900	1,633
19-4	4/15 of £4,900	1,307
19-5	3/15 of £4,900	980
19-6	2/15 of £4,900	653
19-7	1/15 of £4,900	327
		£4,900

13. The methods compared

A table showing the effects on profit of each method is:

	Straight Line £	Reducing Balance £	Sum of Digits £
19-3	980	2,713	1,633
19-4	980	1,241	1,307
19-5	980	568	980
19-6	980	259	653
19-7	980	119	327
	4,900	4,900	4,900

The overall effect on profits for the whole five year period is the *same* but the distribution or allocation to each year within the five year period is different.

The profit shown by the business will be the same for the whole five year period, *but the profits of the individual years will differ according to which depreciation method is chosen.*

WHICH DEPRECIATION METHOD SHOULD BE USED?

14. This is a matter of *policy* on the part of the management of the business. However, *consistency* must be applied. This means:

(a) All similar assets should be depreciated by the same method.
(b) The same method should be used in successive years.

15. Factors to be taken into account include:

(a) Ease of calculation. Clearly, the reducing balance method, in theory, means applying the formula to possibly thousands of separate items of plant. In practice, this is overcome by adopting a blanket rate, say 25%, and ignoring the estimated lives and salvage values.

(b) A view that the *benefit to the business* of a new fixed asset is greater than an older fixed asset. As depreciation is in effect a charge against profit for using an asset, depreciation should be greater in the earlier years of life.

(c) Repairs and maintenance increase through the life of an asset and thus depreciation should reduce. This is a specious argument but is often quoted.

(d) Whether the wearing out of the asset is a function of time (*e.g.* a patent right) or usage (*e.g.* a van).

PARTICULAR FIXED ASSETS

16. The method (Straight line etc.) and the expected lives of fixed assets vary according to the type of fixed asset. For example:

(a) **land.** Land can be said to have an infinite life and, therefore, is not depreciated.

(b) **Buildings.** Buildings do have a limited life. Depreciation should be applied to buildings on the straight line basis over the estimated useful life. Useful life is often taken as forty or fifty years.

(c) **Plant, machinery, equipment etc.** Practice varies widely and both methods of depreciation are found. Estimated lives vary from three to twenty years. It is notable that estimated lives of plant and machinery are falling with the rapid advance of technological change and the onset of early obsolescence.

(d) **Leasehold property.** This asset should be amortised (amortisation is the word used for this asset. It means the same as depreciation), on the straight line method over the period of the lease. Leasehold property, where the lease has more than fifty years to run, is often not amortised.

(e) **Wasting assets.** Wasting assets is a term that can be applied to all assets with a limited life but it is commonly applied to assets such as mines or quarries. If a mine is acquired at cost of say £1 million, it will have a useful life until no more minerals can be extracted economically. Clearly none of the depreciation methods so far explained are appropriate and the usual method is to estimate total extractable quantities, say, 200,000 tonnes and to measure the output each year.

Thus, if 25,000 tonnes were extracted, then $\dfrac{25,000}{200,000}$ x £1,000,000 = £125,000

- this is the depreciation.

This method is known as the *depletion* method.

DISPOSALS OF FIXED ASSETS

17. The methods described work well if in fact the van does last five years and is sold for £100, but in the majority of cases this does not happen.

Example:

Alf commences in business on 1st January 19-4.

On that day he bought a van for £4,000. He estimated its useful life to be four years and its salvage value as £400. The depreciation policy chosen was the straight line method. Profit will, therefore, be reduced by including depreciation on the van as follows:

	£
Cost	4,000
Depreciation in 19-4	900
Net book value 31.12.-4	3,100
Depreciation in 19-5	900
Net book value 31.12.-5	2,200
Depreciation in 19-6	900
Net book value 31.12.-6	1,300
Depreciation in 19-7	900
Estimated salvage value at 31.12.-	400

18. In fact, Alf sold the van at the end of 19-6 for £1,900. Thus the actual loss on the van was £4,000 - £1,900 = £2,100. The usage of the van was in the three years 19-4, 19-5 and 19-6. By the time the vehicle was sold, the Accounts for 19-4 and 19-5 had been prepared with depreciation of £900 in each and these Accounts cannot be altered. Consequently, profit has been reduced by £1,800 and the remainder of the loss (£300) will be regarded as depreciation in 19-6. Thus the depreciation will be allocated to account years as:

	£
Cost	4,000
Depreciation	900
Net book value 31.12.-4	3,100
Depreciation in 19-5	900
Net book value 31.12.-5	2,200
Depreciation in 19-6	300
Actual salvage value	1,900

19. Had the proceeds of sale been £2,350, then the depreciation in 19-6 would have been a negative figure of £150. That is, it would have been a revenue and not an expense.

20. The depreciation in the year of sale is thus the net book value at the beginning of the year less the proceeds of sale. Depreciation is based on estimates but in the year of sale, estimates are not required as the actual loss is known.

21. Depreciation in the year of sale is sometimes known as depreciation adjustment and sometimes as profit on sale (or loss on sale).

ENTRIES IN FINANCIAL STATEMENTS

22. (a) **Profit and Loss Account**

Depreciation is an expense and appear in the list of expenses, usually at the end of the list.

Depreciation can appear as a single figure, *e.g.*

	£
Depreciation	42,620

or it may be itemised, *e.g.*

Depreciation:		£
Buildings	10,200	
Plant	19,320	
Vehicles	13,100	42,620

(b) **Balance Sheet**
Fixed assets usually appear as:

	Cost	Accumulated Depreciation	Net Book Value
	£	£	£
Land	100,000	–	100,000
Buildings	231,000	40,700	190,300
Plant	168,904	72,308	96,596
	499,904	113,008	386,896

23. The accumulated depreciation is all the depreciation that has been debited to profit and loss account up to the date of the balance sheet. For example, if a machine was depreciated on the reducing balance method at 30% as:

	£
Cost in 19-4	1,000
Depreciation 19-4	300
Net book value 31.12.-4	700
Depreciation 19-5	210
Net book value 31.12.-5	490
Depreciation 19-6	147
Net book value 31.12.-6	343

It would be included in successive balance sheets as:

	Cost	Accumulated Depreciation	Net book value
	£	£	£
31.12.-4	1,000	300	700
31.12.-5	1,000	510	490
31.12.-6	1,000	657	343

24. Net book value is that part of the original cost which has not yet been included in the profit and loss account. It is thus the unused part of the original cost. It is *not* the amount that would be realised if the asset were sold. This is counter to the expectations of those unversed in accounting. Note it well.

THEORY AND CRITICISM

25. When a Fixed asset is acquired (say for £10,000), it is presumed to be capable of giving the business £10,000 of use. If part of this is recoverable at the end of its useful life (the salvage value, say £2,000), then the *use* over its life is presumed to be worth £8,000. As this use value is applied over several accounting periods, a means has to be found of spreading the use over the relevant accounting periods. The depreciation process is this means.

26. The depreciation process is a consequence of the *matching* convention whereby revenue and profit dealt with in the profit and loss account are matched with associated costs and expenses by including in the same account the costs incurred in earning them.

Part of the cost of earning the sales of the year will be the use of the representatives' cars. The depreciation process provides part of the original cost of the cars as an expense associated with those sales.

27. The depreciation process is also related to the *going concern* convention. The value of a fixed asset on a balance sheet is not the potential selling price of the asset. You may wonder why. The reason is that it is assumed that the business will continue in operational existence for the foreseeable future. Therefore, there is no *intention* or *necessity* to sell the fixed assets. The likely proceeds of sale if the assets were sold is, therefore, an irrelevant piece of information. It is, in any case, subjective and accountants like to be objective.

28. Students wonder why the resale value cannot be used to determine net book value when the resale value can be fairly estimated as it can be with, for example, cars. The answer is that the net book value is not the realisable value (= the value to an outsider who might buy it) but its *value to the business*. The value to the business is considered to be that part of the original cost which has not yet been exhausted.

29. The managers of a business have a choice of:

straight line	reducing balance
sum of digits	several other methods we have not discussed.

Each method will give a different measure of profit and value to fixed assets. This means that the management can, within limits, select the profit they desire.

30. In addition, estimates of:

useful life	salvage value

will vary according to the subjective views of the persons making the estimates. Consequently, profits and asset values will also vary for this reason.

31. For both the above reasons, comparisons of profit and capital employed can only be made between businesses with knowledge of the depreciation *methods* and *estimates* used. *Disclosure* in notes attached to the accounts is required. Here is an example:

"the cost of leasehold property is amortised on a straight line basis over the period of the lease. Other fixed assets are depreciated at 25% a year on cost."

Statement of Standard Accounting Practice No. 2 requires disclosure of all material accounting policies (see Chapter on Accounting Conventions).

PROBLEMS OF IMPLEMENTATION

32. Depreciation in year of purchase

If the year end is 31st December 19-4 and a fixed asset was acquired on 1st January 19-4, then in the 19-4 accounts, a full year's depreciation will be taken. If the fixed asset was acquired on 20th March, should a full year's depreciation or only a proportion of a year's depreciation be taken? The proportion being 286/365 where 286 is the number of days use in 19-4.

Practice varies. Some companies apportion depreciation in the year of purchase; others take a full year. Each company is said to have an *accounting policy* on the matter. In examinations, instructions are given or if they are not, take a full year's depreciation and state that you have done so, in the absence of instructions.

33. Depreciation in the year of sale

Common practice is to regard depreciation in the year of sale as the net book value at the beginning of the year less the proceeds of sale. Some accountants (and examiners) continue to depreciate up to the date of disposal and then make a depreciation adjustment of the net book value at that date less the disposal proceeds.

34. Use of fully depreciated assets

If it is estimated that a fixed asset will last four years and have a nil salvage value and the policy is to use straight line depreciation, then at the end of the fourth year, the asset will be fully depreciated and have a net book value of nil. However, it may be that the asset is not then disposed of, but continues in use. In that case, no depreciation of that fixed asset will appear in the profit computations of later years.

SUMMARY OF DEPRECIATION METHODS

Method	Formula	Remarks
Straight line	$\dfrac{C - S}{n}$	Exam requirement is often x% of COST
Reducing Balance	$100 \left(1 - \sqrt[n]{\dfrac{S}{C}}\right)$	Exam requirement is often x% of NET BOOK VALUE
Sum of Digits	$\begin{array}{ll} 5 & 5/15 \\ 4 & 4/15 \\ 3 & 3/15 \\ 2 & 2/15 \\ \underline{1} & 1/15 \\ 15 \end{array}$	Rarely found in practice

(if n = 5)

Key: C = Cost
S = estimated salvage value
n = estimated life

SUMMARY

35. (a) Capital expenditure is expenditure on items which will give benefit over more than one year - fixed assets.

(b) If such assets have a limited life, then their cost is an expense of each year in which they are used.

(c) Life limitation is caused by use, wear and tear, obsolescence or the effluxion of time.

(d) There are numerous methods of allocating the expenditure to specific time periods - the depreciation process. Methods include straight line and diminishing balance.

(e) Estimates are required of life and salvage value.

(f) A balance sheet shows the cost less accumulated depreciation which gives that part of the cost which has not yet been expensed to the profit and loss account.

(g) Disposals of fixed assets give rise to a depreciation charge (or credit) which is the difference between the net book value at the beginning of the year and the disposal proceeds.

(h) The depreciation process is a consequence of the *matching* convention.

(i) The showing of fixed assets in a balance sheet at unamortised cost is possible because of the going concern convention. It is assumed that the business is not going to be closed down and that therefore the fixed assets are not going to be sold. Thus there is no purpose to showing the amount they could be sold for. It is better to show the amount of value in use still to be enjoyed. Value in use is a proportion of the original cost.

(j) The method of depreciation used and the estimation of life used should be disclosed in notes to the Accounts.

(k) Choice of depreciation policy gives some flexibility to management in measuring the profit.

POINTS TO NOTE

36. (a) The expression "net book value" is often replaced by the expression "written down value".

(b) The taking of part of the cost of a fixed asset and including it in the profit and loss account is often called "providing" for depreciation and the accumulated amount of depreciation is called the provision for depreciation.

(c) The inclusion of an amount in the profit and loss account is sometimes called writing off. If an asset has a net book value of £100 and is scrapped with no salvage recovered, then the asset is said to be written off to profit and loss account.

(d) The meaning of capital expenditure should be particularly remembered.

(e) The formula for computing the rate for reducing balance depreciation is not known by all accountants of the older generation. In practice, many accountants use reducing balance but take an arbitrary percentage, such as 25%.

(f) The depreciation in the year of sale or disposal is often called a depreciation adjustment or a profit or loss on sale.

(g) We have seen that it is possible to manipulate the profit measurement by selecting a particular depreciation policy. However:

(i)   The method, once chosen must be used consistently.
(ii) The estimates made must be reasonable. They have to be acceptable to *auditors*.

(h) In examination questions, examiners often require depreciation to be n% of cost. This means using the straight line method.

(i) I cannot emphasise enough that net book value is not an estimate of saleable value.

(j) Property generally does not depreciate in value, although the limited life of buildings requires that the buildings part should be subject to depreciation. Some businesses *revalue* their property at intervals and change the net book value to the new (usually higher) valuation. This is permissible although full disclosure must be made. The new higher building value is then depreciated. The effect of this is that the assets are increased in value and profits are then diminished (because depreciation is based on a higher figure).

(k) If there is a revision of the estimated useful life of an asset, the unamortised cost should be charged over the revised remaining useful life.

(l) Statement of Standard Accounting Practice Number 12 – Accounting for depreciation covers many of the items in this chapter.

(m) An item in a balance sheet:

	Cost	Accumulated Depreciation	Net Book
Vehicles	200,000	74,000	126,000

this includes numerous vehicles bought at different times. The depreciation is the sum of the depreciations on each vehicle. Some vehicles will have one years depreciation, some several.

(n) In this chapter you have met the straight line method, the reducing balance method, the sum of digits method and the depletion method. Another method, much loved by theorists but little used in practice is the annuity method. It works by assuming the asset earns a rate of interest which is added to profit (via an "interest and depreciation" account). The depreciation is based on the straight line method and is sufficient to write off the asset cost and the added interest over the life of the asset.

Note:
(i) An interest rate has to be decided upon.

    (ii)   The actual depreciation can only be calculated from actuarial tables.

    (iii) The interest is calculated annually on the written down value of the asset.

    (iv) The profit and loss charge is the depreciation (the same each year) less the interest which *reduces* each year (as it is on the written down value). Thus the overall charge against profit is an *increasing* one.

SELF TESTING QUESTIONS

1.   *What is a fixed asset? Give examples. (3).*
2.   *What is capital expenditure? Give examples from your own household. (4).*
3.   *What are the causes of an asset having a limited life? (6).*
4.   *State three depreciation methods and illustrate them. (8–12).*
5.   *What if the formula for computing "r" in the reducing balance method? (11).*
6.   *How is the depreciation of a fixed asset calculated in the year of disposal? (18).*
7.   *How do fixed assets appear in a balance sheet? (22).*
8.   *Define net book value. (24).*
9.   *What is the connection between (a) the matching convention and (b) the going concern convention, and the depreciation process?*

Exercises (Answers being on page 453)

1.   *Compute the annual depreciation for each year and the year end net book value for the following vehicles:*

	Cost	Estimated Life	Estimated Salvage Value
	£	years	£
1.	8,000	5	200
2.	16,000	4	5,000
3.	7,500	3	0
4.	14,300	5	2,800

under the

    (a) Straight line method.   *(c) Sum of digits method.*
    (b) Reducing balance method.

Show the entries to be made in the Annual Accounts. (Assume all were acquired in 19-4 and the year end is 31st December).

2.   *A machine was purchased on 1.7.-4 for £10,000. Depreciation policy is 20% on cost (assuming a nil salvage value).*

Calculate the depreciation provisions in all years to 31st December 19-1 on the basis of:

    (i)   A full year's charge in 19-4.
    (ii) A half year's charge in 19-4.

and assuming (independently)

    (i)   The machine was sold on 31.5.-7 for £4,500.
    (ii) The machine was sold on 31.5.-7 for £2,600.
    (iii) The machine was sold on 31.12.-1 for £500.
    (iv) The machine was scrapped (no salvage) in 19-7.

3.   *The balance sheet of Zed at 31.12.-6 showed:*

	Cost	Accumulated Depreciation	Net Book Value
Vehicles	142,000	76,000	66,000

Depreciation policy is 20% on cost.

During 19-7
    Vehicle A which had been purchased on 1.1.-3 for £16,000 was sold for £2,000.
    Vehicle B which had been purchased on 1.1.-9 for £6,000 was sold for £500.
    Vehicle C was bought on 1.1.-7 for £20,000.
        Compute the depreciation for 19-7, including the adjustments required for vehicles A and B

4. Yucky Products Ltd acquires the following assets in 19-8:

    (a) A piece of land next to its factory for £10,800.

    (b) A factory extension built on the land. The extension is estimated to have a useful life of 30 years. The
         original factory has already been depreciated for 12 years of its estimated life of 30 years. The cost of the
         extension was £70,000 plus architects fees of £3,500.

    (c) A leasehold warehouse in Darlaston with 6 years left on the lease. The cost of the lease was £4,000 plus
         legal fees £340. The annual rent is £400.

    (d) A machine costing £16,000. The machine was purchased in July 19-8 and first used in October 19-8. Its
         estimated life is 10 years with a residual value of £2,000.

    (e) A quarry in Shifnal for £62,000. The quarry contains about 600 tons of the rare mineral hedonite. In 19-8 the
         amount extracted was 30 tons. It is estimated that without the minerals the quarry would have cost only
         £2,000.

Yucky's year end is 31 December. Suggest suitable depreciation methods for each asset and calculate the 19-8 charge.

What is an alternative phrase for "acquires the following assets"?

5.   What are the causes of limited life in the following assets:

A fork lift truck, a lease of a shop, a copper mine in Zambia, a freehold factory, a machine for making electronic
devices, machinery in a gold mine in South Africa, a wind turbine in Northern Scotland, a patent to make an unusual
kitchen appliance, the copyright in a celebrated textbook.

Exercises without answers
6.   Complete the annual depreciation for each year and the year end carrying value for the following vehicles:

	Cost	Est Life	Est Salvage Value
1	23,200	5	4,000
2	6,000	3	1,200
3	7,200	9	50
4	7,600	4	nil

under the:

    (a) Straight line method
    (b) Reducing balance method
    (c) Sum of digits method

Show the entries in the accounts for 19-6, 19-7 and 19-8, assuming all were purchased in 19-6 and the year end is
December 31.

7.   Alf purchased two lorries:

    A.   June 30 19-9   17,100
    B.   Sept 23 19-9   16,300

He sold them:

    A.   on July 16 19-2 for   3,000
    B.   on Aug 24 19-3 for   8,400

Calculate depreciation and profit/loss on sale on the following separate assumptions:

    (a) Straight line depreciation over 6 years is used with nil salvage value and depreciation is calculated from
         the date of purchase and to the date of sale.

(b) Reducing balance depreciation is used at 25% a year with a full year's charge in the year of purchase and no charge in the year of disposal. Year end is 31 December.

8. Alisa charges depreciation on her vans right up to the date of sale. Ben suggests that she should depreciate her vans in the year of sale. Would there be any difference in profit?

9. G. Chen commenced business on 1st January 1978 with S$6,200 in his bank account. He traded from rented premises, for which the quarterly rental was S$300. As business progressed in the first trading year, Chen prepared the following quarterly accounts:

3 months ended	31.3.78 S$	30.6.78 S$	30.9.78 S$	31.12.78 S$
Receipts from customers	2,800	4,100	6,200	6,900
Opening Stock	–	800	920	1,080
Cash paid to suppliers	3,200	2,600	4,220	4,090
	3,200	3,400	5,140	5,170
Closing Stock	800	920	1,080	960
	2,400	2,480	4,060	4,210
Drawings	1,000	1,080	1,100	1,200
Rent paid	300	300	300	–
Other expenses paid	180	275	202	166
Delivery vehicle bought for cash	2,000	–	–	–
	3,480	1,655	1,602	1,366
Net Profit/(Loss)	(3,080)	(35)	538	1,324

At the end of his first year's trading, Chen explains to you that, having no bookkeeping training, he is not sure if his profit statements are satisfactory, and admits that he is quite unable to prepare a balance sheet as at 31st December 1978.

You establish that end-of-quarter stock valuations have been correctly made at cost, but that outstanding amounts have not been taken into account, including:

31st December 1978 S$
        owing from customers   785
        owing to suppliers   233

Chen anticipates a five-year life for his vehicle with no residual value.

Required:
Using Chen's draft accounts, the additional information, and correcting any obvious unmentioned errors, prepare:

(a) A Trading and Profit and Loss Account for G. Chen for the year ended 31st December 1978. Quarterly figures are not required.

(b) A balance sheet as at 31st December 1978.   (LCCI)

16. Bookkeeping for Fixed Assets and Depreciation

INTRODUCTION

1. Fixed assets are recorded in the double entry system on the debit of fixed asset accounts.

2. There are two methods of dealing with the depreciation of fixed assets.

3. The bookkeeping for disposals requires a disposal account.

FIXED ASSET ACCOUNT

4. Fixed assets are dealt with in double entry systems as:

   (a) Open an account for either:

      (i) each fixed asset - *e.g.* Filing Cabinet.
      (ii) each class of fixed asset - *e.g.* Fixtures and Fittings.

as:

Fixtures and Fittings Account

Dr.					Cr.
Date	Description	£	Date	Description	£

5. Enter acquisitions of fixed assets as:

Fixtures and Fittings Account

		£
5.1.-5	Filing Cabinets	400
28.2.-5	Shelving	582
		982
29.3.-6	Racks	184
		1,166

The double entry is completed by a credit entry on the account of the supplier as:

Filing Cabinet Supply Co. Ltd.

		£
5.1.-5	Filing Cabinets	400

or if there is no invoice and the acquisition is by a simple cash payment, the credit is in the cash book.

DEPRECIATION

6. There are two methods of recording depreciation of fixed assets.

7. **Method 1** is:

Morris Van

		£			£
1.1.-5	Cost (1)	5,600	31.12.-5	Depreciation (ii)	1,250
			"	Balance c/d (iii)	4,350
		5,600			5,600
1.12.-6	Balance b/d	4,350	31.12.-6	Depreciation (ii)	1,250
			"	Balance c/d (iii)	3,100
		4,350			4,350
1. 1.-7	Balance b/d	3,100	31.12.-7	Depreciation (ii)	1,250
			"	Balance c/d (iii)	1,850
		3,100			3,100
1. 1.-8	Balance b/d	1,850	31.12.-8	Depreciation (ii)	1,250
			"	Balance c/d (iii)	600
		1,850			1,850
1. 1.-9	Balance b/d	600			

Note:

(a) Depreciation is over 4 years on the straight line method with an estimated salvage value of £600.

(b) The double entry is completed by:

   (i) a credit to the supplier's account.
   (ii) a debit to the profit and loss account.

(c) The original cost is entered on the debit side. As the van's original cost value (£5,600) is used up, a part of the cost (£1,250) is taken away by an entry on the credit side and placed on the debit side of the profit and loss account where it is an expense.

(d) The remaining, undepreciated part of the cost (iii) is the balance on the account and is the net book value of the asset.

8. **Method II** is slightly more difficult to follow and is much more common in practice. The procedure is:

   (a) Maintain the asset at COST:

Morris Van at cost

	£
1.1.-5 Cost	5,600

This will be the only entry in the account until the van is disposed of.

   (b) When the first depreciation entries are required, open a new account as:

Provision for depreciation of Morris Van

	£
31.12.-5 Profit & Loss a/c	1,250

The double entry is completed by a debit in the profit and loss account.

If the two accounts (Van and provision for depreciation) are looked at as one account, then the bookkeeping is the same as in method I.

   (c) At each subsequent accounting date:

Provision for depreciation of Morris Van

	£
31.12.-5 Profit and loss a/c	1,250
31.12.-6 Profit and loss a/c	1,250
	2,500
31.12.-7 Profit and loss a/c	1,250
	3,750
31.12.-8 Profit and loss a/c	1,250
	5,000

Note:

(i) The net book value at any accounting date is found by (for example at 31.12.-7):

Morris van at cost	*5,600*	
Less Accumulated depreciation	*3,750*	*1,850*

(ii) The cost and also the accumulated depreciation are immediately available using method II.

DISPOSALS – SINGLE ASSETS

9.   The treatment of disposals depends on the method of recording depreciation. We will assume that the van was sold on 31.7.-7 for £2,630.

(a)   **Method I**

Morris Van Account

		£			£
1. 1.-7	Balance b/d	3,100	31. 7.-7	Proceeds of sale (i)	2,630
			31.12.-7	Profit & Loss a/c (ii)	470
		3,100			3,100

Note:

(i)   The double entry is completed by a debit to the person who bought the van or to the cash book.

(ii)   This is the depreciation for the year and is debited to profit and loss account. This entry is sometimes called the depreciation adjustment or profit (or loss) on sale.

(b)   Method II

Morris Van Account

		£			£
1. 1.-5	Cost	5,600	31. 7.-7	Disposal a/c (i)	5,600

Provision for Depreciation on Van Account

		£			£
31. 7.-7	Transfer to Disposal	2,500	1. 1.-7	Balance b/f	2,500

Disposal of Van Account

		£			£
31. 7.-7	Cost (i)	5,600	31. 7.-7	Accumulated Depreciation (ii)	2,500
			31. 7.-7	Proceeds of Sale (iii)	2,630
			31.12.-7	Profit and Loss a/c (iv)	470
		5,600			5,600

Note:

   The double entry (i) and (ii) which removes the vehicle from its own account and the accumulated depreciation from the provision account and enters both on a disposal account. The disposal account now has a balance of (£5,600 – £2,500) which is £3,100 and the net book value. The proceeds of sale (iii) are then entered and the depreciation (or loss on sale) for the year (iv) is found.

DISPOSALS – GROUPED ASSETS

10.   The treatment of disposals in the last section is simple and may seem cumbersome for such small needs, but it becomes more complex when several or numerous fixed assets are grouped into one fixed asset account for a particular type of fixed asset, *e.g.* vehicles or plant and machinery.

11.   Farm equipment in the books of Giles shows:

Farm Equipment at cost

		£		£
1.1.-6	Balance b/f	164,830		

Provision for depreciation on Farm Equipment

		£
1.1.-6	Balance b/f	73,820

Depreciation is at 25% reducing balance. In 19-6, the following transactions took place:

4.10.-6   Acquisition of a new combiner   £36,400
5.11.-6   Disposal of a tractor for £1,000. The tractor had cost £7,200 in 19-2.

Enter these transactions in the books, compute and enter the depreciation for the year and show the balances to carry forward and the entries in the Financial Statements for 19-6.

Farm Equipment at cost

		£			£
1.1.-6	Balance b/d (a)	164,830	5.11.-6	Disposal a/c - Tractor (c)	7,200
4.10.-6	Combiner (b)	36,400	31.12.-6	Balance c/d (d)	194,030
		201,230			201,230
1.1.-7	Balance b/d (d)	194,030			

Provision for depreciation of Farm Equipment

		£			£
5.11.-6	Disposal a/c - Tractor (f)	4,922	1.1.-6	Balance b/d (e)	73,820
31.12.-6	Balance c/d (h)	100,181	31.12.-6	Profit and Loss a/c	
				Depreciation 19-6 (g)	31,283
		105,103			105,103
			1.1.-7	Balance b/d (h)	100,181

Disposal a/c - Tractor

		£			£
5.11.-6	Cost (e)	7,200	5.11.-6	Accumulated Depreciation (f)	4,922
			"	Cash	1,000
			"	Profit and Loss a/c (i)	1,278
		7,200			7,200

Profit and Loss Account for the year ending 31st December 19-6

	£
Depreciation	32,561 (j)

Balance Sheet as at 31st December 19-6

	Cost	Accumulated Depreciation	Net Book Value
Farm Equipment	194,030	100,181	93,849 (k)

Note:

(a) This is all the farm equipment owned at this date at what it originally cost.

(b) This is the new combiner, double entry will be completed by a credit on the supplier's account.

(c) The tractor must be taken out of the account at the value at which it is included in the total of £164,830, viz cost.

(d) This is the historical cost of the farm equipment owned at 31.12.-6.

(e) This is the depreciation charged to profit and loss in all periods up to 31.12.-5 on the assets owned at that date.

(f) This takes out of the £73,820, all the depreciation included for the tractor. It is calculated as:

	£	
Cost	*7,200*	
Depreciation 19-2	*1,800*	*- 1,800*
	5,400	
Depreciation 19-3	*1,350*	*- 1,350*
	4,050	
Depreciation 19-4	*1,012*	*- 1,012*
	3,038	
Depreciation 19-5	*760*	*- 760*
Net Book Value 31.12.-5	*2,278*	
Total depreciation =	*4,922*	

(g) This is the depreciation for the year calculated as:

	£
Cost of assets owned at 31.12.-6 (d)	*194,030*
Accumulated depreciation on those assets - *i.e.* after taking out the item sold (£73,820 - £4,922)	68,898
	125,132
Depreciation at 25% on the *reducing* balance	31,283

(h) accumulated depreciation on the assets owned at that date - including the item bought but after eliminating depreciation on the item sold.

(i) The depreciation on the item sold is calculated in the same way as we have now seen several times (para 9).

(j) The depreciation charge for the year is: £31,283 + (i) £1,278 = £32,561

(k) The net book value of the farm equipment is (d) - (h).

GRAPHING DEPRECIATION AND BOOK VALUES

12. Assume that Joe Acca is not sure what is the best depreciation policy for his parcels delivery service. He has paid £6,000 for the van and expects to keep his van for about five years and then expects the van to be sold for about £1,000.

Alternative policies are:

Straight line: £1,000 a year
Reducing balance: 30% (check this rate with the formula correcting to the nearest whole percent)
Sum of the years digits: year 1 - £1,667, year 2 - £1,333, year 3 - £1,000, year 4 - £667, year 5 - £333.

In order to see the effect of the different methods clearly, it may be desirable to present the information graphically as:

(Note that he expects his profit before depreciation to be about £5,000.)

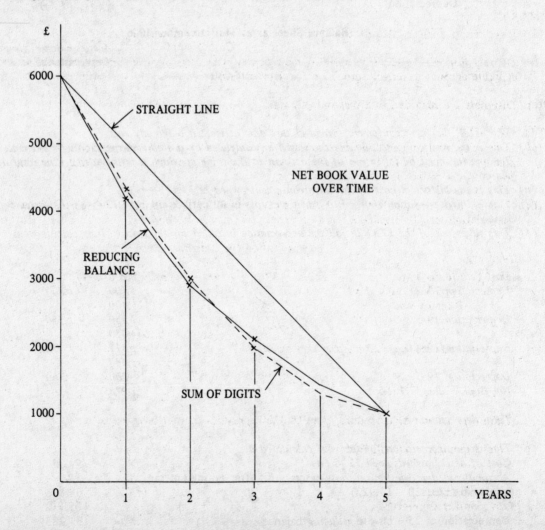

What criteria should he use to choose between the methods?

Possible answers are:

(a) He wishes to show very accurate accounts which reflect:

    (i)   the fact that the resale value of the van diminishes more rapidly in the earlier years.

    (ii) the fact that repairs and maintenance increase as time goes by.

    (iii) sales should be matched with a higher proportion of the costs in the earlier years as the van is newer and thus gives more valuable inputs.

(b) He wishes to show even profits to impress his banker who has lent him money. In particular, he does not want a large depreciation charge in the first year.

(c) He wishes to minimise his tax charge in the first year. (Note that under UK tax rules the depreciation method does NOT affect tax payable but in some countries the depreciation method may affect tax payable in any particular year.)

(d) He wishes to show a high return on capital employed in the first year.

Reading from the graphs and reflecting he can easily see that:

Under criterion (a) reducing balance or sum of digits methods only will suffice.
Under criterion (b) straight line method is best.
Under criterion (c) reducing balance is best (this does not apply in the UK)
Under criterion (d) straight line is best as both return is highest and capital employed is highest.

SUMMARY

13. (a) Fixed assets are recorded on the debit side of the appropriate account.

(b) Depreciation can be recorded on the credit of the asset account or as a credit balance on a completely separate account called the provision for depreciation account.

(c) Disposals are recorded in a disposals account.

POINTS TO NOTE

14. (a) In practice, the grouped fixed asset account (*e.g.* motor vehicles) is more commonly found than individual accounts for each asset and this seems to cause difficulty to students. Remember that the grouped account is really only a collection of individual assets.

(b) If there are several classes of fixed asset or the fixed assets have individual accounts, then the depreciation may be assembled in a "depreciation for year account" as:

Depreciation for Vans for year

19–5		£	19–5		£
Dec 31	Morris Van	826	Dec 31	Profit and Loss a/c	2,076
	Ford Van	520			
	Renault Van	730			
		2,076			2,076

(c) In a trial balance, fixed assets may appear as:

	Dr	Cr
Vehicles	6,430	

If there is no provision account, then £6,430 represents the net book value.

More commonly, you will find:

	£	£
Vehicles at cost	15,820	
Provision for depreciation		9,390

Note that the provision represents accumulated depreciation up to the beginning of the year.

SELF TESTING QUESTIONS

(a) What are the two methods of dealing with depreciation in a double entry system? (6).

(b) How are disposals dealt with? (9).

(c) What is the purpose of transferring the accumulated depreciation on an asset to a disposal account on disposal of that asset? (11f).

(d) Distinguish between a provision for depreciation account and a depreciation expense account. (13b).

Exercises (Answers begin on page 454)

1. Tasmin purchased a lorry for the business costing £12,000 on 1st January 19-8. She estimated its salvage value at £1,000 after the end of its useful life of 6 years. She sold it on 31 December 19-1 for £2,300. Her year end is 31 December.

Show these items in double entry accounts.

2. David commenced in business on 1.1.-4. In his first three years he bought three lorries:

		Cost £
1.1.-4	Dodge	15,800
1.7.-5	Foden	30,400
1.3.-6	Mercedes	28,920

Assuming that depreciation is 20% on cost, with no salvage value, and that depreciation in the year of purchase is apportioned, show for the first three years:

(a) Lorries Account (all lorries on one account) with depreciation on the same account.

(b) Lorries at cost Account (all lorries on one account) with depreciation on a separate provision for depreciation account.

(c) Separate accounts for each lorry with depreciation on the same account.

(d) Separate accounts for each lorry with separate provision for depreciation accounts.

Exercises without answers

3. Graham has motor vehicles in his balance sheet as at 31st December 19-4 as:

	£
Motor Vehicles at cost	684,936
Less Accumulated Depreciation	413,726
Net Book Value	271,210

In 19-5, the following occurred:

Acquisitions	
Renault	7,100
Audi	8,620
Disposals	
Fiat (original cost in 19-2 £6,000)	1,500
Peugeot (original cost in 19-0 £4,300)	500

Depreciation policy is straight line with estimated life four years and nil salvage value. A full year's depreciation is charged in the year of acquisition.

Show:

(a) The vehicles (at cost) account for 19-5.

(b) The provision for depreciation on vehicles account for 19-5.

(c) The disposals account in 19-5.

(d) The profit and loss account and balance sheet entries in the 19-5 accounts.

4. Neil has office equipment in his balance sheet at 30th June 19-4 as follows:

	£
Office Equipment at cost	98,924
Less Accumulated Depreciation	46,818
	52,106

Depreciation policy is 20% on the reducing instalment method with a full year's depreciation in the year of acquisition.

In the year 19-4/5, the following transactions occurred:

Acquisitions		£
18.12.-4	*Computing Equipment*	*1,600*
19. 3.-5	*Filing Cabinets*	*4,380*

Disposals
19. 1.-5	*Computing equipment which had cost £6,000 on 23.4.-2*	*100*
20. 4.-5	*Word processing equipment which had cost £4,600 on 13.11.-0 250*	
20. 6.-5	*Adding Machine which had cost £800 on 13.5.-9 was scrapped*	

Show for the year ending 30.6.-5:

(a) *The office equipment (at cost) account.*
(b) *The provision for depreciation on office equipment account.*
(c) *The disposals account.*
(d) *The entries in the profit and loss account and the balance sheet.*

5. *The balance sheet of Howard showed for vehicles:*

	£
Vehicles at cost	*30,000*
Accumulated depreciation	*19,000*
Net book value	*11,000*

Depreciation policy is straight line over 5 years with nil residual value.

Pop on seeing these figures asks why the accumulated depreciation figure is not a multiple of £6,000. Answer him.

6. *Herbert commenced business on 1.1.-4. In his first three years he bought four machines:*

		£
1.1.-4	*Press*	*7,120*
31.8.-4	*Lathe*	*2,491*
30.9.-5	*Milling Machine*	*3,980*
31.3.-6	*Guillotine*	*6,705*

Assuming that depreciation is at 25% on the reducing balance method with full depreciation in the year of purchase, show for the first three years:

(a) *Separate accounts for each machine with depreciation in the same account.*
(b) *Separate accounts at cost for each machine with depreciation in a separate provision account.*
(c) *Machines (altogether) account with depreciation in the same account.*
(d) *Machines at cost account with depreciation in a separate provision account.*

7. *In Question 2 above, the Dodge truck was sold on 15.5.-7 for £2,600. Give the entries to record this event on each alternative (a-d).*

8. *In Question 6 above, the Lathe was sold on 18.6.-7 for £1,000. Give the entries to record this event on each alternative (a-d) and calculate the depreciation for all machines for 19-7 assuming there were no acquisitions or other sales in 19-7.*

9. *Gill is considering what depreciation method to use for his concrete making machine costing £40,000, lasting 8 years and having a salvage value of £4,000. Graph annual depreciation, net book value, net profit (profit before depreciation is £12,000), return on capital employed (net book value each year without the machine is £20,000) using straight line, reducing balance and sum of digits methods.*

Repeat the exercise using £50,000, 6 years and £8,000.

10. *Twuck Ltd are haulage contractors. Their lorries account at 31.12.-7 showed:*

	£
Lorries at cost	364,000
Accumulated depreciation	154,000
Net Book Value	210,000

In 19-8 the following transactions occurred:

Purchases: Lorry number 64 - £23,000, 65 - £41,000, 66 - £39,500.

Disposals: Lorry number 38 - £2,000, 41 - £3,700, 53 - £5,900.

Lorry 38 was purchased in 19-3 for £12,000, 41 in 19-5 for £15,000 and 53 in 19-7 for £10,000.

Lorries are depreciated on the straight line method over 5 years assuming a nil salvage value.

Lorries (excluding 38) costing £23,000 had been purchased in 19-3 or earlier.

Required:
  (a) Show the lorries account, the provision for depreciation account and the lorries disposal account for 19-8.
  (b) Show these accounts on the assumption that the reducing balance method is used at a rate of 30%.
  (c) Give two alternative expressions for Net Book Value.

11. *A company's plant and machinery account at 31st December 1978 and corresponding depreciation provision account broken down into years of purchase, are as follows:*

Year of purchase	Plant and machinery at cost	Depreciation provision
	£	£
1962	20,000	20,000
1968	30,000	30,000
1969	100,000	95,000
1970	70,000	59,500
1977	50,000	7,500
1978	30,000	1,500
	300,000	213,500

Depreciation is at the rate of 10% per annum on cost. It is the company's policy to assume that all purchases, sales or disposals of plant occurred on 30th June in the relevant year for the purposes of calculating depreciation, irrespective of the precise date on which these events occurred.

During 1979 the following transactions took place:

1. *Purchase of plant and machinery amounted to £150,000.*
2. *Plant that had been bought in 1968 for £17,000 was scrapped.*
3. *Plant that had been bought in 1969 for £9,000 was sold for £500.*
4. *Plant that had been bought in 1970 for £24,000 was sold for £1,500.*

You are required to:

  (a) Calculate the provision for depreciation of plant and machinery for the year ended 31st December, 1979. In calculating this provision you should bear in mind that it is the company's policy to show any profit or loss on the sale or disposal of plant as a completely separate item in the profit and loss account.

  (b) Show the following ledger accounts during 1979:

   (i)   Plant and machinery, at cost.
   (ii) Depreciation provision.
   (iii) Sales or disposals of plant and machinery.

  (c) Show at 31st December 1979 the breakdown under years of purchase of the balances on the:

   (i)   Plant and machinery at cost account.
   (ii)   Depreciation provision account.   *(CIMA)*

PRACTICAL BOOKKEEPING

In theory a double entry bookkeeping system consists of a finite series of separate accounts. It would be possible to include all the accounts in one large book or *ledger*. In practice, several problems would occur with this approach because:

(a) Some accounts have a large number of entries (*e.g.* cash) and some very few (vehicles).

(b) Some accounts must be kept up to date at all times (*e.g.* debtors and creditors) and some need only be entered at intervals (*e.g.* sales and purchases)

(c) If the system can be broken down into sections, errors can be detected more easily.

(d) Entries in sales and purchases accounts would be so numerous that some marshalling of the data before the entry in the accounts is desirable.

(e) Control over the account recording the asset (or liability!) cash at bank can be effected with the *bank statement*.

(f) Separate responsibility for different sections of the system is often desirable.

(g) A dynamic system is required for:

   (i)   Handling the primary documents.
   (ii) Initial recording of the primary documents.
   (iii) Entering the double entry accounts.
   (iv) Verifying accuracy with a trial balance.
   (v)   Correcting errors.

Chapter 17 deals with books of prime entry and deals with problems (a), (d) and (g)(ii).

Chapter 18 is concerned with the cash book and Chapter 19 shows how the cash book can be verified by reconciling it with bank statements.

Chapter 20 describes how a bookkeeping system can be broken down into sub-systems to facilitate error correction and control (b), (c) and (f).

Chapter 21 demonstrates the special entry system that is applied to small cash payments.

Chapter 22 discusses, in more detail than Chapter 9, the trial balance and deals with (g)(iv) and error correction (g)(v).

17. Books of Prime Entry

INTRODUCTION

1. The early writers on bookkeeping including Pacioli recognised that the recording process involved several steps:

   (a) The transactions.
   (b) Evidencing the transactions in the form of documents.
   (c) Entering the details of each transaction in a primary book or journal.
   (d) Entering the details of each transaction in the double entry accounts.

Modern systems of bookkeeping follow this pattern and this chapter shows you how the most common transactions are recorded.

TRANSACTIONS AND DOCUMENTAL EVIDENCE

2. The most frequent transactions that need to be recorded together with the documentary evidence that is usually available are:

Transaction	Documentary evidence
(a) Credit sales	Copy sales invoices
(b) Purchases and expenses made or incurred on credit	Suppliers' invoices
(c) Cash sales	Till rolls
(d) Receipts from customers	Bank paying-in book counterfoil
(e) Payments to suppliers of goods and expenses on credit	Cheque stubs
(f) Wages payments	Wages records

SALES DAY BOOK

3. Sales on credit to customers are evidenced by sending invoices to the customers. A copy is kept and the invoice and the copy contain details of the sale including:

   (a) The number of the invoice - consecutive and put on by the printer when the invoice sets are printed.
   (b) Name and address of the customer.
   (c) Date.
   (d) Details of goods sold, price, and the monetary total of the invoice.

4. The details of the invoices are entered into a book known as the sales day book. A typical ruling is:

SALES DAY BOOK

Date	Invoice Number	Customer	Gross £
28.7.-3	100	John	71.76
28.7.-3	101	David	34.50
29.7.-3	102	Philip	30.13
29.7.-3	103	XY Co. Ltd.	161.00
			297.39

5. Procedures are:

   (a) Invoices are typed as and when the sales occur.
   (b) The sales day book is entered daily from the copy invoices.
   (c) The customer's account in the double entry system is debited with the entry, *e.g.*

Dr		John		Cr
23.7.-3	Invoice 100		71.76	

   (d) Weekly or monthly the sales day book is totalled and the totals entered on the credit side of the sales account:

Dr		Sales Account		Cr
		31.7.-3	Sales day book	71.76

6. The sales day book is known as a book of *prime entry* (prime = first). It is simply a list of sales invoices. *It does not form part of the double entry system.* The double entry is the subsequent entries in the customer accounts and the sales account.

The sending of the invoice is the final stage in a fairly complex process (see Fig. 17.1).

The system for recording sales invoice data is outlined in Fig. 17.2.

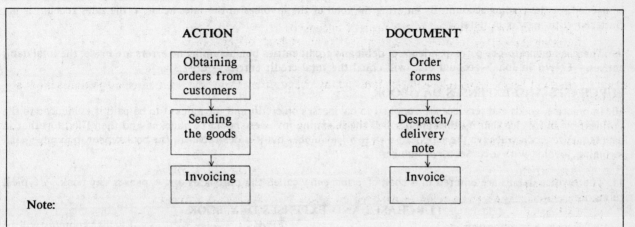

ACTION

- Obtaining orders from customers
- Sending the goods
- Invoicing

DOCUMENT

- Order forms
- Despatch/ delivery note
- Invoice

Note:

(a) Orders can be obtained through the efforts of representatives or agents or orders may be received from satisfied customers or as a result of advertising or reputation.

(b) Despatch/delivery notes serve at least two functions: as a despatch note to record the sending of goods to a customer from which an invoice can be made out: as a delivery note to advise the customer of the nature of the goods delivered.

Fig. 17.1

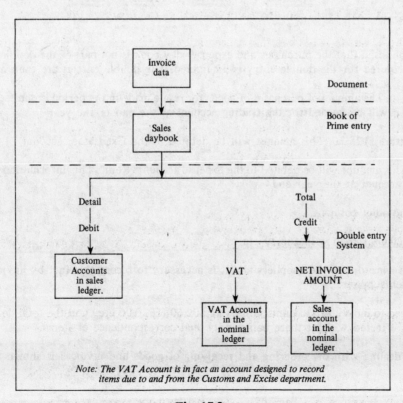

Note: The VAT Account is in fact an account designed to record items due to and from the Customs and Excise department.

Fig. 17.2

7. The amount of each invoice appears on the debit of a customer's account thus recording that the customer owes the firm some money.

8. The total of all sales appears on the credit of the sales account. At the year end the total of this account will be needed for the trading account. By entering the total of the invoices in the sales account, the sales account is not cluttered with a mass of detail.

9. There is no one-to-one correspondence of debit and credit entries but, assuming no errors are made, the total debit entries - £71.76 in John's account etc., will equal the total credit entries - £297.39.

PURCHASES AND EXPENSES DAY BOOK

10. In practice, goods and services are supplied to businesses on credit and the amount to be paid is evidenced to the business by an invoice sent by the supplier. All the incoming invoices should be checked and then filed together in date sequence. Each will have the supplier's own invoice number but it is desirable for the bookkeeper to number each incoming invoice with a consecutive number.

11. The invoice details are entered in a book of *prime entry* called the purchases and expenses day book. A typical ruling is:

PURCHASES AND EXPENSES DAY BOOK

Date	Supplier	Invoice No	Net	Purchases	Fixed Assets	Rent	
30.7.-3	Brown	201	620.00	620.00			Further columns will be
30.7.-3	Green	202	68.20		68.20		provided here so that
30.7.-3	White	203	500.00			500.00	all expense headings
31.7.-3	Gray	204	37.40	37.40			in the profit and loss
31.7.-3	Puce	205	100.00				account are catered
31.7.-3	Black	206	60.00		60.00		for.
31.7.-3	Gas Board	207	72.00				
31.7.-3	Magenta	208	45.00				
			1,502.60	657.40	128.20	500.00	

12. It must be emphasised that the purchases and expenses day book is not part of the double entry. It is a medium wherein the data required for the double entry is assembled. The double entries are then made as follows.

Dr purchases £657.40. The amount of purchases of goods for resale made in the period is debited to purchases account. This information will be needed for the trading account at the end of the year.

  Capital expenditure £128.20. This amount will be debited to the fixed asset account.

  Rent £500.00. This amount will be debited to the expense account "Rent". This information will be needed for the profit and loss account at the year end.

  Similarly for the other columns.

Cr Brown with £620.00, Green with £68.20 etc.

  These items are sums due to the suppliers and it is necessary to record this fact by having individual creditor accounts for each supplier.

13. The total credited to individual accounts will be £1,502.60 (£620.00 etc.) and the total debited £1,502.60. Thus the double entry is effected without there being individual correspondence of items.

14. The system of dealing with the ordering and receiving of goods and invoices is shown in Fig. 17.3.

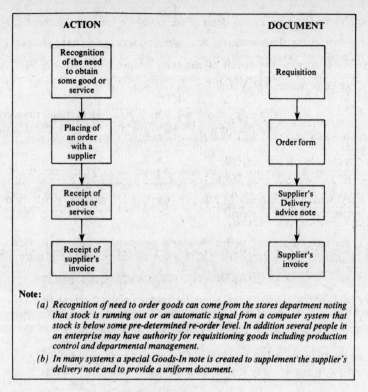

Note:
(a) *Recognition of need to order goods can come from the stores department noting that stock is running out or an automatic signal from a computer system that stock is below some pre-determined re-order level. In addition several people in an enterprise may have authority for requisitioning goods including production control and departmental management.*

(b) *In many systems a special Goods-In note is created to supplement the supplier's delivery note and to provide a uniform document.*

Fig. 17.3

15. See Fig. 17.4 for the system for recording suppliers' invoices.

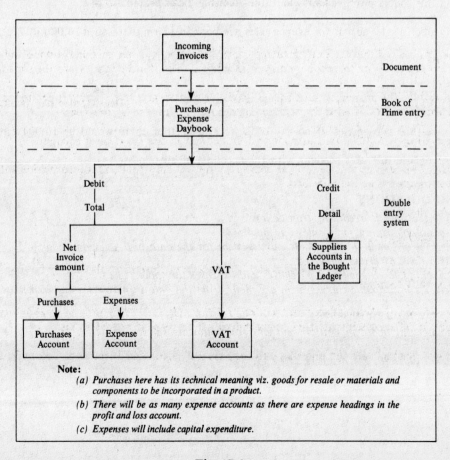

Note:
(a) *Purchases here has its technical meaning viz. goods for resale or materials and components to be incorporated in a product.*

(b) *There will be as many expense accounts as there are expense headings in the profit and loss account.*

(c) *Expenses will include capital expenditure.*

Fig. 17.4

SUMMARY

16. (a) Before making entries in double entry accounts, bookkeepers have found it helpful to make lists of transactions in books of prime entries.

   (b) Two common books of prime entry are:

   the sales day book which is a list of sales invoices;
   the purchase and expenses day book which is a list of suppliers' invoices.

POINTS TO NOTE

17. (a) The procedures required to capture transactions on paper or magnetic media and to enter them in permanent records are part of a subject called business systems. Such systems in practice include procedures called "internal controls" which are intended to detect or prevent fraud and error. A manual of this kind can only discuss one or two aspects of systems.

   (b) The books of prime entry discussed in this chapter are commonly found but often with variations. They are not always given the names I have given them. Other names are: invoice registers, journals, invoice books, sales books etc.

   (c) The sales day book is not always kept. Some businesses simply retain the copy sales invoices on a file and *post* the double entry direct from the invoices. This is known as the slip posting system. The total of all the invoices has still to be found for posting to the sales account. This is done on an adding machine.

   (d) I have discussed the "purchases and expenses day book" as I have found this to be the most commonly used. Some businesses keep two separate day books, one for purchases and one for expenses.

   (e) Be clear about the difference between a book of prime entry and the actual double entry system.

   (f) Many books of prime entry contain an extra column labelled Folio or Fo (Latin for leaf). This column shows the page in the double entry ledger where the item has been posted.

   (g) The effect on a sales account of using a sales day book in a firm that issues 10,000 invoices a year would be:

SALES ACCOUNT

19-4		£	19-4		£
Dec 31	Trading Account	1,243,621.13	Dec 31	Sales day book total	1,243,621.13

There are thus two entries. If no day book were used, then there would be 10,001 entries!

Do not confuse the sales account with the accounts of customers.

SELF TESTING QUESTIONS

   (a) What are the steps in recording transactions? (1).
   (b) Draft a suitable ruling for a sales day book. (4).
   (c) What entries are made in the double entry system for the data in a sales day book? (5).
   (d) What is a book of prime entry? (6).
   (e) Draft a ruling for a combined purchases and expenses day book. (12).
   (f) What entries in a double entry system are made from the data in purchases and expense day book? (13).

Exercises (Answers begin on page 454)

1. Draw up a sales day book for William and enter the following sales:

Carver £600, DK Ltd £340, Elf Brothers £720.25.

2. Draw up a suitably ruled purchases and expense day book for Nathan, a dealer in agricultural machinery and enter:

19X9		£	Goods/Services supplied
March 1	Twinset Limited	14,300	Ploughs
March 9	MEB	2,300	Electricity
March 14	DP Publications Ltd	240	Books
March 18	Eton Ltd	11,300	Harrows
March 20	Rembrandt Ltd	2,000	Repainting premises
March 27	Redemport Ltd	46,000	Tractors
March 30	Thule TV Plc	2,000	Advertising

3. J. Brooks, a sole trader, has the following transactions during the month of September 1983.

6 Sept	Bought on credit from S. Knight 3 carpets at £90 each less 10% trade discount.
9 Sept	Sold on credit to M. Toft 2 carpets at £140 each less 5% trade discount.
14 Sept	Purchased on credit from F. Church 4 carpets at £85 each less 5% trade discount.
16 Sept	Sold on credit to J. Aspin 1 carpet at £135 and 1 at £100 – no trade discount allowed.
21 Sept	Purchased on credit from K. Good 2 carpets at £120 each less 10% trade discount.
28 Sept	Sold on credit to A. Best 1 carpet at £105 and 1 at £115 less 5% trade discount on the complete sale.

Required:

(i) Enter the above transactions in the Sales Day Book and Purchases Day Book as appropriate.

(ii) Post the transactions from the Day Books to the Personal Accounts concerned in the ledger. You should design the system for the documents to the books and include specimen rulings.

(iii) Total the two Day Books and post the totals to the appropriate impersonal accounts in the ledger.

(LCCI)

Exercises without answers

4. Draw up an appropriate ruling for a sales day book and enter the following amounts, adding 15% VAT in each case:

19-4		£
August		
12	A.J.M. Ltd.	260.40
14	PMM Plc	100.00
16	Defoe & Co	1,420.66
20	Lucas Eng Ltd.	49.00

Sum up the columns and state in which accounts the double entries would be made.

5. Draw up an appropriate ruling for a purchase and expense day book for Alan Widgets Ltd., widget wholesalers, with suitable analysis headings and enter the following invoices received:

August 19-4		£	Type of goods/ service
1	Albert & Victoria	138.00	Widgets
1	Edward Ltd.	4,600.00	Delivery van
	George & Co.	59.80	Heating oil
7	Charles Publishing	37.40	Books
9	William & Partners	883.20	Widgets
12	Electricity Board	431.00	Electricity
14	Daily Gazette	200.00	Advertising

Sum the columns and state in which double entry account the items should be posted.

6. *Draw up an appropriate ruling for a purchase and expense day book for Sheila Ltd., motor cycle retailers, with suitable analysis headings and enter the following invoices received:*

Sept 19-4		£	Type of goods/service
1	Eden	6,246	Motor cycles
3	Fredric	134	Posters
9	Gas Board	431	Gas
11	Georgina Ltd	1,984	Motor cycle
15	J.J. Builders	1,046	Repairs to premises
19	Daily News	500	Advertising
24	Kim Fuels Ltd	624	Heating Oil

Sum the columns, test the cross cast and state in which double entry accounts the items should be posted.

18. The Cash Book

INTRODUCTION

1. This chapter is about a book of prime entry which is *also* an account in the double entry system. From the beginnings of double entry businesses have found that a very large number of transactions consisted of receiving and paying sums of money. In earliest times these transactions involved actual payment and receipt of *cash*. Hence the cash of cash book. It was also found that the transactions were so numerous that a page in the ledger was insufficient, so that a separate book had to be devoted to these transactions. So we have the phrase - cash book.

2. In later times, while cash was still used, payments and receipts came to be made by cheque through a bank account. Cash is still the pattern in many countries but in the UK business transaction are almost wholly settled by cheque or some other bank *instrument* such as a *direct debit*. Such cash transactions as do happen are recorded in the petty cash book. Thus a cash book is now used to record bank transactions but it is still called the cash book.

3. You will appreciate that the cash book is a double entry account kept in a separate book. But it is also a *book of prime entry*.

4. Retail transactions by, for example, shops are still carried out using cash, or more correctly a mixture of cash, cheques and credit cards. These can still be regarded as bank transactions as at the end of each day the retailer will count the takings (cash, cheques etc) and pay the lot into the bank.

COLUMNAR CASH BOOKS

5. In practice the usual cash book rulings are in columns as follows:

Dr. RECEIPTS				PAYMENTS			Cr
Date Source	Discount	Amount	Banking	Date	Payee	Discount	Amount
1.8.-3 Balance b/f			1,231.64	2.8.-3	Oxford	31.30	968.20
3.8.-3 Wellington	24.31	839.20		2.8.-3	Keele		131.00
3.8.-3 Stowe	4.60	182.20		2.8.-3	Cash - Wages		1,240.00
3.8.-3 Westminster		313.00	1,334.40	2.8.-3	Gas Board		61.30
4.8.-3 Loan - XY Ltd.		1,000.00		3.8.-3	AHM plc	21.20	761.40
4.8.-3 Eton	21.30	763.00	1,763.00	4.8.-3	Brown		313.20
4.8.-3 Cash Sales			500.00	4.8.-3	Balance c/d		1,353.94
	50.21		4,829.04			52.50	4,829.04
4.8.-3 Balance b/d		1,353.94					

Fig.18.1

NOTE:

(a) The documentary evidence from the debit side is the counterfoil paying-in book provided by the bank. An example follows.

FRONT				
Date _____		Date _____ **BANK GIRO CREDIT**		401—74—59
Credit _____		**QUARRY BANK plc**		
£50		1 High Street		
£20		Cloghampton	Cash	
£10			Cheques	
£5			£	
50p				
Silver				
Bronze		Credit ___ Financial Chicanery Ltd		
Total				
Cheques		⑈000000⑈ ⑊0⑈4713⑊ 61014579⑈ 84		
£				

─────── COUNTERFOIL ───────

REVERSE					
Cheques etc £		£50			Cheques etc
		£20			
		£10			
		£5			
		£1			
		50p			
		Silver			
		Bronze			
Total Cheques carry over		Total Cash Carry over		£	
				carry over	

(b) Two columns are required - one for the individual cheques or amounts paid in, the other for the totals of the bankings.

(c) Many businesses allow their customers to deduct a small percentage of the sum due if they pay by a specified time. This is known as a cash or settlement account and is further discussed in a later chapter. When a cheque is received from a customer who has deducted a discount, the discount is entered in the discount column.

(d) As the cash book is both a book of prime entry and a part of the double entry (a ledger account) the debit side of the cash book is one leg of the double entry and the other leg is a credit to a customer's account (e.g. Wellington) or other account (e.g. sales account for the cash sales).

(e) The discount column is not part of the double entry and the actual double entry will be:

Dr Discount allowed account - this is an expense account.
Cr The individual customer's account (Wellington etc.).

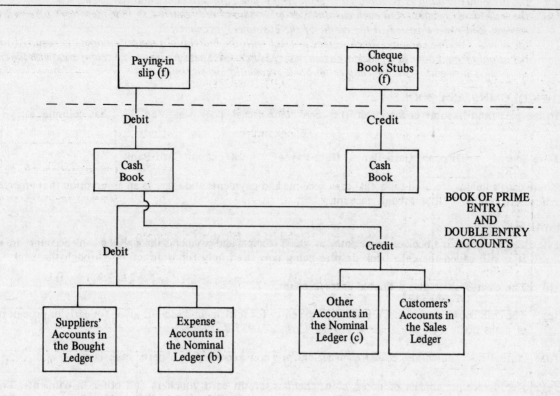

Fig. 18.2

Notes:

(a) *The cash book in which these transactions are entered is nearly always so called but it is really the Cash at Bank Account in the double entry system.*

(b) *The majority of cheque payments are debited to suppliers' accounts. However some payments (notably wages) are debited to expense accounts in the nominal ledger.*

(c) *The majority of receipts are credited to customers' accounts but a few receipts (for example loans) are credited to accounts in the nominal ledger.*

(d) *The treatment of settlement discounts has been omitted from this diagram. The subject is treated fully in a later chapter.*

(e) *All entries are of individual transactions.*

(f) *Some entries are initiated from sources other than the paying-in slips and cheque book stubs e.g. traders' credits and bank interest.*

(f) *The documentary evidence for the credit side is the cheque book stubs. The amount column is both a book of prime entry and part of the double entry. The corresponding debit will be on suppliers' account (Oxford etc.) or on an expense account (e.g. wages).*

(g) *The discount column is solely a prime entry and the subsequent double entry is:*

Dr   The supplier's account (Oxford etc.).
Cr   Discount received account – a revenue account required for the year end profit and loss account.

(h) *It is necessary to have three columns on the debit side because:*

(i)   the discounts column is required as a prime entry place for discounts allowed;

(ii) the individual cheques from each customer or other source are required so that they form a record of such receipts and can be posted to the credit of the customers' accounts;

(iii) the actual banking column (which agrees in total with the individual receipts column) is required to record the actual amount banked on each occasion money is banked. These figures can be compared with the entries in the bank statements - see the chapter on bank reconciliation statements.

THREE COLUMN CASH BOOKS

6.   In the past (and in some countries still) a *three column* cash book was used. This has columns as:

Dr   Cr
Date Source   Discount Cash Bank   Date Payee   Discount Cash Bank

These cash columns are used for actual cash receipts and payments and there is an assumption that an *actual cash balance* is kept as well as a bank account.

SUMMARY

7.   (a)   The cash book is a book of prime entry in which receipts and payments through the bank accounts are entered. It is still called the cash book despite being now used only for transactions through the bank.

(b)   The cash book is also a double entry account.

(c)   The cash book also provides a book of prime entry for settlement discounts given for early or prompt payment of sums due.

(d)   Actual cash (notes and coins) transactions are now recorded in a petty cash book.

(e)   Retail receipts consist of notes, coin, cheques, credit card vouchers and other instruments. These are regarded as bank transactions as the total takings are normally totalled and paid intact into the bank.

POINTS TO NOTE

8.   (a)   Be sure you realise that the cash book is both a book of prime entry and a ledger account.

(b)   The traditional three column which is now rare in UK should really have four columns on the debit:

Discount   Cash   Bank   Actual
detail   banking

(c)   Note that receipts (money etc into the bank) goes on the debit and payments (cheques etc) go on the credit.

SELF TESTING QUESTIONS

(a)   How does the cash book differ from other books of prime entry? (3)
(b)   Draw up an appropriate ruling for a retailer's cash book. (5)
(c)   State the double entry from the debit of the cash book. (5)
(d)   State the double entry from the credit of the cash book. (5)
(e)   What are columns in a three or four column cash book? (6)

Exercises (answers begin on page 454)

1.   *Draw up a cash book and enter the following transactions:*
     Receipts   *Payments*

		Discount	Cheque				Discount	Cheque
January 2	*Richard*	*23.34*	*267.90*	*January 5*	*Gray*		*2.34*	*100.45*
January 4	*David*	*10.87*	*254.45*	*January 6*	*Dove*			*45.32*
January 5	*Hugh*		*68.65*	*January 6*	*Gas board*			*189.09*
				January 7	*Wages*			*432.95*

The above were paid in the bank on January 6.

January 6	*Cash sales*		*674.76*
January 9	*Access vouchers*		*234.76*

The above two items were paid in on January 8 and 10 respectively

The cash book balance at 1 January was £1,643.

Exercises without answers

2.   *Enter the following transactions in a properly ruled cash book:*

(Note that all amounts are after deducting discount, if any)

Paid Joan £237.21 (discount £2.56), received cheque from Dan £345.00, paid Lionel £200, received cheque from Henry £459.00 (discount £12.08), paid in cheques received so far, paid Ken £298.77 (discount £3.90), received and banked cash sales £570.00.

The opening balance at 1.1.-8 was £39.00 overdrawn and the above transactions happen on successive days.

3.   *David owns and manages a seaside cafe. All sales are for cash and a till with till rolls is maintained. Half his expenditure is also made by cash for such items as drawings, wages, eggs, vegetables etc, to local farmers. These payments are made from cash takings before he banks the takings daily. He is able to take settlement discounts from a number of his suppliers.*

Draw up a suitable ruling for his cash book and make twenty specimen entries.

19. Bank Reconciliation Statements

INTRODUCTION

1. The cash book of an enterprise records the monies paid into the bank and the sums drawn from the bank through the media of cheques etc. The data for these entries comes from the paying-in book and the cheque book stubs.

2. The bank also records these items in its own books and issues its customer with a statement summarising the transactions between the bank and the customer.

3. To the business, the bank statement forms an external check on the accuracy of the cash book. However there are usually differences between the cash book and the bank statement and this chapter explores these differences and shows how extra entries should be made in the cash book and a bank reconciliation statement prepared.

TIMING DIFFERENCES

4. Consider the following sequence of events:

1.1.-8	John draws a cheque in favour of Ted and an entry is made in the cash book
2.8.-8	Cheque is mailed to Ted
5.8.-8	Cheque received by Ted
6.8.-8	Ted pays the cheque into his bank account
8.8.-8	The bank deals with the matter through the *clearing* system and the transaction appears on John's bank statement.

There is a timing difference of seven days between John's cash book entry and the corresponding entry on the bank statement.

5. Common timing differences include:

    (a) Cheques drawn (as illustrated above) - delays can be months if recipients of cheques fail to pay them in.

    (b) Payments into the bank - usually only a matter of a day or two.

    (c) Errors by the bank - banks can and do make mistakes and students do not always realise that these are in fact timing differences. George pays in a sum to his bank on July 14th and this is credited in error to Guy. The error is discovered and corrected on August 7th. In effect George's cash book has July 14th as the date and the bank statement will have August 7th.

INFORMATIONAL DIFFERENCES

6. Businessmen commonly write up their cash books from their paying-in books and their cheque book stubs. However, there are transactions which are not found from these sources. Examples are:

    (a) Dividends credited direct to the bank.

    (b) Payments by customers which are paid direct to the bank (*e.g.* traders' credits).

    (c) Bank charges and interest.

    (d) Cheques paid in by the business which have been dishonoured (colloquially "bounced").

    (e) Standing orders (an order made to the bank to make a regular payment - *e.g.* mortgage or hire purchase instalments).

    (f) Cash point withdrawals.

    (g) Direct debits - an arrangement whereby a person's account is debited with a sum at the direction of a supplier with, of course, the account holders prior permission.

The business is usually informed of these transactions but tends to overlook them until a bank statement is received pointing them out. The entries should then be made in the cash book.

BANK RECONCILIATION STATEMENTS

7. Here is the cash book of Pip, a trader, for March 19-4:

19–4 March		£	19–4 March		£
8	Brown	164	1	Balance b/d	2,064
8	Jones	347	2	Walter	39
8	Robinson	163	4	Cash	610
8	Cash Sales	20	7	Hughes	38
14	Hubert	830	9	Williams	915
14	Wilkes	910	14	Noll	37
21	Hinks	34	21	Graham	620
26	Lowe	1,013	28	Wem	99
26	Little	2	30	Xavier	12
30	Howe	137			
31	Balance c/d	814			
		4,434			4,434

The bank statement for the same month showed:

NORTHERN BANK Plc

Pip – Account Number 1342692

1.3.–4	Balance			2064	D
3.3.–4	106284	39		2103	D
5.3.–4	106285	610		2713	D
8.3.–4	Cash and Cheques		694	2019	D
10.3.–4	Cash point	50		2069	D
11.3.–4	106287	915		2984	D
15.3.–4	SO U.D.T. Ltd.	67		3051	D
16.3.–4	Cheques		1740	1311	D
17.3.–4	106288	37		1348	D
20.3.–4	Dividend ICI Plc		24	1324	D
22.3.–4	Cheque		35	1289	D
23.3.–4	106289	620		1909	D
24.3.–4	251332	30		1939	D
27.3.–4	Cheques		1015	924	D
30.3.–4	Charges	36		960	D
	Interest	63		1023	D

N.B. D = Overdrawn

You will note that:

(a) The balance is given after each transaction.
(b) The entries are on the reverse side to the cash book.
(c) Payments in are not detailed.
(d) Cheques are distinguished by numbers only – information not often given in the cash book.

PROCEDURES

8. (a) **Compare the entries** in the cash book with those in the bank statement by ticking them. You should find that unticked items are:

Place	Item			Reason and Action
Cash book	Hinks	34	)	Error in amount, presume bank is
Bank Statement	Cheque	35	)	correct – alter cash book
Cash Book	Howe	137		Timing difference
Cash Book	Hughes	38		Timing difference
Cash Book	Wem	99		Timing differences
Cash Book	Xavier	12		Timing differences
Bank Statement	Cash point	50		Enter in cash book
Bank Statement	SO U.D.T. Ltd	67		Enter in cash book
Bank Statement	Dividend	24		Enter in cash book
Bank Statement	251332	30		Error by bank – timing difference
Bank Statement	Charges	36		Enter in cash book
Bank Statement	Interest	63		Enter in cash book

(b) **Complete the Cash Book**

		£			£
20.3.-4	Dividend ICI Ltd.	24	31.3.-4	Balance b/d	814
21.3.-4	Hinks	1	10.3.-4	Cash point	50
31.3.-4	Correct		15.3.-4	SO U.D.T. Ltd	67
	Balance c/d	1,005	31.3.-4	Bank Charges	36
			31.3.-4	Bank Interest	63
		1,030			1,030

(c) Reconcile the difference between the *adjusted* cash book balance and the bank statement balance as:

Bank Reconciliation Statement as at 31st March 19-4

	£	
Balance per cash book *as adjusted*	1,005	OD
Deduct error by bank – adjusted in April	30	
	1,035	OD
Deduct payments in credited after date	137	
	1,172	OD
Add Cheques presented after date		
Hughes 38		
Wem 99		
Xavier 12	149	
Balance per bank statement	1,023	

THEORY

9. The adjusted balance of the cash book is the balance which is included in the balance sheet. Thus, the balance sheet item at 31st March 19-4 "Bank overdraft £1,005" is not the balance according to the bank (which is £1,023). This has the effect that all transactions effected with the bank by the year end are reflected in the bank balance, despite the fact that the bank may not have recognised them by that date.

A second effect is that for example the cheque drawn in favour of Xavier £12 is reflected in the bank balance and therefore must be reflected in the account of Xavier to complete the double entry.

PRACTICAL DIFFICULTIES

10. This subject does not present many difficulties to students, providing they have grasped the *two* stages:

(a) Adjust the cash book.
(b) Prepare the bank reconciliation statement.

However, in some examination questions and nearly always in practice, the opening balance of the cash book differs from the opening balance of the bank statement. For example:

1.3.-4	Balance per cash book	£639

Extract from bank statement:

		£	£
1.3.-4	Balance		1,146
2.3.-4	110311	460	686
3.3.-4	110313	38	648
3.3.-4	110312	47	601

The technique is to tick off the £639 against 1,146 - 460 - 47 = 639, both the 460 and 47 being in the cash book in February and in the bank reconciliation at 29.2.-4.

11. When presented in the form I have used in this chapter, a student or a cashier can verify that he or she has the right answer because the two balances reconcile. To avoid this facility, some examiners limit the data given and may for example omit the bank statement balance and ask the examinee to calculate it. The solution then is to write out the bank reconciliation statement and insert all known figures. The single unknown can then be found.

SUMMARY

12. (a) The cash book balance can be proved by comparing it with the bank statement.

(b) Two kinds of differences occur.

    (i)   Timing differences.
    (ii)   Transactions which need to be entered in the cash book.

(c) The three stages are therefore:

    (i)   Ticking over the cash book with the bank statement to identify differences.
    (ii)   Adjusting the cash book by making further entries.
    (iii) Preparing a bank reconciliation statement to demonstrate that the two balances are the same, apart from timing differences.

POINTS TO NOTE

13. (a)   Many people keep a note of the current balance of their own bank account on the cheque stubs, altering the balance after each transaction. No doubt my readers do. They will find also that the bank statement balance disagrees. Bank reconciliation statements prepared on the receipt of a bank statement will soon familiarise students with this simple technique.

     (b)   I still have momentary difficulty in knowing whether to add or subtract in the bank reconciliation statement. The trick is to remember that if there are, for example, unpresented cheques then the bank statement balance will be larger than the cash book balance.

     (c)   Some businessmen may wish their balance sheet to show a position which is different from that shown by a strict application of accounting principles.

        For example, drawing a large number of cheques immediately before the year end (but not sending them to the creditors) will mean

        reduced creditors – the businessman does not wish to show that the business owes a great deal of money

        increased overdraft – a large apparent overdraft may indicate that the bank has confidence in the business.

This technique of showing a more attractive position than the proper one is known as window dressing. Correctly, cheques should only be entered in the cash book if and when they are actually sent to the creditors.

SELF TESTING QUESTIONS

    (a) List some typical timing differences between the cash book and the bank statement. (5).
    (b) List some typical informational differences between the cash book and the bank statement.
    (c) Draft the format for a bank statement. (7).
    (d) What balance for "cash at bank" should be included in a balance sheet? (9).
    (e) Summarise the procedures for preparing a bank reconciliation statement. (10).
    (f) Explain window dressing. (13c).

Exercises (Answers begin on page 454)

1. The cash book of Juliet for January 19-7 showed

Dr		£			Cr £
1.1.-7	Balance b/f	234	1.1.-7	Cray	320
2.1.-7	Harris	1,560	3.1.-7	Richardson	45
5.1.-7	Lowe	810	6.1.-7	Wages	1,800
14.1.-7	Gibbon	865	8.1.-7	Bowman	200
17.1.-7	Lizzie	2,340	10.1.-7	Aleric	1,567
21.1.-7	Xavier	54	15.1.-7	Visitis	311
27.1.-7	Younghusband	124	24.1.-7	Lewis	98
31.1.-7	Alice	1,566	28.1.-7	Guy	234
			31.1.-7	LEB	540
			31.1.-7	Balance c/d	2,438
		7,553			7,553

The bank statement showed for the same month:

Jan 1	Balance b/f			234	C
3	624	320		86	D
4	Sundries		1,560	1,474	C
6	625	45		1,429	C
6	626	1,800		371	D
7	Sundries		810	439	C
11	627	200		239	C
11	628	1,567		1,328	D
12	British Gas	100		1,428	D
15	Sundries		865	563	D
17	629	311		874	D
18	Sundries		2,340	1,466	C
22	Sundries		54	1,520	C
23	Wolvborough BC		1,000	2,520	C
27	630	98		2,422	C
31	Sundries		124	2,546	C

Tick over the two records and identify differences. Which differences are informational and which are timing? Complete the cash book and prepare a bank reconciliation statement as at 31.1.-7.

2. The cash book of Bowes for the month of July 19-7 showed:

4.7.-7	Hardwick	684	1.7.-7	b/f		39
8.7.-7	Benbow	72	4.7.-7	Ludwig	721	100
15.7.-7	Dwight	143	11.7.-7	Hart	722	84
15.7.-7	Grahame	93	1.7.-7	Gimlet	723	639
30.7.-7	Walters	116	20.7.-7	Dews	724	22
			24.7.-7	Cowes	725	58
			29.7.-7	Drain	SO	100
			31.7.-7	c/f		66
		1,108				1,108

1.7.-7	Balance			103	C
2.7.-7	719	87		16	C
4.7.-7	Sundries		146	162	C
5.7.-7	Sundries		684	846	C
6.7.-7	721	100		746	C
7.7.-7	720	201		545	C
17.7.-7	Sundries		236	781	C
18.7.-7	722	84		697	C
19.7.-7	723	639		58	C
20.4.-7	Orchestral Society	60		2	D
22.7.-7	Dividends		439	437	C
26.7.-7	725	58		379	C
30.7.-7	Charges	71		308	C
31.7.-7	Drain	100		208	C

Note: £72 was credited to the deposit account by the bank in error.

Correct the cash book and prepare the bank reconciliation statement.

3. The accountant of Summerbee Ltd is attempting to reconcile the bank statements with the cash book as at 31.12.-7. The cash book shows a balance in hand of £578. After ticking over the two documents he finds:

(a) Cash paid into the bank of £489 has been entered in the cash book as £459.
(b) A transfer to the company's deposit account of £1,000 has not been entered in the cash book.
(c) A cheque drawn for £45 has been entered into the cash book as £54.
(d) Cheques for £390 and £231 in the cash book in December had not been presented by the year end.
(e) The cash book debit side page 24 £8,760 total had been carried to page 25 as £7,860.
(f) A standing order for £100 to the Association of Explorers had been omitted from the cash book.

(g) Bank charges of £412 had been omitted from the cash book.

(h) A credit to the bank from George had not been entered into the cash book - £250.

(i) Cheques paid in on 31.12.-7 in the amount of £4,988 has not been credited by the bank at 31.12.-7.

(j) In error the bank had charged the company £26 for a foreign transaction which had not taken place.

Required:

(a) An amended cash book.

(b) A bank reconciliation at 31.12.-7.

Note that you will have to calculate the bank statement balance.

Exercises without answers

4. Croak is trying to balance his cash book against his bank statements at June 30 19-7. The cash book balance is £400 overdrawn. He discovers:

(a) Cheques paid in on 29.6.-7 totalling £580 have not yet come through the bank statements.

(b) A credit recorded by Croak on 24.6.-7 in the amount of £360 from a customer had been credited by the bank in error to another account.

(c) Bank Interest and Charges of £72 had not been included in the cash book.

(d) A cheque from Howe for £23 had been returned marked "account closed" and entered on the debit side of the bank statement on 30.6.-7.

(e) A cash point withdrawal of £50 on 12.6.-7 had not been entered in the cash book.

(f) Cheques in the cash book in June totalling £937 had not been presented to the bank.

(g) Dividends paid directly to the bank £431 had not been entered in the cash book.

(h) A lodgement of cheques on 25.6.-7 had been wrongly added and entered in the cash book as £2,567 instead of £2,557.

Required: an amended cash book and a bank reconciliation statement. You will have to calculate the bank statement balance.

5. The cash book of Dilley for March 19-8 showed:

1.3.-8	b/f		636					
5.3.-8	Hughes Ltd		3,712	3.3.-8	Brown Ltd	648		126
5.3.-8	Walls & Co		6,838	5.3.-8	Cudd	649		39
16.3.-8	Dain		1,520	7.3.-8	Loo Bros	650		4,311
16.3.-8	Eastoe		100	11.3.-8	James	651		87
16.3.-8	Filip		1,391	21.3.-8	Pooter Ltd	652		682
31.3.-8	Godley		1,100	26.3.-8	Fiona	653		1,249
31.3.-8	c/f		374	27.3.-8	Grange	654		737
				28.3.-8	Claas	655		8,000
				31.3.-8	Young	656		440
			15,671					15,671

The bank statement showed:

1.3.-8	Balance			636	C
5.3.-8	648	126		510	C
6.3.-8	Sundries		10,550	11,060	C
7.3.-8	649	39		11,021	C
9.3.-8	650	4,311		6,710	C
10.3.-8	A.A.A.	50		6,660	C
12.3.-8	651	87		6,573	C
14.3.-8	Cash point	40		6,533	C
17.3.-8	Sundries		3,011	9,544	C
18.3.-8	Johns & Co		540	10,084	C
22.3.-8	652	682		9,402	C
22.3.-8	Dishonoured cheque	100		9,302	C
27.3.-8	653	1,249		8,053	C
28.3.-8	Rogers & Co Ltd		240	8,293	C
29.3.-8	654	737		7,556	C
30.3.-8	655	8,000		444	D

Note: the £240 credited by Rogers and Co was an error by the bank.

Correct the cash book and prepare a bank reconciliation statement.

6. The bank account of Fuller Ltd. prepared by the company's bookkeeper, was as shown below for the month of October 1986.

Bank Account

1986 October		£	1986 October	Cheque No	£
1	Balance b/d	91.40	2 Petty cash	062313	36.15
3	McIntosh and Co.	260.11	3 Freda's Fashions	062314	141.17
3	Malcolm Brothers	112.83	6 Basford Ltd	062315	38.04
3	Cash sales	407.54	8 Hansler Agencies	062316	59.32
14	Rodney Photographic	361.02	9 Duncan's Storage	062317	106.75
17	Puccini's Cold Store Ltd	72.54	9 Aubrey plc	062318	18.10
20	Eastern Divisional Gas Board - rebate (August direct credit)	63.40	10 Secretarial Services Ltd	062319	28.42
22	Grainger's Garage	93.62	14 Trevor's Auto Repairs	062320	11.75
29	Cash sales	235.39	15 Wages cash	062321	115.52
31	Balance c/d	221.52	16 Towers Hotel	062322	44.09
			17 Bank charges (September)	-	12.36
			20 Broxcliffe Borough Council	SO	504.22
			21 Eastern Area Electricity Board	DD	196.83
			24 Eastern Divisional Gas Board	DD	108.64
			28 Petty cash	062323	41.20
			30 Wages cash	062324	119.07
			31 Salaries transfers	-	337.74
		1,919.37			1,919.37

		November	
		1 Balance b/d	221.52

In early November, the company's bank sent a statement of account which is reproduced below.

Statement of account with Lowland Bank plc

Account: Fuller Ltd Current Account No. 10501191
Date of issue: 1 November 1986

1986 October	Description	Debit £	Credit £	Balance £
1	BCE			90.45
2	CR		175.02	265.47
2	062310	111.34		154.13
3	062312	9.18		144.95
3	062309	15.41		129.54
3	CR		780.48	910.02
7	062313	36.15		873.87
10	ADJ		12.90	886.77
15	062315	38.04		848.73
16	062314	141.17		707.56
17	CR		443.56	1,151.12
20	SO	504.22		646.90
21	062317	106.75		540.15
21	DD	196.83		343.32
21	062320	11.75		331.57
22	141981	212.81		118.76
22	ADJ	10.00		108.76
22	062319	28.42		80.34
22	062320	11.75		68.59
22	CR		93.62	162.21
24	ADJ		212.81	375.02
27	INT (loan account)	26.35		348.67
27	062321	115.52		233.15
28	062322	44.09		189.06
28	DD	108.64		80.42
30	CGS	9.14		71.28
31	ADJ		11.75	83.03

Abbreviations: BCE = Balance; CR = Credit; ADJ = Adjustment; SO = Standing Order; DD = Direct debit; INT = Interest; CGS = Charges. Balances are credit unless marked OD.

Required:
Prepare the company's bank reconciliation statement as at 31 October 1986. *(ACCA)*

7. At the close of business on 31 May 1985, the Bank Statement of Amos Jones, a sole trader, showed that his balance with the bank amounted to £1,960. This does not agree with the bank balance according to his Cash Book, and the following transactions account for the difference:

(1) On 31 May the bank allowed Jones interest amounting to £76, but this had not yet been entered in the Cash Book.

(2) During May 1985 the bank had paid on behalf of Jones, under a banker's standing order, the rent of his business premises amounting to £110. This had not been entered in the Cash Book.

(3) On 31 May, William Smith, a debtor of Jones paid direct to Jones' account with his bankers the sum of £89, but this had not yet appeared in the Cash Book.

(4) During May, Jones had drawn several cheques but, at the close of business on 31 May 1985, the following three cheques had not yet been presented for payment:

£21, £44 and £39.

Required:
Commencing with the Bank Statement balance of £1,960, prepare the Bank Reconciliation Statement of Amos Jones as at 31 May 1985, ending with the correct bank balance as shown in his Cash Book.   *(LCCI)*

8.   At the close of business on 29 February 1984, the balance of cash at bank as shown in the Cash Book of Joseph Williams, a sole trader, did not agree with his bank statement. On comparing the two, Williams discovered that the following matters accounted for the difference:

(1) During February the bank had allowed Williams bank interest amounting to £27. This had not yet appeared in the Cash Book.

(2) The following cheques, issued by Williams during February, had not yet been presented for payment:

                £38, £42 and £17.

(3) During February the bank had paid, under a banker's standing order, rent of Williams' shop amounting to £65, which did not appear in his Cash Book.

(4) On 29 February Williams paid into his bank cash amounting to £74. The item had been entered in Williams' Cash Book but had not yet appeared on his bank statement.

(5) The Cash Book balance at 29 February 1984 showed cash at bank £634.

Required:
   (i)   Draw up the bank column of the Cash Book of Williams for the end of February 1984, commencing with the figure of £634 given in (5) above. Enter the omitted items, and carry down the balance.

   (ii) Prepare the Reconciliation Statement as at 29 February 1984. This should commence with the final bank balance as in (i) and end with the balance as shown on the bank statement.   *(LCCI)*

9.   Lloyd keeps a cash book which shows a balance of £2,400 in hand at 31 December 19-9. He receives a bank statement which shows a balance of £806 overdrawn. The difference puzzles him but on investigation, he finds:

   (a) A cheque for £37 had been entered in the cash book as £73.
   (b) A cheque drawn in favour of Brown £100 had been entered on the debit side of the cash book.
   (c) Cheques for £380 in total drawn at the end of December did not appear in the bank statements.
   (d) Bank charges of £132 had not been entered in the cash book.
   (e) A lodgement of £3,000 on 31 December 19-9 did not appear in the bank state-ment.
   (f) The bank had debited his account with a standing order of £180 in error.
   (g) The penultimate page of the cash book had been over-added on the debit side by £110.

Correct the cash book and prepare a bank reconciliation statement.

20. Control Accounts

INTRODUCTION

1. Some double entry systems record many thousands of transactions, and errors detected by a difference on the trial balance may be difficult to find. Breaking the system into sections will facilitate the discovery of errors.

2. In large systems, the bulk of the entries are in two areas:

   (a) Credit sales.
   (b) Purchases and expenses incurred on credit.

Therefore the sections kept separate from the rest of the system are these two. The sales system is explained first and then the purchases and expenses system.

SALES LEDGER

3. In a double entry system where there are a large number of accounts and in particular a large number of credit customers, the personal accounts of the credit customers are kept together in a book called the *sales ledger*. The sales ledger may be kept on media other than a book, a magnetic disk for example.

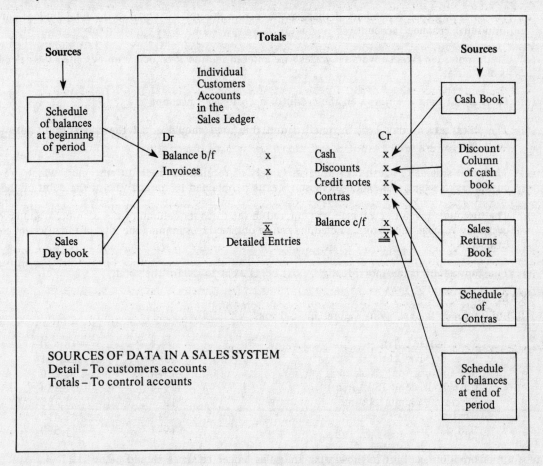

SOURCES OF DATA IN A SALES SYSTEM
Detail – To customers accounts
Totals – To control accounts

4. A typical sales ledger account may appear like this (in the books of AB, a trader):

CD Account

		£			£
1.4.-4	Balance b/f	282	5.4.-4	Cash	195
4.4.-4	Goods	341	5.4.-4	Discount	5
7.4.-4	Goods	262	14.4.-4	Credit note	28
19.4.-4	Goods	999	19.4.-4	Contra	49
			30.4.-4	Balance c/f	1,607
		1,884			1,884

The story told by this account is:

> At the beginning of April CD owed AB £282.
> In April, CD bought further goods totalling £1,602.
> This mean that CD had to pay or settle £1,884 in total.
> In April, he paid £195, was allowed discount £5 for paying the £195 promptly, returned goods value £28, settled £49 in contra - total £277.
> At the end of the month CD still owed £1,607.

Note that contra's (Latin = against) occur when a credit customer also *sells* on credit to a business. Instead of exchanging cheques the two indebtednesses are set against each other and one cheque only is sent. If A owes B £20 and B owes A £5, it is convenient for A to pay B £15.

5.   A system for entering the sales ledger accounts may be as follows:

(a)   Sales invoices are entered in the sales day book.

(b)   Each sales invoice is entered on the debit of a customer account.

(c)   The sales day book is totalled. If there are no errors this total is equal to the total amount entered on the individual customer account.

(d)   Credit notes (in effect reverse invoices) are entered in a book of prime entry called the sales returns day book.

(e)   Each credit note is entered on the credit of a customer's account.

(f)   The sales returns day book is totalled and this total should equal the total credit notes entered on customers' accounts.

(g)   The debit side of the cash book consists largely of receipts from credit customers which are credited to customers' accounts. The total of these receipts is obtained by an analysis of the debit of the cash book.

(h)   The discounts given to customers are entered in the discount column of the cash book and credited to the customers' accounts. The total so credited can be obtained by summing the total of the discount column in the cash book.

(i)   The contras are made individually. A list being kept to obtain the total.

AN EXAMPLE

6.   J.T. Ltd. includes the following figures in its books:

		£
Sales ledger balances	1.1.-4	16,420
Sales day book total	19-4	82,761
Sales returns day book total	19-4	1,210
Cash book debit (S.L. item)	19-4	71,329
Discount column total	19-4	1,785
Contras	19-4	2,410
Bad debts	19-4	560

Produce a memorandum account to show what the sales ledger balances should be at 31.12.-4.

Memo Sales Ledger Control Account y/e 31.12.-4

	£		£
Balance 31.12.-3	16,420	Sales Returns DB	1,210
Sales Day Book	82,761	Cash	71,329
		Discount	1,785
		Contras	2,410
		Bad debts	560
		*Balances 31.12.-4	21,887
	99,181		99,181

*obtained by balancing this account.

The next stage is to extract a list of the individual sales ledger accounts. Suppose this came to £21,981, clearly some errors have occurred and an extensive search revealed:

(a) Two balance were omitted from the list: £136 and £240.
(b) The sales day book was under cast by £100.
(c) An invoice for £62 in the sales day book was posted in error to two customers' accounts.
(d) An invoice for £46 correctly entered in the sales day book, was posted to the the customer's account as £64.
(e) A discount of £20 correctly entered in the customer's account was omitted from the discount column of the cash book.
(f) A contra of £200, included in the list had not been entered on the customer's account.
(g) A customer had overpaid by £100 and a cheque had been sent to reimburse him. This had been correctly entered in his account.
(h) A customer had paid his account and subsequently been given a credit note. His account was thus in credit by £55 and this had been wrongly put on the list as a debit balance.

There are two sorts of error here:

(i) Errors that affect the memorandum total account (errors in the books of prime entry).
(ii) Errors that affect the individual ledger accounts and hence the list of balances.

ANSWER

The revised memorandum control account should show:

	£		£
Balances 1.1.-4	16,420	Sales return DB	1,210
Sales day book total (b)	82,861	Cash	71,329
Credit balance 31.12.-4	55	Discount (e)	1,805
Cash	100	Contras	2,410
		Bad debts	560
		Dr Balances 31.12.-4	22,122
	99,436		99,436

The list of balances total should be:

	£	£
Original list		21,981
Add (a)		376
		22,357
Less (c)	62	
Less (d)	18	
Less (f)	100	
Less (h)	110	290
		22,067

The total of £22,067 is composed of Dr balances £22,122 less Cr balances £55. Item (d) is an example of transposition of figures, a very common error. Note that the difference is always divisible by 9.

PURCHASE LEDGER

7. If you have understood the sectional balancing of the sales ledger, then the sectional balancing of the purchase ledger will present no difficulties as it is the mirror image of the sales ledger. Simply, the entries on the memorandum purchase ledger control account go on the opposite side to their counterparts on the sales ledger.

8. A common examination question which combines knowledge of both sales and purchase ledgers control accounts is:

Good Books Ltd. include the following items in their books for 19-5:

	£
Balances 31.12.-4	
Dr Sales ledger	16,220
Cr Sales ledger	141
Cr Purchase ledger	6,310
Sales day book	101,005
Purchase day book	52,666
Sales returns day book	1,040
Contras	1,551
Bad debts	2,150

Cash Book Debit:
    Sales ledger items   96,434
    Purchase ledger items   152
Cash Book Credit:
    Purchase ledger items   49,200
    Sales ledger items   1,400

	£
Cash Book Debit:	
Sales ledger items	96,434
Purchase ledger items	152
Cash Book Credit:	
Purchase ledger items	49,200
Sales ledger items	1,400
Dr Side Discount column	1,920
Cr Side Discount column	867
Purchase ledger Dr balance 31.12.-5	65
Sales ledger Cr balance 31.12.-52	44

Prepare memorandum control accounts for the sales ledger and the purchase ledger.

ANSWER

Memorandum sales ledger control account y/e 31.12.-5

	£		£
Balances 31.12.-4	16,220	Balances 31.12.-4	141
Sales	101,005	Sales returns	1,040
Cash	1,400	Contras	1,551
Balance 31.12.-5	244	Bad debts	2,150
		Cash	96,434
		Discounts	1,920
		Balance 31.12.-5	15,633
	118,869		118,869

Memorandum purchase ledger control account y/e 31.12.-5

	£		£
Contras	1,551	Balance 31.12.-4	6,310
Cash	49,200	Purchases	52,666
Discount	867	Cash	152
Balances 31.12.-5	7,575	Balances 31.12.-5	65
	59,193		59,193

SUMMARY

9. (a) Large bookkeeping systems need to be broken down into sections to facilitate the detections of errors.

    (b) A common sectioning is the creation of sales ledger sub-system and the purchase and expense ledger sub-systems.

    (c) The balance owing by customers or suppliers can be devised in two ways:

        (i)   In total using the totals of the books of prime entry.
        (ii) In detail by extraction from the sales ledger and the purchase ledger.

Differences between these two totals should be investigated and the explanation found.

POINTS TO NOTE

10. (a) Students find this material very difficult to grasp in an academic way as it is really an extremely practical matter. Practice is needed to familiarise students with the ideas and the jargon. Bookkeepers and accountants spend a lot of time balancing the books and seeking differences. The coming of the computer which balances accounts automatically has largely eliminated the work (and the fascination) of error investigation but has introduced new sorts of errors.

    (b) Some points to watch are:

        (i)   The total accounts (also known as control or summary accounts) are memorandum only. The real double entry is in the individual ledger accounts.

        (ii) The total entries in the control accounts go on the same side as the entries in the detail accounts.

        (iii) In the sales ledger, the debit entries set up the sums due by the customers and the credit side shows how these sums have been reduced or settled.

(iv) The purchase ledger entries are on the opposite side to those of the sales ledger.

(v) Errors may be in the books of prime entry and thus affect the memo total account or in the individual accounts and thus affect the total extracted from the ledger.

(c) The purchase and expenses ledger may be called the *bought ledger*.

(d) Where separate bought and sales ledgers are kept, together with the cash book, all other accounts (real, nominal and some personal) are kept in a ledger called the *nominal, private* or *general* ledger.

SELF TESTING QUESTIONS

(a) What is the purpose of keeping a sales ledger? (3).
(b) What is a contra? (4).
(c) List the books of prime entry in which entries on a customer's account are first entered. (5).
(d) Write out a typical sales ledger control account. (6).
(e) What is a general ledger?

Exercises (Answers begin on page 455)

1. *From the following data prepare sales ledger and bought ledger control accounts for 19-5:*

	Edward's business £	Jane's business £
Debtors 1.1.19-5	23,678	116,745
Creditors 1.1.19-5	15,438	34,780
Purchase daybook	124,324	154,780
Sales day book	98,710	763,243
Cash received	96,450	732,100
Payments to suppliers	123,789	149,980
Discounts received	1,670	1,453
Discounts allowed	880	21,579

Balance the control accounts and bring down the balances.

What would be the effect on the balances of errors in the primary records from which the data was obtained?

2. *Prepare control accounts from the following data for the year ending 19-2:*

	Alice's business £	Kewal's business £
Customers' Dr balances 1.1.-2	3,469	32,500
Customers' Cr balances 1.1.-2	34	1,435
Suppliers' Cr balances 1.1.-2	6,548	23,801
Suppliers' Dr balances 1.1.-2	45	678
Sales day book	63,257	134,902
Sales returns day book	3,780	1,439
Purchase daybook	82,456	278,030
Purchase returns day book	1,272	2,453
Cash paid to suppliers	78,329	241,000
Cash paid to customers	780	1,547
Cash received from customers	58,340	110,456
Cash received from suppliers	1,459	86
Bad debts	872	249
Contras	1,322	756
Interest charged to customer	23	146
Discounts allowed	897	1,680
Discounts received	432	657
Customers' Cr balances 31.12.-2	54	435
Suppliers' Dr balances 31.12.-2	50	324

Balance the control accounts and bring down the balances. Explain the transactions - cash received from suppliers, contras, bad debts, interest charged to customer. How can a debit balance arise on a supplier's account.

3. Prepare a control account for the sales ledger for 19–4 from the following:

	Jean's business £	Akbar's business £
Balances 1.1.-4	6,500	3,530
Sales day book	86,540	34,987
Cash from customers	87,341	31,678

<u>For Jean's business</u>

The list of balances totalled £8,751 and the following errors were found:

(i)   The sales day book was under added by £340.

(ii)   The cash from customers included, in error, a loan to the business from Ted of £3,000.

(iii)   The list did not include the balance due from William of £279.

(iv)   The list included the balance due from Jenny at £345 instead of £354.

<u>For Akbar's business</u>

The list of balances totalled £7,683 and the following errors were found:

(i)   The list included Frank's balance £129 twice.

(ii)   The list was overadded by £200.

(iii)   A page of the daybook was omitted in the summary. Its total was £320.

(iv)   A refund to a customer, who had overpaid, of £195 should have been included in the control account.

For both businesses, amend the control account and the list of balances and show that the ledger now balances.

4.   April Showers sells goods on credit to most of its customers. In order to control its debtor collection system, the company maintains a sales ledger control account. In preparing the accounts for the year to 30th October 1983, the accountant discovers that the total of all the personal accounts in the sales ledger amounts to £12,802, whereas the sales ledger control account balance discloses a balance of £12,550.

Upon investigating the matter, the following errors were discovered:

(a)   Sales for the week ending 27th March 1983 amounting to £850 had been omitted from the control account.
(b)   A debtor's account balance of £300 had not been included in the list of balances.
(c)   Cash received of £750 had been entered in a personal account as £570.
(d)   Discounts allowed totalling £100 had not been entered in the control account.
(e)   A personal account balance had been undercast by £200.
(f)   A contra item o9f £400 with the purchase ledger had not been entered in the control account.
(g)   A bad debt of £500 had not been entered in the control account.
(h)   Cash received of £250 had been debited to a personal account.
(i)   Discounts received of £50 had been debited to Bell's Sales Ledger Account.
(j)   Returns inwards valued at £200 had not been included in the control account.
(k)   Cash received of £80 had been credited to a personal account as £8.
(l)   A cheque for £300 received from a customer had been dishonoured by the bank, but no adjustment had been made in the control account.

Required:

(i)   Prepare a corrected sales ledger control account, bringing down the amended balance as at 1st November 1983.
(ii)   Prepare a statement showing the adjustments that are necessary to the list of personal account balances so that it reconciles with the amended sales ledger control account balance.

                                                                                                    (AAT)

Exercises without answers

5. From the following data prepare sales ledger and bought ledger control accounts for 19-6:

	Kevin's business £	Fiona's business £
Debtors 1.1.19-6	12,658	23,145
Creditors 1.1.19-6	16,780	40,123
Purchase daybook	134,670	234,876
Sales day book	230,091	89,011
Cash received	231,000	84,000
Payments to suppliers	120,765	220,120
Discounts received	1,560	
Discounts allowed		2,450

Balance the control accounts and bring down the balances.

6. Prepare control accounts from the following data for the year ending 19-7:

	Hubert's business £	Evan's business £
Customers' Dr balances 1.1.-7	23,679	43,901
Customers' Cr balances 1.1.-7	167	
Suppliers' Cr balances 1.1.-7	40,567	23,139
Suppliers' Dr balances 1.1.-7		200
Sales day book	156,900	345,345
Sales returns day book	2,678	3,657
Purchase daybook	211,456	132,678
Purchase returns day book	3,200	
Cash paid to suppliers	201,900	126,543
Cash paid to customers	200	673
Cash received from customers	145,006	320,760
Cash received from suppliers		1,500
Bad debts	2,600	1,234
Contras	1,500	700
Interest charged to customer	54	
Discounts allowed	234	1,387
Discounts received	700	256
Customers' Cr Balances 31.12.-7	321	124
Suppliers' Cr Balances 31.12.-7	590	298

7. Prepare the control account for the bought ledger for 19-4 from the following:

	Brenda's business £	Simone's business £
Balances 1.1.-4	12,500	4,532
Purchase day book	74,098	34,982
Cash to suppliers	71,567	33,450

For Brenda' business

The list of balances totalled £15,277 and the following errors were found:

(i) The purchase day book was over added by £100.
(ii) The cash to suppliers included, in error, a payment of wages £487.
(iii) The list did not include the balance due to George of £231.
(iv) The list included the balance due to Agnes at £540 instead of £450.

For Simone's business

The list of balances totalled £6,656 and the following errors were found:

(i)   The list included June's balance £329 twice.
(ii)   The list was under added by £180.
(iii)   The total of a page in the day book £278 was carried forward to the next page as £287.
(iv)   A refund from a supplier, who had been overpaid, of £452 should have been included in the control account.

For both businesses, amend the control account and the list of balances and show that the ledger now balances.

8.   From the following data prepare purchase ledger control accounts for:

	Angel Ltd £	Michael Ltd £	Gabriel Ltd £
Opening balances	3,675	2,789	13,667
Purchases	25,666	72,890	43,901
Purchase returns	1,546	–	2,549
Cheques paid	23,600	71,453	40,786
Cheque received for overpayment	–	–	437
Discounts received	1,698	678	–
Cheque dishonoured	–	1,000	3,561
Contras	1,040	326	–

9.   From the following data prepare sales ledger control accounts for:

	Cain Bros £	Abram & Co £	Solomon & Son £
Opening balances	12,666	3,890	4,651
Sales	102,667	43,900	98,764
Sales returns	3,784	–	1,200
Discounts allowed	238	1,677	908
Cheques received	92,544	43,890	92,877
Cheque paid as refund	3,677	–	500
Bad debts	400	324	20
Contras	1,050	100	–
Interest charged to customer	–	–	56
Bill accepted by customer	–	600	–

10.   From the following data prepare sales ledger and purchase ledger control accounts for:

	Owen £	Blunt £	Brooke £
Opening debtors	23,770	3,890	44,000
Opening creditors	16,334	4,700	24,900
Sales	101,678	98,000	143,766
Purchases	72,678	56,900	87,982
Sales returns	2,679	1,432	2,890
Purchase returns	678	537	742
Cheques in	97,877	75,988	140,809
Cheques out	66,832	51,823	80,234
Bad debts	700	1,766	2,890
Contras	1,046	1,000	874
Discounts received	345	983	540
Discounts allowed	784	651	1,034
Customer's cheque dishonoured	–	–	500
Bill of Exchange accepted by customer	800	–	700

11. The purchase ledger control account of Hopeless does not balance at 31.12.-8. Errors found were:

   (a) The credit side of Hill's account had been overcast by £100.
   (b) Graham's balance £290 had been omitted from the list.
   (c) Howe's balance had been included in the list at £370 instead of £307.
   (d) Burgon's balance £202 was in fact a debit one but it had been included in the list as a credit one.
   (e) A contra of £400 had been omitted from the control account.
   (f) The list had been undercast by £100.
   (g) A cheque paid to Harper of £490 had been entered in his account at £890.
   (h) The additions of the purchase returns book were too much by £1,000.
   (i) A page in the purchase day book had been omitted in the summary thus omitting £4,520.

Required: a revised list of creditors; a revised control account. Note that the original list had a total of £14,735. You will have to calculate the original control account balance.

12. The sales ledger control account of Locke does not balance. On inspection the following errors were found:

   (a) An invoice to Hobbes has not been posted to his account £240.
   (b) The balance due from Marx was omitted from the list of balances £632.
   (c) The sales day book total was overcast by £600.
   (d) A contra of £657 was omitted from the control account.
   (e) Weber's balance of £650 had been brought down as £560.
   (f) Discount allowed £34 had been debited to Popper's account.
   (g) The debit side of Plato's account had been overcast by £60.
   (h) A bad debt entered on Engels' account had not been entered into the control account £100.
   (i) A cash refund had been made to Bentham and entered onto his account and in the control account but no credit note had been raised £36.

Required: A revised list of balances; a revised control account. Note that the total of the list of balances was £23,680 and that the original control account balance was £25,871.

13. The sales ledger control account of Mildred showed:

	£		£
b/f	16,400	Cash	97,000
Sales	103,765	Discount	2,510
Interest on		Bad debt	1,200
overdue a/c	650	Sales returns	2,428
		Contras	1,200
c/f	120	c/f	15,597
	120,935		120,935

The list of balances showed a total of £16,844.

The following errors were found:

   (a) The list omitted £370.
   (b) The list included a balance of £540 twice.
   (c) A credit balance £20 was included as a debit balance.
   (d) The sales day book was undercast by £700.
   (e) The cash book debit analysis overlooked a receipt of £800 from a credit customer.
   (f) A refund was made to a credit customer £200 and correctly debited to his account.
   (g) A bad debt of £120 was omitted from the journal from which the control account was written up.
   (h) The cash above (£97,000) included a sum (£57) from a debtor whose debt was written off in 19-4.

Show that the control account now balances.

14. The book-keeper of Excel Stores Ltd prepared a schedule of balances of individual suppliers' accounts from the creditors ledger at 30 June 1984 and arrived at a total of £86,538.28.

He passed the schedule over to the accountant who compared this total with the closing balance on the Creditors Ledger Control account reproduced below:

Creditors Ledger Control

1984		£	1984		£
June 30	Purchases returns	560.18	June 1	Balance b/d	89,271.13
30	Bank	96,312.70	30	Purchases	100,483.49
30	Balance c/d	84,688.31	30	Discount received	2,656.82
			30	Debtors ledger control (contras)	3,049.75
		£192,561.19			£195,261.19
			July 1	Balance b/d	84,688.31

During his investigation into the discrepancy between the two figures, the accountant discovered a number of errors in the control account and the individual ledger accounts and schedule. You may assume that the total of each item posted to the control account is correct except to the extent that they are dealt with in the list below:

(1) One supplier had been paid £10.22 out of petty cash. This had been correctly posted to his personal account but has been omitted from the control account.

(2) The credit side of one supplier's personal account had been under-added by £30.00.

(3) A credit balance on a supplier's account had been transposed from £548.14 to £584.41 when extracted on to the schedule.

(4) The balance on one supplier's account of £674.32 had been completely omitted from the schedule.

(5) Discounts received of £12.56 and £8.13 had been posted to the wrong side of two individual creditors' accounts.

(6) Goods costing £39.60 had been returned to the supplier but this transaction had been completely omitted from the returns day book.

Required:
(a) Prepare a statement starting with the original closing balance on the creditors ledger control account then identifying and correcting the errors in that account and concluding with an amended closing balance; and

(b) Prepare a statement starting with the original total of the schedule of individual creditors then identifying and correcting errors in that schedule and concluding with an amended total.   (ACCA)

21. Petty Cash Books

INTRODUCTION

1.   The majority of payments between commercial and industrial concerns and their customers are settled by cheque or other bank medium. The only significant cash (notes and coin) movement in business is in retail sales and even there, payment by cheque and credit card is increasingly important. Cash received from retail sales is usually banked intact and hence becomes in effect a bank transaction.

2.   However, most businesses have a need to make small cash payments for such items as tips, bus fares, casual wages (*e.g.* cleaning), tea and coffee. These small payments are dealt with through a petty cash book (petty is from the French, small or little). The specific system commonly used is called the *imprest* system (from the Latin - to lend).

THE IMPREST SYSTEM

3.   The system requires the following procedures:

   (a)   The appointment of a person who is responsible for petty cash - the petty cashier.

   (b)   The giving to the petty cashier by the cashier from the bank of a sum of cash called the imprest or the float - say £100.

   (c)   The payment of petty cash expenses by the petty cashier against authorised and approved vouchers.

   (d)   The entry of all these transactions in the petty cash book which is both a book of prime entry and a part of the double entry system.

   (e)   At intervals the cashier will examine the supporting evidence for the payments, take away and file this evidence and draw from the bank the total amount of payments. Thus if payments made totalled £64.25, then the cash remaining should total £35.75 and further cash will be given to the petty cashier of £64.25 making the float or imprest up to £100 again.

   (f)   At random intervals, a senior official should check the petty cash book, vouchers and balance. The petty cashier should always have a total of £100 in cash or in approved vouchers.

THE PETTY CASH BOOK

4.   A typical petty cash book ruling is shown in Fig. 20.1.

The petty cash book is a double entry account. The double entry of the credit side items will be completed by debit to:

Tips expense A/c	Tips	£5.00
Sundry expenses A/c	Sundries	£7.10
etc		

SUMMARY

5.   (a)   Most cash movement today is through bank accounts.

   (b)   Small cash payments are dealt with through the petty cash system kept on an imprest system.

   (c)   Petty cash transactions are recorded in a petty cash book, which is part of the double entry system, as well as a book of prime entry.

SELF TESTING QUESTIONS

   (a)   Why are cash sales not dealt with in the petty cash book?
   (b)   What payments are put through petty cash?
   (c)   What is the imprest system?

Dr   **PETTY CASH BOOK**   **Cr**

				Total	Tips	Sundries	Stationery	Travelling expenses	Tools
			£	£	£	£	£	£	£
1.1.-4	Balance in hand	34.75	2.1.-4	Bus fares	4.13				4.13	
2.1.-4	Cash from bank	65.25	3.1.-4	Tips	2.00	2.00				
			4.1.-4	Tools	9.20					9.20
			6.1.-4	Petrol	11.50				11.50	
			7.1.-4	Tips	3.00	3.00				
			8.1.-4	Cleaning materials	4.60		4.60			
			9.1.-4	Tea/sugar	2.50		2.50			
			10.1.-4	Books	15.09			15.09		
			12.1.-4	Train fare	25.00				25.00	
					77.02	5.00	7.10	15.09	40.63	9.20
			12.1.-4	Balance c/d	22.98					
		100.00			100.00					

12.1.-4 Balance in hand 22.98
12.1.-4 Cash from bank 77.02

Fig 20.1

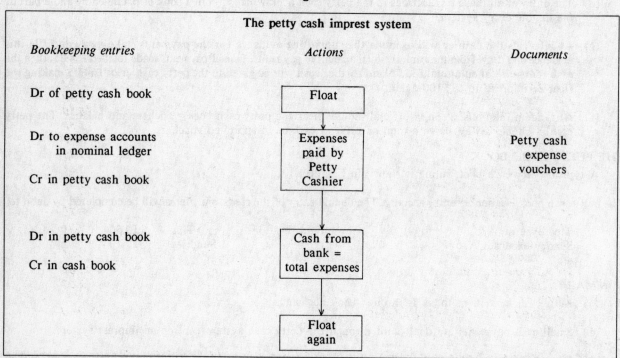

The petty cash imprest system

Bookkeeping entries / Actions / Documents

Dr of petty cash book — Float

Dr to expense accounts in nominal ledger
Cr in petty cash book — Expenses paid by Petty Cashier — Petty cash expense vouchers

Dr in petty cash book
Cr in cash book — Cash from bank = total expenses

Float again

Exercises (Answers begin on page 455)

1.   Camp maintains a petty cash book with columns for travel, post, stationery, motor, sundries, credit accounts. At 19.1.-7 the balance was £16.44. The imprest is £100. In the week ending 24.1.-7 the following payments were made: tea bags £3.78; bus fares £2.33; milk £1.37; posters £4.11; petrol £5.00; taxi £2.44; envelopes £2.11; gift to nuns £5.00; oil filter £4.10; stamps £5.00; parcel £3.20; bus fare £1.50; petrol £6.00; settlement of credit account – Walters Ltd £12.00.

On 20.1.-7 the imprest was made up resulting from the balance at 19.1.-7.

Show the petty cash book for the week and indicate the double entries required.

2.   Clunk maintains his petty cash on the imprest system with an imprest of £80. At 16.1.-7 his balance in hand was £32.12.

In the ensuing week the imprest was made up and the following payments made: paid credit account of Brown £5.90; invoice books £6.23; petrol £4.87; bus fares £1.20; train fare £2.00; loan to Clunk £5.00; sandwiches for auditor £3.80; petrol £7.63; advert £3.00; mileage payment to manager £12.00; leaflet printing £4.00; antifreeze £7.79.

Write up a suitably analysed petty cash book for the week indicating the double entries required.

Exercies without answers

3.   *The Oakhill Printing Co Ltd operates its petty cash account on the imprest system. It is maintained at a figure of £80 on the first day of each month.*

At 30 April 1987 the petty cash box held £19.37 in cash.

During May 1987, the following petty cash transactions arose:

Date		Amount
1987		£
MAY		
1	Cash received to restore imprest	to be derived
1	Bus fares	0.41
2	Stationery	2.35
4	Bus fares	0.30
7	Postage stamps	1.70
7	Trade journal	0.95
8	Bus fares	0.64
11	Correcting fluid	1.29
12	Typewriter ribbons	5.42
14	Parcel postage	3.45
15	Paper clips	0.42
15	Newspapers	2.00
16	Photocopier repair	16.80
19	Postage stamps	1.50
20	Drawing pins	0.38
21	Train fare	5.40
22	Photocopier paper	5.63
23	Display decorations	3.07
23	Correcting fluid	1.14
25	Wrapping paper	0.78
27	String	0.61
27	Sellotape	0.75
27	Biro pens	0.46
28	Typewriter repair	13.66
30	Bus fares	2.09
JUNE		
1	Cash received to restore imprest	to be derived

Required:
Open and post the company's petty cash account for the period 1 May to 1 June 1987 inclusive and balance the account at 30 May 1987.

In order to facilitate the subsequent double entry postings, all items of expense appearing in the 'payments' column should then be analysed individually into suitably labelled expense columns.   *(ACCA)*

4.   *Joy maintains a petty cash book on the imprest system with a float of £100. The balance at 31.1.-8 was £23.64. The float was made up on 2.2.-8 and the following payments made in the week ending 7.2.-8:*

Travelling	12.24; 6.38; 2.39
Sundries	1.34; 7.26; 60p; 1.49
Stationery	2.74; 8.64; 10.01
Wages	6.00; 9.00
Postage	13.00; 2.00
Purchase ledger account	8.00

Rule and enter up a suitable petty cash book. Show where the corresponding double entries will be made.

5.   *Charles Evans is a sole trader who keeps his petty cash on the Imprest system – the Imprest amount being £40. The petty cash transactions for the month of May 1980 are as follows:*

    May
    1   Petty cash in hand £5.17.
    1   Petty cash restored to Imprest account.
    6   Bought notepaper £3.28.
    7   Paid wages £9.14.
    14   Bought postage stamps £3.75.
    16   Paid to J. Thomas, a creditor, £5.36.
    21   Paid wages £9.28.
    23   Bought envelopes £4.37.
    27   Bought postage stamps £2.10.

Required:
Draw up the petty cash book for the month of May 1980, recording the above transactions. You should also give the entry on 2nd June 1980, restoring the petty cash to the Imprest amount.

Note:
    Your analysis columns should be for:
    (a) Stationery   *(c) Postages*
    (b) Wages   *(d) Ledger*   (LCCI)

22. Trial Balances and The Journal

INTRODUCTION

1.   A trial balance is simply a listing, divided into debit and credit columns, of the balances on all the accounts in a double entry system. Its objective is to determine or prove the accuracy of the bookkeeping. The trial balance has come also to be used in the preparation of final accounts and this is also discussed in this chapter.

A difference is often encountered on extraction of a trial balance and a suspense account opened for the difference. Correction of these differences and the errors which cause them is discussed and we continue with the use of the Journal.

2.   Two areas related to the preparation of Accounts from trial balances are presented finally - commissions based on profit and goods on sale or return.

TRIAL BALANCE USES

3.   The following uses are made of trial balances:

   (a)   Testing the accuracy of some aspects of the double entry. Not all errors are revealed by a difference on a trial balance. Errors that are revealed include:

   (i)   Non-correspondence of debit and credit entries by omission of one side, both entries on one side or differences in amount between the entries.
   (ii)   Errors in computation of the balances of the accounts.
   (iii)   Omission of an account balance.
   (iv)   Errors in extraction of the trial balance.

   Errors that are not revealed include:

   (i)   Omission of transactions altogether.
   (ii)   Entries on the wrong accounts.
   (iii)   Compensating errors.

   (b)   The preparation of the financial state-ments.

Following business practice, many examination questions consist of a trial balance, a list of notes on adjustments to be made, and a requirement to prepare final accounts.

EXAMPLE

Trial balance of H. Flashman, bicycle dealer, at 31.12.-9.

	Dr £000	Cr £000
Capital 31.12.-8		68
Stock 31.12.-8	46	
Purchases	234	
Sales		288
Expenses	37	
Drawings	8	
Debtors	48	
Creditors		40
Bank		51
Fixed assets at cost	132	
Depreciation to 31.12.-8		58
	505	505

Notes:
   (a)   Stock at 31.12.-9 was valued at £58,000.
   (b)   Depreciation is 15% straight line.
   (c)   Expenses include prepayments at 31.12.-9 of £12,000 and omit accruals of £23,000.

Required:
Prepare trading and profit and loss account for the year ending 31st December 19-9 and balance sheet at that date.

ANSWER

There are many ways of tackling this type of question. One way which many people find simple is to use a matrix as follows:

H. Flashman

	Trial Balance Dr	Trial Balance Cr	Adjustments Dr	Adjustments Cr	Trading & P&L a/c Dr	Trading & P&L a/c Cr	Balance Sheet Assets	Balance Sheet Liabilities
	£000	£000	£000	£000	£000	£000	£000	£000
Capital		68	8					60
Stock	46		58	46	46	58	58	
Purchases	234				234			
Sales		288				288		
Expenses	37		23	12	48		12	23
Drawings	8			8				
Debtors	48						48	
Creditors		40						40
Bank		51						51
Fixed Assets	132						132	
Depreciation		58		20	20			78
	505	505	89	86	348	346	250	252

The resulting trading and profit and loss account will be:

	£000	£000
Sales		288
Less Cost of Sales		
- opening stock	46	
- purchases	234	
	280	
- closing stock	58	222
Gross Profit		66
Expenses	48	
Depreciation	20	68
Net loss		2

and Balance Sheet as at 31st December 19-9

	£000	£000
Fixed Assets at cost		132
Less accumulated depreciation		78
		54
Current Assets		
Stock	58	
Debtors	48	
Prepayments	12	118
		172
Less Current Liabilities		
Creditors	40	
Accruals	23	
Bank overdraft	51	114
		58
Capital at 1.1.-9		68
Net loss for year		2
		66
Drawings		8
		58

TRIAL BALANCE DIFFERENCES

4. Suppose a trial balance is extracted from the books of I. Legge, a wholesale fruiterer, at 31.12.-9 as:

	£	£
Capital 1.1.-9		41,200
Sales		132,380

Purchases	66,410	
Stock 1.1.-9	4,300	
Overheads	19,204	
Debtors	8,760	
Creditors		12,244
Fixed Assets at cost	30,000	
Depreciation		11,000
Drawings	9,100	
Bank	63,240	
	201,014	196,824

Clearly the trial balance does not balance and there is a difference of £4,190. To make it balance an account can be opened called a "suspense account" thus:

Suspense Account

	£
31.12.-9 TB difference	4,190

Inserted in the trial balance, the trial balance now balances.

5. The difference was caused by errors, and on investigation the following errors were found:

(a) A credit note to Lemon of £264 was entered in the books as £246.
(b) A purchase from Pear of £320 was entered on Pear's account but omitted from purchases account.
(c) A receipt from Apple of £3,000 being a bad debt recovered was entered in the cash book but not credited to any account.
(d) A drawing of £200 was debited to drawings account as £2,000.
(e) A credit to Nutt of £136 was omitted from the books altogether.
(f) An invoice for £290 from G. Plum was credited in error to both G. Plum and H. Plum.

Correcting these errors will require bookkeeping entries as:

Dr			Cr	Dr			Cr
	Sales				**Lemon**		
	Lemon		18	Sales	18		
	Nutt		136				

Dr			Cr	Dr			Cr
	Suspense				**Purchases**		
Bad debt recovered		b/f	4,190	Suspense	320		
	3,000	Purchases	320				
Drawings	1,800	H. Plum	290				
	4,800		4,800				

	Bad debts received				**Drawings**		
	Suspense		3,000			Suspense	1,800

	Nutt				**H. Plum**		
Sales	136			Suspense	290		

Note:

(a) I have omitted all entries on the above accounts except those arising out of the correction of errors.

(b) The suspense account has now been eliminated.

(c) An entry on the suspense account was only required when the error involved a non correspondence of debit and credit entry - items (b), (c), (d) and (f).

(d) The trial balance now balances:

	£	£
Capital		41,200
Sales		132,534
Purchases	66,730	

Stock	4,300	
Overheads	19,204	
Debtors	8,914	
Creditors		11,954
Fixed Assets and depreciation	30,000	11,000
Drawings	7,300	
Bad debts recovered		3,000
Bank	63,240	
	199,688	199,688

THE JOURNAL

6. The majority of transactions are first entered in one of the following books of prime entry:

> Sales day book
> Sales return day book
> Purchases and expenses day book
> Purchases and expenses returns day book
> Cash book (and discount columns)
> Petty cash book

Some transactions, especially those of a non-routine nature are not appropriate for the above books of prime entry. For them, a special book of prime entry is maintained called the journal.

EXAMPLE

Carl, a dealer in antiques, acquired the assets of a rival business owned by Robin for £20,000. The deal was financed by Carl paying cash £10,000 and leaving the remainder on loan from Robin at 15%. The assets acquired were valued as: leasehold premises £3,000; delivery van £2,500; fixtures and fittings £1,500; rent and rates prepaid £500 and stock £7,650.

This transaction has to be entered in Carl's double entry system but first transactions are entered in the journal as:

			£	£
1.	Dr.	Leasehold premises	3,000	
		Delivery van	2,500	
		Fixtures & Fittings	1,500	
		Rent and Rates	500	
		Stock	7,650	
		Goodwill (see (g) below)	4,850	
	Cr.	Purchase of Robin's business A/c		20,000

Being the assets acquired on the acquisition of Robin's business per agreement dated . . . . . .

2.	Dr.	Purchase of Robin's business A/c	20,000	
	Cr.	Cash		10,000
		Loan A/c Robin		10,000

Being consideration given for the purchase of Robin's business.

Note:

   (a) Each journal entry is numbered.

   (b) The debit entries to be entered in the ledger are given first and then the credit.

   (c) One to one correspondence of double entry is not required but the total *debits and credits for any journal entry must be the same.*

   (d) Each entry is accompanied by a narrative *which explains the entry.*

   (e) Each entry is ruled off.

(f) Cash entries appear in the book of prime entry, the cash book but it is customary to include them in the journal to complete a series of entries such as those on the purchase of a business.

(g) Goodwill is the extra paid for the business over the physical assets. It is treated as a Fixed asset.

7. The journal is also used in the correction of errors. Here are the journal entries for the example in paragraph 5.

JOURNAL			Dr £	Cr £
101	Dr	Lemon A/c	18	
	Cr	Sales A/c		18

Being correction of erroneous entry of a sales invoice as £246 instead of £264.

102	Dr	Purchases A/c	320	
	Cr	Suspense A/c		320

Being completion of entry of purchase invoice, entry in the purchases account having been omitted.

103	Dr	Suspense A/c	3,000	
	Cr	Bad debts recovered A/c		3,000

Being completion of the entry of £3,000, a bad debt recovered.

104	Dr	Suspense A/c	1,800	
	Cr	Drawings A/c		1,800

Being correction of erroneous entry in the drawings account, £2,000 instead of £200.

105	Dr	Nutt A/c	136	
	Dr	Sales A/c		136

Being entry of a credit sale invoice, previously omitted.

106	Dr	Plum A/c	290	
	Cr	Suspense A/c		290

Being removal of £290 credited in error to H. Plum as well as to G. Plum

Note that the journal is used as a book of prime entry for any sequence of transactions which are non-routine. Examples are in issue of shares, the purchase or disposal of a business, a change in a partnership or, as here, the correction of a set of errors after extraction of the trial balance.

The journal entries form a connected story and thus items which might properly be included in other books of prime entry (*e.g.* item 105 above) are included for the sake of completeness.

8. Commission based on profit
This is a good point to explain a matter which is frequently found in practice and in exams but which students find difficult.

Many firms pay managers or others a *commission* based on a percentage of the profit. Clearly this is done as an incentive to the manager. The problem is that the commission is based on a percentage of the profit before or *after* *deducting* the commission. If it is before deductions of the commission then:

Phil's business pays a commission to Ted of 10% of the profit:

	Without Commission	£		*With Commission*	£
Gross profit		64,000			64,000
Expenses		42,000		42,000	
Commission		-		2,200	44,200
		22,000			19,800

Remember to include the commission in current liabilities.

But if the commission is on the profit *after charging* the commission:

	Without Commission	£		*With Commission*	£
Gross profit		64,000			64,000
Expenses		42,000		42,000	
Commission		-		2,000	44,000
		22,000			20,000

The procedure for finding the commission is:

(a) Express the percentage as a fraction, i.e. 10% as 1/10, 5% as 1/20, etc.
(b) Add one to the denominator i.e. 1/11, 1/21.
(c) Apply the fraction to the profit.

Alternatively

(a) Calculate 100 + the percentage, i.e. 10 gives 110, 15 gives 115.
(b) Apply the fraction 10/110, 15/115 etc to the profit.

9. Goods on sale or return

Some businesses sell their goods through agents on what is called a goods on sale or return arrangement. The business invoices the agent with the goods and the agent tries to sell them but if he cannot do so he can return them to the business. The goods belong to the business until they are sold by the agent and any unsold goods are thus stock in hand.

EXAMPLE

Sally invoices £1,000 of goods to Nigel on a goods on sale or return basis on 10th December 19-7. Bookkeeping entry: Dr Nigel £1,000; Cr Sales £1,000. The goods had cost Sally £600.

On 11th December Nigel has sold 40% of the goods for £750.

The year end entries should be:

1. As Sally has £1,000 in sales and only £400 have actually been sold, Dr Sales A.c with £600 and Cr Nigel with £600 as he owes only £400.

2. Include £360 in stock. This is the cost (to Sally) price of the unsold goods.

SUMMARY

10. (a) The trial balance is used to test the accuracy of bookkeeping and also as the starting point in the preparation of final accounts.

(b) Final accounts can be prepared from a trial balance using a matrix approach.

(c) The difference on a trial balance is often entered in a suspense account. The discovery and correction of the errors leads to the progressive closing of the suspense account.

(d) The journal is a "catch all" book of prime entry used for entries which do not go through the routine books of prime entry.

(e) Commission based on profit can be calculated *before* or *after* deducting the commission.

(f) Goods invoiced on sale or return agreements must be included in stock at *cost* if unsold at the accounting date.

POINTS TO NOTE

11. (a) Students find correction of errors and the suspense account difficult. The secret of success is:

     (i)   Visualise the correct entry.
     (ii)   Consider how the actual entry differs.
     (iii)   Correct the difference.
     (iv)   Where one-legged entries are concerned (*i.e.* where total Dr and Cr do not correspond) include an entry in the suspense account.

     (b) In recent times the journal has tended to fall out of use. However, the advent of computerised bookkeeping has brought a revival. Computer systems usually contain routines for: credit sales and returns, credit purchases and returns, credit expenses and returns, cash and cheque receipts, cash and cheque payments and wages. All other transactions go through a journal.

SELF TESTING QUESTIONS

     (a) What is a trial balance? (1).
     (b) What are the uses of a trial balance? (3).
     (c) When is a suspense account used? (4).
     (d) What does a credit balance on a suspense account indicate?
     (e) What is the journal used for? (7).
     (f) How is the commission on profit after charging the commission calculated? (8).
     (g) What is the year end treatment of goods on sale or return? (9)

Exercises (Answers begin on page 455)

1. The trial balances of Dick and Doris at 31.12.-8 showed:

	Dick Dr	Dick Cr	Doris Dr	Doris Cr
Capital 1.1.-8		12,608		23,876
Stock 1.1.-8	2,567		3,510	
Purchases and sales	15,908	28,981	40,700	70,432
Expenses		6,200	17,500	
Drawings	5,700		10,322	
Debtors and creditors	3,400	2,300	15,680	5,600
Fixed assets at cost	12,700		10,438	
Depreciation to 31.12.-7		6,230		3,428
Bank	4,006		4,810	

For Dick, the following errors were found:

(i) Drawings of £200 were debited in error to expenses.
(ii) Purchases from Fred, a supplier £36 were debited to his account.
(iii) The sum due from Alf was omitted from the trial balance – £80.
(iv) Fixed asset purchases of £380 were entered as £830 in the fixed asset account.
(v) Drawings by Dick of stock valued at £45 were made in June 19-8 and not recorded in the books.
(vi) A payment of casual wages £80 was entered in the cash book but the double entry was not completed.

For Doris, the following errors were found:

(i) The account of Joshua, a customer was extracted in error as £354 instead of £454.
(ii) A payment for advertising £190 was credited in the expenses account.
(iii) An invoice for goods purchased for resale from Wally £278 was omitted from the books altogether.
(iv) The sales invoice to Hodge was correctly entered in the sales day book as £560 but entered in Hodge's account as £650.
(v) The payment of an advertising account to Noos Ltd £50 was debited in the expenses account and also in Noos Ltd acount. The original invoice was correctly entered in Noos Ltd's account.
(vi) The balance of Geoff's account was entered as £320 Dr. In fact the two sides of his account totalled:
     Dr £890   Cr £534

Required: (for each business)

(a)   Compute the difference on the trial balance.
(b)   Identify which errors cause the difference.
(c)   Place each error including the ones identified in (b) in the list of the Chapter paragraph 3.
(d)   Produce an amended trial balance and show that it now balances.

2.   The trial balance of Donal did not balance at 31.12.-8 and a suspense account balance of £3,776 was inserted on the debit side to make it balance. Subsequent investigations showed:

(a)   Discounts allowed £1,480 had been entered on the wrong side.
(b)   The bank statement balance £498 overdrawn had been included instead of the cash book balance £36 debit.
(c)   June purchases £17,900 had not been posted to the purchases account.
(d)   A cheque for £1,200 for car repairs had been posted to the building repairs account.
(e)   The petty cash balance of £46 had been included as £64.
(f)   Provision for depreciation account £6,800 had been entered on the wrong side of the trial balance.
(g)   A loan from Bob of £4,000 had been omitted from the trial balance.

Show that the trial balance now balances.

3.   The trial balance of Donna does not balance at 31.12.-8 and a suspense account was opened to make it balance. Subsequent investigation showed:

(a)   Discount received £487 had been entered on the wrong side.
(b)   A bad debt of £500 had been entered in the customers account but not in the bad debts account.
(c)   The provision for doubtful debts account £1,700 had been entered on the wrong side.
(d)   The rent received account had been undercast by £400.
(e)   The scrapping of an old lorry net book value £430 had been omitted from the books.
(f)   The expense account balance rent £730 had been omitted from the Trial balance.
(g)   A stationery invoice £23 had been entered in the motor expenses account.
(h)   A new car £4,500 had also been entered in the motor expenses account.
(i)   The sales account had been undercast by £100.

The trial balance now balances. What was the balance on the suspense account?

4.   A difference on the trial balance of Singh at 31.12.-8 was resolved by opening a suspense account. The profit and loss account was then prepared and showed a profit of £12,600. The suspense account was included in the balance sheet to make it balance. Subsequent investigation disclosed:

(a)   A page of the sales day book totalling £576 had not been posted to the sales account.
(b)   An accrual of rates £371 had not been taken account of.
(c)   A repayment of part of the loan from Patel £300 had been entered on the loan interest account.
(d)   The petty cash balance had been included as £57 instead of £75.
(e)   A bad debt £120 had been entered in the customer's account but not in the expense account.
(f)   Drawings £200 had been entered in the sundry expenses account.
(g)   An invoice for car repairs £380 had been entered in the wages account.
(h)   The rent received account balance £600 had been entered on the wrong side of the trial balance and the profit and loss account.
(i)   Advertising account with a balance of £2,759 had been omitted altogether.
(j)   Closing stock had omitted some items valued at cost at £2,000.

Required:
Frame the journal entries to clear the suspense account (narratives not required). Prepare a statement showing the corrected amount of the profit.

Exercises without answers

5.   The trial balances of Diane and Donal at 31.12.-8 showed:

	Diane Dr	Diane Cr	Donal Dr	Donal Cr
Capital 1.1.-8		6,568		2,678
Stock 1.1.-8	5,600			12,540
Purchases and sales	45,879	81,432	34,671	60,430
Expenses	5,790		3,712	
Drawings	6,000		8,200	
Debtors and creditors	10,500	4,563	9,800	6,740
Fixed assets at cost	22,500		13,600	
Depreciation to 31.12.-7		4,600		8,300
Bank		822		4,385

<u>For Diane</u>, *the following errors were found:*

(i)   *The stock was brought down erroneously. It should have been £6,500.*
(ii)   *A payment to Gina, a supplier, was not entered on her account - £760.*
(iii) *A receipt £87 from Tim, a customer, was debited on his account.*
(iv)   *Cash drawn by Diane £500 was entered in her account correctly but in the cash book as £50.*
(v)   *The fixed asset account was balanced off using a debit side which was added up as £27,200 which was £100 too much.*
(vi)   *The balance of the account of Alan, a customer, was omitted - £780.*

<u>For Donal</u>, *the following errors were found:*

(i)   *An invoice from Lisa, a supplier, was omitted altogether - £700.*
(ii)   *The bank's charges for the final quarter (£260) were entered on the purchases account.*
(iii) *A drawing of £50 was entered on the credit of the expense account and a cash sale of £50 was entered on the debit of sales account.*
(iv)   *The proceeds of sale of a fixed asset were entered in sales instead of a disposal of fixed assets account - £70.*
(v)   *The debit of drawings account was under added by £10.*
(vi)   *Wages were debited in error to sales account - £95.*

Required: (for each busines)

(a)   *Compute the difference on the trial balance.*
(b)   *Identify which errors cause the difference.*
(c)   *Place each error including the ones identified in (b) in the list in the Chapter paragraph 3.*
(d)   *Produce an amended trial balance and show that it now balances.*

6.   The balance sheet of Hewitt at 31.12.-7 showed:

Capital b/f	19,369	Fixed Assets Cost	24,000
Profit	18,760	Depreciation	12,540
	38,129		11,460
Trade creditors	12,680	Stock	21,000
Accruals	2,721	Debtors	20,400
		Cash at Bank	3,100
	53,530		55,960

Upon investigation the following errors are found:

(a)   *The balance on the provision for doubtful debts account £1,300 had been omitted from the balance sheet.*
(b)   *Bad debts of £400 need to be written off and then the provision for doubtful debts made equal to 5% of debtors.*
(c)   *A trade creditor of £320 had been omitted.*
(d)   *A fixed asset purchase of £2,000 had been debited to repairs. Depreciation is 20% reducing balance.*
(e)   *The proceeds of sale of a fixed asset (cost in 19-4 £3,000) for £900 had been credited to motor expenses.*
(f)   *The stock had been undervalued by £570.*
(g)   *The bank statement balance had been included instead of the cash book balance £2,690.*
(h)   *Discounts allowed £800 had been credited to the profit and loss account.*

(i) Sales of £2,000 had been debited to debtors but omitted from sales account.

(j) The rent expense in the profit and loss account included the whole of the rent for the half year to 28.2.-8 £900.

Prepare the corrected balance sheet.

7. Consider the balance sheet in the previous question. The following separate set of errors were found:

(a) Rent received of £570 had been debited in the profit and loss account.

(b) In July the proprietor had taken goods for his own use £780.

(c) A purchase of goods for resale £800 had been debited to motor expenses.

(d) A purchase on credit of £4,000 had been credited to the supplier but omitted from purchases.

(e) The rates expense did not include any part of the rates for the half year to 31.3.-8 £1,230.

(f) The stock sheets were overcast by £900.

(g) The proceeds of sale of a fixed asset (cost in 19-3 £3,000) £680 were credited to motor expenses. Depreciation on all fixed assets is 25% reducing balance.

(h) The cost of new fixed asset £5,000 had been debited to purchases.

(i) Bad debts of £500 should be written off and a provision made for doubtful debts of 4% of debtors.

(j) A loan of £5,000 and accrued interest £290 had been omitted from the balance sheet only.

Prepare the corrected balance sheet.

8. Various sorts of errors can be made when the accounts of a business are in course of preparation. Some of these errors become apparent when the trial balance is extracted and fails to balance, but others are not revealed in this way.

Required:

(a) List six different types of error and devise an actual (numerical) example of each by way of illustration.

(b) State, with reasons, which of the errors you have listed and illustrated in (a) above would result in the trial balance failing to balance.

(c) State the procedure you would apply to correct the errors you have identified in (b) above, using a suspense account.

(d) Open and post a suspense account on the basis of your answer to (c) and using the actual figures, as appropriate, given in your answer to (a).

(N.B. The opening balance of the suspense account will have to be derived accordingly).   (ACCA)

9. The bookkeeper of the company which employs you as its accountant, has consulted you about some transactions for which he does not know the appropriate accounting treatment. The company's accounting year ended on 31 March 1986 and draft accounts have already been prepared.

The transactions are:

(1) an account for goods bought on credit from Dominion Supplies Ltd for £127.54. This transaction, which is to be settled in contra against that company's account in the debtors ledger, has not yet been recorded at all;

(2) the company has sold a vehicle which had originally cost £7,800 and on which £4,500 depreciation had been provided, for £2,700. The bookkeeper has debited bank account and credited vehicles account with the sale proceeds but has not effected any other entries;

(3) the company has traded-in another vehicle which had originally cost £8,300 and on which £6,900 depreciation had been provided, at an agreed valuation of £1,800. The only ledger entry made by the bookkeeper so far has been a debit to vehicles account and a credit to the supplier's account of the difference of £8,700 between the cost of the new vehicle and the trade-in value of the old vehicle;

(4) the company had acquired additional warehouse space from 1 October 1985 at an annual rental of £3,000, payable quarterly in advance. The actual payments have been made on the due dates (1 October 1985 and 3 January 1986) but in preparing the draft accounts for the year ended 31 March 1986 the bookkeeper mistakenly thought that these payments were made in arrear and had raised an accrual;

(5) the company has sub-let part of the premises referred to in (4) above at a quarterly rental of £240, payable in advance from 1 January 1986. the tenant paid the rental for the March 1986 quarter on 3 January 1986 and for the June 1986 quarter on 21 March 1986. The bookkeeper has debited both the amounts to bank account and has credited them to premises account.

Required:

Open the company's Journal and make the appropriate entries for the above transactions.

Note:
The narrative is an integral part of each journal entry and must be shown.   *(ACCA)*

10. The first draft of the final accounts of Torkard Traders disclosed a net profit of £41,004 and a capital employed of £352,600, before providing for the manager's efficiency bonus, but including £8,928 (credit balance) for errors held in suspense.

H. Huthwaite, the manager, receives a basic salary plus an annual bonus of £300 for every complete percentage point by which the net profit to capital employed percentage exceeds 10%. In this context, net profit is before charging the manager's bonus, and capital employed is defined as fixed assets plus working capital. The bonus calculation is not carried out until the figures have been audited.

During the course of the audit, it was discovered that:

(i)   discounts allowed, £536, had been credited to discounts received;

(ii)   the sale for cash, of some disused fixtures and fittings which had been completely written off in a previous year, had been credited to Fixtures and Fittings, £470;

(iii)   an amount of £380 owed by M & Co. for goods supplied had been settled in contra against an amount of £850 owing to M & Co., but the ledger entries had not yet been made;

(iv)   a glass carboy containing chemicals, which was kept in the warehouse, had sprung a leak. The resultant seepage had caused irreparable damage to stock valued at £800 but no account has yet been taken of this fact;

(v)   due to an oversight, credit sales for the last three days of the accounting year, amounting to £1,575, have been completely omitted from the Sales Day Book;

(vi)   in the Purchase Day Book, a sub-total of £27,183.54 had been carried forward as £37,183.54. Creditors, however, had been correctly posted;

(vii)   a credit sale invoice of £978 had been entered in the Sales Day Book as £789;

(viii) a credit note from a supplier for £21 in respect of faulty goods, had not been posted;

(ix)   the proprietor of Torkard Traders sometimes, for his convenience, abstracts cash from the till for personal purposes. During the year, this has amounted to £86. The bookkeeper states that he has 'reduced cash sales so that the cash book balances'.

Required:

(a)   Recalculate the net profit and capital employed figures after the above errors have been corrected.
(b)   Calculate the manager's bonus.
(c)   Open the Suspense account and post the eliminating entries.   *(ACCA)*

11. To enable work to proceed on a firm's draft year end accounts a difference found in the trial balance was entered into a suspense account opened for the purpose. The draft Profit and Loss Account subsequently showed a profit for the year of £102,108 and the Suspense Account was shown in the draft balance sheet.

During audit the following errors were found which when corrected eliminated the Suspense Account entry:

(a) One of the pages of the Sales Day Book totalling £5,138 had not been posted to Sales Account.
(b) The year end stock sheets had been overcast by £1,100.
(c) The last page of the Purchases Day Book totalling £7,179 had been posted to Purchases Account as £1,779.
(d) No account had been taken of electricity consumed since the last meter reading, the estimated amount being £246.
(e) An invoice for £64 entered correctly in the Sales Day Book had been posted to the customer's account as £164.
(f) An entry in the Purchases Day Book of £82 had not been posted to the supplier's account.
(g) An error had been made in balancing the Petty Cash Book, the correct amount being £250, not £25.
(h) Loan interest paid amounting to £500 had been posted to the Loan Account.

Required:

(i) Frame the necessary journal entries to clear the Suspense Account (narrative not required).
(b) Prepare the Suspense Account showing the amount of the original difference.
(c) Prepare a statement showing the correct profit/loss for the year.

(AAT)

Some Accounting Complexities

The next part of the manual introduces some accounting complexities. All foundation syllabuses are likely to include the subject matter of Chapter 23 Discounts and Chaper 24 Bad and Doubtful Debts. However some may not include the material in Chapter 25 Value Added Tax, Chapter 26 Hire Purchase Transactions and Chapter 27 Bills of Exchange.

23. Discounts

INTRODUCTION

1.   There are three types of discounts of interest to accountants. These are:

   (a)   Trade discounts which include bulk and quantity discounts.
   (b)   Settlement or cash discounts.
   (c)   Discounts on bills of exchange.

I will deal with the first two. Discounts on bills of exchange I will leave until I deal with Bills of Exchange.

TRADE DISCOUNTS

2.   Trade discounts are literally *reductions of price*. A business may have a standard price for a product. The business may then give trade discounts to a particular customer or to particular classes of customer so that it sells to them at lower prices. The reasons for selling at lower prices to some customers are many and include bulk buying, regular buying, selling to wholesalers when sales are usually made retail, sales to staff or shareholders, sales to members of a particular group, etc.

In some cases, trade discounts are given to all customers as in so-called discount stores!

INVOICES

3.   The effect of trade discounts on invoices is often:

	£
1 dozen Mark IV widgets at £20	240.00
Less Trade discount at 20%	48.00
	£192.00

Alternatively, as the price is effectively £16 a widget, the invoice may simply record:

	£
1 dozen Mark IV widgets at £16	192.00

Where traders have a standard price and a specific range of trade discounts to particular types of customer and they wish each customer to be aware of the discounts given, the discount will probably be shown in the invoice. In other cases, realising that a trade discount actually means a different (lower) price, a trader will simply invoice as in the second example.

Bookkeeping

4.   There is a simple rule for dealing with trade discounts in the books of account and in financial statements. The *net price* only is entered in the books. In our example, £192 would be entered in the books.

CASH DISCOUNTS

5.   A trader may sell his goods on credit, marking his invoices "nett thirty days". This means that he requires his customer to pay the amount of the invoice within thirty days of the invoice date. In practice, if the customer ignores this requirement and always pays three months after the invoice date, there is very little that the trader can do. Legal action is expensive, takes time and upsets the customer who even if he takes a long time to pay is still giving profitable business. Refusing to sell further goods to the customer hurts the trader more than the customer.

A way of inducing customers to pay more quickly is to offer a settlement or cash discount to them. If a trader marks on his invoices "cash discount 5% for payment within 10 days, otherwise net 30 days", then *some* customers will pay their invoices within the ten-day period but will deduct 5% from the sum due. Effectively, the cash discount is a cost to the trader but gives him the benefit of earlier receipt of money from his customers.

In practice, cash discount rates vary from 1% to 15% or more, and periods from 5 days to "the end of the calendar month following the date of invoice".

Bookkeeping

6. There are two categories of cash discount to a trader:

Discounts received - those given by his suppliers to the trader.
Discounts allowed - those allowed to his customers.

Entries are:

(a) For discounts received:

Dr. Suppliers Account (a personal account)
Cr. Discount Received Account (a revenue account).

Thus the supplier's account will look like this (for example):

Widget Supply Co. Ltd.

		£			£
19-5			**19-6**		
Jan 5	Cheque	187.20	Dec 30	Invoice	192.00
Jan 5	2½% discount	4.80			
		192.00			192.00

As all discounts received are posted to the discounts received account, this account will, in a financial year, accumulate all discounts received on *payments made* in that year.

(b) For discounts allowed:

Dr. Discounts Allowed (an expense account).
Cr. Customer's Account.

As all discounts allowed are posted to the discounts allowed account, that account will, in a financial year, accumulate all discounts allowed against *cash received* from customers in that year.

FINANCIAL STATEMENTS

7. (a) At the end of each year, the totals of the discounts allowed and discounts received accounts will be transferred to the *profit and loss account* as an expense and a revenue respectively. Note that they are *not* trading account items. A cash discount is *not* a reduction in price, it is an allowance given to induce earlier payment.

(b) Note that if:

(i) A sale is made by a trader on 30th December 19-4.
(ii) His year end is 31st December.
(iii) Payment is made less 2½% discount on 5th January 19-5, that is, in the financial year following the sale then:

(i) The gross profit on the sale will be in the Accounts of 19-4.
(ii) The discount allowed will be an expense in the Accounts of 19-5.

SUMMARY

8. (a) Trade discounts are reductions in *price*.
(b) Cash discounts are reductions in *payments* given for early payment.
(c) The net amount of an invoice, after deduction of trade discount, is entered in the books.
(d) Cash discounts can be discounts received which are revenues, or discounts allowed which are expenses.

POINTS TO NOTE

9. (a) Cash discounts as expenses or revenues are found in the *profit and loss account*. They are regarded as stemming from financial considerations, not from trading considerations.

(b) In the profit and loss account, the common practice is to show discounts received and discounts allowed. However, some accountants show a net sum.

(c) Remember that the books of prime entry for settlement discounts are the discount columns in the cash book.

(d) Some texts recommend that settlement discounts *to be given* on debtors at balance sheet date should be provided for in the profit and loss account.

For example if debtors at 31.12.-4 are £64,000 and settlement discounts of £1,340 will be given when the debtors pay in 19-5, then £1,340 should be regarded as an expense in the profit and loss account of 19-4 and debtors will be shown in the balance sheet as (£64,000 - £1,340) £62,660. The practice is rare and is not recommended. The theory is that as settlement discounts are an expense incurred to obtain the *use of money* then they should fall into the period in which the money is obtained.

SELF TESTING QUESTIONS

(a) List reasons for giving trade discounts. (2).
(b) What is the bookkeeping procedure for trade discount? (4).
(c) What is the objective of giving settlement discount? (5).
(d) In what part of the Trading and Profit and Loss Account do settlement discounts appear? (7).
(e) Is it possible for the profit on a sale to appear in the trading account of one year and the discount allowed on payment by the customer to appear in the Profit and Loss Account of the next year?

Exercises (Answers begin on page 456)

1.   John sold 4,000 hinges to Paul at his standard retail price of 6p a hinge. However, as Paul is a wholesaler he allowed him a 20% trade discount. As Paul was not satisfied with that price John agreed to a further discount of 5% off the standard price net of the trade discount.

Make out the invoice and show how it would appear in Paul's personal account and the Sales Account in John's books.

2.   Dave sold Jim a storage tank for £600 on 31st June allowing him 5% cash discount for payment within 10 days. Jim duly paid on 8th July taking the discount.

Show the entries in Dave's books.

3.   Enter the following transactions in ledger accounts:

(a) Sold 6 widgets to George on credit at £74 each less trade discount of 25%.
(b) Sold goods to Joan on credit for £200.
(c) Bought goods from Dindle on credit £700 less trade discount of 10%.
(d) Received cheque from Joan for the goods bought on January 2nd less settlement discount of 5%.
(e) Paid for the goods bought from Dindle less 7% cash discount.

4.   The ledger of RBD & Co. included the following account balances.

	At 1 June 1984 £	At 31 May 1985 £
Rents receivable:		
prepayments	463	517
Rent and rates payable:		
prepayments	1,246	1,509
accruals	315	382
Creditors	5,258	4,720
Provision for discounts on		
creditors	106	94

During the year ended 31 May 1985, the following transactions had arisen:

	£
Rents received by cheque	4,058
Rent paid by cheque	7,491
Rates paid by cheque	2,805
Creditors paid by cheque	75,181
Discounts received from creditors	1,043
Purchases on credit	to be derived

Required:

Post and balance the appropriate accounts for the year ended 31 May 1985, deriving the transfer entries to profit and loss account, where applicable.   (ACCA)

Exercises without answers

5.   George sold Fred 200 widgets at £60 each less 10% trade discount on 4 September 19–8. Fred paid less 5% settlement discount on 9 December 19–8.

In what books of prime entry would these items appear?

Show the entries in the ledgers of both parties.

How would the items appear in the trading and profit and loss accounts of both parties?

6.   Walter Gardner, a sole trader, enters all his cash and bank transactions in a three column Cash Book. His transactions for the month of February 1984 were as follows:

1 Feb	Cash in hand £37. Cash at bank £194.
4 Feb	Received cash from H. Robins £47, in full settlement of a debt of £51.
10 Feb	Paid by cheque to F. Johnson the sum of £152, in full settlement of a debt of £160.
11 Feb	Received from N. Wilson a cheque for £2, in full settlement of a debt of £37. This cheque was paid into the bank the same day.
12 Feb	Paid wages in cash £44.
22 Feb	Drew a cheque for £50 for office cash.
25 Feb	Drew a cheque for £60 in favour of "Self", being in respect of drawings.
26 Feb	Paid wages in cash £42.
29 Feb	Paid salaries by cheque £51.
29 Feb	Paid by cheque to R. Church the sum of £65 in full settlement of a debt of £70.

Required:

   (i)   Draw up the three column Cash Book of Gardner to record the above transactions.

  (ii)   Balance the Cash Book as at 29 February 1984 and carry down the balances.

 (iii)   Total the two discount columns and state to which accounts in the ledger these should be posted and also on which side of the ledger each entry should be made.

(LCCI)

NOTE: Ledger Accounts are NOT required.

7.   The following is a list of balances taken from the ledger of Mr Banda, a sole trader, as at 31 July 1986 – the end of his most recent financial year.

LIST OF BALANCES AS AT 31 JULY 1986

	£
Stock at 1 August 1985	5,830
Plant and Machinery:	
at cost	36,420
accumulated depreciation	14,568
Purchases	48,760
Sales	101,890
Discounts allowed	1,324
Discounts received	1,150
Returns to suppliers	531
Returns from customers	761
Wages and salaries	15,300
Other operating expenses	21,850
Trade creditors	4,380
Trade debtors	6,340
Cash on hand	199
Cash at bank	2,197
Drawings	8,465
Capital	24,927

The following additional information as at 31 July 1986 is available:

(a) Stock at the close of business was valued at £6,140.
(b) Certain operating expenses have been prepaid by £172 and others have been accrued by £233.
(c) Plant and Machinery has still to be depreciated for 1986 at 20% per annum on cost.
(d) Other operating expenses include the following:

	£
Carriage inwards	650
Carriage outwards	1,540

Required:
Prepare for Mr Banda's business a Trading and Profit and Loss Account for the year ended 31 July 1986 and a Balance Sheet as at that date. (AAT)

24. Bad and Doubtful Debts

INTRODUCTION

1. It is common business practice to sell goods on credit. Ownership and possession of the goods is transferred at the time of sale and the vendor is left with a debt due from his customer. He hopes that this will be paid and within a reasonable period of time.

2. In practice, most credit sales do result in cash being received from the customer. However, some customers do not pay. Reasons for non-payment include:

   - The customer disappears without trace.
   - The customer becomes insolvent.

If a debt is irrecoverable, it is said to be a bad debt.

3. At a year end, a business may have a large number of debtors. Most of these will be good, that is collectable, but some will prove to be bad. The prudence convention in accounting requires that debts which are *doubtful* should be valued at *net realisable value*. To this end, a deduction is made from debtors so that the debtors are shown at the amount that is expected to be received. This deduction is known as the *provision for doubtful debts*.

CREDIT CONTROL

4. Businesses who give credit to their customers, have to institute systems to ensure that bad debts are minimised. Such systems involve three stages:

   (a) **The decision to grant credit to prospective customers**
   Before granting credit to a new customers, the customer's *credit worthiness* must be established. Methods of determining this include:

   (i) Requesting references from:
   - the customer's bank
   - other suppliers who have given credit to the customer
   - trade associations (*e.g.* national association of widget manufacturers)

   (ii) Inspecting financial statements, which can be obtained by requesting the prospective customer to supply these, or in the case of a company, from Companies House.

   (iii) Impressions gained by representatives or agents who visit the prospective customer.

   Usually, a decision is made either to refuse credit or to grant credit facilities up to a maximum of £x.

   (b) **Continuous review of credit worthiness**
   Once credit has been granted to a customer, continuous review must be made of credit worthiness by:

   (i) Ensuring that each proposed sale does not take credit granted over the agreed limit.
   (ii) Watching that the credit *period* taken does not lengthen.
   (iii) Receiving reports from trade associations and credit rating agencies.
   (iv) Receiving financial statements if available.

   (c) **Debt Collection**
   Once a credit sale has been made, the vendor must have a system to ensure all that can be done is done, to collect the debt. Elements of such a system include:

   (i) Prompt preparation and submission of invoices.
   (ii) Prompt attention to customer queries to prevent non-payment due to disputes over the quality of the goods.
   (iii) A system to ensure that the customer acknowledges receipt of the goods, *e.g.* by signing delivery notes.
   (iv) Prompt preparation of monthly statements of account.
   (v) A system of polite but firm letters to slow payers.
   (vi) Preparation of an aged analysis of debtors, *i.e.* one month in arrear, two months in arrear, etc.
   (vii) Request a review of all accounts to ensure credit limits have not been exceeded.
   (viii) A system for instigating legal action rapidly after other collection methods have failed.

BOOKKEEPING FOR BAD DEBTS

5.   If the sales ledger contains an account as:

Herbert

Dr.   *Cr.*
31.8.-4   Balance b/f   £800

and it has become clear that this debt is uncollectable, then entries should be made as:

Herbert Account

31.8.-4   Balance b/f   £800   1.9.-4   Bad Debt   £800

Bad debts Account

1.9.-8   Herbert   £800

At the year end (31.12.-4), the bad debts account may contain more than one bad debt as:

Bad Debts Account

		£		£
1.9.-4	Herbert	800	31.12.-4 Profit and Loss a/c	2,550
15.10.-4	Denry	350		
30.11.-4	Andrew	1,400		
		£2,550		£2,550

The profit and loss account will include an expense bad debts - £2,550. The balance sheet figure of debtors will *not* include the sums due from Herbert, Denry or Andrew.

BOOKKEEPING FOR DOUBTFUL DEBTS

6.   At each year end, the debtors' account should be reviewed and any that are *definitely* bad, should be *written off* to the bad debts account as explained in paragraph 5.

7.   Some of the debtors may not be *definitely* bad, but may be *doubtful*. In such cases a provision for doubtful debts account should be opened:

The debtors ledger of Frank at 31.12.-4 contains four accounts only whose balances are:

	£
Alan	6,320
Bertram	4,190
Carl	3,000
Davina	1,392
Total	14,902

At the year end, Frank reviews these accounts and forms the conclusion that Carl is in financial difficulties and it is probable that only half the £3,000 will be paid, and that the other half is unlikely to be received.
The bookkeeping entries are:

Provision for doubtful debts

		£
	31.12.-4 P&L A/c	1,500

The effect of this is:

(a)   The profit and loss account will contain an *expense*.

(b)   The balance on the provision account must be included in the balance sheet and is shown as a deduction from debtors:

	£	£
Debtors	14,902	
Less Provision for doubtful debts	1,500	13,402

(c)   The full debt (£3,000) remains in the books as the system for chasing debtors will still be applied until the debt is *definitely* bad.

(d)   The balance sheet entry is composed of the sums due from debtors *less* the credit balance on the provision account.

8. **At the following year end – 31st December 19-5**

(a) Debtors comprised:

		£
Hugh		4,891
Erica		1,340
Fiona		9,820
George		630
Total		£16,681

(b) During 19-5, Carl paid his £3,000 in full so that the 19-4 year end provision was unnecessary. However, the account remains at:

Provision for doubtful debts

		£
31.12.-5 Balance b/f		1,500

(c) In reviewing his debtors at 31.12.-5, Frank forms a conclusion that the debt due from Hugh is doubtful, *i.e.* it will probably not be paid. The entry required is:

Provision for doubtful debts

	£
31.12.-5 Balance b/f	1,500
31.12.-5 P&L A/c	3,391
	£4,891

9. This entry can be seen in two ways:

(a) The entry in the profit and loss account was unnecessary and the profit in 19-4 was wrongly calculated. Therefore, an adjustment must be made to the 19-5 profit - a credit of £1,500. A charge must be made in the 19-5 profit and loss account of £4,891 to reflect the expected loss on the debt due from Hugh. The net effect is a charge of £3,391.

(b) The provision must be *topped up* to £4,891 so that the balance sheet will include:

	£	£
Debtors	16,681	
Less Provision for doubtful debts	4,891	11,790

PERCENTAGE PROVISIONS FOR DOUBTFUL DEBTS

10. Some businesses have a large number of debtors and a review of each debt at the year end to determine which debts are doubtful may be economically impossible. However, it may be that from a statistical analysis of past experience, it appears that some percentage (say 5%) of the debts are likely to prove bad. In such cases, a provision may be made not for specific debts, but for debts in general.

11. Mary's business at 31.12.-4 has 1,400 debtors whose total indebtedness is £183,400. From previous experience she expects 3% to be bad and sets up a provision account as:

Provision for doubtful debts

	£
31.12.-4 P&L A/c	5,502

(a) The profit and loss account will contain an expense:

	£
Provision for doubtful debts	5,502

(b) The balance sheet will include in current assets:

	£	£
Debtors	183,400	
Less Provision for doubtful debts	5,502	177,898

12. At the end of 19-5, the debtors totalled £171,900 and the books *still* contained the balance on the provision account at £5,502. If the estimate of 3% of doubtful debts is maintained, then the provision account will need to be adjusted:

Provision for doubtful debts

		£			£
31.12.-5	Profit and Loss A/c	345	31.12.-4 Balance b/f		5,502
31.12.-5	Balance c/f	5,157			
		£5,502			£5,502

Note:

(a) The profit and loss account will contain a credit entry of:

Adjustment to provision for doubtful debts   £345

(b) The balance sheet will include:

	£	£
Debtors	171,900	
Less *Provision for doubtful debts*	5,157	166,743

(c) Any *actual* bad *debts incurred in 19-5 will* also *appear in the profit and loss account as bad debts £x.*

SUMMARY

13. (a) Trading on credit involves a risk that some customers will be unable to pay.

(b) Actual bad debts are written off to the profit and loss account in the year that the debt is recognised as bad.

(c) At any year end, some of the debtors will be doubtful. In order to include the expected or probable loss on such accounts in the profit and loss account and to value such debts at net realisable value, a provision for doubtful debts account should be opened.

(d) The provision for doubtful debts account (a credit balance) should be adjusted each year to reflect the amount of doubtful debts at that year end.

(e) The requirement for a provision is a consequence of the prudence convention in accounting.

POINTS TO NOTE

14. (a) Two common, but doubtful methods of establishing credit worthiness are:

(i) The use of pro-forma invoices. The vendor sends a pro-forma invoice but no goods. If the invoice is paid then the goods are despatched. The vendor may then decide that the customer is creditworthy and grant credit for future orders.

(ii) Insisting on cash with order for a period of time before granting credit.

(b) One method of trading which may assist debt collection, is to sell goods with *reservation of title*. This method of selling is named after the Romalpa case in 1976. Goods are invoiced and supplied in the normal way, but the title to the goods is expressed or agreed to pass only on *payment*. In practice, it may be difficult to establish ownership of goods which may have been sold by the customer or incorporated into a product.

(c) Actual bad debts can be written off to a bad debts account and subsequently to the profit and loss account. Or actual bad debts may be written off against the provision for doubtful debts account. The effect on profit measurement is the same because if bad debts are written off to the provision account, the provision account will have a smaller balance and any adjustment required to bring it up to the year end requirement will be greater by the amount of bad debts.

(d) A combination of a specific and a general (percentage) provision is possible.

(e) Disclosure of debtors in a balance sheet may be:

	£	£
Debtors	31,428	
Less Provision for doubtful debts	826	30,602

or simply:

Debtors		30,602

(f) Note that the profit on a sale may be taken to profit in a year and the subsequent bad debt be a charge against profit in the following year.

(g) The real loss incurred on a bad debt is not the amount of the bad debt, but the cost of the goods sold. Thus if Jayne sells goods (which cost her £600) to Keith for £900 and the debt proves bad, the actual loss is only £600. However, the profit and loss account shows a bad debt of £900. The profit element of £300 is included in gross profit but is, of course, not shown separately. Note that the VAT element is recoverable on bad debts.

(h) After a debt has been written off as a bad debt, any subsequent receipt should be credited to bad debts recovered account and at the year end, any balance on the bad debts recovered account should be credited to the profit and loss account.

(i) Students find the subject of provision for doubtful debts exceedingly difficult. Remember that:

   (i)   The balance sheet must show the correct amount of provision at the balance sheet date.

   (ii) The profit and loss accounts taken over several years must reflect the *actual* bad debts and *current* provision.

SELF TESTING QUESTIONS

(a) What is a bad debt? (2).
(b) How should doubtful debts be valued in a balance sheet? (3).
(c) List the stages in credit control. (4).
(d) Summarise the bookkeeping entries for bad debts. (5).
(e) Summarise the year-end procedures for dealing with doubtful debts, giving sample entries in the bookkeeping system and the financial statements. (7).
(f) What accounting convention requires provisions for doubtful debts? (13e).
(g) What is a Romalpa sale? How does this method of trading reduce bad debts? (14b).
(h) How do the gross profit on a sale and a subsequent bad debt match in successive accounting periods? (14f, g).
(i) What are the bookkeeping entries for subsequent receipts from customers whose debts have been written off as bad? (4b).

Exercises (Answers begin on page 456)

1. The trial balance of Alice at 31.12.-4 con-tained a debit balance: debtors £161,314. On reviewing the debts, Alice determined that the debts of Betty £3,104 and Carol £520 were bad and that the debt of Diane £610 and 60% of the debt of Elsie £830 were doubtful.

Give the bookkeeping entries and extracts from the financial statements which reflect these matters.

2. The trial balance of Fred at 31.12.-4 included:

	Dr	Cr
	£	£
Debtors	88,880	
Provision for doubtful debts at 31.12.-4		3,420
Bad debts	2,618	

At the year end review, Fred determined that £1,240 of the debts were also bad and that £3,519 of the remaining debts were doubtful.

Give the bookkeeping entries and extracts for the financial statements to reflect these matters.

3. The trial balance of Gail at 30.6.-5 included:

	£
Debtors	431,920
Bad debts	6,380
Provision for doubtful debts at 30.6.-4	15,219

At the year end review, Gail decided that:

(a) A further £1,520 of the debtors were bad.
(b) A specific provision of £4,800 was required against three doubtful debts.
(c) A general provision of 3% was required against the remainder of the debts.

Show the bookkeeping entries and extracts from the financial statements to reflect these decisions.

Exercises without answers

4. Dolly has five customers. Balances and transactions with these were:

	Balance 31.12.-7	Sales 19-8	Cash 19-8	Sales 19-9	Cash 19-9	Sales 19-0	Cash 19-0
	£	£	£	£	£	£	£
A	243	736	824	960	864	931	720
B	618	930	362	260			
C	1,243	2,738	2,346	1,362	1,480	630	
D	390	1,074	888	1,024	320		400
E		1,034	1,011	840	786	2,200	1,143

At 31.12.-8, Dolly made a provision for doubtful debts against the debt due from B.

At 31.12.-9 the provision for doubtful debts was solely against the debts due from C, and B's and D's were written off as bad.

At 31.12.-0, the provision for doubtful debts was solely against E's debt and C's debt was written off as bad.

Enter all these transactions in suitable double entry accounts and show the postings to profit and loss account.

5. at 31.12.-7 Lev had £240,320 of book debts.

He decided that £1,654 were bad and that a specific provision of £3,666 was required and also a general provision of 5% of the remainder.

At 31.12.-8 his book debts were £250,800. He decided that £15,620 were actually bad and that a specific provision of £15,200 was required and also a 5% general provision against the remainder. Also in 19-8 £240 was received from the estates of debtors previously written off as bad.

Enter these transactions in suitable double entry accounts. Show the entries in the financial statements for 19-7 and 19-8.

6. George is a wholesale retailer, and the following information relates to the year ending 30th September 1982:

(a) Goods are sold on credit terms, but some cash sales are also transacted.

(b) At 1st October 1981, George's trade debtors amounted to £30,000 against which he had set aside a provision for doubtful debts of 5%.

(c) On 15th January 1982, George was informed that Fall Limited had gone into liquidation, owing him £2,000. This debt was outstanding from the previous year.

(d) Cash sales during the year totalled £46,800, whilst credit sales amounted to £187,800.

(e) £182,500 was received from trade creditors.

(f) Cash discounts allowed to credit customers were £5,300.

(g) Apart from Fall Limited's bad debt, other certain bad debts amounted to £3,500.

(h) George intends to retain the Provision for Doubtful Debts Account at 5% of outstanding trade debtors as at the end of the year, and the necessary entries are to be made.

Required:
Enter the above transactions in George's ledger accounts, and apart from the cash and bank and profit and loss accounts, balance off the accounts and bring down the balances as at 1st October 1982.   (AAT)

7.   Certain balances in a company's ledger at 30th June, 1980 were:

	£
Debtors	20,000
Provision for bad debts	1,000
Stock of coke	630
Electricity accrued	920

During the year to 30th June, 1981, the following transactions occurred:

	£
Sales on credit	200,000
Cash received from debtors	193,000
Certain debtors became bankrupt, and their debts were written off against the provision	3,000
Certain debts which had been written off as bad in previous years were recovered in cash and transferred to the provision	1,000
Purchases of coke	8,000
Payments for electricity for the year ended 30th April, 1981	6,000

At 30th June 1981 the stock of coke was valued at £750, and the provision for bad debts was adjusted to be equal to 5% of the debtors. On 6th August 1981 the company paid its electricity account of £1,010 for the quarter ended 31st July 1981.

You are required to show the debtors, provision for bad debts and lighting and heating accounts in the company's ledger for the year ended 30th June 1981.   (CIMA)

25. Valued Added Tax

INTRODUCTION

1. This chapter is concerned with VAT - value added tax. It appears in many accounting and bookkeeping syllabuses and is of immense importance in the UK and other parts of the European Economic Community.

The chapter begins with an outline of the tax and then how VAT is entered in the books of prime entry and the ledger accounts. Finally we see how the tax affects final accounts.

AN OUTLINE OF VALUE ADDED TAX (VAT)

2. Any *person (person* = sole trader, partnerships, limited companies, clubs, associations, charities etc.) who is carrying on a business which has a turnover greater than the limit currently in force (*i.e.* all but very small businesses) must *register* for VAT and be given a *VAT number*.

VAT registered persons in making *taxable supplies* of goods or services (effectively all sales) must add VAT at the standard rate (15% at the time of writing). Sales are termed *outputs* and the tax added is called *output tax*.

Example
Jason, a trader in sheepskin coats, sells a dozen coats to Homer at £60. The taxable supply is 12 x £60 = £720, but the invoice must be for:

	£
12 sheepskin coats at £60	720
VAT at 15%	108
Total amount of invoice	828

Note:
- (a) *Homer must pay £828.*
- (b) *Jason keeps the £720 (when and if Homer pays the £828 due).*
- (c) *The tax, £108, is payable by Jason to H.M. Customs and Excise.*

3. In some businesses, for example, take away food shops, the output and output tax is determined as:

(a) Count the takings, *e.g.* £346.32
(b) Apply the fraction 100/115 giving £301.15, this is the output (sales).
(c) Apply the fraction 15/115 giving £45.17, this is the output tax.

	£
Thus output (sales)	301.15
plus VAT at 15%	45.17
Gives the cash paid by the customers	346.32

Jason also buys sheepskin coats and pays expenses. Many of these are invoiced in the form:

	£
6 Sheepskin coats at £40	240.00
VAT at 15%	36.00
Amount payable by Jason	276.00

The VAT suffered by Jason on his purchase and expenses is called *input* tax. It is recoverable from H.M. Customs and Excise.

4. Jason thus owes the Customs and Excise *output* tax and H.M. Customs and Excise owe Jason the *input* tax he has suffered. Clearly the correct way to deal with this is for Jason to send the Customs and Excise a cheque for the output tax less the input tax. Occasionally, input tax is greater than output tax and the Customs and Excise will send Jason a cheque for the difference.

The details of outputs, inputs, output tax and input tax are entered on a *VAT return* which is sent *quarterly* to the Customs and Excise office at Southend-on-Sea. Each taxable person has four accounting dates a year when a return is to be sent, for example, at the end of February, May, August, November. Note that from 1.10.87, traders with a turnover less than £250,000 can account annually and on a cash basis.

Final consumers, *e.g.* the member of the public who buys a sheepskin coat suffers VAT but cannot recover it.

5.   Some businesses add output tax at a special rate, viz., zero, on some or all of their outputs. Zero rated outputs include:

(a)   Most foodstuffs (but not meals, take away meals, drinks in public houses etc.)
(b)   Books, newspapers, maps etc.
(c)   Fuel and power.
(d)   Construction of buildings for residential use.
(e)   Transport.
(f)   Drugs, medicines etc.

Persons who have zero rated outputs can nonetheless recover input tax suffered.

6.   Some supplies are *exempt* supplies. Thus no VAT is added on selling them. Exempt supplies include:

(a)   Land.
(b)   Provision of Insurance cover. Thus insurance premiums are an exempt supply.
(c)   Postal services.
(d)   Betting, gaming and lotteries.
(e)   Finance. Thus interest is an exempt supply.
(f)   The supply of medical services, *e.g.* by doctors, dentists, opticians.

Suppliers of *exempt* supplies *cannot* recover input tax suffered on inputs which relate to the exempt supplies.

BOOKKEEPING

7.   **Output tax** - credit customers.

Invoices should be listed in a sales day book as:

Date	Invoice No	Customer	Net £	VAT £	Gross £
15 May 19-4	361	Alfred	220.00	33.00	253.00
4 June 19-4	362	Ben	82.34	12.35	94.69
5 July 19-4	363	Claud	461.17	69.17	530.34
Total for quarter			763.51	114.52	878.03

The double entry is:

Dr. The customers with the individual *gross* amount *e.g.*:

Dr		*Alfred*		Cr
15 May 19-4 Goods		253.00		

Cr. (i)   *Sales* account with the total £763.51. This sum will form part of the sales figure in the trading account.

(ii)   Customs and Excise Account with £114.52. The Customs and Excise are then a creditor for this sum.

8.   **Output tax** - cash sales.

Gross receipts should be agreed with till rolls and entered on the *debit* of the cash book as:

			Net	VAT	Gross
Dr 8 June 19-4	Cash Sales		346.00	51.90	397.90

Note that it is £397.90 which is received and this goes into the cash book balance.

Credit entries are:

(a)   £346.00 to sales.
(b)   £51.90 to the Customs and Excise account.

9. Input tax

Incoming invoices should be listed in an analysed purchase and expense day book as:

Date	Supplier	Gross £	VAT £	Net £	Purchases £	Rent £	Motor... £
13 May 19-4	Don	27.60	3.60	24.00	24.00		
3 June 19-4	Eddie	100.00	–	100.00		100.00	
2 July 19-4	Frank	58.65	7.65	51.00			51.00
9 July 19-4	Gregory	85.00	11.09	73.91	73.91		
Total for quarter		271.25	22.34	248.91	97.91	100.00	51.00

Note that rent is an exempt supply and so no VAT was added.

Entries in the double entry accounts are:

Debits   £
    Purchases A/c   97.91   To form part of the trading
    Rent A/c   100.00   and profit and loss total
    Motor exp A/c   51.00

    and H.M. Customs and Excise account for the Input VAT £22.34
    Customs and Excise are thus a debtor.

Credits
    Credit the accounts of each supplier with the gross sum due, *e.g.*

Dr	Don	Cr
	13 May 19-4 Goods 27.60	

10. Accounting for the tax due and recoverable

The account of H.M. Customs and Excise will now appear as:

Dr	H.M. Customs & Excise	Cr
31.7.-4 Input tax 22.34	31.7.-4 Output tax	114.52

A credit balance of £92.18 remains and the procedure is to:

(a) Complete the VAT return form for the quarter ending 31st July 19-4.

(b) Submit the form and a cheque for £92.18 to H.M. Customs and Excise by 31st August 19-4.

VAT AND FINANCIAL STATEMENTS

11. Profit and Loss Account

All items in the trading and profit and loss account are net of VAT. Thus in the case of Jason, sales would include just the £763.51 and purchases just the £97.91.

Balance Sheet

The only item appearing in the balance sheet for VAT will be the sum due to or from H.M. Customs and Excise which will be entered under current liabilities or current assets.

Debtors and creditors will appear in the balance sheet gross of VAT since those are the amounts receivable or payable.

Exempt suppliers

Businesses that are:

(a) Exempt suppliers.
(b) Not registered for VAT as having less than the minimum turnover.

Should include inputs gross if the VAT is irrecoverable.

For example, Sid, a driving school proprietor who is not registered for VAT received an invoice for car repair:

	£
Repair	80.00
VAT	12.00
Sum due	£92.00

Since the VAT cannot be recovered, Sid will include £92.00 in his profit and loss item, car repairs.

SUMMARY

12. (a) Value added tax is a very complex tax which affects all businesses to some extent.

(b) Businesses add VAT at the standard rate or zero rate to their outputs. This "output" tax is payable to Customs and Excise.

(c) Businesses can recover VAT suffered on their inputs.

(d) Some supplies are exempt from VAT. Input tax related to them is not recoverable.

(e) Bookkeeping entries are:

Amount	*Dr*	*Cr*
Outputs		
Gross sum due	Customer	
VAT		Customs and Excise
Net amount of supply		Sales
Inputs		
Gross sum due		Supplier
VAT	Customs and Excise	
Net amount of supply	Purchases or expenses	

(f) In the profit and loss account, all items are net of VAT.

(g) In the balance sheet, the sum due to or from the Customs and Excise is shown as a creditor or debtor.

(h) Debtors and creditors are shown gross as the amount due includes VAT.

POINTS TO NOTE

13. (a) Students are sometimes confused by the difference between zero rated and exempt supplies. The effective difference is that tax suffered on inputs related to zero rated supplies can be recovered and that related to exempt supplies is not recoverable.

(b) Much emphasis is placed in practice on the VAT invoice. VAT on inputs can only be recovered if a proper VAT invoice is obtained and kept. A VAT invoice is one that gives full information.

(c) Proper records must be kept by all registered persons and the Customs and Excise make periodic inspections of the books of registered persons.

(d) VAT is a tax ultimately borne by the final retail consumer. However, its collection is from all traders. The correct way to think of the relationship between a business and value added tax is that the business acts as an unpaid tax collector for the Customs and Excise.

SELF TESTING QUESTIONS

(a) Who must register for VAT? (2).
(b) What is output tax? (2).
(c) What is input tax? (3).
(d) What is the effect of the quarterly accounting to H.M. Customs and Excise? (4).
(e) What items are zero rated? (5).
(f) What items are exempt supplies? (6).
(g) What is the difference between zero rated and exempt supplies? (6).
(h) Describe the bookkeeping entries for VAT transactions. (7)

(i) What is the effect of VAT on financial statements:
    (i)   In the trading and profit and loss account.
    (ii)   In the balance sheet? (11)

Exercises (Answers begin on page 457)

1. Enter the following items for the quarter ending 28.2.-8 in the double entry system of Horne. You should show only the sales, purchases, motor expenses, and Customs and Excise Account.

    Sales invoices £45,800 + VAT at 15%
    Cash sales £8,970 including VAT at 15%
    Purchase invoices £34,799 + VAT at 15%
    Zero rated purchase invoices £360
    Motor expenses £830 + VAT at 15%
    Zero rated motor expenses £200

How much is due to Customs and Excise? When will this be paid? How will all these items appear in the financial statements if the year end is 28.2.-8?

Exercises without answers

2. Enter the following items for the quarter ending 31.8.-7 in the double entry system of Gillian whose year end is 31.8.-7.:

Show only the accounts for sales, purchases and Customs and Excise.

    Balance due to Customs and Excise at 1.6.-7 £2,900
    Paid to Customs and Excise on 23.7.-7 £2,000
    Sales invoices £17,600 + VAT at 15%
    Purchase invoices £8,280 including VAT at 15%
    Cash sales £5,750 including VAT at 15%

How much is due to Customs and Excise? When will this be paid? How will these items appear in the Financial Statements?

3. Enter the following amounts in a petty cash book ruled with a VAT column:

Balance 1.1.-9 £34.00, received from bank 2.1.-9 £66.00, paid for postage £5.40, paid petrol £7.40*, paid tea and milk £3.70, paid cleaning materials £7.00*, paid ledger account R Jones & Co £6.98, paid purchases £7.21*, paid petrol £9.80*, paid train fare £30.70.

* = includes VAT at 15%.

(a) What is the amount required to make up the imprest?
(b) Why are some items not subject to VAT?
(c) State the double entry for all items including VAT?

4. In the three months ending 30 June 19-8 the books of Laura contained the following amounts re VAT:

	£
Purchase day book	16,240
Cash book credit	680
Petty cash book	1,345
Sales day book	35,789
Cash book debit	345

How much is now owing to the Customs and Excise?

How will this appear in the Balance Sheet at 30.6.-8?

Assuming all sales day book items are subject to VAT at 15%, what were the total sales to which VAT was added? What figure will appear as Sales in the Trading Account?

Of the sales £24,809 remained unpaid at 30.6.-8 and will appear in the Balance Sheet. Will the item in the balance sheet include or exclude VAT?

5.   The annual financial statements of Hugues include the following:

Bills receivable, bills payable, discounting charges.

How will these items appear

    (a) in the trial balance and on which side
    (b) in the financial statements?

6.   Write brief answers to all the following questions regarding VAT:

    (a) When did VAT first come into operation in the UK?
    (b) What is a "Registered trader" for VAT purposes?
    (c) What Government department is responsible for the administration and collection of VAT?
    (d) What are the differences between "exempt supplies" and "zero rated supplies"?
    (e) (i)   What is Input tax?
        (ii) What is Output tax?

                                                                       (RSA)

26. Hire Purchase Transactions

INTRODUCTION

1. Hire purchase is a very common method of financing the purchase of commodities and services. The law relating to HP is very complicated and we shall not pursue it here. The bookkeeping aspects however are often included in bookkeeping and accounting syllabuses.

HIRE PURCHASE TRANSACTIONS

2. In substance, hire purchase transactions proceed as:

    (a) Antony, whose year end is 31st December, buys a car from Brenda on 15th July 19-4 for £3,000.

    (b) Antony has only £1,000, so he borrows the balance from Car Finance Ltd., under an agreement as:

	£
Price of car	3,000
Deposit	1,000
Amount borrowed	2,000
Interest	400
Total amount due	£2,400

    Payable in twenty-four monthly instalments of £100 each beginning on 15.8.-4.

    (c) From Antony's point of view, he has bought a car for £3,000, paying £1,000 immediately and the balance plus interest over twenty-four months.

    (d) From Brenda's point of view, she has sold the car and been paid immediately in full (£1,000 by Antony and £2,000 from Car Finance Ltd.).

    (e) From Car Finance Ltd.'s point of view, they have lent £2,000 and will be repaid plus interest over two years.

BOOKKEEPING ENTRIES:

3. **In the books of Antony:**

Motor Vehicles Account

	£		£
15.7.-4 Car Finance Ltd (i)	3,000		

Car Finance Ltd. Account

	£		£
15. 7.-4 Cash (i)	1,000	15.7.-4 Car (i)	3,000
15. 8.-4 -			
15.12.-4 Five instalments (ii)	500	15.7.-4 Interest (iii)	400
31.12.-4 Balance c/d (iv)	1,900		
	£3,400		£3,400
		1. 1.-5 Balance b/d (iv)	1,900

Hire Purchase Interest Account

	£		£
15.7.-4 Car Finance Ltd (iii)	400	31.12.-4 Profit and Loss a/c (v)	83
		31.12.-4 Balance c/d (vi)	317
	£400		£400
1.1.-5 Balance b/d (vi)	317		

Cash Book

			£
		15.7.-4 Deposit (i)	1,000
		15.8.-4 -	
		15.12.-4 Five instalments (ii)	500

Note:

(i) The amount borrowed is £2,000 being £3,000 less the deposit £1,000.

(ii) The instalments of £100 are paid monthly on 15th August, 15th September etc. (probably by standing order with the bank).

(iii) The interest added is debited to an expense account.

(iv) At the year end, £1,900 remains outstanding.

(v) The interest charge is an expense of the years in which any part of the loan is outstanding (that is, to 15.7.-6). The proportion relating to 19-4 is:

$$\frac{5}{24} \times £400 = £83$$

and this is debited to profit and loss account.

(vi) The remainder of the interest is an expense of 19-5 and 19-6 and will be charged in the profit and loss accounts of those years:

$$\frac{12}{24} \times £400 = £200 \text{ in } 19\text{-}5, \text{ and } \frac{7}{24} \times £400 = £117 \text{ in } 19\text{-}6$$

(vii) The car is a fixed asset and will be depreciated in the usual way.

(viii) In the balance sheet at 31st December 19-4, Current liabilities will contain:

Hire Purchase commitment   1,583
(£1,583 = £1,900 - £317)

Note that alternatively and especially if the hire purchase commitment was *material*, the balance sheet entries would be:

In current liabilities
    Hire purchase commitment   £1,900

In current assets
    Hire purchase interest in advance   £317

SUMMARY

4. (a) Hire purchase transactions involve a vendor, a buyer and a finance company. The finance company lend the buyer a proportion of the purchase price. Interest is added and the buyer pays the amount borrowed plus the interest by equal instalments.

(b) Bookkeeping entries record the loan and the interest expense account. The interest is charged to the profit and loss account over the period in which the loan is outstanding.

POINTS TO NOTE

5. (a) The bookkeeping entries in the books of the finance company are traditionally found in a more advanced text.

(b) Some vendors both sell goods and finance the hire purchase transactions themselves.

(c) In law, the *ownership* of goods subject to hire purchase is transferred by the vendor *to the finance company*. Only when the *final* instalment has been paid is the ownership of the goods passed to the purchaser.

However, in our example, the transaction has been treated as if the ownership was given to the buyer immediately. Thus the *form* of the transaction is that ownership passes on the payment of the final instalment. Instalments are in law, hire charges. The *substance* of the transaction is that the ownership passes on the signing of the agreement and the instalments are repayments of the loan. This is an example of the accounting convention "*substance over form*". The substance of a transaction is reflected in the accounts even though the legal form is different.

SELF TESTING QUESTIONS

(a) What is the substance of a hire purchase transaction? (2).

(b) What is the relationship between the parties? (2).

Exercises (Answers begin on page 457)

1. Douglas bought a car from Etty for £7,000 on 15.4.-8. He gave his old car (cost £7,000, accumulated depreciation £5,230) in part exchange at £2,000. The deal was financed by Claud who advanced £5,000 + interest £900 to be settled by 24 monthly instalments of £245.83 beginning 15.5.-8.

The instalments were met on time but on 14.2.-0 he paid off the amount owing with a settlement figure of £720.

Enter all the items in double entry accounts in Douglas's books.

Show how all these items would appear in the Financial Statements for all years ending 31 December.

Why might Douglas wish to pay off the outstanding sum due early?

2. James, whose year end is 31st December, bought a car from Julia. The invoiced dated 4th October 19-5 showed:

	£
Purchase price	7,000
One year's tax	85
Tankful of petrol	22
	£7,107

James paid a deposit of £1,107. The balance was financed by Bernard. The agreement provided for interest of £600 and payment by twelve monthly instalments of £550, beginning on 4th November 19-5.

Required:
Record the transaction in the books of James for all relevant years, and show relevant extracts from the profit and loss accounts and balance sheets.

Exercises without answers

3. Harriet, whose year end is 31st March, purchased a car from Philip for £8,000 (including one year's car tax £85) on 14th July 19-5. The finance was by Robert, who provided £6,000. Interest was £960 and repayment was to be £290 a month beginning on 14th August 19-5. The deposit was a car whose book value in Harriet's books was £2,630.

On 3rd February, 19-7, Robert allowed Harriet to pay £1,640 in full settlement.

Required:
Record these transactions in the books of Harriet for all relevant years. Give also the profit and loss account and balance sheet entries.

4. Davies' business purchased a van on Hire Purchase on 13.4.-8 on the terms:

Price of Van £6,000, deposit paid £1,200, interest £1,860, 24 monthly instalments of £277.50 beginning 10.5.-8.

Write up all appropriate accounts assuming all instalments are paid on time.

How will these items appear in the annual accounts at 31.12.08?

5. T. Prince is a sole trader. His financial year ends on 31st March, 1982.

On 1st January 1982 he purchased a piece of office equipment from S.J. Dixon Ltd., under a hire purchase agreement.

The cash price was £2,600, but the terms of the hire purchase agreement were:

(a) A cash deposit of £200 to be paid on 1st January 1982.

(b) 24 equal monthly instalments, to include interest at 12% per annum, calculated on the balance of the cash price outstanding on 1st January 1982. The first instalment was payable on 31st January 1982 and subsequent instalments on the last day of each month.

A full year's depreciation is to be charged on the equipment at the rate of 10% per annum on cost.

All payments were made by T. Prince as and when they became due.

Required:

(i) *Draw up the account of S.J. Dixon Ltd., as it appears in the ledger of T. Prince from 1st January 1982 to 31st March 1982. Balance the account and carry down the balance.*

Note:
All calculations must be shown.

(ii) *Show extracts from the Balance Sheet of T. Prince as at 31st march 1982. You are required to calculate the appropriate figures in respect of the above hire purchase transactions.* (LCCI)

6. *On 1 April 1980, J. Fisher, a publisher, bought a new printing press, the cash price of which was £8,000, from the Ajax Company, under a hire purchase agreement. He paid a cash deposit of £2,000 on 1 April 1980 and agreed to pay six half-yearly instalments, commencing on 30 September 1980, of £1,000 plus interest calculated on the balance of the cash price outstanding on 1 April 1980. The rate of interest was 20% per annum.*

The financial year of J. Fisher ends on 31 December.

Required:
(i) *Draw up the account of The Ajax Company as it appears in the ledger of J. Fisher from 1 April 1980 to 1 October 1981; it is to be balanced half-yearly.*

(ii) *Draw up an Interest Account from 30 September 1980 to 1 January 1982.* (LCCI)

27. Bills of Exchange

INTRODUCTION
1. Some bookkeeping and accounting syllabuses include Bills of Exchange and many, who do not, include mention of Bills in questions such as those on control accounts. So it is desirable for you to know what a bill is, some of the jargon connected with Bills and the bookkeeping and accounting entries found.

2. The essential thing about a Bill of Exchange is that it is a piece of paper to which are attached various rights and obligations. The bill can be bought and sold and the rights and obligations transferred.

WHAT IS A BILL OF EXCHANGE?
3. The Bills of Exchange Act 1882 defines a bill of exchange as:

"an unconditional order in writing, addressed by one person to another, signed by the person giving it, requiring the person to whom it is addressed to pay on demand, or at a fixed or determinable future time, a sum certain in money to or to the order of, a specified person or to bearer".

4. Here is a specimen:

Wolverhampton 24th June 19-4

Three months after date pay to my order the sum of Two hundred and fifty pounds sterling for value received.

To: George, London   Fred

---

5. The procedures concerning this bill may be:

(a) George owes Fred £250.

(b) Fred makes out the bill in the form shown and sends it to George. Fred is called the *drawer* of the bill.

(c) George writes "accepted" on the bill, signs it, and sends it back to Fred. George was the *drawee* but having accepted it, he becomes the *acceptor*.

(d) Fred no longer has a *debt* due from George. He now has a bill of exchange instead.

(e) Fred now sells the bill to his bank for £240. The difference is called the *discount* or *discounting charges* and Fred is said to have *discounted* the bill with his bank. He is said to have *negotiated* it to his bank. The bill is a *negotiable* instrument in that it can be sold by its *holder* to another person.

(f) On 24th September 19-4, the bank *present* the bill to George who will pay the £250 due to the bank.

(g) Should George be unable to pay, the bill will be said to be *dishonoured* and the bank will have *recourse* to Fred who sold it to them. Fred will have to pay.

BOOKKEEPING
6. Bookkeeping entries for bills of exchange are exemplified by:

19-5
Jan 31   John owes Mary £1,000
Feb 1   Mary sends John a three month bill of exchange which John accepts
Feb 2   Mary discounts the bill with the bank, receiving £965.
May 1   John is unable to pay and the bank seek recourse to Mary, who pays them.

ANSWER

In the books of Mary:

Dr   John Account   *Cr*
31.1.-5   Balance b/f   1,000   1.2.-5   Bill receivable (i)   1,000
1.5.-5   Bill dishonoured (iv) 1,000

Bills Receivable Account
1.2.-5   John (i)   1,000   4.2.-5   Cash (ii)   965
                                          4.2.-5   Discount (iii)   35
                                  1,000   1,000

Cash Book (Bank)
2.2.-5   Bill discounted (ii)   965   1.5.-5   Payment of bill (iv)   1,000

Discounting Charges Account
2.2.-5   *re* John's bill (iii)   35

Note:

(i)   *The debt due from John is replaced by another asset - the bill of exchange.*
(ii)   *The asset, bill of exchange, is replaced by another asset, cash with a loss (iii).*
(iii)   *The loss, £35, will be written off in the profit and loss account at the year end.*
(iv)   *On dishonour of the bill, Mary has to pay up and we are back to the original debt which in fact appears to be a bad debt.*

7.   You are likely to see Bills of Exchange either as a credit balance (Bills Payable) or as a debit balance (Bills Receivable) in a trial balance.

SUMMARY

8.   (a)   A bill of exchange is a piece of paper (an *instrument*) which has value in that it gives the *holder* the right to receive from the *acceptor* a sum of money at a specified date.

(b)   A bill is *negotiable* in that it can be sold to others including the bank.

(c)   A bill has several parties - the drawer, the drawee, who is also the acceptor, the payee who may be the drawer *or* some other person, the holder who may be the drawer or some person who has acquired from the drawer or holder.

(d)   Bills may be dishonoured, in which case the holder has *recourse* to previous holders or to the acceptor.

POINTS TO NOTE

9.   (a)   Bills of exchange are extensively used in foreign trade where they are known as foreign bills.

(b)   Bills are less common in ordinary commerce when they are known as inland bills.

(c)   The benefit to a creditor is that a bill of exchange is itself evidence of a debit (he can "sue on the instrument") whereas a trade debt may require proof that money is owing.

(d)   A bill is not due on the due date but within three days thereof. The three days are called *days of grace*.

(e)   Our example was seen from the point of view of Mary. To her the bill is a bill receivable. From John's point of view, the bill is a bill payable.

(f)   In balance sheets, bills receivable are a separate item in current assets and bills payable are a separate item in current liabilities.

(g)   If dealing in bills is extensive, then separate books of prime entry should be maintained - a bills receivable day book and/or a bills payable day book.

(h) Another negotiable instrument, similar to a bill of exchange is a promissory note which is defined as an "unconditional *promise* in writing made by one person to another, signed by the maker, engaging to pay on demand or at a fixed or determinable future time, a sum certain in money to or to the order of a specified person or to bearer".

SELF TESTING QUESTIONS

(a) Define a bill of exchange. (3).
(b) Draft a specimen bill of exchange. (4).
(c) What relationship have the following to a bill:
  (i) Drawer; (ii) Drawee; (iii) Acceptor; (iv) Holder? (5).
(d) What do the following terms mean:
  (i) discounting; (ii) negotiable instrument; (iii) presentation; (iv) dishonour; (v) recourse? (5).
(e) Summarise the bookkeeping entries required in respect of a bill of exchange. (6).
(f) What are days of grace? (9).
(g) Define a promissory note. (9).

Exercises (Answers begin on page 457)

1. *Delia is in business and makes extensive use of bills of exchange. The following are some of her transactions in the year ending 31 December 19-4.*

			£
Jan	3	Sold goods to Ed	800
Jan	15	Purchased goods from Frances	925
Jan	18	Sold goods to Gavin	1,526
Jan	31	Accepted a three-month bill drawn by Frances	925
Feb	28	Ed accepted a one-month bill	400
Mar	19	Ed paid the remainder of his account	
Mar	31	Ed paid on presentation of the bill	
Apr	22	Sold goods to Hal	300
Apr	29	Hal accepted a two-month bill	300
May	1	Sold goods to Iona	750
May	2	Iona accepted a three-month bill	750
May	3	Paid Frances' bill	
May	10	Discounted Iona's bill – net receipt	720
June	30	Hal's bill dishonoured. Hal has no assets	
Jul	16	Gavin is made bankrupt. His estate pays 50p in the pound	
Aug	18	Sold goods to jack	1,830
Sept	1	Jack accepts a one-month bill	1,830
Sept	3	Jack's bill is discounted – net receipt	1,680
Sept	15	Delia buys, with a cheque, a bill for £800 due from Tom on Oct 31st	760
Oct	31	Tom pays his bill	
Nov	4	Sells goods to Ken	300
Nov	7	Ken accepts a three-month bill	150
Nov	13	Buys goods from Lena	220
Nov	30	Accepts Lena's bill at three months	220

Required:
(a) Enter all these items in double entry accounts.
(b) Show the entries in the profit and loss account and balance sheet for 19-4.

Exercises without answers

2. *Harold is in business and has the following transactions in 19-5:*

			£
Jan	1	Sold goods to Paul	2,300
Jan	5	Purchased goods from Ron	250
Jan	5	Paul accepted a bill at four months	2,000
Jan	10	Paul's bills discounted – net receipt	1,900
Feb	5	Purchased goods from Simon	950
Feb	18	Paid Ron	
Feb	22	Accepted Simon's bill at three months	800
Apr	4	Paul paid balance due	
Apr	16	Paid Simon the amount due on his account	
May	25	Paid Simon's bill	
Jun	30	Purchased a bill (paying by cheque), of £1,000 due from Will at three months, from Trevor 910

Jul	8	Sold goods to Una	1,210
Jul	10	Una accepts a four-month bill	1,210
Jul	15	Sells Una's bill to Victor	1,170
Jul	30	Sells goods to Xavier	900
Sept	10	Will pays his bill	
Sept	11	Xavier accepts a four-month bill	900
Oct	8	Sells goods to Ben	340
Nov	3	Buys goods from Adam	328
Nov	5	Accepts Adam's bill at three months	164
Dec	19	Sells goods to Ben	620

Required:
(a) Enter all these items in double entry accounts.
(b) Show the entries in the profit and loss account and balance sheet for 19-5.

3. John Teh is an exporter. On 1 January 1983 he exported the following:

		Cost of goods sold	Selling price
		£	£
Customer	A	3,000	3,900
	B	2,000	2,400
	C	8,000	9,000

In each case Teh drew a 3-month Bill of Exchange on his customer in the sum of the stated selling price. Each customer accepted the bill drawn on him.

Bill details were then as follows:

Bill accepted by customer:

A   Discounted with Midshires Bank. Net proceeds £3,750. Honoured on maturity.
B   Retained to maturity. Honoured in full.
C   Discounted with Midshires Bank. Net proceeds £8,680. Dishonoured on maturity. Customer C agreed to make an immediate payment of £2,500 and to accept another 3-month bill for £6,900. In due course this bill was honoured in full.

Required:
(a) Prepare the following accounts in the books of Teh to record the information given:
  (i)   Cash (bank column);
  (ii)   Customer A;
  (iii) Customer B;
  (iv)   Customer C;
  (v)   Bills receivable.
(b) Compute the total profit made by Teh on the three transactions.   (LCC)

4. During the year 1982 the following transactions took place:

Apr	1	Jones purchased goods from Vernon £2,000 and sold goods to Parry £1,200.
Apr	2	Jones drew a Bill of Exchange (1) on Parry for £900 at 3 months and Parry accepted it.
Apr	8	Parry drew a Bill of Exchange (2) on Bradburn for £200 at 3 months which Bradburn accepted.
Apr	12	Parry endorsed bill (2) over to Jones and on 16th April Jones endorsed this bill over to Vernon.
Apr	22	Jones accepted Bill of Exchange (3) drawn by Vernon for £1,820 at 3 months in settlement of his account including interest.
Apr	24	Vernon discounted bill (3) at his bank, Lloyds, Fenton.
Jul	12	Vernon informed Jones that Bradburn's acceptance had been dishonoured, Jones thereupon sent a cheque for £200 to Vernon.
		Jones' bank was Barclays, Stoke.
		The other bills were duly paid.
Jul	16	Jones received a cheque from Parry for half the amount due from him.

Required:
Make the necessary entries in the ledger of Jones (including a bank account but not purchases and sales accounts) to record the above mentioned transactions.

Note: Entries should include dates, narrations and amounts.

(LCCI)

Putting it all together

The next part summarises what you have learned about capital and profit measurement. Some golden rules to help you with bookkeeping are then suggested.

28. Capital and Profit

INTRODUCTION

1. The balance sheet measures the amount of capital using money as the standard of measure. The profit and loss account measures, for a period, the effect of one cause of change in the amount of capital. Other causes of change are new capital introduced and drawings.

2. Capital is not a physical thing but a concept which is different from the idea most people concerned in accounting imagine it to be. Profit is a similarly difficult concept to grasp. In this chapter we shall discuss what capital and profit are and what they are not. We shall also discuss how they are related.

3. In conclusion we will examine an important but difficult concept, that of materiality in accounting.

WHAT IS CAPITAL?

4. The Capital of a business is composed of two elements

    - Assets
    - Liabilities

5. The assets included are not all the assets of the business. To be included, assets must:

    (a) Have had a *cost* to the business some time in the *past*.
    (b) Be capable of giving some benefit to the business some time in the *future*.

6. Some assets are thus not included. Exclusion may be:

    (a) Goodwill unless this has been purchased. Goodwill is the value attached to customers who will continue to buy from the business.

    (b) The value of patents, trade marks, licensing agreements, franchising agreements, agency agreements and other contractual or agreed arrangements which will give benefit in the future, unless there are identifiable historical costs associated with them.

    (c) Orders received but not yet exercised.

    (d) Valuable employees.

7. Clearly a business which has numerous contented customers, valuable patents created by brilliant research staff, an agreement to the exclusive distribution rights of an imported product in great demand and a full order book is more valuable than a business with none of these and yet those assets do not appear on the balance sheet.

8. The methods of valuation of assets vary according to the type of asset:

    (a) **Fixed assets** are valued by the depreciation process on the basis that:

        (i)   An asset is capable of giving benefits over its useful life equal to its original cost.
        (ii) It steadily gives up this value over its useful life.
        (iii) The balance sheet value is that part of the original cost which has yet to expire.

        This value is in no way indicative of what the asset would realise if it were sold.

    (b) **Stock** is valued at the lower of:

      (i)   Historical cost.
      (ii)   Net realisable value.

      This odd mix of values excludes valu-ation methods which might be expected, *e.g.* selling price or replacement value.

    (c) **Debtors** are valued at the amount which is expected to be received which may be the sum due or if a debt is doubtful, some lesser sum.

9.   Liabilities are simpler to grasp, in that all liabilities that are due for future payment and related to benefits already received, *must* be included. However, some liabilities that will not be payable except in special circumstances, *e.g.* redundancy payments, are excluded.

10.   Thus, *capital* is arrived at by:

    (a) Ascribing values by arbitrary and unlikely methods to *some* of the assets of the business.
    (b) Totalling these values.
    (c) Deducting the total of liabilities.

11.   What does the measurement of capital mean? Firstly, it does *not* indicate:

    (a) The value of the whole business if it was sold.
    (b) What would be left if the assets were realised and the liabilities paid off.

Both (a) and (b) would be useful facts, but are *not* given because deriving them would involve *estimates* and guesses which accountants deride as subjective.

12.   The accountants method of measuring capital is largely objective (there are not too many estimates), but it is very easy to argue that it gives very little *information* of use or relevance.

WHAT IS PROFIT?

13.   Like capital, profit is a very elusive concept. It is not a physical thing. It cannot be spent!

14.   Profit for a wholesaler (a simple business to grasp), is measured as:

    (a) The total of sales made in the period.
    (b) Less the *cost* of goods sold, destroyed, stolen or otherwise lost in the period.
    (c) Less the cost of expenses computed on the accruals basis.

15.   This simple view is complicated by adoption of accounting practices such as:

    (a) Prudence where the cost of sales is affected by opening and closing stock, valued in part at net realisable value.

    (b) The depreciation process.

16.   Thus measured, profit is the result of a complex process and is subject to conventions (realisation, accruals, etc) which are not apparent to those unversed in accounting and to a multitude of different methods of application of those conventions (F.I.F.O or AVCO; straight line or reducing balance depreciation).

THE RELATIONSHIP BETWEEN CAPITAL AND PROFIT

17.   Profit can be defined as the amount that can be withdrawn from a business during a period while remaining as well off at the end of the period as at the beginning. This means that:

    (a) Drawings reduce capital (by reducing one of the assets, cash).
    (b) Profit increases capital.
    (c) If capital is the same at the beginning as at the end, then profit = drawings.
    (d) If profit is greater than drawings, then capital will increase by the excess.
    (e) If profit is less than drawings, then capital will be reduced by the shortfall.

18.   The result of a given amount of profit is an increase in capital of that amount. Since capital *is* assets less liabilities then the result of a profit is an increase in the overall amount of assets less liabilities. It is *not* an increase in one particular asset (*e.g.* cash) but of the overall total of the assets.

19. Capital can also be increased by capital introduced and reduced by drawings.

ACCOUNTING AS A MEASUREMENT PROCESS

20. The distance from London to Wolverhampton is 200 kilometres. This idea is easily understood. The profit made to Bill's business in 19-4 was £23,240. This could be read as Bill's business making £23,240 pound notes which Bill has at the end of the year, and many non-accountants will see it that way. In fact, a profit is *measured* in pounds in the same way as distance is measured in kilometres.

REPORTING AND MATERIALITY

21. Financial statements are produced for people to *use*. The management of a business is *reporting* through the medium of the financial statements on his actions to interested classes of people - owners, shareholders, the Inspector of Taxes, the bank and other lenders, creditors, potential buyers of the business etc. Each class of user may have different informational needs, but the Accounts are more or less drawn up in a single form. The business may well have thousands or even millions of transactions during the year and the financial statements *summarise* the results (profit) for the year and the position at the end of the year (the balance sheet).

22. The summarising process requires that all transactions (sales, purchases, expenses etc.) and balances (debtors, creditors, stock, plant etc.) are put into categories, the total only of each category is shown.

23. Decisions have to be made as to what category a transaction or balance is in and whether a category should be shown as a single total or distinguished into sub-categories.

EXAMPLES

(a) **Stocks.** Should stocks of a manufacturing enterprise be shown as stocks £680,243 or should this total be broken down into:

	£
Raw materials	124,620
Work in progress	231,303
Finished goods	322,980
Consumable stores	1,340

Commonly, today the breakdown is shown, but only in notes to the Accounts.

(b) **Creditors.** Should creditors be shown as Trade Creditors £186,991, or should this be broken down into amounts due, for, say, raw materials, plant and equipment, expense items etc. Commonly, this breakdown is not given and this causes difficulty in calculating the ratios which users of Accounts need to make sense of the numbers.

24. Whether sub-categorisation is given, depends on the concept of *materiality*.

25. Materiality is usually thought of in terms of significant or essential. Thus, if stock is a significant amount in a business's Accounts, say 25% of total assets, then a breakdown is essential to an understanding of the *view* given by the Accounts. However, if the stock is very small in relation to other assets, showing a breakdown will have the effect of:

(a) Filling the Accounts with figures which are trivial.
(b) Drawing attention away from the important figures in the accounts.
(c) Preventing the reader of Accounts seeing the wood (the overall impression of the health of the business) because of the trees (endless details).

26. In an accounting sense, a matter is material if its non-disclosure, mis-statement or omission would be likely to *distort the view given by the Accounts.*

An example:

During 19-4 Giles' Wholesale Meat Co., suffered a burglary when large amounts of meat were lost. The loss was uninsured. The effect on the Accounts was:

(All in £000)	*19-2*	*19-3*	*19-4*
Sales	1,342	1,439	1,562
Less cost of Sales	937	1,002	1,164
Gross Profit	405	437	398
Gross Profit percentage	30.2	30.4	25.5

The view given by the Accounts is that turnover was steadily increasing in line with inflation, but that in 19-4 the business suffered an alarming decline in gross profit margin.

In fact, if the loss caused by the burglary was disclosed as:

	£	
Sales	1,562	
Less cost of Sales	1,084	Gross Profit percentage 30.6
Gross Profit	478	
Less Expenses		
Loss due to burglary	80	
Rent etc...........		

The loss is so material (= significant), that the view given by the Accounts is distorted unless the item is disclosed separately.

27. In practice, materiality causes great difficulty to accountants who, in preparing accounts:

  (a) Are summarising large numbers of transactions and balances.
  (b) Wish to present their financial statements in a form which is easily digested *i.e.* avoids too much detail.
  (c) Fear that omission of some detail may distort the view given by the Accounts.

SUMMARY

28. (a) The capital of a business is not a physical thing, but an accounting measurement of the *assets* less the liabilities of a business.

  (b) Some assets are excluded and those included are valued in a variety of arbitrary ways.

  (c) The result is not indicative of the value of the business as a whole nor of the amount to be obtained if the assets were realised and the liabilities paid off. What information is given by the accounting calculation of capital is difficult to discern.

  (d) Profit for a period is also not a physical thing nor a sum of money, but a measurement of the gain in capital arising out of trading. Its measurement is a function of the accounting conventions which are not made clear to lay readers of Accounts.

  (e) Profit and capital are connected in that the result of profit is an increase in the net assets (= capital) of the business.

  (f) Accounting for and the reporting of results is a summarising process. The extent of detailed disclosure is the subject of a very difficult idea in accounting - the materiality convention.

POINTS TO NOTE

29. (a) The methods used in drawing up the financial statements of an enterprise are often seen as very unlikely and rather odd by new students of accounting. This is because the accounting conventions followed were not determined by an objective search for methods which would give the most useful information to a range of users, the accounting conventions were developed by historical accident.

  (b) The balance sheet came first on the principle that:

  (i) Investors give the management a sum of money (the initial capital).

  (ii) This sum is added to by lenders, and suppliers of trade credit.

  (iii) The resultant resources are invested in assets (fixed assets and stock), some of which have limited lives.

  (iv) Some of the assets are exchanged for debts (credit sales) or cash (cash sales and credit sales ultimately).

  (v) The balance sheet shows what *has happened* to the initial capital invested. It will have become:

    - fixed assets which if they have limited lives must be shown at cost less depreciation

- stock	- cash
- debtors	etc.

(c) The profit and loss account came later. It summarised the changes to overall capital.

(d) It is essential to realise that capital and profit are accounting measures and not, in themselves, real things or actual money.

(e) Whenever you prepare a set of financial statements, consider carefully the level of detail required and if there is a need to disclose or emphasise any particular items.

SELF TESTING QUESTIONS

(a) What is the capital of a business? (4).
(b) What is an asset? (5).
(c) List some assets which are excluded from a balance sheet. (6).
(d) How are fixed assets valued? (8).
(e) How is stock valued? (8).
(f) What is a liability? (9).
(g) What information is given by the measurement of capital? (11, 12).
(h) What is profit? (13 - 16).
(i) How are profit and capital related? (18).
(j) What is the effect of the materiality convention in accounting? (25).
(k) Historically what are the origins of the modern balance sheet? (29b).
(l) Knott's business has made a profit of £16,000 in 19-8. Mrs Knott hears this and makes plans to spend the £16,000. Discuss.

Exercises (Answers begin on page 458)

1. *Which of the following would be included in the balance sheet of a trader:*

   (a) the goodwill of the hundreds of clients the firm has.
   (b) the excess of purchase price over net tangible assets of a business purchased for cash in the year.
   (c) orders received but unstarted.
   (d) orders received and part finished.
   (e) a property which cost £40,000 in the year (land £5,000, building £35,000) which is expected to last for 35 years.
   (f) a piece of land which cost £3,000 many years ago. The land has not been used but is now worth £20,000.
   (g) stock in trade which cost £12,000 which is marked for sale at a total of £16,500.
   (h) a debt due from Paul £3,900 which is disputed by him. The matter is in court and the lawyer says we have a 50% chance of getting paid.
   (i) probable cost of correcting some faulty goods £3,274 sold in the year.
   (j) redundancy payments to staff accrued £4,800. It is expected that about 20% of the staff will actually be made redundant in the coming year.

Comment on your opinion and where there is more than one possibility of valuation say which would be used and why.

2. *Comment on the following statements:*

   Profit is a sum to be spent.

   We can use the profit made this year to renew the fixed assets.

   Capital is an asset of the business.

   Capital is an asset of the proprietor.

   As capital has increased in the year there must have been a profit.

   Two accountants prepared a profit and loss account of Holmes independently but used the same data. They produced quite different measurements of profit.

   John, a bank clerk, sees that a customer of the bank Miles Rich has died and left £2 million. John knows that Rich has an overdraft at the bank.

Walter's business owes me £3,000 but this does not seem to appear on his balance sheet.

My car business has some stationery stock £430 but this does not appear on the balance sheet.

Isaiah imports gold jewellery from Germany which he wholesales from his inner city warehouse. His gross profit ratio has fallen this year compared with last year despite a 50% increase in sales.

Auntie May, a little old lady, has deposited £4,000 with the High Street branch of The Boring Bank plc. Each year she calls at the bank and asks to see her money.

Exercises without answers

3.   *In preparing the annual accounts of the medium sized business by which you are employed as assistant accountant, the following items require to be dealt with at the financial year end, 31 March 1987.*

(1) There is a stock of unused postage stamps which had cost £3.

(2) A customer had paid his outstanding account by cheque, £35. Your company's bank has now returned this cheque marked 'Refer to drawer – insufficient funds'.

(3) The company's office block has been extended to house a computer installation. The company's own workmen carried out the building work at a wages cost of £764 and used materials which had cost £2,681.

(4) The computer equipment is rented at an annual rental of £19,200, paid quarterly in arrears on the last day of January, April, July and November.

(5) A contract has been signed for the removal of the existing heating system from the company's premises and its replacement by a new one, at a total cost of £22,700. Work is not scheduled to start until July 1987.

Required:
State the accounting treatment, including available alternative treatments, you could apply to each of the above items.
                                                                                          (ACCA)

4.   *Rudolf is reviewing his annual financial statements for 19–8. He remarks:*

(a) I see the goodwill in Charley's business which I bought in July is included but surely I have more goodwill than that.
(b) My plant is surely worth more than the book value of £4,500.
(c) I can sell my stock for £8,000 at least, so why is it included at only £5,000.
(d) I have made a profit of £16,000 and drawn only £11,000 but my overdraft has gone up.
(e) Where are my weekly wages of £200 a week. The wages only seem to be Fred and June's.
(f) I can't see the £20 owing to Lola.

Comment on these remarks.

5.   *Wallace is entitled to a commission of 10% on the profit after charging the commission of Julie's business which he manages. He sees the annual accounts and objects to:*

(a) Depreciation on Julie's Jaguar (20% on cost of £24,000).
(b) Interest of £2,600 on a loan taken out to buy the Jaguar.
(c) Loss on sale of some goods £1,200 which Wallace only bought on Julie's insistence.
(d) A bad debt of £300 incurred on Rowan's account. Wallace only sold to Rowan on Julie's insistence. The mark up on cost is 40% on cost.

The original accounts show a commission due to Wallace of £3,400. Julie agrees to adjust the accounts for (c) and (d) and allow a half charge only on (a) and 9b).

Calculate Wallace's adjusted commission.

6.   *Samantha is preparing the accounts for her wholesale fruit business for the year ending 30 September 19–8. The following problems arise:*

(a) She has bought a fork lift truck at auction for £1,000. She has obtained it very cheaply and considers it to be worth at least £2,000.

(b) She has imported at a cost of £1,500 a special machine for treating coconuts but finds it does not work. She cannot get her money back or sell it and it is just rusting away in a corner.

(c) She has recently negotiated a special import concession from an enterprise in Poland which has enabled her to undercut her rivals.

(d) She has just negotiated a very advantageous firm contract to supply a supermarket chain for a period of one year.

(e) Her property had cost £30,000 ten years ago and the buildings part £22,000 is being depreciated over 40 years. She has had the property valued and the valuer says it is worth £85,000.

(f) She has a stock of imported exotic tinned fruits which cost £7,000 and which can be sold for £11,600.

(g) She supplied some fruit which is alleged to have caused food poisoning. The sufferer is suing her for damages and the sum of £10,000 + costs of £8,000 has been mentioned. Her own costs in the case are estimated to be £6,500. She is vigorously disputing the action.

(h) She has twelve employees and if they all were dismissed she would have to pay £6,900 in redundancy pay.

(i) At the year end creditors (excluding anything mentioned elsewhere in this question) amount to £45,000 (previous year £31,000) but this includes £12,100 for a new delivery van.

(j) During the year her refrigeration equipment broke down at a weekend and she lost stock costing £5,500. Her turnover is £580,000 with a gross profit percentage of about 30%.

Comment on these items and explain the correct treatment to accord with accounting conventions. State which conventions are involved.

She is hoping to borrow from the bank to expand into another line of business. Comment on the utility to the bank of her accounts in the light of the information above.

She may decide to sell the business instead. Comment on the usefulness of her accounts to a prospective buyer in the light of the information above.

She is not sure how much she can draw from her business. Comment on the usefulness of annual accounts in making decisions on how much can be drawn from a business.

29. Bookkeeping – Golden Rules

INTRODUCTION

1.   Bookkeeping has often been seen, at least by University Accounting departments as a technique unworthy of serious study. In practice, students who attempt to learn bookkeeping in a classroom or from books, find it exceedingly difficult. As a technique it is essential at the routine level of maintaining records and as a basis of the preparation of financial statements. It is also powerful as a tool in solving problems in such areas as group accounts, budgeting and standard costing.

2.   This chapter gives a few rules which may help in the learning process. However, there is no doubt that the best strategy for learning bookkeeping is constant practice.

DEBIT OR CREDIT

3.   Once a student has memorised which side is the debit and which the credit, the problem is to decide which side of an account an entry should be made.

4.   Accounts can be divided into four categories:

(a)   **Real Accounts.** Real accounts are accounts which record physical assets such as land, buildings, vehicles, plant, cash, investments etc.

Additions to real accounts are always made on the *debit*. Reductions (dis-posals, depreciation etc.) are entered on the credit side. Note that stock is a special sort of real account which has a debit entry only at accounting year ends which is removed by a credit at the next succeeding year end.

WHICH SIDE?

DEBIT	CREDIT
Profit and Loss Account Items	
- Expenses	- Sales
- Purchases	- Revenues
- Depreciation (for year)	
Balance Sheet Items	
- Assets	- Liabilities
- Drawings	- Capital
	- Provisions:
	depreciation
	doubtful debts

Note:
Provision for depreciation on the credit side is accumulated depreciation.

Fig. 23.1

(b)   **Personal accounts.** These accounts show the dealings with and the balances due to or from persons or institutions. Examples are customers, suppliers, lenders, the bank and capital.

Transactions which increase the amount *due* to a person by the enterprise are entered on the credit side. A purchase of goods by the enterprise from a supplier requires an entry of the amount due on the credit side of the supplier's account.

Transactions which reduce the amount due to a *creditor* are entered on the debit side of the creditor's account.

Transactions which increase the amount due *from* a person by the business are entered on the *debit* side of that persons account. For example, sales invoices are entered on the debit side of a customer's account.

Transactions which *reduce* the amount due from a person to the business are entered on the credit side of that person's account.

The cash book is an example of a personal account. It is the account which records dealings with and the balance due to or from the bank. The easy way to remember on which side entries are to be made, is that receipts (payments into the bank) go on the debit and payments (cheques drawn etc.) go on the credit.

The capital account is also a personal account - the account of the proprietor. Profit is credited as it increases the sum due to the proprietor and drawings are debited as they reduce the amount due.

(c) **Nominal accounts.** These accounts *accumulate* the data required for the trading and profit and loss accounts. Examples are sales, purchases, rent, rates, discounts etc.

Revenue items are accumulated on the credit side of their accounts. Revenues include sales, rent receivable, discount receivable and interest receivable.

Expense items are accumulated on the debit side of their accounts.

(d) **Valuation accounts.** Examples are provision for depreciation and provision for doubtful debts. It is the custom to record fixed assets in their real accounts at *cost*. However, the book value is cost less depreciation. In order to retain the cost figure on the debit of a real account, a provision for depreciation account on the credit is maintained. Similarly if debtors' personal accounts are retained at the sum due, but are shown in the balance sheet at the estimated realisable value, a valuation account on the credit - provision for doubtful debts is required.

TRIAL BALANCES - DEBIT AND CREDIT BALANCES

5. A trial balance is a list of the balances in a double entry system. It is a mix of:

    (a) Balance sheet items - personal, real and valuation accounts.
    (b) Trading and Profit and Loss Accounts - the nominal accounts.

6. **Debit balances** will be:

    (a) Assets - Balance sheet.
or (b) Expenses - Profit and Loss Account.

7. **Credit balances** will be:

    (a) Revenues - Profit and Loss Account.
or (b) Liabilities - Balance Sheet.
or (c) Valuation accounts - Balance Sheet.

SUMMARY

8. (a) Accounts in a double entry system can be categorised into:

    (i) Real Accounts - physical assets - debit balances.
    (ii) Personal Accounts - debit balances for debtors - credit balances for creditors.
    (iii) Nominal Accounts - profit and loss items - debit balances for expenses - credit balances for revenues.
    (iv) Valuation Accounts - credit balances reducing assets held at cost to net book value.

  (b) A trial balance is a mix of balance sheet items and trading and profit and loss account items as:

Debit Balances	*Credit Balances*
Assets	Liabilities
Expenses	Revenues
	Valuation Accounts

POINTS TO NOTE

9. (a) In bookkeeping exercises, always remember that every debit must have an equal credit and vice versa.

(b) In real accounts, debits record increases in the asset. Credits record decreases. Remember that the *balance remaining* must be meaningful, so that credits must reduce what is in the debit. For example, if an asset is at cost, credit entries reducing the asset must *also* be at cost or if at disposal price, an adjustment must be made.

(c) A good points of reference in determining which side an entry should go, is the cash book. Remember:

Dr. Receipts   **Cr. Payments**

Consequently, the corresponding entries must be:

Debits - assets and expenses.
Credits - revenues and liabilities.

(d) A favourite trick of examiners, is to include bank balance in a trial balance on the credit side. It is thus a liability and should appear as bank overdraft under current liabilities.

SELF TESTING QUESTIONS

(a) What categories of accounts are there? (4).
(b) What accounts will be on the (i) debit side, (ii) credit side of a trial balance? (5 - 7).
(c) How can the cash book be used as a reference point for double entry posting? (9c).
(d) If the bank balance in a trial balance is on the credit side, where should the item appear in the balance sheet? (9d).

Exercises (Answers begin on page 458)

1. *Which of the following accounts are real, personal, valuation, nominal:*

Cash in hand, bank overdraft, wages, rent and rates, depreciation expense, provision for depreciation, lorries at cost, sales, purchases, a debtor, capital, discount received, stock in trade, accrued electricity, drawings, advertising?

In each case state whether the account will be a debit or a credit balance.

2. *A trial balance of Eggbert's business at 31.12.-7 included the following entries:*

	Dr	Cr
Gross Profit		232,766
Stock in Trade	567,300	
Lorries at cost	870,300	
Depreciation for year	178,900	
Provision for depreciation of lorries		432,569

At what date is the stock in trade £567,300?

Up to what date is the provision for depreciation?

3. *Hartley opens a shop on 1.1.-8 and the following transactions occur in the first month:*

January
1 *Opened a bank account with £20,000 drawn from the building society and introduced his car to the business value £1,900.*
2 *Bought goods on credit from Harold £3,900.*
3 *Bought goods by cheque from Lowe £2,700*
4 *Paid rent by cheque for first quarter £500*
5 *Cash sales into bank £1,522*
6 *Bought shop fittings on credit from Hummel £670*
7 *Bought goods on credit from Harold £380*
8 *Received credit note from Harold £311*
9 *Bought goods from Downs on credit £690*
10 *Sold goods to Bonser on credit £570*
11 *Sold goods on credit to Gibbon £800*
12 *Paid wages by cheque £140*
13 *Took £1,800 in cash sales, paid stationery therefrom £40 and banked the remainder*
14 *Drew a cheque for Horizontal Holidays plc £370*
16 *Gibbon paid less 5% settlement discount*

19 Bought goods from Bonser on credit £60
20 Contra'd the two accounts of Bonser
24 Sold some of the shop fittings which had cost £100 for £120 on credit to Lewis
31 Cash sales banked £2,700

Enter all the above in double entry accounts, balance off accounts where necessary and extract a trial balance.

Exercises without answers

4. James opens a shop on 1st July 1982, and during his first month in business, the following transactions occurred:

1982

1 July   James contributes £20,000 in cash to the business out of his private bank account.

2 July   He opens a business bank account by transferring £18,000 of his cash in hand.

5 July   Some premises are rented, the rent being £500 per quarter payable in advance in cash.

6 July   James buys some second-hand shop equipment for £300 paying by cheque.

9 July   He purchases some goods for resale for £1,000 paying for them in cash.

10 July   Seddon supplies him with £2,000 of goods on credit.

20 July   James returns £200 of the goods to Seddon.

23 July   Cash sales for the week amount to £1,500.

26 July   James sells goods on credit for £1,000 to Frodsham.

28 July   Frodsham returns £500 of the goods to James.

31 July   James settles his account with Seddon by cheque, and is able to claim a cash discount of 10%.

31 July   Frodsham sends James a cheque for £450 in settlement of his account, any balance remaining on his account being treated as a cash discount.

31 July   During his initial trading, James has discovered that some of his shop equipment is not suitable, but he is fortunate in being able to dispose of it for £50 in cash. There was no profit or loss on disposal.

31 July   He withdraws £150 in cash as part payment towards a holiday for his wife.

Required:
(a) Enter the above transactions in James' ledger accounts, balance off the accounts and bring down the balances as at 1st August 1982.

(b) Extract a trial balance as at 31st July 1982.   (AAT)

5. During the month of January 1987 John Agar's trading transactions on credit were as follows:

January		£
1	Sales to C. Badman	196.00
5	Purchases from T. Mason	*512.00
6	Sales to R. Cooper	237.00
9	Returns from C. Badman	13.00
13	Sales to J. Davies	175.00
15	Purchases from S. Parfitt	**680.00
22	Sales to R. Cooper	314.00
27	Returns from J. Davies	46.00
30	Received credit note from S. Parfitt in respect of goods with a list price (excluding VAT) of	30.00

*   Subject to 25% trade discount
**   Subject to 30% trade discount

Note: All purchases, sales and returns are subject to Value Added Tax at 10%.

You are required to:

(a) write up Agar's Sales, Purchases, Sales Returns and Purchases day books for the month of January 1987;
(b) write up all of Agar's ledger accounts which were concerned with the transactions with Mason and Parfitt.

There were no balances on the accounts at 1 January.

Do not balance the accounts at the end of January.   (RSA)

6.   Herbert Emery, a sole trader, extracted a Trial Balance at the close of business on 31 October 1984. This did not balance but he prepared Trading and Profit and Loss Accounts for the year ended 31 October 1984 and these showed a Net Profit of £2,190.

Subsequently, Emery discovered the following errors which accounted for the total difference in the Trial Balance:

(1) Salaries paid during the year included an item of £130. The correct entry had been made in the Cash Book but the double entry had not been completed.

(2) A sale of £216 to W. Jones had been entered correctly in the Sales Day Book but the entry in the personal account of Jones was £261.

(3) In the Sales Day Book the total at the bottom of one page was £3,460. This had been carried forward to the next page as £3,760.

(4) In the Trading Account the Stock in Trade at 31 October 1984 was quoted as £2,290. It has now been discovered that due to an error in the stock valuation sheets the figure should have been £2,480.

Required:
    (i) Indicate how each of the above errors affected the original Trial Balance. Your answer should be in the form of the following table:

Error	Excess Dr	Excess Cr	If No Effect write No Effect
(1)			
(2)			
(3)			
(4)			

    (ii) Calculate the correct Net Profit.

NOTE: Calculations must be shown.

(LCCI)

Final Accounts

The next part is concerned with final accounts. Final accounts is a phrase meaning the Income Statements (profit and loss accounts etc) and the Balance Sheet. Other statements such as the statement of source and application of funds may be included in practice. Chapter 30 looks at final accounts produced from an orthodox bookkeeping and a trial balance. Chapter 31 considers a matter of great examination significance - the preparation of final accounts from incomplete records.

30. Final Accounts

INTRODUCTION

1. This chapter introduces nothing new but brings together what has been learned so far in the preparation of final accounts - a trading and profit and loss account and a balance sheet.

EXAMPLE

2. The trial balance of the business of Harbridge, a wholesaler of widgets at 31 December 19-3 showed:

	Dr £	Cr £
Capital		73,928
Drawings	6,800	
Stock	24,700	
Land at cost	13,000	
Buildings at cost	64,800	
Equipment at cost	17,200	
Buildings depreciation provision		23,410
Equipment depreciation provision		6,800
Debtors	23,230	
Creditors		18,970
Sales		96,900
Purchases	51,000	
Discounts allowed and received	1,300	890
Overhead expenses	28,540	
Carriage inwards	2,100	
Bank balance		4,872
Loan from June at 15%		6,000
Provision for doubtful debts		900
	232,670	232,670

Note:

(a) Stock at 31.12.-3 was valued at £26,800.

(b) Harbridge had drawn goods to the value of £600 during the year and these had not been reflected in the records.

(c) Harbridge had received £60 cash from a debtor included in the debtors in the trial balance. He has kept the cash for himself.

(d) An invoice for some new equipment bought on 15 December 19-3 £4,200 has not been included in the trial balance.

(e) Depreciation is at 4% on the cost of the buildings.

(f) Depreciation is at 30% reducing balance on all equipment owned at the year end.

(g) Overheads includes motor insurance for the year ending 31.3.-4 £680 but does not include the rates for the half-year ending 31.3.-4 £1,530.

(h) Bad debts are to be written off £390 and a specific provision made against £280 of debts and a general provision of 3% against the remainder.

(i) No interest or capital payments have been made in respect of the loan which was made on July 1 19-3.

Prepare a trading and profit and loss account for the year ending 31 December 19-3 and a balance sheet as at that date.

ANSWER

3.   Before beginning the answer note a few points.

(a)   The stock in the trial balance is as at 31 December 19-2.
(b)   The depreciation provisions and the provisions for doubtful debts are also as at 31 December 19-2.
(c)   The bank balance is an overdraft since it is on the credit side:

Answer:
Harbridge
Trading and Profit and Loss account for the year ending 31 December 19-3.

	£	£
Sales		96,900
Less cost of goods sold:		
Opening stock	24,700	
Purchases	50,400	
Carriage inward	2,100	
	77,200	
Closing stock	26,800	
		50,400
Gross profit		46,500
Discounts allowed	1,300	
Discounts received	(890)	
Loan interest	450	
Bad debts	390	
Additional provision for doubtful debts	55	
Overheads	29,135	
Depreciation on buildings	2,592	
Depreciation on equipment	4,380	
		37,412
Net profit		9,088

BALANCE SHEET AS AT 31 DECEMBER 19-3

Fixed assets	Cost	Depreciation	Net book value
	£	£	£
Land	13,000	–	13,000
Buildings	64,800	26,002	38,798
Equipment	21,400	11,180	10,220
	99,200	37,182	62,018
Current assets			
Stock		26,800	
Debtors		21,825	
Prepayments		170	
		48,795	
Current liabilities			
Creditors		23,170	
Accruals		1,215	
Bank overdraft		4,872	
		29,257	
			19,538
			81,556
Capital as at beginning of the year			73,928
Net profit			9,088
			83,016
Drawings			7,460
			75,556
Loan			6,000
			81,556

Workings and notes

(a) Purchases = £51,000 - £600.

(b) Carriage inwards goes in the trading account part of the income statement.

(c) Discounts received could be put in other parts of the income statement.

(d) Loan interest - 1/2 year accrued - put in accruals also.

(e) Bad debts - see note (h).

(f) Debtors can be seen by a double entry account:

Dr		*Cr*	£
b/f	23,230	Bad debts	390
		Cash (Dr to drawings)	60
		c/f	22,780
	23,230		23,230

The provision is £280 + 3% of (£22,780 - £280) = £955.

Debtors on the balance sheet are £22,780 - £955 = £21,825.

(g) Overheads are £28,540 + £765 (Rates for ¼ year to 31 March) - £170 (motor insurance for ¼ year to 31 March) = £29,135.

(h) Depreciation on buildings is 4% on the cost of £64,800.

(i) Depreciation on equipment is 30% on (£17,200 + £4,200 - £6,800) = £4,380.

(j) Fixed assets are in a three column form. Note that depreciation is accumulated. That is, it is this year's plus the brought forward depreciation of earlier years.

(k) Do not forget the prepayment in the balance sheet.

(l) Creditors should include the new equipment.

(m) Accruals is shown as one figure and is the loan interest due + the rates.

(n) Drawings is £24,700 + £600 + £60 = £25,360.

(o) Note that in this problem we have used the following conventions:

- the business entity - Harbridge's personal affairs have been excluded;
- money measurement;
- historical cost - all the assets are valued at or by reference to historical cost and the inputs to profit and loss account are at cost;
- going concern - we have assumed the business will continue into the future and can thus give a value to the equipment which may not be realisable on sale;
- periodicity - annual accounts;
- realisation convention - no profit has been taken on the closing stock but gross profit has been included on items sold which had not at 31.12.03 resulted in cash (ie the debtors at that date);
- the matching convention - profit has been calculated by sales less costs incurred in earning those sales;
- accruals - note the overheads;
- conservatism or prudence - the doubtful debt provision;
- materiality - the accounts are in a summarised form. In particular the list of expenses seems very odd with a large item (overheads) and some very small items (provision for doubtful debts and bad debts). In practice the overheads would be detailed.

SUMMARY

4. In this chapter a set of final accounts were prepared and the conventions used in their preparation were considered.

POINTS TO NOTE

5. (a) This was a straightforward preparation of final accounts but you will have realised that it took time and patience to get it fully right. Some points were tricky - notably the doubtful debts provision. Remember when preparing accounts:

- items affecting the trading and profit and loss account often also affect the balance sheet;
- depreciation can be straight line (x% on cost) or reducing balance;
- depreciation in the balance sheet must be the accumulated depreciation;
- accruals and prepayments must be carefully calculated. In any set of students, some will include the whole year or half year as a prepayment or accrual;
- accruals and prepayments must appear in the balance sheet;
- the bank balance must be on the right side.

(b) In an actual exam, students find there is not enough time to complete all that is required. A way round this problem is to ignore complications that take a long time (eg the doubtful debt provision) but you will of course lose the marks given for these complications. On the other hand the extra time available may allow you to gain marks on a matter you find easier.

(c) In an exam, you will find that your final accounts do not balance. Do not let this worry you. Very few accounts balance first time in the real world. Simply ignore the fact that your accounts do not balance and go on to the next question. You will waste much time looking for differences you may not find. If you do find a difference it may be because of a trivial error and you will gain perhaps one mark at the expense of time which could have earned you perhaps 5 marks. In the real world, of course, differences have to be found but there is adequate time for the search.

SELF TESTING QUESTIONS

6. (a) In a trial balance, the bank overdraft is a debit. Is this cash in the bank or an overdraft? (3)

(b) What should be done in an accounting exam if a balance sheet does not balance? (5)

Exercises without answers

1. The following trial balance was extracted from the books of R T Shore on 31 October 1988.

	£	£
Sales		550,000
Stock at 1 November 1987	16,500	
Purchases	432,400	
Returns inwards and outwards	600	800
Carriage inwards	700	
Carriage outwards	300	
Discounts received and allowed	400	200
Light and heat	4,400	
Rates and insurance	6,100	
Wages	68,400	
Motor expenses	6,300	
Premises	62,000	
Vehicles (at cost)	12,000	
Fittings and fixtures (at cost)	6,400	
Provision for depreciation		
Fittings and fixtures		2,600
Vehicles		4,800
Bad debts	200	
Cash in hand and at bank	6,600	
Drawings	22,800	
Capital		90,300
Debtors and creditors	41,000	38,400
	687,100	687,100

The following information is also available.

1. Stock in trade on October 31 1988 amounted to £18,400.
2. 20% of the cost price of the vehicles and 10% of the cost price of the fittings and fixtures is to be written off as depreciation.
3. £1,300 of the motor expenses are deemed to have been for Shore's own use.
4. Rates have been prepaid by £200 and there is an account of £450 outstanding for heating.
5. A provision for bad debts equivalent to 2% of debtors is to be created.

You are required to:

Prepare the trading and profit and loss accounts of Shore for the year ended 31 October 1988 and a balance sheet as at that date.

NB: You accounts should be in vertical format and should clearly show:
    (i) Cost of goods sold;
    (ii) Working capital.   *(RSA)*

31. Incomplete Records

INTRODUCTION

1. The ideal method for preparing the annual final accounts for a business is illustrated in the attached diagram.

2. In practice, many businesses fail to record all their transactions in a double entry bookkeeping system and accountants have to prepare the accounts from whatever information is available. Sometimes this information is fragmentary and considerable ingenuity has to be used to determine all the figures in the accounts.

3. Questions are often set on this subject which is sometimes called *single entry* as double entry records are not available.

4. The stages in preparing accounts from incomplete records are on the attached diagram. In examination questions, some of these stages are not required, for example, the opening balance sheet may be given.

EXAMINATION TECHNIQUE

5. Before working an example, consider the following points:

   (a) Incomplete records questions present a large amount of unsorted information.
   (b) This information has to be used to prepare specific financial statements.
   (c) An essential intermediate stage is the preparation of *working papers* in which:
       (i) Proper headings must be given.
       (ii) The work is neat.
       (iii) All amounts must be adequately described.
   (d) It is essential to concentrate on one matter at a time.
   (e) Be patient, thorough and painstaking.

ACCOUNTS PREPARATION FROM DOUBLE ENTRY RECORDS

Transactions
|
Documents
|
Books of prime entry
|
Double entry accounts
|
Trial balance at year end
|
Adjustments for accruals, prepayments, depreciation etc.
|
Profit and loss account and balance sheet

ACCOUNTS PREPARATION FROM INCOMPLETE RECORDS

(a) Establishment of opening balance sheet.
(b) Reconstruction of bank transactions.
(c) Reconstruction of cash transactions.
(d) Preparation of debtors summary.
(e) Preparation of creditors summary.
(f) Preparation of any other required working schedules.
(g) Completion of profit and loss account and balance sheet.

6. An example:

Mr T. Bone runs a butcher's shop. All his takings are in cash, which he pays into the bank after deducting:

(a) £50 per week in drawings.
(b) Wages and expenses also paid in cash. During the year to 30th June 19-5 these were as follows:

	£
Assistants' wages	4,420
Sundry expenses	1,050

A summary of his bank account for the year revealed the following:

	£		£
Balance b/f 1st July 19-4	850	Rent	2,900
Shop takings banked	29,270	Rates	1,020
		Electricity	490
		Sundry expenses	280
		New fittings	4,800
		Purchases	19,400
		Balance c/f 30th June 19-5	1,230
	30,120		30,120

You discover the following additional information:

	30th June 19-4 £	30th June 19-5 £
Fittings at cost	6,300	?
Accumulated depreciation	2,900	?
Accrued electricity	50	60
Prepaid rates	100	140
Stock	1,820	2,600
Debtors	530	880
Creditors for meat	1,380	1,934
Cash in the till	100	90

Depreciation of fittings is at 20% on the reducing balance basis.

Required:
(a) Prepare a statement of Mr Bone's capital as at 1st July 19-4.
(b) Prepare a trading and profit and loss account for the year ended 30th June 19-5.
(c) Prepare a balance sheet as at 30th June 19-5.

7. Answer:
(a) Statement of Mr Bone's capital at 1st July 19-4:

	£	£
Assets		
Fittings at cost		6,300
Less Depreciation		2,900
Net book value		3,400
Stock		1,820
Debtors		530
Prepaid rates		100
Balance at bank		850
Cash in hand		100
Total assets		6,800
Liabilities		
Creditors	1,380	
Accrued electricity	50	1,430
Capital		5,370

Notes:

(a) This statement is usually called a "statement of affairs". It is essentially a balance sheet without the trimmings.

(b) The statement is produced by searching all the data for matters which give information on assets and liabilities at 1st July 19-4.

(b) Before the profit and loss account and balance sheet can be prepared, working schedules must be drawn up:

Cash in the till

Receipts	£	Payments	£
Balance at 1.7.-4	100	Drawings 52 x 50	2,600
From customers (a)	?	Wages	4,420
		Sundry expenses	1,050
		Payments into bank	29,270
		Balance 30.6.-5	90
	37,430		37,430

Notes:

(a) Mr Bone started with £100 in his till. During the year, his customers paid him some unknown amount. From this he paid out £2,600 to himself, £4,420 as wages, £1,050 for cleaning and put £29,270 into the bank. He still has £90 in the till at the year end.

(b) The amount he must have received to do all this is the balance of the account (a). You can calculate this. It is £37,330.

(c) We now have cash received from customers in the year.

Customers

Due from customer	£	How the customers settled	£
Balance at 1.7.-4	530	Cash	37,330
Sales made (b)	?	Balance at 30.6.-5	880
	38,210		38,210

Notes:

(a) Customers owed £530 at the beginning of the year. Sales were made in the year of some unknown amount.

(b) As the customers paid £37,330 and still owed £880 at the year end, the sales must have been the balance of the account (b) which you will calculate at £37,680.

(c) We now have the figure of sales for the trading account.

Suppliers

How Bone settled	£	Due to Suppliers	£
Payments	19,400	Balance at 1.7.-4	1,380
Balance at 30.6.-5	1,934	Purchases (c)	?
	21,334		21,334

Notes:

(a) This account is similar to the account for customers but appears on opposite sides.

(b) The balance on the account (c) is the amount purchased during the year £19,954 and this figure is required for the trading account.

We are now ready to prepare the trading and profit and loss account:

T. Bone – Butcher

**Trading and profit and loss account for the
year ending 30th June 19-5**

	£	£
Sales		37,680
Less Cost of goods sold:		
Opening stock	1,820	
Purchases	19,954	
	21,774	
Less Closing stock	2,600	19,174
Gross Profit		18,506
Less expenses:		
Assistants' wages	4,420	
Sundry expenses (a)	1,330	
Rent	2,900	
Rates (b)	980	
Electricity (c)	500	
Depreciation (d)	1,640	11,770
Net profit		£ 6,736

Notes:

(a) Some sundry expenses were paid by cash £1,050 and some by cheque £280, the total is £1,330. Marks will be deducted if these figures appear separately in the profit and loss account.

(b) Rates is calculated as:

	£		£
Prepayment b/f	100	Expense of year	?
Cheques	1,020	Prepayment c/f	140
	1,120		1,120

This can be seen as:

	£
On debit - paid in previous year	100
paid this year	1,020
	1,120
of which, relates to next year	140
therefore relates to this year	980

(c) Electricity is similarly calculated:

	£		£
Cheques	490	Accrual b/f	50
Accruals c/f	60	Expense of year	?
	550		550

(d)

	£
Net book value of fittings at 1.7.-4	3,400
Additions in year	4,800
	8,200
Depreciation at 20%	1,640

The balance sheet can now be prepared as:

T. Bone – Butcher
Balance sheet as at 30th June 19–5

	£	£	
Fixed assets			
Fittings at cost		11,100	(a)
Less Accumulated depr		4,540	(b)
Net book value		6,560	
Current assets			
Stock	2,600		
Debtors	880		
Prepayments	140		
Cash at bank	1,230		
Cash in hand	90	4,940	
		11,500	
Less **Current liabilities**			
Trade creditors	1,934		
Accruals	60	1,994	
		9,506	
Capital:			
as at 1st July 19–4		5,370	(c)
Add Net profit		6,736	
		12,106	
Less Drawings		2,600	
		9,506	

Note:

	£
(a) Fixtures at cost 1.7.–4	*6,300*
Purchased in the year	*4,800*
	11,100
(b) Accumulated depreciation at 1.7.–4	*2,900*
Depreciation in the year	*1,640*
	4,540

(c) Derived from our opening statement of affairs.

THEORY

8.   There is no theory which is specific to incomplete records. However, incomplete records questions form a good medium for illustrating the accounting conventions. The going concern, realisation, matching and accruals conventions have been applied to the question in paragraph 6. In addition, the prudence convention is often applied in such questions, in stock valuation, and provisions for doubtful debts.

PROBLEMS IN IMPLEMENTATION

9.   The number of variations and complications that can be put into an incomplete records question is endless. It is not possible to discuss them all. Many will appear in the working schedules which may need expansion in some or all of the following ways:

(a)   **Cash in till account**

Receipts		Payments	
Balance b/f	x	Drawings	x
Cash/cheques from customers	x	Expenses	x
Cash drawn from the bank	x	Fixed assets	x
Proceeds of sale of fixed assets	x	Income tax (1)	x
		Paid into bank	x
		Balance c/f	x
	x		x

(1) Treat income tax as drawings

Note that any of these items can be the unknown. A favourite trick of examiners is to give cash received from customers (or require it to be derived from other information), and for the drawings to be unknown. Drawings is then calculated by treating it as the balancing figure in the cash account.

(b) **Total customers account**

Due from customers		*Settlement by customers*	
Balance b/f	x	Cash received	x
Sales in year	x	Settlement discounts	x
		Returns	x
		Bad debts	x
		Balance c/f	x
	x		x

Note that provisions for doubtful debts do *not* appear in this account.

(c) **Total creditors account**

Settlement		*Due to suppliers*	
Cash/cheques paid	x	Balance b/f	x
Returns	x	Purchases	x
Settlement discounts	x		
Balance c/f	x		
	x		x

(d) The trading account:

Sales			x
Less Cost of goods sold:			
Opening stock		x	
Purchases		x	
Available for sale		x	
Less Goods taken by proprietor for his own use	x		
Closing stock	x	x	x
Gross profit			x

Examiners often require the following logical sequence:

(a) The purchases is computed say £20,000.

(b) Cost of goods sold is computed by adjusting for stocks giving say £21,000.

(c) The question gives the information that gross profit on sales is 20%. From this sales *and* gross profit can be found thus:

	£	%
Sales	?	100
Cost of sales	21,000	?
Gross profit	?	20

If gross profit on sales is 20% of sales, then cost of sales is 80% of sales. Therefore if cost of sales is £21,000, sales must be £26,250 and gross profit is £5,250.

(d) Further unknowns can be calculated once sales is known.

SUMMARY

10. (a) Not all businesses keep perfect records on double entry principles. Many traders have incomplete records. Preparing accounts from such records poses the accountant with logical problems which may tax his ingenuity.

(b) Such problems are overcome by patience, concentration on one item at a time, and careful recording of all steps taken.

(c) The steps to be taken are:
 (i) Prepare opening statement of affairs.
 (ii) Prepare working schedules.
 (iii) Prepare accounts.

POINTS TO NOTE

11. (a)   Students find incomplete records difficult. The only way of mastering the subject is constant practice and rigid following of the steps in paragraph 5. Neat work with adequate descriptions of all figures is essential.

SELF TESTING QUESTIONS

(a)   List the stages on the preparation of financial statements when proper bookkeeping methods are employed. (5).

(b)   When financial statements are prepared from incomplete records what working papers may be required? (5).

(c)   What is a statement of affairs? (7a).

(d)   What will appear in the "Cash in till" working paper? (9a).

(e)   What is the relationship between sales in the trading account and cash received from customers? (9b).

(f)   What are the essential requirements for success in incomplete records preparation? (5d, e).

Exercises (Answers begin on page 459)

1.   The following data relates to the businesses of Hugh and Heather and Munro at 31 December 19-4:

	Hugh	Heather	Munro
Stock	23,670	146,549	23,211
Debtors	13,652	98,762	35,327
Cash in hand	2,543	1,548	Nil
Creditors	42,411	69,820	28,567
Bank	Dr 21,783	Cr 2,540	Cr 1,321
Fixed assets at cost	54,844	38,700	50,050
Accumulated depreciation	17,540	21,734	41,450
Accrued electricity	641		105
Prepayment of rates		1,580	

Calculate for each the capital at 31 December 19-4.

2.   The capitals of the businesses of Hengist and Horsa at 31 March 19-5 were £34,830 and £76,110.

In the year ending 31 March 19-6:

Profit of Hengist was £21,860 and his drawings £20,100.

The drawings of Horsa were £12,099 and his capital at 31 March 19-6 was £80,200.

Calculate, for Hengist his capital at 31 March 19-6 and for Horsa, his profit for the year ending 31 March 19-6.

3.   The following relate to the businesses of Alan, Beth and Claire:

	Alan	Beth	Claire
Debtors at 31 December 19-2	12,650	34,768	20,800
Sales 19-3	102,650	?	102,500
Cash received from debtors	98,500	41,820	?
Discounts allowed	4,300	830	1,762
Contras	2,699	–	1,004
Debtors at 31 December 19-3	?	36,391	22,500

Calculate the amounts labelled "?".

4.   The following relate to the businesses of Leon, Mary and Sue

	Leon	Mary	Sue
Cash in till at 31 December 19-4	1,600	Nil	2,490
Payments into bank in total in 19-5	102,564	96,450	64,237
Payments into bank which were not from customers	10,000	6,400	2,000
Total sales	114,004	99,700	?
Cash payments from till for expenses	7,400	4,320	3,100
Cash in till 31 December 19-5	1,350	1,500	800
Drawings in cash	?	6,800	8,000
Debtors at 31 December 19-4	Nil	7,500	2,431
Debtors at 31 December 19-5	Nil	?	2,800

Calculate the items labelled "?".

5. The following data relates to the business of Geoff, Winnie and Ron:

	Geoff	Winnie	Ron
Sales in 19-8	100,060	?	154,800
Stock 31 December 19-7	23,859	14,542	32,692
Stock 31 December 19-8	?	16,740	27,750
Purchases in 19-8	74,610	?	?
Gross profit/sales ratio	25%	30%	?
Creditors 31 December 19-7	Nil	28,590	16,560
Creditors 31 December 19-8	Nil	31,562	18,630
Payments to creditors in 19-8	74,610	176,932	92,400

Calculate the items labelled "?".

6. Hunter is a wholesaler of furniture. A balance sheet of his business at 1st January 1979 showed the following figures:

	£		£
Capital	9,420	Fixed assets – cost	6,000
Furniture suppliers	2,300	Depreciation	2,500
Rent	100		3,500
		Stock	6,200
		Debtors	1,500
		Bank	620
	11,820		11,820

Proper books were not kept but an analysis of his bank statements revealed:

	£
Lodgements	
From customers	15,180
Legacy	1,100
Sale of motor car	400
Cheques drawn	
To suppliers	9,730
Rent	700
Other overheads	2,050
Drawings	2,200
New car	2,600

A small black book was kept and this showed that before banking the cash and cheques received from customers, £1,000 was paid out for purchases and £200 for personal drawings.

Rent is £1,000 a year.

At 31st December 1979, the following figures were computed:

Debtors	£2,300
Stock	£7,800
Creditor for furniture	£3,950

Depreciation is at 15% on the reducing instalment method. The original cost of the car sold was £1,500 and its written down value was £500.

Required:
(a) A trading and profit and loss account for the year ending 31st December 1979.
(b) A balance sheet as at that date. (RSA)

7.   Ken Jones, who has not kept a complete set of books for his business. has asked you to prepare his accounts and has been able to provide the following information:

	31st May	
	1982	1983
	£	£
Plant and machinery	31,500	35,350
Stock in trade	15,120	17,255
Trade debtors	11,396	13,020
Trade creditors	6,020	6,468
Rates paid in advance	-	350
Rent accrued	910	1,750
Expenses accrued	840	1,050

Jones pays all cash received into the bank and makes all payments by cheque. A summary of his bank statements for the year is shown below:

	£		£
Balance b/f	1,834	Creditors	119,112
Cash sales	116,592	Wages	18,669
Debtors	57,134	Rent	5,250
		Rates	1,750
		Expenses	11,382
		New machinery	7,000
		Drawings	7,560
		Balance c/f	4,837
	175,560		175,560

Jones had noted during the year that he had allowed discounts of £2,205 to debtors and had been allowed to deduct £4,578 for early payment of suppliers' accounts.

Required:
Prepare Ken Jones' trading and profit and loss accounts for the year ended 31st May 1983, and his balance sheet at that date.
                                                                                    (AAT)

Exercises without answers
8.   The following data relates to the businesses of Ian Bryan and Miller at 31 December 19-4:

	Ian	Bryan	Miller
Stock	1,567	12,547	?
Debtors	3,658	5,929	17,543
Cash in hand	100	652	786
Creditors	6,430	2,431	43,537
Bank	Cr 104	Dr 4,328	Cr 9,435
Fixed assets at cost	20,000	7,490	23,657
Accumulated depreciation	12,000	3,459	8,542
Accruals	768	1,432	1,809
Capital	?	?	3,457

Calculate for each the item labelled "?" at 31 December 19-4.

9.   The capitals of the businesses of Wat and Tyler at 31 March 19-5 were £54,690 and £43,260.

In the year ending 31 March 19-6:

The loss of Wat, was £15,547 and his drawings £19,400.

The drawings of Tyler were £7,600 and his capital at 31 March 19-6 was £48,769.

Calculate, for Wat, his capital at 31 March 19-6 and for Tyler, his profit for the year ending 31 March 19-6.

10. *The following relate to the businesses of Minnie, Mo and Mell:*

	Minnie	Mo	Mell
Debtors at 31 December 19-2	65,760	35,239	43,918
Sales 19-3	?	102,454	194,000
Cash received from debtors	201,657	93,509	?
Discounts allowed	3,436	Nil	1,522
Contras	1,200	768	333
Debtors at 31 December 19-3	71,345	?	51,999

Calculate the amounts labelled "?".

11. *The following relate to the businesses of Harpo, Chico and Groucho:*

	Harpo	Chico	Groucho
Cash in till at 31 December 19-4	23	1,543	2,400
Payments into bank in total in 19-5	105,399	9,700	33,295
Payments into bank which were not from customers	12,544	2,000	4,321
Total sales	?	18,000	51,00
Cash payments from till for expenses	2,400	?	7,600
Cash in till 31 December 19-5	76	240	3,129
Drawings in cash	5,000	6,600	?
Debtors at 31 December 19-4	3,200	4,500	23,100
Debtors at 31 December 19-5	4,300	2,345	22,470

Calculate the items labelled "?".

12. *The following data relates to the businesses of Berry, Blue and Carol:*

	Berry	Blue	Carol
Sales in 19-8	?	74,500	?
Stock 31 December 19-7	17,500	23,581	22,456
Stock 31 December 19-8	18,439	19,760	24,782
Purchases in 19-8	?	36,100	67,890
Gross profit/sales ratio	20%	?	40%
Creditors 31 December 19-7	23,456	10,400	?
Creditors 31 December 19-8	27,589	?	22,456
Payments to creditors in 19-8	78,799	34,690	66,231

Calculate the items labelled "?".

13. John Emery is a sole trader who does not operate a full double entry system of bookkeeping, but the records he does keep are accurate, and from them the following figures have been extracted:

	30 Sept 1980	30 Sept 1981
	£	£
Fixtures and fittings	400	360
Stock	1,280	1,490
Cash at bank	720	940
Cash in hand	30	40

On 30th September 1980, debtors amounted to £1,460. Cash received from debtors for the year ended 30th September 1981 - £6,390. Sales for the same period totalled £5,950.

On 30th September 1980, creditors amounted to £1,040. Cash paid to creditors for the year ended 30th September 1981 - £4,130. Purchases for the same period totalled £3,980.

During the year ended 30th September 1981 no bad debts were incurred. In addition there was no discount allowed or received.

Required:
  (a) Calculate debtors and creditors as at 30th September 1981.
  (b) Calculate John Emery's capital as at 30th September 1980 and 30th September 1981.
  (c) Calculate John Emery's net profit for the year ended 30th September 1981, allowing for the fact that his drawings during that period amounted to £1,250.   *(LCCI)*

14. *David Denton set up in business as a plumber a year ago, and he has asked you to act as his accountant. His instructions to you are in the form of the following letter.*

Dear Henry,

I was pleased when you agreed to act as my accountant and look forward to your first visit to check my records. The proposed fee of £250 pa is acceptable. I regret that the paperwork for the work done during the year is incomplete. I started my business on 1st January last, and put £6,500 into a business bank account on that date. I brought my van into the firm at that time, and reckon that it was worth £3,600 then. I think it will last another three years after the end of the first year of business use.

I have drawn £90 per week from the business bank account during the year. In my trade it is difficult to take a holiday, but my wife managed to get away for a while. The travel agents bill for £280 was paid out of the business account. I bought the lease of the yard and office for £6,500. The lease has ten years to run, and the rent is only £300 a year payable in advance on the anniversary of the date of purchase, which was 1st April. I borrowed £4,000 on that day from Aunt Jane to help pay for the lease. I have agreed to pay her 10% interest per annum, but I have been to busy to do anything about this yet.

I was lucky enough to meet Miss Prism shortly before I set up on my own, and she has worked for me as an office organiser right from the start. She is paid a salary of £3,000 pa. All the bills for the year have been carefully preserved in a tool box, and we analysed them last week. The materials I have bought cost me £9,600, but I reckon there was £580 worth left in the yard on 31st December. I have not paid for them all yet. I think we owed £714 to the suppliers on 31st December. I was surprised to see that I had spent £4,800 on plumbing equipment, but it should last me five years or so. Electricity bills received up to 30th September came to £1,122, but motor expenses were £912, and general expenses £1,349 for the year. The insurance premium for the year to 31st March next was £800. All these have been paid by cheque but Miss Prism has lost the rate demand. I expect the Local Authority will send a reminder soon since I have not yet paid. I seem to remember that rates came to £180 for the year to 31st March next.

Miss Prism sent out bills to my customers for work done, but some of them are very slow to pay. Altogether the charges made were £29,863, but only £25,613 had been received by 31st December. Miss Prism thinks that 10% of the remaining bills are not likely to be paid. Other customers for jobs too small to bill have paid £3,418 in cash for work done, but I only managed to bank £2,600 of this money. I used £400 of the difference to pay the family's grocery bills, and Miss Prism used the rest for general expenses, except for £123 which was left over in a drawer in the office on 31st December.
Kind regards,
Yours sincerely,
David.

Required:
Draw up a profit and loss account for the year ended 31st December, and a balance sheet as at that date. (ACCA)

15. *Whilst Jim Pond, a retailer, does not maintain a full set of accounting records, the following information has been obtained concerning his business activities during the year ended 31st March 1980.*

  (a) Payments to suppliers which totalled £24,440, covered not only goods purchased but also goods costing £500 withdrawn from the business by Jim Pond for his own use and not included in the cost of goods sold or sales.
  (b) Gross profit has been at a uniform rate of $33\frac{1}{3}$% of the cost of goods sold.
  (c) Staff wages paid amounted to £3,200.
  (d) Rent, rates, light and heat payments totalled £960.
  (e) Administrative expenses paid were £660.
  (f) There were no disposals of fixed assets during the year.
  (g) On 31st March 1980, Jim Pond received a loan of £2,000 for his business from uncle, Tom Stream.
  (h) With the exception of the loan, the source of all cash received was trade debtors.
  (i) All cash received has been banked in the business account except for £4,800 taken by Jim Pond for his cash drawings.

Fixtures and fittings, amounted to £2,500 at 31st March 1979, and £3,400 a year later, the provision for depreciation was £750 at 31st March 1979.

Depreciation is provided annually at the rate of 10% on the cost of assets held at each accounting year end.

Jim Pond's net current assets at 31st March 1979, and 1980 were as follows:

31st March		£	£	£	£
Stock in trade, at cost			4,000		3,000
Trade debtors			3,800		2,180
Prepayments – rent			70		120
Balance at bank			–		620
			7,870		5,920
Less	Bank overdraft	2,040		–	
	Trade creditors	3,310		3,870	
	Amounts accrued due – elect	40	5,390	30	3,900
			2,480		2,020

Required:

(i)   Jim Pond's bank account for the year ended 31st March 1980 in as much detail as possible.

(ii)   Jim Pond's trading and profit and loss account for the year ended 31st March 1980, and balance sheet as at that date.

(iii) Why is it important to distinguish between fixed and current assets in accounting?   (ACCA)

16. *The summarised balance sheet at 30th September 1978, of John Bowers, retailer, is as follows:*

	£		£	£
Capital account		Fixtures and fittings:		
J. Bowers	15,600	At cost	11,000	
		Less Aggregate		
		depreciation	6,600	4,400
		Stock in trade		9,000
Trade creditors	2,130	Trade debtors		2,100
Accrued charges (electricity)	230	Prepayments (rates)		260
		Balance at bank		2,200
	17,960			17,960

Although Jim Bowers does not keep a full set of accounting records, his business transactions during the financial year ended 30th September 1979 are summarised as follows:

(a) *Sales totalled £95,830 and sales returns £880; trade debtors at 30th September 1979, amounted to £4,400.*

(b) *Gross profit amounted to 2/9th of net sales revenue.*

(c) *Stock in trade, at cost, at 30th September 1979, shows an increase of £6,000 over that of a year earlier.*

(d) *Trade creditors at 30th September 1979, amounted to £3,970; discounts received from suppliers totalled £450 for the year under review.*

(e) *Payments for rent, rates, light and heat totalled £6,830 and wages payments £8,250 for the year ended 30th September 1979.*

(f) *At 30th September 1979, rent prepaid amounted to £320 and electricity charges accrued due were £270.*

(g) *On 30th September 1979, a loan of £2,000 was received from L. Pond.*

(h) *Additions to fixtures and fittings during the year cost £1,500 cash.*

(i) *Cash drawings amounted to £4,000 and, in addition, John Bowers withdrew from the business goods for his own use which had cost £310. Whilst these goods were paid for in the payments made to suppliers, the goods withdrawn by John Bowers for his own use were not included in the cost of the goods sold or sales.*

(j) *It has been decided to make a provision for doubtful debts at 30th September 1979, of 2¼% of trade debtors.*

(k) *Depreciation is provided annually on fixtures and fittings at the rate of 10% on the cost of assets held at the relevant accounting year end.*

Required:
   (i) From the figures and information above compile John Bowers' trading and profit and loss account for the year ended 30th September 1979, and a balance sheet as at that date.

   (ii) Give reasons which could be advanced to John Bowers in favour of keeping a full set of accounting records.
                                                                                        (ACCA)

17. *Since commencing business several years ago as a cloth dealer, Tom Smith has relied on annual receipts and payments accounts for assessing progress. These accounts have been prepared from his business bank account through which all business receipts and payments are passed.*

Tom Smith's receipts and payments account for the year ended 31st March 1980 is as follows:

	£		£
Opening balance	1,680	Drawings	6,300
Sales receipts	42,310	Purchases payments	37,700
Proceeds of sale from grandfather clock	870	Motor van expenses	2,900
Loan from John Scott	5,000	Workshop: rent	700
Closing balance	1,510	rates	570
		Wages – John Jones	3,200
	51,370		51,370

Additional information:
   (a) The grandfather clock sold during the year ended 31st March 1980 was a legacy received by Tom Smith from the estate of his late father.

   (b) The loan from John Scott was received on 1st January 1980; interest is payable on the loan at the rate of 10% per annum.

   (c) In May 1980 Tom Smith received from his suppliers a special commission of 5% of the cost of purchases during the year ended 31st March 1980.

   (d) On 1st October 1979, Tom Smith engaged John Jones as a salesman. In addition to his wages, Jones receives a bonus of 2% of the business's sales during the period of his employment; the bonus is payable on 1st April and 1st October in respect of the immediately preceding six month's period.

   Note: *It can be assumed that sales have been at a uniform level throughout the year ended 31st March 1980.*

   (e) In addition to the items mentioned above, the assets and liabilities of Tom Smith were as follows:

At 31st March	1979	1980
	£	£
Motor van, at cost	4,000	4,000
Stock in trade, at cost	5,000	8,000
Trade debtors	4,600	12,290
Motor vehicle expenses prepaid	-	100
Workshop rent accrued due	-	200
Trade creditors	2,900	2,200

   (f) It can be assumed that the opening and closing balances in the above receipts and payments account require no adjustment for the purposes of Tom Smith's accounts.

   (g) As from 1st April 1979, it has been decided to provide for depreciation on the motor van annually at the rate of 20% of the cost.

Required:
The trading and profit and loss account for the year ended 31st December 1980, and a balance sheet at that date of Tom Smith.
                                                                                        (ACCA)

Accounting Systems and Electronic Data Processing

This part of the manual has but one Chapter and is concerned with the impact of computers on accounting and bookkeeping.

32. Computerised Accounting

INTRODUCTION

1.   Traditionally businesses have produced their business documents, kept their books and prepared their annual accounts manually. In recent years the computer has been used in many businesses to perform some or all of these tasks.

2.   The basic principles of business documentation, books of account and annual financial statements remain *unchanged* by the advent of the computer.

3.   Procedures are in some ways different in computer systems from those in manual systems.

4.   Computer processing speeds have meant that more information can be obtained from computer systems. Some examples are given later in the chapter.

5.   This chapter considers computerised accounting under the following heads:

- Manual and computerised systems compared
- Files
- Terminology
- New facilities

6.   The difference between manual systems and computer systems can be easily seen by diagrams:

Manual Systems

1	Document preparation	Sales invoices, purchase invoices, cheque stubs, paying-in book counterfoils, etc.
2	Enter in books of prime entry	Sales day book, purchase day book, cash book, etc.
3	Post to ledger accounts	Sales ledger, purchase ledger, nominal ledger
4	Extract trial balance (and find difference!)	
5	Prepare list of adjustments	Prepayments, accruals, depreciation, etc.
6	Prepare annual accounts	Profit and Loss Account Balance Sheet

7.   *Computerised systems*
While one manual system does not differ much in practice from other manual systems, computerised systems vary a great deal both in the extent of computerisation and in method. A typical sales ledger system is shown in Fig. 32.1.

8.   Note the principal difference between this and a manual system:

(a)   Minimal data (customers name *or* code and items sold) need to be input.

(b)   The use of files (customer details, stock details) with frequently used information on disc which the computer can access.

(c)   Automatic (and 100% accurate) calculation.

(d)   Automatic printing of invoices and other documents.

(e)   Automatic updating of files (eg. outstanding invoices, cash book, nominal ledger accounts) held on disc.

(f)   Automatic balancing.

(g)   to some extent, the computer can check the validity of input data (e.g. consecutive numbers of documents, customers are on customer file, stock sold is on stock file) but will always do exactly as it is programmed to do. For example, if the docket says 1,000 typewriters sold to XYZ plc when it should be 10, then 1,000 will be invoiced but in a manual system the invoice typist would query the number.

---

1.   Prepare pre-numbered sales dockets manually indicating customer, customer order number, items sold.

2.   *Batch* the dockets daily and input the data into the computers on a *terminal* with a visual display unit (*VDU*).

3.   The computer will:

    (a)   Check the data by: (for example)

        - Consulting *files* to see if the customer is a recognised one and the items sold are items on the stock file.
        - Verifying the consecutiveness of the sales docket numbers.

    (b)   Calculate the amount of the invoice by:

        - Obtaining prices from the price *file*
        - Extending price x quantity
        - Sum the items
        - add VAT

    (c)   Print the invoice set using the data above and the name and address of the customer from the customer *file*.

    (d)   Store the information in an outstanding invoices file.

    (e)   Update the sales account.

    (f)   Update the "items in stock" file.

4.   On receipt of cash the data (cash and discount) will be input to the computer which will:

    (a)   Match the cash and discount information to the outstanding invoices file and eliminate items which correspond.

    (b)   Update the cash book file.

Fig. 32.1 – A computer sales ledger system

(h)   Information is held on magnetic media which is not available for inspection unless called up on the VDU. This is, of course, easily done.

(i)   Much information is only held temporarily: e.g. the outstanding invoice file is emptied of paid invoices.

(j)   The information can be input by staff ignorant of bookkeeping and the bookkeeping is done by the computer whereas manual systems require trained staff.

(k)   Other systems (e.g. continuous inventory) can be updated simultaneously at no cost.

You will note that this system does not keep conventional sales ledger accounts for individual customers but only a file of unpaid invoices. This is a common approach but conventional sales ledger accounts can be kept by computer systems.

FILES

9.   Computerised accounting requires the maintenance of numerous *files*. A file is a collection of *records*. Examples of files found in accounting systems include:

File	*Records*
Sales Ledger Balances	Individual customers balances
Customer	Details of individual customers (e.g. name, addresses, credit limit, credit status, etc)
Price	Price of each product
Supplier	Individual supplier's details
Outstanding invoices	Individual unpaid sales invoice details
Personnel	Details of each employee
Stock	Details of balance of each stock line

All the above are sometimes called *master* files.

Other files are called *transaction* files, e.g.

File	*Records*
Sales invoices	Details of individual invoices
Debit bank	Details of bankings
Credit bank	Details of cheques drawn
Payroll	Details of a weeks wage payments

The difference between *master* files and transaction files are:

(i)   Master files contain data in current use, e.g. outstanding balances, pay rates, prices, whereas transaction files are of utility in preparing a profit and loss account but are essentially of a historical nature.

(ii)   In computer systems, master files are kept in magnetic files (usually now discs) but transaction files are retained only in the form of print outs.

TERMINOLOGY

10.   Many students are put off computing by the problem of *terminology*. In practice some ideas and things found only in computing systems must be found names (e.g. boot up, magnetic disc) and some computer people enjoy using a vocabulary which mystifies other people. Here are a few words which may be useful:

Applications - particular computer program or set (suite) of computer programs applied to a specific area, e.g. sales or wages.

Application controls - controls designed to aid the completeness, accuracy and validity of processing in a particular application.

For example, if details of advice notes are input with details including the serial number, the computer can check that all serial numbers are present thus ensuring the completeness of processing.

Back-up - procedures for copying and storage of data, programs and files so that recovery can be made from loss of data from systems malfunction, errors or sabotage.

BASIC - a very common high level language used in micro systems.

Batch processing - a system of processing where similar data are grouped together and processed at one go. For example, all the week's invoices might be processed on Friday afternoon.

This method can be used in manual systems also and commonly is so. Contrast real time and on line systems.

Disc - A device looking like a gramophone record which is used to store data in magnetic form. Discs can be hard (and expensive) or floppy (and cheap). They are used with a disc drive.

Distributed processing - the use of more than one computer to do a firm's processing. Methods vary and may involve every department having its own micro and suite of programs.

Dumping - the copying of computer held files onto separate magnetic media or on to a print out. The objective is to aid in the recovery of data lost due to error, malfunction or sabotage.

Field - an item of data within a record, e.g. the invoice number or the customer code on an invoice.

File conversion - the process of converting files (e.g. sales ledger balances) from manual records to magnetic form.

Floppy discs - small flexible discs for storage of data and files.

Front end processing - the use of one computer for limited processing (e.g. validity check) before transmission to a larger computer for processing proper.

General controls - a somewhat vague term meaning the use of procedures designed to maintain a high standard of discipline within the computer environment. They relate to proper development and implementation of applications, and the integrity of program and data files, and of computer operations. They may be manual or programmed.

Grandfather, father, son - a rule whereby files are not overwritten for three generations. For example, a disc carrying the sales ledger balances each month could be overwritten but if three discs (say January, February, March) are retained the loss of one can be recovered by using the previous one.

This highlights one of the differences between manual and computer systems. Manual systems produce permanent *hard copy* records (ledgers, day books, etc), which are hard to destroy or lose (except by fire or theft). Computer systems produce magnetic discs which can be *overwritten* or lost or destroyed by excessive dust, heat or magnetic devices.

Hardware - the physical equipment both mechanical and electronic.

Hash total - a total which is useful (e.g. it can be compared with a total derived elsewhere) but which has no meaning. An example is the sum of all invoice numbers in March. If these are totalled in the invoicing department and then again by computer, it will be known if all the invoices have been processed.

Computers can do sequence checks or add up a series of numbers easily and quickly so that accuracy and completeness are more easily maintained than on manual systems.

Integrity - the state of being correct, complete or uncorrupted. Computer held files can be altered: in error, invalidly, or with moral turpitude.

Alterations to manual records are more obvious.

Interactive - a mode of processing which involves a series of prompts from the computer to which the user responds and in which the user can condition the way the computer processes data.

This is why less skilled staff can be used.

Keyboard - the typewriter-like device through which data can be input to the computer or instructions given to it.

Language - a coding system by a programmer which can be translated into a series of operations by the computer. Well known languages include Cobol, Algol, Fortran, BASIC.

Logs - a record of applications processed on a computer, often produced automatically by the computer.

Magnetic media - storage devices for computer data or files. In commercial systems discs are used but domestically tapes are still common.

Main frame computers - large computers with many connections, e.g. numerous terminals, hard disc drives, printers, etc. Often they require special environments such as air-conditioning, temperature control, etc.

Menu - choices of processing offered to a user on a monitor.

Micro - a small cheap computer. They are now so powerful that for many applications, large main frames are becoming obsolete.

Operating system - the permanently held programs which control the use of applications programs and provide standarised facilities to the facility, such as copying files and giving choices of menu.

On line - a system of processing whereby each transaction can be input when it occurs. Compare with batch processing.

> Manual systems can be entered in this mode, e.g. every sales invoice can be entered in the day book as it is typed. But *batch* processing is more common.

Packaged programs - a set of programs written by a software house and sold to users to provide standard processing facilities.

Parallel running - where new programs are used to process data but manual processing continues until it can be certain that the computer program is successful.

Pilot running - implementation of a new system in small stages to ensure each works satisfactorily before the next stage is tried.

> Manual systems generally work from day one as human beings are very flexible and adaptable. Computer systems are much harder to get to work reliably and smoothly. Thus the *implementation* of computer systems is difficult, costly and takes time.

Program - a set of instructions which a computer can follow to carry out processing. Programs can be written in machine code or in high level languages.

Real time - a system of processing where transactions are input, processing is done and files up-dated as the transactions occur. Examples include airline bookings.

> The great advantage of real time systems is that 100% up to date files are available (e.g. what is in stock? What is a customer's balance?). Contrast on-line with real time. On line does not necessarily mean that *all* files are immediately updated.

Record - a sub division of a file. For example a sales ledger file consists of a set of customers' accounts.

Remote terminal - a terminal that is geographi-cally separate from a computer it interacts with. Connection will be by land line, telephone line or some more exotic method.

Run to run controls - a control whereby data (e.g. a real or hash total) is calculated for a file and checked again by the computer each time that file or set of data is processed.

Service bureau - an organisation offering data processing facilities to others.

Software - programs and systems.

Systematic errors - errors caused by program faults or hardware malfunction. They tend to recur as there is no human intervention in processing.

Systems analysis - the art, science or profession of investigating, analysing, designing and implementing computer systems.

Terminals - devices usually consisting of typewriter-like keyboards and TV-like screens (the monitor) for interacting with a computer.

Test packs - sets of data used by an auditor to test the operation of a client's computer program. It may consist of a set of typical transactions processed by the program under test.

Turn key - a total package sold to an organisation by a software house comprising hardware and user programs. In theory the user merely has to turn a key to start processing.

Users - any users of computer programs. Often used to distinguish people or departments responsible for a function (e.g. wages, purchasing) from the computer department who process for them.

Utility program - a generalised computer program providing common facilities to computer users. Examples are copying files or programs, sorting files and text editing.

Visual Display Unit (VDU) - a device similar to a TV screen on which information on computer files can be displayed.

NEW FACILITIES

11. A feature of computerised accounting is the ability of the systems to produce new information rapidly and very cheaply. Examples are:

   (a) Invoices can be analysed to produce data on sales: by type and quantity, to different types of customer, sales by region, by value, etc.

   (b) Outstanding invoices can be analysed by date, customers, region, etc.

   (c) Stock records can be maintained so that management or operational personnel can instantly determine the amount of every item in stock.

   (d) Automatic signalling of important information can be made, e.g. overdue accounts, stocks at re-order levels.

   (e) *Models* can be built. For example, the effect on stock levels, debtor levels, bank balance and creditor levels can be forecasted at different levels of activity by building a set of accounts on a *spread sheet* program.

All of these functions can be produced by manual systems but the cost in terms of time and wages is often too great. For example stock records in a firm wholesaling 2,000 different types of product is desirable but prohibitively expensive by hand as it would require a full time clerk who would often be behind with the recordings. However a computer system can do it easily, quickly and cheaply, in effect, as a by-product of the processing of purchase and sales invoices.

SUMMARY

12. (a) Bookkeeping is still done manually in many firms but the computer can now be used for bookkeeping and has become very common.

   (b) The basic principles of bookkeeping are unchanged by computer systems.

   (c) There are many differences between computer and manual bookkeeping systems including:

- minimal data entry	- retention of data
- use of master data files	- corruptibility of data
- accuracy of calculation	- integrity of data
- automatic printing	- batch, on-line and real time processing
- one-step up date of files	- complexity of systems
- automatic balancing	- difficulty in designing and implementing systems
- validity checks (completeness, accuracy, authorisation	- remote access to data
	- use of service bureau
- problem of access to data	- extra facilities
- temporary storage	
- use of unskilled staff	

   (d) The concept of separate files (master and transaction) is important to computer systems.

   (e) Computer people use a vocabulary which can (is perhaps designed to) confuse mere accountants.

(f) New facilities can be obtained using computers, e.g.:

- analyses
- stock records
- real time systems – these are especially used in banks and other financial service companies and in the holiday, hotel and airline industries.
- remote access. A cash point in Newcastle can give me instant bad news about my bank balance in Wolverhampton.
- automatic signalling of important data
- model building.

POINTS TO NOTE

13. (a) Many syllabuses now include computerised accounting. Examiners have not found it easy to design suitable questions but questions are likely to increase in sophistication as time goes on. Courses with continuous assessment nearly always include the use of standard accounting software (eg Pegasus or Sage Soft and the use of a spreadsheet package.

(b) It is true that bookkeeping can be done on a menu driven interactive computer system by people ignorant of bookkeeping. However, some knowledge of bookkeeping is required to interpret much of the output, e.g. overdue accounts listing, and even more in trying to match unpaid sales invoices with unmatched credit notes, cash and discounts. At the level of accounts preparation and management accounting, professional accountants will be in even greater demand as more facilities become available, e.g. more frequent production of financial statements, greater analyses of data and model building.

(c) Computer systems can do many more things than manual systems and do them more quickly. However, they also cause far more chaos unless they are carefully designed and implemented. In particular:

   (i) Off the peg systems do not always work well.

   (ii) Implementation takes time (often many months) and care.

   (iii) File conversion (e.g. the manual sales ledger file to a computer file) has to be carefully done and checked.

   (iv) Master file data (e.g. a price or a wage rate) will be used forever until it is changed. If it is wrong then serious consequences can occur. In manual systems the clerk will often recognise an item in error, using that marvel of nature, the human mind. Computer systems, unless specially programmed to recognise particular errors, cannot recognise an error when it sees one.

(d) An advantage of computer systems is that they can maintain stock records. If they can be done in value terms then total stock value can be obtained from the computer. This enables financial statements such as trading and profit and loss accounts and balance sheets to be produced much more frequently, perhaps weekly. This seems to be good for businesses who can take remedial action if they know results are unsatisfactory and for accountants who become even more centre stage.

(e) Analysis is cheap and easy. Two examples:

   (i) A weekly list with cumulative annual totals of the four principal customers of our 24 best selling products.

   (ii) A list of all customers who have not purchased product X in the last six months.

Both these lists can be produced manually at great cost but can be produced almost cost free on the computer.

SELF TESTING QUESTIONS

(a) What changes in principle occur on a switch from manual to computer book-keeping and accounting? (2).

(b) State the meaning and the implications for bookkeeping of the following terms:

- *batch*
- *terminal*
- *VDU*
- *files*
- *update*
- *input*
- *output*
- *matching of data*
- *minimal data input*
- *real time*
- *hard copy*
- *software*

- *interactive*
- *implementation*
- *systematic errors*
- *users*
- *spread sheets*
- *automatic signalling*
- *automatic action*
- *validity*
- *completeness*
- *authorisation*
- *master file*
- *transaction files*

- *records*
- *applications*
- *on-line*
- *file conversion*
- *hardware*
- *hash totals*
- *menu*
- *remote terminals*
- *fraud*
- *model building*
- *analysis of data*

(c) List the differences between manual and computer bookkeeping systems mentioned in this chapter.

(d) Contrast the roles of bookkeepers and accountants in manual and computer systems.

Exercises (Answers begin on page 459)

1.   The following is a sample purchase ledger computer application.

(a) Purchase invoices are batched monthly by Janet who:

(i)   Compares the details with goods inward notes.
(ii)   Checks correspondence with approved copy orders.
(iii)   Writes on consecutive numbers.
(iv)   Writes on the supplier code from a list (e.g. J724 for Thomas Jones & Son Limited).
(iv)   Writes on the expense code from a list (e.g. 24 for raw material purchases, 37 for heating and lighting).

(b) The details are input to the computer by Jim on a terminal. Input details are:

(i)   Consecutive number.
(ii)   Supplier's code.
(iii)   Expense code.
(iv)   Invoice net amount.
(v)   VAT.
(vi)   Invoice gross amount.

(c) The computer:

(i)   Checks the number is consecutive.
(ii)   Puts the suppliers name on the screen.
(iii)   Checks the expense code exists.
(iv)   Compares invoice net, VAT and invoice gross.

(d) The computer then:

(i)   Updates the nominal ledger file.
(ii)   Updates the Customs and Excise balance file.
(iii)   Updates the invoices payable file.
(iv)   Prints "remittance advices" for each supplier listing the invoices payable and the total due.
(v)   Prints cheques to be sent with the remittance advices. These are signed by two directors.

Required:
(a) Outline a manual system to do the same thing.
(b) List the ways in which the computer system differs from the manual system.

2. A sample spread sheet program has cells as follows:

Jamie and Co

Forecast trading Account for the next three periods

		A	B	C	D	E	F	G
1.	Sales			9,000		C1 x 1.05		E1 x 1.06
2.	Op.St.		1,500		B5		D5	
3.	Purchases		B4 – B2		D4 – D2		F4 – F2	
4.			B5 + C5		D5 + E5		F5 + G5	
5.	Cl.St.		B2 x 1.2	C1 – C6	D2 x 1.2	E1 – E6	D5 x 1.1	G1 – G6
6.	Gr. Prof			C1 x .4		E1 x .38		G1 x .37

Required:
(a) Complete the numbers in this spreadsheet (e.g. E1 will be 9,450).
(b) Consider how the use of a spreadsheet like this demonstrates a changing role for accountants in business.

Exercises without answers

3. James is in charge of the computerised accounting system of Philip. The system is completely computerised up to the trial balance.

In what ways will James use his knowledge of accounting and bookkeeping?

How might the system assist in ensuring the completeness of processing?

In what ways would a similar manual system incorporate controls to detect the accuracy of processing? Why is a computer system likely to be more accurate.

4. Julia's invoice payment system works like this:

(a) Amanda checks each incoming against goods inward notes and copy order forms and stamps a grid on it.

(b) The grid has spaces on it for supplier code; nominal code; consecutive number; cash discount offered/not offered; cash discount rate; cash discount latest date; cash discount; net payment. Amanda fills all these in.

(c) Sam enters the invoice details into the computer;

Invoice number; supplier code; nominal code; net amount; VAT; gross amount; discount; net payable.

(d) The printer prints cheques for those payments which attract discount and also produces a disk file for unpaid invoices. All the files (nominal ledger, cash book etc) are updated.

What errors might occur? How can these be avoided/detected?

Design a manual system to do the same things? How would it differ from the computer system?

Manufacturing and Accounting

The next part of the manual considers the measurement of profit and capital in a manufacturing business and also shows how the information collected in a costing system can be used both in measuring profit and in decision making.

Chapter 33 shows how profit is measured in a manufacturing enterprise using a manufacturing accounting.

Chapter 34 shows how stock is valued and the effect of differing valuation methods on profit measurement and on decision making.

Chapter 35 considers labour costs in calculating total costs used in profit measurement.

Chapter 36 is on the subject of overhead costs.

Chapter 37 deals with work in progress and its valuation in manufacturing accounts. This chapter also considers the valuation in accounts of long term contracts.

Finally Chapter 38 introduces marginal costing. The valuation of stocks and work in progress is considered and the uses of marginal costing in decision making are briefly reviewed.

33. Manufacturing Accounts

INTRODUCTION

1. Manufacturing businesses can be carried on by sole traders, partnerships, limited companies or with other modes of ownership. The specific problems of accounting for manufacturing activities are not affected by mode of ownership and as we have not yet dealt with partnership or companies we will prepare manufacturing accounts for sole traders.

2. The objectives of a manufacturing enterprise are:

   (a) To make a saleable product.
   (b) To sell the product.

Activity (b) is the same activity as that carried on by the trader. The difference is that instead of buying in saleable products from outside suppliers, the manufacturer makes the products himself. *The accountant therefore needs to substitute for purchases, the costs of goods manufactured.* This cost is derived from an account called the manufacturing account and shall begin with the preparation of a manufacturing account.

3. A special problem with manufacturing is the valuation of year end stocks of finished goods and work in progress, and we shall discuss this in later chapters.

THE MANUFACTURING ACCOUNT

4. The format of a manufacturing account is:

Richard, trading as The Widget Manufacturing Co
Manufacturing Account for the year ending 31 December 19-4

		£'000
Raw materials and components		
Opening stock		26
Purchases		134
Carriage on purchases		6
		166
Closing stock		30
Consumption		136
Direct labour		288
Other direct costs		16
Prime cost		440
Works overheads		
Rates	30	
Insurance	15	
Indirect labour	82	
Indirect materials, heat, light, power	16	
Repairs	14	
Miscellaneous	19	
Depreciation of factory	12	
Depreciation of plant	39	
		227
Factory inputs in the year		667
Add: Opening work in progress		19
		686
Less: Closing work in progress		24
Works cost of finished goods output		662

5. (a) *Raw materials and components* are those physical things which will actually form part of the finished product, eg wood, plastic, screws, glue, varnish, glass and cabinet fittings in a furniture factory.

   (b) *Direct labour* is the remuneration paid to production workers for work directly related to production. It will not include supervisory or clerical labour.

   (c) *Other direct costs* are costs incurred specifically for a particular product. Examples include royalties paid per unit for a copyright design and plant or tool hire charges for a particular job.

(d) *Prime cost* is an important concept in costing and consists of direct materials, direct labour and other direct costs.

(e) *Direct costs* are all those costs which can be directly identified with particular jobs, batches or products. For example, in the production of brass castings, direct costs are brass and the wages of the workers who tend the furnace, cast the brass, and clean, polish and pack the brass castings.

(f) *Works overheads* are all those costs which are incurred in operating the works but which cannot be identified directly with a particular job, batch or product. The heating and lighting in a pin factory is clearly related to production in general but is in practice impossible to relate to particular pins or batches of pins.

(g) *Indirect* labour will include remuneration paid to supervisors, clerks, maintenance people, cleaners etc.

(h) *Indirect materials* will include lubricating oil, spare parts for machinery, cleaning materials, maintenance materials etc.

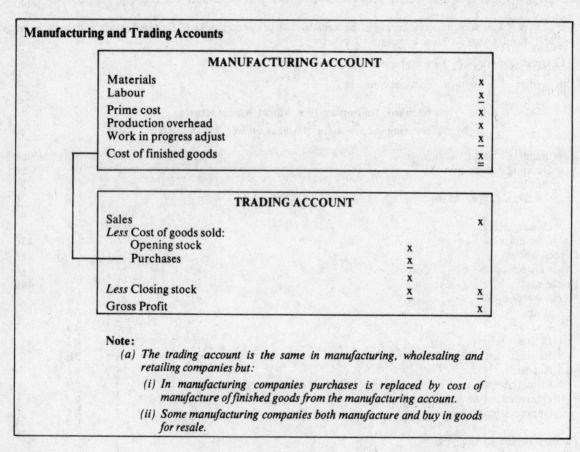

Fig. 33.1

(i) *Work in progress.* Some manufacturing processes are completed very quickly, for example, bread making or pin making. Some products take a long time to complete – we say that they have a long manufacturing cycle. Examples are aircraft, ships and heavy machine tools. Where the manufacturing cycle is longer than a day, there will always be some products at the day's end which are incomplete. These items are called work in progress. It is very difficult to value work in progress and we will cover this in a later chapter.

THE TRADING ACCOUNT OF A MANUFACTURING BUSINESS

6. In the previous section, the manufacturing account was used to build up and demonstrate the cost of the output of finished, saleable products from the factory. This output can be seen as being transferred to a warehouse where the goods are stored until they are sold.

7. The format of a trading account is:

Trading Accounting for the year ending 31st December 19–4

	£
Works cost of finished goods output transferred from the manufacturing account	662
Finished goods bought from outside supplier	104
Opening stock of finished goods	109
Available for sale	875
Less closing stock of finished goods	162
Cost of goods sold	713
Sales	1,138
Gross profit	£425

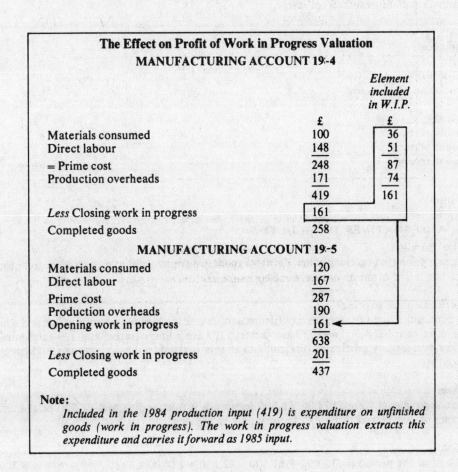

The Effect on Profit of Work in Progress Valuation
MANUFACTURING ACCOUNT 19–4

	£	*Element included in W.I.P.* £
Materials consumed	100	36
Direct labour	148	51
= Prime cost	248	87
Production overheads	171	74
	419	161
Less Closing work in progress	161	
Completed goods	258	

MANUFACTURING ACCOUNT 19–5

	£
Materials consumed	120
Direct labour	167
Prime cost	287
Production overheads	190
Opening work in progress	161
	638
Less Closing work in progress	201
Completed goods	437

Note:
Included in the 1984 production input (419) is expenditure on unfinished goods (work in progress). The work in progress valuation extracts this expenditure and carries it forward as 1985 input.

Fig. 33.2

8.   **Finished goods bought from outside suppliers**

(a) Many manufacturers also sell goods made by other manufacturers or imported from abroad, in addition to their own product.

(b) Stocks of finished goods are difficult to value and again we will deal with this subject in a later chapter.

THE PROFIT AND LOSS ACCOUNT OF A MANUFACTURING BUSINESS

9.   As a manufacturing business tends to be more complex in its administration than a purely trading business, non-manufacturing overheads are usually analysed into categories and sub-categories.

Here is a possible format:

	£	£
GROSS PROFIT		425
Administrative expenses		
Rates	6	
insurance	4	
Salaries	28	
Telephone	14	
Miscellaneous	19	
Depreciation	3	
	£74	
Selling expenses		
Salaries	26	
Commissions	31	
Advertising	43	
Motor expenses	16	
Depreciation of representatives' cars	26	
	£142	
Distribution costs		
Salaries	20	
Transport costs	41	
Depreciation of vehicles	30	
	£91	
Financial costs		
Loan interest	8	
Discount allowed	14	
Discount received	(3)	
	£19	
		326
NET PROFIT		£99

EXCEPTIONS, ALTERNATIVES, DIFFICULTIES

10. (a) **Physical parallels**

The assumption that on completion, finished goods are transferred to a separate warehouse to await sale is useful but is not often an accurate reflection of reality.

(b) **Apportionment of expenses**

Some examination questions require apportionment of overheads between manufacturing and other overheads. For example, rates are £18,000 and 7/9 are factory, 1/9 are administrative and 1/9 sales administration. This does not present any particular difficult but if this is combined with accruals and prepayments, care is required.

Example

Insurance payments were £15,000. £1,500 insurance is outstanding and £2,500 of the cost is in advance. Insurance is considered to be 4/5 factory and 1/5 office.

Solution

Total cost of the period is £15,000 + £1,500 − £2,500 = £14,000. Factory overheads will include £11,200. Office overheads will include £2,800.

(c) **Separate profit centres.** Some questions require the transfer of finished goods from the manufacturing account to the trading account to be at some arbitrary figure and not at cost. This transfer price may be based on some externally derived data such as the cost of competing products or it may be based on cost plus a percentage. Assuming the transfer is above cost, there will be profit in the manufacturing account and a reduced gross and net profit. The object of this process may be:

(i)   To compare the cost of production with some bench mark such as the possible buying in price.

(ii) To provide an incentive to the different sections of the enterprise.

(iii) To determine the separate contributions of the various sections to overall profit.

This process does present a small difficulty in that the closing stock of finished goods will be valued at above cost. This is appropriate in the manufacturing and trading accounts but not in the overall profit computation or in the balance sheet. Thus the excess of valuation over cost of finished stock must result in an entry:

Dr. Profit and loss account   (1)

Cr. Provision against profit in stock   (2)

The finished stock in the balance sheet will be valued at valuation less the provision. The opening stock will probably also be at above cost and an entry as:

Dr. Opening provision against profit in stock   (3)

Cr. Profit and loss account   (4)

will be required.

In practice entries (1) and (4) will appear as increase/(decrease) in provision against profit in finished goods stock.

SUMMARY

11. (a) Profit measurement in a manufacturing business is achieved through a series of accounts viz:

   The manufacturing account
   The trading account
   The profit and loss account.

(b) Manufacturing costs include direct materials, direct labour and other direct costs which collectively are called the prime cost. Manufacturing costs also include works (production or, manufacturing, or factory) overheads or indirect costs.

(c) The preparation of a manufacturing and trading account involves the valuation of:

   - Stocks of raw materials
   - Work in progress
   - Stock of finished goods

(d) Non-manufacturing costs are usually categorised into types. A division into administration costs, selling costs, distribution costs and financial costs is one such categorisation.

POINTS TO NOTE

12. (a) I have included separate manufacturing trading and profit and loss accounts in this chapter to emphasise the stages in the measurement of profit. In practice, these accounts can be separate or joined together as:

Herman Engineering
Manufacturing, Trading and Profit and Loss Account for the year ending 31st March 19--

	£
Raw materials consumed	x
Direct labour	x
Other direct costs	x
Prime cost	x
Works overheads	x
Total works input	x
Work in progress adjustment	x
Cost of finished goods produced	x
Finished goods bought in	x
Finished goods stock adjustment	x
Cost of goods sold	x
Sales	x
Gross profit	x
Non-manufacturing overheads	x
Net profit	x

(b) The provision against profits in stock discussed in paragraph 15(c) is considered difficult by students. In fact it is analogous to the provision for doubtful debts although I suppose that does not make it any easier!

(c) Many accountants consider that a global summary of all manufacturing operations for a whole year as illustrated in this chapter is of little value. They would prefer the accounts to be broken down into separate manufacturing accounts for individual products or groups of products or for the individual departments. Examiners usually ask for global accounts but segmented accounts are sometimes asked for.

(d) The manufacturing account concept draws upon the framework developed by cost accountants. This framework assumes that costs can be categorised into:

       Direct costs

       Indirect costs

Very often the distinction is clear in theory but difficult to make in practice. For example, electricity to power a machine may, in theory, be directly related to a specific item made on the machine but finding the quantity of electricity used requires data collection methods which would cost more than any possible benefit.

(e) The framework also assumes that the indirect costs can be categorised into:

       Manufacturing overheads

       Non-manufacturing overheads.

In practice a manufacturing concern is very complex and the sections of the enterprise - manufacturing, warehousing, the offices, selling and distribution - are not as separate and distinct as the framework assumes. Many costs, for example, rent and rates, can only be categorised by arbitrary assumptions.

SELF TESTING QUESTIONS

13. *(a) What is the relationship between 'purchases' in a trading business and 'cost of goods manufactured' in a manufacturing business? (2)*

(b) Draft a manufacturing account. (4)

(c) What is the meaning of the phrase 'direct costs'? (5)

(d) Give examples of indirect (i) labour, (ii) materials. (5)

(e) What is prime cost? (5)

(f) What are the difficulties involved in treating manufacturing and trading as separate profit centres? (10)

(g) What are the arguments against a global manufacturing account? (12)

(h) What assumptions underly the preparation of a manufacturing, trading and profit and loss account? (12)

EXERCISES (answers begin on page 461)

1. *From the following data prepare manufacturing, trading and profit and loss accounts for the businesses of Terri, Vic and Aled:*

	Terri	Vic	Aled
Stock of raw materials 1.1.-5	134	68	219
Work in progress 1.1.-5	68	108	245
Finished goods stock 1.1.-5	234	27	160
Purchases of raw materials	764	453	865
Stock of raw materials 31.12.-5	237	55	189
Work in progress 31.12.-5	73	123	221
Finished goods stock 31.12.-5	255	64	178
Direct labour	324	541	132
Direct expenses	39	54	21
Plant and machinery at cost	654	320	941
Accumulated depreciation	389	101	431
Indirect labour	106	238	98
Works overheads	254	381	120
Goods purchases for resale	103	76	642
Sales	2,500	2,720	2,800
Administrative overheads:			
Rent and rates	31	88	64
Salaries	91	56	78
Sundry	102	143	154
Selling and distribution:			
Advertising	221	129	35
Salaries	143	151	60
Transport	121	39	143
Sundry	74	32	78

	Terri	Vic	Aled
Interest on loans	154	40	12
Bank interest	63	23	165

For Terri
(a) There is an accrual of direct labour – £12
(b) Depreciation is 15% on cost
(c) Rent and rates includes £3 in advance.

For Vic
(a) Depreciation is 25% reducing balance
(b) There is an accrual of £23 and a prepayment of £11 on rent and rates. 10% of the rent and rates should be regarded as selling and distribution.

For Aled
(a) The transfer from manufacturing account to trading account should be made at cost + 10%.
(b) Depreciation is 20% straight line.

(a) In the case of Aled, the closing stock of finished goods is valued at cost + 10%. Assuming that the opening stock was valued at cost, what should be the Dr to profit and loss a/c and the Cr to 'provision for unrealised profit in stock'. What value should appear in the balance sheet at 31.12.-5 for finished goods? (Assume all the stock was manufactured internally.)

(b) Repeat (a) but assume that the opening stock was also valued at cost + 10%.

Exercises without answers

2. The Flinge Manufacturing Co Ltd have been manufacturers of flinges for many years. At 31st December 1982, their trial balance included the following items.

	£'000
Stocks at 31.12.81:	
Raw materials	100
Work in progress	120
Finished goods	85
Raw material A imports	35
Raw material purchases	350
Factory rates and insurance	78
Sales	1,125
Administrative expenses	73
Factory salaries	60
Direct wages	165
Plant at cost	200
Depreciation on plant to 31.12.81	80
Selling and distribution expenses	55
Factory sundry overheads	55
Factory at cost	600
Depreciation on factory to 31.12.81	240
Carriage on raw materials	40

Notes:

(a) Raw materials in the factory at 31.12.82 were valued at cost at £102,000. During the year the company had bought raw material A in a foreign country and after holding it in a warehouse abroad had imported it into this country. Transactions had been recorded on a LIFO basis, but for manufacturing account purposes stocks are to be valued on a FIFO basis. Details are:

1982

July	Purchase 5 tonnes at £4,000 a tonne
Aug	Purchases 3 tonnes at £5,000 a tonne
Sept	Exported to UK 4 tonnes
Oct	Purchases 2 tonnes at £8,000 a tonne
Dec	Exported to UK 2 tonnes.

(b) Work in progress at 31.12.82 was counted and valued at cost as:

	£'000
Raw materials	50
Direct labour	12

For accounts purposes, work in progress is to be valued at total absorption cost and works overheads are to be added at 150% of direct labour cost.

(c) Finished goods stock in the factory at 31.12.82 was valued at full cost at £95,000. However, this included some items that were valued at cost at £20,000 but which were damaged and would fetch on sale only £10,000 subject to a sales commission of 10%.

(d) Depreciation on the plant is at 20% a year on the reducing balance method. An item of plant was purchased on credit in December 1982 for £40,000 but not included in the books or trial balance. A full year's depreciation is to be charged on this item in 1982.

(e) Depreciation on the factory is at 4% a year on cost.

(f) Sales included £20,000 to Dodgy Ltd on sale or return. This sale was priced at cost plus 25%. In fact, Dodgy Ltd were unable to effect any sales themselves and the goods were returned to Flinge in January 1983, and resold at a profit to Tophole Ltd.

(g) Selling and distribution expenses includes £10,000 licence fees for the company's lorries for the year ending 30 June 1983.

Required:
A Manufacturing Trading and Profit and Loss account for the year ending 31 December 1982 showing clearly prime cost, cost of goods sold, and gross and net profit.

(RSA)

3. The following trial balance was extracted from the books of G. Ashcroft at 31 October 1986.

Trial Balance at 31 October 1986

	£	£
Capital		251,990
Drawings	25,700	
Trade debtors and creditors	42,800	14,600
Purchases of raw materials	208,000	
Manufacturing wages	150,600	
Factory expenses (excluding depreciation)	42,440	
Selling and distribution expenses	12,800	
Administration expenses	42,000	
Sales		630,000
Stocks at 1 November 1985		
Raw materials	18,000	
Finished goods	48,500	
Work in progress	2,700	
Bad debts	1,900	
Provision for bad debts		2,350
Plant and machinery at cost	190,000	
Office furniture and equipment at cost	28,000	
Premises at cost	150,000	
Bank	18,500	
Provision for depreciation		
Plant and machinery		76,000
Office furniture and equipment		7,000
	981,940	981,940

You are given the following additional information:

(i) Stocks at 31 October 1986

Raw materials	17,800
Finished goods	41,900
Work in progress	3,200

(ii) Depreciation is written off fixed assets as follows:
  Plant and machinery: 25% per annum using the reducing balance
  Office furniture and equipment: 10% per annum using the straight line basis.
(iii) Part of the premises consist of a small flat which Ashcroft occupies privately. It was decided to charge £2,000 of the administrative expenses to Ashcroft's drawings to allow for this.
(iv) The provision for bad debts is to be reduced to 5% of debtors outstanding on 31 October 1986.

You are required to:

Prepare Ashcroft's manufacturing, trading and profit and loss account for the year ended 31 October 1986 and his balance sheet as at that date. Your accounts should be in vertical form and should clearly show:
  (a) Prime cost.
  (b) Cost of manufacture.
  (c) Cost of goods sold.   *(RSA)*

4. The following information is extracted from the books and records of Hudson Ltd, a manufacturing company, in respect of the year ended 31 December 1983.

		£
Stocks of raw materials:	at 1 January 1983	103,700
	at 31 December 1983	126,500
Work in progress:	at 1 January 1983	74,800
	at 31 December 1983	66,200
Finished goods:	at 1 January 1983	203,800
	at 31 December 1983	271,400
Payments to suppliers		417,300
Receipts from customers		924,100
Discounts received		3,600
Discounts allowed		5,700
Bad debts written off in respect of 1983 sales		4,000
Trade debtors:	at 1 January 1983	168,500
	at 31 December 1983	172,100
Trade creditors:	at 1 January 1983	101,200
	at 31 December 1983	126,500
Depreciation of plant		26,000
Sundry indirect factory costs		107,300
Direct manufacturing wages		259,100
Rent and rates		12,000

The figure for rent and rates is considered to relate to the factory, two-thirds, and office accommodation, one third. Work in progress and finished goods are valued on the basis of total factory cost.

Required:

(a) Calculations of the figures for sales and purchases.
(b) The manufacturing and trading accounts of Hudson Ltd for 1983 using the relevant information listed above and the results of your calculations under *(a)*.

34. Stock and Materials

INTRODUCTION

1.   The majority of businesses include among their assets stock and work in progress. Measuring the quantity and value of this asset is difficult, subject to differing methods, time consuming and there is much potential for error.

This chapter considers stock under a number of headings:

(a) Stock and the matching convention.
(b) Types of stock.
(c) Inclusions in cost.
(d) Valuation methods, FIFO etc.
(e) Net realisable value and the prudence convention.
(f) Stocktaking.
(g) For cost accounting purposes.

2.   The valuation of stock and work in progress is covered by Statement of Standard Accounting Practice Number 9 (as revised in 1988).

STOCK AND THE MATCHING CONVENTION

3.   Consider the accounts of a retailer and a manufacturer in the illustration. The objective in each case is to match the cost of the goods sold with the sales made in the year. The cost of any unsold or unconsumed stocks will have been incurred in the expectation of future revenue and closing stock is included in the accounts in order to take out of the costs those costs which should be matched with sales of the following year. The problem is which costs relate to the following period and are thus taken out by the inclusion of closing stock.

A Retailer
Trading Account for the year ending 31 December 19-5

	£	£
Sales		134,820
Less cost of goods sold:		
Opening stock	20,871	
Purchases	86,382	
	107,253	
Less closing stock	24,693	
		82,560
Gross profit		£52,260

4.   In the case of the retailer, the cost of his unsold stock is relatively straightforward and the stock takes out that part of purchases which relates to unsold stock.

5.   The matter is more complicated with a manufacturer because costs of manufacture of work in progress and finishing goods are not simply the bought in cost of goods but include prime cost and some proportion of the indirect production costs. The idea to grasp is that closing work in progress and finished goods stock:

(a) Take out those costs included in prime cost and indirect production costs which relate to incomplete or unsold goods which can then be *matched* with sales of the following year.

(b) Leave the sales of this year to be matched with the costs of producing the goods sold *this* year.

A Manufacturer
Manufacturing and Trading Account for the year ending 31 December 19-5

	£
Materials consumed	60,700
Direct labour	73,400
Prime cost	134,100
Indirect production costs	141,700
	275,800
Add opening work in progress	69,720
	345,520
Less closing work in progress	92,720
Finished goods output	252,800
Add opening stock of finished goods	101,910
	354,710
Less closing stock of finished goods	143,560
Cost of goods sold	211,150
Sales	401,175
Gross profit	£190,025

TYPES OF STOCK

6. Stocks of incomplete, unsold or unconsumed items can be categorised as:

(a) Finished goods held for resale.
(b) Goods purchased for resale.
(c) Work in progress.
(d) Raw materials and components purchased for incorporation into products for sale.
(e) Consumable stores - lubricants, cleaning materials, fuel, spare parts etc.

7. The balance sheet should show the stock analysed into these categories either on the balance sheet proper or preferably in a note attached to the balance sheet.

INCLUSIONS IN COST

8. Stock is normally valued at cost. However, the term 'cost' needs some precise definition. In SSAP9, cost is defined as:
"That expenditure which has been incurred in the normal course of business in bringing the product or service to its present location and condition."

9. Cost should include:
(a) Cost of purchase including import duties, transport and handling costs (eg carriage in) and any other directly attributable costs less trade discounts, rebates and subsidies.

(b) Cost of conversion.

10. Cost of conversion comprises:
(a) Costs which are specifically attributable to units of production, ie direct labour, direct expenses (eg royalties payable on production) and sub-contracted work.

(b) Production overheads.

(c) Other overheads (eg of administration), if any, attributable to the particular circumstances of the business to bringing the product or service to its present location and condition. In practice, few of these costs are ever included.

11. **Production overheads** are *overheads* incurred for production, based on the normal level of activity. Overheads to be included are all those related to production (eg rent of factory, depreciation of machinery, salary of works manager) not withstanding that these may accrue wholly or partly on a time basis.

This means that expenses such as rent which accrue strictly on a time basis can be taken out of production overheads by inclusion of part of the cost in the value of work in progress or finished goods. This subject is taken further in the chapter on overheads.

VALUATION METHODS – FIFO etc

12. The cost of an item in stock should be measured as nearly as possible to the actual historical cost of that particular item.

For example, in a shop there are in stock 160 widgets. The most recent purchases of widgets were:
   Dec 4   150 at £25 each
   Dec 13   50 at £26 each
   Dec 19   90 at £30 each

How much did the 160 widgets cost? The answer clearly depends on which consignment the individual widgets arrived in and this may not be known as the widgets are undistinguishable one from another (the technical expression is that they are fungible assets).

13. In practice firms use one of the following methods of stock *rotation* for *actually* dealing with stock.
(a) The oldest are used up first – obviously essential for perishable items like foodstuffs.
(b) The latest arrivals are used first. This seems unlikely but if the goods are stacked in a bin as:

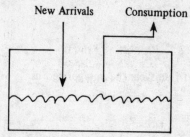

it will be seen that this can occur.

(c) Consumption is from old and new stocks selected randomly. This happens with liquids as old and new stock mix up completely and selection for consumption must be of the mixture. It can also happen with solid items that are stacked randomly so that it is not known which is old and which is new.

14. For *valuation* of the year end stock, a method is selected which approximates to 13(a), (b) or (c). The *method chosen may not actually follow precisely the reality* but it should do so as nearly as possible. The methods to correspond with 13 (a), (b) and (c) are:

(a) First in, first out – FIFO
(b) Last in, last out – LIFO
(c) Average cost – AVCO

15. In *some* businesses, the amount and cost of stock is recorded continuously and we will illustrate FIFO etc as if it were so recorded. In practice, most businesses do not have continuous stock recording but stock must be valued following the same principles. For each illustration we will assume:

	Stock item		*small widgets*
Stock at	1.12.-5	–	20 at £5 each
Purchases:			
	2.12.-5	–	30 at £6 each
Consumed	9.12.-5	–	35
	18.12.-5	–	10

consumed can mean used in production or sold but *never* use the sale price in these calculations.

FIFO

16.

Date	*In*	*Out*	*Balance*
1.12.-5			20 at £5 = £100.00
2.12.-5	30 at £6 =£180.00		⎰ 20 at £5 = £100.00
			⎱ 30 at £6 = £180.00
9.12.-5		⎰ 20 at £5 = £100.00	
		⎱ 15 at £6 = £90.00	15 at £6 = £90.00
18.12.-5		10 at £6 = £60.00	5 at £6 = £30.00

Note:

(a) The account balances as to quantity: 20 + 30 − 35 − 10 = 5
and cost value (£)   100 + 180 − 100 − 90 − 60 = 30

(b) When the 35 were consumed, the oldest stock (20 @ £5) were assumed to be used first and the balance must have come from newer stock.

(c) The method is cumbersome in that the cost of an item sold is a mix of different prices and individual stock items may have different prices.

(d) Stock is valued at the latest price (£6).

LIFO

17.

Date	In	Out	Balance
1.12.-5			20 at £5 = £100.00
2.12.-5	30 at £6 = £180.00		{ 20 at £5 = £100.00
			{ 30 at £6 = £180.00
9.12.-5		{ 30 at £6 = £180.00	15 at £5 = £75.00
		{ 5 at £5 = £25.00	
18.12.-5		10 at £5 = £50.00	5 at £5 = £25.00

Note

(a) The account balances as to quantity: 20 + 30 − 35 − 10 = 5
and cost value (£):   100 + 180 − 180 − 25 − 50 = 25

(b) When the 35 were consumed, the newest stock (30 @ £6) were assumed to have been used and the balance only came from earlier purchases.

(c) The method is cumbersome in that consumption and stock can be at multiple prices.

(d) Stock is valued at the earliest price (£5).

(e) In times of inflation, LIFO gives a lower value to stock.

AVCO - weighted average cost

18.

Date	In	Out	Balance
1.12.-5			20 at £5 = £100.00
2.12.-5	30 at £6 = £180.00		50 at £5.60 = £280.00
9.12.-5		35 at £5.60 = £196.00	15 at £5.60 = £84.00
18.12.-5		10 at £5.60 = £56.00	5 at £5.60 = £28.00

Note:

(a) On the purchase at 2.12.-5, a weighted average cost is calculated by dividing the total cost (£100 + £180 = £280) by the number of items in stock (20 + 30 = 50). This gives a cost of £5.60 which is part way between £5 and £6, but nearer £6 because more weight is given to the 30 items (at £6) than the 20 items (at £5).

(b) The calculation of average cost occurs only at purchases. In practice issues are much more frequent than purchase.

(c) Issues and stock are all at one price.

(d) All the stock are valued at the same, average price.

(e) In times of inflation, weighted average cost gives a value of stock and profit, between that of LIFO and FIFO.

19. Other stock valuation methods are possible - unit cost, base stock, replacement cost, standard cost, adjusted selling price.

(a) **Unit cost** where the stock is divisible into individual units and the cost of each unit can be reasonably found then this cost should be used and approximation such as LIFO and FIFO are not required.

PROFIT WITH AVCO AND FIFO AND LIFO
Trading Account 19-4

	AVCO		LIFO		FIFO	
Sales		100		100		100
Opening stock	10		10		10	
Purchases	70		70		70	
	80		80		80	
Closing stock	15		13		18	
		65		67		62
Gross profit		35		33		38

Note:

(a)   In periods of rising prices stock values under LIFO will be lower than AVCO prices which will be lower than FIFO values.

(b)   The effect on profit can be seen in the examples. Instinctively, a lower asset value at the year end must mean a lower profit.

Trading Account 19-5

	LIFO		AVCO		FIFO	
Sales		110		110		110
Opening stock	13		15		18	
Purchases	77		77		77	
	90		92		95	
Closing stock	11		13		14	
		79		79		81
		31		31		29

Note:

When opening stock and closing stock are similar in size the effect of the different stock value methods becomes negligible.

(b)   **Base stock.** This method assumes that a certain minimum stock is always held and that this minimum quantity should be valued at some historically based (and therefore low) fixed unit price. All stock held in excess of base stock will be valued on LIFO, FIFO or some other acceptable method.

Base stock is not acceptable under SSAP9.

(c)   **Replacement price** should not be used as it does not measure the cost of the stock. However, it can be used in the special circumstances described in paragraph 24.

(d)   **Standard cost** is a measure of cost arrived at as part of a system of management accounting called standard costing. A standard cost is a predetermined budgeted cost. It is not acceptable as an actual cost but frequently by applying variances (differences between budget and actual cost) actual cost can be approximated.

(e)   **Adjusted selling price** can be used. In supermarkets the cost price is difficult to determine but selling price is of course marked on all items. If the stock is evaluated at selling price and then marked down by the normal gross profit margin, then actual cost is approximated providing all stock is fairly fast moving.

NET REALISABLE VALUE AND THE PRUDENCE CONVENTION

20.   Most items of stock will be sold at a price higher than their cost. However, some items may have to be sold at prices which are lower than their cost. Reasons include damage, obsolescence, buying errors, deliberate policy (eg to clear out old stock), technological change, market changes etc.

21.   Such items should be valued at net realisable value. Net realisable value of an item is defined as the amount which the item can be disposed of without creating either profit or loss in the year of sale. It is easier thought of as the:

estimated proceeds of sale

less all further costs to completion; and

less all costs to be incurred in marketing, selling and distributing directly related to the item.

For example

A widget had cost £500 to place it in its present location and condition. However, a new model had been put in production and it is estimated that it can only be sold for £450. Completion costs will be £45 and selling and distribution costs (including sales commission) directly related will be £64.

Net realisable value will be: 450 – 45 – 64 = £341

22. Each item in stock should be reviewed to determine if net realisable value is less than cost and if it is, net realisable value should be the value used. Thus all items of stock are valued at the lower of cost and net realisable value.

23. The valuation of some stock items at net realisable value is an example of the use of the prudence convention, sometimes called the conservatism convention. The convention requires that:

"Revenue and profits are not anticipated, but are recognised by inclusion in the profit and loss account only when realised in the form either of cash or of other assets, the ultimate cash realisation of which can be assessed with reasonable certainty; provision is made for all known liabilities (expenses and losses) whether the amount of these is known with certainty or is a best estimate in the light of the information available."

All this means, is that:

(a) Items not sold in a year are valued at cost. If they were valued at selling price, a profit would be counted.

	Stock at cost		Stock at selling price	
	£	£	£	£
Sales		1,000		1,000
Less cost of goods sold:				
Purchases	800		800	
Less closing stock	200		300	
		600		500
Gross profit		400		500

The higher profit is because of the higher value of closing stock.

Profit must not be anticipated. Only sales (giving rise to cash or a debt) can give a countable profit.

(b) Items of stock that will be sold at a price less than cost must be valued at the *net realisable value*. Effect on profit:

	Stock at cost		Stock at lower of cost and n.r.v.	
	£	£	£	£
Sales		1,000		1,000
Less cost of goods sold:				
Purchases	800		800	
Less closing stock	200		170	
		600		630
		400		370

The lower profit is because of the lower valuation of stock.

(c) The expected profit (a) is not counted but any expected losses (b) are counted.

(d) Net realisable value is not always known with certainty and estimates have to be made.

24. In some cases a good surrogate (= substitute) for net realisable value is replacement price. If replacement price is used, it is being used not as the valuation method, but as a reasonable equivalent or surrogate for net realisable value.

STOCK: COST OR NET REALISABLE VALUE

200 Good Widgets
    Cost £20 each   £4,000   Select cost
    Net realisable value (selling price)   as NRV is   £4,000
    £30 each   £6,000   higher

10 Damaged Widgets   £200
    Cost £20 each   Select NRV
    Net realisable value   as NRV is   £100
    £10 each   £100   lower

Note:

(a) Net realisable value is defined as that value which will give no profit or loss in the year of sale.

(b) Thus, if selling price (realisable value) were £15 each and £2 needed to be spent to put the widgets in saleable condition and transport and commission on sale was £3 each, then net realisable value would be £10 each.

STOCKTAKING

25. In practice, stock is difficult to determine both as to quantity and to value. Errors are easily made. The needs specifically are:

(a) Identifying precisely each item of stock.
(b) Counting, weighting or measuring accurately.
(c) Entering the details on stock sheets.
(d) Ensuring all stock sheets are included.
(e) Determining cost for each item.
(f) Extending quantity x price accurately to give value.
(g) Identifying and valuing items which need to be valued at net realisable value.
(h) Summing the values.
(i) Ensuring accurate cut-off.

26. Good stocktaking procedures would include:

(a) Good, early planning of the stocktaking operation.
(b) Issue and discussion of instructions to staff.
(c) Division of the stock into manageable areas for control purposes.
(d) Proper instructions for counting, weighing, measuring and checking.
(e) Two persons to be involved in counting each item.
(f) Procedures for marking items which have been counted.
(g) Control of movement during the stock take.
(h) Cut off procedures.
(i) Procedures for identifying damaged, obsolete and slow moving stock.
(j) Identification of stock on the premises owned by third parties, and of stock held by outside parties.
(k) Control over the issue of blank stock sheets and the return of completed and unused stock sheets.

STOCK RECORDS AND MANAGEMENT ACCOUNTING

27. Continuous inventory is very important in management accounting. Management accounting is the use of accounting information for management purposes and continuous inventory provides a great deal of information for management. Some of the uses are:

(a) Where companies have a wide variety of items in stock which are for sale or for use in the manufacturing process, it is important to maintain adequate stocks of each item. Otherwise customers' needs cannot be met or the manufacturing process comes to a halt. It is possible to set a re-order level for each item so that when stocks go down to this level, the ordering process is triggered off. Having written records, regularly updated, of what is in stock, facilitates this process. Computerised stock records can set the re-order process going automatically. Setting the optimum re-order level is an interesting subject beyond the scope of this book.

(b) Customers enquire about buying items in stock. Having continuous stock records enables instant answers to be given about the availability of stock without physical inspection. Where stock is held at several locations, customer service is greatly helped by knowing instantly what is in stock and where it is. Similar benefits arise to production controllers who need to know what raw materials and components are in stock.

(c) When continuous inventory records also the cost of each item estimators can know the cost of the materials to use in preparing their estimates. For example, Dave is an estimator at Grainger Equipment Ltd. Cook a customer requires a price quotation for a widget of a particular specification and Dave has to collect the expected costs, add on an element of profit and quote a selling price. Dave can estimate the type and quantity of materials which will be needed. The continuous inventory assists him in informing him if the items are available in stock and what each cost. The costs are of course FIFO, LIFO or average costs and these costs may not be seen as being the best for this purpose. Some companies use other prices in making estimates. These include:

HIHO - highest in highest out. The highest recorded input price is used.

NIFO - next in next out. The estimator uses the price of the next delivery. Clearly this information is not available from the stock records but is usually available from catalogues etc.

(d) Many firms collect the costs of all their products. The reason may be for comparison with expected or budgeted costs. Sometimes the cost collection process is carried out on double entry principles. What ever method is used materials and other inputs must be valued at cost. With materials, this cost is based on LIFO, FIFO or AVCO and collected costs are thus a function of the recording process. Different costs will be given depending on whether LIFO, FIFO or AVCO are used.

(e) Management need to know the profit made by the enterprise overall as well as that made (see (d) above) on individual products. This is of course done in the annual accounts but management like to know the profit more frequently perhaps monthly. The difficulty of measuring profit lies in the counting and pricing at cost of stock. Where continuous inventory is maintained at cost then (if computerised) the total stock at cost is available at the touch of a button.

SUMMARY

28. (a) The objective of the valuation of stock and work in progress is to remove from costs of the year, those costs that relate to stocks at the year end in order to match the remaining costs with the sales of the year.

(b) Stock should be valued at the lower of cost and net realisable value.

(c) Cost is the expenditure incurred in bringing the stock items to their present location and condition.

(d) Cost includes cost of purchase and cost of conversion.

(e) Cost of conversion includes direct costs and a proportion of production overheads including costs which vary on a time basis.

(f) Valuation methods include FIFO, LIFO and weighted average cost.

(g) The valuation of stock at net realisable value is an example of the use of the prudence convention.

(h) Continuous inventory provides information for management including: re-order levels, what is in stock and where it is, costs for pricing and estimating, costs for cost collection and comparisons with budgets and standard costs, end of period total stock at cost.

POINTS TO NOTE

29. (a) The measurement of profit on a regular basis is highly desirable. For many businesses this is done infrequently, perhaps only once a year, because of the difficulty of stocktaking. However, computers have made stock recording within the reach of many more businesses.

A benefit of computerised stock records is that stock can be valued with relative ease at any time.

(b) You should note that a higher closing stock means a higher profit. This is sometimes difficult to see because of difficulty in visualising the double negative - 'less cost of goods sold' incorporating 'less closing stock'.

(c)   The various alternative stock valuation methods are not all acceptable. SSAP9 recommends FIFO or AVCO and condemns LIFO and base stock. LIFO is also not acceptable in the UK to the tax authorities and if LIFO is used, then adjustments have to be made to represent the Accounts using FIFO or AVCO. LIFO is commonly used by American companies.

(d)   Students should note that adoption of say FIFO does not mean that goods are physically kept in that way but the method used should as far as possible, accord with what actually happens.

(e)   Weighted average cost takes into account the differing quantities of stock at each price. An alternative is to use simple average cost, eg if prices are £2.50 and £3.50, simple average is £3.00. Weighted average is to be preferred.

(f)   The use of LIFO can lead to stock being valued at prices which are many years old. In practice, stock varieties change and there are occasions when a stock line is reduced to nil, so that very old prices are rarely found.

(g)   Different stock valuation methods lead to different profits. However, both opening and closing stocks must be valued using consistent methods. If opening and closing stocks are similar in value then the effect of different stock valuation methods is not material.

(h)   The SSAP9 requirement for the valuation of manufacturing work in progress and finished goods at full or total absorption cost is not universally popular. Some companies value such stock using another method called marginal cost.

(i)   The expected loss on goods which have to be valued at net realisable value is automatically counted in the profit measurement by their being so valued. There is no need to include the expected loss specifically as an expense.

SELF-TESTING QUESTIONS

30. *(a) What is the relationship between stock and the matching convention? (3-5)*
     (b) What categories of stock can be found in a balance sheet? (6)
     (c) Define 'cost' in relation to stock. (8-10)
     (d) Define 'cost of conversion' (10)
     (e) What overheads should be included in stock, and on what basis? (11)
     (f) What are fungible assets? (12)
     (g) What should be the relationship between stock rotation and stock valuation methods? (14)
     (h) What is (i) FIFO; (ii) LIFO; (iii) AVCO? (14)
     (i) When should selling prices be used in stock recording systems using LIFO, FIFO etc? (15)
     (j) Describe the stock valuation methods:
          (i)   unit cost;
          (ii)   base stock;
          (iii) replacement cost;
          (iv)   standard cost;
          (v)   adjusted selling price.
          When can these methods be used? (19)
     (k) What is the relationship between net realisable value and the prudence convention? (20)
     (l) Define net realisable value. (21)
     (m) List the management accounting uses of continuous inventory. (27)

EXERCISES (Answers begin page 461)

1.   *What is the correct valuation for the accounts, of the following items in stock:*

     (a) 200 widgets invoiced at £40 each less 20% trade discount. The goods were delivered to head office with a carriage charge of £500 for the consignment. Since purchase, the goods have been transported to a branch at a cost of £405 and the widgets have been rust proofed at a cost of £3 each. The invoice from the supplier was paid less a settlement discount of 5%.

     (b) 40 brockets which had been invoiced at £30 each. They have been replaced in the catalogue and the proposal is to sell them off at £32. On sale, commission of 10% and a carriage charge of £1 each will have to be paid.

(c) An upper sprocket which cost:

	£
Raw materials	4.00
Direct labour	2.50
Packing	.50

Production overheads attributable to the product are £4.20.

2. *Show continuous stock records for the following on:*
(a) FIFO;
(b) LIFO;
(c) Weighted average costs methods

		Business A	Business B	Business C
1.1.-5	Stock	200 at £12	50 at £71	40 at £30
6.1.-5	Purchase	400 at £17	40 at £56	50 at £40
9.1.-5	Sale	300 at £30	20 at £100	80 at £65
15.1.-5	Sale	250 at £32	25 at £95	10 at £60
17.1.-5	Purchase	100 at £18	30 at £41	50 at £35
21.1.-5	Sale	60 at £32	5 at £60	10 at £70

3. *Janet is preparing the estimated price to be quoted to Fred, a customer, for a special widget. The widget includes three Boggets. On consulting the bogget record, she sees the following:*

	Boggets			
1.	b/f			20 at £5 £100
2.2	In	30 at £5.50 £165.00		50 at £5.30 £265
6.2	Out		13 at £5.30 £68.90	37 at £5.30 £196.10
9.2	In	5 at £5.20 £26.00		42 at £5.29 £222.18

Required:
(a) What measurement methods for cost records do the company use?
(b) What cost should be included for the boggets if the company use:
(i) the stock record as it stands;
(ii) HIFO;
(iii) NIFO (the supplier has quoted £60 a dozen less 5% for orders greater than 10 dozen + delivery of £5 an order + VAT at 15%).
(iv) FIFO;
(v) LIFO.

Exercises without answers

4. *What is the correct valuation for the accounts of the following items of stock:*

(a) 150 frames which had been invoiced at £40 each, less a trade discount of 15%. The goods were delivered with a carriage charge of £500 the lot. Since purchase, the goods have been painted at a cost of £2 each and transported to stores at a cost of £700 the lot. The invoice was paid, less a settlement discount of 2%.

One frame was damaged in transit to the store and it is proposed to sell it for £30. This will involve expenditure of £5 for repairs.

(b) 500 bearings which cost to make (each):

Raw materials	£7.00
Direct labour	60p
Production overheads:	
2 machine hours at £4 an hour	
3 labour hours at £1 an hour	

5. The following information relates to the acquisition and issue of material 2XA by Roe Limited, a small manufacturing company, for the three months to 31 March 1984:

Material 2XA

Date	Acquisitions Quantity Kg	Price per Kg £	Issues Quantity Kg
1.1.-3	100	3.00	
15.1.-3	200	4.00	
29.1.-3			150
17.2.-3	400	4.50	
5.3.-3			450
16.3.-3	100	5.00	
31.3.-3			50

Note: There was no material in stock at 1 January 19-3.

Required:

(a) Calculate the closing stock value of Material 2XA using each of the following methods of pricing the issue of stock to production:
   (i)   First-in, first-out (FIFO);
   (ii) Last-in, first-out (LIFO);
   (iii) Periodic simple average;
   (iv) Periodic weighted average;
   (v)   Weighted average.

(b) Examine the effect on gross profit of using the first-in-first out (FIFO) and last-in, first-out (LIFO) methods of pricing the issue of stock to production assuming that price levels are rising.   (AAT)

6. (a) Name five groups into which business stocks can be categorised. State the general rule for the accounting treatment of stock and relate that rule to the concepts or conventions on which accounting is based.

   (b) Explain how best accounting practice, embodied in Statement of Standard Accounting Practice 9, follows the general rule.

   (c) Baggaley Leather Goods operate a shop selling ladies shoes and handbags. Until recently they had always purchased goods for resale, but have decided to make all the handbags they sell, from 1 January 1981.

   The trading account for the year to 31 December 1981 shows the following figures for handbag sales through the shop:

	£
Opening stock at cost (500 x £30)	1,500
Received from workshop at transfer price (10,000 x £4)	40,000
	41,500
Less closing stock (1,000 x £4)	4,000
Cost of sales	37,500
Gross profit	22,500
Sales	£60,000

Mr Baggaley comments that buying the bags from his own workshop at £4 each was a mistake, since he could have bought them through the trade at £3.80. However, he says the workshop did well to produce them at £3.50 each and show a profit of 50p on each one.

Show how the stock of handbags would appear in the balance sheet as at 31 December 19-1.   (AAT)

7. An evaluation of a physical stock count on 30 April 1982 in respect of the financial year ending on that date at Cranfleet Commodities has produced a figure of £187,033.

   The firm's bookkeeper has approached you, as the accountant, for assistance in dealing with the following matters to enable him to arrive at a final figure of closing stock for inclusion in the annual accounts:

(a) 320 components included at their original cost of £11 each can now be bought in for only £6 each due to over production by the manufacturer. This drop in price is expected to be only temporary and the purchase price is expected to exceed its original figure within 12 months. Cranfleet Commodities intends to continue selling the existing stock at the present price of £15 each.

(b) It has been discovered that certain items which had cost £5,657 have been damaged. It will cost £804 to repair them after which they can be sold for £6,321.

(c) On one stock sheet a sub-total of £9,105 has been carried forward at £1,095.

(d) 480 units which cost £1.50 each have been extended at £15.00 each.

(e) The firms has sent goods with a selling price of £1,500 (being cost plus 25%) to a customer on a sale or return basis. At 30 April 19-2, the customer had not signified acceptance, but the goods have not been returned, and consequently had not been included in the physical stock count.

(f) Included in stock were goods bought on credit for £4,679 from Byfleet Enterprises. At 30 April 19-2, Cranfleet Commodities had not paid this account.

(g) Byfleet Commodities had also sent some free samples (for advertising purposes only). These have been included in stock at their catalogue price of £152.

Required:
Taking account of such of the above facts as are relevant, calculate a closing stock figure for inclusion in the 1982 annual accounts of Cranfleet Commodities, giving reasons for the action you have taken in each individual case.

8. Megalot Ltd made the following purchases and sales of stock item C4321 during May 1986:

May 10   Purchased 3,000 units at £6.00 each
May 15   Sold 2,500 units at £9.00 each
May 16   Purchased 1,000 units at £6.60 each
May 23   Sold 900 units at £9.70 each

Assume there were no units of Stock item C4321 in stock as at 1 May 1986.

Required:
(a) Compute the values for sales and purchases of stock item C4321 for May.
(b) How many units should there be in stock at the 31 May 1986?
(c) Compute the value of closing stock on each of the following bases:
    (i) FIFO; and
    (ii) LIFO.
(d) Calculate the gross profit earned on this item during May if closing stock were to be valued under each of the two bases in *(c)* above.
(e) Suppose that a physical check of the number of items of C4321 in stock as at the end of May 1986 revealed a number different to what you had calculated in *(b)* above. What factors might account for the difference.

(AAT)

9. *(a)* The results of a company's stocktaking at the financial year end were:

Item	Category	Cost £	Net realisable value £
1	X	20	21
2	X	30	28
3	X	10	9
4	Y	70	73
5	Y	90	88
6	Y	100	102
7	Z	200	210
8	Z	250	240
9	Z	280	270

Required:

(i)   *Give three values, conforming to the formula 'cost or net realisable value, whichever is the lower', which could be placed upon the stock for balance sheet purposes.*

(ii)   *State briefly and with reasons, which of these three values the company should, in your opinion, adopt.*

(b)   *A company's financial year ended on 30 June 1982, which happened to be a Wednesday. It was not possible to take stock on that day, and stocktaking therefore took place on Saturday and Sunday 3rd and 4th July 1982, when the works were closed. The value, at cost, of the raw material stock was £93,206. However, during Thursday and Friday, 1st and 2nd July 1982, the following transactions occurred:*

Raw materials costing	£10,417 were received from suppliers
Raw materials costing	£235 were returned to suppliers
Raw materials costing	£8,991 were issued from the stores
Raw materials costing	£546 were returned from the factory to the stores in good condition.

Certain items included in the stocktaking valuation at a cost of £7,832 were found to have a net realisable value of £6,724. These items were not part of the four transactions occurring on 1st and 2nd July.

You are required to state the value which should be placed on the company's raw materials stock at 30th June 1982, for balance sheet purposes.

(CMA)

10. *M Hague has been in business for three years. The purchase and sales of goods have been as follows:*

		Purchases		Sales
Year 1	January	40 at £20 each	November	50 at £30each
	September	30 at £21 each		
Year 2	February	20 at £23 each	December	30 at £36 each
	May	10 at £24 each		
	October	24 at £25 each		
Year 3	April	12 at £26 each	September	70 at £40 each
	August	50 at £30 each		

You are required to calculate the gross profits for each of the three years using:

(a)   *The first-in, first-out method of stock valuation.*
(b)   *The last-in, first-out method of stock valuation.*

You should show all of your workings.

(RSA)

35. Labour Costs

INTRODUCTION

1. This chapter is concerned with various aspects of labour costs. From the financial accounting point of view, labour represents a cost in the profit and loss account but it also enters into the cost of producing finished goods which may be in stock at a period end.

2. From the costing point of view labour is a major cost which forms part of the cost of products. Determining the cost of products is a principal aim of costing and the costs so determined are used in pricing and other decisions.

3. This chapter looks at the following aspects of labour costs:

    (a) labour as a part of product costs;
    (b) types of labour - direct and indirect;
    (c) payments systems and the total cost of labour.

PRODUCT COST

4. The cost of a product can be divided into three major parts or elements:

    (a) materials and component parts;
    (b) direct labour;
    (c) overheads.

Materials were considered in the last chapter and overheads are considered in the next chapter. SSAP9 considers product costs in terms of:

    (a) cost of purchase;
    (b) cost of conversion.

Essentially, the cost of purchase is the materials and components which are bought from suppliers to form part of the product. Examples are wood, screws, paint and brass fittings which form the physical substance of a piece of furniture. SSAP9 defines the purchase price as including import duties, transport and handling costs and any other directly attributable costs less trade discounts, rebates and subsidies.

The cost of conversion is the cost of turning the raw materials and components into a saleable finished product. Costs of conversion are the direct labour and overheads.

Direct costs are those costs which can be directly identified with a job, batch, product or service. Direct costs can be contrasted with indirect costs (= overheads). To illustrate the difference, screws used in making a particular lock can be used only in that lock and the cost of the screws can be traced directly as a part of the cost of that lock. When the key to the lock is assembled from separate parts by means of an electric arc welder, a small amount of electricity is used and the cost of that electricity is technically a direct cost of producing the key. However, in practice, the cost of electricity is traceable only as a monthly charge for the whole factory and it is not feasible to trace the cost of electricity used to individual products. More obviously, the cost of cleaning the factory is clearly a part of the cost of production but it is not feasible to ascribe the cost of particular cleaning materials or cleaner's wages to particular products. The costs of cleaning are shared by all the products.

Thus: *Direct costs can be traced exclusively to particular products. Indirect or overhead costs are shared by more than one product.* Examples of direct costs include direct labour (eg the wages of a worker who is assembling a particular lock), direct expenses (eg the cost of hallmarking the cost of a particular piece of gold jewellery) and sub-contracted work (eg the cost of blister wrapping the finished lock which is done by local housewives in their own homes).

TYPES OF LABOUR

5. Labour in factory can perform many functions, eg:

    (a) On the shop floor:
       - making the product
       - supervising the manufacture
       - cleaning
       - repair and maintenance of the machinery
       - clerical
       - transporting materials and products within the factory.

(b) In the offices:
-       accounting both cost and financial
-       management
-       selling and marketing
-       personnel work

(c) In other activities:
-       selling
-       transport
-       grounds maintenance
-       research and development.

Most of these labour costs are indirect or overheads. Only labour which has direct contact with products can be considered to be direct. In Adam Smith's famous pin factory (In the Wealth of Nations 1776) the workers each did one only of eighteen distinct operations on the pin and the direct labour cost of each whole pin was thus easily determined. This division of labour still exists today, but many production processes are automated and a worker may control several machines so that it is difficult to trace his wage to particular products.

PAYMENT SYSTEMS

6.   There are basically three payment systems found in practice:
-       an hourly (or weekly or monthly) rate
-       payment according to output - piece work
-       complex systems.

(a) Where direct labour is paid by the hour, the problem for costing systems is to collect data on the time spent on each individual product. This can be achieved by time sheets and diaries.

(b) Where payment is by piecework. Collection of the data is relatively easy. For example, in a lock factory, the workers are often paid x pence per operation performed. The number of operations performed can be entered in an operation card signed by the worker and the foreman. Subsequently, the amount of work paid for should be reconciled with output.

(c) In complex systems it is much more difficult to collect the precise direct labour costs of each product.

THE TOTAL COST OF LABOUR

7.   The cost of labour is not as simple as may appear. In the UK and most other countries the gross pay (eg hourly rate x hours worked) is not the only cost. There is also the cost of national insurance and other social security and pension costs. In addition each worker costs extra for holiday pay and pay while absent during sickness and training. All these extra costs are generally regarded as indirect.

All work paid for does not result in work chargeable to particular products. Workers are paid also for idle time. Idle time arises for many reasons - getting from the gate to the workbench, toilet and refreshment breaks, machine breakdown, shortage of parts or work, illness at work, accidents etc. Idle time is usually regarded as an indirect cost. One of the advantages of piece work payment systems is that idle time is not paid for.

OVERTIME

8.   Many workers work overtime. This presumes that there are standard hours established for work and that any hours worked beyond those hours are paid at a higher rate - for example, double time on Sundays. The overtime premium is the extra amount paid over the standard rate. For example if the standard rate is £4 an hour and time and a half is paid for Saturdays then the premium is £2 an hour. Overtime premiums are usually regarded as indirect costs. However, in special circumstances they can be direct costs. For example Jim wants his widget made in a hurry and Ron agrees to make it on a Sunday if Jim will pay a higher price. In this case the overtime is specific to the widget and is thus direct.

SUMMARY

9.   (a) Product costs can be divided into direct materials, direct labour and overheads.
(b) SSAP 9 considers product costs as being cost of purchase plus the cost of conversion.
(c) The cost of conversion is the cost of turning the product into a saleable product.
(d) Direct costs are those costs that can be reasonably traced to particular products. Indirect costs are all other costs. The essence of an indirect cost is that it is shared by more than one product.
(e) Labour costs can be direct or indirect. Only the wages paid to workers whose work can be directly related to particular products are direct.
(f) There are many payment systems. The simple ones are directly related to time worked or to output.

(g) The total cost of labour includes social security and holiday pay and idle time. Additions such as national insurance and holiday pay are regarded as indirect costs as is idle time.

(h) The overtime premium is usually regarded as indirect.

POINTS TO NOTE

10. (a) Reference has been made in this chapter to products. In practice products may be made singly or may be made in batches. A product can thus be a single product (eg a set of double glazed windows for a customer), a particular job (eg the construction of a garage for a customer), a batch (eg a batch of yoghurts), or a service (eg the production of a set of accounts for a client).

    (b) The distinction between direct and indirect costs is important because a particular cost will, if direct, be ascribed to a particular product and, if indirect, be shared amongst all the products (the next chapter explains how). This means that although the total costs are the same whether they are direct or indirect the total costs will be shared out amongst the products in ways which depend on the relative treatment of costs between direct and indirect. If a product cost is measured in different ways by different accountants then different decisions (eg on pricing) will be taken. Also the costs enter into the valuation of work in progress and finished goods and thus affect the measurement of profit.

    (c) The measurement of product cost is simple in theory but exceptionally difficult in practice.

SELF-TESTING QUESTIONS

11. *(a) What are the elements of cost? (4)*
    (b) State the view of product cost set down by SSAP9. (4)
    (c) Define the cost of purchase. (4)
    (d) What is the conversion cost? (4)
    (e) Define direct costs. (4)
    (f) What are indirect costs? (4)
    (g) What labour costs can be considered as direct? (5)
    (h) How can the labour cost of particular products be measured? (6)
    (i) What costs are additional to hourly rate or piece work payments. (7)
    (j) How are such costs treated? (7)
    (k) How is overtime costed? (8)

EXERCISES (with answers page 461)

1. *Woad Ltd manufacture paint in standard batches of 1,000 tins. The direct labour employed on manufacture of a batch is:*

   Ron who is paid 20p a box to pack the tins in boxes of four tins.

   Les and Doug who are paid £3.50 an hour each to mind the machines which produce the paint. Each batch varies in time of manufacture but batch 34 took four hours.

   Hugh who is paid £6 an hour to set up the machines. Batch 34 took him 1.6 hours.

   (a) What is the direct labour cost of batch 34:
   - per batch
   - per tin.

   (b) What other costs would be incurred in producing batch 34?

   (c) What would be the direct labour cost if batch 34 happened to be produced on a Saturday. Regular Saturday overtime is worked.

   (d) What would the direct labour cost be if batch 34 had been produced on a Saturday (time is paid at 1.5 times normal rate) in response to an order from a customer who agreed to pay extra for immediate delivery?

2. *What is the cost to be included in the closing stock of a part finished trailer whose costs had been:*

   Parts £32 + £4 carriage from Glasgow less 5% for payment within seven days:
   Paint 2 gallons at £16 a gallon
   Direct labour: 4 hours at £5.20 an hour
   *   32 operations at an average cost of 43.1p an operation.*

   (ignore overheads).

Exercises without answers

3.   Jack is a landscape gardener. On job number 765 he employs:
        Sid who is paid £4 an hour for 13 hours
        Will who is paid £3 an hour also for 13 hours.
Sid is paid for 2,000 annual hours of which he actually works on jobs for 1,600.

Will is paid for 1,800 annual hours of which he works 1,560. The cost of both men's wages is the hourly rate + national insurance at 10.5%.

What is the direct labour cost of job 765 (ignore overheads)?

What would the cost be if Sid had had an exceptionally busy week and four of his hours chargeable to job 765 had been in overtime at time + 1/3?

4.   Which of the following are direct labour in a coffee plantation:

    Bean pickers   Coffee plant planters   Truck drivers
    The general manager   Drying machine minders   Irrigation workers
    Canteen workers   Sacking machine operators

36. Overheads

INTRODUCTION

1. The cost of manufacture of finished goods is defined in SSAP9 as the cost of purchase (materials) + the cost of conversion. Cost of conversion is:

- costs which are specifically attributable to units of products (eg direct labour, direct expenses and sub-contracted work)
- production overheads
- other overheads - but only in certain circumstances.

Overheads are shared among all the products made and it is difficult to assign an appropriate share to each product. Cost accountants have devised a method of doing this which is rather arbitrary. Students find this very difficult but it is not that impossible to grasp.

PRODUCT AND OTHER OVERHEADS

2. Overheads can be classified according to function. They can be:
- production
- administration
- selling and delivery.

Whether an overhead is production, administration or selling is not always obvious. Consider the following expenses:

rent of the premises	advertising
the cost of the accounts department	interest
production director's salary	audit fee

If the premises consist of the factory (production), the offices (admin), the sales department and the transport section (delivery) then the cost of running the premises will have to be split in some way between the functions.

Advertising is easier, it is obviously a selling overhead. Note that this means that it is not part of the cost of producing a product.

The cost of the accounts department is also an overhead split amongst the functions. The accounts department will do at least the following:

- paying production wages and dealing with production purchases (production)
- dealing with the sales ledger (selling)
- preparing the annual accounts (admin)

Interest is usually regarded as an administrative expense although a case can be made for part of it (say the interest on money borrowed to buy extensive stocks of raw materials) being production.

The production director's salary appears to be a production expense but part of his time will be spent on general directorial matters and attending board meetings. These are administration matters.

The audit fee is generally regarded as an admin expense.

You will see that splitting overhead by function is not easy and different accountants may take different views. In that case the cost of products both for decision making (eg pricing) and for inclusion in the annual accounts will differ, albeit marginally.

PRODUCTION OVERHEADS AND COST CENTRES

3. The first step, as we have seen is to classify overheads by function. We are then only concerned with the production expenses. The next step is to associate the production overheads with cost centres prior to assigning them to products.

4. The term cost centre can be defined as 'a location function, or item of equipment in respect of which costs may be ascertained and related to cost units for control purposes'. For example, in a factory making galvanised sheeting the factory may be divided into departments as: the shearing shop (where sheet steel is cut into appropriate sizes, the pressing shop (where it is pressed into the required shapes), the galvanising shop (where it is coated with zinc), the packing shop (where it is packed ready for delivery to customers). Each department is regarded as a cost centre. These cost centres are locations. Functional cost centres may be appropriate in a merchant bank (which also produces a product - a service) eg share dealing, portfolio advice, corporate finance and venture capital. The number of cost

centres in a business is a matter of opinion as much as a matter of fact. Some are regarded as having just a few (like the galvanising factory) but some have very many. It is possible to regard each machine in a factory as a separate cost centre. The level of detail chosen affects the amount of work involved for the cost accounting staff.

SPLITTING OVERHEADS AMONG COST CENTRES

5.   Suppose a factory has the following departments with some statistics about them also given:

	Area metres^2	Number of employees	Value of plant	Stores requisitions made
Press shop	25	36	£230,000	165
Assembly shop	37	51	£65,000	456
Packing shop	50	26	£10,000	341
Stores dept	40	12	£35,000	–
Maintenance dept	8	5	£21,000	138

Note that all these cost centres are to do with production but that stores and maintenance do not produce anything but provide services to those departments that do.

	Pr	As	Pa	St	Ma	Shared
Rates						38,000
Heating						26,000
Employer's liability insurance						2,500
Canteen costs						5,000
Labour – direct	15,400	25,100	12,000			
Labour – indirect	4,900	7,200	4,000	7,800	4,230	
Depreciation 12% pa on the value of plant						

Note:

(a)   I have put in seven expenses – there would be many more in practice.

(b)   The first four items are shared amongst the departments. The others are not. They are said to be allocated to the departments where the costs are incurred. The other first four items will need to be apportioned.

(c)   I have included direct wages. This is not an overhead – it is a direct cost.

(d)   These costs are expected or budgeted costs. Costs are useful if they can be foreseen and decisions made accordingly. After the event actual costs can be compared with budgeted costs and useful lessons learned.

The costs can be apportioned as follows;

Expense	Basis	Total £	Pr £	As £	Pa £	St £	Ma £
Rates	metres^2	38,800	6,062	8,973	12,125	9,700	1,940
Heating	metres^2	26,000	4,062	6,013	8,125	6,500	1,300
EL ins	gross pay	2,500	652	989	490	239	130
Canteen	No of workers	5,000	1,385	1,962	1,000	461	192
Indirect labour	Allocated	28,130	4,900	7,200	4,000	7,800	4,230
Depreciation	Allocated	3,610	2,300	650	100	350	210
Total		104,040	19,361	25,787	25,840	25,050	8,002

Note:

(a)   Make sure your totals cross-cast.

(b)   Rates have been apportioned on the basis of floor area. This is usual for rent, rates, building insurance and heat and light. However heat and light may be apportioned in other ways – volume, or number of workers or using special knowledge. For example, some shops may need no heating because heat is produced by the process.

(c)   Employer's liability insurance premiums are based on the total payroll.

(d)   Canteen costs have been apportioned using the number of workers in each department – this seems a rational procedure.

(e) Direct labour is excluded. It is included in product costs as a direct cost, not as a part of overheads.

(f) Depreciation is 1% on value as this is a one month period.

(g) You will realise that there are several very inexact areas here. Depreciation is an estimate. The apportionment bases are matters of opinion. Consequently, in practice, very elaborate apportionment schedules are no more 'accurate' than less detailed ones.

6. There is a further step. We must ascribe all production overheads to producing departments. So we further apportion the service departments to the producing departments as:

	Pr	As	Pa	St	Ma	Sum
From schedule	19,361	25,787	25,840	25,050	8,002	104,040
Stores	3,757	10,384	7,766	(25,050)	3,143	
Subtotal					11,145	
Maintenance	7,801	2,229	1,115		(11,145)	
Total	30,919	38,400	34,721			104,040

Note

(a) A rational way of apportioning the costs of the stores department is by reference to use by the other departments. A reasonable indication of use is the number of stores requisitions raised.

(b) The use by each department of maintenance is not easily determined. In examination questions the basis of apportionment is usually given to examinees. I have assumed that an investigation has revealed an apportionment on the basis of 7:2:1 as rational.

(c) You will note that some of the stores department costs have been reapportioned to the maintenance department. It would also be possible then to reapportion some of the maintenance department costs back to the stores. This would require further apportionment of stores to maintenance and from maintenance to stores ...... This problem is called the reciprocal service department problem. There are several ways of solving it but I will refer you to a text specialising in costing for the solutions.

OVERHEAD ABSORPTION

7. Now that we have all the production overheads allocated or apportioned to the production departments, we need to find out how much of these overheads is absorbed or shared by each product.

Suppose that in the press shop, the main activity is the pressing of the product into different shapes using machines. The machines are, of course, operated by workers but the use of the machines is the main determinant of product use of the department. Essentially, the more machine time is spent on a product, the larger share it has of the overheads.

If we estimate that in the month, there will be an average of 200 hours of usage out of each of the 20 presses. That is a total of 2,400 *machine hours*. So the overheads of the department are £30,919 and are spent to provide 2,400 machine hours. You can thus say that each machine hour cost £30,919/2,400 = £12.99 (or say £13 as the figures are full of assumptions, opinions and estimates. We say we have a machine hour rate of £13 and that is the *overhead* cost of using a machine for one hour.

With the assembly shop the primary purpose is to enable *direct labour* to work. Thus if we estimate that 45 of the employees in the assembly shop are direct labour and they will work on products for a total of 7,200 hours in the month then the overhead cost of each worker is £38,400/7,200 = £5.33. This is called a *labour hour rate*. The overhead cost of one direct worker for one hour in the assembly shop is £5.33. Note that is *in addition* to his/her wage.

Similarly, in the packing shop, if total direct labour hours are estimated to be 3,360 then the labour hour rate is £34,721/3,360 = £10.33.

8. These rates – machine hour and labour hour are called absorption rates. If it takes say four machine hours in the press shop, 5 labour hours in the assembly shop and 3.5 labour hours in the packing shop to make a particular product then the total overhead cost or total overhead absorbed is 4 x £13 + 5 x £5.33 + 3.5 x £10.33 = £114.80. This information might be used in:

(a) determining the price to be charged for the product;
(b) controlling costs by determining, after the event, how many hours were actually used on manufacture.

PRODUCT COSTS

9.   In the factory discussed in the paragraphs above, a customer has made an enquiry for a product of a particular specification. The estimator discovers that the probable costs of manufacture will be:

	In the press shop	In the assembly shop	In the packing shop
Direct costs:			
Materials	£187	£31	£24
Labour	12 hours at £4	15 hours at £3.50	6 hours at £3.60
Overheads:			
Machine hours	15		

The company has a policy of charging cost + a profit sufficient to give a 25% gross profit on selling price.

Calculate the estimated selling price.

The estimated selling price can be derived as: £

Material cost	£187 + £31 + £24		242.00
Direct labour costs			122.10
Overheads : press shop	15 x £13	195.00	
: assembly shop	15 x £5.33	79.95	
: packing shop	6 x £10.33	62.00	336.95
Total cost			701.05
Profit margin 25/75 x £701.05			233.68
Estimated selling price (rounded)			935.00

Notice what a large proportion of the total cost is provided by overheads. This is a common experience.

LEVELS OF ACTIVITY

10.   In the example above the level of activity chosen for the press department was 2,400 hours. This assumes that the department will be able to provide 2,400 hours and that there will be enough work available to need 2,400 hours. If less than 2,400 hours are worked – say only 2,100 hours of work were possible – then the machine hour rate would be £30,919/2,100 = £14.72. Thus all products will cost a little more as the overheads have to be divided over fewer products. SSAP 9 requires the level of activity taken to be *the normal* level of activity taken *one year with another*. In deciding upon *normal*, account should be taken of intended levels of production for which the facilities were designed and the budgeted level and the levels achieved in recent periods.

SUMMARY

11.   (a)   The cost of a product at any given stage in its production is the costs incurred up to that point in bringing the product to its present location and condition.

   (b)   This cost is the cost of purchase (materials) + the cost of conversion.

   (c)   Cost of conversion includes direct costs and some appropriate proportion of the overheads or indirect costs.

   (d)   Only production overheads should normally be included in the cost of production of a product.

   (e)   Production overheads are allocated or apportioned to cost centres.

   (f)   A total overhead for each cost centre can be obtained.

   (g)   Service department costs are then apportioned to the producing departments.

   (h)   An absorption method is developed to share these overheads amongst the products. These methods include machine hour rates and labour hour rates.

   (i)   A product cost is the direct costs + the overheads absorbed.

   (j)   In deriving absorption rates, a normal level of activity should be used.

POINTS TO NOTE

12.   (a)   Production overheads include expenses which accrue on a time basis such as rent. Thus if rent is incurred in year 1 and the rent is included in the overheads of a cost centre and the overheads are a part of the cost of manufacturing widget x and the widget is in stock at the year end *then* part of the rent will become an expense of year 2.

   (b)   When overheads are absorbed into a product they are said to be *recovered*. This means in essence that the costs are recovered from the customer. If insufficient products are made to absorb all the overheads then those overheads are lost. For example, if the overheads of department Z are £20,000 and the expected machine hours are 5,000 then the recovery rate is £4 an hour. If only enough products are made to absorb 4,000 hours then only £16,000 is recovered and £4,000 is under-recovered or lost. Really, the absorption rate should have been £5 an hour.

(c) Remember that a *labour hour rate* is overheads. The wage paid is additional.

(d) I have covered only machine hour rates and labour hour rates.

There are several others in use including:

- percentage on materials (used in restaurants);
- percentage on direct labour costs (used in garages);
- percentage on prime cost.

(e) This method of finding the *total cost* of a product is called *total absorption costing*. It contrasts with marginal costing which we will meet later. Total absorption costing is required by SSAP 9 for inventories.

(f) The value of 'cost' found in this way is subject to many uncertainties, opinions and estimates. It is thus very imprecise. Scientifically educated readers will recognise the concept of error in scientific experiment. Note that accountants never say 'the costs is expected to be £36 ± £4.20'. We have an undeserved reputation for accuracy!

(g) Overheads other than production overheads can occasionally be included in costs but only in rare circumstances. For example, where firm sales contracts have been entered into for the provision of goods or services to customer's specification, overheads relating to design, and marketing and selling costs incurred *before* manufacture, may be included in arriving at cost.

(h) The method of costing described in this chapter was originally developed for the manufacture of things but it is used equally in the manufacture of services.

(i) Never include direct costs in overheads.

SELF TESTING QUESTIONS

(a) Define cost of manufacture. (1)
(b) What functions of a firm absorb overheads? (2)
(c) What functional costs are included in the cost of production? (1)
(d) Define cost centre. (4)
(e) Suggest some bases of apportionment? (5)
(f) Distinguish allocation from apportionment. (5)
(g) What is the reciprocal service department cost problem? (6)
(h) Explain the derivation of two absorption rates. (7)
(i) Explain the derivation of a product cost. (9)
(j) What level of activity should be used in deriving the denominator in absorption rate calculations? (10)
(k) How does under recovery of overheads occur? (12)
(l) What other methods of overhead recovery exist? (12)
(m) Distinguish labour rates from labour hour rates. (12).

Exercises (Answers begin on page 462)

1. Which of the the following costs are likely to be classified as:

(a) Production   (b) Direct

(a) Production	(b) Direct
Rates of the premises	Cleaning materials
Canteen subsidy	Repairs to machinery
Travelling expenses	Paint
Foremen's wages	Employer's national insurance
Lubricating oil	Lathe operator's wages
Accounting software	Commissionaire's wages
Royalties	Packing materials

2.   Deskout Ltd is a manufacturer of office furniture. Budgeted data for period 24 is:

Direct materials	£24,000
Direct labour 15,000 hours at £4 an hour	
Rates	£28,000
Machinery depreciation	£18,000
Electric power	£38,400
Supervision	£9,000

Statistics about the three manufacturing departments (cutting, joining, finishing) are:

	Cutting	Joining	Finishing
Area in square meters	1,200	1,000	600
Machinery value	£600,000	£240,000	£60,000
Number of employees	40	20	15
Machine hours	12,000	6,000	1,200

(a) Prepare an overhead apportionment schedule for the three production cost centres.

(b) Calculate a machine hour absorption rate for the cutting department.   (RSA)

3.   The Widget Manufacturing Co Ltd make widgets to order.

A customer has requested a price for a widget and you have been asked to prepare an estimate for that customer.

You determine the following:

(a) The widget will use 13 kilograms of Hedonite at £2.50 a kg, 4 metres of tube at £5.25 a metre and £9 worth of sundry material.

(b) Direct labour costs will be:

in the machine room – 18 hours at £3 per hour
in the assembly shop – 6 hours at £2 an hour
in the packing shop – 4 hours at £2.50 an hour.

(c) The manufacture of the widget will include five hours' use of a machine in the machine room.

(d) Overheads are absorbed as follows:

in the machine room, by a machine hour rate of £6.50
in the assembly shop, by a labour hour rate of £3
in the packaging shop at 150% of direct labour cost.

(e) A profit margin is to be added such that the profit margin is $33\frac{1}{3}$% of the selling price.

Required:
The estimated selling price which will be quoted to the customer. You should set out your answer in the form of a statement with sub-total of direct costs, overheads and total cost.   (RSA)

Exercises without answers
4.   Which of the following costs are likely to be classified as:

(a) Production   (b) Direct

in a furniture factory?

Fork lift truck costs	Screws
Electricity	Letterheads printing
A sales convention	Settlement discount
Carriage on imported hardwood	Labels
Telephone	Maintenance foreman's wages
Carpenter's wages in overtime	Varnish
New racking for stores	Repairs to gate.

5. *Shafto Ltd uses process costing. There are three departments, preparation, moulding and painting. The preparation departments are labour intensive, whilst the moulding department employs expensive machinery. The company therefore uses a machine hour rate for overheads in the moulding department, whilst the other departments use a labour overhead rate.*

The following are the estimates of overheads, hours worked and cost of labour:

	Preparation	Moulding	Painting
Indirect labour	£27,000	£5,000	£26,000
Other indirect expenses	£23,000	£55,000	£14,000
Labour hours worked	12,500	2,500	8,000
Machine hours worked	2,000	4,000	1,000
Cost per hour of direct labour	£3	£5	£4

You are to find the cost of producing 500 units given the following information:

(a) *Raw materials costing £6,780 were taken into the preparation department, processed in 320 labour hours and then passed on to the moulding department.*

(b) *In the moulding department 58 machine hours and 76 labour hours were spent on them.*

(c) *The items are completed in the painting department where £375 materials are used, and 170 labour hours spent on them.* (RSA)

6. *AHM Engineers Ltd manufacture metal tanks to order, each tank being made in accordance with the customer's specification. The company operates a total absorption costing system and the budgeted indirect factory overheads are as follows for the year to 31 December 1979:*

	£
Indirect materials	20,000
Rent	20,000
Depreciation of machinery	70,000
Supervisory salaries	92,000
Power	64,200
Heat and light	15,000

There are three production departments (P1, P2, P3) and two service departments (S1 stores and S2 maintenance).

Statistics relating to these departments are:

	P1	P2	P3	S1	S2
Number of employees	60	80	40	10	10
Floor space in square feet	3,600	5,100	4,200	600	1,500
Indirect material requisitions	130	120	75	25	50
Value of machinery (£'000)	100	50	180	6	14
HP of machinery	500	600	800	40	60
Machine hours in year (in '000)	20	10	20	1	1

You may assume that S1 supplies S2 and both supply all three production departments.

Required:

(a) *A statement showing budgeted factory overhead cost for each of the three production departments. You should use whatever methods of allocation or apportionment seem appropriate.*

(b) *Outline the uses to which management may put your statement.* (RSA)

7. *What is the appropriate level of activity for overhead recovery purposes of the machining shop of Gail's factory given that:*

(a) *The machinery can at maximum deliver 21,100 machine hours in normal working time but was expected to deliver only 19,000 because of breakdowns, maintenance etc.*

(b) Actual annual hours delivered recently have been:

17,600
24,020 - boom year when much overtime was worked
18,600
17,800
15,000 - recession year
18,800

(c) Current indications are that the present year will be exceptionally good and overtime will need to be worked again. How will the choice of activity level affect:

(i)   pricing decisions;
(ii) work in progress and finished goods stocks value?

8.   The factory of the Finchfield Manufacturing Co Ltd is divided into five cost centres viz, three manufacturing departments A, B and C, and two service departments, stores and factory administration.

Data concerning the cost centres are:

	A	B	C	Stores Administration	Factory Administration
Floor area (metres²)	800	1,600	1,600	400	400
Number of employees	14	21	28	7	14
Number of machines	26	22	-	-	-

Factory overheads for the month of October 1984 are budgeted at:

Allocable	£
A	500
B	450
C	380
Stores	100
Factory administration	140
Rates	9,600
Employer's liability insurance	1,440
Power	2,400
Canteen costs	1,680
Heat and light	4,800
	21,490

Required:
(a) Prepare a schedule showing the total overheads attributable to each cost centre.
(b) Reapportion the service department costs on the basis that factory administration is equally apportionable to each of the other four cost centres and the stores department costs are divisible: A 40%; B 40%; C 20%.   (RSA)

9.   Gerk Ltd has two productive departments - cooking and pickling. Costs are recovered: in cooking by use of a machine hour rate and in pickling by a labour hour rate.

The budget for the ensuing year showed:

	Cooking	Pickling
Overheads	£408,000	£200,000
Direct labour hours	20,000	40,000
Machine hours	3,000	-

The product 'onions' has a direct cost per gross boxes of:

Materials	£520
Direct labour : cooking	10 hours at £2 an hour
: pickling	30 hours at £2 an hour
Machine time in cooking	1 hour 15 minutes

Produce a job cost statement for 'onions'.

(RSA)

37. Work in progress

INTRODUCTION

1.   In many businesses, there will be products in stock at the year end which are only partly finished. These products are called work in progress. Work in progress can be industrial products such as part finished furniture or tractors or computers but can also be part completed services such as half completed audits or conveyances. They all need to be valued for inclusion in the income statement.

2.   In most businesses the business cycle is short so that the work in progress will be finished early in the following financial year. For example, a manufacturer of road signs might find that the whole process of manufacture takes at most two weeks. Some businesses make products which have a much longer manufacturing cycle. Examples are construction (a motorway may take two or more years to build) and shipbuilding (a ship may take three years to build).

3.   Products with short cycles are usually valued at cost as explained in the previous chapter. In rare instances they may need to be valued at net realisable value.

4.   Products with long cycles are treated differently in accordance with SSAP 9's requirements on *long-term contracts*.

ORDINARY WORK IN PROGRESS

5.   Ordinary work in progress in a manufacturing or service business must be valued at total absorption cost as explained in the last chapter. As examples:

   (a)   Horace manufactures hardwood doors to order and for stock. One of these doors was part finished. Expenditure to date had been:

	£
Materials	40.00
Direct labour hours 2.5 at £5.20	13.00
Overheads : .5 machine hours at £7.80	3.90
: 2.5 labour hours at £7.10	17.75
	74.65

   Note:
   (i)   That this is the cost so far. Further costs will be incurred before completion and will be included in the following year.
   (ii)   The 2.5 labour hours at £7.10 is not labour cost but the overheads associated with the direct labour hours.
   (iii) Where this item occurs in a manufacturing account and how this represents a taking – out of the costs in the manufacturing account and placing them in the following manufacturing account as opening work in progress.

   (b)   Ted is a chartered accountant. He has a member of staff (Emma) who has worked on Job No 246 – the audit or Leon's accounts. Expenditure to date is:

	£
Emma's wages 52 hours at £6.10	317.20
Associated overheads 52 x £3.20	166.40
Direct costs: travelling expenses	17.40
	501.00

   Note:
   No element of profit is included. Some accountants value work in progress at charge out rates but that would include an element of profit.

ITEMS AT NET REALISABLE VALUE

6.   William has a business making special bicycles to order. One order was for a special bicycle and William sadly underestimated the costs and quoted £300 only. At this year end data is:

	£
Contract price	300.00
Cost to date	240.00
Estimated costs to completion	103.00

The bicycle would be valued at £197 which is its net realisable value and which is lower than its cost (£240.00).

LONG TERM CONTRACTS

7.   Owing to the length of time taken to complete many long term contracts (eg roads, power stations, aircraft etc), to defer taking profit into account until completion may result in the profit and loss account reflecting not so much a true and fair view of the results of the business's actual activity in the year but rather the results relating to contracts *finished* in the year. This would distort the year on year results.

8.   Accordingly SSAP 9 allows that *when the outcome of contract can be foreseen with reasonable certainty* a portion of the expected profit can be included in the profit. Conversely, if it is expected that a loss will be incurred on a contract then *the whole expected loss* should be accounted for straight away.

9.   Some examples: (All figures in £'000)

Project	A	B	C
Total costs incurred	564	730	35
Value of work done	620	720	45
Cumulative payments on account received	430	525	–
Expected costs to completion	240	134	920
Contract total price	915	835	1,200

Project A:

Include in *turnover* in the profit and loss account	£620
Include in *cost of sales*	£564
Thus profit taken =	£ 56
Include in debtors £620 – £430	£190

Note that in accordance with SSAP 9 as revised in October 1988, the part finished contract, which is expected to make an overall profit, is included in turnover and debtors and not as work in progress.

Project B:

Include in turnover	£720
Include in cost of sales £730 + £19	£749

(The £19 is the expected loss on the contract being £835 – (£730 + £134) – £10 already taken).

Thus include in the profit and loss account a loss of £29.

Include in the balance sheet as debtors £720 – £525	£195

Include in balance sheet as accrual/provision for loss	£19

Contract C:

This contract has hardly started so no profit can be taken as the outlook for the contract cannot reasonably be foreseen so early. The cost of the work done £35 should be included in long term contract balances in stocks.

10.   Note that in example A, the amount to be included in the turnover (ie in sales) is the *value* of the work done to date. This can normally be ascertained on a long term contract. The profit to be included is the profit earned to date, that is, the value of work done to date less the cost of carrying out that work. Ultimately, the remaining turnover and profit on the contract will be included in the years when the work is done. The value on the balance sheet (in debtors) is the work done to date less money already received. It is usual for customers to pay for long term contracts as they go along and not wait until completion.

11.   In contract B, the contract is expected to make a loss of £29 and the whole of this loss not just the £10 lost so far must be included in the profit and loss account. In this case SSAP 9 paragraph 30c requires including the net value of the contract in stocks but separately disclosed.

SUMMARY

12.   (a)   Work in progress should be valued in profit and loss accounts and balance sheets at total absorption cost in accordance with SSAP 9.

(b) Work in progress that will ultimately be completed and show a loss should be included at net realisable value if that is lower than cost.

(c) Long term contracts should be valued to include that part of the expected profit which has been earned to date as 'attributable profit'. This should occur only if the outcome of the contract can reasonably be foreseen.

(d) If an attributable profit is included then the work done to date should be included in turnover and the cost + attributable profit – amount received to date should be included as a separate item in debtors.

(e) If a loss is expected on a contract then the *whole* expected loss should be included in the accounts. The work done to date should be included in turnover and the value of work done less the cash received on account should be included in a separate item in stocks. Further the provision for the loss should be included in current liabilities.

POINTS TO NOTE

13. (a) In estimating costs to completion, all expected costs must be considered including rectification and guarantee work and bearing in mind the effects of inflation on future costs.

(b) Many contracts are agreed at a total price for the job and a sale price for the work done so far can only be estimated. However some jobs do have separate prices for separate stages and usually, for stage payment purposes, quantity surveyors certify the value of the work done.

(c) SSAP9 states that if the stage payments received exceed the value of work done (this seems unlikely) then the excess should be separately included in current liabilities as payments on account.

(d) The material in this chapter on long term progress is new having been promulgated in October 1988. At the time of writing it has not been fully absorbed by the profession.

Exercises (Answers on page 462)

1. *What should be the value in the accounts of the following work in progress items:*

	A	B	C	D
Materials cost to date	£200	£700	£500	£250
Direct labour to date	24 at £7	16 at £4.5	–	£870
Machine hours to date	12	–	40	–
Overhead labour hour rates	£9	–	–	–
Overhead machine hour rates	£21	–	£19	–
Overhead recovery		80% on prime cost		120% on labour costs
Expected costs to completion	£412	£30.4	£400	£290
Selling price	£1,400	£1,800	£1,900	£2,400

2. *What should be included in the accounts for the following long term contracts:*

	A	B	C	D	E
Total contract price	2,000	386	375	750	843
Value of work done	650	300	200	80	500
Cost of work done to date	450	305	160	74	450
Estimated cost of work to completion	1,059	100	120	?	480
Payments on account	400	230	300	nil	450

Exercises (without answers)

3. *What should be the value in the accounts of the following work in progress items:*

	A	B	C	D
Materials cost to date	200	342	342	100
Direct labour to date	64 at £6	76 at £4	121 at £5	3 at £3
Machine hours to date	37	12	–	–
Overhead labour hour rates	£14	£7	£7	
Overhead machine hour rates	£23	£15	–	
Overhead recovery				150% on labour
Expected cost to completion	£74	£354	£200	£60
Selling price	£2,800	£1,598	£2,100	£290

4. What should be included in the accounts for the following long term contracts:

	A	B	C	D	E
Total contract price	754	643	385	900	376
Value of work done	390	180	325	50	200
Cost of work done to date	351	170	284	45	190
Estimated cost of work to completion	299	420	40	?	220
Payments on account	350	200	280	nil	170

38. Marginal costs

INTRODUCTION

1.   Costs can be categorised in many ways. We have already considered categorisation into materials, labour and overheads, into production, marketing and distribution and general administration and into direct and indirect costs. Another very useful categorisation is into fixed and variable costs. Another word for variable is marginal and the subject of marginal costing is concerned with this categorisation.

2.   The valuation of stocks and work in progress is now, under SSAP 9, always at total absorption cost. However, many companies used to value stocks at marginal cost and questions on the effect of the different bases of valuation are still found, so we will review this issue.

3.   The division of costs into fixed and variable categories enables a number of decisions to be made rationally. We will briefly look at this aspect.

FIXED AND VARIABLE COSTS

4.   A *fixed cost* is one which, within certain output limits, tends to be unaffected by variations in the level of activity.

A *variable cost* is one which tends to vary in direct proportion to variations in the level of activity.

Examples of fixed costs are rent and rates. Examples of variable costs are materials, labour paid on piece rates and power consumption.

A good way of thinking about which category a cost falls into is to consider a particular level of activity (say on output of 5,000 widgets a month) and then to see which costs would change if output was increased (to say 6,000 widgets a month). The rent and rates of the factory would not change although if production was to rise very substantially additional premises would need to be taken on. However, rent and rates tend to be fixed for likely output levels and in the short term. Labour costs are likely to increase pro rata to output if the workers are paid piecework and possibly also if extra hours have to be worked by workers paid an hourly rate. In practice it is difficult to determine the effect on other costs. Would the telephone costs or heating costs be different at different levels of output?

MARGINAL COSTS

5.   Marginal cost is the additional cost incurred by the production of one extra unit. This idea is related to the division between fixed and variable costs. If a factory was producing 4,000 widgets in a period, what would be the *additional* cost of producing just one more. The extra cost may be in materials, piecework labour and perhaps a tiny amount of electricity, lubricating oil and other manufacturing costs. Many costs (salaries, rent, rates, insurance etc) will stay the same.

STOCKS AND WORK IN PROGRESS

6.   Under SSAP 9 stocks should be valued at total absorption cost eg:

Widget 642 cost in materials £76, in direct labour £24 and in overheads 13 machine hours at £12 an hour = a total of £256.

However some of the overheads included in the machine hour rate are fixed costs. Suppose 70% of these costs are fixed, then the variable or marginal cost of widget 642 would be £76 + £24 + 30% (13 x £12) = £146.80.

7.   Suppose Downland Clogs Ltd commenced business on 1.1.-4 and achieved the following figures in 19-4 and 19-5.

	£	£
Sales	24,656	36,419
Materials	5,321	8,543
Direct labour	7,800	12,300
Fixed manufacturing costs	4,533	4,720
Variable manufacturing costs	2,500	3,300
Non-manufacturing costs	1,890	2,200

Stocks at year ends were:

	£	£
if valued at full (= TAC) cost	3,500	5,200
if valued at variable cost	2,950	4,700

Measure profit for each year on a total cost stock value basis and a marginal cost stock value basis.

	TAC 19-4 £	MC 19-4 £	TAC 19-5 £	MC 19-5 £
Sales	24,656	24,656	36,419	36,419
Materials	5,321	5,321	8,543	8,543
Direct labour	7,800	7,800	12,300	12,300
VMC	2,500	2,500	3,300	3,300
		15,621		24,143
Opening stock				2,950
				27,093
Closing stock		2,950		4,700
		12,671		22,393
FMC	4,533		4,720	
	20,154		28,863	
Opening stock			3,500	
			32,363	
Closing stock	3,500		5,200	
	16,654		27,163	
Gross profit	8,002	11,985	9,256	14,026
FMC		4,533		4,720
NMC	1,890	1,890	2,200	2,200
Net profit	6,112	5,562	7,056	7,106

Notes:

(a) The profit in year 1 is larger if stock is valued higher (that is at total absorption cost). The difference is £550.

(b) The total profits of the two years are respectively £13,168 on a TAC basis and £12,668 on a marginal cost basis. The difference is £500 which is the difference in the values of stock at 31.12.-5.

(c) The profit in year 2 is different because of the different values of opening and closing stocks.

(d) In the income statement, the stock adjustment is made after *all* manufacturing costs in a TAC values statement and only *after* variable manufacturing costs in a marginal costs value statement.

(e) Under SSAP 9 the TAC approach should always be used but for *internal* purposes many companies use the marginal approach.

MARGINAL COSTS AND DECISION MAKING

8. Knowledge of marginal costs is very useful in decision making. In this section we will look at four decisions that can be made using this costing approach.

(a) **How to make**

P Ltd can make their widgets on a labour intensive method (the L method) or by a capital intensive method (the C method). Figures are:

	L	C
Selling price per item	£20	£20
Variable cost per item	£12	£8
Total fixed cost	£20,000	£60,000

How should the item be made if output is expected to be:

(i) 4,000 units;
(ii) 12,000 units.

The approach is to work out the *contribution* in both cases. Contribution is simply selling price less variable costs. In this case it is £8 for the L method and £12 for the C method.

Profits will be:

	4,000 output		12,000 output	
	L	C	L	C
	£	£	£	£
Total contribution	32,000	48,000	96,000	144,000
Fixed costs	20,000	60,000	20,000	60,000
Profit (loss)	12,000	(12,000)	76,000	84,000

Clearly at 4,000 units the labour method is the most profitable but at 12,000 units the capital method gives higher profits.

A useful idea is the *break even point*. This is were total contribution equals fixed costs and no profit or loss is made. In the case of the L method:

If breakeven output is y then: $8y = £20,000$ and $y = 2,500$, whereas for the C method: $12y = £60,000$ and $y = 5,000$.

(b) Limiting factor

G Ltd have a choice of making either or both of two products A and B.

	A	B
Facts are:		
Contribution	£24	£40
Usage of scarce labour	½ hour	1 hour

There are only 400 hours of the *limiting factor* or scarce resource available. What should be made if sales are unlimited?

The technique is to calculate the contribution per unit of scarce resource. This is £48 an hour for A and £40 an hour for B. Thus if an hour of the scarce labour is used to make an A the contribution will be £48 and if making a B then it will be £40.

It is obviously more profitable to make A's and a total of 800 A's should be made as this will exactly use up all the limited labour available.

If only 700 A's could be sold then output should be 700 A's using 350 hours and 50 B's to use up the remaining hours.

In some cases there are two or more constraints (= limiting factors) and to solve the output problem *linear programming* methods are required. These are beyond the scope of this book.

(c) Special orders

Grue Ltd have been asked to quote for the supply of 100 of their unique widgets to a company in Sweden. The price needs to be extremely low to land the order. The cost of each widget is:

	£
Materials	15
Direct labour	13
Variable overheads	8
Fixed overheads	6
	42

The normal home price is £55 and this will be unaffected by the export order if that order is received.

If the order is accepted, there will need to be a payment to a supervisor of £400 for the time he spends on the manufacture. There will also be an extra packing cost of £1 an item.

The *marginal* cost of the 100 widgets will thus be:

		£
Materials	100 x £15	1,500
Direct labour	100 x £13	1,300
Variable overheads	100 x £8	800
Packing	100 x £1	100
Supervisor		400
Total cost		4,100

Notes:
(a)   The costs calculated above are marginal costs. They are *extra* costs that will be incurred by the firm if the 100 widgets are made.
(b)   Any selling price above £4,100 will be of benefit to the firm.
(c)   In this calculation, the fixed costs can be ignored as they will be incurred if Grue makes the widgets or if it does not.
(d)   Selling at marginal costs can be dangerous, in that although the firm may receive more than it pays out as a result of a low price sale, other customers who are paying full price may want a reduction also.

(d) **Make or buy decisions**

Trater Ltd manufacture a flinge which costs:

	£
Materials	51
Direct labour	40
Variable overheads	23
Fixed overheads	39
	153

They have been quoted £105 each for the supply of the flinges from a firm in Korea. Transport costs will be £5 an item. There will be a saving of £2,000 a year in fixed costs if the flinges are not manufactured by Trater. Output is 1,000 a year.

The reduction in costs if the 1,000 flinges are not made will be:

1,000 x (51 + 40 + 23) + £2,000 = £116,000.

The costs of importing the 1,000 items will be:

1,000 x (£105 + £5) = £110,000

Thus it is more profitable to import than to manufacture. Note however, that there are many other arguments - continuity of supply, price variations due to exchange rates and other factors, delivery problems etc.

SUMMARY

9.   (a)   Fixed costs remain the same at different levels of activity or output - at least within certain output levels and in the short term.
(b)   Variable costs tend to vary in direct proportion (= linearly) to variations in levels of activity.
(c)   A marginal cost is the additional cost of producing one more of a product.
(d)   Stocks should be valued at total absorption cost under SSAP 9. Some exam questions are set to show the different profits measured if marginal costs are used to value stocks.
(e)   Marginal costs can be usefully employed in decision making.

POINTS TO NOTE

10.   (a)   Direct costs, variable costs and marginal costs can be equivalent. However, some variable costs (eg power) are often not included in direct costs because of the difficulty of measurement. Variable cost is a term used to describe the *behaviour* of costs. Marginal costs are strictly as defined in the summary. In practice some people are very particular about terminology but it is perhaps more important to understand the concepts and use them intelligently.

(b)   In practice the *behaviour* of costs is very difficult to determine. Even direct materials are not strictly linearly variable as quantity discounts may be obtained.

EXERCISES (answers begin on page 462)

1. *Describe the behaviour of the following costs:*

Fire insurance, employers' liability insurance, depreciation of plant, repairs to buildings, cleaning materials, telephone, metered water.

2. *Jam Ltd manufacture glogs and their figures for 19-6 and 19-7 are:*

Sales	87,600	89,450
Materials consumed	23,700	24,710
Direct labour	20,800	21,500
Variable manufacturing costs	8,690	9,320
Fixed manufacturing costs	18,600	17,500
Non-manufacturing costs	6,800	8,200

Finished goods stock was:	31.12.-5	31.12.-6	31.12.-7
If valued at total absorption cost	15,000	16,800	17,400
If valued at marginal cost	11,500	12,000	12,400

Calculate profits for both years on both bases of stock valuation.

3. *Doe makes his socks by labour intensive methods and his costs are:*

Materials £30, direct labour £60, variable production costs £10. (All these are for 200 pairs), fixed production costs £40,000 a year. If output is:

(a) 400,000 pairs;
(b) 600,000 pairs;

would it pay him to employ capital intensive methods if production costs increased to £110,000 a year. The selling price is 70p a pair.

Would your answer to (a) be different if (i) getting sales was very difficult (ii) sales were expanding fast.

4. *Hong can make three products whose contributions and potential sales and usage of scarce resource F are:*

Product	J	K	L
Contribution (per unit)	£24	£16	£60
Potential sales (units)	20,000	16,000	5,000
Usage of F (per unit)	12	10	32

Supply of F is limited to 30,000 units.

What should he make?

Exercises without answers

5. *Saeed makes a gong which costs - prime cost £39 + variable overheads £11 + fixed overheads £26. he sells it for £100. He has been asked to quote very keenly for the supply of 4,000 of these to a wholesaler (he normally supplies retailers). He reckons the extra sales will add £40,000 to his fixed costs but will reduce his prime costs to £37 for all his output (viz: his normal output of 30,000 + the 4,000).*

What is the lowest price he can accept?

6. *Facts as in 5 above. Saeed has been offered a supply of gongs at £52 each. Acceptance of the supply will reduce his fixed overheads by £50,000. Should he make or buy?*

7. *Perton Ltd manufacture special machinery to customers orders. The cost estimation department have costed an enquiry received from Shipley Ltd at £15,200 on a total absorption cost basis and have suggested a selling price of £17,000. Shipley decline to give an order at this price and propose that £14,000 is all they are willing to pay.*

Required:
Discuss this problem from Perton's point of view. Your essay should include a description of alternative costing principles that might allow Perton to accept the order at £14,000 and an indication of the criteria which Perton might take into account in deciding whether or not to accept the order.   *(RSA)*

8.   *John Gale has been in business for two years. He has not yet prepared any final accounts. Details of his trading for these two years can be summarised as follows:*

		Year 1	Year 2
(i)	Sales	400 units at	500 units at
		£12 each	£13 each
(ii)	Production	500 units	600 units
(iii)	Fixed factory overheads	£1,000	£1,050
(iv)	Cost of direct labour and materials	£4 per unit	£4.50 per unit
(v)	Variable overheads	£2 per unit	£2 per unit

From these figures, assuming the first-in, first-out method, you are required to calculate gross profits for each year using:

   (a)   *Marginal approach to valuing stocks.*
   (b)   *Absorption approach to valuing stocks.*   *(RSA)*

9.   *Electro-Cute Ltd has a division which manufactures and sells a patented electronic device. All the parts can be obtained by either (a) making them in Electro-Cute's own factory or (b) by having them made by another manufacturer. Cost and other data include:*

(i)	At selling price of	£200	£210
	Sales are expected to be (in units)	1,000	800

		Fixed	Variable
(ii)	Costs are expected to be:		
	if made in own factory	£65,000	£80 each
	if made outside	nil	£150 each

Advise Electro-Cute on:

   (i)   *whether to make the device themselves or to buy in; and*
   (ii) *the selling price giving the maximum profit.*   *(RSA)*

10. *Concrete Slabs Ltd, can make a variety of moulded concrete products. Their products are in great demand but production for July 1983 will be limited by the number of hours they can use the mixing machine. The following data may be relevant in planning production for that month:*

   (a)   *Four products are proposed and their prices, costs and machine usage are:*

	Large lintels	Small lintels	Slabs	Blocks
Prices (in £)	6.50	4.50	3.25	2.60
Variable costs (in £)	4.50	3.30	2.45	1.10
Machine usage (minutes)	2	1.5	0.5	2.5

   (b)   *The maximum sales achievable are:*

   slabs – 6,000 units; blocks – 20,000 units; the lintels – unlimited.

   (c)   *Sales of the products are quite independent except that volume of production of the small lintels must be at least 25% of that of large lintels.*

   (d)   *The total hours available on the mixing machine in July 1983 will be 145.*

Required:
A table showing what products and in what quantities Concrete Slabs Ltd, should make in July 1983 to make the highest possible profit.
                                                                                            (RSA)

PROFIT AND CAPITAL MEASUREMENT IN DIFFERENT TYPES OF ENTERPRISE

The fascination of financial accounting is that it deals with businesses and there are an infinite variety of types of business. So far we have formulated some general rules which apply to all enterprises but we have applied them only to sole traders who trade in goods. In this section, we will look at some enterprises which differ in mode of ownership and/or in type of activity carried on.

In Chapter 39 we look at clubs, societies and other non-trading and non-profit making enterprises. In Chapter 40 we look at service industries. In Chapter 41 we look at departmental accounts.

39. Non Trading Bodies

INTRODUCTION

1. Retailers, wholesalers, manufacturers and other commercial and industrial organisations have, as a primary objective, the making of a profit. The profit (or loss) is measured in the profit and loss account.

2. For clubs, societies and charitable bodies, the objectives are not to make profits, but to supply a service to members or the beneficiaries of the charity.

3. Nonetheless, clubs, societies and charitable bodies must have, at least in the long term, sufficient income to meet expenditure and annual (or more frequent) accounts must be produced to show members and others, the financial affairs of the organisation.

4. The format for reporting financial affairs of a club, society or charitable body is:

   - An Income and Expenditure Account
   - A Balance Sheet

The Income and Expenditure account, which is the equivalent of the profit and loss account of a business, contain sub-divisions such as a bar trading account.

PREPARATION OF ACCOUNTS

5. Here is an example:

The Tettenhall Accountants Club was formed on 1st January 19-4 to provide an opportunity for Accountants to meet together and also to amass sufficient money to endow a scholarship fund for accounting students without grants.

At the end of the first year the treasurer summarised the bank account as follows:

Receipts	£	Payments	£
Members subscriptions	1,250	Purchase of 10 years lease of	
Donations to scholarship fund	1,180	building	2,000
Grand draw receipts	1,425	Rent for first 15 months	560
Bar takings	2,763	Bar purchases	1,934
Interest on Building Society		Overheads	620
Account	12	Deposited in Building Society	1,000
Loan at 10% on 1.1.-4 from		Equipment	340
wealthy member	2,000	Books for library	147
		Grand Draw prizes	710
		Part time bar staff - wages	290
		Grants made to students	580

You ascertain that:

(a) The equipment should last at least five years.

(b) At 31st December 19-4:

	£
Bar Stocks	325
Creditors – bar purchases	327
Accrued overheads	13
Subscriptions in arrears	20
Subscriptions in advance	60

(c) The profit on the grand draw is to be credited to the scholarship fund.

Required:
(i) Income and Expenditure Account for the year ending 31st December 19-4.
(ii) Balance Sheet as at 31st December 19-4.

6. ANSWER

The Tettenhall Accountants Club
Bar Trading Account for the year ending 31st December 19-4

	£	£
Sales		2,763
Less Cost of goods sold:		
Purchases (a)	2,261	
Less Closing stock	325	1,936
Gross Profit		827
Wages – Bar staff		290
Net Profit		£ 537

Note:

(a) *Purchases is obtained from payments (£1,934) and year end creditors (£327).*

(b) *This Account is drawn up on conventional lines. It is clearly important for the members to know the finanical contribution made by the bar and for them to apply elementary appraisal techniques such as computing the gross profit percentage (30%) to see that it is reasonable.*

Income and Expenditure Account for the year ending 31st December 19-4

	£	£	
Income			(a)
Net profit on bar		537	
Subscriptions		1,210	(b)
Building Society interest		12	
		1,759	
Expenditure			(c)
Rent	448		
Overheads	633		
Books for Library	147		(d)
Amortisation of lease	200		(e)
Depreciation of equipment	68		(f)
Interest on loan	200	1,696	
Surplus of income over expenditure for year		63	(g)

Note:

(a) *In the Accounts of clubs etc., there are usually several sources of income, unlike businesses where gross profit is the main source of income.*

(b) *Subscriptions must be the subscriptions for 19-4 and receipts have to be adjusted for receipts in arrear and in advance.*

(c) *Expenditure categories are included using the accruals convention. In this example:*

(i)   *Rent is adjusted for a prepayment.*
(ii) *Overheads are adjusted for an accrual.*

(iii) No interest has been paid on the loan but interest has accrued over the year and is thus an expense of the year.

(d) It is arguable that as the books will be of use over more than one year, their cost could be capitalised (= treated as a fixed asset) and depreciated over their useful life. In practice most accountants would write them off (= treat them as an expense in the year of purchase).

(e) Lease depreciation is termed amortisation.

(f) I have adopted a depreciation policy of straight line with no salvage value.

(g) Since the club does not have as a primary aim the making of a profit, the difference between income and expenditure for the year is called a surplus, or, if expenditure exceeds income, a deficit.

Income and Expenditure Account of Scholarship Fund for the year ending 31st December 19-4

	£	£	
Income			
Donations		1,180	
Grand draw: Receipts	1,425		(b)
Prizes	710	715	
		1,895	
Expenditure			
Grants to students		580	
Surplus for the year		1,315	

Notes:

(a) The club has two principal aims, a social one and a philanthropic one. In this case, it is desirable to measure the income and expenditure of each separately because:

(i) Social section income must, in the long run, exceed or equal social section expenditure.
(ii) The amount of grants which can be made, depends on there being sufficient income for this purpose.

(b) Members could be interested in knowing:

(i) The income from the draw;
(ii) The outlay on prizes;
(iii) The surplus achieved.

The Tettenhall Accountants Club
Balance Sheet as at 31st December 19-4

	Cost £	Accumulated Depreciation £	Net Book Value £	
Fixed Assets				(a)
Leasehold premises	2,000	200	1,800	
Equipment	340	68	272	
	2,340	268	2,072	
Current Assets				
Bar stocks		325		
Subscriptions in arrear		20		
Prepayments		112		
Building Society Deposit		1,000		
Cash at Bank		449	1,906	
			3,978	
Less **Current Liabilities**				
Bar Creditors		327		
Accruals		213		
Subscriptions in advance		60	600	
			3,378	
Less **Long term Liabilities**				
Loan at 10%			2,000	
			1,378	

Accumulated Fund
    Surplus for year   63   (b)
Scholarship Fund
    Surplus for year   1,315   (c)
                                           £1,378

Note:

(a) *The balance sheet is drawn up on conventional lines as far as assets and current and long term liabilities are concerned. The sections, accumulated fund and scholarship fund are peculiar to clubs and societies and charitable bodies.*

(b) *This is equivalent to "capital" in a business balance sheet.*

(c) *The idea of separate funds is not easy to grasp. The club has assets of £3,978 and liabilities to specific external persons of £2,600 so that the net assets are £1,378. Of the net assets, £1,315 is held so that grants may be paid to students. Only the remainder of the net assets £63 properly belongs to the members.*

THEORY

7. The Accounts of many clubs, societies and charitable bodies consist simply of a *Receipts and Payments Account*. This has the merit of simplicity and is easy for non-accountants to prepare and for non-accountants to understand. Where the organisation has few assets other than cash in hand and at bank, this approach is acceptable.

8. When an organisation has assets other than cash, a simple receipts and payments account fails to give the relevant information which members are entitled to and leads to lack of comparability between successive years as income and capital items are not separated.

9. In consequence, clubs, etc., in their accounts normally adopt an income and expenditure account which uses the accounting conventions:

(a) Realisation –   for bar trading.
(b) Matching –   Income of a year is matched with expenditure of the year.
(c) Accruals –   Receipts and payments are adjusted for accruals and prepayments.
(d) Going concern – As the organisation is expected to continue into the foreseeable future, the fixed assets can be valued at unamortised cost.
(e) Prudence –   This convention can be applied to value stocks and also to debtors (subscriptions in arrears for example) whose collectability is in doubt.

10. Finally, there is the item of net assets being divided into separate funds indicating that the net assets are held or owned for different purposes.

PROBLEMS IN IMPLEMENTATION

11. **Life members.** Subscriptions are often received from *life members*. Life members pay a once and for all subscription which entitles them to membership facilities for the rest of their lives. Clearly, the accounting convention of matching requires that such subscriptions should be credited to income and expenditure, not as they are received, but over the *life times* of such members.

In practice, if life member subscriptions are small, they are credited to income as received but if they are significant in amount, then they should be credited in equal parts over the *estimated active* club membership of such members.

12. **Entrance Fees.** Similar problems are encountered with *entrance fees*. In practice, most accountants take entrance fees to income and expenditure account as they are received.

13. **Separate activities.** In the example, chosen, the bar represents a *separate activity* of a fairly complex nature and a separate account is drawn up to measure the income from the source. It is possible that other activities (*e.g.* the grand draw) may be sufficiently complex to require a separate account away from the income and expenditure account proper. In all cases where sources of income have associated expenditures, the income and expenditure should be put together and the surplus or loss on that particular activity should be shown.

14. **Separate funds and separate investment.** In the example chosen, the monies received for the benefit of the scholarship fund, were paid into the general club bank account and assets acquired therefrom for general club use. The effect of this is that, although the scholarship fund stands at £1,315, actual cash is not available to make grants of that amount.

To prevent monies given or raised for a particular purpose being used for other purposes, it is possible to *invest* such sums in specific investments. In such cases, a choice can be made between:

(a) Showing the fund and its associated investments in separate parts of the general balance sheet.

(b) Having a separate balance sheet for the fund and its associated investments.

SUMMARY

15. (a) Clubs, societies, charitable bodies and other organisations that do not trade with a view to profit, must prepare annual accounts to present to members and other interested parties.

(b) The financial statements produced are:

- An Income and Expenditure Account.
- A Balance Sheet.

(c) The Income and Expenditure Account may be supported by separate accounts such as a Bar Trading Account.

(d) The *capital* of a business balance sheet is, in a non-trading body, called the Accumulated Fund.

(e) Where the net assets are held or earmarked for specific purposes, the balance sheet may show separate *funds* in addition to the Accumulated Fund.

POINTS TO NOTE

16. (a) Clubs, Society and Charity Accounts, are an example of *stewardship* accounting. The committee, council, trustee or whatever the management are termed, receive, spend and invest monies belonging to others and it is right they should give an account of their dealings with the funds entrusted to their care.

(b) Members of a club or society or a person concerned with a charity, can appraise the performance of the management body in many ways. Financially this may include:

(i) Assessing the bar trading account for adequacy of gross profit margin, appropriateness of pricing or sufficiency of contribution to the organisation's finances.

(ii) Assessing income and expenditure to determine whether, taking one year with another, income matches expenditure. Note that, in these organisations, non-recurring income or expenditure can occur and regular income should be sufficient to meet regular expenditure.

(iii) Assessing future policy on such matters as subscription levels and charitable giving.

(c) Receipts and Payments Accounts are often presented horizontally as:

Dr   Receipts   *Payments   Cr*

Some income and expenditure accounts are also presented horizontally, in which case the two sides are the reverse of those of receipts and payments:

Dr   Expenditure   *Income   Cr*

(d) In examination questions, workings must be given, preferably in double entry form. For example, if the calculation of subscriptions for the year is complex:

Subscriptions Account

Dr			*Cr*
Subscriptions in arrear b/f	110	Subscriptions in advance b/f	286
Income and Expenditure A/c	?	Cash receipts	3,240
Subscriptions in advance c/f	813	Receipts by cheque	4,860
		Subscriptions in arrear c/f	140
	£8,526		£8,526

From this account, the subscriptions for the year can be calculated as £7,603.

SELF TESTING QUESTIONS

(a) What are the objectives of clubs, societies, and charitable bodies? (2).

(b) What financial requirements do such bodies have? (3).

(c) What financial statements should be produced by such bodies? (4).

(d) What is the term used for the capital of a non-trading body? (6).

(e) What is the relationship between "funds" and "net assets"? (6).

(f) Contrast a Receipts and Payments Account with an Income and Expenditure Account. (7-9).

(g) How should (i) life member subscriptions and (ii) entrance fees be accounted for? (11,12).

(h) Distinguish between separate funds and separate investment. (14).

(i) How can a member of a club use the financial statements to appraise the performance of the management body? (16).

EXERCISES (Answers begin on page 463)

1. The following is the receipts and payments account of Twood Climbing Club for the year ending 31.12.-7.

Receipts and Payments Account of Twood Climbing Club
for the year ending 31.12.-7

	£		£
Subscriptions	5,600	Clubhouse overheads	4,540
Bar takings	4,530	Bar Purchases	3,180
Donations	100	New equipment	1,200
Annual Dinner tickets	850	Cost of Annual Dinner	1,070
Collection for Prize Fund	970	Prizes purchased	865
		Petty cash	100
b/f	1,030	c/f	2,125
	13,080		13,080

Balances at 31.12:	19-6	19-7
	£	£
Subscriptions in advance	135	240
Subscriptions in arrear	200	320
Bar Stocks	780	543
Bar purchases creditors	650	728
Prize Fund	1,600	?
Clubhouse overhead accruals	238	143
Clubhouse overhead prepayment	100	57
Equipment at cost	3,600	?
Equipment accumulated depr	1,400	?
Prize Stock	300	327
Petty cash	30	51

One quarter of the clubhouse overheads is apportionable to the bar.
Depreciation is at 30% reducing balance.
Petty cash is used only for postage and stationery.

Required: bar trading account; income and expenditure account; balance sheet; a commentary on the results and the treasurer's proposal to increase subscriptions by 5%.

2. The Anglo India Cricket and Hockey Club has two sections – cricket and hockey. Its receipts and payments account for the year ending 31.12.-7 showed:

	£		£
Subs - Hockey 67 x £30	2,010	Bar purchases	4,600
Subs - Cricket 58 x £40	2,320	Hockey dinner costs	623
Dinner - Hockey section	456	Cricket dance costs	520
Dance - Cricket section	561	Barman's salary	1,100
Bar takings	6,790	Development fund raffle prizes	200
Raffle for development fund	880	General overheads	3,100
		Hockey section costs	1,168
		Cricket section costs	653
		Government Bonds	2,000
b/f	1,543	c/f	596
	14,560		14,560

Balances at 31 December were:

	19-6	19-7
Bar debtors	132	247
Bar creditors	780	903
Bar stocks	580	435
Subs in advce – hockey	3 mbrs	2 mbrs
– cricket	12 mbrs	18 mbrs
Subs in arrear – hockey	5 mbrs	12 mbrs
– cricket	0 mbrs	1 mbr
General overheads creditors	120	238
General overheads prepmts	100	350
Stock of raffle prizes	140	138
Club premises at cost	24,000	24,000
Premises accumulated depreciation	3,000	?
Development Fund balance	4,700	?
Hockey section balance	2,170	?
Cricket section balance	2,305	?
Loan on Mortgage	13,000	13,000

Note: The cost of the clubhouse (£20,000) is being depreciated over 20 years. The bar profit is credited 50% to the hockey section and 50% to the cricket section. Depreciation and general overheads are debited similarly.

Prepare income and Expenditure Account and Balance Sheet. Comment on the club's financial affairs.

Exercises without answers

3.   *The following is a summary of the receipts and payments of the Miniville Rotary Club during the year ended 31 July 1986:*

Miniville Rotary Club
Receipts and Payments Account
for the year ended 31 July 1986

	£		£
Cash and bank balances b/f	210	Secretarial expenses	163
Sales of competition tickets	437	Rent	1,402
Members' subscriptions	1,987	Visiting speakers' expenses	1,275
Donations	177	Donations to charities	35
Refund of rent	500	Prizes for competitions	270
Balance c/f	13	Stationery and printing	179
	3,324		3,324

The following valuations are also available:

as at 31 July	1985	1986
	£	£
Equipment	975	780
(original cost £1,420)		
Subscriptions in arrears	65	85
Subscriptions in advance	10	37
Owing to suppliers of competition prizes	58	68
Stocks of competition prizes	38	46

Required:
  (a) Calculate the value of the Accumulated Fund of the Miniville Rotary Club as at the 1 August 1985.
  (b) Reconstruct the following accounts for the year ended 31 July 1986:

    (i)   the Subscriptions Account,
    (ii)   the Competition Prizes Account.

  (c) Prepare an Income and Expenditure Account for the Miniville Rotary Club for the year ended 31 July 1986 and a Balance Sheet as at that date.
                                                                                                    (AAT)

4.   (a)   S. Nastuti runs a business with a financial year ending on 31 March of each year. The business premises are rented at an annual rental of £6,000 payable quarterly in advance on the 1 April, 1 July, 1 October and 1 January of each financial year.

The rent payable on 1 April 1985 was paid by cheque on 25 March 1985. During the financial year ended 31 March 1986 S. Nastuti made two further rental payments by cheque.

		£
25 June 1985		1,500
20 October 1985		1,500

Required:
Reconstruct the Rent Account for the financial year ended 31 March 1986 showing how the account would be balanced and closed off at 31 March 1986.

(b)   The Scenium Drama Club runs a bar to help swell club funds. The following information is available for the year ended 31 May 1986:

		£
Bar sales		19,366
Bar staff wages		2,574
Owing to bar suppliers	at 31 May 1985	1,114
	at 31 May 1986	1,571
Paid to bar suppliers		14,680
Other bar expenses		1,104
Bar stock	at 31 May 1985	2,597
	at 31 May 1986	3,155

Required:
Prepare a Bar Trading Account for the year ended 31 May 1986.

(c)   After preparing its draft Final Accounts for the year ended 31 March 1986 and its draft Balance Sheet as at 31 March 1986 a business discovered that the stock lists used to compute the value of stock as at 31 March 1986 contained the following entry:

Stock Item	Number	Cost per unit	Total Cost
Y 4003	100	£1.39	£1,390

Required:
(1)   What is wrong with this particular entry?
(2)   What would the effect of the error have been on:

(i)   the value of stock as at 31 March 1986?
(ii)   the cost of goods sold for the year ended 31 March 1986?
(iii) the net profit for the year ended 31 March 1986?
(iv)   the total for Current Assets as at 31 March 1986?
(v)   the Owner's Capital as at 31 March 1986?

(AAT)

5.   As treasurer of your local tennis club you have just prepared a draft Receipts and Payments account, which is reproduced below.

The club committee decides, however, that it wishes its financial statements for 1983 and subsequent years to be in the form of an Income and Expenditure Account accompanied by a balance sheet and requests you to amend the 1983 account accordingly.

Receipts and Payments account for the year ended 31st December, 1983

		£
Receipts: *Cash in hand at 1 January 1983*		*100*
Cash at bank at 1 January 1983:		
Current account		*1,160*
Deposit account		*2,000*
Members' subscriptions:	*1982*	*620*
	1983	*8,220*
	1984	*125*
Interest on deposit account		*85*
Entry fees for club championship		*210*
Tickets sold for annual dinner/dance		*420*
Bank overdraft at 31st December 1983		*4,000*
		16,940
Payments:		
Groundsman's wages		*4,000*
Purchase of equipment (on 30th June 1983)		*8,000*
Rent for year to 30th September 1983		*2,000*
Rates for year to 31st March 1984		*1,800*
Cost of annual dinner/dance		*500*
Secretarial expenses		*400*
Prizes for club championship		*90*
Miscellaneous expenses		*100*
Cash in hand at 31st December 1983		*50*
		16,940

Additional information:

1. *At 31st December 1983 £700 was outstanding for members' subscriptions for 1983.*
2. *During 1982, £230 was received in respect of members' subscriptions for 1983.*
3. *The cost of equipment purchased in previous years was:*

	£
30th June 1972	*5,000*
1st January 1977	*1,000*
30th September	*1,000*

4. *The committee decides that equipment should be depreciated at the rate of 10% per annum on cost.*
5. *Rent has been at the rate of £2,000 per annum for the last two years and is not expected to change in the immediate future.*
6. *Rates of £750 for the six months to 31st March 1983 were paid on 2nd November 1982.*
7. *Interest of £250 on the bank overdraft had accrued at 31st December 1983.*
8. *Taxation is to be ignored.*

You are required to prepare:
   (a) the club's Income and Expenditure account for the year ended 31st December 1983; and
   (b) its balance sheets as at 31st December 1982 and 31st December 1983. *(CIMA)*

6. *The Hon. Secretary of the Hanford Social Club kept a cash book in which he recorded the day-to-day transactions of the club. An analysis of the transactions for the year 1985 produced the following information:*

	£
Subscriptions - 136 members @ £20 per annum	*2,720*
Entrance fees - new members 20 x £15	*300*
Life membership subscriptions - 20 x£100	*2,000*
Members' loans to New Pavilion Fund	*140*
Gaming machine licence (1 year)	*500*
Hire of gaming machine (1 year)	*200*
Secretarial costs inc Honorarium	*240*
Telephone	*85*
Repairs & Maintenance - pavilion	*1,680*
Gas and Electricity	*850*
Fire Insurance	*60*
Wages - part-time caretaker	*600*
Sundry Expenses	*190*
Gaming machine income	*1,500*
Net proceeds - fund-raising efforts	*720*

The following balances existed in the accounts named at the dates stated:

	31/12/84	31/12/85
	£	£
Stoke Suburban Building Society (5½% Ord shares)	1,000	1,055
National Bank - current a/c	40	510
New Pavilion Fund - loans from members	850	940
Post Office Investment a/c	–	1,500
Life Membership Suspense a/c	1,400	2,250
(Life Membership subscriptions were treated as subscriptions for five years)		

There were the following prepayments and accruals:

Members' subscriptions in arrears	200	180
Members' subscriptions prepaid	40	30
Telephone Account, received 25/12/85, not paid	–	15

Provide for one year's depreciation of £1,000 on the pavilion.

Required:
Prepare an Income and Expenditure Account for the Hanford Social Club for the year 1985.

Note: In a horizontal account Income should be on the credit side.   (LCCI)

7.   *The following Trial Balance was extracted from the books of the ABC Social Club as at 31 October 1983:*

	Dr	Cr
	£	£
Creditors for Refreshment supplies		990
Refreshment stocks 1 Nov 1982	1,760	
Subscriptions received		1,970
Accumulated Fund 1 Nov 1982		5,090
Freehold premises	5,500	
Income from social events		470
Rates and Insurance	610	
Wages and Salaries	3,790	
Furniture and Fittings	860	
Refreshment Purchases	8,640	
Cash	60	
Income from special events		2,460
Repairs	160	
Refreshment Sales		10,180
Sundry Expenses	470	
Discount received		130
Bank Overdraft		560
	21,850	21,850

NOTES

(1) Refreshment Stocks 31 October 1983 - £1,920.

(2) £600 of Wages and Salaries should be debited to the Refreshment Trading Account.

(3) Rates prepaid 31 October 1983 - £70.

(4) Subscriptions due but unpaid at 31 October 1983, £110.

(5) Provide for depreciation of Furniture and Fittings £80.

Required:
Draw up the Refreshment Trading Account and General Income and Expenditure Account for the year ended 31 October 1983 together with a Balance Sheet as at that date.

(LCCI)

8. The following is a summary of the bank account of the Northminster Arts centre for the year ended 31 December 1986.

Bank summary

	£		£
Balance at bank @ 1.1.86	7,200	Payments for bar supplies	56,100
Bar takings	84,200	Rates	3,600
Rents received	6,400	Equipment	30,400
Members subscriptions	7,800	Light and heat	3,800
Overdrawn balance @ 31.12.86	2,700	Telephone	1,800
		General expenses	2,900
		Administrator's salary	9,700
	108,300		108,300

You are able to ascertain the following:

(i)   Weekly wages for part-time bar staff amounting to £60 per week are paid in cash before takings are banked.
(ii) Suppliers' invoices for crisps, tobacco etc which have been resold in the bar amount to £4,900. These have been paid in cash.
(iii) Ten members have prepaid their 1987 subscriptions of £5 each.
(iv) Equipment is to be depreciated by £7,500.
(v)   Bar stocks on 31 December had increased by £200 since 1 January whilst creditors for the bar purchases had fallen by £100 in the same period.

Assets and liabilities on 1 January 1986 were as follows:

	£
Premises (at cost)	60,000
Equipment (book value)	50,000
Bar stocks	8,100
Creditors for bar supplies	6,200

You are required to:
Prepare a bar trading and an income and expenditure account for the year ended 31 December 1986 and a balance sheet as at that date.   (RSA)

9. The Allied Bowls Club presents you with the following data for the year ended 31 December 1987.

Receipts	£	Payments	£
Subscriptions received	34,000	Rates	1,200
Dance takings	15,000	General expenses	28,000
		Dance expenses	8,000

You are also advised that:

	31.12.86	31.12.87
	£	£
Subscriptions owing	1,400	1,200
Subscriptions pre-paid	200	300
Premises (at cost of £90,000)	40,000	36,000
Fixtures and fittings (at cost of £20,000)	6,000	4,000
Bank	2,000	13,800

You are asked to:
(a) Present the income and expenditure account for the year ended 31 December 1987, highlighting the surplus/deficit of the dance.
(b) Calculate the accumulated fund as at 31 December 1986 and at 31 December 1987.   (RSA)

40. Service Industries

INTRODUCTION

1. So far, in this manual, we have considered the trading and profit and loss accounts of manufacturers, retailers and wholesalers, and the income and expenditure accounts of clubs and societies.

2. The profit and loss account of businesses in service industries measures the profit earned by the business and this chapter considers appropriate layouts for such statements.

3. Particular problems of accounting measurement arise in service industries and these are reviewed.

PROFIT AND LOSS ACCOUNTS IN A SERVICE INDUSTRY

4. Service industries are those in which the enterprises supply, not a good or commodity but a service. Examples are professional services (accountants, lawyers etc.); personal services (hairdressing, driving schools); transport; entertainment; travel and holidays; restaurants and hotels. It is probable that service industries will grow rapidly in the future as manufacturing declines.

5. A suitable format for the profit and loss account of an accounting practice might be:

	£000	£000
Fees invoiced		440
Less		
Costs and expenses:		
Wages and salaries	180	
Rent, rates, insurance	46	
Professional indemnity		
insurance	8	
Motor and travelling	31	
Printing and stationery	36	
Sundries	12	
	313	
Work in progress at beginning	38	
	351	
Less work in progress at end	44	307
Net Profit		£133

Note:

(a) *There is no gross profit stage to the statement. Gross profit as an idea is difficult to define precisely, but might be considered to be goods or services supplied less the* direct *cost of the goods or services supplied. Net profit can then be derived by deducting overhead expenses which are not part of the direct cost of the goods or services supplied.*

(b) *In an accounting practice, it is impossible to satisfactorily distinguish between which expenses are part of the cost of service supplied and which are overheads, not directly related to the service.*

(c) *The matching convention which underlies the profit computation requires that:*

    Revenue dealt with in the profit and loss account is matched with associated costs and expenses by including in the same account the costs incurred in earning them.

(d) *The objective of including work in progress is to eliminate from the costs and expenses those costs and expenses, which although incurred in the year, should be matched with revenue of the following year. The problem is how to value work in progress.*

6. A suitable format for a travel agent might be:

		£000
Commissions earned:		370
Less Costs and expenses		
Wages and salaries	104	
Rent, rates, insurance	59	
Telephone	34	
etc., etc.	52	249
Net Profit		121

7.   In this case, there would be no work in progress.

8.   In some service industries, the activities can be divided into *segments*. For example, a hotel may offer room lettings, a dining room and a bar. The gross profit on the bar can be determined but a gross profit on a dining room is more difficult. The cost of the goods offered, meals, is not simply the material cost, but the cost of labour in waiting and serving the meal and the cost of providing the dining room and kitchen facilities.

9.   In most service industries, an approach to devising an appropriate and informative profit and loss account might:

   (a)   Consider if the activities can be segmented.
   (b)   Consider if the concept of a gross profit is appropriate for all or any of the activities.
   (c)   Consider what categories and sub-categories the overheads can be analysed into.
   (d)   Consider if work in progress exists and how it might be measured.

ACCOUNTING POLICIES

10.   In all businesses, a profit has to be measured for each separate accounting year. The accounting conventions are recognised as the way in which decisions are made about which accounting year, the profit or loss on a particular transaction is entered.

Examples are the realisation convention which indicates that profits are taken on all items sold in a year whether or not cash has been realised in the year, and the prudence convention which requires that expected losses, but not expected gains, are taken into account in the year that its expectations are recognised.

11.   Many expense items relate, not to particular revenue earning transactions, but to revenues in general. For example, the depreciation process is required to allocate fixed asset consumption to specific time periods and the accruals convention allocates revenue expenses (*e.g.* rent) to specific accounting periods.

12.   There are many revenues and expenses where the application of the conventions requires the adoption of a choice among a limited selection of possible accounting *policies*. For example, depreciation of plant can be based upon any of the following depreciation *policies:*

   - straight line   - sum of digits
   - reducing instalment   - usage as a proportion of maximum lifetime usage etc.

13.   The problem of *annual* profit measurement in terms of accounting *policy* selection is illustrated by the following question:

On 1st January 19-3, Meg Tape started in business as a software designer and computer bureau operator. She started her business bank account with £2,500 taken from her building society account and £6,200 borrowed at £20% from her brother. Her first year transactions were:

(1)   On 1.1.-3 she purchased the remaining sixty years of a lease on an old property for £20,000 taking a mortgage of £18,000 at 16%. Instalments with interest were due on 30th June and 31st December and in 19-3 were met on time. The capital part of each instalment was £1,000.

(2)   Computing and other equipment was bought for £10,000 using a temporary overdraft. Expected life of the equipment is very uncertain because of the probability of obsolescence.

(3)   Sundry overheads of £26,300 were paid of which £200 was in advance at 31.12.-3. A further £1,280 was outstanding at 31.12.-3.

(4)   Drawings were £4,400.

(5)   She paid various independent programmers £4,800 to write programs for her including £2,600 for a program which can be sold to numerous potential clients. No sale of such a program has yet been made.

(6)   She wrote various programs for clients including one suite of programs which has general applicability and of which twenty copies have already been sold to clients.

(7)   Sales of £46,000 were made of which £5,300 was outstanding at 31.12.-3.

Required
- (a) The cash book summary for 19-3.
- (b) Profit and Loss Account for 19-3.
- (c) Balance Sheet at 31.12.-3.
- (d) A statement of accounting policies to accompany the accounts. You should select policies which accord with generally accepted accounting principles. Any assumptions made should be stated.

Part (a) is relatively simple:

Dr	Cash Book Summary 19-3		Cr
	£		£
Cash introduced by proprietor	2,500	Lease	20,000
Loan from brother	6,200	June mortgage instalment	2,440
Mortgage	18,000	December mortgage instalment	2,360
Sales receipts	40,700	Computing equipment	10,000
Balance c/f 31.12.-3	2,900	Sundry overheads	26,300
		Drawings	4,400
		Programmers	4,800
	70,300		70,300

Part (b) requires the development of appropriate accounting policies in the following areas:

(i) **Depreciation of lease.** Many businesses do *not* amortise (= depreciate) leases with more than 50 years to run. We will select a policy to amortise the cost of the lease on a straight line basis.

(ii) **Depreciation of computing equipment.** Estimation of life and salvage value is exceedingly difficult in industries with fast changing technology. In addition several depreciation policies are possible. A *prudent policy* may be to use the reducing balance method at say 50% a year.

(iii) **Independently written programs.** It appears from the question that £2,200 (£4,800 - £2,600) was for work done that is to be matched with some of the revenues (£46,000) and is, therefore, an expense of 19-3. the £2,600 cannot be matched with 19-3 revenues. But can it be carried forward to 19-4 and subsequent years? The answer depends on the likelihood of future revenues and these are uncertain. A prudent *policy* may be to regard all such expenses as expenses of the year in which they are incurred. We will do so.

(iv) The ideal accounting policy here would be to determine the cost of the suite of programs (say £2,000) and charge that sum in the profit and loss accounts in those years when copies were sold. If for example, sales were 20 in 19-3, 30 in 19-4, 40 in 19-5 and 10 in 19-6, then the costs (£2,000) would appear in the accounts as:

	Sales (Units)	Costs (£)
19-3	20	400
19-4	30	600
19-5	40	800
19-6	10	200
		£2,000

In practice, two problems arise:

- (a) What are the cost of the programs? Presumably a proportion of the overheads, depreciation of equipment etc. But estimating this is both difficult and arbitrary.
- (b) At the end of 19-3, it is not known what sales would be made in later years.

Thus, the prudent policy is to allow all the costs of production of the suite of programs to fall into 19-3.

Meg Tape

**Profit and Loss Account for the year ending
31st December, 19-3**

	£	£
Sales		46,000
Less Costs and expenses:		
Amortisation of lease	333	

Mortgage interest		2,800	
Depreciation of computing equipment		5,000	
Sundry overheads		27,380	
Programs written		4,800	
Loan interest		1,240	41,553
Net Profit			£ 4,447

Balance Sheet as at 31st December, 19-3

	Cost	*Depreciation*	*Net*
	£	£	£
Fixed Assets			
Lease	20,000	333	19,667
Equipment	10,000	5,000	5,000
	30,000	5,333	24,667
Current Assets			
Debtors		5,300	
Prepayments		200	5,500
			30,167
Current Liabilities			
Creditors		1,280	
Loan interest accrued		1,240	
Bank overdraft		2,900	5,420
			£24,747
Capital Introduced			2,500
Profit for year			4,447
			6,947
Drawings			4,400
			2,547
Loans - mortgage		16,000	
- brother		6,200	22,200
			£24,747

Statement of Accounting Policies

(a) Leasehold property is amortised on the straight line basis over its remaining life of 60 years.

(b) Computing and other equipment is depreciated on the reducing balance method at the rate of 50% a year.

(c) Costs of programs written by independent programmers are written off as the expenditure is incurred. The costs of programs created internally are also written off as incurred.

14. The profit for 19-3 has been measured at £4,447, but this is after charging all the costs of producing programs which, without further cost, may produce revenue in succeeding years. Thus, if the programs mentioned in notes 5 and 6 produce large sales in 19-4, the split of profit earned in the two years to 31st December 19-4 will be distorted.

SUMMARY

15. (a) There are service industries as well as trading, manufacturing and non-profit organisations.

(b) The format of the Profit and Loss Account of a business providing a service, may or may not include a "half way stage" in terms of measuring a gross profit.

(c) Gross profit is an elusive idea which implies that costs and expenses can be separated into those directly incurred in creating a good or service and those not related or apportionable to the product.

(d) In businesses where two or more different services are provided, *segmented* profit measurement is desirable.

(e) In many service industries, the preparation of *annual* profit measures requires careful selection of appropriate accounting policies to relate revenue and expenses to particular financial years.

POINTS TO NOTE

16. (a) The two stage, income statement – gross profit and then net profit, is firmly established in the practice of preparing accounts for trading and manufacturing businesses. It does not usually work so well in service industries and you should be very sure that costs are distinguishable between those directly concerned with a product and those which are not, before deciding to compute a gross profit.

(b) Many of the accounting policy problems relate to the idea of work in progress. For example, in the accounting practice (paragraph 5), work in progress has been included. This means that, that part of the salaries, motor expenses etc, which relate to work done but not invoiced until the following year, has to be taken out of the profit and loss account (as closing work in progress). The conceptual problem of valuing work in progress is very difficult. Very often an arbitrary approach of say 50% of selling price is taken.

(c) All published accounts include a list of accounting policies used. It is a good idea to look at some.

(d) The problems of accounting measurement and the selection of suitable accounting policies is common to *all* businesses. However, the problem is most frequently met with in service industries.

SELF TESTING QUESTIONS

(a) *List some examples of service industries. (4).*
(b) *When can a gross profit be calculated?*
(c) *When is segmental reporting desirable? (8).*
(d) *What is an accounting policy? (12).*
(e) *What is the purpose of a statement of accounting policies? (13).*

Exercises (Answers begin on page 464)

1. *The Balance Sheet of Sparks, a Certified Accountant in private practice was, on 31.12.-8:*

	£			£
Capital	11,433	Equipment at cost		3,900
Creditors	1,367	Depreciation	1,500	2,400
Bank Overdraft	10,800	Car at cost	8,000	
		Depreciation	2,800	5,200
		Work in progress		9,800
		Debtors		6,200
	23,600			23,600

His cash book summary for 19-9 showed:

Receipts	£	Payments	£
From clients	50,700	Staff costs	28,590
Legacy from Aunt	5,000	Drawings	12,600
		Taxation – Schedule D	3,611
		Office occupancy costs	5,620
		Motor and other overheads	6,300

At 31.12.-9, his work in progress was valued at £12,800 and debtors amounted to £8,800.

He is depreciating his car, which he bought in 19-6, over 5 years on the straight line basis and his equipment at 20% reducing balance.

Creditors are all for office occupancy costs and the corresponding figure for 19-9 is £1,230.

Prepare an Income Statement and a Balance Sheet.

What do you think are Sparks' problems?

Could you design an Income Statement for Sparks with an intermediate or Gross Profit?

How would Sparks value his work in progress?

2.   Partridge bought 40 acres of farmland and turned the estate into a series of boating and fishing lakes to provide amenities for tourists who came by the day or stayed in his farmhouse. Most day visitors also ate in his farmhouse restaurant/cafe. He charged for the use of all facilities and also made money from the sale of fishing and boating gear and souvenirs.

He spent large sums on building additions to the farmhouse, roads, excavating the lakes, and planting trees.

At the end of the first year he is very concerned to know if the venture if profitable and if any part should be developed or any part reduced.

Required:
(a) Design a suitable sectionalised Income Statement.
(b) Consider suitable depreciation policies and rates for the capital expenditure.

Exercises without answers

3.   Write an essay on the concept of gross profit. Under what conditions may a gross profit be a valid concept for a service industry?

4.   List as many service industries as you can. In each case state the form of income which is equivalent to sales.

5.   Draft a skeleton form for the Income Statement and Balance Sheet for a dental surgeon.

6.   In what ways might a segmented Income statement be appropriate for a hotel business? What segments might be included?

7.   In 19-8 Ratbag, a pop group, spent a material amount of money on making an album. Costs were:

Creating the master disc, recording studio etc £6,500
Pressing 20,000 albums, sleeves etc   £40,000

In 19-8 they sold 4,000 at £8 each.

They expect to sell a further 10,000 albums in 19-9 and perhaps the rest later.

How much did they make out of the album in 19-8?

41. Departmental accounts

INTRODUCTION

1.   Some businesses are essentially two or more businesses. For example, a departmental store is really a collection of separate businesses - toiletries, ladies fashions, perfumes, furniture etc. In this book you have learned to prepare income statements to measure and demonstrate the profit earned by a business. Usually the income statement is prepared for the business. However, management find it useful to know the profit earned by each department or section of the business if there are separately identifiable sub-divisions of the enterprise. There are a few difficulties with this process so this chapter shows how to prepare departmental accounts and how these might be useful.

PREPARING DEPARTMENTAL ACCOUNTS

2.   The primary difficulty in preparing departmental accounts is that many expenses are *shared*. For example, in the business of John, there are two sections - books and toys. Many of the expenses are shared - rent, rates, insurance and general management. A possible format for departmental accounts might be:

John - Trading and profit and loss account for year ending 31 December 19X7

	Books	Toys	Total
Sales	68	54	122
Cost of goods sold	48	37	85
Gross profit (a)	20	17	37
Other direct costs (b)	7	6	13
Contribution (c)	13	11	24
Shared overheads (d)			15
Net profit			9

Notes:

(a)   It is relatively simple to keep separate records of the sales, purchases and stocks of the two departments and so separate gross profits can be calculated.

(b)   Some overheads can be considered to be direct costs of one or other of the departments. For example, the wage of an assistant who only works in the book department is wholly an expense of the book department.

(c)   The gross profit of a department less the costs which are exclusive to overall profit and shared overheads. Note that if the book department was closed down the business as a whole would not have to spend £7,000 (the direct expenses) and would thus be worse off by the contribution £13,000. (However, this is not quite all the story and we will discuss this further later).

(d)   No attempt has been made to split shared overheads between the two departments.

SHARED OVERHEADS

3.   In the example of John, the shared overheads were not split between the two departments but this can be done if some rational means can be found. In the above example, the shared overheads were:

Rent, rates and insurance	9.3
Telephone	1.1
Motor expenses	2.6
Other expenses	2.0
	15.0

It is felt that these costs can be split as:

Rent etc on floor area occupied (53 m^2: 37 m^2)

Telephone ($\frac{2}{3}$: $\frac{1}{3}$) - more to books as they have more telephone contact with customers

Motor expenses ($\frac{1}{4}$: $\frac{3}{4}$) mostly to toys as toy supplies are often bought at cash and carry warehouses and have to be transported back to the shop.

Other expenses - equally.

Thus the income statement may now appear as:

	Books		Toys		Total
Gross profit		20.0		17.0		37.0
Allocated costs	7.0		6.0		13.0
Apportioned costs:					
Rent etc	5.5		3.8		9.3
Telephone	0.7		0.4		1.1
Motor	0.7		1.9		2.6
Other	1.0		1.0		2.0
Net profit		14.9		13.1		28.0
		5.1		3.9		9.0

Notes:

(a) This profit and loss is more traditional in that it distinguishes the gross profit and then shows the overheads in detail. The additional words (allocated and apportioned) do alert the reader to the artificial nature of the split of the apportioned expenses.

(b) The management can now see the overall profit of £9,000 came from books £5,100 and toys £3,900. However, this division of profit is artificial and different accountants may well have apportioned the overheads differently and got a different division of the profit.

(c) One decision that could be made is to close down one department – say toys. What would the effect of this be?

-   loss of gross profit   £17,000
-   saving of direct costs   £6,000
-   saving of some of the shared costs   ?

It is not clear what shared costs would be saved if the toys department was closed down. The rent and rates etc would not change unless the space vacated by the toy department could be let. The motor expenses include a number of fixed costs (eg tax and insurance) which would not be saved.

Finally, some customers come into the shop to buy toys and then buy a book as well. This trade would be lost to the book department if the toy department were closed down.

Thus, the departmental accounts, whether in the first form shown or the second, do not show the effect of closing down one of the departments. They do however, help in any real analysis of the effects of a closure of a department.

DECISION MAKING

4. As many businesses are compartmentalised and prepare departmental accounts, one must suppose that such accounts are useful. One such use has been identified (the closure decision) and the matter has been seen to be rather more difficult than appears at first sight. Other uses include:

(a) Knowing which part of a business is more profitable. Suppose Sid has a business which is divided into (i) stamp dealing and (ii) publishing a monthly magazine about stamp dealing. It is really essential to know which part of this dual business is more profitable. This enables decisions about expansion and contraction of parts to be made.

(b) Paying commissions or shares of profits to management or staff of the separate departments based on departmental profits.

(c) In many partnership businesses, one section is run by one partner and one by another (up to any number of partners) and partnership profit sharing may use a formula taking into account departmental profits.

SUMMARY

5. (a) Some businesses are divisible into separate parts or departments or sections or divisions.

(b) It may be of use to break down the overall profit departmentally.

(c) This can be done by showing separate gross profits or separate contributions with shared overheads also broken down or not broken down.

(d) Decisions about expansion and contraction, closing down divisions or starting new divisions, partner or management remuneration, can be made.

POINT TO NOTE

6. (a) Goods can be transferred between departments. Such transfers should normally be made at cost by a Dr to purchases of the transfer in department and a Cr to purchases of the transfer out department.

    (b) In this chapter I have talked of departments, divisions and sections. Other words are *classes* of business, *components* of the business and *segments* of the business. I have also used the expression *shared costs*. It is also possible to use the term *common costs*.

    (c) It is possible to have a departmentalised balance sheet but this is not usually of great use. However, some managements like to know the separate *fixed assets* and *working capital* employed by the departments.

Exercises (Answers begin on page 465)

1. Prepare departmental accounts for Simone's business which has two parts – letting caravans and selling caravans:

	Letting	Selling	Unspecified
Sales	135,000	264,700	
Purchases		137,000	
Stock 1.1.-4		43,600	
Stock 31.12-4		58,700	
Caravans at cost 1.1.-4	145,000		
Depreciation on caravans to 31.12-3	60,300		
Land at cost	220,000		
Buildings at cost			146,000
Depreciation of buildings at 31.12.-3			37,000
Wages	43,000	34,000	13,300
Rates etc			15,000
Other overheads	24,700	20,100	12,800

Notes:

(a) During the year some caravans which had been let were sold. These had cost £50,600 and had been depreciated by £15,600.

(b) Depreciation policy is 20% straight line on caravans and 4% straight line on the buildings.

(c) The manager of the caravan sales department is entitled to a commission of 10% of the net profit of the department after charging the commission.

(d) The buildings are estimated to be used 4/5 by caravan sales and 1/5 by letting.

(e) Unspecified wages and other expenses are to be divided equally.

Required:

(a) A departmental profit and loss account.

(b) Assess the impact of closing down either department.

(c) Would you be happy with the accounts if you were the manager of the caravan sales department?

Exercises without answers

2. Fingle is in business as a DIY Superstore. He has three departments, A, B and C. His figures for 19-7 were: (in £'000)

	A	B	C	Common
Stocks 1.1.-7	120	84	100	
Stocks 31.12.-7	158	76	130	
Purchases	689	840	562	
Sales	1,031	1,150	954	
Labour	104	60	101	48
Occupancy costs				215
Buildings at cost				870
Administration expenses	23	15	30	129
Equipment at cost	123	53	120	160

Note:

(a) Depreciation is 15% on cost for equipment and 5% on cost for buildings.

(b) Common depreciation is to be divided in proportion to other equipment.

(c) Occupancy costs are to be divided in proportion to sales.

(d) Common administration costs are to be shared equally.

(e) Each department head is entitled to a commission of 5% of gross profit + 3% of net profit after deducting both types of commission.

Required:
(a) Prepare a departmental profit and loss account.
(b) Comment on the apportionment methods.

3. Yeegods plc own an upmarket department store. They operate an accounting system such that all costs are allocated or apportioned to departments and a separate profit and return on capital employed figure is obtained for each department. This is used to make decisions about expanding, contracting and closing departments. The figures for the candle department on the fourth floor are:

Gross profit	£134,800
Wages	61,000
Allocated costs	16,700
Apportioned costs	40,100
Working capital	55,000
Fixed assets (net)	30,000
Return on capital target	25%

Support the manager of the department who is appealing against the decision to close the department. You make whatever assumptions you like but must state them.

Partnerships

This part of the manual is concerned with businesses owned and managed by two or more persons in common. Chapter 42 describes the legal and commercial aspects of partnerships. Chapter 43 is concerned with the partnership aspects of financial statements – the balance sheet and the appropriation section of the profit and loss account. Chapter 45 looks at the accounting aspects of changes in partnerships. While Chapter 44 deals with the dissolution of partnerships.

42. Partnership – Legal and Commercial Aspects

INTRODUCTION

1.   This chapter is concerned with what partnerships are; some of the things the law says about partnerships; and finally some of the ways in which partners can share the profits of their businesses.

DEFINITION

2.   The Partnership Act 1890 defines partnership as:

"The relationship which subsists between persons carrying on a business in common with a view to profit."

Thus:

(a)   Partnership is a relationship. In fact is is a relationship requiring the utmost trust and cooperation between the partners.

(b)   Partnership, in this manual, is a business relationship. It is concerned with two or more people who jointly own and manage a business.

(c)   The objective of the partnership is to make a profit which has to be shared in some ways by the partners.

THE AGREEMENT

3.   The essence of a partnership is the *agreement*. Partners must agree about all aspects of the conduct of the business and of the relationship between the partners. Some of the aspects which must be covered by the agreement are:

(a)   Who the partners are.
(b)   How much each should contribute to the partnership capital.
(c)   When the partnership should commence.
(d)   How long the partnership should last.
(e)   How profits should be shared.
(f)   How much each partner may draw from the business.
(g)   Hours of work, holidays etc.
(h)   What happens if a partner dies, retires, becomes bankrupt, medically incapable or insane.
(i)   The extent to which partners can engage in other business activities.
(j)   Commercial matters – products, premises, rate of expansion, employment policy etc.

4.   The agreement may be a formal one – a deed drawn up by a solicitor and signed by all the partners – or it may be written less formally, perhaps in the form of the exchange of letters or minutes of a meeting, or it may merely be the *conduct of the parties*.

The assumption behind the latter is that the agreement is what the partners do.

For example, if the written partnership agreement says that the partners may take two weeks holiday each a year but they actually take four weeks each, then their agreement is not what the written agreement says but what they do.

5.   In practice, failure to agree *in advance* on some aspect of the partnership affairs may lead to acrimony and even collapse of the partnership. I recall two partners who differed in their opinion of the length of the working day. No agreement was reached in advance and it became impossible for the ambitious partner who wished to work a fourteen-hour day to continue in partnership with his partner who felt that eight hours were sufficient.

THE LAW

6.　Partnership law is a considerable subject and I do not intend to even outline it. It is sufficient for our purposes to know that the general law was codified in the Partnership Act 1890 and that relations between partners are governed by their partnership agreement whether this be expressed, or implied by the conduct of the parties.

7.　The number of partners in a partnership permissible in law is restricted to 20 except for certain professional partnerships – accountants, doctors, solicitors, chartered loss adjusters etc.

8.　A section of the Partnership Act 1890 of particular interest to accounting students is Section 24 which states how profits are to be shared in the *absence of agreement*. This will be discussed in the next chapter.

PROFIT SHARING

9.　Partners can share the profits of their business in any way they like. Many partnerships share profits in ways which reflect the differing contributions made by the partners to the business, for example:

(a)　Capital invested.
(b)　Time spent on partnership business.
(c)　Expertise or experience.
(d)　Seniority.

10.　Some profit sharing arrangements are complex. For example, in the partnership of Dick, Eddie and Fred they agreed that:

(a)　Each should have a part of the profit equivalent to 10% of their capitals at the beginning of the year. This reflects the different amounts of capital each has tied up in the partnership business.

(b)　Dick should have £7,000 of the profit to reflect the fact that he alone works full time on the business and thus foregoes the salary he could have earned elsewhere.

(c)　Eddie should have a share of the profit equal to 2% of the sales to reflect the special expertise he has in obtaining customers.

(d)　Any remaining profit should be shared equally.

SUMMARY

11.　(a)　Partnership is defined in the Partnership Act as the relationship which subsists between persons carrying on a business in common with a view to profit.

(b)　The rules governing partnership are found in the partnership agreement. This may be expressed in a written agreement or implied by the conduct of the partners.

(c)　The number of partners in a partnership is limited to 20. Some professional partnerships are exempted from this rule.

(d)　All partnerships must have some arrangement for sharing profits and this may be complex to reflect the differing contributions of the partners.

SELF TESTING QUESTIONS

(a)　Define partnership. (2).
(b)　What matters might be included in a partnership agreement? (3).
(c)　What factors may influence profit sharing arrangements? (10).
(d)　What is the maximum number of partners in a partnership? What partnerships does the rule not apply to? (7).

Exercises (Answers begin on page 466)

1.　Alice, Brenda and Carla are meeting together to discuss the formation of a partnership between them. The business would be the importation of expensive textiles from Europe and selling them to fashion manufacturers in England. Payment would be required for the goods immediately on importation to the UK, substantial stocks would be carried and customers would on average take some 2 to 3 months to pay.

Alice, a retired lecturer in fashion, is 67 years old, has some £20,000 of capital available, has a good pension, speaks several European languages and loves travel. She does not wish to work full time in the business as she likes to spend time with her dogs.

Brenda is 34 and has passed the Level 2 Certified Accountants exams and works with a firm of export/import agents. She has agreed to give 3 months notice to her employers. She has an overdraft facility with her bank for £3,000 and her current overdraft is £600. She likes hard work.

Carla who is 44 is a partner in a fashion shop and wishes to retain this connection at least part time. Her former employment was with a firm of fashion manufacturers as a buyer. She is married with 3 children. She has £2,000 in a building society account and her husband is a wealthy man with inherited capital.

Draw up a partnership agreement. (In class this exercise could be used as a role play exercise.)

2.   *Gordon, Frank and Ed ware considering going into business as specialist car kit makers.*

Gordon is already doing this successfully but on a very small scale. He could only bring in the net assets of the business worth about £3,500. He is 58 and has a heart condition.

Frank is 24, is well known in the car racing and rallying world, receiving a good salary. He has no capital. He is a good rally driver and receives a good fee for entering rallies with works cars.

Ed is 37 and has recently been made redundant from his job as a works manager. He has £20,000 in cash from his savings and redundancy money. He is married and has 4 children.

Draw up a possible partnership agreement.

Exercises without answers

3.   *Bee, Cee and Dee have been holding preliminary discussions with a view to forming a partnership to buy and sell antiques.*

The position has now been reached where the prospective partners have agreed the basic arrangements under which the partnership will operate.

Bee will contribute £40,000 as capital and, up to £10,000 as a long-term loan to the partnership, if needed. He has extensive other business interests and will not therefore be taking an active part in the running of the business.

Cee is unable to bring in more than £2,000 as capital initially, but, because he has an expert knowledge of the antique trade, will act as the manager of the business on a full-time basis.

Dee is willing to contribute £10,000 as capital. He will also assist in running the business as the need arises. In particular, he is prepared to attend auctions anywhere within the United Kingdom in order to acquire trading stock which he will transport back to the firm's premises in his van. On occasions he may also help Cee to restore the articles prior to sale to the public.

At their next meeting, the three prospective partners intend to decide upon the financial arrangements for sharing out the profits (or losses) made by the firm and have approached you for advice.

Required:
Prepare a set of explanatory notes, under suitable headings, of the considerations which the prospective partners should take into account in arriving at their decisions at the next meeting.
(ACCA)

4.   *Why do partnerships need an agreement?*

5.   *List the heads of agreement between the prospective partners of a firm of Certified Accountants.*

6.   *Suggest a profit sharing agreement for Adam, Bernard and Carla, interior decorators:*

Adam will put up most of the capital £20,000 required. He will work full time in the business but has no expertise except in the commercial and accounting aspects of the business.

Bernard is impecunious but has expensive tastes. He is the artistic partner who will provide the necessary technical and design expertise. He will work full time.

Carla is the partner with the contacts. She will introduce most of the customers. She is involved with another business and will work only half time. She has some design and technical ability.
Does your agreement allow for low profits or losses?

43. Accounting for Partnerships

INTRODUCTION

1. This chapter describes the use of the *appropriation* account in computing and demonstrating the division of the profit or loss among the partners. The use of partners' capital and current accounts is then introduced and finally the formats for profit and loss accounts and balance sheets are discussed.

THE APPROPRIATION ACCOUNT

2. We will demonstrate this with an example:

Andrew, Guy and Martin are in partnership as camping equipment retailers. Their trial balance at 31.12.-3 was:

Dr	£	Cr	£
Fixed Assets at cost	24,300	Depreciation provision 31.12.-2	4,750
Stock 31.12.-2	16,720	Sales	112,220
Debtors	1,340	Andrew – Capital 31.12.-2	12,020
Overheads	7,105	Guy – Capital 31.12.-2	7,001
Purchases	78,626	Martin – Capital 31.12.-2	1,000
Drawings: Andrew	4,800	Creditors	9,820
Guy	7,100		
Martin	5,600		
Bank	1,220		
	146,811		146,811

Note:

(a) Stock at 31.12.-3 was valued at £22,300.
(b) Depreciation is at 20% a year on the reducing balance.
(c) The partnership agreement provides that profit shall be shared:

> *Interest on capital 15%*
> *Salaries: Guy £3,000, Martin £2,000*
> *Balance: 5:4:3*

Required:
Prepare trading and profit and loss and appropriation accounts for the year ending 31.12.-3.

The answer

Andrew, Guy and Martin
Trading and Profit and Loss Account
for the year ending 31st December 19-3

	£	£
Sales		112,220
Less Cost of Sales:		
Opening stock	16,720	
Purchases	78,626	
Available for sale	95,346	
Closing stock	22,300	73,046
Gross Profit		39,174
Overheads	7,105	
Depreciation	3,910	11,015
Net Profit		£28,159

Appropriation Account

	Andrew	Guy	Martin	Total
	£	£	£	£
Interest on Capital	1,803	1,050	150	3,003
Salaries	–	3,000	2,000	5,000
Balance	8,398	6,719	5,039	20,156
	10,201	10,769	7,189	28,159

Note:

(a) The first stage in these questions, is to prepare the trading and profit and loss account in exactly the same way as with the accounts of a sole trader.

(b) With a sole trader, all of the profit belongs to the sole trader, but in a partnership the profit is shared among the partners. Consequently an additional account is required to show the appropriation of the profit among the partners.

(c) The profit is shared in accordance with the agreement.

Note that despite reference to interest on capital and salaries these are not interest on capital or salaries, they are part of the profit sharing formula.

(d) In this case the profit sharing formula divides the profit among the partners as Andrew £10,201, Guy £10,769 and Martin £7,189.

3.   The profit sharing *formula* agreed on by Andrew & Co. divided the profit of £28,159 in a unique way. But suppose the business had a bad year and the profit earned was only £7,000. How would this be divided? There are at least two possibilities:

(a)

	Andrew £	Guy £	Martin £	Total £
Interest on Capital	1,803	1,050	150	3,003
Salaries	-	3,000	2,000	5,000
Balance (loss)	(418)	(334)	(251)	(1,003)
	1,385	3,716	1,899	7,000

(b)

	Andrew £	Guy £	Martin £	Total £
Interest on Capital	1,803	1,050	150	3,003
Salaries	-	2,398	1,599	3,997
	1,803	3,448	1,749	7,000

The salaries have been reduced so that total salaries absorb the remainder of the profit. Each salary has been reduced proportionately.

Whichever is correct, depends on a legal interpretation of the partnership agreement. To avoid difficulties of this sort, the wording of the formula must be precise and unambiguous and be able to cover all sizes of profit or loss.

PROFIT SHARING IN THE ABSENCE OF AN AGREEMENT

4.   It may be that the partners in a business failed to agree in advance how they should share profits. This is not necessarily a problem, as they could come to an agreement in arrear. However, if they are still unable to agree, the Partnership Act 1890, Section 24 provides that:

(a) 5% interest on *loans* to the partnership by partners.
(b) No interest is to be allowed on capital.
(c) Balance of profit to be divided equally.

Notes:

(i) Loans to the partnership by partners are possible but normally any monies put into the business by a partner as regarded as part of that partner's capital.

(ii) Section 24 is rarely invoked in practice.

CAPITAL AND CURRENT ACCOUNTS

5.   Some partnerships have capital and current accounts. Some have only capital accounts.

(a) **Capital accounts where there are also current accounts**
At the formation of a new partnership, the partners may agree to put into the partnership from their private resources, cash and/or other assets to an agreed value. The amount of such resources put in by a partner is his capital. Usually the partners agree that no partner will withdraw resources from the partnership in such

a way that the capital is reduced. A partner's capital account will only change by agreement or on the occurrence of events such as a change in the profit sharing ratio or on the death or retirement of a partner or the admission of a new partner.

(b) Current accounts

If a profit is made by a partnership, it means that the net assets of the partnership have increased by the amount of the profit. Each partner's share of the profit is credited to his current account. The balance standing to the credit of a partner's current account represents the maximum amount that the partner can withdraw from the partnership assets. Thus a partner can only make drawings up to the amount of his accumulated share of profits. The current account represents undrawn profits.

(c) Capital accounts without current accounts

Many partnerships simply have capital accounts without partners' current accounts. In these cases, the capital account represents a mixture of capital subscribed and undrawn profits. There is therefore no maximum put on partners' drawings by the division between capital and current accounts and restriction of another sort has to be agreed upon. (Perhaps a weekly amount and an annual drawing when profits have been calculated).

In the question in paragraph 2, the partners' capital accounts would appear thus: (in columnar form as is usually asked for in examinations).

	Andrew £	*Guy* £	*Martin* £		*Andrew* £	*Guy* £	*Martin* £
31.12.-3 Drawings	4,800	7,100	5,600	31.12.-2 Balance	12,020	7,001	1,000
31.12.-3 Balance	17,421	10,670	2,589	31.12.-3 Profit	10,201	10,769	7,189
	22,221	17,770	8,189		22,221	17,770	8,189

FORMATS

6. Formats for a partnership *trading and profit and loss account* are the same as for sole traders. The additional feature for partnerships is the *appropriation account* and a suitable format has already been given in paragraph 2.

7. An alternative is:

	Interest £	*Salary* £	*Balance* £	*Total* £
Andrew	1,803	–	8,398	10,201
Guy	1,050	3,000	6,719	10,769
Martin	150	2,000	5,039	7,189
	3,003	5,000	20,156	28,159

Other formats are possible but any format should show the total share of profit given to each partner.

8. The *balance sheet* formats of a partnership are the same as for sole traders. The difference is that instead of a single capital account for the proprietor, there are several accounts (and perhaps current accounts), one for each partner. In simple cases, the full accounts can be given, showing separately, opening balance, share of profit, drawings, closing balance. But in more complex cases, the detail is usually put in a separate *schedule* and only the final balances put on the balance sheet.

An example

Katie and Brennan are in partnership as tree surgeons sharing profits 3:2. Their trial balance after computing profit at 31.12.-4 showed:

	£		£
Fixed Assets at cost	20,000	Creditors	6,280
Debtors	15,400	Capital: Katie	10,000
Cash at bank	1,100	Brennan	7,000
Stock	8,400	Current A/c 31.12.-3 Brennan	3,100
Current A/c 31.12.-3 Katie	180	Loan at 15% Brennan	10,000
Drawings: Katie	4,600	Profit 19-4	10,200
Brennan	5,200	Depreciation 31.12.-4	8,300
	54,880		54,880

Note:

During 19-4, each partner had subscribed an additional £3,000.

Required:
Draw up the balance sheet at 31.12.-4.

Katie and Brennan
Schedule of Capital and Current Accounts
year ending 31st December 19-4

	Katie £	*Brennan* £	*Total* £
Capital Accounts			
As at 31.12.-3	7,000	4,000	11,000
Additions in 19-4	3,000	3,000	6,000
As at 31.12.-4	10,000	7,000	17,000
Current Accounts			
As at 31.12.-3	(180)	3,100	2,920
Profit share in 19-4 (3:2)	6,120	4,080	10,200
	5,940	7,180	13,120
Drawings in 19-4	4,600	5,200	9,800
	1,340	1,980	3,320

Total interest in the net assets of the partnership at 31.12.-4   11,340   8,980   20,320

Balance Sheet as at 31st December 19-4

Fixed Assets at cost		20,000
Less Accumulated depreciation		8,300
		11,700
Current Assets		
Stock	8,400	
Debtors	15,400	
Cash at bank	1,100	
	24,900	
Current Liabilities		
Creditors	6,280	18,620
		30,320
Partners' interests – as schedule		20,320
Long term liability		
Loan at 15%		10,000
		30,320

Note:
The schedule is *often expressed as being* attached to *and* forming part *of the balance sheet.*

9.   To complete the chapter and to show a balance sheet format without a schedule, we will complete the question in paragraph 2.

Andrew, Guy and Martin
Balance Sheet as at 31st December 19-3

	£	£
Fixed Assets at cost		24,300
Less Accumulated Depreciation		8,660
		15,640
Current Assets		
Stock	22,300	
Debtors	1,340	
Bank	1,220	
	24,860	
Current Liabilities		
Creditors	9,820	15,040
		£30,680

Capital Accounts

	Andrew	*Guy*	*Martin*	*Total*
	£	£	£	£
as at 1.1.-3	12,020	7,001	1,000	20,021
Net Profit Share	10,201	10,769	7,189	28,159
	22,221	17,770	8,189	48,180
Drawings	4,800	7,100	5,600	17,500
	17,421	10,670	2,589	30,680

SUMMARY

10. (a) In a partnership, profit is shared amongst the partners in accordance with the *formula* in the agreement.

(b) The computation of the profit sharing is demonstrated in the *appropriation* account.

(c) In cases of dispute where there is no agreement on how to share profit, s.24 of the Partnership Act 1890 gives directions.

(d) Partnerships may distinguish between permanent capital and undrawn profits by keeping separate capital and current accounts for each partner. Alternatively the partners may maintain only capital accounts for each partner.

(e) The balance sheet of a partnership may show movement on the capital accounts of the partners in detail in the balance sheet. Alternatively, the capital (and current accounts if kept) may be summarised in a separate schedule which is attached to and forms part of the balance sheet.

POINTS TO NOTE

11. (a) It is important to realise that partners' salaries and interest on capital are not salaries and interest but part of the profit sharing formula.

(b) Consequently, partners' salaries and interest on capital do *not* appear in the profit and loss account. Interest on partners' *loans*, if any, will appear as an expense in the profit and loss account.

(c) Partners' drawings have nothing to do with the profit and loss account or the appropriation account.

(d) The format of a balance sheet is a matter of the best means of carrying information from the accountant who prepares it to the partners and others who need it. As a general rule, a partnership balance sheet (in conjunction with a schedule if desired) must clearly show separately fixed assets, current assets, current liabilities, the net total of all these and how this was financed by showing long term liabilities and the net interest each partner has in the net assets of the business.

(e) Partnership is entirely a matter of mutual trust and agreement among the partners. This is well illustrated by the famous story of business ethics. A partner in a retail business received £100 overpayment from a customer due to a misunderstanding. The ethical problem is: should he tell his partner?

SELF TESTING QUESTIONS

(a) What information will appear in a partnership appropriation account?

(b) In what part of the profit and loss account of a partnership should partners (i) interest on capital, (ii) salaries, appear? (3).

(c) Which section of which Act applies in the absence of agreement among partners? (4).

(d) Distinguish between partners' capital and current accounts. (5).

(e) How are capital and current accounts expressed on a partnership balance sheet? (8, 9).

Exercises (Answers begin on page 467)

1. *Gaynor, Amanda and Samantha started in part-nership as office cleaners on 1.1.-7. Their verbal agreement was:*

(a) 10% interest on capitals.
(b) 16% interest charged on drawings.
(c) 5% commission on turnover to Gaynor to reflect her ability to get business.
(d) A salary to Amanda of £3,000 to reflect her longer work time on partnership affairs.

(e) Balance of profit to be divided 2:2:1.

Samantha has made a loan to the partnership of £10,000 at 16%.

At the end of the first year turnover was found to be £40,000 and net profit (after loan interest paid to Samantha) £14,640.

Capitals were:

	Introduced 1.1.-7	Introduced 30.6.-7	Withdrawn 30.6.-7
Gaynor	£2,000	£6,000	
Amanda	£6,000		£1,000
Samantha	£5,000		

Drawings were:

	31.3.-7	30.6.-7	30.9.-7
Gaynor	£500	£900	£1,000
Amanda	£800	£800	£700
Samantha	£900	£200	£900

Required:

(a) The partnership appropriation account for the year ending 31.12.-7.

(b) The partners' capital AND current accounts for the same period.

(c) Recast (a) and (b) on the basis that the interest on capital was at 7%, interest on drawings was 20% and interest on the loan was at 8%.

(d) Recast (a) and (b) on the basis that profit was not £14,640 but only £2,600.

(e) Recast (b) on the basis that all transactions go through the capital accounts. How would this affect the profit sharing?

2.   *Karl and Stanley have formed two separate partnerships. Their profit sharing agreements and other information are:*

	Partnership 1	Partnership 2
Interest on capital	10%	15%
Interest on loans	15%	12%
Salary - Karl	2,000	
Salary - Stanley		4,000
Capital - Karl 1.1.-8	15,000	6,000
Capital - Stanley 1.1.-8	7,000	2,000
Profit 19-8 after loan interest	26,500	23,980
Loan from Karl	20,000	
Drawings 19-8 - Karl	6,500	4,700
Drawings 19-8 - Stanley	3,000	4,100
Residual Profit Share		
- Karl	3/5	2/5
- Stanley	2/5	3/5

Required:

(a) Appropriation Account for 19-8 for each partnership.
(b) Capital accounts for each partner. No current accounts are kept.
(c) Recast (a) and (b) on the basis that the profit before interest was - Partnership 1 £4,000, Partnership 2 £6,000.

Exercises without answers

3.   *(a) The current accounts of three partners, Able, Baker and Delta at 31 December 1980 were as follows.*

	A £	B £	D £		A £	B £	D £
Balance at 1 Jan	–	500	–	Balance at 1 Jan	350	–	800
Drawings	2,100	2,300	2,400	Salary	800	–	–
Goods	210	–	–	Interest on capital	600	400	300
Balance at 1 Dec	1,940	100	1,200	Share of Profits	2,500	2,500	2,500
	4,250	2,900	3,600		4,250	2,900	3,600

Required:
Give a brief explanation of each type of entry, and suggest reasons why the partnership agreement has allowed for salary, interest on capital and a share of profits, and not just for a share of profits.

(b) Further investigation of the accounts of Able, Baker and Delta reveals that:

(i) Interest on capital was credited at 5% but the partnership agreement had allowed for 8%.

(ii) A provision for doubtful debts had been increased by £100 but should have been decreased by the same amount.

(iii) Goods taken by Able were at sales value (£210) and not at cost (£110).

(iv) The business's cars were shown at a net book value at 31 December 1980 of £4,500 (original cost £10,000, accumulated depreciation £5,500) but the current year's depreciation had been charged in error at 10% on the written down value at 1 January 1980 instead of on a straight line basis. No cars had been bought or sold during the year, and there was no expected residual value.

(v) The closing stock included some goods (cost £800) which had been invoiced to a customer for £1,000 on 31 December 1980, but which had not been despatched until 2 January 1981.

Required:
Draw up an extract from the Balance Sheet as at 31 December 1980 showing the Partners' capital accounts and revised balances on their current accounts.
(ACCA)

4. (a) For a number of years you have been employed in a senior position by a firm of certified accountants.

The two partners, Checke and Tikk, have now offered to take you into the firm as a junior partner with effect from 1 April 1985.

Hitherto the partners have contributed capital thus:

	£
Checke	50,000
Tikk	30,000

on which they received interest at 5% per annum. They have shared profits (and losses) in the ratio of 3:2 respectively.

After admission to the partnership you will be expected to continue managing the practice for which you will receive exactly half your present annual salary of £14,000 as a partnership salary. You will also be expected to contribute £20,000 as capital (on which you will receive interest at 5% per annum).

The profit sharing ratio will then be altered to give you a one sixth share of the profits and losses, without disturbing the relative shares of the other two partners.

For the year ended 31 March 1985, the total amount appropriated by the two partners was £34,000.

Required:
Prepare a statement showing the details of the amounts appropriated by Checke and Tikk during year ended 31 March 1985 together with details of the amounts which would have been appropriated if you had been taken into partnership on 1 April 1984.

(b) The financial arrangements between the members of a partnership are usually contained in an agreement.

Required:
State:

(a)   *The position where a partnership agreement contains financial arrangements which conflict with the requirements of the Partnership Act 1890*

and

(b)   *the requirements of the Partnership Act 1890 regarding*

      (i)   *interest on capital*
      (ii)   *interest on loans made by partners*
      (iii) *remuneration of partners*
      (iv) *sharing of profits and losses*   *(ACCA)*

Note: Part (b) is now excluded from the syllabus.

5.   *Brushe, Payperr and Paynte are in process of drawing up an agreement for the painting and decorating partnership which they are proposing to form.*

They have estimated that after the partnership has become properly established, annual net profit should not be less than £28,200 but is unlikely to exceed £36,400.

Various arrangements for appropriating the net profit have been suggested but the prospective partners have now narrowed down the choice to two:

Arrangement (A)

(1)   drawings to be permitted throughout the year but no interest to be charged on them;
(2)   interest to be credited at 5% per annum on partners' capitals;
(3)   partnership salary to Brushe of £2,000 per annum;
(4)   residual profits and losses to be shared 3:5:2 between Brushe, Payperr and Paynte respectively.

Arrangement (B)
(1)   drawings to be permitted only after the profit for the year has been ascertained;
(2)   interest to be credited at 10% per annum on partners' capitals;
(3)   no partnership salaries to be paid;
(4)   residual profits and losses to be shared 4:3:3 between Brushe, Payperr and Paynte respectively.

Capital introduced by the partners will be Brushe £10,000, Payperr £14,000 and Paynte £20,000.

One of the prospective partners, Brushe, has asked you which alternative arrangement would be the more beneficial to him.

Required:
    (a)   *Prepare, in tabular format, your calculations of the amounts which individual prospective partners would receive at each of the two stated profit levels.*

    (b)   *State what advice you would give to Brushe, as the result of your calculations in (a).*   *(ACCA)*

6.   *Eric and Janet are in partnership sharing profits 3:1 after a salary to Janet of £4,000 and interest on their capital at the beginning of the year of 15%.*

At 31.1.-8 the capitals were Eric £32,500 and Janet £18,400.

In 19-8 the profit was £33,635.

Drawings in 19-8 were Eric £9,254 and Janet £8,709.

Show the appropriation account and the partners' capital accounts.

Repeat the exercise with a profit of £8,200 and a loss of £2,865.

7. *Grahame, Margo and Raj set up in partnership together some years ago with capitals of £50,000, £30,000 and £15,000 respectively. The following are summaries of the partners' Current Accounts for the year ended 31 December 1985. Study these carefully and then answer the questions which follow.*

Grahame – Current Account

1985			£	1985			£
		Drawings	13,031	Jan 1		Balance b/f	366
Dec 31		Share of Balance	200	Dec 31		Interest on Capital	6,000
Dec 31		Balance c/f	135	Dec 31		Salary	7,000
			13,366				13,366

Margo – Current Account

1985			£	1985			£
		Drawings	10,640	Jan 1		Balance b/f	264
Dec 31		Share of Balance	120	Dec 31		Interest on Capital	3,600
				Dec 31		Salary	6,500
				Dec 31		Balance c/f	396
			10,760				10,760

Raj – Current Account

1985			£	1985			£
Jan 1		Balance b/f	133	Dec 31		Interest on Capital	1,800
		Drawings	7,598	Dec 31		Salary	5,500
Dec 31		Share of Balance	80	Dec 31		Balance c/f	511
			7,811				7,811

Required:
(a) Reconstruct the appropriation scheme Grahame, Margo and Raj have agreed for the division of profits and losses.

(b) Calculate the Net Profit of the partner-ship for the year ended 31 December 1985.

(c) How would the partners have shared this profit had they made no formal agreement as to the division of profits?

(d) What would the partners' shares in profit have been had the net profit for the year ended 31 December 1985 been £60,000? *(AAT)*

8. *Barr and Carr have been trading in partnership for several years under an agreement providing for interest on partners' capital at the rate of 5% per annum, a salary of £2,000 per annum to be credited to Barr, and interest being charged on drawings at the rate of 5% per annum and the balance of the net profit/loss divided between Barr and Carr in the ratio of 3:2 respectively.*

However, as from 1st November 1979, it was agreed that Barr's salary should be increased to £4,000 per annum, the interest on partners' capital and the interest on drawings to continue at the same rates as previous but the balance of the net profit/loss to be divided equally between the partners.

The following trial balance as at 30th April 1980, has been extracted from the books of the partnership:

		£	£
Capital accounts at 30.4.79:	Barr		15,000
	Carr		12,000
Current accounts:	Barr		3,258
	Carr		1,632
Freehold property, at cost		10,000	
Fittings, at cost		7,000	
Prov for depr 30.4.79			3,500
Motor vehicles at cost		4,000	
Prov for depr 30.4.79			1,000
Stock in trade, at cost		12,000	
Purchases		93,000	
Sales			120,000
Salaries		11,900	

Drawings: Barr	4,500	
Carr	2,500	
Administrative expenses	3,460	
Establishment expenses	2,500	
Balance at bank	1,200	
Petty cash	140	
Trade debtors	14,000	
Trade creditors		9,810
	166,200	166,200

Additional information:

(a) Partner's salary totalling £3,000 has been debited to salaries and credited to Barr's current account.

(b) Depreciation is provided on the cost of the fixed assets held at the end of each financial year as follows:

| Fittings | 5% |
| Motor vehicles | 25% |

(c) Interest on partners' drawings is to be charged as follows:

	£
Barr	100
Carr	70

It can be assumed that a half of the interest in each case is attributable to the six months to 31st October 1979.

(d) Accrued administrative expenses at 30th April 1980, amounted to £190.

(e) Establishment expenses prepaid at 30th April 1980, amounted to £400.

(f) It has been decided to create a provision for doubtful debts of 5% of the trade debtors at the accounting year end.

(g) Stock in trade at 30th April 1980, was valued, at cost, at £8,000.

(h) It can be assumed that the net profit/loss arose uniformly throughout the year.

Required:

(i) The partnership's trading and profit and loss account for the year ended 30th April 1980, and a balance sheet at that date.

(ii) The partners' current accounts for the year ended 30th April 1980.   (ACCA)

9.   James, Moon and Brady are in partnership, sharing profits and losses in the ratio 3:2:1 respectively. Their agreement, also allows the following:

(a) Interest is allowed on fixed capitals at 8% per annum.
(b) Moon is to receive a partnership salary of £4,000, and Brady a partnership salary of £3,000.
(c) James is entitled to interest of 10% per annum on loan.

At 31 December the following information is available.

	James		Moon		Brady
Fixed capital accounts	25,000		10,000		5,000
Current accounts	210	(Dr)	156	(Dr)	70
Drawings	8,500		8,300		5,200
Loan account	10,000				

The net profit of the partnership at 31 December 1985 was £22,200, after charging loan interest to James.

Required:

(i) A profit and loss appropriation account for the year ended 31 December 1985.

(ii) Columnar current accounts of the partners, showing the transactions posted to it and the balances brought down.   (LCCI)

44. Dissolution of Partnerships

INTRODUCTION

1. This chapter is concerned with the accounting aspects of the dissolution of partnerships.

2. The dissolution of partnerships may be caused by many factors including:

(a) Insolvency - the inability to continue because the partnership cannot meet its financial obligations.
(b) A decision of the partners not to continue, in order perhaps that each may go his own way.

3. There is a special, but exceedingly rare, situation when a partner owes money to the partnership in dissolution and is unable to pay. The matter was dealt with in the legendary case of Garner v Murray 1904 which is the concluding subject in this chapter.

THE REALISATION ACCOUNT

4. The dissolution of a partnership involves the disposal (= realisation) of the assets. Inevitably the amounts realised will differ from the book value and a profit or loss will result. The bookkeeping is:

(a) Debit the realisation account with the book values of the assets being realised.
(b) Credit the realisation account with the proceeds of disposal.
(c) Distribute the overall difference (profit or loss) among the partners in the profit sharing ratio.
(d) Complete the dissolution by paying to the partners, the balances on their capital/current accounts.

5. **An example:**

The balance sheet of Vanessa and Julie at 31.12.-4 showed:

	£		£	£
Capital accounts		Fixed assets		14,000
Vanessa	10,000	Current assets		
Julie	9,000	Stock	6,800	
Current accounts		Debtors	4,750	
Vanessa	1,900	Cash	150	
Julie	1,700			11,700
Creditors	3,100			
	£25,700			£25,700

The partnership was dissolved at 31.1.-5.

(a) The motor cars included in fixed assets were taken by the partners at agreed values as Vanessa £2,000, Julie £3,000.
(b) The remainder of the fixed assets were sold for £12,000.
(c) The stock was sold at auction for £4,300.
(d) The debtors realised £4,600.
(e) The creditors were paid off less a 5% discount.
(f) Expenses of realisation were £250.
(g) The profit sharing formula is: 10% interest on capital, balance 3:2.

Show relevant accounts in the dissolution
Answer

Realisation Account

		£		£
Fixed assets		14,000	Car taken by V	2,000
Stock		6,800	Car taken by J	3,000
Debtors		4,750	Proceeds of sales of fixed assets	12,000
Creditors		2,945	Proceeds of sales of stock	4,300
Expenses		250	Debtors	4,600
Profit on realisation:			Creditors	3,100
V	153			
J	102	255		
		£29,000		£29,000

Cash

	£		£	£
Balance b/d	150			
Proceeds from fixed assets	12,000	Creditors		2,945
Proceeds from stock	4,300	Expenses		250
Proceeds from debtors	4,600	Vanessa	10,053	
		Julie	7,802	17,855
	£21,050			£21,050

Capital account

	V £	J £		V £	J £
Cars	2,000	3,000	Capital b/f	10,000	9,000
Cash	10,053	7,802	Current accounts b/f	1,900	1,700
			Share of profit on realisation	153	102
	£12,053	£10,802		£12,053	£10,802

Notes

(a) Assets to be realised are debited to realisation account.

(b) The proceeds of the realisation are credited to realisation account and debited to cash or in the case of the partners' cars to the partners.

(c) Creditors are usually put through the realisation account if a profit or loss is involved, as here.

(d) There are often some expenses of realisation.

(e) The profit/loss is shared in profit/loss sharing ratio – the interest on capital part of the formula is irrelevant as no effluxion of time is involved.

(f) There is no need to show the account of the assets realised as they are simply (eg):

Stock

	£		£
Balance b/f	6,800	Transfer to realisation a/c	6,800
	£6,800		£6,800

(g) The capital and current accounts are put together in a dissolution since their difference is no longer relevant. As a going concern capital accounts are not payable to partners as they are permanent capital. Current accounts are payable to partners as they are undrawn profits.

(h) When all the assets have been realised and the creditors paid off, there are only three balances left:

An asset – cash		£17,855
Two liabilities:	Vanessa	£10,053
	Julie	£7,802

The asset just matches the liabilities and can be used to pay them off, leaving no balance at all in the double entry system.

GARNER V MURRAY

6.   A complication arises in dissolution when one partner finishes up in debit (ie owing the partnership money) and has no assets.

Example

Tom, Roger, Harry and James are in partnership sharing profits 5:4:4:3. Their balance sheet at 31.5.-4 was:

	£		£
Tom	3,500	Fixed assets	6,006
Roger	3,500	Stock	9,500
Harry	300	Debtors	7,800
James	116		
Creditors	6,250		
Overdraft	9,640		
	£23,306		£23,306

On 1st June 19-4 the partnership was dissolved and the following happened:

(a)   The assets were sold to RPH Ltd for £20,000 only. The consideration was £15,000 cash and 5,000 shares in RPH Ltd.

(b)   The creditors were settled for £6,000.

(c) It was agreed that the shares in RPH Ltd should be taken by Tom and Roger only in equal shares.

(d) James was declared bankrupt with no assets.

Answer

Realisation Account

	£			£
Fixed assets	6,006	RPH Ltd – Cash		15,000
Stock	9,500	– Shares		5,000
Debtors	7,800	Creditors		6,250
Cash paid to creditors	6,000	Loss on realisation		
		T	955	
		R	764	
		H	764	
		J	573	
				3,056
	£29,306			£29,306

Cash

	£		£
RPH	15,000	b/f	9,640
Harry	483	Creditors	6,000
Tom	174	Roger	17
	£15,657		£15,657

Shares in RHP Ltd

	£		£
Realisation account	5,000	Tom	2,500
		Roger	2,500
	£5,000		£5,000

Partners' Accounts

	T £	R £	H £	J £		T £	R £	H £	J £
Share in loss	955	764	764	573	b/f	3,500	3,500	300	116
Shares in RPH Ltd	2,500	2,500			Cash	174		483	
G v M	219	219	19		G v M				457
Cash		17							
	£3,674	£3,500	£783	£573		£3,674	£3,500	£783	£573

Notes:

(a) The first step is to open a realisation account and transfer to it all the assets to be disposed of.

(b) The proceeds of sale £20,000 are credited to the realisation account with £15,000 debited to cash and £5,000 debited to a new asset account: shares in RPH ltd.

(c) The creditors and the amount paid to them are put through the realisation account since a gain is involved.

(d) The balance on realisation account (a loss) is transferred to capital accounts in the profit/loss sharing ratio.

(e) The asset, shares in RPH Ltd, is debited to Tom and Roger equally as agreed.

(f) The partners' capital accounts are now as in the balance sheet less their share of the loss on realisation and in the case of Tom and Roger, less the assets (shares in RPH Ltd) taken by them.

(g) James' account is in debit. This means that he owes the partnership £457. He should pay this amount to the partnership but cannot do so because he is bankrupt and has no assets. The amount due is therefore a bad debt of the partnership and must be written off. The obvious method of writing it off is to debit the remaining partners in profit/loss sharing ratio and this would be done in most countries including the USA. However in the United Kingdom, the loss is debited to the partners in the ratio of their last agreed capital accounts (ie as in the balance sheet at 31.5.-4). This follows the rule in the famous case of Garner v Murray 1904.

(h) Debiting the loss £457 to Tom, Roger and Harry in the proportion 3,500:3,500:300 gives debits of £219, £219 and £19 respectively.

(i) Tom's account and Harry's account are now in debit in the sum of £174 and £483 respectively, and they must bring these amounts of cash into the partnership which they do.

(j) Finally, Roger's account is in credit £17 and the only asset left is cash £17 which is paid to Roger.

SUMMARY

7. (a) Partnerships may dissolve when the following happens:
    (i) The assets are realised, usually at a profit or a loss.
    (ii) The external liabilities (creditors etc) are settled.
    (iii) The balance of cash or other assets remaining are distributed to the partners by settling the balances on their capital accounts.

    (b) In a dissolution, assets are debited to a realisation account and the proceeds of disposal credited. Any difference is debited or credited to partners' capitals in the profit/loss sharing ratio.

    (c) If the account of a partner finishes up as a debit balance and the partner has no assets, the balance is written off to the debit of the other partners' account in the ratio of their last agreed capital accounts following the rule in Garner v Murray 1904.

POINTS TO NOTE

8. (a) Be careful to maintain double entry in these cases. The debits and credits are equal in the opening balance sheet and care should be taken to ensure all debit entries have corresponding credit entries and vice versa.

    (b) The distinction between capital and current accounts is no longer relevant in dissolution.

    (c) The profit and loss on realisation is shared between the partners in profit/loss sharing ratio ignoring interest on capital, partners' salaries etc.

    (d) At the conclusion of the dissolution, the remaining assets (usually just cash) is paid to the partners to settle their capital accounts. Students who distribute the remaining cash in profit/loss sharing ratio are advised to take up manual work!

    (e) The Garner v Murray rule applies to a type of situation which is exceedingly rare in practice. However, knowledge of the case distinguishes accountants from other people.

    (f) The complication of there being final assets other than cash (for example, shares in a company) is common in partnership dissolution questions. The question should indicate how the asset is to be distributed to the partners.

SELF TESTING QUESTIONS

(a) What factors may lead to the dissolution of a partnership? (2)
(b) List the accounting procedures required in a dissolution. (4)
(c) What is the relevance of capital and current account separation in a dissolution? (5(g))
(d) How should the final cash balance be distributed among the partners? (5(h))
(e) When does the rule in Garner v Murray 1904 apply? (6)
(f) How is the rule applied? (6(g))

Exercises (Answers begin on page 467)

1. *John and Mary are in partnership sharing profits equally. Their balance sheet at 31.3.-5 showed:*

	£		£
John	15.352	Fixed assets	16,435
Mary	11,530	Stock	8,762
Creditors	12,465	Debtors	12,900
		Bank	1,250
	£39,347		£39,347

On 1.6.-5 they dissolved the partnership and the following events occurred:

	£
The fixed assets were sold for	15,000
The stock was sold for	7,500
The debtors realised	12,450
The creditors were paid off for	12,200

Required: All accounts to close the partnership books.

2.   Harry, James and Roger are in partnership sharing profits 3:2:1. Their balance sheet at 1.10.-4 showed:

	£	£
Fixed assets		23,875
Stock		24,567
Debtors		13,546
		61,988
Current liabilities		
Creditors	38,970	
Overdraft	13,456	
		52,426
		£9,562

Partners' accounts

	Capital	Current	
	£	£	£
Harry	3,000	102	3,102
James	4,000	860	4,860
Roger	1,000	600	1,600
	£8,000	£1,562	£9,562

The partnership was dissolved on 2.10.-4 when the following events occurred:

	£
The fixed assets were sold for	20,000
The stock was sold for	18,000
The debtors realised	13,000
The creditors were paid off for	38,965

Note: Roger has no private assets and is therefore unable to contribute to the assets of the partnership.

Required: All accounts to close the partnership books.

Exercises without answers

3.   Bridget, Mac and Olga are in partnership sharing profits 3:4:2. Their balance sheet at 30.9.-4 showed:

	£		£
Bridget	13,800	Fixed assets	24,780
Mac	25,000	Stock	13,552
Olga	16,075	Debtors	32,780
Creditors	14,567		
Overdraft	1,670		
	£71,112		£71,112

On 1.10.-4 they dissolved the partnership and the following events occurred:

	£
Bridget took one of the fixed assets (a car with net book value of £1,000) for her own use at an agreed value of	800
The remainder of the fixed assets were sold for	20,000
The debtors realised	28,000
The creditors were paid off for	13,500
Expenses of realisation were paid	750

Required: All accounts to close the partnership books.

4.   John Graham, Bill Murphy and Bob Wilkins are trading in partnership together, sharing profits and losses equally. The balance sheet of the business as at 31 December 1983 is as shown below:

	£	£
Capital		
Graham		70,000
Murphy		35,000
Wilkins		21,000
		126,000
Current accounts		
Graham	5,000	
Murphy	8,000	
Wilkins	(3,000)	
		10,000
Loan account – Mrs Wilkins		100,000
		£236,000

	£	£
Represented by:		
Fixed assets, at book value		
Land and buildings		450,820
Plant		77,115
Vehicles		18,065
		546,000
Current assets		
Stock	37,000	
Debtors	51,000	
	88,000	
Less current liabilities		
Trade creditors	(91,400)	
Hire purchase on car	(3,000)	
Overdraft	(303,600)	
Working capital		(310,000)
Net assets		£236,000

The partnership business has made losses in recent years, and the bank and trade creditors are pressing for repayment of funds advanced to the business. Graham and Murphy consider the suggestion that they should inject more capital into the business, but decide against this plan. Wilkins is now bankrupt so cannot advance more funds. The partners decide to sell the business as at 31 December 19-3 to Exodus Plc, a company in the same trade.

The terms of the sale are as follows:

(a) Exodus Plc agree to purchase the land and buildings, plant, two of the vehicles, and the stock, all for £501,000.

(b) The third vehicle, a car, which has a book value of £6,000, is to be taken by Murphy as part of his capital repayment. The price agreed for the car is £4,000, but Murphy also agrees to settle personally the hire purchase debt owing on the car.

(c) The partners collect the debts of their business, but because of their haste, £4,000 of bad debts are incurred, and £2,000 of cash discounts are allowed.

(d) The consideration is to be partly settled by Exodus Plc by the payment of £368,600 in cash, and the assumption of the trade creditors (all except a personal contact of Graham who is owed £10,000 and is paid separately by the partnership). The balance of the consideration is to be settled by the issue of £1 ordinary shares in Exodus Plc at par to the partners.

Required: Draft ledger accounts to close the books of the partnership.   (*AAT*)

5.   The following trial balance has been extracted from the books of Gain and Main as at 31 March 1982; Gain and Main are in partnership sharing profits and losses in the ratio 3:2.

	£	£
Capital accounts:		
Gain		10,000
Main		5,000
Cash at bank	1,550	
Creditors		500
Current accounts:		
Gain		1,000
Main	2,000	
Debtors	2,000	
Depreciation: Fixtures and fittings		1,000
Motor vehicles		1,300
Fixtures and fittings	2,000	
Land and buildings	30,000	
Motor vehicles	4,500	
Net profit (for the year to 31 March 19-2)		26,250
Stock, at cost	3,000	
	£45,050	£45,050

In appropriating the net profit for the year, it has been agreed that Main should be entitled to a salary of £9,750. Each partner is also entitled to interest on his opening capital account balance at the rate of 10% per annum.

Gain and Main have decided to convert the partnership into a limited company, Plain Ltd, as from 1 April 1982. The company is to take over all the assets and liabilities of the partnership, except that Gain is to retain for his personal use one of the motor vehicles at an agreed transfer price of £1,000.

The purchase consideration will consist of 40,000 ordinary shares of £1 each in Plain ltd, to be divided between the partners in profit sharing ratio. Any balance on the partners current accounts is to be settled in cash.

Required: Prepare the main ledger accounts of the partnership in order to close off the books as at 31 March 1982.

(AAT)

45. Goodwill and Changes in Partnerships

INTRODUCTION

1. Changes can occur in partnerships including:

    (a) Changes in profit/loss sharing ratio.
    (b) Introduction of a new partner.
    (c) Retirement of a partner.

2. Most of these changes involve the valuation of *goodwill* and the chapter begins with a discussion of goodwill.

3. Some general rules on the bookkeeping in partnership changes are then derived.

GOODWILL

4. Goodwill has been judicially described as "the probability that the customers of a business will continue to patronise the business on a change of ownership".

5. That goodwill has value can readily be seen by an example. Cooper is a newly qualified accountant who wishes to commence private practice. He could do so by renting some offices and advertising his services in the press. However, finding clients is difficult and takes time. It may be that Price has a block of clients and wishes to retire. Clearly it would pay Cooper to buy the clients from Price. The intention of the clients to patronise a particular accounting practice is known as the goodwill of the practice. Such intention is usually transferable and hence has value.

6. Goodwill, like any other scarce commodity, is worth what a willing buyer will pay a willing seller. The value, or price if it is to be sold, is normally reached by negotiation or in cases of dispute by independent arbitration.

7. Although the value of goodwill is reached by agreement after negotiation amongst the interested parties, there are some guidelines as to how the value may be estimated in certain industries and also in general. These include:

In particular

    (a) n times the grosss annual fee income – accounting practices. n is usually 1 to $1\frac{1}{4}$.
    (b) x times the annual gallonage of beer sold – public houses.

In general

    (a) n times the average net profit. This is often described as n years purchase of the average annual net profit.
    (b) Capitalisation of super profits (super = above). An example:

John owns a wholesale clothing business. Annual profits are £30,000. Capital tied up in net assets is £50,000. Philip is interested in buying the business. He might consider that if he bought it, he would have to pay £50,000 for the physical net assets thus losing say £7,500 of interest he is currently earning from the £50,000 which is invested in stock exchange securities. He would also lose the £14,000 he is currently earning as a factory supervisor. He would thus lose £21,500 but gain £30,000. How much is the extra (super) income of £8,500 worth? To put it another way, how much would Philip be prepared to invest to earn an extra £8,500.

Suppose that Philip felt that the £8,500 was a fairly risky source of income and required a 20% return on investment (*i.e.* for every £100 invested, he requires an income of £20), then the £8,500 a year is worth £42,500 and that is the value to Philip of the goodwill.

Valuation of goodwill of John's business from Philip's point of view:

	£
Income if business not bought	
From investments	7,500
From salary	14,000
	£21,500
Income if business is bought – profit	£30,000
Difference – super profits	8,500
Value of super profits $\frac{100}{20}$ x 8,500	42,500

Notes:

(a) *Philip will have to borrow the £42,500 at a rate of interest. If he borrows at say 16% he will earn £8,500 and pay out £6,800. This seems a good bargain but the £6,800 is certain and the £8,500 is risky.*

(b) *In effect Philip is saying:*

	£
The business will earn me	*30,000*
But I will lose my salary	*14,000*
Leaving me	*16,000*
Just enough to earn:	
15% on my investment in tangible assets	*7,500*
20% on my investment in intangible assets	*8,500*

I need a higher return on the investment in intangible assets because I am unlikely to recover it if things go wrong.

PARTNERSHIP CHANGES

8.   When a change occurs in a partnership which is a going concern such that goodwill has value then the following procedures are required:

   (a)   Agree on the value of goodwill.

   (b)   Write up the goodwill account, by debiting goodwill and crediting the pre-change partners in the pre-change profit/loss sharing ratio.

   (c)   Write down the goodwill to nil, by crediting goodwill account and debiting the post-change partners in the post-change profit/loss sharing ratio.

   (d)   Assets other than goodwill are sometimes involved and are treated in the same way.

Example 1

The partners, Graham and Keith of Truckbits, share profits equally and the partnership balance sheet at 30.6.-4 was:

	£		£
Capital: Graham	30,000	Fixed assets	35,000
Keith	18,500	Current assets	28,000
Current liabilities	14,500		
	63,000		63,000

On 1.7.-4, the partners agreed that as Graham wished to take a smaller part in the partnership business, the profit sharing ratio should change to 2:3 with a salary of £5,000 a year to Keith. For the purpose of the change only, goodwill was agreed at a value of £30,000 and fixed assets at a value of £47,000. These changes in value were not to be incorporated in the books.

Answer

Goodwill Account

	£		£
Graham (a)	15,000	Graham (b)	12,000
Keith (a)	15,000	Keith (b)	18,000
	30,000		30,000

Fixed Assets

	£		£
b/f	35,000	Graham (b)	4,800
Graham (a)	6,000	Keith (b)	7,200
Keith (a)	6,000	c/f	35,000
	47,000		47,000

CAPITAL ACCOUNTS

	Graham	Keith		Graham	Keith
	£	£		£	£
Goodwill (b)	12,000	18,000	b/f	30,000	18,500
Fixed assets (b)	4,800	7,200	Goodwill (a)	15,000	15,000
c/f	34,200	14,300	Fixed assets (a)	6,000	6,000
	51,000	39,500		51,000	39,500

Notes:

(a) Goodwill and fixed assets are written up to their agreed values (£30,000 and £47,000) by credits to the partners' accounts in the old profit sharing ratio (equal shares).

(b) Goodwill and fixed assets are written down to their continuing book values (nil and £35,000) by debits to the partners' accounts in the new profit sharing ratios (2:3).

(c) The salary part of the profit sharing formula is irrelevant for this purpose.

Example 2

Jonathan and Diane are in partnership sharing profits equally and with a balance sheet at 31.7.-5 as:

	£		£
Capital: Jonathan	60,000	Net assets	100,000
Diane	40,000		
	100,000		100,000

On 1.8.-5 Tina was admitted to the partnership and brought in £30,000 cash. Profit sharing was to be in equal shares. It was agreed that goodwill was worth £24,000 and that no goodwill account was to be maintained in the books.

Answer

Goodwill Account

	£		£
Jonathan	12,000	Jonathan	8,000
Diane	12,000	Diane	8,000
		Tina	8,000
	24,000		24,000

CAPITAL ACCOUNTS

	J	D	T		J	D	T
	£	£	£		£	£	£
Goodwill	8,000	8,000	8,000	b/f	60,000	40,000	
c/f	52,000	32,000	22,000	Cash			30,000
	60,000	40,000	30,000		60,000	40,000	30,000

RETIREMENT OF A PARTNER

9. In theory, the retirement of a partner from the partnership involves the dissolution of the partnership and the setting up of a new partnership of the non-retiring partners from the old partnership. In practice the assets and liabilities of the old partnership are usually carried through to the new partnership and the books continued.

10. The steps required on the retirement of a partner are:

(a) Determination of the value of the goodwill.

(b) Writing up the value of the goodwill as:

Dr Goodwill
Cr Partners in their profit sharing ratio

(c) Charging any assets taken by the retiring partner to his account.

(d) Making any required adjustments to the value of any assets or liabilities with corresponding entries on the capital accounts of any profits/losses in profit sharing ratio.

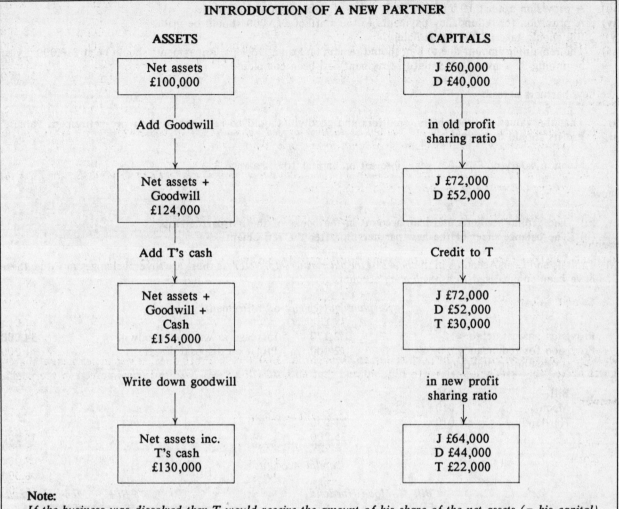

INTRODUCTION OF A NEW PARTNER

Note:
If the business was dissolved then T would receive the amount of his share of the net assets (= his capital) plus his share of the proceeds of the sale of the goodwill i.e. £22,000 + £8,000 = £30,000 which he put in. Always check answers this way.

(e) Writing down value of goodwill to nil by:

     Dr   Capital accounts of remaining partners
     Cr   Goodwill

     in new profit sharing ratio.

(f) Re-titling the capital (together with current account) of the retiring partner as a loan to the new partnership.

11. Example of retirement of a partner

Bill, Moon and Hartland are in partnership sharing profits equally. On 31 January 1988 their balance sheet showed:

	B £	M £	H £	£		£
Capitals	28,000	15,000	11,000	54,000	Plant and vehicles	28,000
Current Account	3,100	2,000	900	6,000	Stock	14,000
Creditors				10,500	Debtors	21,700
					Cash at Bank	6,800
				70,500		70,500

On 1st February 1988, Bill retired and it was agreed that, in accordance with the partnership agreement:

(i) Goodwill was valued at £34,000.

(ii)   Bill should take a car (written down value £2,800) at a valuation of £4,000.
(iii) A provision against 10% of the book value of debtors should be made.
(iv)   A provision for redundancy payments to the staff of £12,000 should be made.
(v)   Bill should take £5,000 immediately.
(vi)   The remaining amount due to him should remain on loan at 15% pa. Repayments should be at £10,000 a year beginning 31 January 1989 until repayment had been completed.

The new partners agreed:

(i)   That the values of the debtors, creditors and goodwill should be returned to their pre-retirement values.
(ii)   Profits should be split:

Moon, a salary of £3,000 a year, interest on capital 10%, balance 3:2.

Show:

(a)   The capital accounts and loan account in the books of the old partnership.
(b)   The balance sheet of the new partnership after the retirement.

(a)   Capitals and Loan Accounts in the *books of the old partnership. Note:* As there are several changes in value, these have been summarised in a *revaluation* account.

Revaluation Account on retirement

	£		£
Provision against debtors	2,170	Increase in value of goodwill	34,000
Provision for redundancy	12,000	Profit on disposal of car	1,200
Net surplus on revaluation:			

Bill	7,010		
Moon	7,010		
Hartland	7,010	21,030	
		35,200	35,200

Capital Accounts

	Bill £	Moon £	Hartland £		Bill £	Moon £	Hartland £
Car withdrawn	4,000			Balance b/f	28,000	15,000	11,000
Cash	5,000			Share of surplus	7,010	7,010	7,010
Transfer/s loan	26,010	22,010	18,010				
	35,010	22,010	18,010		35,010	22,010	18,010

Loan Account – Bill

	£		£
Balance c/f	29,110	Capital Account	26,010
		Current Account	3,100
	29,110		29,110

(b)   In the books of the new partnership, we must first restore the balances to their pre-retirement levels:

Revaluation Account

	£			£
Goodwill	34,000	Provision against debtors		2,170
		Provision for redundancy		12,000
		Adjustment to Capital:		
		Moon	11,898	
		Hartland	7,932	19,830
	34,000			34,000

Capital Accounts

	Moon £	Hartland £		Moon £	Hartland £
Write down	11,898	7,932	b/f	22,010	18,010
c/f	10,112	10,078			
	22,010	18,010		22,010	18,010

Finally we can prepare the:

Balance Sheet of the new partnership

	Moon £	Hartland £	Total £		£
Capitals	10,112	10,078	20,190	Plant Vehicles	25,200
Current A/c	2,000	900	2,900	Stock	14,000
Creditors			10,500	Debtors	21,700
Bill - loan			29,110	Cash at Bank	1,800
			62,700		62,700

Note:
The goodwill etc. is written down in the new profit sharing ratio ignoring the salary to Moon.

To complete the matter, let us look at the situation one year hence when the trial balance showed:

		Dr £	Cr £
Plant and vehicles		23,900	
Stock		18,700	
Debtors and Creditors		22,600	22,380
Loan Account - Bill			19,110
Net Profit for year			*22,600
Drawings	- Moon	8,350	
	- Hartland	7,900	
Capitals	- Moon		10,112
	- Hartland		10,078
Current a/c	- Moon		2,000
	- Hartland		900
Cash at bank		5,730	
		87,180	87,180

* After charging interest paid on the loan from Bill, £4,366.50.

The appropriation account will be:

Net Profit   22,600

	Moon £	Hartland £	Total £
Salary	3,000		3,000
Interest on Capital	1,011	1,008	2,019
Balance	10,549	7,032	17,581
	14,560	8,040	22,600

The partners current accounts will be:

	Moon £	Hartland £		Moon £	Hartland £
Drawings	8,350	7,900	b/f	2,000	900
c/f	8,210	1,040	Share of profit	14,560	8,040
	16,560	8,940		16,560	8,940

and the final balance sheet:

	Moon £	*Hartland* £	*Total* £			£
Capital Account	10,112	10,078	20,190	**Fixed Assets** Plant etc.		23,900
Current Account	8,210	1,040	9,250			
				Current Assets		
				Stock	18,700	
	18,322	11,118	29,440	Debtors	22,600	
				Cash	5,730	47,030
Loan - Bill			19,110			
Current Liabilities						
Creditors			22,380			
			70,930			70,930

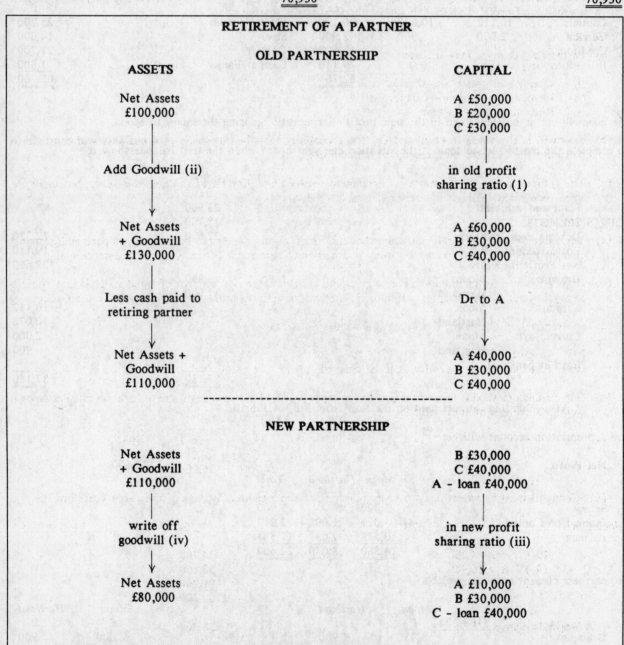

RETIREMENT OF A PARTNER

OLD PARTNERSHIP

ASSETS	CAPITAL
Net Assets £100,000	A £50,000 B £20,000 C £30,000
Add Goodwill (ii)	in old profit sharing ratio (1)
Net Assets + Goodwill £130,000	A £60,000 B £30,000 C £40,000
Less cash paid to retiring partner	Dr to A
Net Assets + Goodwill £110,000	A £40,000 B £30,000 C £40,000

NEW PARTNERSHIP

Net Assets + Goodwill £110,000	B £30,000 C £40,000 A - loan £40,000
write off goodwill (iv)	in new profit sharing ratio (iii)
Net Assets £80,000	A £10,000 B £30,000 C - loan £40,000

(i)   Equal shares
(ii) And any adjustments to other assets or liability values
(iii) B ⅔ and C ⅓
(iv) And any adjustments to other asset or liability values

THEORY

12. The theory on the treatment of goodwill in partnership changes can be summarised as:

    (a) Profit is any increase in the *net* assets of a business other than from an injection of capital.

    (b) In a partnership profits are credited to capital accounts in profit sharing ratio.

    (c) The net assets of the partnership are equal to the sum of the partners' capital accounts.

    (d) There is usually an asset, goodwill, which is not normally included in the net assets on the balance sheet.

    (e) The recognition of this asset (and any other incorrectly valued asset or liability) would, in a dissolution, involve a credit to the partners' capitals in profit sharing ratio. Effectively the creation of a new asset is a profit, and profit is shared in the partnership profit sharing ratio.

SUMMARY

13. (a) Partnership changes may include:

    (i)   Changes in profit/loss sharing ratio.
    (ii) Introduction of a new partner.
    (iii) Retirement of a partner.

    (b) Goodwill is the value to be placed on "the probability that the customers of a business will continue to patronise the business on a change of ownership".

    (c) The value of goodwill is a matter of agreement between a willing buyer and a willing seller, but there are some recognised methods of arriving at such a value.

POINTS TO NOTE

14. (a) The value of goodwill is relevant only when a business or an interest in a business (*e.g.* a partnership share) changes hands. In such cases, the value is a matter of agreement between the parties concerned.

    (b) However, there are a number of accepted methods of achieving a first estimate of value which is then subject to nego-tiation. In this chapter, a number of methods of arriving at the first esti-mate have been discussed.

    (c) In examination questions, the usual approach is either:

    (i) To give the value.
    (ii) To explain how the value is to be derived.

    (d) One common method is to give the profits (or super profits) for recent years and to base the calculation on a weighted average of these profits, *e.g.*

	19-0	19-1	19-2
	£	£	£
(i) Profits	24,200	26,900	30,400

    (ii) Goodwill is to be valued at two years purchase of the weighted average of the three years profits.

Calculation

		£
19-0	1 x 24,200 =	24,200
19-1	2 x 26,900 =	53,800
19-2	3 x 30,400 =	91,200
	6	£169,200

Weighted average = $\dfrac{£169,200}{6}$ = £28,200

Two years purchase = 2 x £28,200 = £56,400

Note that more *weight* has been given to the later years.

SELF TESTING QUESTIONS

(a) What changes in partnerships can occur? (1).
(b) What is goodwill? (2).
(c) How should goodwill be valued? (4).
(d) What methods are found in practice to assess the value of goodwill? (7).
(e) What are super profits and how might they be calculated? (7).
(f) List the accounting procedures on a change in a partnership. (8).
(g) What is the relationship between capital, net assets, goodwill and profit? (12).
(h) What is a weighted average? (14).

Exercises (Answers begin on page 468)

1.   *Alec and Ben are in partnership as bakers. Their profit sharing formula is Alec - salary £5,000, the balance to be shared equally. Their balance sheet at 31.12.-4 was:*

		£		£
Capital:	Alec	23,000	Goodwill	5,000
	Ben	22,000	Other net assets	40,000
		45,000		45,000

As from 1.1.-5, the profit sharing ratio is to be Alec - salary £10,000, Ben 2% commission on sales, balance 3:2. Goodwill at 1.1.-5 was agreed at £30,000. After 1.1.-5, the goodwill account is to be written out of the books.

Required:
(a) Alec and Ben's capital accounts.
(b) Goodwill account.

2.   *Felix and Gemma are in partnership sharing profits equally. Their balance sheet at 31 May 19-8 is:*

		£		£
Capitals	Felix	35,000	Net Assets	58,920
	Gemma	20,000		
Current Accounts				
	Felix	3,100		
	Gemma	820		
		58,920		58,920

(i)   *From 1st December 19-8, profit sharing is to be - Felix, salary £6,000 a year, remainder Felix 3/5, Gemma 2/5.*

(ii)   *Profit in the year ending 31st May 19-9 was £24,000. It accrued evenly during the year.*

(iii)   *Goodwill is to be valued at £20,000 and no account is to be maintained for goodwill in the books.*

(iv)   *Drawings in the year to 31st May 19-9 were Felix £12,700, Gemma £9,250.*

(a) Prepare the appropriation account for the year ending 31st May 19-9.
(b) Show capital and current accounts for the same period.
(c) What are the net assets at 31 May 19-9?

3.   *Louise, Manuel and Nathan are in partnership sharing profits 2:2:1 with balance sheet at 31 October 19-8:*

	£		£
Louise	14,300	Net Assets	26,300
Manuel	6,800		
Nathan	5,200		
	26,300		26,300

(i)   *On 1 November 19-8, Manuel retires on the basis that his share of the good-will is credited to him and the balance of his capital account is transferred to a loan account carrying interest at 15% with repayments of the loan being as soon as possible but no later than 31.12.19-5.*

(ii)   *Goodwill is valued at £36,000 but no account is to be maintained in the books.*

(iii) As from 1 November 19–8, Louise and Nathan will share profits as 10% interest on capital, remainder 3/5:2/5.

Show the capital and loan accounts of the partners at the retirement of Manuel.

(i) On 31 October 19–9, the partnership had made a profit of £28,400 before interest to Manuel.
(ii) On 30 April 19–9, £3,000 had been paid to Manuel together with interest to that date.
(iii) The partners had drawn: Louise £6,200, Nathan £4,100.

Show the appropriation account for 19–8/–9, the current accounts of the partners and the balance sheet as at 31 October 19–9.

Exercises without answers
4. Windle and Zengle are in partnership sharing profits 7:3 with balance sheets at 31.12.–7 as:

	£		£
Windle	24,620	Net Assets	43,350
Zengle	18,730		
	43,350		43,350

(i) On 1 January 19–8, Windle retired and goodwill was valued at £11,000.
(ii) Zengle borrowed from his bank to pay half the amount due to Windle.

Show the balance sheet of Zengle after these transactions.

5. Lorraine, Steel and Wilkes are in partnership sharing profits – 10% interest on capital and balance 5:5:4. Their balance sheet at 31.1.–8 showed:

	£		£
Lorraine	31,000	Net Assets	61,300
Steel	23,500		
Wilkes	6,800		
	61,300		61,300

(i) On 1 February 19–8, Barker was admitted as a partner and the profit sharing was changed to 15% interest on capital and the balance in equal shares.

(ii) Goodwill was valued at £28,000 but no goodwill account was to be maintained in the books.

(iii) Barker bought in £20,000 as his capital and his share of the goodwill.

Show their capital accounts.

At the end of the year ending 31 January 19–9, profit was £58,000, drawings were: Lorraine £7,300, Steel £12,200, Wilkes £8,700 and Barker £5,350.

Show:
(a) The appropriation account for the year.
(b) The partners' capital accounts for the year.

6. James and John are in partnership sharing profits equally. Their balance sheet at 31.5.–7 shows:

	£		£
James	2,400	Net Assets	6,700
John	4,300		
	6,700		6,700

On 1.6.–7 Mary is admitted to the partnership bringing in £2,000. The new profit sharing ratio is to be James 2/5, John 2/5 and Mary 1/5. Goodwill is to be valued at £5,000 but no account is to be maintained on a permanent basis in the books.

Required:
(a) Capital accounts of the partnership, and the balance sheet after admission of Mary.
(b) Repeat under a new profit sharing ratio of equal shares.

7.   Dwin and Dell are in partnership sharing profit 3/5:2/5 with Dwin having a salary of £6,000.

Their balance sheet at 30.6.-7 shows:

	£		£
Capitals		Net Assets	25,700
Dwin	13,000		
Dell	10,000		
Current A/cs			
Dwin	1,400		
Dell	1,300		
	25,700		25,700

On 1.7.-7 Gain is admitted bringing in £6,000 so that the partnership profit sharing ratio is 4:3:3, with all partners having 10% interest on capital and Gain having a salary of £4,000.

Goodwill is valued at £12,000.

In the year ending 30.6.-8 the profit was £28,000 and drawings were Dwin £6,800, Dell £8,300, Gain £7,200.

Required:
(a)   the balance sheet of the partnership at 30.6.-8.
(b)   Repeat under the basis that the new profit sharing ratio is equal shares with no interest on capital or partnership salary.

8.   Peter, Quinney and Roland are in partnership sharing profit equally. The balance sheet at 31.12.-7 shows:

	£		£
Peter	12,000	Other Assets	25,400
Quinney	11,000	Bank	14,100
Roland	4,500		
Creditors	12,000		
	39,500		39,500

On 1.1.-8 Quinney retires on the following basis:

(i)   Goodwill is valued as £24,000.
(ii)   Quinney is to be paid 20% of the sum due to him.
(iii) The remainder is to stay as a loan to the partnership at 10% pa interest.

Required:
(a)   Show the partners' capital accounts on the dissolution on the assumption that the new profit sharing ratio will be Peter 3/5 and Roland 2/5.

(b)   After 12 months the profit earned was £18,000 and drawings were Peter £7,000, Roland £5,600. Creditors totalled £13,000 and cash at bank was £3,200. Draw up an appropriation account and a balance sheet.

(c)   Recalculate on the basis that the original P,Q,R profit sharing had been 4:4:2.

(d)   Recalculate on (i) the original basis and (ii) on the (c) basis, on the assumption that the new profit sharing ratio is equal but Roland has a salary of £2,000.

9.   Hubert and Lambert are in partnership sharing profits 6:4 with capital accounts at 30th June 19-8, Hubert £24,700 and Lambert £26,300.

On 1 July 19-8, Constance was admitted to the partnership on the basis that:

(i)   Goodwill was to be valued at £30,900.

(ii)   Constance would bring in £25,000.

(iii) New profit sharing ratio was to be 10% interest on capital, Constance a salary of £6,000 a year and the balance in equal shares.

On 1 January 19-9, Greig was to be admitted to the partnership on the basis that:

(i) Goodwill was to be valued at £35,000.

(ii) Greig would bring in £30,000.

(iii) New profit sharing ratio was to be 15% interest on capital, salary to Constance £8,000 a year, salary to Greig £4,000 a year and the balance in equal shares.

Given that:

(i) Profit in the year ending 30 June 19-9 was £53,000. This profit accrued evenly over the year.

(ii) Drawings in the year were Hubert £4,300, Lambert £7,200, Constance £2,900 and Greig £1,950. All drawings were taken evenly over the period in which the person was a partner.

(a) Show the appropriation account for the year ending 30th June 19-9.
(b) Show the capital accounts of all the partners for the same period.

10. Eagle and Falcon are partners sharing profits in the ratio 3:1 respectively. On 31st December 1982 their balance sheet showed:

		£		£
Capital:	Eagle	18,000	Premises	16,000
	Falcon	12,000	Vehicles	5,800
		30,000		21,800
Current:	Eagle	300		
	Falcon Dr Bal	(700)	Stocks	1,500
		29,600	Debtors	6,200
Creditors		1,800	Bank	1,900	9,600
		31,400		31,400

At the date of the balance sheet, Falcon retires and Hawk is admitted to partnership with Eagle. Eagle and Hawk will now share profits in the ratio 4:1. On Falcon's retirement the following revaluations were made:

Goodwill	6,000
Premises	18,000
Vehicles	6,000

Falcon will take a vehicle valued at £2,800 and will take the balance of the amount due to him in cash.

Hawk will introduce £10,000 cash as fixed capital, but he will not introduce any payment for goodwill.

Required:
(a) Prepare (in columnar form) the capital accounts of Eagle, Falcon and Hawk, including the adjustments necessary upon the retirement of Falcon and the admission of Hawk.

(b) Prepare the opening balance sheet of the new partnership. The value of goodwill is to be shown in this balance sheet. (LCCI)

11. Alan and Brian are in partnership sharing profits as:

Alan - salary of £4,000 pa
Balance - Alan 5/8:Brian 3/8.

Their balance sheet at 30th April 1985 showed:

		£000		£000
Capitals	Alan	80	Goodwill	2
	Brian	116	Fixed tangible assets	148
Current liabilities		34	Cash at bank	6
			Other current assets	74
		230		230

On 1st May 1985, Colin was admitted to the partnership with the following agreement:

(i)   Goodwill is to be valued at one year's purchase of the weighted average profits of the preceding three years which were 1982/3: £25,000; 1983/4: £34,000; 1984/5: £37,000.

(ii) Colin is to bring £50,000 cash and his car valued at £10,000 into the partner-ship.

(iii) The profit sharing ratio from 1st May 1985 is to be:
      Alan: salary of £6,000 a year
      Colin: salary of £10,000 a year
      Balance: Alan 5/17   Brian 6/17   Colin 6/17

Required:
Record the changes resulting from the change in the partnership by showing:
  (a) The goodwill account - the balance of this account is to be written off immediately after the admission of Colin.
  (b) The partners' capital accounts in columnar form.
  (c) The balance sheet after the admission of Colin.   (RSA)

Limited Companies

The next part of the manual is concerned with limited companies formed under the legal requirements of the Companies Act 1985.

Chapter 46 introduces the legal and commercial aspects of companies. Chapter 47 describes the company balance sheet and the mysteries of its financing section. Chapter 47 deals with share capital and debentures. Chapter 49 describes the profit and loss account and its appropriation section.

46. Limited Companies

INTRODUCTION

1. A business can be owned by an individual personally (a sole trader), several people in common (a partnership), or by a *company* registered under the Companies Act. This chapter outlines:

    (a) The historical development of the limited company to meet business needs.
    (b) Some of the particular legal characteristics of companies.
    (c) The distinction between sole traders, partnerships and limited companies.
    (d) The accounting requirements for companies.
    (e) Different sorts of companies likely to be met with in practice.

HISTORY

2. Before the nineteenth century, businesses were generally small and were not capital intensive. They did not need large amounts of fixed assets or working capital. Individuals were lightly taxed and it was perfectly possible for entrepreneurs, either alone or in partnership, to find the necessary capital from their private resources. A few businesses were larger and they required so much capital that many individuals had to pool their resources and employ professional management. Such *companies* were formed under a *Royal Charter* or by *special Act of Parliament*. Examples are the East India Company and the Hudson's Bay Company.

3. In the nineteenth century, the industrial revolution and colonial expansion caused the formation of many more business ventures requiring large capital outlay beyond the resources of a few individuals and the devices of Royal Charter and special Acts of Parliament proved insufficient. Consequently a series of Acts of Parliament providing general machinery for the formation of companies were passed. The principal Act was the Companies Act 1862 on which modern company law is founded.

4. Since then, many companies acts have updated the law. At the time of writing, the Act in force is the Companies Act 1985.

CHARACTERISTICS OF LIMITED COMPANIES

5. These include:

    (a) **Legal personality.** A company is regarded as having separate legal personality. It is an *artificial* person that can own property, make contracts, sue and be sued. The company is a separate entity distinct from those who own it.

    (b) **Perpetual succession.** As a company is a separate entity, its ownership can change without changing the company itself.

    (c) **Limited liability.** The owners of a company (known as its *members* or its *shareholders*) are not liable for the debts of the company.

6. To illustrate these ideas, consider Antony who owns a home in which he lives and a building in which he carries on a restaurant business. He is considering forming a company, Antony Ltd., so that he and his wife will own the company and the *company* will own the restaurant building and operate the restaurant business. The effect of the change on certain events will be:

Event	Effect if A is a sole trader	Effect if A transfers the restaurant to A Ltd.
Death of Antony	Property and business pass to his heirs including legal conveyance of property.	A Ltd shares pass to his heirs.
Sale of business	Business transferred to new owners, property (if also sold) must be conveyed legally.	Shares in A Ltd sold to new owners.
Failure of business	Creditors of business can look to satisfy sums due to them from business assets and *also* Antony's private assets including his house.	Creditors of business can look *only* to the assets of A Ltd.

By trading as a limited company:

(a) Transfers of ownership of a business are facilitated.
(b) Antony's private assets are safeguarded.

7. COMPANIES COMPARED WITH SOLE TRADING AND PARTNERSHIPS

	Sole Trader	Partnership	Companies
Regulating Acts	-	Partnership Act 1890	Companies Act
Rules	-	Partnership agreement	Memorandum and Articles of Association
Business is a separate legal entity	No	No	Yes
Liability of proprietor	Unlimited	Unlimited	Limited
Ownership	Sole trader	Partners	Members
Management	Proprietor	Partners	Directors
Number of owners	1	1 to 20 (a)	minimum 2 maximum unlimited
Books required	No (b)	No (b)	Companies Act requirements
Annual accounts	No (b)	No (b)	Companies Act requirements
Audit	No (b)	No (b)	Companies Act requirements
Information available to the public	None	None	Publicly available file on companies
Profit division	All to proprietor	As partnership agreement	Decision of directors subject to approval of members
Profit withdrawal	Drawings	Drawings	Dividends

(a) Partnerships are limited by law to twenty members except for certain professional partnerships (*e.g.* lawyers, doctors, accountants who can have as many members as they wish).

(b) Sole traders and partners may, *if they so wish,* keep books, prepare accounts and have the accounts audited. In practice because of legal requirements to PAYE, statutory sick pay, VAT and income tax *all* businesses do these things.

8. Note that:

(a) The owners of a company are called *members* of the company or *shareholders.* The capital of a company is usually divided into a fixed number of shares and each member will have a particular number of shares.

(b) Each year, the members meet at an Annual General Meeting where the members elect or re-elect the *directors* and transact other business.

(c) The rules of a company are legal documents called the Memorandum of Association. The *memorandum* contains the following clauses:

(i) The name of the company.
(ii) The domicile of the company which means Scotland or England and Wales.
(iii) The objects of the company - usually this clause runs to many pages to enable the company to do virtually anything.
(iv) A statement that the liability of the members is limited.
(v) Details of the share capital which the company is *authorised* to issue.
(vi) A public company will also have a clause stating that it is a public company.

The articles contain regulations on such matters as:

The issue of shares.	The appointment and duties of directors.
The transfer of shares.	The use of the company seal.
General meetings.	Accounts and audit.
Voting at meetings.	Etc., etc.

Most companies adopt a model set of Articles called "Table A" (with some modifications), which are to be found in the Companies (Table A to F) Regulations 1985.

(d) All companies must file information about themselves (*e.g.* share capital, names of directors etc.) including their accounts with the Registrar of Companies and this file is open to the public. They must make an *annual return* to the registrar which includes a copy of the annual accounts.

9. DIFFERENT TYPES OF COMPANY

(a) Public companies
A public company is one which:

(i) States in its memorandum that it is a public company.
(ii) Ends its name with "public limited company" or p.l.c.
(iii) Has a minimum share capital of £50,000.

(b) Private companies
A private company is any company which is not a public company. Private companies end their names with the word "limited".

The differences between the two types of company are numerous. As examples:

Public companies must have at least two directors and private companies need only have one.

A private company cannot offer its shares or debentures to the public and thus cannot obtain a stock exchange listing.

(c) Small, medium and large
To be small or medium sized, a company must satisfy *two* or *more* of the following criteria:

	Small	Medium sized
Turnover not exceeding	£1.4m	£5.75m
Balance sheet total not exceeding	£700,000	£2.8m
Average number of employees does not exceed	50	250

Small and medium sized companies are permitted to file modified accounts, giving less information, with the registrar of companies.

(d) Unlimited companies
These are relatively rare private companies where the liability of the members is unlimited.

(e) Companies limited by guarantee
Most companies have a share capital. A company may instead have the liability of its members limited by the Memorandum to such amounts as the members may guarantee to contribute to the assets of the company in the event of its being wound up. Guarantee companies are usually trade associations, professional associations or clubs or societies.

(f) Quoted companies also called listed companies
These are public companies whose shares are traded on the stock exchange. As shares are bought and sold on the stock exchange, the shareholders change and thus the ownership of the company is continually changing.

In addition to companies whose shares are listed on the stock exchange there are many companies who shares are quoted on the *unlisted securities market* (U.S.M.) or on the third market. There is little difference in practice between the market for shares in companies with a full stock exchange listing and those quoted on the U.S.M. or the third market.

10. ACCOUNTING REQUIREMENTS FOR COMPANIES
The Companies Act requires companies to maintain proper accounting records, maintain statutory books and lay before the shareholders financial statements in a particular format, showing additional information in the form of notes.

(a) Accounting records
All companies must maintain proper accounting records which record:

(i)   Entries from day to day of all *sums of money* received and expended and the matters about which these receipts and payments book place, *i.e.* a cash book.
(ii) *Assets* and *liabilities*.
(iii) Where the company *deals* in *goods* then:

- Statements of stock held at each financial year end.
- Statements of stock takings from which these were prepared.
- Except for retail sales, statements of all *goods bought and sold* with names of buyers and sellers, *i.e.* purchase and sales day books and ledgers.

The books must be sufficient to show, with reasonable accuracy, at any time the financial position of the company and enable the directors to ensure that any profit and loss account or balance sheet produced both shows a *true and fair* view and complies with the requirements of the Companies Acts.

(b) Statutory books
In addition to the accounting records, all companies are required to keep certain other records known as the statutory books (*i.e.* books that the statute requires to be kept).

These include:

(i)   *A register of members* (= shareholders) (CA 1985 s352-354).
      This must contain, for each member, name and address, date of becoming a member, the shareholding. The register must have an index if there are more than 50 members. It must be kept at the registered office or some other place within the country of registration (*i.e.* England and Wales or Scotland).

(ii) *A register of directors and secretaries* (CA 1985 s.288-290)
      This must list full particulars (for directors, names and former names, address, nationality, business occupation and particulars of other directorships and, for secretaries, names and former names and address) of directors and secretaries. The register must be available for inspection by members of the company without charge at least two hours a day and to members of the public for a charge not exceeding 5p.

(iii) *A register of charges* (CA 1985 s.407)
      This lists all charges both fixed and floating on the property of the company (see chapter on debentures). This must also be available for inspection on the same terms as the register of directors but inspection must be free to creditors.

    (iv) *Minute books* (CA 1985 s382-383)

          Minutes of all proceedings at meetings of the company (*i.e.* shareholders) of directors and of managers must be maintained. The minutes of shareholders' meetings must be available for inspection by any member of the company.

    (v) *Register of directors' interests*

          In shares and debentures of the company and those of his/her spouse, infant children and certain other persons, trusts and companies connected with him/her. (CA 1985 s324-325). It must be available for inspection in the same way as the register of members. It should be indexed.

    (vi) Public companies must keep a register of shareholders who have an interest of 5% or more in the nominal value of the voting share capital (CA 1985 s211).

In addition every company must make a *return (the annual return)* to the Registrar of Companies at least once in every year, containing details of the registered office, the register of members and debenture holders, shares and debentures, indebtedness, past and present members and the secretary. The annual accounts are also included. (CA 1985 s363 and Sch 15.)

(c) **Annual accounts**

    The directors must cause to be produced annually:

    (i)   A profit and loss account.
    (ii)   A balance sheet.
    (iii) Notes attached to forming part of, and amplifying (i) and (ii).
    (iv)   A directors' report with specific content.
    (v)   The auditors' report.

In the case of non-trading companies (*e.g.* clubs), an income and expenditure account is required instead of a profit and loss account.

These accounts must be *laid* before the members at each Annual General Meeting. Normally they are circulated in advance with other documents in the Annual Report and Accounts.

The accounts must also be *delivered* to (filed with) the Registrar of Companies in Cardiff.

Both these presentations must be within ten months (for private companies) or seven months (for other companies), of the accounting reference date (= company year end).

The accounts must give a *true and fair view* and comply with the accounting requirements of the Companies Act.

11. The accounting requirements of the Companies Act are now very detailed. They include:

    (a) Use of specified formats.
    (b) Use of specified accounting principles - going concern, realisation, prudence, accruals.
    (c) Giving of particular detailed information about each item in the accounts.

12. **SUMMARY**

    (a) Companies provide a mode of ownership of a business whereby a company owns the assets, owes the liabilities and is in turn owned by its shareholders.

    (b) The characteristics of a company include:

        - Legal personality
        - Perpetual succession
        - Limited liability on the part of its shareholders.

    (c) Companies are regulated by the Companies Act 1985.

    (d) The Registrar of Companies in Cardiff maintains a file on every company. Each file contains information about the company including the accounts and is available to the public.

    (e) The Companies Act requires companies to maintain or prepare:

(i)   Proper accounting records – receipts and payments, assets and liabilities, stocktakings, suppliers' and customers' ledgers.

(ii) Statutory books.

(iii) Annual accounts consisting of:

- a profit and loss account (or income and expenditure account).
- a balance sheet
- notes attached to and forming part of these two documents.
- a directors' report.
- the auditors' report.

13. POINTS TO NOTE

(a) Companies range in size from the very small, the corner shops, to the very large, the multi national companies. Many small companies are owned by a man who has ninety-nine shares and is the sole director, and his wife with one share. In such cases ownership and management are in the same hands. In public companies there are typically many thousands of shareholders with a board of directors who themselves own a negligible number of shares.

(b) There are some 870,000 companies on the register, of which only 8,000 are public companies. However, many of the private companies are subsidiaries of (they are owned by) public companies.

(c) The Companies Act regulates the formation, conduct, and liquidation of companies with two principal objectives:

(i)   To protect creditors of the companies.
(ii) To protect investors.

(d) The requirement to file information and accounts at Companies House has led to the saying "public disclosure is the price paid for limited liability".

SELF TESTING QUESTIONS

(a) List and explain three characteristics of limited companies. (5).

(b) Give another name for shareholders. (8a).

(c) Who elect the directors of a company? (8b).

(d) What are the documents called that regulate a particular company? (8c).

(e) What clauses appear in the memorandum of a company? (8c).

(f) What criteria establish whether a company is small or medium sized? (9).

(g) What accounting records must a company keep? (10).

(h) What are the time restrictions on the laying and delivery of accounts? (10c).

(i) Contrast a sole trader, a partnership and a limited company from the point of view of:

- legal entity   – records requirements   – management
- statutory control   – annual accounts   – number of owners
- proprietorial liability   – audit requirement   – profit division
- ownership   – public information   – profit withdrawal (7).

(j) what is Table A? (8).

(k) What is the purpose of and principal contents of:

- a register of members   – a register of directors' interests
- a register of directors and secretaries   – minute books
- a register of charges   – an annual return

Exercises without answers

1. *Explain the following terms:*

Companies Act	Company	Delivered to
Act of Parliament	Legal Personality	Royal Charter
Limited Liability	Members	Perpetual Succession
Memorandum	Articles	Shareholders
Audit	Dividends	Director
Registrar of Companies	Domicile	AGM
Public company	Authorised capital	Objects Clause
Limited	Private Company	Table A
Unlimited	Listing	PLC
Accounting Records	Guarantee	Quoted
Registrar of Members	True and Fair	Statutory Books
Minute Book	Secretary	Charges
Laid before	Annual Return	Annual Accounts
		Small and medium

2. *Distinguish between:*

Partnerships and sole traders	Ownership and management
Partnerships and limited companies	Public and private companies
Dividends and drawings	Quoted and unquoted companies
Agreements and Memorandums and Articles	Institutional and private shareholders

3. Why should A and B who are in partnership as importers of toy guns wish to incorporate their business into a company? Note that their mode of business is to buy the goods for cash as they are landed in the UK, hold them in stock until sold and then sell on credit to retailers.

4. Why are limited companies tightly regulated when partnerships are not?

47. The Company Balance Sheet

INTRODUCTION

1.   The Companies Act 1985 requires that a company balance sheet for filing with the registrar and sending to shareholders should be in one of two formats given in the Act. One of the formats is the vertical form and the other is the same but in horizontal form. In practice virtually all companies use the vertical form. Format 1 is given at the end of the Chapter. It contains many headings which are rarely found in practice and we will concentrate in this chapter on a simplified version.

2.   The company balance sheet differs from the balance sheet of a sole trader or a partnership in a number of ways. Primarily, this is a matter of vocabulary and this chapter introduces and explains a number of words of importance in a company balance sheet.

3.   Among the words is the word "reserves" which causes special difficulties to beginning students. Make sure you fully understand the concepts involved.

PREPARATION OF A COMPANY BALANCE SHEET

4.   The trial balance of Bangle Wholesalers Limited at 31 December 19-7 *after* preparing the profit and loss account of the year ending on 31 December 19-7 showed:

	Dr £000	Cr £000
Land and buildings at cost	500	
Land and buildings depreciation provision		84
Plant at cost	32	
Plant depreciation provision		17
Stock	164	
Debtors and Creditors	183	102
Prepayments and Accruals	26	14
Bank		16
Corporation Tax		35
Proposed dividends		27
Ordinary Share Capital - £1 shares		200
7% Preference Share Capital - £1 shares		100
Reserves		180
12% Debentures (20-4 - 20-7)		130
	905	905

5.   Firstly, we will assemble this information into the form of a balance sheet. Note that there are no nominal accounts in this trial balance as the profit and loss account has already been prepared and all nominal account balances (sales, purchases, expenses, etc) have been transferred to it. Remember that:

(a)   Debit balances are assets.
(b)   Credit balances are either valuing accounts (the depreciation provisions) or LIABILITIES.

BANGLE WHOLESALERS LIMITED
Balance Sheet as at 31 December 19-7

Fixed Assets	Cost	Accumulated Depreciation	£'000 Net Book Value
Land and buildings	500	84	416
Plant	32	17	15
	532	101	431

Current Assets		
Stock	164	
Debtors	183	
Prepayments	26	
	373	

Creditors: amounts falling due within one year		
Creditors	102	
Accruals	14	
Bank Overdraft	16	
Corporation Tax	35	
Proposed Dividends	27	
	194	

Net current assets		179
Total assets less current liabilities		610

Creditors: amounts falling due after more than one year		
12% Debentures (20-4 to 20-7)		130
		480

Capital and reserves		
Ordinary Share Capital		200
Preference Share Capital		100
Reserves		180
		480

6.   Much of this will be familiar to you - all the fixed and current assets and the creditors, accruals and bank overdraft in the current liabilities. I hope you realised that a bank balance on the credit side of a trial balance is an overdraft. The other words may be new to you and I will explain them in some detail.

Note also:
(a)   The Act uses the term 'Creditors: amounts falling due within one year' instead of 'current liabilities' but reverts to 'Current liabilities' in the term 'total assets less current liabilities'.

(b)   Net current assets are often known colloquially as working capital. We shall explore this term in the chapter on Funds Flow.

(c)   Long term liabilities are described as 'Liabilities: amounts falling due after more than one year'.

(d)   The expression 'capital and reserves' is the difficult one. It helps to regard it as one sum and as the equivalent of capital in a sole trader or a partnership.

ORDINARY SHARE CAPITAL

7.   When a company is formed by its *promoters*, it has no assets or liabilities. On its incorporation, the *memorandum* allows or *authorises* the company to *issue* any number of *shares* in the company up to the maximum stated in the memorandum. Issue means giving the new shareholders, shares in the company in exchange for valuable consideration. The consideration can be in the form of cash or other assets, for example, a business.

Suppose XYZ Limited was formed on 1st June 19-8 and issued 500 ordinary shares of £1 each, for cash, then its balance sheet would show:

Assets	£
Cash	<u>500</u>

Liabilities	
500 ordinary share capital	<u>500</u>

When it starts to trade, the cash will be changed into fixed assets stock etc. but the ordinary share capital will remain as 500 ordinary shares of £1 each - £500 in successive balance sheets unless more shares are issued.

What does it mean

(a) The company is divided into 500 shares or parts. Any particular shareholder can own one or more shares. There must be at least two shareholders. In effect the owner of one share owns 1/500th of the company.

(b) The company owes the shareholder collectively £500 because that was the amount they originally *subscribed* for the shares. This is thus a *liability* of the company to the shareholder. It is however a rather peculiar liability in that the company are not allowed (except in special circumstances) by company law to pay the liability.

8. Partly paid shares

The company could issue £1 shares for payment by instalments. For example the company may issue £1 shares with 50p payable on *application* and the balance payable when the company *call* for it some time in the future. In that case the balance sheet would show:

500 Ordinary Shares of £1 each (50p paid)	£250.00

The company may issue partly paid shares so that it can call upon the shareholders for the balance when needs for more money (*e.g.* for development) arise in the future.

9. Note that the "£1" records the amounts paid on the share in the past if it is fully paid, or the amount paid in the past plus payable in the future for partly paid shares. It does not indicate the *value* of the share which depends on the balance of supply and demand for the share.

PREFERENCE SHARES

10. The ordinary shareholders are in effect the owners of the company. But some companies also issue preference shares. Preference shareholders are technically part-owners of the company but their interest in the company is more like that of lenders than owners.

11. Preference shareholders are entitled to a fixed rate of dividend which is specified in the memorandum. In the case of Bangle Wholesalers, the preference shareholders receive an annual payment called a dividend at the rate of 7%. This means that the owner of a £1 preference share would receive a dividend of 7p a year and all the preference shareholders together would receive £7,000 which is 7% of £100,000.

ORDINARY AND PREFERENCE SHARES COMPARED

12.

	Ordinary Shares	*Preference Shares*
Risk	Will receive high dividends if the company does well or no dividend if the company loses money.	Dividend is at a fixed rate (but usually not payable if company makes a loss).
Right to vote at meetings	Yes	Usually not
Rights to dividend	As declared by the company. Rate will vary, inter alia, with profit.	A fixed rate of dividend which must be paid before any ordinary dividend can be paid.
Rights in a liquidation	Right to all that is left (if anything) after all other claims have been met.	Rights to return of capital subscribed after all claims except those of the ordinary shareholders have been met.

Notes:

(a) Some *preference shares are* participating *that is they have some claim on profits in addition to their fixed dividend.*

(b) *Preference shares are normally cumulative. That is if in a year no profit is made, and no dividends (preference or ordinary) are paid then before any ordinary dividend can be paid in future years the arrears of preference dividend must be made good.*

(c) *Some investors prefer the lower risks attached to preference shares and are content with the more limited prospect of rewards. Thus a company may issue preference shares to obtain access to funds available from such investors.*

DIVIDENDS

13. Each year, a company prepares its balance sheet and profit and loss account to determine and report to shareholders and others, the state of affairs at the year end and the profits for the year. This preparation of financial statements of course takes place *after* the year end. If a profit is shown then the directors may *propose* that the shareholders approve the payment of a dividend to the shareholders. These dividends are paid in the year after the profit was earned but are none the less put into the accounts of the year when the profit was earned. In the case of Bangle, the dividends will be decided upon and paid in 19-8 but appear in the 19-7 balance sheet as current liabilities. The dividends proposed will be:

Ordinary - 10p a share on 200,000 shares	20,000
Preference - 7% on 100,000 £1 shares	7,000
	£27,000

SHARE PREMIUM

14. A share with a *nominal* value of £1 will normally be sold *by the company* at that price on the formation of the company and will remain on the balance sheet as a liability of the company of £1. If the company is successful, then the *market* value of the share may be much higher. You should realise that the market value is the *real* value of the share and the *nominal* value is fundamentally of historical interest only and yet it is the nominal value which appears in the balance sheet.

15. If a successful company later wishes to issue more shares, it will be able to sell its £1 shares at a price in excess of £1. The excess is called the *share premium.* Thus if the company in paragraph 6 had signed a valuable contract (which would not appear on the balance sheet) and each share had a market value of £2.50, the company could sell *new* shares at £2.50. If 100 were so sold, the balance sheet would appear as:

	£
Assets - Cash (100 + 100 x 2.50)	350
Share Capital	200
Share premium	150
	£350

16. Notes:

(a) *The buyers of the new shares have acquired* half *the company. It is right that they should pay more for their shares than the original shareholders.*

(b) *"Share premium" is a liability of the company to* all *its ordinary shareholders.*

(c) *Like share capital, share premium is a liability which cannot be paid because of the doctrine of capital maintenance.*

RESERVES

17. This word has caused more misunderstandings than any other in accounting. Abandon *all* of your present understandings of the word (perhaps you think of something being held back for future use or for emergency use). In accounting the words means: "the amount by which assets exceed specific liabilities".

Consider Stan Ltd at 31st December 19-4:

The company has fixed assets including land, £100,000; current assets, £60,000 and current liabilities, £45,000. Its share capital is £20,000 and share premium stands at £10,000. Its balance sheet would show:

	£
Fixed assets	100,000
Current assets	60,000
	160,000
Less Current liabilities	45,000
Total assets *less* current liabilities	115,000
Share capital	20,000
Share premium	10,000
Reserves (a balancing figure)	85,000
	115,000

The reserves are £85,000 because the company has assets £160,000 and specific liabilities (current liabilities £45,000, share capital £20,000 and share premium £10,000) £75,000.

18. Reserves are *not* assets but are *represented* by assets – some part of the fixed and current assets.

19. You will see that the word "reserves" in Bangle's balance sheet indicates that the company has more assets (£431,000 + £373,000 = £804,000) than specific liabilities (£194,000 + £200,000 + £100,000 + £130,000 = £624,000). The surplus being £180,000. Far from being an asset (like something held back) it is in fact a *liability* to the *shareholders*.

20. If a company has more assets than liabilities then there must be a *historical* cause. In the case of Stan Ltd., suppose the causes were:

(a) Increase in the fixed assets by an upward revaluation of the land £20,000.
(b) Trading profits over the years of £65,000.

Then part of the balance sheet could be amplified as:

	£
Share capital	20,000
Share premium	10,000
Revaluation reserve	20,000
Other reserves:	
Profit and loss account	65,000
	115,000

21. Thus the balance sheet shows in its various sections:

	£
The assets:	
Fixed assets	100,000
Current assets	60,000
	160,000
Liabilities to third parties	45,000
Net assets belonging to shareholders	115,000

and how that quantity of net assets came about:

	£
By original subscription from the shareholders	30,000
By revaluing an asset	20,000
By profitable trading	65,000
	115,000

22. The reserves can also be seen as *liabilities to the shareholders*. There are two kinds:

(a) **Capital reserves** - liabilities to shareholders which because of the capital maintenance doctrine cannot be repaid. Revaluation reserve is one.

(b) **Revenue reserves** - liabilities to shareholders which can be paid. Profit and loss account is the typical revenue reserve. Payment can be made by paying to the shareholder a *dividend*. For Stan Ltd., a maximum legal dividend would be £65,000. In *practice* it may be difficult to pay as the assets are not in *liquid* form. (The company has not enough cash.)

23. CORPORATION TAX
A company that makes profits, pays a tax on those profits called corporation tax.

The procedure is:

(a) Calculate profits for the year by preparing a profit and loss account. This will be done *after* the year end.
(b) Calculate the corporation tax payable.
(c) Include the corporation tax liability in the profit and loss account for the year and in current liabilities in the balance sheet.

Corporation tax is normally payable nine months after the year end to which it relates.

Thus:

Profits year end 31 December 19-8
Corporation tax on those profits payable 1 October 19-9.

DEBENTURES
24. In the case of Bangle Wholesalers Limited, the appearance of 12% Debentures on the balance sheet indicates that:

(a) The company has borrowed £130,000 some time in the past from a person or persons who are then called debenture holders.

(b) The £130,000 will be repaid to the debenture holders some time in the period 20-4 to 20-7. The company will *redeem* (= repay) the debentures at the earliest opportunity (20-4) if interest rates have fallen below 12%. (The company could borrow at a lower interest rate, redeem the debentures and pay the lower rate of interest to the new lenders.) If interest rates rise then the company will delay redemption until the latest date (20-7).

(c) Interest is payable to the debenture holders at the rate of 12% a year, so Bangle will have to pay £15,000 a year to its debenture holders.

25. Some company balance sheets contain a class of LIABILITY called *provisions*. These are defined in the Companies Act as:

"A Provision is any amount retained as reasonably necessary for the purpose of providing for any liability or loss which is either likely to be incurred, or certain to be incurred but uncertain as to amount or as to the date on which it will arise."

Thus provisions are:

(i) Amounts retained - this is a very confusing term. Think of retained meaning "is a liability".
(ii) Where there is doubt about whether the liability exists at all.
(iii) Where it is certain that a liability does exist but that amount or the date of payment are uncertain.

Examples of provisions are:

An employee of A. Ltd. damaged some property of B, a customer. The matter is subject to a court action sometime in the future. There is a probability that A. Ltd. will have to pay damages (thus a liability exists), but the amount and date of payment are uncertain. B. Ltd. guarantee their products for twelve months from the date of sale by retailers. At any balance sheet date there is a liability to put right faulty products arising out of the guarantee. The amount of this liability and the date of payment are uncertain. A best estimate has to be made to quantify the liability.

Thus provisions are liabilities which are uncertain as to:

existence *or* amount *or* date of payment.

You will have realised that the word provision also occurs in the phrase "provision for depreciation". A depreciation provision is within the definition of a provision as it is "an amount retained as reasonably necessary for the purpose of providing for any *loss* which is certain to be incurred but *uncertain* as to amount (cost less estimated residual value) or as to the date on which it will arise (date of disposal)".

26. *Retention* in these circumstances is not easy to grasp. Suppose X Ltd starts in business with £1,000 of capital and trades profitably for one year so that its balance sheet shows:

Liabilities:	£	Assets:	£
Share Capital	1,000	Fixed Assets at cost	3,000
Profit and Loss Account	4,500	Current Assets	8,000
Current Liabilities	5,500		
	11,000		11,000

The company now has net assets of £4,500 more than the net assets provided by the shareholders. Thus the company can pay a dividend of £4,500. However, no depreciation has been charged. If it had (say at 20%) then profit would have been £3,900 only. Thus the dividend could be £3,900 only. It can be said that the depreciation reduces the legal maximum of dividend and so forces the company to *retain* resources in the business.

PUBLISHED COMPANY BALANCE SHEETS

27. Below is the full Companies Act Format 1:

		£'000	£'000	£'000
A.	Called up share capital not paid			10
B.	Fixed assets			
I	Intangible assets			
	1. Development costs	15		
	2. Concessions, patents, licences, trade marks and similar rights and assets	25		
	3. Goodwill	100		
	4. Payments on account	10	150	
II	Tangible assets			
	1. Land and buildings	680		
	2. Plant and machinery	1,204		
	3. Fixtures, fittings, tools and equipment	600		
	4. Payments on account and assets in course of construction	50	2,534	
III	Investments			
	1. Shares in group companies	40		
	2. Loans to group companies	150		
	3. Shares in related companies	650		
	4. Loans to related companies	100		
	5. Other investments other than loans	40		
	6. Other loans	50		
	7. Own shares	100	1,130	3,814
C.	Current assets			
I	Stocks			
	1. Raw materials and consumables	810		
	2. Work in progress	430		
	3. Finished goods and goods for resale	518		
	4. Payments on account	34	1,792	

II	Debtors			
	1.	Trade debtors	739	
	2.	Amounts owed by group companies	143	
	3.	Amounts owed by related companies	26	
	4.	Other debtors	54	
	5.	Called up share capital not paid	-	
	6.	Prepayments and accrued income	<u>137</u>	1,099
III	Investments			
	1.	Shares in group companies	103	
	2.	Own shares	15	
	3.	Other investments	<u>340</u>	458
V	Cash at bank and in hand			<u>136</u>
				3,485

D.	Prepayments and accured income			
E.	Creditors: amounts falling due within one year			
	1.	Debenture loans	400	
	2.	Bank loans and overdrafts	324	
	3.	Payments received on account	61	
	4.	Trade creditors	458	
	5.	Bills of exchange payable	78	
	6.	Amounts owed to group companies	49	
	7.	Amounts owed to related companies	84	
	8.	Other creditors including taxation and social security	61	
	9.	Accruals and deferred income	<u>134</u>	1,649
F.	Net current assets (liabilities)			1,836
G.	Total assets less current liabilities			5,660
H.	Creditors: amounts falling due after more than one year			
	1.	Debenture loans	1,000	
	2.	Bank loans and overdrafts	260	
	3.	Payments received on account	10	
	4.	Trade creditors	104	
	5.	Bills of exchange payable	38	
	6.	Amounts owed to group companies	44	
	7.	Amounts owed to related companies	59	
	8.	Other creditors including taxation and social security	624	
	9.	Accruals and deferred income	<u>17</u>	2,156
I.	Provisions for liabilities and charges			
	1.	Pensions and similar obligations	726	
	2.	Taxation, including deferred taxation	444	
	3.	Other provisions	<u>39</u>	1,209
J.	Accruals and deferred income		-	3,365
				2,295
K.	Capital and reserves			
I	Called up share capital			500
II	Share premium account			260
III	Revaluation reserve			500
IV	Other reserves			
	1.	Capital redemption reserve	100	
	2.	Reserve for own shares	50	
	3.	Reserves provided for by the articles of association	110	
	4.	Other reserves	<u>58</u>	318
V	Profit and loss account			717
				£2,295

Called up share capital not paid can appear at A or C.II 5.
Prepayments and accrued income can appear at D or C.II 6. C.II 6 is preferred.
Accruals and deferred income can appear at J or at either E9 or H9. E9 or H9 are preferred.

Notes:
(a) *I have included figures to make it easier to follow.*
(b) *Some of the items are rarely found in practice.*
(c) *Greater detail can be shown, eg under B.II 1. Land and buildings could be shown separately.*
(d) *Headings where there are no amounts can be omitted, eg if there is no called up share capital not paid (C.II 5)
     then the words can be omitted.*
(e) *The actual letters (A etc), roman numerals (II etc) and arabic numbers (1, 2 etc) are nearly always omitted.*
(f) *In respect of each item, the corresponding amount for the previous year should also be shown.*

SUMMARY

28. (a) The Companies Act 1985 requires companies to publish their balance sheets in particular formats.

    (b) Ordinary shareholders are fundamentally the owners of a company. The ordinary share capital gives information
         on the capital submitted some time in the *past*.

    (c) Some companies also issue preference shares. Preference shareholders are part owners of the company but
         receive a fixed rate of dividend if the company is profitable.

    (d) A company can pay dividends to its shareholders. The dividends for a year are *declared* and paid after the
         year end but put back into the accounts of the year and appear in current liabilities.

    (e) 'Reserves' is a confusing term. It is a liability to the shareholder which arises out of the fact that a
         company has more assets than it has specific liabilities. This surplus arises out of profitable trading and
         other causes, *e.g.* revaluing a fixed asset.

    (f) Corporation tax payable on the profit of a year is included in the current liabilities for the year.

POINTS TO NOTE

29 (a) Shares can be of any denomination, *e.g.* 10p, 20p, 50p, £1 or any other amount. You may see:

         Ordinary Share Capital 10p shares   £500,000

         This will indicate that the company is divided into 5 million shares of 10p each.

    (b) Ordinary shares are frequently called equity shares.

    (c) The word reserves is often used as a heading and other words appear instead, *e.g.* profit and loss account,
         fixed asset revaluation reserve etc.

    (d) Some ordinary shares and most preference shares are *redeemable*. This means that the company *can* at some time
         redeem or pay back to the shareholders the sums originally subscribed. This is not simply a matter of drawing
         the cheques as there are some legal formalities to observe.

    (e) Note the meanings of the words authorised, issued and paid up capital.

The memorandum of association authorises Jake Thing PLC to issue 5,000,000 50p ordinary shares. That is the
authorised share capital. In fact it has issued 4,000,000 to ordinary shares with 30p payable on application. The
issued capital is thus 4,000,000 shares and these are partly paid. The paid up share capital is £1,200,000.

    (f) There is a difference between a nominal value of a share and its market value. If Mendel Genes PLC issued
         their £1 shares in 1970, the £1 is the nominal value. In 19-7 the shares are changing hands on the Stock
         Exchange at amounts between £2.80 and £3.00. As an analogue, I bought my antique table for £150 in 1980. It
         is now worth about £600. Note, however, that the nominal or *par* value is what appears in the balance sheet.

    (g) The nature of a company balance sheet is confusing to students and company directors alike. If you still
         think that a company with reserves has some hidden assets then please reread the chapter. The company balance
         sheet can be interpreted in at least three ways as shown on the following page.

(h)   Remember that reserves are a measure of the amount by which assets exceed specific liabilities. Specific liabilities include share capital and share premium. Reserves could reasonably be shown as a simple figure but are usually broken down. Sometimes the breakdown is shown for statutory reasons, for example, to show reserves arising out of the revaluation of fixed assets or out of the redemption of share capital. Sometimes the breakdown has no obvious purpose. For example between:

> General Reserve
> Profit and loss account.

This division is still found in examinations although very rarely in real life. It is devoid of meaning.

(i)   The definition of a provision should be learned.

(j)   Remember that balance sheets always balance. Any change in the amount under any heading *must* have a corresponding change elsewhere.

(k)   The company balance sheet is a mystifying document. This is not a conspiracy by accountants but an historical accident. The key to the mystery is to remember that:

(i)   The balance sheet must balance.
(ii)   There are numerous liabilities to shareholders.
(iii)   Reserves are liabilities to shareholders.

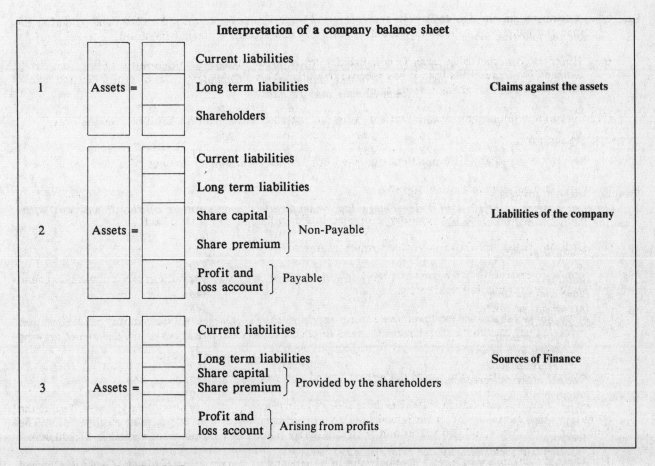

Interpretation of a company balance sheet

SELF TESTING QUESTIONS

(a)   *What are (i) promoters; (ii) subscribers; (iii) authorised capital? (7).*
(b)   *What is the nominal or par value of a share. (6).*
(c)   *Why is share capital a liability of a company which cannot normally be paid? (7).*
(d)   *Distinguish between ordinary shares and preference shares. (12).*
(e)   *What is the meaning of (i) participating; (ii) cumulative; (ii) arrears? (12).*
(f)   *What is a share premium? (14).*
(g)   *Distinguish between the market value and the nominal value of a share. (14).*

(h)   Share premium on a balance sheet is a liability: to whom? (16).
(i)   Give a simple definition of reserves. (17).
(j)   What is the relationship between reserves and assets? (18).
(k)   Distinguish capital reserves from revenue reserves. (22).
(l)   Define provision. (25).
(m)   Draft an outline company balance sheet. (5).
(n)   In connection with share capital what are applications and calls? (8).
(o)   What is a partly paid share? (8).
(p)   W Ltd. proposed at a directors meeting in March 19-7 to declare a dividend of 4p a share on its share capital of 10,000 ordinary shares of 30p each for the year ending 31.12.19-6. How would this appear in:

        - the trial balance at 31.12.-6
        - the balance sheet at 31.12.-6 (13).

(q)   Pow PLC has calculated that the corporation tax arising out of its profit for the year ending 31.12.-6 will be £300,000. How will this appear in the:

        - trial balance at 31.12.-6
        - balance sheet at 31.12.-6   When will it be paid? (23).

(r)   What is a debenture? What does redeem mean? Why are two redemption dates given? (24).

Exercises (Answers begin on page 469)

1. Complete the following table:

Company	Fixed assets	Current assets	Creditors due in less than 12 mths	Creditors due in more than 12 mths	Share Capital	Reserves
	£	£	£	£	£	£
A	1,000	540	462	500	620	
B		720	243	50	200	325
C	1,461	372	431	0		525
D	1,264	890	462		400	692

Exercises without answers

2.   The trial balance at 31.12.-4 of Foley Things Ltd., manufacturers and importers of play things, was, after preparing the profit and loss account:

	£000	£000
Goodwill at wdv	1,200	
Land	520	
Buildings	1,624	
Plant and machinery	846	
Investments at cost	348	
Stocks at 31.12.-4		
Raw materials	144	
Work in progress	221	
Finished goods	369	
Trade debtors and creditors	542	468
Prepayments	62	
Cash at bank	24	
Bank overdraft		647
Accruals		31
Taxation and social security due before 31.12.-5		144
Debenture loan due 30.6.-4		550
Issued share capital - 20p shares		1,400
Share premium account		600
Profit and loss account at 31.12.-4		2,060
	5,900	5,900

Required: Prepare a balance sheet.

3.   The trial balance of Wood Toys plc at 31.12.-4 after extracting the profit and loss account for the year ending 31.12.-4 was:

	£000	£000
Bank balance		644
Share capital – 25p shares		2,000
Investment at cost	850	
Share premium account		285
Goodwill at wdv	100	
Premises at cost	1,326	
Trade debtors and creditors	1,442	889
Plant and machinery	626	
Prepayments and accruals	104	251
Debenture loan due 31.7.95		500
Stocks at cost:		
Raw materials	237	
Saleable goods	638	
Profit and loss account		754
	5,323	5,323

Required: Prepare a balance sheet at 31.12.-4.

48. Shares and Debentures

INTRODUCTION

1. Companies are financed by:

   (a) People who take an *equity* or risk taking stake in the company. Such people are termed the *members* or shareholders in the company.

   (b) People or institutions who lend to the company. Such people are termed loan creditors or sometimes, debenture holders.

SHARES

2. People who subscribe for shares in a company are issued by the company with share certificates - see the example.

3. Subscription can be:

   (a) In cash or by other assets (*e.g.* a business).
   (b) In one single payment or by instalments.
   (c) At par or at a premium. Shares cannot in general be issued at a discount.

ORDINARY 25p SHARE CERTIFICATE

FINANCIAL CHICANERY public limited company

incorporated under the companies acts 1862 to 1900

Certificate No.
8342

No of ordinary shares
of 25p each - 240

This is to certify that Mrs Mary Smith

is/are the registered holder(s) of:

   two hundred and forty

Ordinary shares of twenty-five pence each fully paid and subject to the memorandum and Articles of the Company.

Given under the common seal of the company
this 16th day of December 19-3

Note - no transfer of any of the Shares comprised in this certificate will be registered until this Certificate has been delivered at the Company's Transfer Office.

ISSUE OF SHARES

4. Daft Ltd have a balance sheet at 31 December 19-8 as:

Liabilities	£	Assets	£
Share Capital in 50p shares	2,000	Net assets	2,600
Profit and loss account	600		
	2,600		2,600

On 1st January 19-9 the company issued 1,000 additional shares at 75p each for cash. The new shares are to rank pari passu with the existing shares (= they are to be equal in all respects and have identical rights and obligations).

The balance sheet will now show:

Liabilities	£	Assets	£
Share Capital in 50p shares	2,500	Net assets	3,350
Share premium	250		
Profit and loss account	600		
	3,350		3,350

Notice that the assets have increased as the company have received 750 in cash and that the *liabilities* must go up correspondingly. In this case, the additional liabilities (Share Capital and Share premium) are to the shareholders as a body.

5.   (a)   The bookkeeping entries for this issue of shares are:

Cash at Bank			Issued Share Capital		
	£				£
1.1.-9 Shares 750				1.1.-9 Cash	500

Share Premium		
	£	
1.1.-9 Cash	250	

(b) It is possible to issue shares for payment by instalments. In such cases an intermediate account called an application and allotment account is usually set up. Sometimes this account is split into two so that there is an application account and an allotment account. It is also possible for shareholders to default on payment of an instalment. In such cases, the shares can be forfeited. To illustrate both these points, here are some bookkeeping entries in the form of journal entries:

Issue of 20,000 ordinary shares of 50p each at 70p each, payable by instalments:

On application	1st April 1985	10p
On allotment	3rd May 1985	30p (to include the premium)
On first and final call	4th Sept 1985	30p

Notes:
(i) 35,000 shares were applied for - applications for 10,000 shares were allotted in full, applications for 20,000 shares were granted half, applications for 5,000 were refused. Applicants for 100 shares did not pay the call. These shares were forfeited on 10th November 1985 and sold again at 80p each on 6th December 1985.
(ii) The company year end is 30th June.

Journal	Dr	Cr	Commentary
	£	£	
Applications account	2,000		
Share capital account		2,000	An application account is a debtor
being sum due at 10p a share on issue of			account. This amount is due from
20,000 shares of 50p each, 10p a share			unspecified persons who may wish to
payable on application			be shareholders.
Cash	3,500		
Applications account		3,500	More shares were applied for than
being cash received from applications for			were for sale
35,000 shares at 10p a share			
Applications account	500		
Cash		500	Unsuccessful applicants have their
being return of cash to unsuccessful applicants			money returned

Applications account	1,000		
Allotment account		1,000	Applicants for 20,000 shares received only 10,000 shares. Extra paid used for sums due on allotment

being utilisation of overpayment by some
applicants to pay for sums due on allotment

Allotment account	6,000		
Share capital		2,000	Set up of debtors, sums due on allotment. Note that some has been paid on application
Share premium account		4,000	

being sums due on allotment of 20,000 shares
at 30p a share

Cash	5,000		
Allotment account		5,000	10,000 shares at 30p
			10,000 shares at 20p

being sums paid on allotment

at this point the balance sheet would show:

Current assets
Cash   £8,000

Share capital
20,000 ordinary shares of 50p each
20p paid   4,000
Share premium   4,000
                                                         £8,000

Journal

Call account	6,000		
Share capital account		6,000	Sets up a debtor account - sums due on first and final call

being amount due on first call

Cash	5,970		
Call account		5,970	All paid except applicant for 100 shares

being sums received on first call

Share capital	50		
Forfeited shares account		50	The forfeiture means that the shares are no longer in issue and must be taken out of share capital. Forfeited shares account is a capital reserve

being forfeiture of 100 shares

Cash	80		
Share capital		50	The forfeited shares are resold. Note that the company have received 40p a share from the original applicant (which he has forfeited) and 80p from the new shareholder
Share premium account		30	

being resale of forfeited shares at 80p each

Forfeited shares account	50		
Share premium account		50	Since the forfeited shares account measures sums paid above the nominal amount, this is in effect share premium

being transfer of forfeited shares account
to share premium account

REDEEMABLE SHARES

6.   A company can issue *redeemable* shares. These can be preference or equity (ordinary) shares. The capital maintenance concept means that share capital is a non-payable liability and redeemable means that share capital will be paid back to the shareholders. In practice the capital maintenance concept is not infringed as we will see. The legislation is in the Companies Act 1985 and there are some restrictions:

(a) Authorisation must be given in the articles.

(b) There must always be some non-redeemable share capital (or the company could have no share capital).

(c) Only fully paid up shares can be redeemed.

(d) Payment must be made at the same time as the redemption. Thus redemption cannot take place without simultaneous payment.

(e) Redeemable shares may only be redeemed out of distributable profits *or* out of the proceeds of a fresh issue of shares made for the purposes of redemption.

(f) Any premium on redemption must be paid out of distributable profits.

(g) Where the redeemable shares were issued at a premium, any premium payable on redemption may be paid out of the proceeds of a fresh issue up to the lesser of:

    (i)   Premiums received on the issue of the shares redeemed.
    (ii) The current balance on share premium account.

7.   Thus, the assets representing the original capital subscribed by the redeemable shareholders cannot be paid back to them, but:

    (a) The capital can be replaced by a new issue of shares.
or
    (b) The assets representing profits can be paid to the redeemable shareholders.

8.   Where profits are so used, the portion of the reserve "profit and loss account" (a payable liability) used must be renamed "capital redemption reserve" (a non-payable liability).

BALANCE SHEET ENTRIES ON REDEMPTION OF SHARE CAPITAL

9.   The share capital of Thin Ltd. is:

	£
1,000 ordinary shares of £1 each, 50p paid	500
1,000 redeemable preference shares of £1 each fully paid	1,000
Share premium account	100

On 1st January 19-5, the redeemable shares were redeemed at £1.15 out of:

    (a) A new issue of 200 ordinary shares of £1 each at £1.05 each.
    (b) Profits.

SUCCESSIVE BALANCE SHEETS

1.   Opening:

	£
Net assets	2,750
Cash	950
	3,700
1,000 ordinaries 50p paid	500
1,000 redeemable preference	1,000
Share premium	200
Profit and loss account	2,000
	3,700

2.   On new issue:

	£
Net assets	2,750
Cash (950 + 210)	1,160
	3,910
1,000 ordinaries 50p paid	500
1,000 redeemable preference	1,000
200 new ordinaries	200
Share premium (200 + 10)	210
Profit and loss account	2,000
	3,910

3.   On redemption: £
     Net assets   2,750
     Cash (1,160 - 1,150)   10
                                                                                 2,760

     1,000 ordinaries 50p paid   500
     1,000 redeemable (1,000 - 1,000)   -
     200 new ordinaries   200
     Share premium (210 - 150)   60
     Profit and loss account   2,000
                                                                                 2,760

4.   On required transfer to capital redemption reserve   £
     Net assets   2,750
     Cash   10
                                                                                 2,760

     1,000 ordinaries 50p paid   500
     200 new ordinaries   200
     Share premium   60
     Capital redemption reserve   1,000
     Profit and loss account (2,000 - 1,000)   1,000
                                                                                 2,760

RIGHTS ISSUES

10. Martin Ltd., has a balance sheet as:

| | Before rights issue | | After rights issue | |
	£	£	£	£
Fixed assets		65,000		65,000
Current assets				
Stock	36,200		36,200	
Debtors	48,800		48,800	
Cash at bank	1,600	86,600	31,600	116,600
		151,600		181,600
Creditors - amounts falling due				
within one year		38,600		38,600
Total assets Less Current liabilities		113,000		143,000
Capital and reserves				
Share capital £1 shares		40,000		60,000
Share premium		15,000		25,000
Profit and loss account		58,000		58,000
		113,000		143,000

If Martin Ltd wishes to raise cash by issuing *new* shares, then it must, by the requirements of the Companies Act 1985 (although there are numerous exceptions allowed), first offer the new shares to the existing shareholders pro rata (= in proportion to) their present holdings. Such issues of shares are called *rights issues* because the existing shareholders have *pre-emption rights to the new shares. The shareholders may prefer not to subscribe for the new shares, in which case they can give away or sell their rights.* Suppose Martin plc makes a new share offer of 20,000 new £1 shares at £1.50 each. Then each shareholder would be offered 1 share for each 2 shares held (a 1 for 2 offer).

The effect of a rights issue is:

(a) Increase the cash resources of the company because money flows from the shareholders to the company.
(b) Increase the liabilities to the shareholders by the same amount.

11. BONUS ISSUES

It is possible for a company to increase its share capital by *giving* new shares to its existing shareholders. Suppose that A Ltd., has a share capital of 100,000 ordinary shares of £1 each and a balance sheet as:

	£
Ordinary share capital	60,000
Profit and loss account	123,000
	183,000
Net assets	183,000

The company makes a bonus issue of 30,000 new ordinary shares of £1 each. Each shareholder will be given one new share for every two held. This is called a one for two issue. George who has twenty-four shares will be given twelve new shares and finish up with thirty-six shares.

The effect on the balance sheet will be:

	£
Ordinary share capital	90,000
Profit and loss account	93,000
	183,000
Net assets	183,000

Notes:

(a) The share capital has increased from £60,000 to £90,000.

(b) The net assets remain unchanged. The shares have been given *and the shareholders have paid no money to the company. Contrast a Bonus Issue with a Rights Issue where the shareholders* pay *for their new shares.*

(c) Since the balance sheet must balance, the reserves must be reduced by the amount of the increase in the share capital. The effect on the ability of the company to pay dividends is that the legal maximum dividend is reduced from £123,000 to £93,000. £30,000 of the payable *liability to shareholders (Profit and Loss Account) has been changed to an unpayable liability to shareholders (Share Capital).*

12. The reasons why a company make a Bonus issue may include:

(a) To bring the nominal value of each share nearer to its intrinsic value. In this case the net assets per share were £3.05 and after the Bonus Issue they had become £2.03.

(b) To fix the net assets representing the profit and loss account in the company. In theory the company could have paid a dividend of £123,000. Now the company can only pay £93,000. This means that creditors are sure that the assets less liabilities of the company to which they can look for, now has a larger irreducible minimum. New and potential lenders may be more inclined to lend if this happens.

(c) By tradition the announcement of a Bonus Issue is a "bull" point. It means that the directors are signalling to investors that the company has good prospects.

13. Bonus Issues are also called Capitalisation Issues, Scrip Issues and in the United States Stock (= share) dividends.

14. The effect on the market price:

B Plc have a share capital of 50,000 shares of 25p each quoted at £2.10 each. A Bonus Issue of one for two is made, the total value of the company before the Bonus issue was 50,000 x £2.10 = £105,000. After the Bonus issue, the value of the company remains at £105,000 but as the company is now divided into 15,000 shares, each share will be worth, and hence the quotation will move to, £105,000/75,000 = £1.40. John who has fourteen shares worth £2.10 each with a total value to his investment of £29.40 will, after the Bonus issue have twenty-one shares worth £1.40 each worth in all £29.40.

15. Bonus Issues effect very little change and yet they are common and shareholders receiving free shares are usually very pleased. Probably they do not understand the empty nature of the happening. Because of the negligible effect, Bonus Issue have been jokingly called *Bogus Issues*.

16. A Bonus Issue always involves an equivalent transfer from *reserves* to share capital. Any reserves whether capital or revenue can be used for this purpose.

DEBENTURES

17. A debenture has been judicially defined as a *document* which creates or acknowledges a debt. Thus a debenture (from latin debere = to owe) is not a loan but a document which *evidences* a loan. It will normally be under the company's seal and contain clauses on:

  (a) Interest rate and dates of payment of interest.
  (b) Repayment - dates; whether at par, at a premium or at a discount.
  (c) Security or collateral.

In common commercial speech, loans are referred to as debentures although technically the document only is the debenture.

18. Loans can be:

  (a) Unsecured ("naked debentures"). This means that debenture holders have the same rights in a liquidation as any unpaid supplier of goods or services.

  (b) *Secured* by a *fixed charge* on a *specific asset*. These loans are often called *mortgage* debentures.

  Example:
  A Ltd., wish to buy a property for £100,000. The company can find £20,000 and to obtain the balance, they borrow £80,000 from the Ineffective Assurance Co. Plc, giving the assurance company a *fixed charge* (or mortgage) on the property.

  The effect of the charge is:

  (i) The deeds of the property will be deposited with the assurance company.

  (ii) This means that the property cannot be resold by A. Ltd., without first paying off the loan.
  (iii) If A. Ltd., fail to pay the interest on the loan or due instalments of the capital, then the assurance company can seize the property (technically they appoint a *receiver* to act for them), sell it and use the proceeds of sale to repay the loan due to them. Any surplus is returnable to the company where it can be used for the benefit of other (unsecured) creditors.

  (iv) Thus, as long as the value of the security (the property) exceeds the loan, a lender with a fixed charge cannot lose. A fixed charge can be taken over any asset, but in practice fixed charges are taken only over interests in land, ships and aircraft.

  (c) *Secured by a floating charge* over the *assets generally*.

  Example:
  B. Ltd., borrow £20,000 from the Muddy Bank Plc who evidenced the loan with a debenture giving a floating charge on the assets. This means that if B. Ltd. default on the interest or capital payments then the bank can seize (or appoint a receiver to do this for them), all the assets of the company, sell the assets and use the proceeds to repay the loan. Any surplus goes to the company for the benefit of unsecured creditors. Thus, as long as the company has assets with a value greater than the loan, the bank cannot lose. However, unlike the holder of a fixed charge who can prevent the company disposing of the subject (property) of the fixed charge, the holder of a floating charge can only hope that the assets he seizes will be sufficient. The *floating* charge is said to *crystallise* on the occurrence of an event (default on payment etc.) foreseen in the debenture deed.

ISSUE OF LOANS EVIDENCED BY DEBENTURES

19. Loans can be issued at:

  (a) *par e.g.* C. Ltd. borrowed £50,000 on a 10% debenture (1996-1999). 1996 is the *earliest* date the company will redeem (= repay) the loan.

  1999 is the *latest* date the company can redeem the loan.

Journal	Dr £	Cr £
Cash	50,000	
10% Debenture Loan Account		50,000

(b) *At a premium e.g.* D. Ltd. borrowed £40,000 at 105 on a 11% debenture repayable in 2005.

Journal	Dr	Cr
	£	£
Cash	42,000	
10% Debenture		40,000
Debenture Premium Account		2,000

It may seem strange that £42,000 can be borrowed and only £40,000 repaid but the interest rate may be higher to attract investors in these circumstances. The £2,000 is in effect a gain to the company and the Debenture Premium account becomes a reserve. In theory it could be transferred to profit and loss account but this is not normally done.

(c) *At a discount e.g.* E. Ltd. borrowed £60,000 at 98 on a 9% debenture repayable in 1999.

Journal	Dr	Cr
	£	£
Cash	58,800	
Debenture Discount	1,200	
9% Debenture		60,000

The objective of borrowing £58,800 and owing back £60,000 is to make the loan issue attractive to investors.

The debenture discount account is in effect an expense. It is customary to write if off to:

(i) Profit and loss account   *or*   (ii) Share premium account.

SUMMARY

20. (a) Companies are financed by shareholders who take an equity interest in the company and lenders to the company who may be called debenture holders.

(b) People who subscribe to shares in a company may pay in cash or other assets, e.g. a business.

(c) Shares can be issued at a premium above the nominal or par value of the share.

(d) Share capital can, with many restrictions, be redeemed.

(e) Redemption can only be made out of a new issue of shares made for the purpose or out of profits. If redemption is made out of profits then there must be a transfer from profit and loss account to capital redemption reserve.

(f) Rights issues are new issues of shares to existing shareholders. Rights issues involve a real transfer of money to the company from the shareholders.

(g) Companies can make bonus issues. These are free issues of shares to the shareholders. Simple book entries are made debiting reserves or share premium and crediting share capital. No real money flows to the company.

(h) Companies can borrow money and issue a debenture in exchange. Debentures can be naked (unsecured), secured by a floating charge or secured by a fixed charge.

POINTS TO NOTE

21. (a) All liabilities which are secured by a fixed or floating charge must be registered in the company's file at Companies House.

(b) Loans can be made under debenture deeds to a company by a single person or institution, or collectively by a large number. Where there are a large number of debenture holders, a trustee (usually a Bank or an Insurance Company) will be appointed to look after their affairs.

(c) Debenture loans can be *quoted* on the stock exchange in which case the *debentures* (documents with rights to interest and capital repayment) will be bought and sold.

(d) Once a share premium account is opened, it can only be reduced by:

  (i)   A bonus issue of new shares.
  (ii) The premium or costs of issue or redemption of shares or debentures.

(e) Once a capital redemption reserve has been set up it can only be reduced by a bonus issue of new shares.

SELF TESTING QUESTIONS

(a) How can companies be financed? (1).
(b) What are the possible terms of issue of shares? (3).
(c) What are the restrictions on redeeming share capital? (6).
(d) What is a debenture? (17).
(e) What terms are usually found in a debenture? (17)
(f) What is a fixed charge and what is its effect? (18).
(g) What is a floating charge and what is its effect? (18).
(h) What are the bookkeeping entries on the redemption of share capital? (9).
(i) Can debentures be listed on a stock exchange? (21).
(j) What is a rights issue? (10).
(k) What is a bonus issue? (11).
(l) What is the effect of a rights issue?
(m) What is the effect of a bonus issue?

Exercises (Answers begin on page 469)

1. In order to raise more capital the firm of B Taylor Ltd issued 200,000 ordinary shares of £1 each at £1.20 payable 40p on application, 50p on allotment (including the premium) and 30p on call. Payment was required as follows:

On application	*1st April 1983*
On allotment	*9th April 1983*
On first/final call	*1st June 1983*

All these shares were subscribed, allotted and paid for by the due dates. There was no over-subscription.

Required: Show by journal entries the recording of the above share issue in the books of the company.

Note: Narrations are not required, but cash entries should be journalised.   *(LCC)*

2. JHP Limited is a company with an authorised share capital of £10,000,000 in ordinary shares of £1 each, of which 6,000,000 shares had been issued and fully paid on 30 June 1981.

The company proposed to make a further issue of 1,000,000 of these £1 shares at a price of £1.40 each, the arrangements for payment being:

(a) 20p per share payable on application, to be received by 1 July 1981.
(b) Allotement to be made on 10 July 1981, and a further 50p per share (including the premium) to be payable.
(c) The final call for the balance to be made, and the money received, by 30 April 1982.

Applications were received for 3,550,000 shares and were dealt with as follows:

(i) Applicants for 50,000 shares received an allotment in full.
(ii) Applicants for 300,000 shares received an allotment of one share for every two applied for; no money was returned to these applicants, the surplus on application being used to reduce the amount due on allotments.
(iii) Applicants for 3,200,000 shares received an allotment of one share for every four applied for; the money due on allotment was retained by the company, the excess being returned to the applicants.
(iv) The money due on final call was received on the due date.

You are required to record these transactions (including cash items) in the journal of JHP Limited.   *(CMA)*

3. *Wallis plc has a balance sheet as at 31.12.-7 as:*

	£		£
Ordinary 20p (10p paid)	60,000	Net Assets	240,000
Profit and Loss Account	180,000		
	240,000		240,000

The following transactions occurred:

(a) *The company issue 80,000 50p preference shares at 90p each.*
(b) *The company issued 40,000 16% debentures at 105.*
(c) *The company called up the amount unpaid on its ordinary shares at par.*
(d) *The company redeemed 20,000 of its preference shares.*

Prepare successive balance sheets to show the effect of these transactions.

4. *Jimboy Limited has a balance sheet as at 31.12.-7 as:*

	£		£
Share Capital		Net Assets	31,600
Ordinary 10p	10,000		
10% preference £1	8,000		
Share premium	2,600		
Profit and loss account	11,000		
	31,600		31,600

The following transactions occurred:

(a) *A rights issue of 1 for 4 was made at 24p a share.*
(b) *A bonus issue of 1 for 5 was made on the enlarged capital from profit and loss account.*
(c) *The company issued £6,000 14% debentures at 98.*
(d) *The company redeemed half the 10% preference shares at par out of:*

(i) *A new issue of 4,000 8% preference shares at par.*
(ii) *Profits.*

Prepare successive balance sheets to show the effect of these transactions.

Exercises without answers

5. *Woden Gnomes Plc had a balance sheet at 31.12.-6 as:*

	£'0000		£'000
Ordinary shares (20p each)	600	Other assets (net)	4,180
Share premium	1,435	Cash	635
Profit and loss account	2,780		
	4,815		4,815

(a) *On 1.1.-7 the company made a bonus issue of 4 for 1 out of profits otherwise available for dividend.*

Required: Show the balance sheet after the bonus issue.

(b) *On 2.1.-7 the company made a public issue of shares on the following terms:*

10 million shares were offered at 95p each payable:
- *20p on application*
- *20p on allotment*
- *55p on 1st call*
(The latter two payments are considered to be the premium.)

15.5. million shares were subscribed for and the shares were allotted:
to applicants for 6 million shares - in full
to applicants for 7 million shares - 50% of application
to applicants for 2 million shares - 25% of application
to applicants of 0.5 million shares - allotment was refused and the application monies returned.

The surplus monies paid by applicants who received less shares than they applied for were retained against sums due on allotment or first call.

All sums due on allotment were received on the due dates.

All sums due on first call were received on the due date except for the sums due from shareholders who subscribed for 10,000 shares and who had received a 100% allotment. These shares were forfeited and resold for £1.20 each.

Required:
(a) Show by double entry accounts (or journal entries) this series of transactions.
(b) Show the balance sheet after this series of transactions (assume there were no other transactions in the period).

6.   *Mouldy Breads Ltd had a balance sheet as at 31.12.-7 as: (all in £'000)*

	£'000		£'000
Ordinary shares (30p each)	240	Net assets other than cash	780
Preference shares (£1)	100		
Share premium	60		
Profit and loss	310		
Overdraft	70		
	780		780

The the following occurred:

A bonus issue of one ordinary share and one preference share for every six ordinary shares held was made.

A right issue of one new ordinary share at 60p for every seven ordinary shares held was made on the enlarged capital.

The preference shares were redeemed at a premium of 5% partly out of the proceeds of the rights issue and partly out of the profits. An overdraft was obtained for the purpose.

The costs of the various issues and redemptions was £20,000 and was paid by cheques.

Required: *Show this series of transactions by (a) successive balance sheets, or (b) journal entries or (c) double entry accounts. Prepare a balance sheet at the end.*

7.   *The following are balances in the ledger of Gooee Soups Ltd at 31.12.-8:*

	£	£
Land & buildings at cost	23,567	
Plant & vehicles at cost	45,800	
Prov for depr on land etc		6,580
Prov for depr on plant etc		17,540
Investments at cost	3,000	
Stocks	11,654	
Debtors and Provision for doubtful debts	22,500	1,500
Cash in hand	1,200	
Bank balance		4,351
Trade creditors		14,300
Accruals and prepayments	2,400	3,100
Proposed dividends		5,200
Prov for Corporation Tax		3,600
Profit and Loss a/c at 31.12.-7		9,400
Ord share capital in 20p shares		30,000
6% Pref share capital in 20p shares		1,000
Retained profit for 19-8		1,550
Share premium		2,000
General reserve		10,000

An error occurred, in that the provision for doubtful debts should have been 5% of debtors.

Correct the error with a journal entry, then prepare a balance sheet in good form.

8.   Using the date in question 7 only:

Show journal entries for the following transactions:

Purchase by cheque of a vehicle for £6,000 (note that the marketing director has requested that this comes out of the general reserve).

Issue of 5,000 ordinary shares at 35p each to rank pari passu (equal in all respects) with the existing shares.

Issue of £10,000 16% Debentures at par.

Revaluing the land and buildings at £33,000.

Produce the revised balance sheet.

9.   Twoddle Limited had a balance sheet as:

	£		£
Share Capital 20p ordinaries	60,000	Net Assets	250,000
Share Premium	30,000		
Revaluation Reserve	40,000		
Profit and Loss Account	120,000		
	250,000		250,000

The following transactions occurred:

(a) A bonus issue of 1 for 3 was made out of revaluation reserve.
(b) A rights issue of 1 for 8 on the enlarged capital was made at 55p a share.

Required:
(a) Show successive balance sheets to demonstrate the effect of these transactions.
(b) The share price before the two transactions was 60p. What might be the effect on its price of the two transactions?

10. Ilpsim plc has a balance sheet at as 31.12.-7 as:

	£		£
Ordinary shares (50p each)	100,000	Other assets	350,000
Preference shares (20p each)	30,000	Cash at bank	27,000
Share premium account	43,000		
Profit and loss account	62,000		
14% Debentures	10,000		
Creditors etc	132,000		
	377,000		377,000

Required:
Show successive balance sheets after the following events:

(i)   A rights issue of 2 ordinary shares for every 4 held at 85p each.
(ii)   An issue of £20,000 16% debentures at par.
(iii)   Redemption of one half of the prefer-ence shares at par. (Note that a transfer to capital redemption reserve is required.)
(iv)   A bonus issue of 1 new ordinary share for every 5 held out of profits.

11. Diddy Limited have a balance sheet as:

	£		£
Ordinary share capital 20p	100,000	Net assets	241,000
6% Preference shares £1	50,000		
Share premium	13,000		
Profit and loss account	48,000		
16% Debentures	30,000		
	241,000		241,000

The following transactions occurred:

(a) *The Company redeemed the preference shares at par out of:*

    (i) *A new issue of 25,000 ordinary shares at 50p each.*
    (ii) *Profits.*

(b) *A rights issue of 1 for 3 at 56p on the enlarged capital.*

(c) *The debentures were redeemed at 106.*

Show successive balance sheets to demonstrate the effects of these transactions.

12. *At the end of the Annual General Meeting of the Better Brewers Ltd., you, as chairman, have to answer three questions from shareholders. They are:*

(a) *Mr Jacklin asks, "Why does the company leave so much money in the General Reserve? Surely it would be better to spend it to modernise our machinery."*

(b) *Miss Faldo says, "The value of the company's shares would be much higher on the stock exchange if we had shown higher profits. Couldn't we stop any transfers to reserves and thus show higher net profits?"*

(c) *Mrs Crenshaw asks, "Why should we use so much of the cash in our reserves in giving away so many bonus shares? Wouldn't it be better to spend it on other things?"*

How would you reply to the shareholders?   *(RSA)*

13. *The Newstead Trading Estate Co Ltd had an authorised capital of 400,000 shares of £1 each, divided equally between ordinary shares and 8% redeemable cumulative preference shares. The issued capital was 150,000 ordinary shares and 100,000 preference shares.*

It was decided to:
(1) Issue the remainder of the ordinary shares at a premium of 25%.
(2) Issue 50,000 8% debentures of £1 each at a discount of 5%, redeemable at par in 1996.
(3) Use the proceeds of the above two issues to redeem all the preference shares.

The ordinary shares were applied for with full cash on 25 February 1985 and allotted on 1 March 1985, as were the debentures, the dates being 25 March and 1 April 1985, respectively. The preference shares were redeemed in cash at par on 1 May 1985. On 1 September 1985 the company paid an interim dividend of two pence per share on the whole of its ordinary share capital. On 1 October 1985 the company paid the first half yearly instalment of its debenture interest.

Required:
(i) Show by means of journal entries (including cash items) how you would record the above in the books of the Newstead Trading Co Ltd.
(ii) Indicate whether the debenture interest should be a charge against profits or an appropriation of profits.
                                                              (LCCI)

14. *Beet and Root plc has an authorised capital of 500,000 ordinary shares of £1 each and an issued and paid-up capital of £300,000. It has also issued £200,000 12% debentures.*

The directors decided to:
(1) Issue the remaining 200,000 ordinary shares at £1.40 per share.
(2) Redeem the 12% debentures at a discount of 10%.

The payment for the shares was received as follows: 50p on application, 50p on allotment and the balance on first and final call. Applications were received for exactly 200,000 shares and all monies due on application, allotment and call were received by the due dates. The cash due on allotment included the amount of the premium.

The debentures were subsequently redeemed.

Required:
(i) Show by means of journal entries the recording of the issue of shares and the redemption of the debentures.
(ii) After the above transactions have taken place show the part of the balance sheet which gives details of the shareholders' interest.

Notes:
(1) All cash receipts are to be journalised.
(2) Narrations are not required.   *(LCCI)*

15. Charter Pressings Ltd has an authorised capital of 6,000,000 ordinary £1 shares of which 4,200,000 have been issued. 2,000,000 of the shares were issued at par when the company was formed a number of years ago, and the remainder were issued in 1983 at a premium of 60p per share. The share premium balance has not been applied for any purpose.

In the year ended 31 December 1984, the company made a profit (after all interest charges) of £1,800,000. An interim dividend of 5p per share was paid in June 1984 and the directors are now proposing a final dividend of 10p per share.

Balances remaining in the ledger of the company at 31 December 1984, other than those to which reference has already been made are:

	£'000
Profit and loss credit balance – 1 January 19-4	3,810
Fixed assets at written down value	9,180
10% loan stock repayable 19-5	2,200
Stocks	1,915
Trade debtors	3,730
Bank loans and overdrafts	600
Trade creditors	1,165
Cash in hand	60

Required:
(i) Prepare the balance sheet of Charter Pressings Ltd in vertical form as at 31 December 1984.
(ii) On 1 January 1985, the company issued 1,200,000 shares at £2.10 each payable in full on application. The proceeds were used to repay the 10% loan stock (there was no accrued interest), and the balance to purchase fixed assets.
Prepare journal entries to record these transactions.

Note: Narrations are not required.   *(LCCI)*

49. The Company Profit and Loss Account for Internal use and for Publication

INTRODUCTION

1. Almost every company has to prepare a profit and loss account every year. The only exceptions are non-trading companies (such as charities and clubs) which prepare an income and expenditure account and dormant companies (companies which do not trade because they have ceased to do so or have never started).

2. The first stage is to produce a detailed profit and loss account for internal purposes. This may take the form of a manufacturing, trading and profit and loss account or a trading and profit and loss account. These are very much like the income statements of sole traders and partnerships but do exhibit special features which I will discuss. Some exam syllabuses only require company profit and loss accounts for internal purposes.

The next stage is to shorten the internal profit and loss account to accord with the Companies Act requirements for laying accounts before the shareholders and filing them with the Registrar of Companies. We will see how to do this.

PROFIT AND LOSS ACCOUNT FOR INTERNAL USE

3. The following is the trial balance at 30th June 19-8 of Guy Wholesale Ltd., a company wholesaling frozen foods:

	£000	£000
Purchases and sales	1,032	1,760
Carriage inwards	19	
Settlement discounts	23	68
Wages and salaries	96	
Advertising	34	
Insurance	16	
Cost of delivery to customers	78	
Debenture interest	13	
Commission to salesmen	41	
Rent and rates	90	
Light and heat	47	
Director's salaries	100	
Repairs and maintenance	11	
Interim dividend at 2.5p a share paid 27.3.-8	30	
Fixtures & fittings at cost	154	
Provision for depreciation on fixtures & fittings		83
Motor vehicles at cost	72	
Provision for depreciation on motor vehicles		51
Trade debtors and creditors	460	160
Goodwill at cost	320	
Share capital 25p shares		300
Stock at 30.6.-7	285	
Profit and loss account		107
Share premium		150
Bank		42
13% debenture loan 2004/2006		200
	2,921	2,921

Notes:
(a) Prepayments and accruals at 30.6.-8 are (in £000):

	Prepayments	Accruals
Wages		6
Insurance	4	
Commission to salesmen		5
Auditor remuneration		13

(b) Corporation tax on the profit for the year is expected to be £68,000.

(c) Depreciation is at 10% straight line for fixtures and fittings, and 25% reducing balance for motor vehicles.

(d) Stock at 30.6.-8 is valued at £314,000.

(e) There was a bonus issue of one share for every three held on 1st December 19-8.

(f) A final dividend, on the enlarged share capital, at 4p a share is proposed.

Prepare a trading and profit and loss account for the year ending 30th June 19-8 for presentation to the directors, and a balance sheet as at 30 June 19-8.

4. ANSWER:

Guy Wholesale Limited

Trading and profit and loss account for the year ending 30th June 19-8

	£	£
Sales		1,760
Less Cost of goods sold:		
Stock 30.6.-7	285	
Purchases	1,032	
Carriage inward	19	
Available for sale	1,336	
Stock 30.6.-8	314	1,022
Gross profit		738
Occupancy costs		
Rent and rates	90	
Insurance	12	
Light and heat	47	
Repairs and maintenance	11	
Depr of fixtures & fittings	15	
	175	
Administration costs		
Wages and salaries	102	
Directors' remuneration	100	
Auditor's remuneration	13	
	215	
Selling and distribution costs		
Advertising	34	
Commission	46	
Delivery	78	
Depreciation of vehicles	5	
	163	
Financial costs		
Discount allowed	23	
Discount received	(68)	
Debenture interest (13% x £200,000)	26	
	(19)	534
Net profit on trading for the year		204
Corporation tax on the profit for the year		68
Net profit after tax		136
Dividends:		
Paid - Interim at 2.5p a share	30	
Proposed - Final at 4p a share	64	94
Retained profit for the year		42
Retained profit from previous years b/f		107
		149
Bonus issue during the year		100
Retained profit carried forward		49

Guy Wholesale Limited
Balance Sheet as at 30 June 19–8

Fixed Assets	Cost	Accumulated Depreciation	Net Book Value
	£000	£000	£000
Goodwill	320	–	320
Fixtures & fittings	154	98	56
Motor vehicles	72	56	16
	546	154	392

Current Assets		
Stock		314
Debtors		460
Prepayments		4
		778

Current Liabilities		
Creditors		160
Accruals		37
Bank Overdraft		42
Corporation Tax		68
Proposed Dividend		64
		371

Working Capital		407

Net Assets employed		799

Financed by:		
Ordinary Share Capital 25p shares		400
Share premium		150
Reserves		49
Shareholders funds		599
13% Debenture 2004/6		200
		799

5.   Much of this profit and loss account is exactly as you have prepared for sole traders and partnerships. The division of overheads between occupancy, administration etc., is arbitrary and another division might be preferable.

6.   **Some items are unique to companies:**

(a) **Directors' remuneration**
Directors are regarded as *employees* of the company and as such their remuneration is an *expense* in the same way as any wages and salaries are expenses. This applies even if the shareholders and directors are the same people.

(b) **Debenture interest**
Interest payable on debenture loans is an expense of the company in the same way that interest on any loan is an expense in any business profit and loss account.

(c) **Corporation tax**
Companies are required to pay a tax called *corporation tax* on their profits. The computation of the tax payable is complicated and outside the scope of this manual. In questions, the amount of corporation tax payable on the profit of the year is normally given as it is here. Note that the corporation tax is not regarded as an expense, but as an *appropriation* of profit. Thus the net profit is calculated first, the corporation tax follows and the difference is shown as the net profit *after* tax.

(d) **Dividends**
The owners of companies (the shareholders) do not have drawings. They receive dividends.

The mechanics of dividend payments are:

(i) The directors decide whether a dividend should be paid and the amount. The decision is based on whether the company has made a profit, the amount of previous dividends and other criteria.

(ii) In the case of *interim* dividends (those paid before the end of the year), the directors *declare* that a dividend should be paid and it is then paid.

(iii) In modern practice, a dividend is always x pence a share. So that if a dividend is 2.5p a share and if a shareholder has 100 shares, he will receive £2.50.

(iv) In the case of final dividends, the directors *recommend* a dividend and the recommended dividend is *approved* by the members at the AGM. Dividends are also *appropriations* of profit.

(e) **Bonus issue**

Bonus issues were discussed in the previous chapter.A bonus issue is a *free gift* of new shares to the existing shareholders and as this involves an increase in the share capital liability to shareholders, it must also involve a *decrease* in the retained profit (revenue reserves) liability to shareholders.

RESERVES

7. The trial balance at 30 June 19-8 includes the term profit and loss account which was the balance at 30 June 19-7. This was the reserves at 30 June 19-7 and indicated that the assets exceeded the specific liabilities at that date by £107,000.

In the year to 30th June 19-8, the company made a profit after tax of £136,000. The company propose dividends of £94,000 so that the retained profit for the year was £42,000. This means that the assets less liabilities increased by £42,000.

This is saying that the reserves (= assets - liabilities) increased by £42,000 to £149,000. In the balance sheet the words profit and loss account or retained profits may be used instead of the word reserves.

Part of the liability to shareholders "reserves" was re-named share capital which is also a liability to shareholders. There is very little substance in this happening but it does now mean that part of payable liability has now become a non-payable liability.

TRANSFERS TO RESERVE

8. Some boards of directors feel that if the reserves (= retained *profits*) seem large, the shareholders may demand higher dividends. To discourage this part of the profit and loss account balance is sometimes *renamed* as

Reserve for future contingencies
General reserve
Fixed asset replacement reserve etc.

Transfers to reserve, as this *renaming* is called, has no practical effect but note the bookkeeping involved:

Dr Profit and Loss Account
Cr Appropriate reserve account.

All such entries are freely reversible. You must appreciate that *no* other accounts are involved.

FIXED ASSET REVALUATION RESERVE

9. Fixed assets are normally valued at cost less depreciation as in the following balance sheet:

	£		Cost £	Depn £	NBV £
Share capital	800	Premises	2,700	700	2,000
Profit and Loss Account	2,194	Plant	1,120	270	850
Current liabilities	1,126	Current Assets			1,270
	4,120				4,120

The directors are worried that the balance sheet does not show the "true" value of the premises and commission a valuation. The valuer gives them a certificate valuing the premises at £3,200. It is permissible to alter the balance sheet as:

	£		£
Share capital	800	Premises at valuation	3,200
Premises Revaluation Reserve	1,200	Plant at net book value	850
Profit and Loss Account	2,194		
Current Liabilities	1,126	Current Assets	1,270
	5,320		5,320

Note:

The assets have increased in *carrying* value (the value in the books and balance sheet) and to make the balance sheet balance, the liabilities side must be increased to compensate.

The increase in assets is an increase in "assets less liabilities", that is an increase in reserves. Reserves are a liability to shareholders and it is clearly right to indicate that the increase in the value of the premises belongs to the shareholder.

PUBLISHED PROFIT AND LOSS ACCOUNTS

10. There are four formats given in the Companies Act 1985. Of these 1 and 3, and 2 and 4 are the same but in vertical and horizontal form respectively. As the vertical form is the common usage in the UK, we will ignore formats 3 and 4. In this chapter we will concentrate on Format 1.

11. Format 1 is:

Profit and loss account
Format 1

1. Turnover
2. Cost of sales
3. Gross profit or loss
4. Distribution costs
5. Administration expenses
6. Other operating income
7. Income from shares in group companies
8. Income from shares in related companies
9. Income from other fixed asset investments
10. Other interest receivable and similar income
11. Amounts written off investments
12. Interest payable and similar charges
13. Tax on profit or loss on ordinary activities
14. Profit or loss on ordinary activities after taxation
15. Extraordinary income
16. Extraordinary charges
17. Extraordinary profit or loss
18. Tax on extraordinary profit or loss
19. Other taxes not shown under the above items
20. Profit or loss for the financial year.

12. Adapting the question in paragraph 3 the Format 1 requires an analysis of the expenses into:

(a) Cost of sales
(b) Distribution costs
(c) Administrative expenses

The Act does not state which expenses are to be classified under the three headings but a common division is:

Cost of sales: Opening stocks and work in progress
                          Direct materials and expenses
                          Direct labour
                          Fixed and variable production overheads including depreciation
                          Research and development costs
                          Less: closing stocks and work in progress

Distribution costs: Sales salaries and commissions
                          Advertising
                          Warehousing costs of finished goods
                          Travelling and entertaining

> Carriage out including depreciation of vehicles
> Overhead costs of sales outlets
> Discounts allowed

Administrative expenses: Salary costs of administrative personnel (eg accounting function, directors and general management)
Overhead costs of administration buildings
Professional fees
Bad debts

This division is clearly appropriate for a manufacturing company but can be adapted for trading companies (like Guy Wholesale Ltd) and service providing companies. Essentially the cost of sales is the cost of making the product whether it be a thing or a service.

For Guy Wholesale Ltd I have analysed the expenses as:

	Cost of sales £	Admin. £	Distribution £
Purchases	1,032		
Stock adjust	(29)		
Carriage in	19		
Occupancy	150	10	15
Wages and salaries	72	10	20
Directors	50	30	20
Auditor's fees		13	
Selling and distribution			163
Discounts	(68)		23
	1,226	63	241

You will be able to recognise some of these as being in the list (eg purchases and discounts allowed) but some (eg wages and salaries) I have distributed arbitrarily. In practice some analysis of expenditure is necessary. For example, the rent and rates can be apportioned on the basis of floor area occupied by sales and distribution and administration. The rest of the floor area will be considered as part of the cost of sales.

In examinations, the basis of the analysis should either be given or be readily apparent.

13.   **Guy Wholesale ltd**
Profit and loss account for the year ending 30 June 19-4

	£'000
Turnover	1,760
Cost of sales	1,226
Gross profit	534
Distribution costs	241
Administrative expenses	63
	304
	230
Interest payable	26
Profit on ordiary activities	204
Tax on profit on ordinary activities	68
Profit on ordinary activities after tax	136
Dividends	94
Retained profit for the year	42
Retained profit brought forward	107
	149
Bonus issue	100
Retained profit carried forward	49

14. The format allows for the inclusion of items which are only found in the largest public companies (eg income from shares in group companies) and where there is no income or charges under these headings, the headings can be omitted. The format does not include space for dividends and these have to be added.

15. In addition to the relatively few lines of the format, the Act requires a large number of *notes attached to and forming part of the profit and loss account*. A set of notes which complies with the requirements are:

Notes attached to and forming part of the profit and loss account.

(a) *Accounting policies*
Fixtures and fittings are depreciated on the fixed instalment method over a period of ten years.
Motor vehicles are depreciated on the reducing balance method at a rate of 25% a year.

(b) *Interest* - is that paid on the 13% debenture loan 1989/92.

(c) *Profit* - is stated after charging the following items:
Auditors remuneration £13,000
Depreciation of fixed assets £20,000
Directors' emoluments £100,000
of which the chairman received £36,000 and the range of directors' emoluments and the number of directors within each range was:
£15,001 - £20,000 - 2
£30,001 - £35,000 - 1

(d) Tax payable is corporation tax on the profits of the year at 52% less marginal relief.

(e) The average number of employees during the year was sixteen. Their remuneration was:
Wages and salaries - £95,000
Social security costs - £9,000

SUMMARY

16. (a) The profit and loss account of a company is similar to that of partnerships and sole traders but has some unique features:

- Directors' remuneration
- Dividends

- Debenture interest
- Corporation tax

(b) The profit and loss account is divided into sections as:

the computation of profit	
less Corporation tax	
	Appropriations
Dividends	
= Retained profit for the year	
Balance brought forward	Statement of retentions
Bonus issue	
Balance carried forward	

(c) Published profit and loss accounts, *i.e.* those laid before shareholders and filed at Companies House must be in one of four formats.

(d) As an addition to the profit and loss account, which is a relatively short document, there are notes attached to it which form part of the profit and loss account.

POINTS TO NOTE

17. (a) The preparation of a company profit and loss account for internal management purposes is simple provided you remember to produce the profit and loss account *first*, treating directors' remuneration and debenture interest as expenses, and *follow* with the appropriation section - corporation tax and dividends.

(b) The brought forward profit and loss account balance is usually added to the retained profit of the year and then follow any odd entries, *e.g.*

- bonus issues
- transfers to capital redemption reserve
- transfers to reserves

(c) In the company accounting world today, companies do not usually transfer amounts from profit and loss account to general or other reserves but examiners often do so still.

(d) Remember that such transfers are mere book entries. There are *no* changes in real things like bank accounts.

SELF TESTING QUESTIONS

(a) How is directors' remuneration dealt with in company accounts? (6a).
(b) How is corporation tax dealt with in company accounts? (6c) and (7).
(c) What is a dividend? (6d).
(d) List the mechanics of dividend payment. (6d).
(e) How are dividends treated in company accounts? (6d iv) and (7).
(f) Write out Format 1 profit and loss account.

Exercises (Answers begin on page 470)

1. Bustle Ltd a retailer of high class ladies dresses has the following items among its trial balance entries at 31.12.86:

	Dr £'000	Cr £'000
Interim dividend paid	3	
Purchases and sales	210	290
Stock 1.1.86	40	
Advertising	7	
General distribution costs	12	
Agents' commission	3	
General administration costs	15	
Audit fee	4	
Van running expenses	8	
Accounting office costs	6	
Bad debt	5	
Loss on shoes division closure	13	
Share capital in 10p shares		50

Notes:

(a) Stock at 31.12.86 was valued at £60,000.
(b) The van is used to take dresses to customers' homes.
(c) The bad debt was caused by the bankruptcy of a customer.
(d) The van running expenses include licence fees for the year ending 30 June 1987 of £2,000.
(e) Advertising includes the cost (£3,000) of a series of advertisements in a monthly magazine running from November 1986 to April 1987 inclusive.
(f) The shoe sales division, which had been a significant part of the business was closed down because it had become unprofitable.
(g) Tax on ordinary activities is expected to be £12,000.
(h) A final dividend of 1p a share is proposed.

Prepare the profit and loss account in Format 1 of the Companies Act 1985 (copy attached). You should omit lines in which no amount for Bustle would appear but include line 14.

(Note: Item f is an extraordinary item) (RSA)

Exercises without answers

2.   The trial balances of Ams Ltd and Trad Ltd as at 31.12.-8 are:
(Ams Ltd make pottery articles - at the year end there were no stocks of raw materials or work in progress)
(Trad Ltd are importers of brass ware which they package - there were no stocks of packaging material).

(All figures in £'000)

	Ams Ltd		Trad Ltd	
	£	£	£	£
Land at cost	240		160	
Buildings at cost	650		315	
Buildings depreciation		180		68
Plant at cost	175		28	
Plant depreciation		131		10
Stock	54		75	
Debtors and creditors	62	47	76	50
Purchases and sales	350	895	280	680
Production overheads	81		31	
Direct labour	57		43	
Discounts	6	10	4	3
Warehousing costs			70	
Warehousing labour			62	
Interim dividend	20		10	
Advertising	38		12	
Cost of sales office	15		13	
Salesmen's remuneration	39		26	
Delivery van costs	28		14	
Administration costs	44		20	
Legal charges	5			
Bad debts	12		14	
Research and development			21	
Bank		12	87	
Share capital - Ords 20p		100		80
Share capital - Pref £1 - 10%		50		100
Share premium		80		65
Capital redemption reserve				120
Profit and loss account		171		105
15% debentures		200		80
	1,876	1,876	1,361	1,361

For Ams Ltd:
(a) Depreciation is Buildings 2% on cost: Plant 25% reducing balance.
(b) A doubtful debt provision of 3% of debtors is to be set up.
(c) Auditor's remuneration of £15,000 is to be provided for.
(d) Interest on the debentures is to be provided for from the date of issue on 1.7.-8.
(e) The delivery van costs include licences for the year ending 31.3.-9 of £8,000.
(f) A bonus issue of one ordinary share for every four held is to be put through at 31.12.-8.
(g) The dividend on the preference shares is to be provided.
(h) An ordinary dividend of 10p on the ordinary share capital is proposed. The bonus shares do not rank for this dividend.
(i) Closing stocks were £62,000.
(j) Corporation tax of £52,000 is to be provided on the profits of the year.

Required:

(a) Prepare a profit and loss account in Format 1 and a balance sheet as at 31.12.-8.
(b) 'Why cannot we put money aside in a general reserve like other companies?' asks the production director. Anwer his question.

For Trad Ltd:

(a) On 28.12.-8, new plant costing £36,000 was delivered and began to be used. This transaction has not yet been put through the books.
(b) Depreciation is: Buildings 4% on cost: Plant 15% straight line on all plant in use at the year end.
(c) Stock at end is £69,000.

(d) An additional bad debt is to be recognised £3,000.

(e) Warehousing costs include rates for the half year to 31.3.-9 £8,000.

(f) The interim dividend includes the half year dividend on the preference shares to 30.6.-8.

(g) A rights issue of 1 for 5 on the ordinary shares was effected in December 19-8. The price was 55p per share and the monies were held in a special bank account. Costs of £2,000 are to be charged against the share premium account. None of this appears in the trial balance but should now be incorporated in the accounts.

(h) Corporation tax is to be provided at £12,000.

(i) The interest on the debentures for the half year ending 30.6.-8 has been paid and included in the administration costs. The remaining half year should be provided.

(j) The company are being sued by another company for a breach of copyright. The outcome is uncertain but a prudent provision for damages and costs is £10,000.

(k) A final dividend on the ordinary share capital of 7.5p per share is proposed together with the remaining half years preference dividend.

(l) A transfer of £10,000 to preference share redemption reserve is to be made and also a transfer to plant replacement reserve of the same amount.

Required:

(a) A profit and loss account for the year in Format 1 together with a balance sheet as at the year end.

(b) The sales director remarks that having made the transfers in (1) above the company will have the cash available to redeem the preference shares and to buy more plant. Explain why this is not so.

3. Capital Supply Plc has been in business for a number of years trading as wholesale grocers within the Greater London area. The following trial balance was extracted from the books as at 31 March 1984:

	Dr £	Cr £
Sales		3,900,000
Purchases	3,000,000	
Carriage inwards	4,000	
Delivery charges on sales	15,000	
Staff wages (15 employees)	80,000	
Rent and rates of premises	114,000	
Insurance of premises and stock	700	
Lighting and heating of premises	12,300	
Repairs and maintenance	21,200	
Office salaries (10 employees)	50,000	
Commission paid to two salesmen	17,400	
Auditors' remuneration	1,500	
Directors' fees	20,000	
Interim dividend paid on 1 January 1984	4,000	
Provision for depreciation of F & F		32,800
Share capital – fully paid ordinary shares		100,000
Provision for bad debts		8,000
Trade debtors and trade creditors	160,000	250,000
Goodwill, at cost	500,000	
Stock-in-trade at 1 April 19-3	80,000	
Furniture and fittings, at cost	82,000	
Profit and loss account balance at 1.4.83		35,250
Bank interest received		500
Cash at bank on deposit account	10,000	
Cash at bank on current account	154,450	
	4,326,550	4,326,550

You are required to:

(a) prepare a detailed trading and profit and loss account for the year ending 31 March 19-4 in a form suitable for presenting to the directors of the company; and

(b) prepare a profit and loss account for the year ended 31 March 19-4 in a form suitable for submission to the Registrar, with any necessary notes attached.

Use Format 1.

49. The company profit and loss acount
for internal use and for publication

The following additional information is to be taken into consideration in the preparation of the required accounts:

(i) depreciation of furniture and fittings for the current year amounting to £4,100 has not yet been recorded in the books;

(ii) repairs and maintenance includes £3,000 for modernisation of the offices;

(iii) the sum of £2,600 has accrued for salesmen's commission;

(iv) a provision is to be made for corporation tax on the current year's profits amounting to £240,000;

(v) stock in trade at 31 March 19-4 is valued at £100,000;

(vi) a final dividend of £6,000 has been recommended;

(vii) it is considered that one-quarter of the office salaries relate to work done on delivery to customers.

(RSA)

4.   The trial balances of Kith Limited and Kin Limited at 31.12.-7 show:

(Note that all amounts including the notes are in £000).

	KITH Dr	KITH Cr	KIN Dr	KIN Cr
Share Capital Ordinaries £1		100		50
8%/7% Preference shares of 20p		50		100
Share premium account		60		34
Profit and Loss Account		19		8
Fixed asset replacement reserve		100		
Land and buildings at cost	190		200	
Land and buildings depreciation		14		30
Plant at cost	186		204	
Plant depreciation		53		71
Stock 1.1.-7	68		90	
Debtors and Creditors	60	29	120	180
Provision for doubtful debts		2		7
Purchases and Sales	234	331	380	556
Discounts	7	9	12	14
Carriage In	12		18	
Wages 37		53		
Overheads	24		46	
Interim ordinary dividend	5		10	
General Reserve	10			6
Bank balance	21		23	
Goodwill at cost	55			
10% Debentures 2010/2013		80		100
	878	878	1,156	1,156

For Kith Limited

(a) Closing Stock was valued at 104 at cost but that included some items costing 30 which can only be sold for 24.

(b) Overheads includes rates for the half year to 31.3.-8.

(c) Proposed dividends are 8% for the preference and 3p per share on the ordinaries.

(d) The land is to be revalued to 40 and the buildings to 200.

(e) Depreciation is 4% on the buildings as revalued and 15% on cost on the plant.

(f) The provision for doubtful debts is to be 5% of debtors.

(g) The debenture interest is not in arrears.

(h) The directors have decided to transfer 20 to fixed asset replacement reserve.

For Kin Limited

(a) Stock is valued at 125.

(b) Depreciation is at 2% on the buildings (150 at cost).

(c) Depreciation is 20% reducing balance on the plant.

(d) The doubtful debts provision is to be made equal to 5% of debtors.

(e) There is a wages accrual of 5.

(f) No interest has been paid on the deben-tures during the year.

(g) During the year a bonus issue of one for five was made to the ordinary shareholders. This has not been entered into the books.

(h) The proposed dividends are: preference 7% and ordinary 10p a share. The bonus shares do not rank for dividend until the following year.

(i) The company acquired the goodwill but no other assets of a similar business for 30. The consideration was 20,000 ordinary shares. These shares also do not rank for dividend. This transaction has not been entered in the books.

(j) Transfer 3 from General Reserves back to Profit and Loss Account.

Required:
For each company prepare financial statements for internal use.

Interpretation

Financial statements are produced to be used. The next part of the manual explains how users of accounts interpret the information contained in them. Chapter 50 deals with the problems caused by one set of financial statements being produced but many users of the statement have different information needs. Chapter 51 shows the preparation of a relatively new financial statement with great interpretive power - the funds flow statement. Chapter 52 shows how to assess the probability of a business surviving and the ability of a business to pays its liabilities. Chapter 53 shows how to assess the performance of a business. Chapters 54 and 55 deal with the relatively advanced matters of gearing and investment ratios.

50. Uses of Accounting Information to Different Classes of User

INTRODUCTION

1. Financial statements for a business are produced to provide *information* to people who have contact with the business. The information is of an *historical* nature and is in a *summarised* form (*e.g.* net book value of plant is £x, but not a list of items of plant), and is highly *selective* (*e.g.* net book value of plant is given but not its market or replacement values).

2. Despite these disadvantages, financial statements are frequently used:

(a) As a guide to the future.
(b) As a basis for action.

3. This chapter reviews:

(a) The categories of users of financial statements.
(b) The uses to which they might put the financial statements.
(c) The methods of analysing accounts by calculating ratios, examining trends, and making comparisons.
(d) Gives an example to demonstrate the difficulties involved in drawing conclusions from these techniques.

USERS AND THEIR INFORMATION NEEDS

4. Financial statements of an enterprise are used by many categories of people who have contact with the business. This table shows the types of user and lists their particular needs.

Users

Owners who are also managers	(i)	Assessment of past performance.
	(ii)	Whether to cease business, continue as before, expand, etc.
	(iii)	As a basis for detailed future planning.
	(iv)	To show to potential buyers of the business.
Owners who are not managers *e.g.* shareholders in companies	(i)	To assess the performance of the management.
	(ii)	Whether to support or change the management.
	(iii)	Whether to remain as an owner, dispose of the investment or invest still more etc.
Management who are not also owners, *e.g.* company directors	(i)	To assess their own performance.
	(ii)	In the case of companies, to decide on what dividends to recommend.
	(iii)	As a basis for detailed future planning.
Inspectors of taxes	(i)	To assess the taxation which is due.
	(ii)	To determine if all income has apparently been included.
Banks and other lenders	(i)	To assess the management's performance to decide whether lending should be abandoned, reduced, continued or increased.

	(ii)	To determine the terms and conditions of any lending (*e.g.* if security should be offered, if guarantees should be sought from owners, repayment times etc.).
Potential buyers of the business	(i)	Whether the business should be bought or not.
	(ii)	The price it is reasonable to pay.
	(iii)	What detailed actions will need to be taken if the business is bought (*e.g.* changing premises, buying new plant, paying off workers etc.).
Actual and potential suppliers	(i)	How long the business takes to pay its suppliers.
	(ii)	Whether it is likely to stay in business long enough to pay.
	(iii)	What credit limit is reasonable.
Actual and potential customers	(i)	An appreciation of the size of order to be placed compared with the whole turnover of the business.
	(ii)	Appraisal of the long and short term ability of the business to fulfil orders placed.
Employees and potential employees and trade unions	(i)	Ability of the business to pay higher wages and salaries.
	(ii)	Ability of the business to survive in the long term.

5.   Each category of user has his own particular information needs. Some of these information needs can be met from financial statements. Many needs cannot be so met.

The information that users attempt to gain from financial statements is under general headings:

(a) **Liquidity** - the ability of the business to pay its way and survive in the long run.
(b) **Performance** - the quality of management and the rightness of decisions made.
(c) A guide to the future.

ANALYSIS OF FINANCIAL STATEMENTS

6.   Investigation, analysis and appraisal of the figures in a set of accounts is carried out by:

(a) Examining each figure and comparing it with:

(i)   The corresponding figure in previous accounts.
(ii) The figure which was forecast or budgeted.
(iii) The same figure in other similar businesses.

(b) Computing ratios (*e.g.* gross profit to sales percentage) and comparing them with:

(i)   The corresponding ratio in previous accounts.
(ii) The ratios of forecast or budgeted accounts.
(iii) The ratios found in the accounts of other businesses.

AN EXAMPLE OF ACCOUNTS APPRAISAL

7.   Pete owns a chain of hardware shops in suburban shopping centres. Each shop is managed by a manager who makes his own decisions on buying, pricing, employment of staff etc. Some buying is done jointly to obtain the advantages of bulk discounts.

Each year, a trading and profit and loss account and balance sheet is produced for each shop and Pete studies these carefully to make assessments of:

(a) The performance of the managers.
(b) Whether to maintain the shop as it is, expand it or close it.

8.   The trading account of the shop in Smalltown showed:

		19-3		*19-4*
		£000		£000
Sales		110		95
Less Cost of goods sold:				
Opening stock	18		21	
Purchases	72		75	
	90		96	
Closing stock	21	69	30	66
Gross profit		41		29

9. Pete notices that:

   (a) Sales in money terms have reduced from £110,000 to £95,000, a reduction of 13.6%, which is even greater in *real* terms.

   (b) The gross profit to sales ratio has reduced from $\frac{41}{110}$ x 100 = 37.3% in 19-3 to 30.5% in 19-4.

   (c) Stock as a proportion of cost of sales is $\frac{21}{69}$ x 100 = 30.4% at the end of 19-3 and 45.5% at the end of 19-4.

At first sight, the manager's performance is very poor - sales have declined, the profit element of each sale is smaller and stocks have increased. Pete feels inclined to:

   (a) Dismiss the manager and/or   (b) Close the shop.

10. However, Pete asks the manager for an explanation of the results and discovers:

    (a) During 19-4, a cut price competitor opened nearby and therefore, sales were lost to this competitor.
    (b) Prices had to be reduced to meet the competition.
    (c) An extensive housing area near the shop has been demolished under a slum clearance scheme.

11. The manager maintained that he had done well in the circumstances. He also pointed out that:

    (a) At the end of 19-4, the competitor had become bankrupt and had closed his business.
    (b) A new housing estate was under construction in the slum clearance area.
    (c) He had bought large stocks at the end of 19-4 to take advantage of the new custom available from the new estate and the collapse of his competitor, and he had bought most of the stock of his competitor at a very low price.

12. Ratio analysis is used to assess performance and liquidity and to forecast the future by *extrapolating trends*. However, as our example has shown, things are not always what they seem. Ratio analysis should not be used as a basis for decisions but rather as a guide to what *questions* to ask.

SUMMARY

13. (a) Financial statements contain information which is used by several categories of people having an interest in the business including owners, managers, lenders, suppliers, customers, the taxman and employees.

    (b) The utility of this information is limited because accounts are:

        (i)   Historical.
        (ii) Summaries.
        (iii) Selective as to content.

    (c) Users of accounts seek information on:

        (i)   Liquidity and the survival prospects of the business.
        (ii) Performance of the management.
        (iii) Future prospects of the business.

    (d) Financial statement analysis is carried on by comparing detailed figures and *ratios* with:

        (i)   Previous accounts.
        (ii) Budgets and forecasts.
        (iii) Other businesses.

(e) Misleading or false conclusions can be drawn from ratio analysis. Ratio analysis should be used as a pointer to further enquiries rather than a source of data for decision making.

POINTS TO NOTE

14. (a) In appraising financial statements, the figures considered by themselves are rarely useful. The basis of appraisal is the *comparison* of figures and ratios and the *determination* of *trends*.

SELF TESTING QUESTIONS

(a) What are the disadvantages of financial statements to persons seeking information about a business? (1).

(b) List the categories of persons seeking information about a business. (4).

(c) How can investigation, analysis and appraisal of financial statements be carried out? (6).

(d) How should ratio analysis be used? (12).

Exercises without answers

1. In the context of accounting statements comment on the following statements:

(a) We are interested in buying the business but we do not think there is any real goodwill. We are really only interested in the value of the assets.

(b) We want to sell goods to Oh Ltd but we feel their finances are shaky and we do not want to find we do not get paid.

(c) We want to buy the business and we feel the value in it lies in the business deals it is going to do.

(d) My business is run by a manager and I really want to know if he is running it as well as possible.

(e) I am not sure whether to sell my shares in Beerbok plc or to keep them in my portfolio.

2. Hicks is a foreman in the foundry shop of Wenfield Engineering plc. From his point of view and from the point of view of the company discuss whether or not accounting information should be given to Hicks by the company. What information might be given?

3. Comment on the following statements:

Accounting information is only about the past.
The valuations in accounts are absurd.
The valuations in the accounts are useless.
Accounting information is imcomprehensible.
Profit depends not on real performance but on who prepares the accounts.
Accounting information does not help me make decisions.
The accounts do not tell you about what might have been.
Accountants are too pessimistic.
Accountants do not measure the really interesting things like how much we lost from shoplifting.
Accounts pull it all together but it is the detail that is really interesting and that is not there.
Why cannot we have separate accounts for me, the taxman, the bank and my employees?

4. Wibble plc is considering the purchase of the whole share capital of Advourd Limited, an advertising agency and of Reelail Ltd, a small brewery. Discuss the utility of financial statements in evaluating each potential purchase.

5. "In a sense, published financial reports must strive to be all things to all men". Sidebotham. discuss this statement. *(CIMA)*

6. Company financial statements, including profit and loss accounts, balance sheets and statements of source and application of funds, are used by a variety of individuals and institutions for a wide variety of purposes.

Required:
Specify six different types of users of financial statements and explain in each case the aspects of performance or position in which they are interested. *(ACCA)*

7. David is considering introducing a profit sharing scheme into his small company. Draft such a scheme and consider its wider implications.

51. Funds Flow Statements

INTRODUCTION

1.   The balance sheet of an enterprise shows the assets and liabilities at a particular moment in time.

2.   From an inspection of balance sheets of the same enterprise one year apart, it is possible to discover:

  (a) Changes in individual assets and liabilities.
  (b) Changes in total assets.
  (c) Changes in total liabilities.

3.   A *partial* explanation for the changes is the profit and loss account which explains:

  (a) Profit earned in the period.
  (b) Appropriations of profit in the period, *e.g.* drawings in a sole trader or partnership; taxation and dividends in a company.

4.   Another partial explanation is the Funds Flow statement or, more formally, *Statement of Source and Application of Funds*.

This is a *Financial statement* which shows:

I.   (a) Sources of increases in working capital in the year.
      (b) Applications of working capital in the year.
      (c) Net increase (decrease) in working capital in the year.
II.   Net changes in the component parts of working capital over the year.

5.   Funds Flow statements are designed to show the *flow* over *time* of financial resources. They are intended to give information on *liquidity*. The profit and loss account is designed to show *profit* over the the period.

6.   Funds Flow statements are the subject of Statement of Standard Accounting Practice No. 10. "Statements of Source and Application of Funds".

7.   The set of accounts of a business enterprise normally comprise at least:

  (a) Balance sheet.   (c) Funds Flow statement.
  (b) Profit and loss account.

Enterprises where turnover is less than £25,000 a year need not produce a Funds Flow statement.

WORKING CAPITAL

8.   This term is widely used but variously defined. One definition is simply current assets minus current liabilities. Thus if current assets are £800 and current liabilities are £550, then working capital is £250.

9.   For the special purposes of Funds Flow statements, we shall define working capital more precisely as:

  Current assets.
  minus
  all current liabilities *except* for corporation tax and proposed dividends.

10.   Thus, the *components* of working capital are:

Positive:	Stocks	Negative:	Creditors
	Debtors		Accruals
	Prepayments		Bank overdraft
	Cash at bank		
	Cash in hand		

11.   Distinguish between the *component parts* of working capital and the *total* of working capital. Some transactions change two or more components (*e.g.* a debtor paying reduces debtors and increases cash), but leave the total working capital unchanged. Some transactions change one or more components (*e.g.* the buying of a fixed asset increases one component only - creditors) but *also* change the total.

CHANGES IN WORKING CAPITAL

12. The *total* of working capital can be *changed* by:

(a) Gross profit — On a credit sale, stock at *cost* is reduced and debtors at *selling price* are increased.

(b) Expenses used or consumed — Accruals increased or prepayments reduced.

(c) The proceeds of sale of fixed assets — Cash at bank is increased or overdraft reduced.

(d) The proceeds of a new issue of shares or debentures — Cash at bank is increased or overdraft reduced.

The *total* of working capital can be *reduced* by:

(e) Acquisition of fixed assets — Increase in creditors or reduction in cash at bank.

(f) Redemption of shares or debentures — Reduction in cash at bank, or increase in overdraft.

(g) The payment of dividends — Reduction in cash at bank, or increase in overdraft.

(h) The payment of taxation — Reduction in cash at bank, or increase in overdraft.

You will note that (a) and (b) is the *net profit*. However, there is one expense, depreciation, which does not affect working capital.

THE INVESTMENT IN WORKING CAPITAL

13. Joseph commences business on 1.1.-5, his initial transactions are:

1.1.-5   Buys on credit 100 widgets for £5 each.
28.2.-5   Pays for the widgets (2 months after purchase).
31.3.-5   Sells all the widgets.
30.6.-5   Customer pays (3 months after the sale).

Thereafter he replaces all stock sold with a purchase on the same day.

Sales are made at the rate of 100 widgets a month.

The first payment will be made on 28.2.-5 but the first receipt from a customer will not be received until 30.6.-5. Thus:

(a) He must have £500 in cash available on 28.2.-5 to pay for the goods bought on 1.1.-5.
(b) Further, he must have a further £500 in cash available on 31.5.-5 to pay for the goods bought on 31.3.-5.
(c) Thereafter, sufficient cash will be received from customers to pay suppliers unless there are changes in the scale of trading or the relative timing of receipts from customers and the payments to suppliers.

Therefore, he needs to *find the money* to pay for goods:

(a) Held in stock before sale.
(b) Sold but with a longer period of time before receipt from customers than the payment to supplier.

This is called the investment in working capital.

FUNDS FLOW STATEMENTS

14. Perton Ltd.

The balance sheets of Perton Ltd., at 31st December

	19-4 £000	*19-5* £000
Fixed assets at cost	365	581
Less Depreciation	143	201
	222	380
Current Assets		
Stock	186	301
Debtors	204	209

Cash in hand	18	408	22	532
		630		912

*Liabilities – amounts falling due within the year

Creditors	162		204	
Overdraft	35		89	
Corporation tax	60		76	
Dividend	50	307	60	429
		323		483
Share capital £1		160		200
Share premium		80		130
Retained profits		83		153
		323		483

* Abbreviated to current liabilities in the discussion.

The profit and loss account for 19-5 showed:

		£000
Sales		880
Cost of sales		410
Gross profit		470
Distribution costs	80	
Admin expenses	162	242
Net profit		228
Taxation		76
Profit after tax		152
Dividends – interim paid	22	
– final proposed	60	82
Retained		70

Notes:

(a) During 19-5, a fixed asset which had originally cost £60,000 and had a written down value at 31.12.-4 of £23,000, was sold for £20,000.

PERTON LTD.
Statement of Source and Application of Funds for the year ending
31st December 19-5

		£000	
Source of funds			a
Profit before tax		228	a
Adjustments for items not involving the movement of funds:			a
Depreciation	95		b
Loss on sale of fixed assets	3	98	c
Total generated from operations		326	d
Funds from other sources			e
Issue of shares for cash	90		f
Proceeds of sale of fixed assets	20	110	g
		436	
Application of funds			h
Dividends paid - final 19-4	50		i
- interim 19-5	22		
Tax paid	60		
Purchase of fixed assets	276	408	j
Increase in working capital		28	k
Increase in stocks	115		l
Increase in debtors	5		m
Increase in creditors	(42)		n
Movement in net liquid funds:			
Increase in cash balances	4		
Bank overdraft	(54)	(50)	28

a.   **Heading** - never omit the heading. Always write it out in full with no abbreviations.

b. **Units of Account** - the pound has now depreciated in value to the point where most businesses have accounts in at least five or six figures. The common unit for accounting statements is thus £000. The use of £1 units will clutter the statement and obscure its impact.

c. **Profit before tax** - the principal source of new working capital is net profit - gross profit less expenses.

d. **Adjustments for items not involving the movement of funds** - expenses include items (notably depreciation) which have *no effect* on the total or any component of working capital. These must be added back to profit to find the effect of profit on working capital.

e. **Depreciation** - is included in expenses but has no effect on working capital. The effect of depreciation is solely to reduce fixed assets and profit. Depreciation is found by creating a matrix as:

	Cost	Accumulated Depreciation	NBV
	£	£	£
As at 31.12.-4	365	143	222
Disposal (take out of the opening figures)	60	(1) 37	23
	305	106	199
Additions in year	(2) 276		276
Depreciation in year		(3) 95	(95)
As at 31.12.-5	581	201	380

(1) Is simply £60,000 - £23,000.
(2) Is computed from the cost column.
(3) Is computed from the accumulated depreciation column.

This matrix will usually be required in Funds Flow questions and its format should be learned.

f. **Loss on sale of fixed assets** - The *whole effect* of disposal of the fixed assets on working capital is an increase of £20,000 which reduces the bank overdraft but has no effect on any other component. The difference between the book value and the proceeds of sale is a loss which is included in the profit and loss account. This loss reduces the overall profit of the business, and should be added back to determine the source of funds arising from the trading profit.

g. **Total generated from operations** - Profitable trading generates working capital because:

Selling *stock* (at cost) to create *debtors* (at selling price) increases working capital.

and
   Expenses (but not depreciation) reduces working capital.

Operations here means trading in the ordinary course of business.

h. **issue of shares for cash** - the share capital has gone up by £40,000 and the share premium by £50,000. We can assume that 40,000 £1 ordinary shares were issued at £2.25 each to bring in £90,000 cash.

i. **Proceeds of sale of fixed assets** - always use the word "proceeds" to remind you that it is the amount received from the sale of fixed assets which increases working capital.

j. **Dividend paid - final 19-4** - in the balance sheet at 31.12.-4 a liability to pay a final dividend for 19-4 was included in current liabilities and this would have been paid in 19-5, reducing working capital in the process. This years proposed dividend of £60,000 has not yet been paid and does not therefore reduce working capital.

k. **Interim 19-5** - during 19-5 an interim dividend was paid and working capital reduced accordingly. We know that it was paid since it appears in the appropriation account but does not appear in the 19-5 current liabilities.

l. **Tax paid** - the tax appeared as a liability in the 19-4 balance sheet but not in the 19-5 balance sheet. It was, therefore, presumably paid in 19-5. The 19-5 liability is the tax on the 19-5 profits and this appears in the 19-5 appropriation account.

m. **Purchase of fixed assets** – in most questions, the amount paid for the acquisition of fixed assets is found from the matrix in (e) above.

n. **Increase in working capital** – at this point the answer can be checked! Calculate the working capital as:

		19–4		*19–5*
Current assets		408		532
Creditors	162		204	
Overdraft	35	197	89	293
		211		239
Increase			£28	

The increase in working capital means that *more resources* have become available in the year to finance:

Stocks
Debtors who take longer to pay than the period allowed by *our* suppliers.

The statement can be seen as having two distinct parts:

Part one explains the sources and application of working capital.
Part two explains why net liquid funds, a component of working capital has changed.

The increase in the total of working capital of £28,000 allows the components to change. In fact because stocks have increased by £115,000, debtors by £5,000 and creditors by £42,000, *net liquid funds* have been reduced by £50,000.

THEORY

15. The underlying purposes of the funds flow statement is that it measures, explains and demonstrates:

(i)   Financing.
(ii)   Liquidity.
(iii)   Flows.

(a) **Financing**

A business can be seen as having two sorts of assets only:

Fixed assets.
Working capital.

Fixed assets are easily understood and it is clear that any business requires some fixed assets to start and then acquires more as replacements are needed or as the business expands and responds to change.

Working capital as a single asset is a more subtle idea but the concept is little more than the idea that payment for goods must be made before the receipt of money from a customer for the sale of those goods.

Increases in these assets requires new resources. The principal sources are:

Retained profits.   Borrowing.
New injections of capital.   Sales of fixed assets.

The funds flow statement shows the sources of the finance required to obtain new fixed assets and working capital.

In addition the funds flow demonstrates:

(i)   That profit produces financial resources to enable the business to expand by acquiring more fixed assets and working capital.

(ii)   That the effect of profit on producing new resources is reduced by paying taxation and dividends.

(iii) That profit is reduced by depreciation. For this reason dividends are smaller than they would be if the profit was expressed without depreciation reduction. Depreciation has no effect on working capital, but it is sometimes said to be a source of funds in that it prevents the payment of excessive dividends.

(iv) The relative usage of new sources of funds. Historically in the UK retained profit is easily the largest source of new finance for companies.

(v) The relative sizes of the uses of funds - dividends, tax and new investment.

(b) **Liquidity** - Users of financial statements are interested to consider the profit earned in a year but also to consider the ability of the enterprise to stay in business and to pay its bills as they become due.

The funds flow statements indicate if working capital requirements have been met. As stocks and debtors grow (due to inflation, expansion or for other reasons) the growth can be financed by growth in creditors or overdraft *or by an overall increase in working capital.*

- if stocks and debtors grow
- the bank does not allow the overdraft to grow
- working capital does not grow

then creditors must grow and that means not paying bills as they become due and can lead to disaster.

(c) **Flows** - a business is not a static thing as depicted in a balance sheet. it is a *dynamic* entity continually changing. The funds flow statement measures flows and hence helps to emphasise the dynamic nature of business.

ALTERNATIVES

16. In this chapter, I have used the format in the Appendix to SSAP 10. This format is not prescriptive and other formats can be used and are found in practice.

PROBLEMS IN IMPLEMENTATION

17. In the real world, funds flow statements are prepared from the other financial statements and all necessary data is readily available. However, in examinations, students are tested by being denied some data and being required to deduce the missing figures from other figures that are given. In funds flow questions, like my illustration, the depreciation charge for the year and the acquisitions of fixed assets were not given but could be deduced from the matrix.

In some questions the profit and loss account is also omitted and has to be reconstructed. For example:

Wood Ltd.
Balance sheets as at 31st December

		19–4		*19–5*
Fixed assets		85		113
Current assets		59		60
		144		173
Current liabilities				
Creditors	31		26	
Corporation tax	12		30	
Dividend	10	53	15	71
		91		102
Share capital		40		40
Profit and loss account		51		62
		91		102

Note during 19-5, an interim dividend was paid of £6.

Reconstruct the appropriation section of the profit and loss account.

Profit and loss account for the year
ending 31st December 19-5

		£	£	
Net profit on trading			62	the balance of this account after all other
Less Taxation	(1)		30	figures have been entered
Profit after tax			32	
Dividends				
Paid – Interim		6		
Proposed – Final		15 (1)	21	
Retained profit for the year			11	the increase in profit and loss account as per the balance sheet

(1) As per the current liabilities.

SUMMARY

18. (a) The funds flow statement or "Statement of Source and Application of Funds" is a financial statement which accompanies the profit and loss account and balance sheet of all businesses with a turnover greater than £25,000 a year.

    (b) Funds flow statements are the subject of Statement of Standard Accounting Practice No. 10.

    (c) Working capital is defined for the purpose of funds flow statements as:

    Current assets
    Less all liabilities falling due within one year except taxation and dividends.

    (d) Sources of funds can be:

    Net profit before tax and dividends.
    Proceeds of sale of fixed assets.
    Loans received which are repayable more than a year after the balance sheet date.
    Proceeds of issue of share capital (share capital + share premium).

    (e) Application of funds can be:

Trading losses.	Dividends paid.
Acquisition of fixed assets.	Taxation paid.
Repayment of share capital and loans.	

    (f) Net profit is a source of funds after adjusting for items not involving the flow of funds. Depreciation and profit/loss on sales of fixed assets are examples.

    (g) The net figure of sources less applications is the change of working capital over the year and this can be confirmed from the balance sheets.

    (h) The second half of the funds flow statement shows the changes in the *components* of working capital.

    (i) Funds flow statements show the sources of *finance* becoming available in the year and how that finance was used.

POINTS TO NOTE

19. (a) Funds flow statements are a relatively new development in financial reporting. The ideas presented are not easy to grasp but add greatly to the ability of a reader of the financial statements to interpret the success and liquidity of the business.

    (b) Students should *learn* the format.

    (c) New businesses often underestimate the requirement for working capital.

    (d) Funds statements demonstrate very effectively the connection between *profit* and *new investment*. An unprofitable business cannot engage in new capital expenditure.

(e) In this chapter we have examined funds flow statements for companies. Similar statements can be prepared for all types of business. Note that in sole traders and partnerships, dividends in the application section are replaced by drawings.

(f) Students sometimes find difficulty in appreciating the difference between changes in the components of working capital and changes in working capital as a total.

(g) A good technique is to consider each item on the balance sheets except for working capital items and account for all changes especially noting the effect of the changes on working capital.

SELF TESTING QUESTIONS

(a) List principal sources and applications of working capital. (18d, e).
(b) Define working capital. (8, 9).
(c) What statement of standard accounting practice applies to funds flow statements? (6).

Exercises (Answers begin on page 470)

1. What is the effect on (a) profit, (b) working capital, of the following items:

(a) Sale of a motor vehicle (book value £2,600) for £1,500.
(b) Purchase of a new machine for £4,000.
(c) Annual depreciation of plant £16,200.
(d) The sale of stock (cost £64) for £100.
(e) Repayment of a loan £2,000.
(f) Payment of interest on the loan £100.
(g) Issue of 10,000 ordinary shares of £1 each at £2.50 each.
(h) Payment of corporation tax £60,000 on the profits of the year ending 31st December 19-4 on 15th October 19-5.
(i) The granting of overdraft facilities by the bank manager.

2. Show the effect on (a) individual working capital components, (b) working capital as a whole, (c) net profit, of the following:

(a) Purchase of a new machine on credit £800.
(b) Sale of an old machine (cost £1,500, accumulated depreciation £700) for £600 on credit.
(c) Scrapping of a machine with a written down value of £100.
(d) Borrowing £60,000 for repayment in 5 years time.
(e) Sale for £800 on credit of stock which had cost the company £500.
(f) Payment of an interim dividend of £40,000.

3. The balance sheets of Tring, a trader in special oils, at 31 December were:

	19-7 £	19-8 £		19-7 £	19-8 £
Capital b/f	34,679	36,043	Fixed Assets		
Net Profit	18,864	12,699	Cost	41,700	43,860
	53,543	48,742	Depreciation	11,790	17,724
Drawings	17,500	17,300		29,910	26,136
	36,043	31,442			
Creditors	21,543	28,500	Stocks	16,422	13,300
Overdraft	1,352		Debtors	12,606	16,700
			Bank		3,806
	58,938	59,942		58,938	59,942

Note: In 19-8 fixed assets were sold for £1,200. They had cost £2,000 and had been depreciated by £600.

(a) Prepare a statement of source and application of funds statement for 19-8.
(b) Comment on the events of 19-8 so far as you can from the limited data.

Exercises without answers

4. The balance sheets of Norman, a trader in widgets, at 31.12:

	19-7 £	19-8 £		19-7 £	19-8 £
Capital b/f	20,400	28,800	Fixed Assets		
Introduced	10,000	5,000	Cost	10,600	16,600
Net Profit	16,000	23,000	Depreciation	4,700	7,220
	46,400	56,800		5,900	9,380
Drawings	17,600	19,000	Stocks	18,300	18,730
	28,800	37,800	Debtors	12,720	25,920
Creditors	8,200	12,630	Bank	80	
Overdraft		3,600			
	37,000	54,030		37,000	54,030

Note: in 19-8 fixed assets (cost £1,000 WDV £200) were sold for £350).

(a) Prepare funds flow statement for 19-8.
(b) Comment on the events of 19-8.

5. The balance sheets for 31 December of Fiji Widgets Ltd are:

	19-7 £	19-8 £		19-7 £	19-8 £
Share Capital	10,000	15,000	Fixed Assets		
Share Premium	1,000	6,000	Cost	56,000	60,000
Reserves	23,700	32,650	Depreciation	27,200	35,000
				28,800	25,000
Creditors	18,700	22,750	Stock	23,200	31,320
Overdraft	12,400		Debtors	21,000	29,080
Dividend	4,000	5,000	Bank		100
Taxation	3,200	4,100			
	73,000	85,500		73,000	85,500

Notes: In 19-8:

(a) Fixed Assets (cost £7,000, accumulated depreciation £4,200) were sold for £2,050.
(b) Trading profit before tax was £18,050.

Prepare a funds flow statement for 19-8.

6. The Balance Sheets of Hengist Ltd as at 31st December:

	19-7 £	19-8 £		19-7 £	19-8 £
Share Capital			Fixed Assets		
Ordinary	10,000	20,000	Cost	80,000	123,000
Preference	8,000		Depreciation	43,200	59,200
Share Premium	2,000	4,000		36,800	63,800
Capital Redemption Reserve		8,000	Stock	13,000	18,700
Profit and Loss	7,000	4,000	Debtors	6,000	9,000
Debentures		10,000	Bank		200
Creditors	21,000	19,000			
Overdraft		16,500			
Dividend	5,000	4,000			
Taxation	3,000	6,000			
	56,000	91,500		56,000	91,500

Notes: In 19-8:

(a) Fixed Assets (cost £7,000, accumulated depreciation £3,000) were sold for £4,500.
(b) Each £100 of the Debentures was sold for £95. The discount was taken to the profit and loss account.
(c) During 19-8 an interim dividend costing £2,000 was paid.

(d) In 19-8 there was a bonus issue of 1 ordinary share for every two held followed later by a rights issue.

Required:

(a) Calculate the trading profit before tax for the year.
(b) Prepare a funds flow statement for 19-8.

7. The Balance Sheets of Horsa Ltd as at 31 December:

	19-7 £	19-8 £		19-7 £	19-8 £
Share Capital			Fixed Assets		
Ordinary	10,000	20,000	Cost	80,000	97,000
Preference		5,000	Depreciation	43,900	62,000
Share Premium	2,000	5,000		36,100	35,000
Capital Redemption Reserve	8,000	8,000	Stock	23,000	21,200
Profit and loss	12,000	4,000	Debtors	28,400	32,000
Debentures	15,000	10,000	Bank		500
Creditors	24,000	25,000			
Overdraft	8,500				
Dividend	5,000	7,000			
Taxation	3,000	4,700			
	87,500	88,700		87,500	88,700

Notes: In 19-8:

(a) Fixed assets (cost £3,000, accumulated depreciation £2,200) were sold for £1,020.
(b) Each £100 of the redeemed Debentures was redeemed by a payment of £105.
(c) During 19-8 an interim dividend costing £3,000 was paid.
(d) In 19-8 there was a bonus issue of one ordinary share for every one held. There was later a rights issue of one preference share of £1 each at £1.60 for every four ordinary shares held.

Required:
(a) Calculate the trading profit before tax for the year.
(b) Prepare a funds flow statement for 19-8.

8. Discuss the informational content of Funds Flow Statements. Contrast them with other financial statements in this respect.

9. "I cannot understand Income statements and balance sheets but funds flow statements I find really useful." Discuss.

10. Explain why depreciation is added back to net profit.

11. Explain why the loss on sale of an asset is added back to profit and the proceeds of sale are included in sources.

12. Gavin Limited has balance sheets as at 31 December:

£000	19-7	19-8	£000	19-7	19-8
Share Capital (20p)	30	80			
Share premium	–	20	Cost	68	169
Profit and loss	47	37	Depreciation	23	52
12% Debenture	40	20		45	117
Creditors	58	61	Stock	70	73
Dividend	7	9	Debtors	62	57
Taxation	4	7	Bank	9	–
Overdraft	–	13			
	186	247		186	247

(a) Fixed assets (cost £21,000, accumulated depreciation £9,000) were sold for £8,000.
(b) An interim dividend of £4,000 was paid in 19-8.
(c) The partly redeemed debenture was redeemed at 105 and the premium written off to profit and loss account.

(d) A bonus issue of 2 for 3 was made in March 19-8 followed by a rights issue of 3 for 5.

Prepare a funds flow statement for 19-8.

13. You are presented with the following forecasted information relating to Blackley Limited for the three months to 31 March 1987:

Forecasted profit and loss accounts (abridged)
for the three months to 31 March 1987

	January 1987 £000	February 1987 £000	March 1987 £000
Sales	250	300	350
Cost of goods sold	(200)	(240)	(280)
Gross profit	50	60	70
Depreciation	(3)	(20)	(4)
Administration, selling and distribution expenses	(37)	(40)	(42)
Forecasted net profit	10	–	24

Forecasted balances at

	31 December 1986 £000	31 January 1986 £000	28 February 1986 £000	31 March 1986 £000
Debit balances				
Tangible fixed assets at cost	360	240	480	480
Investments at cost	15	5	5	10
Stocks at cost	40	30	40	55
Trade debtors	50	65	75	80
Cash at bank and in hand	80			
Credit balances				
Debentures (10%)	–	–	–	50
Trade creditors	80	120	140	150
Taxation	8	–	–	–
Proposed dividend	15	–	–	–

Additional information:

(1) Sales of tangible fixed assets in January 1987 were expected to realise £12,000 in cash.

(2) Administration, selling and distribution expenses were expected to be settled in cash during the month in which they were incurred.

Required:

(a) Calculate Blackley Limited's forecasted net cash position at 31 January, 28 February and 31 March 1987 respectively; and

(b) prepare a forecasted statement of source and application of funds for the three months to 31 March 1987.

(AAT)

52. Liquidity Ratios

INTRODUCTION

1. Liquidity is the term used to describe the extent to which a business can pay its debts as they fall due.

2. Insolvency is the state of being *unable to pay debts as they fall due*. Insolvency leads to the collapse of the company and the appointment of a receiver or a liquidator.

3. Investors are unwilling to buy shares in or lend money to a company which is insolvent and traders are unwilling to supply goods on credit to companies which are or are likely to become insolvent.

4. Thus actual and potential investors and trade suppliers need to assess the liquidity of a business to determine if it is or is likely to become insolvent.

5. Assessing the financial statements of a business to assess its liquidity is in practice difficult and inconclusive. This is because:

  (a) Financial statements are historical. Liquidity assessment is concerned with the future.

  (b) Financial statements are static displays. Liquidity is concerned with *flows* of resources.

  (c) Financial statements are not designed to give the information required for an accurate liquidity assessment of a business.

  (d) Financial statements are summaries. Effective liquidity assessment requires a detailed breakdown of such items as debtors and stocks.

  (e) Financial statements omit information on important areas such as overdraft facilities agreed but not taken up.

  (f) Year ends are often chosen at dates when balance sheet items had untypical sizes. For example, a shop may choose a year end when stock is usually low, perhaps when winter goods have almost gone and spring goods have not yet arrived.

  (g) Some managements engage in "window dressing".

6. Despite the inherent difficulties, the assessment of liquidity is a very common activity. It is usually done by means of ratios. Some of which are:

Debtors payment period.   Current ratio.
Creditors payment period.   Acid test ratio.
Stock turnover.

The examples of calculations of ratios in this chapter are taken from the accounts of Bingo Manufacturing Co. Ltd. on the following page.

DEBTORS PAYMENT PERIOD

7. This ratio purports to measure the average length of time that credit customers take to pay. The ratio is calculated for 19-3 as:

		£
(a)	Turnover for year	4,800,000
(b)	Divided by 12 to give average monthly turnover	400,000
(c)	Debtors at year end	900,000

  (d) Average debtor is outstanding $\frac{900,000}{400,000} = 2\frac{1}{4}$ months.

From 19-4 and 19-5, the figures are 2.8 months and 1.95 months.

Bingo Manufacturing Co. Ltd.

Profit and loss account for the years ending 31st December

	19-3	19-4	19-5
	£000	£000	£000
Sales	4,800	5,050	5,340
Less Cost of sales	2,600	2,800	3,050
Gross profit	2,200	2,250	2,290
Distribution costs	460	530	495
Administration expenses	1,140	1,220	1,300
Net profit	600	500	495
Taxation	150	160	85
Profit after tax	450	340	410
Dividends	150	150	170
Retained	300	190	240

Balance sheets as at 31st December

	19-3	19-4	19-5
	£000	£000	£000
Fixed assets	1,560	1,753	2,448
Current assets			
Stock – raw materials	200	240	180
Work-in-progress	250	280	210
Finished goods	460	475	560
Debtors	900	1,190	870
Prepayments	54	56	60
Cash in hand	45	32	47
	1,909	2,273	1,927
Creditors – due within 12 months			
Trade creditors	560	760	900
Accruals	70	86	60
Corporation tax	150	160	85
Dividends	150	150	170
Bank overdraft	479	620	670
	1,409	1,776	1,885
Net current assets	500	497	42
Net assets	2,060	2,250	2,490
Share capital – 25p shares	600	600	600
Reserves	860	1,050	1,290
Due to shareholders	1,460	1,650	1,890
Creditors due more than 12 months	600	600	600
	2,060	2,250	2,490

8. The ratio is an indication and should be used with care because:

(a) The debtors are as at the year end, average debtors over the *whole* year are unknown. The year end figures may not be typical.

(b) The debtors may include debtors which are not trade debtors (*e.g.* loans to employees).

(c) The turnover may include *cash sales*.

(d) Turnover is net of VAT, debtors include VAT.

(e) Sales may not be uniform over the year. If sales are smaller than average in the last quarter, the debtors will be from those sales and should be compared with the last quarter's sales and not the sales of the whole year.

INTERPRETATION

9.   The ratio on its own indicates very little. It can be compared with:

(a)   Credit period granted to customers - say 30 days. Customers rarely pay within the time allowed.

(b)   The ratios of other similar businesses. If other companies persuade their debtors to pay more quickly, perhaps Bingo needs to see if they can improve their performance.

(c)   Trends - the ratio has worsened between 19-4 and 19-5 and improved between 19-5 and 19-6. Any change indicates not satisfaction or despair, but a search for explanations, which might be:

   (i)   A genuine change in credit control and credit management.

   (ii)   Deliberate policy to seek sales from less or more credit worthy customers.

   (iii)   Commencement or abandonment of settlement discount offers.

   (iv)   Changes in the seasonal patterns of sales.

   (v)   Averages may conceal changes in the composition of sales and/or debtors.

   (vi)   Window dressing - the company may deliberately date sales invoices before the year end but allow longer credit.

   (vii)   Some other reason not apparent from the published figures.

CREDITORS PAYMENT PERIOD

10.   This ratio measure the average time taken to pay suppliers. It is a very important ratio because:

(a)   Potential suppliers will want to know how long it will be before they get paid.

(b)   Significantly long payment time may mean that the business is about to fail because if creditors sense impending failure or become impatient with waiting, they may sue the company. If material numbers of creditors sue, the company will be unable to pay. Alternatively unpaid creditors may refuse to supply further goods on credit.

(c)   It is the most sensitive indicator of liquidity.

11.   It is measured by:

(a)   Taking annual supplies on credit. This is generally not revealed on financial statements. The figure is not "Cost of sales" since much of this is wages and other costs not supplied on credit. Let us *assume* that the figure is one half of cost of sales plus one half of distribution costs namely 1,300 + 230 = £1,530,000.

(b)   Divide this into £560,000, the outstanding creditors at the year end to give the result, 4.4 months. The corresponding figures for 19-4 and 19-5 are 5.5 months and 6.1 months respectively.

DIFFICULTIES IN MEASUREMENT

12.   These include:

(a)   Supplies on *credit* are not stated separately in financial statements.
(b)   Profit and loss account items are not inclusive of VAT. Trade creditors on the balance sheet include VAT.
(c)   Trade creditors at the year end may not be typical of the whole year.
(d)   Supplies on credit may be seasonal or not uniformly distributed through the year for other reasons.
(e)   The management may window dress the accounts. For example, reducing creditors by increasing bank overdraft *in appearance only* by drawing cheques but not sending them.

INTERPRETATION

13.   (a)   This ratio can be compared with that indicated by other businesses.

(b)   A more useful interpretation is from examining trends. Bingo Ltd., seems to be deteriorating. Care should be taken to investigate the reasons which might be:

(i)   A deliberate policy of financing new investment (note increase in fixed assets) by postponing payment of suppliers.

(ii) A change in policy on settlement discounts.

(iii) Changes in the seasonal patterns of supply.

(iv) Inclusion in creditors of large amounts of special items (*e.g.* capital expenditure) made late in the year.

(v)   Averages may conceal changes in the composition of creditors or suppliers.

(vi) Some other reason, not apparent from the financial statements.

(c)   This is one statistic which does give information in itself. Taking nearly six months to pay suppliers is very dangerous. Collapse of the company may be imminent.

STOCK TURNOVER

14. This ratio is usually given as an indicator of liquidity and indeed *changes* in stock turnover may give indications of better or worse liquidity. It is also a useful indicator of management performance.

The stock turnover rate measures the average length of time that stock is stored before use. In the case of work-in-progress it measures the average length of time between commencement and completion of items produced.

CALCULATION

15. To determine the stock turnover of finished goods stock:

(a)   Take the cost of goods sold £2,600,000.
(b)   Divide by 12 to determine average monthly throughput of finished goods sold. This gives £216,667.
(c)   Divide this figure into the year end stock to give 2.1 months.

The ratios for 19-4 and 19-5 are 2 and 2.2 months.

16. An alternative measure using the same data is: $\dfrac{\text{Cost of goods sold}}{\text{Average year end stock}} = \dfrac{£2,600,000}{£460,000} = 5.6$

This is expressed by saying that the stock is turned over 5.6 times a year.

17. Work-in-progress turnover is measured in the same way by comparing work-in-progress with average monthly throughput of sales at *cost price*, namely cost of sales.

The figures are:

	19-4	19-5	19-6
Months	1.1	1.2	.8

or on the alternative measure

	19-4	19-5	19-6
Times a year	10.4	10	14.5

18. Raw materials turnover is also measured in the same way by comparing the raw material stock with average monthly raw material usage. This is not given in published accounts but will be included in a full manufacturing account. *Assume* in Bingo that raw material usage is:

	19-4	19-5	19-6
	1,300	1,400	1,525

Then the raw material stock represents:

	19-4	19-5	19-6
Months usage	1.8	2.0	1.4

or on the alternative measure

	19-4	19-5	19-6
Times a year	6.5	5.8	8.4

INTERPRETATION

19. Management performance

(a) As a single statistic, the appropriate level of stock is difficult to evaluate. Sales and production management like large stocks to ensure that customers' requirements can be met and production is not halted by shortages. Financial managers like small stocks because stock:

(i) Deteriorates with storage.
(ii) Costs money to store.
(iii) Ties up capital.

(b) Comparison with other businesses are useful. If Bingo's management discovered that a rival company had only one months' requirement of finished goods, that might be an indication that Bingo's finished goods stock was higher than necessary.

(c) Trends. The trends indicated here are:

Raw materials	– a rise in 19-4 and a substantial fall in 19-5.
Work-in-progress	– a rise in 19-4 and a substantial fall in 19-5.
Finished goods	– a small fall in 19-5 and a considerable increase in 19-6.

The causes of these changes might be:

(i) Deliberate changes of policy, *e.g.* to reduce raw materials and work-in-progress and increase finished goods stock.

(ii) A build up of finished goods stock during 19-5 caused by an imbalance between production and sales followed by a reduction of output leading to lower raw material stocks and work-in-progress.

(iii) Improvement in management performance in that production time, as evidenced by lower work-in-progress, has shortened.

(iv) Random fluctuations caused for example by consignments in or out arriving or departing by chance either just before or just after the year end.

(v) Inflationary effects - the same *quantity* of stock may be held but at a higher *cost*.

20. Liquidity

Any increase in stocks decreases liquidity - simply because more money is tied up in stocks. Thus an increase in activity and turnover at the same stock turnover rate will reduce liquidity. Slower stock turnover at the same level of activity will reduce liquidity.

The effects on liquidity of stock turnover changes in the case of Bingo are substantial.

CURRENT RATIO

21. This ratio simply compares the relative sizes of *current assets* and *current liabilities*.

In the case of Bingo, the current ratio at 31.12.-3 is:

$$\frac{\text{Current assets}}{\text{Current liabilities}} = \frac{1909}{1409} = 1.35$$

The corresponding ratios at 31.12.-4 and 31.12.-5 are 1.28 and 1.02.

INTERPRETATION

22. **As a single statistic.** It has, since the 1890's, been a tradition that the current ratio of a business ought to be at least 2. This idea came about because it was felt that current assets would, in liquidation, be used to pay off current liabilities and as on forced sales, current assets would "shrink" then credit or loans should only be granted up to a limit of a current ratio of two. It was then felt that fixed assets were to be considered as giving unknown support to credit or loan applications.

In practice "the current ratio must be at least two" idea is surely an illogical measure of liquidity because:

(a) In the event of liquidation, *all* assets and all liabilities must be taken into account in assessing whether or not a particular creditor will be paid in full.

(b) The possibility that a company may fail is a function of *all* its assets and liabilities and also of dynamic not static factors. Cash flows are measured over time - debtors payment period, creditors payment period and stock turnover are better predictors of failure.

(c) Business A with excessive stocks and slow paying debtors would apparently have a better current ratio than business B with a fast turnover of stocks and efficient credit management. Yet business A is clearly more likely to fail.

(d) On the bank overdraft factor. Bank overdrafts normally appear among the current liabilities. Note that:

   (i) The bank may have advanced the money to pay for capital expenditure.

   (ii) The existence of bank overdraft finance is a random factor. Some businesses may obtain medium term finance, some may use bank overdraft finance, some (which will then have a better current ratio) may be unable to obtain an overdraft.

   (iii) The figure in the balance sheet may be much less than the overdraft facilities (maximum overdraft allowed) granted by the bank.

23. Comparisons with other businesses

Some types of business are likely to have low current ratios. For example, a shop which sells largely for cash will have few debtors. Some types of business will have very high current ratios. For example, civil engineering contractors will have very large work-in-progress. Only comparison of the current ratios of a particular business with others of the *same type* can give indications of liquidity problems.

24. Trends

Downward changes in the current ratio may indicate liquidity problems. However, causes which are not indicative of liquidity problems include:

(a) An overdraft increase to acquire fixed assets.
(b) An overdraft increase to finance increased business which will result in higher stock and debtors.

ACID TEST RATIO

25. This ratio is: $$\frac{\text{All current assets except stock}}{\text{Current liabilities}} = \frac{999}{1409} = .71$$

Ratios for 31.12-4 and 31.12-5 are .72 and .52.

26. This ratio is also historically regarded as a good indicator of liquidity. Many textbooks suggest that the ratio ought to be at least one, in which case Bingo Ltd. appears to be inadequate. However, the arguments against using the ratio in this simple manner are similar to those described for the current ratio.

INTERPRETATION

27. Indications of liquidity problems arising from the acid test ratio include:

(a) Comparison with other businesses. If other businesses in the same industry have higher acid test ratios then this may indicate poor liquidity.

(b) Trends. If the ratio has a downward trend then this again may be an indication of future liquidity difficulties.

OVERTRADING

28. Normally businesses that increase their sales at profit earning prices are rightly considered successful. However, paradoxically success may lead to failure due to liquidity problems caused by *overtrading*, that is, by doing too much business.

Jan 2	Buy goods in anticipation of increased sales.
Feb 28	Pay for them.
Mar 4	Sell the goods on credit.
May 8	Customer pays.

Assume that the goods are over and above normal levels of business then cash must be found to make the payment on Feb 28th.

Unless a new source of cash is found, *e.g.* by borrowing, then the cash used will have to be diverted from some other use. This other use might be payment of creditors in the normal way. Failure to pay may lead to the creditor suing for payment or cutting off supplies.

29. Indications of overtrading include:

(a) Higher turnover.

(b) Increasing debtors.

(c) Increasing stocks.

(d) Longer payment period for creditors.

SUMMARY

30. (a) Liquidity – the extent to which a business can pay its debts as they fall due.

(b) Insolvency describes the inability to pay debts as they fall due.

(c) Investors and trade suppliers are often concerned to assess a business's liquidity from its financial statements.

(d) Investors and trade suppliers are also concerned to detect impending failure of businesses which may come about for illiquidity reasons.

(e) Ratios can be used in assessing liquidity.

(f) Debtors payment period is the average time credit customers take to pay. It is measured by

$$\frac{\text{year end debtors}}{\text{turnover}} \times 12 \text{ (months)}$$

(g) Creditors payment period is the average time taken to pay suppliers on credit. It is measured by:

$$\frac{\text{year end creditors}}{\text{credit supplies}} \times 12 \text{ (months)}$$

(h) Stock turnover measures the average time goods are in stock before sale. It is measured by:

$$\frac{\text{average stock}}{\text{annual throughput}} \times 12 \text{ (months)}$$

or by

$$\frac{\text{annual throughput}}{\text{average stock}}$$

(i) Stock turnover is a measure of liquidity and also a measure of management performance. High stocks indicate poor control over stocks, low stocks may indicate difficulties in continuing production or meeting customers' demands.

(j) The current ratio is simply: $\dfrac{\text{current assets}}{\text{current liabilities}}$

(k) The acid test or quick ratio is measured by: $\dfrac{\text{current assets (less stocks)}}{\text{current liabilities}}$

(l) Overtrading, or doing too much business, can lead to liquidity difficulties and very often to business failure.

(m) Ratios can be used by:

(i) Considering the ratio in isolation and with budgets.

(ii) Comparing the ratios with those of other, similar companies.

(iii) Examining trends.

POINTS TO NOTE

31. (a) The *static* ratios - the current ratio and acid test ratios - are widely used but are unreliable. The *dynamic* ratios are better indicators. A comparison is often made with a reservoir. Does water level really indicate water surplus or shortage? What determines surplus or shortage is the supply (from rain fall) and demand (from consumers) over *time*.

    (b) In all ratio analysis be careful to compare *like with like*. For example:

        (i)   Debtors (at selling prices) with sales (also at selling prices).
        (ii) Stocks (at cost) with cost of sales.

        Where debtors are inclusive of VAT and sales are exclusive, an adjustment must be made.

    (c) I have computed the dynamic ratios in months. It is equally correct to calculate them in days, *e.g.*

        $$\frac{\text{Debtors}}{\text{Sales}} \times 365 \text{ days}$$

    (d) Ratios should not be calculated with excessive precision as the underlying data is not precise.

    (e) In the case of private businesses and partnerships, trade creditors must take into account that the private assets of the proprietor and partners are also available to creditors.

    (f) Limited companies that are part of *groups* may have access to group resources.

    (g) The stock turnover ratio requires the *average* stocks. Average that is over the whole year. The use of an average of beginning of year and end of year stocks is unlikely to be nearer the average than the year end stock.

    (h) The stock turnover ratio can be computed by reference to *purchases* or annual consumption. There is not usually a material difference.

    (i) Window dressing does occur but should be prevented by a competent auditor.

    (j) Overtrading is caused involuntarily by inflation. Each sale of an item of stock requires a replacement at a higher price.

    (k) The assessment of a business's liquidity is immensely difficult in practice. Beware of assuming that the calculation of a few ratios gives any conclusive answers.

SELF TESTING QUESTIONS

    (a) *Define liquidity. (1).*
    (b) *Define insolvency. (2).*
    (c) *Why is the assessment of the liquidity of a business carried out? (4).*
    (d) *What are the limitations of using financial statements in assessing liquidity? (5).*
    (e) *How is the debtors payment period calculated? (7).*
    (f) *List some explanations for a change in the debtors payment period. (9).*
    (g) *How is the creditors payment period calculated? (10).*
    (h) *State two measures of stock turnover. (15, 16).*
    (i) *What criteria are there for deciding on optimum stock levels? (19).*
    (j) *Why is the current ratio a poor tool for assessing liquidity? (22).*
    (k) *How is the acid test ratio calculated? (25).*
    (l) *What is overtrading? (28).*
    (m) *Why does overtrading lead to illiquidity? (28).*

Exercises (Answers begin on page 471)

1. *The turnover of J. Ltd., for 19-5 was:*

	£		£
January	16,000	July	15,100
February	18,500	August	6,800
March	12,500	September	18,200
April	13,100	October	10,100
May	14,200	November	7,400
June	11,900	December	4,800

Total for year £148,600
Debtors at the year end £23,000.

Calculate
The average payment period for debtors based on:

(a) The published figures (i.e. £148,600 and £23,000).
(b) Actual figures given above.

In both cases, adjust for VAT.

2. Cost of sales of K. Ltd., for 19-5 were:

	£		£
January	24,200	July	16,200
February	18,700	August	19,500
March	16,300	September	20,300
April	18,500	October	24,600
May	15,200	November	24,200
June	19,100	December	27,400

Creditors at the year end were £54,000.

Calculate
The average payment period for creditors based on:

(a) The published figures (i.e. annual total).
(b) The actual figures given above.

In both cases adjust for VAT.

3. N. Ltd., are a new wholesale company operating from rented premises with very few fixed assets and a small staff. Their first three years figures showed (in £000):

	19-3		19-4		19-5	
Sales		110		192		360
Opening stock	–		15		51	
Purchases	100		180		315	
	100		195		366	
Closing stock	15	85	51	144	94	272
Gross profit		25		48		88
Overheads		12		22		45
Net profit		13		26		43
At year end						
Debtors		27		56		120
Creditors		26		60		131
Overdraft		10		15		26

Required:
(a) Calculate 5 liquidity ratios for all three years.
(b) What problems of liquidity might N. Ltd. be facing?

Exercises without answers

4. Harley Triumph Limited are a company manufacturing spares for all makes of motor cycles. The balance sheets at 31 December were: (all figures in £000):

	19-6		19-7		19-8	
Fixed Assets		80		68		94
Stock		76		94		69
Debtors		102		116		90
		258		278		253
Creditors	86		95		80	
Overdraft	42		56		40	

Dividend	6		4		4	
Taxation	8	142	9	164	10	134
		116		114		119
Share Capital		100		100		100
Profit and Loss Account		16		14		19
		116		114		119

Profit and Loss Accounts included.

		19-6		19-7		19-8
Turnover		440		430		435
Gross profit		81		84		80
Net profit		19		14		19
Tax	6		9		10	
Dividend	10	16	7	16	4	14
Retained		3		(2)		5
Wages Totals		80		82		84

Required:

(a) Calculate a range of liquidity ratios.

(b) Identify and comment upon the company's actions re. capital expenditure, divi-dends and liquidity.

5.   Al Fresco Limited is a company in the wholesale barbeque equipment industry importing from the far east and also buying in the UK.

Balance sheets at 31 December showed (in £000):

	19-7	19-8		19-7	19-8
Capital	2	2	Fixed Assets	24	28
Reserves	12	26	Stock	28	34
Creditors	37	43	Debtors	57	69
Taxation	6	8			
Dividend	2	4			
Overdraft	50	48			
	109	131		109	131

Profit and loss accounts		19-7		19-8
Turnover		240		290
Cost of sales		144		178
Gross profit		96		112
Distribution	14		15	
Administration	15	29	18	33
		67		79
Directors Remuneration		50		53
		17		26

The Chairman's report states the imports which are paid for on delivery amount to 25% purchases and the notes to the accounts give wages as only £20,000 apart from directors' remuneration.

Required:

(a) You have been asked to quote for the supply of a product to Al Fresco Limited. Why should you consider the liquidity of the company?

(b) On average how long does Al Fresco take to pay its creditors?

(c) Does the company have any "going concern" problems?

(d) Does the current ratio or acid test ratio or change therein have any relevance to anything?

6. *Flotsam Limited is a retail carpet store and Jetsam Limited is a manufacturer of catering equipment. Their working capitals at 31 December 19-8 were:*

		Flotsam £000	Jetsam £000
Stock -	Raw materials components	–	33
	Work in progress	–	41
	Saleable goods	104	98
Debtors		13	180
Creditors		200	43
Overdraft		90	231
Dividend		20	20
Taxation		30	32
Turnover in 19-8		1,000	1,000
Purchases on credit in 19-8		600	500

Calculate suitable liquidity ratios and comment on their meaning for:

(i) a potential supplier to either company.
(ii) a potential maker of an unsecured loan to either company.

7. *Your company is considering supplying goods on credit to T Ltd. You have the accounts of T Ltd for two years and calculate the following:*

	19-4	19-5
Debtors/sales ratio	2.4 months	2.9 months
Creditors/credit purchases ratio	3.1 months	3.8 months
Stock turnover	4 times	3.4 times
Current ratio	1.4	1.2
Acid test ratio	.8	.7

(a) Would you sell on credit to T Ltd?
(b) Each ratio is 'worse' than the previous year. Give explanations for each change which puts the company in a favourable light.

53. Profitability Ratios

INTRODUCTION

1.   The purpose of producing financial statements is to measure the profit earned over the period and the capital employed at the end of the period.

2.   The owners of an enterprise, whether or not they also manage the enterprise, will use the financial statements to appraise the success of the business over the period.

3.   The owners of the enterprise may then take action based upon their appraisal. The actions may be:

(a) Enquire further.
(b) Support, chastise or fire the management.
(c) Expand, maintain or close down the enterprise.

4.   To assist in the appraisal:

(a) The figures may be simply compared with those of previous periods, budgets and forecasts and those of other businesses.
(b) Ratios may be prepared and compared with those of previous years, budgets and forecasts and other businesses.

5.   This chapter gives examples of profitability analysis of:

(a) The trading and profit and loss account of a retail business.
(b) The return on capital employed of a small business owned and managed by a sole trader.
(c) The return on capital employed of a company.

TRADING AND PROFIT AND LOSS ACCOUNT ANALYSIS

6.   Steve owns a newsagency business selling newspapers, magazines, books, records, stationery, tobacco, ice cream, toys and confectionery. His trading and profit and loss account for the three years to 31st December 19-4 shows:

	All in £000		
	19-2	*19-3*	*19-4*
Sales	135.0	158.0	178.0
Cost of sales	95.0	116.0	135.0
Gross profit	40.0	42.0	43.0
Occupancy costs (rent, rates etc.)	6.2	8.3	10.4
Wages and national insurance	14.3	15.9	17.1
Motor expenses	2.7	2.4	2.6
Other overheads (telephone, audit fee etc.)	3.8	4.4	4.9
	27.0	31.0	35.0
Net profit	13.0	11.0	8.0

Steve is concerned that his net profit has declined from £13,000 to £8,000 over the three years and wishes to analyse his trading and profit and loss account to seek possible causes of the decline and to determine what measures can be taken to arrest the decline.

7.   The first step is to calculate the proportions of all items to sales by computing percentages. Restating the data:

	19-2		*19-3*		*19-4*	
	£000	%	£000	%	£000	%
Sales	135.0	100.0	158.0	100.0	178.0	100.0
Cost of sales	95.0	70.4	116.0	73.4	135.0	75.8
Gross profit	40.0	29.6	42.0	26.6	43.0	24.2
Occupancy	6.2	4.6	8.3	5.2	10.4	5.8
Wages	14.3	10.6	15.9	10.1	17.1	9.6
Motor expenses	2.7	2.0	2.4	1.5	2.6	1.5
Other overheads	3.8	2.8	4.4	2.8	4.9	2.8
Total overheads	27.0	20.0	31.0	19.6	35.0	19.7
Net profit	13.0	9.6	11.0	7.0	8.0	4.5

8. The significant variables should also be compared with the corresponding figures for previous years. Again restating the figures:

	19-2	% Increase	19-3	% Increase	19-4
Sales	135.0	17.0	158.0	12.7	178.0
Gross profit	40.0	5.0	42.0	2.4	43.0
Occupancy	6.2	33.9	8.3	25.3	10.4
Wages	14.3	11.2	15.9	7.5	17.1
Motor expenses	2.7	(11.2)	2.4	8.3	2.6
Other overheads	3.8	15.8	4.4	11.4	4.9
Total overheads	27.0	14.8	31.0	12.9	35.0
Net profit	13.0	(15.4)	11.0	(27.3)	8.0

9. Studying the data, the following observations can be made:

(a) Sales have increased by 17% and 12.7% which is above the rate of inflation and appears to be satisfactory. However:

    (i) Percentage increases always seem large if they are from a low base, *i.e.* if 19-2 was a poor year.

    (ii) An increase may seem good but opportunities may have existed for even larger increases.

(b) Gross profit has increased each year (but by only 5.0% and 2.4%) but the gross profit portion of sales revenue has declined from 29.6% in 19-2 to 26.6% in 19-3 and 24.2% in 19-4. This clearly is the major cause of the decline of net profit and the reasons must be sought. Possible explanations include:

    (i) Excessive pilfering of money and/or goods by staff or "customers".

    (ii) Change of sales mix, so that a larger proportion of low margin items (*e.g.* cigarettes) are being sold.

    (iii) Scrapping of unsaleable items *e.g.* magazines.

    (iv) Reductions in selling prices.

(c) Occupancy costs have risen by 33.9% and 25.3% so that they went from 4.6% of sales in 19-2 to 5.8% of sales in 19-4. These are significant increases. The causes are probably unavoidable increases in rent and rates and electricity tariffs.

(d) Wages have increased by 11.2% and 7.5% but as a percentage of sales, they have declined.

(e) Motor expenses seem to be under control.

(f) Other overheads have increased in absolute terms but have remained the same proportion of sales revenue.

(g) Overall, overheads have increased by 14.8% and 12.9% but have declined as a proportion of turnover.

(h) The effect overall is a serious decline in net profit.

10. An examination of past achievements and historical accounting data is without point unless indications for future action are found and followed. The remedies might be:

(a) Careful buying to avoid stocking unsaleable items.

(b) Attention to pricing so that optimum prices can be obtained.

(c) Control over security of stock and cash.

(d) Concentration on high profit lines.

Note that some costs increases (*e.g.* rent and rates) are out of the control of the business. The effect of such increases may be to make the business *unviable* or to inspire the proprietor to greater efforts in increasing turnover and margins and reducing overheads.

RETURN ON CAPITAL EMPLOYED OF A SMALL BUSINESS OWNED BY A SMALL TRADER

11. Return on capital employed is calculated by:

$$\frac{\text{Income derived from the use of capital (the return)}}{\text{The capital used}} \times 100\%$$

In the simple case of an investment in a building society of £100 invested on 1st January. If this will *yield* £8 interest by 31st December, then the return on capital employed is

$$\frac{8}{100} \times 100 = 8\%$$

For a business, the calculation is complicated by several factors:

(a) The "return", the profit, can be calculated in many different ways (*e.g.* by using different depreciation methods).

(b) The capital employed is not a simple building society deposit but a complex mix of assets and liabilities.

(c) The valuation of the assets can be accomplished in many different ways (*e.g.* different depreciation methods or FIFO or AVCO stock valuation methods).

(d) The "capital" of the business is not constant but is varied as profit is made, new capital is introduced and drawings are made.

(e) The profit is not wholly a reward for investing capital. It is also:

  (i) A reward for the proprietor's time in managing the enterprise.
  (ii) A reward for the proprietor's "risk" in engaging in entrepreneurial activity.

12. Vic is the proprietor of Vic's ice cream parlour. His balance sheets at 31st December were (in £000):

	19-3		19-4	
Fixed assets				
Properties		51		55
Equipment		14		17
Vehicles		10		13
		75		85
Current assets				
Stock	6		8	
Debtors	5		9	
Cash	1	12	1	18
		87		103
Current liabilities				
Creditors	15		18	
Overdraft	3	18	14	32
		69		71
Capital				
At 1st January		65		69
Net profit for year		19		22
		84		91
Drawings		15		20
		69		71

Vic is concerned about the profitability of his business and is seeking a measure to indicate this. He estimates that:

- Alternative employment is available to him at about £9,000 a year.

- If the business were wound up, the assets sold and the liabilities paid off, he could invest the remainder at an interest rate of 10%.

Thus, the profit for 19-4 of £22,000 can be seen as:

	£
(a) A reward for Vic's labour in managing the business full time	9,000
(b) A reward for investing his capital in business assets $10\% \times \dfrac{(69 + 71)}{2}$	7,000

(c) The balance a reward for entrepreneurial endeavour   6,000
                                                                      £22,000

13. Note:
   (a) *The notional reward for Vic's time and the 10% interest rate adopted are opportunity costs, that is the best rewards foregone by engaging in business.*

   (b) *The capital employed throughout 19-4 has been taken as the average of the opening and closing figures. In practice it rarely makes much difference whether the opening figure, or the closing figures or the mean of the two is taken.*

RETURN ON CAPITAL EMPLOYED OF A COMPANY

14. Bev Plc has a balance sheet at 31st December as (in £000):

	19-3	19-4
Fixed assets	4,300	4,550
Net current assets	3,200	3,380
	7,500	7,930
Ordinary share capital (£1)	1,000	1,000
Reserves	3,500	3,930
Due to shareholders	4,500	4,930
10% unsecured loan stock	3,000	3,000
	7,500	7,930

The profit and loss account for 19-4 showed:

	£
Net profit before interest	1,030
Interest on loan stock	300
Net profit after interest	730
Dividends	300
Retained profits	430

15. Calculation of the return on capital can be:

   (a) Return on capital employed by *all long term suppliers of capital.*
   (b) Return on capital employed by *ordinary shareholders.*

16. (a) *Return on capital employed by all long term suppliers of capital*

   $$= \frac{\text{Return gained from the use of capital}}{\text{Capital employed}} \times 100\%$$

   $$= \frac{1,030}{(7,500 + 7,930)/2} \times 100\% = 13.35\%$$

   (b) *Return on capital employed by ordinary shareholders*

   $$= \frac{\text{Return gained from the use of capital}}{\text{Capital employed}} \times 100\%$$

   $$= \frac{730}{(4,500 + 4,930)/2} \times 100\% = 15.48\%$$

17. Notes:
   (a) *I have taken the average of opening and closing capital employed. In practice, the opening or the closing figure might be used. It would make little difference.*

   (b) *Capital employed can be seen here as the assets used in the business less all liabilities except those for whom we are measuring the return. Thus in measuring the return to all long term suppliers of capital (ordinary shareholders and loan stock holders), we take: Fixed assets + Net current assets and for return on capital of ordinary shareholders we take: Fixed assets + Net current assets − the unsecured loan stock, which is by definition equal to share capital + reserves.*

(c) The net profit before interest is taken for calculation (16.a) because this sum is the sum to be used to reward both loan stock holders (with £300,000) and ordinary shareholders (with £730,000).

(d) The net profit after interest is taken for calculation (16.b) because only this is available to ordinary shareholders even though £300,000 only is to be paid to them as dividends.

INTERFIRM COMPARISON

18. Many industries and trades have set up interfirm comparison schemes, whereby:

(a) Member firms send in details of their financial statements.

(b) Ratios and other significant data are abstracted and the mean and spread of ratios and other data is calculated. Spread can be measured by standard deviation or the use of quartiles or deciles.

(c) The mean and spread of the ratios and other data is communicated to member firms. The name of member firms is kept confidential.

19. As an example, the Institute of Chartered Accountants in England and Wales run a confidential annual interfirm comparison in which data calculated includes:

- Operating and gross profit as a percentage of fees.
- Salaries as a percentage of fees.
- Overheads as a percentage of fees.
- Profit and remuneration per partner.
- Inflation adjusted profit per partner.
- Growth in fee income.
- Debtors and work-in-progress as a percen-tage of fees.
- Any many others.

20. The major difficulty with interfirm comparisons is that all firms do not use precisely uniform accounting practices in preparing their financial statements. Most schemes detail exactly how financial statements are to be prepared to overcome this problem.

21. An item by item comparison of a firm's data with the average data of firms in the industry will:

(a) Enable management to identify variations from the average.
(b) Direct management to seek causes for variation.
(c) Direct management to take corrective action.

SUMMARY

22. (a) Owners and managers of businesses use financial statements to assess the performance of the business and its management in order to make decisions about the business's future.

(b) Each item of expense and net profit can be expressed as a percentage of sales and the percentage compared with corresponding percentages.

(i) In previous years.
(ii) In budgets and forecasts.
(iii) In other similar businesses.

(c) Changes in corresponding items in the profit and loss accounts of successive years can be converted into percentages to determine trends.

(d) The profit of the business of a sole trader who also manages the business is:

(i) A reward for the use of the capital employed in the business.
(ii) A reward for the time and expertise spent in management.
(iii) The residue being a reward for entrepreneurial endeavour.

(e) The return on capital employed in a company can be measured as:

(i) The return on the capital employed by all long term suppliers of capital. This is

$$\frac{\text{Profit } \textit{before interest}}{\text{Equity} + \text{Debt}} \times 100\%$$

where equity is the sum due to the shareholders (share capital + reserves) and debt is long term loans.

(ii) The return on capital employed by the ordinary shareholders. This is

$$\frac{\text{Profit } \textit{after interest}}{\text{Equity}} \times 100\%$$

POINTS TO NOTE

23. (a) In practice, computations of ratios and comparison between firms is complicated by *taxation*. As this is a Foundation manual, I have simplified the examples by ignoring taxation.

(b) In all matters of comparisons, it is essential to compare *like* with *like* using the same *standard of measure*. For example:

(i) Stock turnover must be computed using stock and cost of goods sold since both are measured at *cost* price.

(ii) In calculating the return on capital employed by all long term suppliers of capital, the return must be the profit *before* interest.

Note that in some examination questions the profit is given after interest and an adjustment has to be made:

For example:

	£000
Net profit for 19-4	600
Dividends	200
Retention	400

Balance Sheet at 31.12.-4

	£000
Fixed assets	2,200
Net current assets	340
	2,540
Share capital	1,000
Reserves	540
	1,540
10% debentures	1,000
	2,540

Return on capital employed by all long term suppliers of capital (debt + equity) =

$$\frac{(600 + 100^*)}{2,540} \times 100\% = 27.6\%$$

*The interest (10% on £1m) which is an expense charged in finding the £600,000 net profit.

Return on capital employed by ordinary shareholders =

$$\frac{600}{1,540} \times 100\% = 39\%$$

(iii) Capital employed by ordinary shareholders is always capital *plus reserves*.

(c) In ratio analysis, the data is often not known. For example stock turnover requires the average stock for the year and return on capital employed requires the average capital employed during the year. In practice, balance sheet figures at the beginning of the year or the end of the year or a simple average of them are used as *surrogates* for the unknown figures. If it is known that the surrogate is a poor substitute, then adjustments must be made. For example, many businesses have year ends when stock is at its lowest.

SELF TESTING QUESTIONS

(a) What are the purposes of calculating profitability ratios? (3).

(b) What comparisons can be made using a particular ratio? (4).

(c) Are ratios, in themselves, indicative of malaise or well-being within the business? (9).

(d) What rewards to a sole trader does his business profit represent? (11e).

(e) What is meant by "opportunity cost"? (13).

(f) How is the return on capital employed by all long term suppliers of capital calculated? (16a).

(g) How is the return on capital employed by ordinary shareholders calculated? (16b).

(h) Why should share capital plus reserves be taken as capital employed by share-holders? (17b).

(i) What are the difficulties of interfirm comparison? (20).

(j) What are the benefits? (21).

Exercises (Answers begin on page 472)

1. The balance sheet of the businesses of Abel, Ben, Cain and Darren show: (all in £000 and all retailers of fashion goods).

	A	B	C	D
Premises	50	-	76	-
Fixtures vehicle	26	41	52	12
Stock	62	87	60	21
Bank	4	-	-	-
Creditors	46	54	40	11
Overdraft	-	39	22	13
Profit and Loss Account:				
Net Profit	24	26	12	18

Note: Abel, Ben and Darren all work full time in the business. Comparable inputs of time, expertise etc. would probably cost at least £15,000 a year. Cain employs a manager and lives in the Bahamas. Abel's premises are at recent valuation but Cain's are now worth £100-£120,000.

Calculate a measure of profitability for these businesses.

2. Amanda owns and manages a retail jewellers shop and Sandra owns and runs a leather goods shop.

Their figures for 19-6, 19-7 and 19-8 were: (in £000).

	Amanda			Sandra		
	19-6	19-7	19-8	19-6	19-7	19-8
Sales	165	169	174	102	124	142
Cost of sales	92	98	110	50	62	69
Gross profit	73	71	64	52	62	73
Occupancy	16	19	23	12	15	16
Wages	24	20	18	14	16	18
Motor expenses	3	3	4	2	3	3
Advertising	4	5	3	7	12	14
Other overheads	9	9	10	6	7	7
Net profit	17	15	6	11	9	15

Make observations on the profitability of their two businesses.

3. Shoe Man plc and Mock Asin plc are both manufacturers of footwear. Their accounts for the year ending 31 December 19-8 show: (£000).

	Shoe Man	Mock Asin
Fixed Assets	280	900
Current Assets	149	460
	429	1,360
Current liabilities	86	380
	343	980

Share capital	120	150
Reserves	123	630
16% Debentures	100	200
	343	980
Net profit after interest	53	115
Taxation	17	40
Dividend	15	20
Retained	21	55

Calculate:
(a) Return on capital supplied by all suppliers of capital (before tax).
(b) Return on capital supplied by equity (i) before tax (ii) after tax.

Exercises without answers

4. Charlie and Davina are both Certified Accountants in sole practice in Loamshire. They belong to an Inter Firm Comparison Scheme operated in their county. Their figures and the means of the sole practitioners in the county are: 19-8 (£000)

	Charlie	Davina	Mean
Fixed assets (excluding vehicles and premises)	18	4	12
Work in progress	5	10	4
Debtors	9	11	6
Current Liabilities	9	12	5
Fees	68	80	50
Salaries	31	27	20
Occupancy	12	6	5
Other overheads	7	12	8
Net profit	18	35	17

Comment on Charlie's and Davina's performance and how they conduct their businesses.

5. The summarised balance sheets of Ritt Ltd at the end of two consecutive financial years were as shown below.

Summarised Balance Sheets as at 31 March

1986			1987	
£000	£000		£000	£000
		Fixed assets (at written down values)		
50		Premises	48	
115		Plant and equipment	196	
42		Vehicles	81	
	207			325
		Current assets		
86		Stock	177	
49		Debtors and prepayments	62	
53		Bank and cash	30	
188				269
		Current liabilities		
72		Creditors and accruals	132	
20		Proposed dividends	30	
92			162	
	96	Working capital		107
	303	Net assets employed		432
		Financed by		
250		Ordinary share capital	250	
53		Reserves	82	
	303	Shareholders' funds		332
	-	Loan capital: 7% debentures		100
	303			432

Turnover was £541,000 and £675,000 for the years ended 31 March 1986 and 1987 respectively. Corresponding figures for cost of sales were £369,000 and £481,000, respectively.

At 31 March 1985, reserves had totalled £21,000. Ordinary share capital was the same at the end of 1985 as at the end of 1986.

Required:

(a) Calculate, for each of the two years, the ratios listed below:

Gross profit/Turnover percentage   Net profit/Net assets employed percentage
Net profit/Turnover percentage   Current assets/Current liabilities
Turnover/Net assets employed   Quick assets/Current liabilties

(Calculations should be correct to one decimal place.)

(b) Comment on each of the figures you have calculated in (a) above, giving probable reasons for the differences between the two years.   (ACCA)

6. Financial statements use such peculiar values that return on capital employed cannot really be measured. Discuss.

7. Cone is in business as a motor factor. His condensed financial accounts for the last three years as summarised below:

Profit and loss accounts for the year to 31st March

	1980 £000	1980 £000	1981 £000	1981 £000	1982 £000	1982 £000
Sales (all on credit)		400		630		870
Less Cost of goods sold:						
Opening stock	20		25		50	
Purchases	325		550		790	
	345		575		840	
Less Closing stock	25	320	50	525	100	740
Gross profit		80		105		130
Less Expenses	40		50		60	
Loan interest	–	40	–	50	10	70
Net profit		40		55		60

Balance sheets as at 31st March

	1980 £000	1980 £000	1981 £000	1981 £000	1982 £000	1982 £000
Fixed assets		89		93		101
Current assets						
Stocks	25		50		100	
Trade debtors	50		105		240	
Cash at bank	10	85	5	160	–	340
		174		253		441
Financed by:						
Capital		100		118		141
Add Net profit for the year	40		55		60	
Less Drawings (all on 31.3)	22	18	32	23	36	24
		118		141		165
Loan		–		–		100
Current liabilities						
Creditors	56		112		166	
Bank overdraft	–	56	–	112	10	176
		174		253		441

Required:
  (a) Compute the following ratios for 1980, 1981 and 1982:

  (i)   Gross profit on sales.
  (ii) Gross profit on cost of goods sold.
  (iii) Stock turnover.
  (iv) Return on capital employed.
  (v)   Current ratio.
  (vi) Liquidity (or quick) ratio.
  (vii) Debtor collection period.

  (b) Comment briefly on the results of the business over the last three years using the ratios you have computed in answer to part (a) of the question. (AAT)

8. Two competing wholesale businesses have accounts for 1986 as:

	Yup Ltd	Arrive Ltd
	£'000	£'000
Sales (all credit)	680	920
Cost of sales	544	773
Gross profit	136	147
Overheads	96	127
Net profit	40	20
Fixed assets at cost	51	60
Depreciation	13	48
	38	12
Stock	90	190
Debtors	56	151
	146	341
	184	353
Creditors	45	188
Overdraft	2	26
	47	214
	137	139
Capital	100	50
Reserves	37	89
	137	139

At 31.12.85, the balance sheets included:

Stock	80	150
Debtors	51	120
Creditors	43	141

  (a) Calculate for each company:
  (i)   gross profit to sales ratio;
  (ii) stock turnover in days
  (iii) debtors average credit time in days
  (iv) creditors average credit time in days.

  (b) Using these ratios, briefly identify the problems facing Arrive Ltd.

  (c) Calculate the ratio of profit to shareholders equity for each company.

  (d) State with reasons which company has the most modern equipment.

(RSA)

9.   The accounts of BHS Ltd, musical instrument retailers for the two years 1984 and 1985 showed: (in £'000)

		1984		1985
Income:				
Cash and credit sales		280		310
Opening stock	65		80	
Purchases	250		273	
	315		353	
Closing stock	80		95	
		235		258
Gross profit		45		52
Overheads		26		29
Net profit		19		23
Working capital		31.12.84		31.12.85
Stock		80		95
Debtors		26		30
Cash		4		5
		110		130
Creditors	42		57	
Overdraft	62		68	
	104		125	
	6		5	

Required:

(a) Give the formula for calculation and calculate for each year:
   (1) rate of stock turnover (in months);
   (2) creditors average credit time (in months);
   (3) gross profit to turnover percentage;
   (4) net profit to turnover percentage.

(b) Explain why, in the absence of further information, it is impossible to calculate the debtors' average credit time.

(c) Calculate for the two years, and comment on, the current ratio and the acid test ratio, in the light of the idea that the current ratio should exceed 2 and the acid rest ratio should exceed 1.

(d) Discuss the rightness of the idea that the current ratio should exceed 2.   (RSA)

54. Gearing

INTRODUCTION

1. This chapter is concerned with the way companies are financed and the proportions of capital provided by risk taking shareholders and by lenders to the company.

GEARING

2. Companies are usually *financed* by:

(a) Short term methods, *e.g.* trade credit (paying for goods a short time after obtaining possession and use of the goods) and bank overdrafts.

(b) Long term borrowing *e.g.* by issuing, in exchange for loans, loan stocks or debentures which are pieces of paper acknowledging the loans and containing terms for repayment etc. Such borrowings are known as *debt*.

(c) Obtaining money from persons or institutions who become *shareholders*. Remember that in effect, shareholders also contribute to the company's funds by allowing profit which belongs to them, to be *retained* by the company. The funds supplied by shareholders by direct subscription and by retained profits are called *equity*.

3. The proportions of capital raised by *debt* and *equity* is the subject of gearing. Gearing is called *leverage* in the USA and this term is becoming used also in the UK. Companies who engage in gearing give an *advantage* to their shareholders in that (See Bev plc in previous chapter):

(a) Money (£3,000,000) can be borrowed.
(b) The money can be invested in assets to produce a profit of 13.35% = £400,000.
(c) Interest is payable to the lenders at 10% - £300,000.
(d) Thus extra profit is produced of £400,000 at a cost of only £300,000. The £100,000 belongs to the shareholders.

4. There is a disadvantage:

(a) Money (£3,000,000) can be borrowed.

(b) The money can be invested in assets to produce a profit of 13.35% = £400,000, but this may *not* happen. Suppose that the extra profit produced is only £200,000.

(c) The funds becoming available to pay interest £300,000 are only £200,000. This can lead to the company failing.

5. Gearing can be measured by: $\dfrac{\text{debt capital}}{\text{all long term capital}} \times 100\%$

In the case of Bev Ltd. (see previous chapter), this is (19-4 figures)

$$\frac{3,000}{7,930} \times 100\% = 37.8\%$$

6. Companies with a *high* proportion of their capital in debt form are said to be *high geared*. Companies with a small proportion of their capital in debt form are said to be *low geared*. No gearing ratio can be considered high or low in general. To determine if a particular company is high or low geared, comparison has to be made with the gearing ratios of other similar companies.

INCOME GEARING

7. It is possible to calculate a measure of gearing to the income of a geared company.

For example:

Puddle plc
Profit and Loss Account year ending 31.12.-7

	£000
Net profit before interest	2,400
Interest on debenture	600
Net profit after interest	1,800

A measure of gearing might be $\dfrac{\text{Interest}}{\text{Net profit before interest}} \times 100 = 25\%$

This interest takes up 25% of income, leaving 75% of income for shareholders.

In appraising the company, commentators would note that a fall in income of say 10% (£240,000) would reduce the shareholders portion of income by 13⅓%.

SUMMARY

8. (a) Companies are financed by:

    (i)   Risk taking shareholders - equity.
    (ii) Lenders to the company - debt.

    (b) The different proportions of the company's capital supplied by equity shareholders and lenders is the subject of gearing.

POINTS TO NOTE

9.   Gearing is measured by the "debt/equity ratio". There are several ways of calculating this but the simple way is:

$$\frac{\text{Long term debt}}{\text{Long term debt + shareholders equity}}$$

Note that shareholders' equity must include *reserves*.

SELF TESTING QUESTIONS

(a) *How can companies be financed? (2).*
(b) *What is gearing or leverage? (3).*
(c) *What are the (i) benefits, (ii) disadvantages of gearing? (3, 4).*
(d) *How can gearing be measured? (5).*
(e) *In measuring gearing, should reserves be included in shareholders equity? (9).*

Exercises (Answers begin on page 472)

1.   *The Accounts for 19-8 of three companies show: (in £000).*

Balance Sheet	Boring plc	Risquee plc	Happee plc
Share capital	1,000	100	1,300
Share premium	100	400	200
Preference Shares 7%	–	300	–
Reserves	200	250	600
Debentures 16%	100	400	800
Net Assets	3,200	1,450	2,900
Profit and Loss			
Net profit after interest	340	400	420
Preference Dividend	–	21	–
Ordinary Dividend	150	80	100
Retained	190	299	320

Calculate measures of gearing for the companies. Which companies are high geared?

2.   *Randaid plc and Spudfix plc have balance sheets as:*

	Randaid	Spudfix
Share Capital	100	400
Reserves	300	700
16% Debenture	–	400
Net Assets	400	1,500
and make profit of (after interest)	60	220

Randaid has an opportunity to invest £200 in assets which will produce an annual return of £40. The company can borrow the necessary money at 15%.

Spudfix have an opportunity to invest £500 in assets which will produce an annual return of £120. The company can borrow the necessary money at 18%.

Contrast the return on the new assets with the return given by them to the shareholders.

Exercises without answers

3.   *The assets employed by limited companies are financed by loans of various sorts and/or by shares.*

All limited companies, apart from those limited by guarantee, must have a share capital. The two most common types of share are preference and ordinary (equity).

The authorised share capital is stated in each company's Memorandum of Association and appears in the balance sheet, together with the issued share capital, which may, or may not, be fully called up. Some of the share capital may be redeemable.

Required:
Answer the following questions which relate to the above statements.

   (a) In what respects are the rights of preference shareholders preferential over the rights of ordinary share-holders?

   (b) For what main reason may a company issue preference shares rather than ordinary shares?

   (c) For what main reason may a company issue redeemable shares rather than those which are irredeemable?

   (d) What form of remuneration do shareholders receive on their holdings?

   (e) How is the remuneration in (d) accounted for in a company's profit and loss account?

   (f) Under what main circumstance may a company's share capital be only partly called up?

   (g) What is the main effect of a preference share issue on the capital structure of a company?   *(ACCA)*

4.   *The chairman of a public limited company has written his annual report to the shareholders, extracts of which are quoted below.*

Extract 1
'In May 1986, in order to provide a basis for more efficient operations, we acquired PAG Warehousing and Transport Ltd. The agreed valuation of the net tangible assets acquired was £1.4 million. The purchase consideration, £1.7 million, was satisfied by an issue of 6.4 million equity shares, of £0.25 per share, to PAG's shareholders. These shares do not rank for dividend until 1987.'

Extract 2
'As a measure of confidence in our ability to expand operations in 1987 and 1988, and to provide the necessary financial base, we issued £0.5 million 8% Redeemable Debenture Stock, 2000/2007, 20 million 6% £1 Redeemable Preference Shares and 4 million £1 equity shares. The opportunity was also taken to redeem the whole of the 5 million 11% £1 Redeemable Preference Shares.'

Required:
Answer the following questions on the above extracts.

(Extract 1)

   (a) What does the difference of £0.3 million between the purchase consideration (£1.7m) and the net tangible assets value (£1.4m) represent?

   (b) What does the difference of £0.1 million between the purchase consideration (£1.7m) and the nominal value of the equity shares (£.6m) represent?

   (c) What is the meaning of the term 'equity shares'?

(d) What is the meaning of the phrase 'do not rank for dividend'?

(Extract 2)

(e) In the description of the debenture stock issue, what is the significance of

(i) 8%?
(ii) 2000/2007?

(f) In the description of the preference share issue, what is the significance of

(i) 6%?
(ii) Redeemable?

(g) What is the most likely explanation for the company to have redeemed existing preference shares but at the same time to have issued others?

(h) What effect will these structural changes have had on the gearing of the company?

(i) Contrast the accounting treatment, in the company's profit and loss accounts, of the interest due on the debentures with dividends proposed on the equity shares.

(k) Explain the reasons for the different treatments you have outlined in your answer to (j) above.   (ACCA)

5. "A high geared company is a high profit company".
    "A high geared company is a high risk company".

Comment.

6. I like to save up for things both at home and in my business.

Comment.

7. Luvabull plc is considering the financing mix for its debut as a quoted company. Possible arrangements are:

	(a)	(b)	(c)
Ord shares of 20p each	1,500,000	2,500,000	1,000,000
Share premium and reserves	1,000,000	1,000,000	1,000,000
15% Debentures	1,000,000	–	1,500,000

Profits are expected to be 600,000 before interest.

(a) Calculate
    (i)   a gearing ratio
    (ii) profits available for dividend in each case.

(b) Assume a 10% reduction in profit before interest. Calculate the percentage change in profit available for dividend in each case.

8. The balance sheet of Arrow Limited, a retail store at 30th June 1979 was:

	£			£
Ordinary shares of 25p each	25,000	Land and buildings at cost		55,000
10% preference shares	40,000	Other fixed assets:		
Capital redemption reserve fund	10,000	Cost	40,000	
Share premium	5,000	Depreciation	31,000	9,000
Revenue reserves	6,000			
16% Mortgage debentures	20,000	Stock		46,000
Creditors	34,000	Debtors		22,000
		Cash at bank		8,000
	140,000			140,000

Required:

(a) What is the asset value of one ordinary share?

(b) The company wish to extend their store at a cost of £10,000. One director suggests using the capital redemption reserve fund. Explain why this is not possible.

(c) Explain why the words "share premium" appear in this balance sheet.

(d) Explain what is meant by 16% "mortgage debenture".

(e) What does this balance sheet tell you about the age of "Other fixed assets"?

(f) This company is highly geared. Compute a measure of gearing.   (RSA)

9. Risky Investments Limited has a balance sheet at 31.12.81 as follows:

	£		£
25p Ordinary shares	100,000	Investments	470,000
20% preference shares	50,000		
Reserves	120,000		
18% loan stock	200,000		
	470,000		470,000

The only income of the company in 1981 was investment income of £100,000.

Required:

(a) A calculation of the return on capital employed in the business.
(b) A calculation of the net return on the shareholders' interest.
(c) A calculation of the net return on the ordinary shareholders' interest.
(d) What would the yield as a percentage be, on the ordinary shares if the shares were quoted at 50p and all income was distributed?   (RSA)

10. The following are the summarised trading and profit and loss accounts for the years ended 31 December 1983, 1984 and 1985 and balance sheets as at 31 December 1982, 1983, 1984 and 1985 of James Simpson, a retail trader.

**Trading and profit and loss accounts years ended
31 December 1983, 1984 and 1985**

	1983 £'000	1984 £'000	1985 £'000
Sales	100	120	140
Cost of sales	60	72	98
Gross profit	40	48	42
Expenses (including loan interest)	20	30	28
Net profit	20	18	14

Balance sheets as at 31 December 1982, 1983, 1984 and 1985

	1982 £'000	1983 £'000	1984 £'000	1985 £'000
Fixed assets	38	48	68	90
Current assets				
Stocks	14	16	20	29
Trade debtors	10	18	40	52
Balance at bank	9	13	39	16
	71	95	167	187
Financed by:				
Capital at 1 January	51	67	87	105
Add net profit for the year	16	20	18	14
	67	87	105	119
Loan (received 31 December 1984)	-	-	50	50
Current liabilities - trade creditors	4	8	12	18
	71	95	167	187

Additional information:

(1) James Simpson, a man of modest tastes, is the beneficiary of a small income from his grandfather and therefore has taken no drawings from his retail business.

(2) Interest of 10% per annum has been paid on the loan from 1 January 1985.

(3) It is estimated that £12,000 per annum would have to be paid for the services rendered to the business by James Simpson.

(4) All sales are on a 30 day credit basis.

(5) James Simpson is able to invest in a bank deposit account giving interest at the rate of 8% per annum.

Required:

(a) Calculate for each of the years ended 31 December 1983, 1984 and 1985 the following financial ratios:
> return on gross capital employed
> acid or quick
> stock turnover
> net profit to sales

(b) Use two financial ratios (not referred to in (a) above) to draw attention to two aspects of the business which would appear to give cause for concern.

(c) Advise James Simpson whether, on financial grounds, he should continue his retail business. **Note:** Answers should include appropriate computations.

(d) Advise James Simpson as to whether it was a financially sound decision to borrow £50,000 on 31 December 1984.

(*AAT*)

11. The following is the balance sheet at 31 March 1985 of Claregate Ltd, a manufacturing company which sells entirely on credit to wholesalers.

	£'000			£'000
Share capital	200	Fixed assets		500
Reserves	175	Current assets		
Debenture at 10%	400	Stocks	490	
Current liabilities	465	Debtors	250	
				740
	1,240			1,240

The profit and loss account for 1984/85 included:

	£'000
Sales	1,000
Net profit before interest	124
Interest	40
Net profit after interest	84

The following ratios were calculated for the year ended 31 March 1984.

(i)	Debtors average credit time	–	70 days
(ii)	Profit to all long term capital employed	–	24%
(iii)	Return on shareholders equity	–	26%
(iv)	Net profit after interest to turnover	–	7%
(v)	Turnover to fixed assets	–	220%

You are required in respect of each ratio to:

(a) Calculate the ratio for the year ending 31 March 1985.
(b) State whether the 1984/85 is better or worse than the 1983/84 ratio.
(c) Give two possible causes for the ratio having changed.

Assume that there are 350 days only in a year. Ignore tax and dividends.   (*RSA*)

55. Investment Ratios

INTRODUCTION

1. The financial statements of quoted companies are appraised by investors and their advisers in order to make investment decisions like buying more of the shares or holding on or selling out. Such decisions are assisted by calculating ratios, and such ratios are calculated and given as well as the quotation for the share, against every share, daily, in the Financial Times.

RATIOS

2. The ratios are: (using Bev plc 19-4 figures):

Bev Plc balance sheets

	19-3	19-4
	£000	£000
Fixed assets	4,300	4,550
Net current assets	3,200	3,380
	7,500	7,930
Ordinary share capital (£1)	1,000	1,000
Reserves	3,500	3,930
Due to shareholders	4,500	4,930
12% unsecured loan stock	3,000	3,000
	7,500	7,930

Profit and loss account for 19-4

	£
Net profit before interest	1,030
Interest on loan stock	300
Net profit after interest	730
Dividends	300
Retained profits	430

(a) **Price Earnings Ratio**
This is simply the:

$$\frac{\text{Price of one share}}{\text{Profit attributable to one share}}$$

The price of a share is the price at which *small parcels* of the shares are bought and sold on the stock exchange. The price changes continually according to supply and demand for the shares. Let us assume that Bev Plc ordinary shares are quoted at £9.20 each. The earnings per share is:

$$\frac{\text{Total profit available to ordinary shareholders}}{\text{Number of shares}} = \frac{£730,000}{1,000,000} = 73\text{p}$$

In practice, there is no need to calculate the earnings per share (eps) as it is given in all published profit and loss accounts.

Thus the price earnings ratio for Bev Plc is: $\frac{£9.20}{73\text{p}} = 12.6$

The price of a share is 12.6 times the annual profits attributable to that share.

What this means is beyond the scope of this manual, but a high PE ratio (12.6 is fairly high) means that investors expect the profits of the company to grow.

(b) **Dividend yield**
This is simply:

$$\frac{\text{Dividend per share}}{\text{Share price}} \times 100\%$$

In Bev Plc's case: $\dfrac{£300,000/1,000,000}{£9.20}$ x 100% = 3.26%

An investor who buys one share at £9.20, the current market price, will receive a dividend of 30p which is equivalent to a return or *yield* of only 3.26%. This is substantially below the yield obtainable for investing in a building society. The yield is low because investors expect the rate of dividend per share to *grow*.

(c) **Dividend cover**
This is: $\dfrac{\text{Profits available to ordinary shareholders}}{\text{Dividend paid}}$

In Bev Plc's case, this is $\dfrac{£730,000}{£300,000}$ = 2.43

This is expressed as the dividend being 2.43 *times covered* by the profits. This is an indication that:

(i)   Profits will have to fall very substantially before the dividend is less than the profit.

(ii) A majority of the profit is *retained* rather than paid out to shareholders as dividends.

(iii) As the company is retaining the larger part of its profit, the company is *growing* and this will lead to *growth* in prospects and dividends in the future.

SUMMARY

3. (a) Investment ratios are used by investors in evaluating the shares of quoted companies as potential investments.

(b) The Price Earnings ratio (PE ratio) is: $\dfrac{\text{Quoted price of the share}}{\text{Earnings per share}}$

(c) The dividend yield is: $\dfrac{\text{Dividend per share}}{\text{Quoted price of the share}}$ x 100%

(d) The dividend cover is: $\dfrac{\text{Profits after tax available to ordinary shareholders}}{\text{Total dividends for the year}}$

POINTS TO NOTE

4. (a) The dividend cover is also known as the payout ratio.

(b) The calculation of the price earnings ratio involves a calculation of earnings per share. This can be very complicated and is covered by Statement of Standard Accounting Practice No. 3.

SELF TESTING QUESTIONS

(a) Why are investment ratios calculated? (1).
(b) What is the price earnings ratio? (2a).
(c) How is the dividend yield calculated? (2a).
(d) How is dividend cover calculated? (2c).
(e) What are earnings per share? (4).

Exercises (Answers begin on page 473)

1. Data about:

	Proton plc £000	Neutron plc £000	Positron plc £000
Share capital in 20p shares	4,000	3,000	12,000
Net profit after tax	1,200	600	4,700
Dividend per share	3p	2p	5p
Share price	60p	32p	96p

Calculate:
(a) Earnings per share
(b) Price earnings ratio
(c) Dividend yield
(d) Dividend cover.

Anticipate plc wish to make a bid for Proton plc. If they offered 60p a share, do you think Proton's shareholders (or at least 50% of them) would accept the offer?

2.   *Here is some data about Wensfield Industries plc:*

> Share capital 6,000,000 ordinary shares of 20p each
> Net Profit after tax   £400,000
> Total dividends   £150,000
> Share quotation   55p

Calculate:
Earnings per share, price earnings ratio, dividend yield, dividend cover, dividend per share.

3.   *Pullit plc, poultry distributors, is a listed company. Data in the Financial Times shows:*

> Share price   80p
> Price earnings ratio   10
> Dividend cover   2.5

The share capital is 1,000,000 ordinary shares of 20p each.

Calculate:
> *(a) Earnings per share.*   *(c) Total dividend payable.*
> *(b) Net profit.*   *(d) Dividend per share.*

Exercises without answers

4.   *Byron Ltd. has an issued capital of 2,000,000 ordinary shares of £1 per share. In order to finance its expansion programme it needs to raise a further £1,000,000.*

At a board meeting, the Marketing Director suggested an issue of 8% debenture stock at par. The Production Director disagreed and proposed the issue of 7% preference shares at par "because we shall save 1% (£10,000) each year". The Managing Director does not favour fixed rate issues and advocated the issue of further ordinary shares at par.

As the meeting progressed the arguments became more heated until the Chairman stopped the proceedings and said that the matter should be held over until the next meeting for a decision. In the meantime the Finance Director should prepare figures for each of these proposals on the basis of the following assumptions.

> *(a) Profits (before tax) of £800,000 per annum on the present basis are likely to continue.*
>
> *(b) There are no debentures or preference shares in issue at present.*
>
> *(c) The employment of the additional funds will bring about an increase of £200,000 per annum in profits before charging interest and tax.*
>
> *(d) Corporation tax is 52%.*
>
> *(e) The current market price of ordinary £1 shares is £2.50 per share. This is likely to remain at the same figure if either debentures or preference shares are issued but to fall to £2 per share if further ordinary shares are issued.*
>
> *(f) The present dividend of 10% on ordinary shares would be maintained, whichever proposal is adopted.*

Required:
Prepare a statement, showing separately for the present arrangement and for each of the proposed schemes:

> *(i)*   *Earnings.*   *(iii) Price earnings ratio.*
> *(ii)*   *Earnings per share.*   *(iv) Dividend yield of ordinary shares.(RSA)*

5.   The net assets of three unconnected companies are financed as follows, as at 31 December 1984:

	X PLC		Y PLC		Z PLC	
	£000	£000	£000	£000	£000	£000
Share capital						
Authorised						
Ordinary shares of £1.00 per share	12,000		–		–	
Ordinary shares of £0.25 per share	–		6,000		6,000	
8% Preference shares of £1.00 per share	–		4,000		4,000	
	12,000		10,000		10,000	
Called up and issued						
Ordinary shares of £1.00 per share £0.75 paid	6,000		–		–	
Ordinary shares of £0.25 per share fully paid	–		4,000		1,000	
8% Preference shares of £1.00 per share, fully paid	–		4,000		2,000	
		6,000		8,000		3,000
Reserves						
Share premium account (raised on issue of ordinary shares)	–		500		200	
General reserve	1,000		–		1,300	
Fixed asset revaluation reserve	2,000		–		–	
Fixed asset replacement reserve	–		1,000		–	
Profit and loss account	1,000		500		1,500	
		4,000		2,000		3,000
Shareholders' funds		10,000		10,000		6,000
10% Debenture stock		–		–		4,000
		10,000		10,000		10,000

For all three companies, the profit before interest and tax is estimated at £5,000,000 for the next 12 months ended 31 December 1985. The capital structure of each company will remain unaltered.

Taxation on profits after interest is an effective rate of 40%. Assume that an ordinary dividend of 12% of the paid up share capital will be paid.

Required:
For each of the three companies,

(a) prepare the estimated profit and loss accounts for the year ended 31 December 1985,

(b) calculate
(i)   basic earnings per share for the year ended 31 December 1985,
(ii) gearing ratio as at 31 December 1984.

(c) briefly explain, in relation to gearing, the effects on earnings of substantial changes in profit after tax.

Marks will be awarded for workings which must be shown.   (ACCA)

6.   The Gravelea Haulage Company plc is an established company which intends to expand its activities from 1982 onwards.

In the opinion of the directors, the only feasible means of financing the expansion programme is by obtaining funds from outside sources.

Over a period of weeks, the directors have been considering alternative ways of raising the £500,000 needed.

They have now narrowed down the choice to one of three possibilities:

Scheme:

(A) an issue of £500,000 7% redeemable debentures 1990/1997 at par;

(B) an issue of 500,000 10% redeemable preference shares of £1.00 per share, at par;

(C) an issue of 400,000 ordinary shares of £1.00 per share, at a premium of £0.25 per share, on which it is hoped to pay an annual dividend of 15% currently paid on existing ordinary shares.

Currently, the company's issued share capital consists of 3,000,000 ordinary shares of £1.00 per share, fully paid.

The Chief Accountant has estimated that the company's profit before interest and tax (without taking account of the additional profit from the expansion programme) is likely to remain static at £574,000 for the next five years. Interest payable on bank overdraft for each of these years has been estimated at £4,000.

It has also been estimated that, after it has been implemented, the programme will produce an annual amount of £130,000 profit before interest and tax, additional to the figure shown above.

Corporation tax has been estimated as an effective rate of 40% on the company's total profit after interest and before tax.

Without taking the expansion programme into account, the company's earnings per share is estimated to be 11.4p, arrived at as follows:

	£
Profit before interest and tax	574,000
Less:	
interest	4,000
Profit after interest before tax	570,000
Less:	
corporation tax (40% x £570,000)	228,000
Profit after tax	342,000
Less:	
Preference dividends	Nil
Earnings (attributable to ordinary shareholders)	342,000
	No
Number of ordinary shares in issue and ranking for dividend	3,000,000
Earnings per share (EPS)(as above)((342,000 x 100)/3,000,000)	11.4p

Required:
Write notes, or produce calculations, as appropriate, to answer the following questions which have been raised:

(a) *In schemes (A) and (B), what is the significance of the term 'redeemable'?*

(b) *For what reasons might the company wish to redeem its shares or debentures?*

(c) *What is the significance of the date 1990/1997 in Scheme (A)?*

(d) *In scheme (C) will the dividend of 15% be calculated on the nominal value (£400,000) of the additional ordinary shares or on the issue value (£500,000)? What is an alternative way in which the dividend could be expressed?*

(e) *What will be the company's annual earnings per share on the basis that:*

   (i)   *Scheme A is adopted?*
   (ii) *Scheme B is adopted?*
   (iii) *Scheme C is adopted?*

   (Earnings per share (EPS) is defined as the profit in pence attributable to each ordinary share after tax and before taking extraordinary items into account. No extraordinary items have been forecast for the next five years.)

(f) *What will be the company's capital gearing in a full year after implementation, separately for each of the schemes?*
                                                                                   (ACCA)

7.   The following balance sheets as at 31 December relate to Crocks plc, wholesale hardware merchants.

£'000 1982		£'000 1982
1,000	Issued share capital (fully paid)	1,000
240	Profit and loss account	200
300	Debenture stock	300
	Current liabilities	
160	Trade creditors	200
£1,700		£1,700
	Fixed assets	
1,500	at cost	1,500
325	less provision for depreciation	400
1,175		1,100
	Current assets	
300	Stock in trade	300
200	Trade debtors	250
25	Cash	50
£1,700		£1,700
	Sales	3,000
	Gross profit	600
	Net profit before tax	300

The Trade Association has published average figures compiled from returns submitted by all members of the Association, in respect of the year 1983. Some of these are:

(i)   rate of stock turnover   10 times
(ii)   debtors average credit time   40 days
(iii) percentage gross profit to turnover   25%
(iv) percentage net profit to turnover   8%
(v)   return on capital employed   15%

You are required to:

(a)   write a short essay to show your understanding of (i) inter-firm; and (ii) intra-firm comparisons and their purpose;

(b)   comment on the performance of Crocks in comparison with the average;

(c)   state two other ratios/percentages you would expect to see if you were a shareholder in Crocks and you were considering whether or not to dispose of your shareholding. Give reasons for your selection and ignore any interim or final dividends which may have been paid during the year.   (RSA)

Accounting Theory

This part of the manual is concerned with the theoretical underpinnings of accounting and the accounting conventions.

56. The Accounting Conventions

INTRODUCTION

1.　The accounting conventions have been discussed or mentioned at many points in this manual. This chapter brings the subject together and reviews all the accounting conventions and discusses their justifications, drawbacks and consequences.

THE BUSINESS ENTITY CONVENTION

2.　The business is seen as an entity separate from its owner(s) or proprietor(s).

(a)　The justification for this convention is that the proprietor and other interested parties (*e.g.* lenders, tax man) are concerned to know the profit earned by and the capital employed in the business (or each business if the proprietor has several).

(b)　The drawbacks of this convention are:

(i)　It is artificial - the assets and liabilities are in law those of the proprietor not of some artificial entity "the business".

(ii)　The accounts do not make clear to creditors what actual assets are available to meet their claims or what other liabilities must be met out of the assets.

(c)　The consequences of the convention include:

(i)　Assets and liabilities are arbitrarily included in a balance sheet on a subjective view of what assets and liabilities are properly those of the business. Some assets, *e.g.* motor cars, are both business and private assets.

(ii)　The capital of the business is seen as a liability of the business to its proprietor.

(iii)　Drawings and losses are regarded as a reduction of this liability.

(iv)　Profits and capital introduced are regarded as an increase in this liability.

THE MONEY MEASUREMENT CONVENTION

3.　Transactions are recorded in money terms. Financial statements are drawn up with revenues, expenses, assets and liabilities being expressed in money terms.

(a)　The justification for this convention is that financial statements are intended to summarise the events of the financial year and the position of the business at the end of the year. To do this effectively, a common unit of measurement must be used and that common unit of *measurement* is money.

(b)　The drawbacks to this convention are that:

(i)　Transactions, events and facts that cannot be recorded in money terms are ignored. For example, relevant facts about a business such as the quantity of orders on hand, the existence of satisfied customers or competent management are not included in financial statements.

(ii)　Financial statements are drawn up from the entries in the books. The entries in the books are made from data concerning individual transactions. This *transaction* based approach to accounting, means that facts about the business which are not derived from transactions are not recorded in the accounting system. For example, purchased goodwill is included in the system since it is derived from a transaction (the purchase), but goodwill acquired from successful trading is ignored.

   (iii) Money, as a unit of measurement, is unstable. Price levels change with inflation (or rarely, deflation). Historical cost accounting implies wrongly that the currency has stable value. Clearly, measurement of say distance using a unit (say the kilometre) whose value fluctuated with time, would be quite unacceptable.

  (c) The consequences of this convention include:

   (i)   Exclusion of non-transaction based facts.

   (ii)   Exclusion of relevant data which are not measurable in money terms.

   (iii) Assumption that it is reasonable to show, for example, fixed assets at written down value £x when x is composed of costs at different times.

   (iv) Focusing attention on the financial aspects of the business when other aspects may be of equal or greater importance.

THE HISTORICAL COST CONVENTION

4.   Assets and expenses are entered into the books at their actual cost to the business.

  (a) The justification for this convention is that historical cost is *objective* and *verifiable*. Any alternative convention (*e.g.* showing assets at realisable value) would be subjective and thus lead to a wide variation in measurement. The cost convention provides a universal, consistent and simple method of recording assets and expenses. An argument used in favour of unamortised cost as the value of fixed assets is that the value required is the value in use represented by its cost and not the value on resale represented by what some hypothetical buyer might value it at.

  (b) The drawbacks of this convention are:

   (i)   Items having no cost are left out of account.

   (ii)   In times of changing price levels, serious distortion occurs when, for example, depreciation based upon the historical costs of earlier years, is set against revenues at current prices.

   (iii) The actual information required by managers, investors, etc. may be current values of assets and values based upon historical costs may be irrelevant for their purposes.

  (c) The consequences of the convention include:

   (i)   Assets are valued at cost or cost derived figures (*e.g.* unamortised cost for fixed assets).
   (ii)   Revenues at current prices are matched with historical costs.
   (iii) Items which had no cost are ignored.
   (iv) Unrealised gains are ignored.
   (v)   Relevant information (*e.g.* the real value of capital employed in the business) is not given.

THE GOING CONCERN CONVENTION

5.   The going concern convention assumes that the enterprise will continue in operational existence for the foreseeable future. The balance sheet and profit and loss account are drawn up on the assumption that there is no *intention* or *necessity* to liquidate or *curtail* significantly the scale of operation.

  (a) The justification for this convention is simply that it is true. If it were not so, then liquidation values would need to be substituted for the historical cost based figures.

  (b) The drawbacks to this convention are that:

   (i)   It may mislead - some firms do cease trading shortly after publication of accounts drawn up on the going concern basis.

   (ii)   Information is not given on the consequences of abandoning the convention. The consequences of such abandonment may be important information to an unsecured lender.

    (iii) Alternative courses of action cannot be evaluated. For example, the use of historical cost based values may indicate a satisfactory return on capital employed whereas knowledge of potential realisable prices for fixed asset may suggest that the business should be wound up and the sums realised invested elsewhere.

(c) The consequences of this convention include:

    (i)   Fixed assets are valued at unamortised costs.
    (ii)   Current assets are valued at lower of cost and net realisable value in the normal course of business.
    (iii) Liabilities that will arise only in the event of liquidation (*e.g.* redundancy pay), are ignored.
    (iv) In company accounts, shareholders funds are divided between payable and non-payable liabilities.
    (v)   Information about the consequences of liquidation is not given.

PERIODICITY

6. This convention requires that a balance sheet and profit and loss account should be produced at regular intervals. Most businesses produce annual accounts and the Companies Acts require annual accounts for companies. Public companies produce half yearly interim accounts and many businesses produce monthly or quarterly accounts for internal purposes.

(a) The justification for this convention is that ongoing information about the business is required at regular intervals for all sorts of purposes - performance evaluation, tax computations etc.

(b) The drawbacks of the convention are:

    (i)   It is assumed that business transactions can be identified with particular periods. In practice, many transactions (*e.g.* buying a fixed asset), have consequences for many periods.

    (ii)   Periodic income determination leads to comparisons of the results of successive periods. As the pattern of business activity changes over time, this comparison may be misleading.

    (iii) A range of conventions have had to be developed (matching, realisation, prudence) to relate transactions to specific time periods. Differing accounting bases (*e.g.* depreciation methods) can cause difficulty in comparing different businesses.

    (iv) In very short period accounting (*e.g.* half yearly or shorter), seasonal variations can mislead.

(c) The consequences of the periodicity convention are:

    (i)   Much effort is required to prepare the periodic accounts.
    (ii)   Arbitrary allocation and apportionment methods are required.

THE REALISATION CONVENTION

7. This convention requires that the profit on any given transaction is included in the accounts of the period when the profit is *realised*. Realisation means when a transaction (*e.g.* a sale) has occurred which gives legal rights to the receipt of money.

(a) The justifications for this convention include:

    (i)   The *critical event* principle. The trader as a businessman is in business to *sell* things. It is suggested that buying goods and collecting debts are relatively easy. The hard bit is selling the goods and consequently it is at that point that the profit is earned.

    (ii)   The *certainty* principle. When goods are bought the profit that will be made is not certain. It is not certain that the goods will be sold and a profit made. When the goods are sold, there is certainty that a profit has been made and how much the profit is.

    (iii) The *asset transfer* principle. On the sale the goods cease to be the property of the trader and become the property of his customer. The trader ceases to have goods; instead he has a debt due to him. The value of the debt is the sum due. The value of the goods was their cost to the trader. Any other value (*e.g.* selling price) would be an estimate and account-ants like to be *objective*.

(b) The drawbacks to this convention include:

(i)   Unrealised or holding gains are ignored. For example, an asset may have increased in value while it has been held by the business but no recognition of this increase is made until the asset is sold.

(ii) Distortions can occur when the trading cycle is long. For example, the profit on long term contracts accrues over the period of the contract and does not occur suddenly on the completion of the contract. In practice, the realisation convention is modified in the case of long term contracts.

(iii) The convention is unnecessarily cautious in waiting until a sale before a profit can be recognised.

(c) The consequences of the convention include:

(i)   Fixed and current assets are valued at cost or cost derived amounts.
(ii) Holding gains and unrealised gains are ignored.

THE MATCHING CONVENTION

8.   The matching convention requires that in an accounting period, costs are matched with related income. Where costs have been incurred and there is no related income in the period or in future periods, with which the costs can be matched, they are treated as an expense of the accounting period.

(a) The justification for this convention arises out of the periodicity convention. The profits of the period are revenues from transactions less all associated costs. Which revenues should be included is determined using the realisation convention. Any costs not associable with the future revenue are written off as they are incurred.

(b) The drawbacks to this convention include:

(i)   The difficulty of determining which costs are associated with particular revenues. The whole business of depreciation and total absorption cost finished goods and work-in-progress valuation are features of the matching convention.

(ii) The use of different matching methods (*e.g.* depreciation methods) by different accountants leads to the results of enterprises not being comparable one with another.

(c) The consequences of the matching conven-tion include:

(i)   Valuations of stock and work-in-progress on a balance sheet which includes time related costs (*e.g.* rent) for expired periods.

(ii) The inclusion on a balance sheet of assets with no tangible value, *e.g.* development costs.

(iii) The inclusion of estimated liabilities where provisions are neces-sary to match costs with revenues.

THE ACCRUALS CONVENTION

9.   The accruals convention is also a consequence of the periodicity convention. Revenues and costs are recognised and included in the profit and loss account as they are accrued (earned or incurred), not as they are paid or received.

(a) The justification for this convention is that receipts and payments are to a degree random as to timing, whereas the earning of a revenue or the consumption of a resource can be accurately related to specific time periods.

(b) The drawbacks to this convention include:

(i)   The work required to apportion expenses to time periods.
(ii) Financial statements become more complex (than say cash flow accounting), with a consequent loss of intelligibility to the layman.

(c) The consequences of the convention include:

(i)   The inclusion of prepayments and accruals in a balance sheet. The meaning of these words is not apparent to the layman.

THE CONVENTION OF CONSERVATISM OR PRUDENCE

10. This convention requires that:

(a) Revenue and profits are not anticipated but are recognised by inclusion in the profit and loss account only when realised in the form of cash or other assets (*e.g.* a debt) the ultimate cash realisation of which can be assessed with reasonable certainty.

(b) Provision is made for all known liabilities (expenses and losses) whether the amount is known with certainty or is a best estimate in the light of information available. As an example, Dick is in business to service cold stores equipment on a contract basis. By 31st December 1985 the following irrevocable contracts had been signed:

A. £5,000 a year for 19-6, 19-7 and 19-8. Expected costs to Dick are in the region of £3,000 a year.
B. £6,000 a year for 19-6 and 19-7. Expected costs to Dick are £7,000 for 19-6 and £7,400 in 19-7.

The prudence convention requires that in the 19-5 accounts:

- The profit on contract A should be ignored. It will fall into 19-6 and 19-7.
- The loss on contract B (£2,400) should be included.

(c) The justification for this convention is that accountants are cautious people. The natural optimism of businessmen needs to be countered by the pessimism of the accountants. It is felt that where doubt exists, it is better to err on the safe side.

(d) The drawbacks to this convention include:

(i) It is unnecessarily pessimistic.
(ii) The tendency to understate asset values tends to lower the appropriate prices for shares on the stock exchange.

(e) The consequences of this convention are that:

(i) Profits are not anticipated.
(ii) Holding gains are ignored.
(iii) Potential losses (even future losses) are fully reflected in the accounts.

CONSISTENCY CONVENTION

11. This convention requires that there is consistency of accounting treatment of like items within each accounting period and from one period to the next. For example, the straight line method of depreciation once chosen for vehicles, should be used for *all* vehicles and for all periods.

(a) The justification for this convention seems self evident if comparability over time is to be achieved. However, its extension to all businesses seem desirable, but has not been achieved.

OTHER CONVENTIONS

12. There are some other ideas which some writers consider to be conventions. These include:

(a) **Materiality**
Accounting is concerned with the measurement of profit and capital and the presentation of the results to interested parties. In essence it is a summarising process. Too much detail in the annual accounts and the view is obscured. Insignificant items are merged with others and are not shown separately. The problem is making a decision as to what is material and what is not material. For example, bad debts always occur to Smith Plc. However, each year the total bad debts is small relative to other items in the accounts and the total is included in cost of sales and not shown separately. However, in 1985 a particularly large bad debt caused a downward jump in profits after several years of increases. To explain the downward jump the bad debt has to be disclosed separately. In practice, decisions on whether items are material enough to affect the view given by the accounts and hence to require disclosure, are very difficult.

(b) **Dual aspect**
The double entry system requires all transactions to have two entries, one on the debit of an account and one on the credit of the same or a different account. This enables balance to be maintained in the accounting equation - capital = assets - liabilities. The detailed application of this convention ensures that balance sheets always balance but does not ensure that the balance sheet is correct in other ways.

(c) **Substance over form**

Some transactions have a legal *form* which is different from the underlying commercial reality or substance. In such cases, for accounting purposes, *the substance is preferred to the form.*

Two examples will illustrate this:

(i) **Hire purchase transactions.** The legal form that the "buyer" of an asset under a hire purchase transaction, hires the asset until the final payment when the ownership is transferred to him. The substance of the transaction is that the asset is acquired by the "buyer" and that he has a loan to assist him in the purchase which he repays over a period of time together with interest.

(ii) **Goods sold subject to reservation of title.** ("Romalpa" transactions). The legal form of these transactions is that goods are sold with the agreement that ownership of the goods does not pass from the vendor to the buyer until payment is made. The substance of the transactions is that they are normal credit sales with the reservation of title clause in the contract for sale being of importance only if the buyer becomes insolvent.

SUMMARY

13. (a) Financial statements measure and demonstrate profit, capital and other ideas. They are drawn up using a number of accounting conventions.

(b) Conventions include:

- business entity
- money measurement
- historical cost
- going concern
- periodicity or continuity
- realisation
- matching

- accruals
- conservatism or prudence
- consistency
- materiality
- dual aspect
- substance over form

POINTS TO NOTE

14. (a) The entity convention is implicit in company accounting where the idea of a separate business is the legal reality.

(b) Separate businesses imply separate double entry systems. Remember that in questions which concern the takeover of one business by another, or an amalgamation of businesses, that you view the matter from the right perspective. Focus on one entity at a time.

(c) Money has been the accountant's method of measurement from time immemorial. However, its problems in times of inflation have led the accounting bodies to seek alternative systems of accounting. SSAP 16 is the latest, but not the last!

(d) The historical cost basis of producing financial statements arose out of the system of double entry bookkeeping, since in a double entry system, assets and expenses are recorded at their cost. It naturally followed that when periodic financial statements were developed, the available data from the double entry system should be used.

(e) The going concern convention has given rise to some discussion in recent years with the closure of large numbers of industrial plants in the UK. It should be noted that while most of an enterprise can be a going concern, a *part* can be measured using liquidation values.

(f) Most of the problems of accounting measurement arise out of the periodicity convention. The difficulty is deciding what revenues and expenses should relate to any particular year. In addition, the labour involved in apportioning expenditure and building up stocks and work-in-progress costs is very considerable. In future with computers able to summarise data on stocks, debtors and creditors at any time, more frequent financial statements will be produced.

(g) The realisation convention which prevents unrealised gains being taken into account, can distort the view given by accounts. The practice of revaluing properties is an exception to the convention and is widespread.

(h) The prudence convention in the past led to the true position being viewed as "at least as good" as that shown. This is in some way comforting, but not to a shareholder who has sold his shares at a price, which is a fraction of that which he could have obtained if the true position had been known.

(i) Where the prudence convention conflicts with other conventions, the prudence convention should prevail.

(j) You may have noticed that many of these conventions seem to overlap. They *do*, and some writers consider that, for example, the accruals convention encompasses what I have called the separate conventions of realisation, matching, accruals and historical cost.

Official recognition of Accounting Conventions:

Statement of Standard Accounting Practice No. 2

1. Going concern

2. Accruals   - matching
                   - accruals

3. Consistency

4. Prudence   - realisation
                   - prudence

Companies Act 1985

1. Going concern

2. Consistency

3. Prudence   - realisation
                   - prudence

4. Accruals

5. Materiality

SELF TESTING QUESTIONS

(a) What is the business entity convention and what is its justification, its drawbacks and consequences? (2).
(b) What is the money measurement convention? List its drawbacks and consequences. (3).
(c) What is the historical cost convention? What is its justification? List its drawbacks and consequences. (4).
(d) Define the going concern convention. What is its justification? List its drawbacks and consequences.
(e) What is the justification for the periodicity convention? What are its drawbacks and consequences? (6).
(f) What is the realisation convention? State the justifications for this convention. What are its drawbacks? (7).
(g) What is the matching convention? What are its drawbacks and consequences? (8).
(h) Define the accruals convention and list its drawbacks and consequences. (9).
(i) Define the prudence convention. List its drawbacks and consequences. (10).
(j) What is the consistency convention? (11).
(k) What is the relevance of materiality to accounting? (12a).
(l) Give two examples of "substance over form". (12c).
(m) What official recognition is given to specific accounting conventions? (14j).

Exercises (Answers begin on page 473)

1. Watkin is in business as a manufacturer of fishing tackle. He is consulting his daughter who is a certified accountancy level 1 student about certain items which puzzle him in connection with his accounts which are in preparation. These are:

    (a) I garage my car at a house down the road as I have no room at my own house. This costs me £5 a week. I use the car about 30% to getting to work, 30% on business and 40% for private motoring.

(b) Due to breakdowns in some machinery which has now been replaced, I have been unable to manufacture as many goods this year as last year. However, my order book is now three times what it was at the end of last year and stands at six months work.

(c) A supplier told me that he was considering cutting off credit to me as my business liabilities are large in comparison with my business assets.

(d) My bank manager tells me my return in capital has been very good but my capital employed includes the property at cost less depreciation which I bought in 1960 for £10,000.

(e) In the last years' accounts there was no figure shown for potential redundancy pay which I know amounts to over £3,000.

(f) I have some special fishing rods which I have had in stock at cost for many years at £100. I am negotiating now to sell these to a Japanese business acquaintance for £1,500. How will these appear in the accounts?

(g) I would like my accounts prepared more frequently than once a year as the way things are, I like to see how I am going month by month.

(h) I have sent 100 rods to an agent in Germany on a sale or return basis. I think he has sold some but I have not yet had any information from him.

(i) I know I had two cheques of £100 each from Harry for part of the factory I let off to him for the second half of the year and which he still rents. However, that covers four months only and in the draft accounts the accountant has put £300 as rent received. Is this right?

(j) I have agreed to buy 50 special rods from a supplier in France at 360 francs each. This was a very high price and now I will get only 9 francs to the pound. I only bought them to please an old customer and I have contracted to sell them to him at £35 and I have carriage of £100 in total on them.

(k) I depreciate my machinery on a straight line basis and this seems to put part of my machinery into a nil value on the balance sheet. Could I change to some other method of depreciation?

(l) Last years' accounts did not seem to include the petty cash in hand of £15 or the loan to my secretary of £70.

(m) The business is buying a van on hire purchase. The agreement says that the van belongs to Carp Van Finance plc until I have paid the last instalment.

(n) I have 2,000 metres of glass fibre tubing in my yard which will not be mine until I have paid GFT Limited, the suppliers, because it says so on their invoice.

Explain these matters to Watkin in terms of the accounting conventions and how they will be treated in the accounts. Comment on the usefulness of the accounts in the light of these matters.

Exercises without answers

2.   "If a business invests in shares, and the market value of the shares increases above cost then, until and unless the business sells them, no profit is made. If the business invests in stock for resale, and the market value of the stock falls below cost then the loss is recognised even though no sale has taken place.

"If a business undertakes an intensive advertising campaign which will probably result in increased sales (and profit) in succeeding years it will nevertheless usually write off the cost of the campaign in the year in which it is incurred."

Required:
Explain the reasoning behind the application of accounting principles in situations such as these and discuss the effect on the usefulness of accounting information in relation to users' needs.   (ACCA)

3.   You are interested in acquiring some shares in Varac PLC and have acquired the most recent set of the company's accounts for appraisal purposes.

The accounts are supported by explanatory notes, extracts of which are reproduced below:

'Turnover
The figure includes only the cash actually received for cash and credit sales less actual and estimated amounts of bad debts.'

'Cost of sales
Stocks
Opening stock is at FIFO cost. Following a policy review the directors have decided that a more accurate valuation would be obtained by a percentage addition for overheads; accordingly closing stock has been valued on this new basis. (See also Purchases below.)

Purchases
Purchases have been accounted for at their gross (catalogue) prices. Trade discounts received on purchases have been included in discounts received and have been credited to profit and loss account.

It is the company's policy to account only for those goods for which it has paid. Goods which the company has received before the year-end, but for which it has not paid, are excluded from purchases, from closing stocks and from creditors.'

'Depreciation
During the current year the level of business activity has been much lower than had been anticipated resulting in a greatly reduced amount of net profit. It has been decided, therefore, that it would be inadvisable to charge any depreciation to profit and loss account as to do so would convert the small net profit into a net loss.

Should this situation recur in the next financial year, the directors propose to transfer a suitable amount from the accumulated provision for depreciation to the credit of profit and loss account in order to maintain the ordinary dividend.'

Required:
Comment on the extent to which Varac PLC's accounts adhere to, or conflict with, recognised accounting principles and practices, so far as can be elicited from the above extracts. (ACCA)

4. An acquaintance of yours, H.Gee, has recently set up in business for the first time as a general dealer.

The majority of his sales will be on credit to trade buyers but he will sell some goods to the public for cash.

He is not sure at which point of the business cycle he can regard his cash and credit sales to have taken place.

After seeking guidance on this matter from his friends, he is thoroughly confused by the conflicting advice he has received. Samples of the advice he has been given include:

"The sale takes place when:

(1) "you have bought goods which you know you should be able to sell easily"
(2) "the customer places the order"
(3) "you deliver the goods to the customer"
(4) "you invoice the goods to the customer"
(5) "the customer pays for the goods"
(6) "the customer's cheque has been cleared by the bank".

He now asks you to clarify the position for him.

Required:
(a) Write notes for Gee, setting out, in as easily understood a manner as possible, the accounting conventions and principles which should generally be followed when recognising sales revenue.

(b) Examine each of the statements (1) to (6) above and advise Gee (stating your reasons) whether the method advocated is appropriate to the particular circumstances of his business. (ACCA)

5.   Consider the following situations

     (a) Maygog is a grocer. In 19-8, he withdrew £2,400 worth (at selling prices) from the shop for his own
          consumption. His average mark up on cost is 25%.

     (b) Soulerby has taken stock in his engineering business. He totals the stock at £43,000 at cost. Of that, £3,500
          consists of obsolete components. He cannot sell them and as they are bulky he finds that he has to agree with
          a scrap merchant to take them away with no payment to or from the scrap merchant.

     (c) Graham is selling his business. He is concerned that his balance sheet includes nothing for the £40,000 (at
          selling prices) sales contracts he had already signed before the year end and for delivery in the next year
          or so.

     (d) Lewis has 150 widgets in stock at his year end. He fits them as a major component in the machinery he makes
          and sells profitably. He bought them for £7 each but a price war has meant that he can now buy them at £4
          each.

     (e) Doda Limited has a factory it bought for £60,000 ten years ago. It has always depreciated the buildings part
          (cost £50,000) on the straight line method over 40 years. The company wish to show a better profit than that
          measured for 19-7 and so commission a valuation of the property which shows a value of land £30,000,
          buildings £140,000. The company decide to incorporate the revaluation in the books in 19-7.

     (f) Halibut Limited, fish dealers, are having a difficult time in their business. The Board are considering
          closing several branches and making several employees redundant.

     (g) Godfrey has started a business as an engineering consultant and his first year's accounts are being prepared.
          He is worried about his tax liability as he is short of cash. This is because he has difficulty in getting
          his clients to pay. They usually do pay after several months but often making reductions from his invoice. He
          suggests that the cash receipts be used to determine his profit.

     (h) The current assets section of Lambert's balance sheet shows:

Trade debtors	£140,000
Prepayments	1,725
Loans to staff	800
Deposits with suppliers	750
Hire purchase interest not accrued	347

     (i) Sawfit Limited do not wish to pay a large dividend as they wish to conserve cash because of a need to make
          extensive repairs to their old premises.

Required:
What accounting conventions are involved? How would these matters be entered in the financial statements? Be precise
and set out your argument logically.

6.   In preparing the accounts of your company, you are faced with a number of problems. These are summarised below:

     (a) The managing director wishes the company's good industrial relations to be reflected in the accounts.

     (b) The long-term future success of the company is extremely uncertain.

     (c) Although the sales have not yet actually taken place, some reliable customers of the company have placed
          several large orders that are likely to be extremely profitable.

     (d) One of the owners of the company has invested his drawings in some stocks and shares.

     (e) At the year end, an amount is outstanding for electricity that has been consumed during the accounting
          period.

     (f) All the fixed assets of the company would now cost a great deal more than they did when they were originally
          purchased.

(g) During the year, the company purchased £10 worth of pencils; these had all been issued from stock and were still in use at the end of the year.

(h) The company has had a poor trading year, and the owners believe that a more balanced result could be presented if a LIFO (last-in, first-out) stock valuation method was adopted, instead of the present FIFO (first-in, first-out) method.

(i) A debtor who owes a large amount to the company is rumoured to be going into liquidation.

(j) The company owns some shares in a quoted company which the accountant thinks are worthless.

Required:

(i) State which accounting rule the accountant should follow in dealing with each of the above problems.

(ii) Explain briefly what each rule means.

(*AAT*)

7.   It would be possible to recognise revenue by bringing it, as such, within the compass of a periodic income statement at a variety of points in the typical transaction history.

Discuss this quotation from "Introduction to the theory and context of accounting" by Roy Sidebotham.   (*CIMA*)

8.   You are required to say briefly how you would deal with each of the following when preparing a company's profit and loss account and balance sheet:

(a) The company is defending in the court an action for damages due to alleged breach of contract.

(b) The goods received records show that various items, properly ordered, have been received in the financial year, but no invoice has yet been received.

(c) The company sells articles which it guarantees to repair, free of charge, during the six months from the date of sale. A large number of such articles has been sold during the last six months.

(d) The company has recently bought an expensive new machine of a kind it has not used before, and you have to establish the straight-line percentage of cost rate of depreciation to use. Of the two senior engineers employed by the company. Mr Smith says that he thinks its maximum life cannot exceed eight years at the most. Mr Jones, however, thinks this far too pessimistic an estimate, and believes that, with proper repairs and maintenance, its life could be as long as twelve years.

(e) At the year-end physical stocktaking of raw materials, each item was valued at its purchase price and also at its net realisable (saleable) value. Separate totals have been obtained for each basis of valuation.

How should the stock of raw materials be valued?

(*CIMA*)

9.   The legal requirement that limited companies must publish annual profit and loss accounts and balance sheets is the cause of many of the problems that beset financial accountants.

Discuss the problems of year-end cut-off points.

(*CIMA*)

Forecast Financial Statements

The next part of the manual – the chapter on forecast financial statements – describes the way in which accounting statements can be drawn up in forecast form, to be used in planning the future. This subject is very frequent in examinations.

57. Forecast Financial Statements

INTRODUCTION

1. The majority of this manual is concerned with the measurement of profit and capital in historical terms. For example, the accounts for the year ending 31st December 19-4 are prepared in 19-5.

2. Increasingly, in recent years, businesses are *forecasting* or *planning* their profit and loss accounts and balance sheets for future periods. The method of this approach is:

(a) Proposed policies for action are formulated.

(b) An expected future profit and loss account and balance sheet is prepared based on the proposed policies.

(c) If the projections seem unsatisfactory, policies can be changed and (a) and (b) are repeated with different policies.

The loop a - c is repeated until satisfactory plans have been formulated.

3. Such forecasting is relatively simple with computer software such as visicalc and its competitors. Examiners are increasingly setting questions of this type in financial accounting papers. To answer them, no new knowledge is required, but some practice is essential.

AN EXAMPLE:

4. Kallagan Ltd. trades in hot air balloons and has just received the accountant's report on its first year of operation:

Trading and profit and loss account for year ended 31st March 19-5

	£	£		£	£
Opening stock	40,000		Sales - cash	50,000	
Purchases	180,000		Sales - credit	150,000	200,000
	220,000				
Less Closing stock	80,000				
		140,000			
Gross profit c/d		60,000			
		200,000			200,000
Administration expenses	20,000		Gross profit b/d		60,000
Selling and distribution exps	9,000				
Depreciation	21,000				
Net profit before tax c/d	10,000				
	60,000				60,000
Tax at 50%	5,000		Net profit before tax b/d		10,000
Net profit after tax c/d	5,000				
	10,000				10,000

Balance sheet as at 31st March 19-5

	Cost £	Depr'n £	Net £
Fixed assets	140,000	21,000	119,000
Current assets:			
Stock		80,000	
Debtors		50,000	
		130,000	
Less Trade creditors		45,000	
Taxation		5,000	
Overdraft		4,000	
		54,000	
			76,000
			195,000
Financed by:			
Share capital (50p shares)			190,000
Net profit			5,000
			195,000

The Chairman of Kallagan Ltd., Arthur Gillscar, and his board have produced the following guidelines for 19-5/-6.

(a) Double turnover.
(b) Expect tax to remain at 50%.
(c) Increase gross profit to sales margin by one fifth.
(d) Increase administration costs by £10,000.
(e) Reduce stock by 25% at the end of the year.
(f) Maintain the ratio of cash:credit sales.
(g) Maintain the depreciation policy at 10% straight line at its present level.
(h) No fixed assets are to be bought or sold.
(i) Reduce the average collection period by one month.
(j) Take three months to pay creditors.
(k) Increase selling and distribution costs by 30% and £20,000 for advertising.
(l) Declare a dividend of 5p a share.

You are asked to prepare budgeted accounts for 19-5/-6 incorporating the above decisions.

ANSWER:

Kallagan Ltd.

Budgeted trading and profit and loss account for the year ending 31st March 19-6   a

	£	£	
Sales		400,000	b
Less Cost of sales:			
Opening stock	80,000		
Purchases	236,000		f
	316,000		
Closing stock	60,000	256,000	e, d
Gross profit		144,000	c
Administration expenses	30,000		g
Selling and distribution expenses	31,700		h
Depreciation	21,000	82,700	i
Net profit before tax		61,300	
Taxation at 50%		30,650	j
Net profit after tax		30,650	
Proposed dividend		19,000	k
Retained profit for the year		11,650	

Kallagan Ltd.

Forecast balance sheet as at 31st March 19–6

	Cost £	Depr'n £	Net £
Fixed assets	140,000	42,000	98,000
Current assets			
Stock		60,000	
Debtors		75,000	l
Cash at bank		?	n
		217,300	
Current liabilities			
Creditors		59,000	m
Dividend		19,000	
Taxation		30,650	
		108,650	
			108,650
			206,650
Financed by:			
Share capital			190,000
Retained profits			16,650
			206,650

a. Forecast or budgeted statements must be so labelled.

b. Gross profit margin in 19-4/-5 was $\frac{60}{200}$ x 100 = 30%.

Gross profit margin in 19-5/-6 will be 30% + 1/5 = 36%.

Gross profit in 19-5/-6 will be 36% x 400,000 = £144,000

d. Cost of sales is computed by deducting gross profit from sales.
e. Closing stock is 25% less than last year.
f. Purchases are obtained by deduction.
g. Administration costs are £10,000 more than last year.
h. Selling expenses are 130% x £9,000 + £20,000.
i. Depreciation is 10% of *cost* of fixed assets.
j. Tax is 50% of net profit.
k. Dividend is 5p a share on 380,000 shares.
l. Collection period in 19-4/-5 was $\frac{50,000}{150,000}$ x 12 = 4 months

Collection period in 19-5/-6 will be 3 months.
Debtors will be $\frac{3}{12}$ x 300,000 = £75,000.

m. Creditors will be $\frac{3}{12}$ x 236,000 = £59,000.
n. The cash at bank is the balancing figure on this balance sheet. You will calculate it as £82,300.

SUMMARY

5. (a) The majority of accounting paper questions are concerned with the preparation of historical accounts.

(b) Increasingly, the same techniques used to prepare historical accounts can be used to prepare forecast or budgeted financial statements.

(c) The effect of different trading and other policies can be tried out by determining the resulting trading and profit and loss accounts and balance sheets.

POINTS TO NOTE

6. (a) Budgeting properly belongs to a work on management accounting. However, the preparation of projected financial statements and cash flow forecasts is increasingly common in financial accounting papers. The techniques used are largely those of financial accounting.

   (b) The profit and loss account and balance sheet can be thought of as models of the firm. Trying out possible trading and other policies using these models is a fast growing technique, now that appropriate computer software is available.

   (c) In working questions involving forecasts in examinations, remember:

      (i) There are no short cuts - work everything out.
      (ii) *Focus on one thing at a time.*
      (iii) Prepare and submit good workings.
      (iv) Ensure that the requirements of the question have been met.

SELF TESTING QUESTIONS

   (a) How can financial accounting be used for planning? (2).

Exercise (Answer on page 474)

1. The Profit and Loss Account for 19-7 of Bangle Limited, a wholesaler of novelty goods with also a retail outlet, is:

	£			£
Administration	44,000	Sales – credit		140,000
Selling and distribution	8,000	Sales – cash		100,000
Depreciation	8,000			240,000
Advertising	6,000	Opening stock	31,000	
Directors' remuneration	20,000	Purchases	155,000	
Net profit	10,000		186,000	
		Closing stock	42,000	144,000
	96,000			96,000

A dividend of 20p a share will be paid.

The Balance Sheet shows:

	£			£
Share capital (10p)	2,000	Fixed Assets		
Reserves	23,000	Cost		40,000
Loan from a director	20,000	Depreciation		24,000
Creditors	26,000			16,000
Overdraft	18,000	Stock	42,000	
Dividend	4,000	Debtors	35,000	77,000
	93,000			93,000

The loan is interest free.

In 19-8 plans are to:

1. Increase cash sales by 40% by volume but prices will be reduced by 5%. Advertising will increase by £5,000 to achieve the cash sales and to achieve an increase in credit sales of 15% at 19-7 prices.
2. Reduce administration costs by 10%.
3. Allow selling and distribution costs to rise by 25%.
4. Increase directors' remuneration by 10%.
5. Pay £15,000 off the loan.
6. Reduce stock by 10%.
7. Campaign to reduce debtors to 2½ months.
8. Maintain the creditors credit payment period.
9. Spend £10,000 on new fixed assets. Depreciation is 20% straight line. No assets have been completely written off.
10. Pay a dividend of 25p a share.

Prepare forecast accounts.

Exercises without answers

2.   For a number of years Martin Smith has been employed as the works' manager of a company which manufactures cardboard cartons.

He has now decided to leave the company and to set up a similar business of his own on 1 January 1986 but, before taking this step he wants to see what his financial results are likely to be for his first year of operations.

In order to do this, he has obtained certain "average industry" ratios from his trade association, the Cardboard Carton Manufacturers' Association (CCMA), which he wants to use as his norm for predicting the first year's results.

At this stage he consults you, asks for your professional assistance and supplies the following information:

	CCMA statistics 1984 (based on year-end figures)
Sales/Net assets employed	2.8 times
Gross profit/Sales	28.0%
Net profit/Sales	10.0%
Fixed assets/Working capital	1.5:1
Current assets/Current liabilities	2.25:1
Debtors collection period	36.5 days
Creditors payment period	58.4 days

He informs you that he is able to contribute £40,000 as capital and has been promised a long term loan of £6,000 from a relative.

Initially, he intends to acquire a stock of materials at a cost of £20,000 but his (simple) average stock for the first year will be £18,500. Purchases of materials for the year, excluding the initial purchase of stock, £20,000, will be £97,800. All purchases and sales will be on credit.

Sundry accruals at 31 December 1986 are estimated at £350 and bank and cash balances at £5,000.

He proposes to withdraw £10,000 during the year for living expenses.

Required:
Prepare, in as much detail as can be elicited from the information supplied, a forecast trading and profit and loss account for Martin Smith's proposed business for the year ended 31 December 1986, and a forecast balance sheet at that date.

All figures should be stated to the nearest £10.

Marks will be awarded for workings which must be shown.   (ACCA)

3.   The balance sheet of Dinah Limited wholesaler of explosives, at 31.12.-7: (in £000)

Share capital - 10p shares	30	Fixed assets	
Profit & Loss	127	Cost	246
Creditors	63	Depreciation	134
			112
Overdraft	34	Stock	78
Corporation Tax	7	Debtors	81
Dividend	10		
	271		271

Given that in 19-8:

1.   Turnover is expected to be £540,000 and overheads other than depreciation £70,000.
2.   Gross profit to sales ratio is 30%.
3.   Stock will be 3 months purchases.
4.   Debtors will be 2 months sales.
5.   Creditors will be 2 months purchases.
6.   Fixed assets (cost £30,000, wdv at 31.12.-7 £12,000) will be sold for £10,000 and new fixed assets purchased for £60,000. Depreciation is 25% reducing balance.
7.   A new issue of 100,000 shares will be made at 50p each.

8. Corporation tax will be 30% of net profit.
9. A dividend of 5p a share is proposed. The new shares do not rank for dividend from the 19-8 profits.

Prepare for the year ending 31 December 19-8:

(a) Forecast trading and profit and loss account.
(b) Forecast balance sheet.
(c) Forecast funds flow statement.

4. G. Toop proposes to commence business on the 1st January 1982.

(a) On the 1st January he will pay the sum of £20,000 into the business bank account.

(b) He will purchase the following assets - motor vehicles £3,200; plant and machinery £4,000 and premises £10,000 on that date.

(c) Purchases for goods will be on credit. £4,000 of goods bought on the 1st January, will be paid for in February. Other purchases will be rest of January £6,400, February, March, April, May and June £8,000 each month. Other than the £4,000 worth bought in January, all the other purchases will be paid for two months after purchase.

(d) All goods are sold on credit. January £8,000, and £10,000 for each succeeding month. Debtors to settle their accounts three months from month of purchase.

(e) Value of stock in trade at the end of June 1982 - £4,000.

(f) Cost of wages and salaries £300 per month payable at the end of each month.

(g) Sundry expenses £100 each month, payable in the month following that in which they were incurred.

(h) It is expected that Toop will receive a sum of £11,000 in April, which will be paid into the business bank account.

(i) The cost of insurance for one year will be £240 which is payable on the 30th June.

(j) Rates – for the period to 31st March 1982, paid on the 28th February 1982. For the 12 months ended 31st March 1983, paid on 31st July 1982. Rates are a fixed amount of £720 per annum.

(k) Monthly drawings £160 per month.

(l) Depreciation is to be charged at the rate of 20% per annum on motor vehicles and 10% on plant and machinery.

(m) Cash at 30th June 1982 will be £3,720.

Required:
Prepare budgeted final accounts for the six months ended 30th June 1982 and a balance sheet at that date.

(RSA)

5. J. Lester tells you of his plans to start a business on 1st January 1983. They can be summarised as follows:

(a) He is to open a bank account with £8,000 of his own money and a loan of £2,000 from a friend.

(b) J. Lester's drawings will be £400 per month cash plus goods from stock at a cost of £80 per month.

(c) Purchases will be on credit, and will be £3,000 per month for the first 3 months and £3,300 per month after that.

(d) It is expected that sales value will be equal each month. Half on credit and half will be cash sales.

Goods will be sold at a uniform profit of 40% on cost.

It is expected that stock on 30th June 1983 will be £3,420.

(e) Expenses will all be paid for by cash £200 per month.

(f) A motor vehicle will be bought by cheque on 1st January for £4,800. Depreciation at the rate of 20% per annum is to be brought into account.

(g) Debtors will pay their accounts two months after they have bought the goods. Creditors will be paid three months after the goods have been bought.

Required:
Draw up Lester's budgeted trading and profit and loss account for the 6 months ended 30th June 1983 and a balance sheet as at 30th June 1983.

Show all of your workings.   (RSA)

6   (a) use Supercalc or similar to prepare trading and profit and loss accounts and balance sheets for the first three years of Humbug's business given that:

    (i)   Sales will be £10,000 in the first year and grow at 15% compound.
    (ii)   Gross profit will be 25% of sales.
    (iii) Debtors at year end will be 2 months of annual sales.
    (iv)   Stock at year ends will be 3 months of annual cost of sales.
    (v)   Creditors will be 1.5 months of purchases.
    (vi)   Overheads (excluding depreciation) will be £6,000 and grow at 10% compound a year.
    (vii) Fixed assets will cost £30,000 at the beginning of the first year.
    (viii) Depreciation will be 25% reducing balance.
    (ix)   Drawings will be £10,000 a year.
    (x)   Initial capital will be £12,000.

    (b) Repeat the exercise as: (each is separate):

    (i)   Sales in the first year of £150,000.
    (ii)   Sales growth at 4% compound.
    (iii) Debtors at 3 months.
    (iv)   Creditors at 1 month.
    (v)   Stocks at 4 months.

MORE ADVANCED MATTERS

For the final two chapters in the manual, we cover two areas of a more advanced nature. The first is the subject of accounting for changing price levels. One of the basic assumptions of traditional accounting is that price levels are constant - there is no inflation. We are all aware that inflation does occur and accountants have tried to develop an accounting response to inflation. The second area is that of accounting regulation. You have already met the Companies Act and we have mentioned SSAPs in passing.

58. Accounting for Changing Price Levels

INTRODUCTION

1. Traditional accounting measures profit by comparing sales with cost of sales and overhead expenses measured at their historical cost. This method is objective and, in times of relatively stable price levels, works well. However, in recent years, when rises in the general level of prices of up to 20% a year have been experienced, the profession has recognised the need for some amendments to historical cost accounting.

2. The major problem is that if *dividends* and *taxation* are based upon profits measured by sales less cost of sales and expenses measured by their historical costs, then there is a possibility that *operating assets will not be maintained* and *capital will be reduced*. Two examples will illustrate this:

		£
(a)	A. Ltd. maintains a stock of ten widgets cost £1 each	10
	They sell these for £1.50 each	15
	and make a profit in historical cost terms of	5
	This permits a dividend (ignore tax) of	£5
	But, prices are rising and A. Ltd. must replace the widgets at £1.20 each	12

If the historical cost profit is distributed in full, it will not be possible to replace the ten widgets at £1.20 each since the operating capital is only £10. To stay in the same position of stocking ten widgets, capital must increase by £2.

A. Ltd.   **Cash Book**

	£		£
Sales receipts	15	Dividends	5
		8⅓ widgets at £1.20	10
	15		15

(b) B. Ltd. operate an ice cream van.
This cost £4,000 in 19-0 and will last four years.

		£	£
Each year -	Sales		10,000
	Cost of sales	3,000	
	Depreciation	1,000	4,000
	Historical cost profit		6,000

If this profit is distributed in full as dividend, then resources available to replace the van will be £4,000 but if by 19-4 the replacement cost is £7,000. Capital has been maintained in money terms at £4,000 but it needs to be £7,000 to be in the same real position.

B. Ltd.   **Cash Book** for four years

	£		£
Sales receipts	40,000	Cost of sale	12,000
		Dividends	24,000
		Available for new van	4,000
	40,000		40,000

BENEFITS OF HISTORICAL COST ACCOUNTING

3.   There are good reasons why accounting is done on an historical cost basis. Some of these are:

(i)   Transactions are entered in the accounting records as they occur at the contractual amounts involved. For example, the purchase of a car for £9,000 is entered in the books in the car account £9,000 and to supplier creditor's account as the same amount. It is difficult to imagine any amount other than £9,000 being used.

(ii)   The financial statements are a summary of the bookkeeping entries and consequently historical cost is the only basis available.

(iii)   Historical cost is objective and verifiable. Any other basis would be an estimate and many estimates are possible. Accountants and other users of financial statements intuitively prefer an objective and verifiable basis.

(iv)   Financial statements began as reports of historical events to the owners of the business. They still are this kind of report but increasingly users of all kinds are using them as a basis of decision making.

(v)   No acceptable alternative to historical cost accounting has yet been identified despite many high powered attempts to find one.

(vi)   It has always been so done and users of accounts understand the ideas involved. This is a dubious fact.

(vii)   Long experience has refined the system. This is also rather a doubtful proposition.

LIMITATIONS OF HISTORICAL COST ACCOUNTING

4.   Some of the consequences of using historical costing accounting can be criticised. These include:

(i)   Fixed assets are included in the balance sheet at historical cost values which bear no relation to current values. For example, property at cost in 1968 – £25,000 may now have a resale value of £275,000. The disparity in value is compounded by depreciating buildings.

(ii)   Stock valued at cost £30,000 may cost £40,000 to replace, yet historical cost is always used.

(iii)   The sum of assets is a sum of mixed values, 1970 pounds, 1987 pounds etc. yet we all know 1987 pounds were worth a fraction of the 1970 pounds.

(iv)   The capital (or capital and reserves of a company) purports to show the net assets employed in a business yet this is meaningless if historical cost values are used.

(v)   On the trading and profit and loss account sales revenue is matched with cost of goods sold and other expenses. Sales are at recent prices but some of the inputs can be at earlier input prices. The difference may of course be small except in very inflationary times.

(vi)   In particular, depreciation is based on a very old value and does not represent the true real value of the resources consumed. To this extent profit may be much overstated.

(vii)   Holding gains are ignored. Thus inflation increases the money value of the assets but this is ignored in income statements.

(viii)   The sum repayable on long term loans and debenture may be much reduced in *real* terms. This is not reflected in historical cost accounts.

(ix)   Dividends and drawings are often based on historical cost profits. If these are distorted so that profit is for example overstated by depreciation on a historical cost basis, then dividend may be less than historical cost profit but may *exceed* real profits. Thus dividends may be paid unwittingly out of capital and *real* capital may not be maintained.

(x)   Dividend cover calculations may be misleading.

(xi) Return on capital employed calculations may be misleading as:

- return is distorted by depreciation using historical cost.
- capital employed does not reflect the real value of assets.

(xii) Decision making based on out of date values will be sub-optimal. As examples:

- J does not know whether to close or enlarge his branch in Tipton.

- P does not know if selling his product at prices based on costings done on the historical costs in inputs producing the product is reasonable.

SOLUTIONS TO THE PROBLEMS OF HISTORICAL COST ACCOUNTING

5. Solutions to the problems of historical costing that have been proposed include:

(a) *Revaluation of fixed assets*
When fixed assets, particularly land and buildings, have potential resale values much above cost based carrying values, then it is possible to revalue the asset. This involves obtaining professional revaluation which is of course an *estimate*. After the revaluation, the balance sheet will show a more realistic value and as the depreciation change will be on the raised value, profits will more accurately reflect resources used.

This approach has been common for many years and is an accepted part of the accounting scene. Some companies call attention to the current value of property by means of a note attached to the accounts instead of incorporating the revaluation in the balance sheet.

(b) *Current Purchasing Power Accounting (CPP)*
This is a complete system for providing financial statements. It works by converting the historical figures to current purchasing power by an appropriate price index. A general index (*e.g.* the retail price index RPI) was considered appropriate.

Advantages of CPP are:

-   It reflects the general increase in the prices of goods and services.

-   Shareholders spend profit and the amount they can buy depends on inflation and therefore the RPI is appropriate.

Disadvantages are:

-   Inflation is not general in nature and prices of different goods, services and assets change at different rates and so a general index is misleading.

-   the RPI is to do with a family budget and has little to do with assets or consumption of goods and services of large companies.

CPP was in vogue in the 1970's.

(c) *Current Cost Accounting (CCA)*
This is also a complete system for preparing financial statements. The CCA system requires the use of specific indices and other ideas for measuring current value so that the adjustment for inflation closely relates to the assets and costs concerned.

6. The basic concepts are:

Profit and Loss Account
The current cost profit is derived by taking the historical cost trading profit and adjusting it by charging an extra item against income. The extra item is the difference between *value to the business* of the assets consumed in generating the income and the historical acquisition costs. *Value to the business* is an elusive term, but is generally expressed by the *replacement costs* of the assets consumed. Four adjustments are made in two stages.

Stage I
(i)   A *depreciation adjustment* being the difference between the proportion of their value to the business (at replacement prices) of the fixed assets consumed in the year instead of depreciation calculated on the historical cost basis.

(ii)   A cost of sales adjustment (COSA) being the difference between the value to the business and historical cost of *stock* consumed in the period.

(iii) A monetary working capital adjustment (MWCA) to reflect the additional working capital (mainly debtors) required in times of rising prices. Additional resources are needed to finance any increase in debtors caused purely by inflation, less any part financed by increasing creditors.

Stage II
The gearing adjustment
When part of the net operating assets is financed by borrowing, a proportional reduction is made to the Stage I adjustments to reflect the gain made by the company from borrowing which will be repaid at some future date, in depreciated currency.

Balance Sheet
The balance sheet should contain:

(a)   Fixed assets and stocks at their value to the business. This usually means at depreciated *replacement* cost.
(b)   Other current assets, and all liabi-lities, at historical cost.
(c)   Shareholders interests divided into:

-    Share capital.
-    Current cost reserve – the adjustments made to profit to arrive at current cost profit and revaluation reserve.
-    Other reserves.

The *advantages* of CCA are:

-    specific indices are used
-    the system is very sophisticated at a detailed level.

The *disadvantages* are:

-    the system is expensive to apply.
-    the ideas are not easy to grasp.

SUMMARY
7. (a)   In times of changing price levels, historical cost accounting can be misleading. In particular, in times of inflation, profits measured in historical cost terms are only sufficient to maintain operating assets in money terms and not to preserve and maintain the level they should be maintained at in real terms.

(b)   Historical cost accounting has many justifications including a natural progression from double entry bookkeeping, objectivity, a long history and it is generally well understood.

(c)   However, it has some limitations including assets at values which bear no relation to current values, profits based on inputs of (low) historical costs, dividends and drawings paid out of capital, capital which is not maintained at real values, ignoring of holding gains, misleading calculations of dividend cover and return on capital employed and sub-optimal decision making.

(d)   Proposed solutions include revaluation of fixed assets, current purchasing power (CPP) and current cost accounting (CCA).

POINTS TO NOTE
8. (a)   Inflation has been with us for a long time and most users of accounts have tended to make *mental adjustments* to the figures in historical cost accounts to allow for it. This subjective approach can lend to different users getting a different view from a given set of accounts.

(b)   CCA and CPP accounts were generally presented as *supplementary* accounts and published in addition to the historical cost accounts. In general accounts showed profits considerably below histo-rical cost profits.

(c)   Historical cost accounts are derived from the double entry system and thus an historical cost system can be described as *transaction* driven.

(d)   CCA was all the rage in the early 1980's but fell into the doldrums when inflation became relatively small and the subject has now been almost abandoned as a practical matter. However, if inflation returns then the subject will be revived.

SELF TESTING QUESTIONS

(a)   *Why do firms using historical cost accounting not maintain operating assets and find their capital is reduced? (2).*

(b)   *List the benefits of historical cost accounting. (3).*

(c)   *List the limitations of historical cost accounting. (4).*

(d)   *What are holding gains? (4).*

(e)   *List three suggested solutions to the problems of historical cost accounting. (5).*

(f)   *What will the effect on depreciation be when assets are revalued? (5).*

(g)   *What are the advantages of CPP? (5).*

(h)   *What is the basic principle of CPP? (5).*

(i)   *What are the disadvantages of CPP?*

(j)   *What are the basic concepts of CCA? (6).*

(k)   *List the four adjustments required by CCA. (6).*

(l)   *What are the advantages and disadvantages of CCA? (6).*

(m)   *What are supplementary accounts? (8).*

(n)   *Why is historical cost accounting said to be transaction driven? (8).*

Exercises without answers

1.   *Consider the following statements:*

(a)   *There is no need to make adjustments to historical cost accounts as users always make mental adjustments.*

(b)   *In appraising the performance of an enterprise over a period of years valid comparisons cannot be made.*

(c)   *I fear we are paying part of the dividend out of capital.*

(d)   *We always seem to be short of working capital.*

(e)   *I like historical cost accounts. They are so objective and verifiable.*

(f)   *We have just sold our four year old Jaguar at the same price we paid for it and made a large profit over original cost on the piece of surplus land.*

(g)   *We can almost pay off our old debenture loans out of petty cash.*

(h)   *We seem to be doing well and yet old Fidget's business makes twice our rate of return on capital employed.*

(i)   *The branch factory at Wodensbury is making a reasonable profit but we don't really know the value of resources tied up in it.*

(j)   *There is no such thing as general inflation, only price changes in specific products.*

(k)   *I just feel that everything seems to be more expensive.*

(l)   *I find historical cost accounts hard to understand and CCA are even harder.*

59. Regulatory Framework of Accounting

INTRODUCTION

1.   Double entry bookkeeping developed by experimentation in Renaissance Italy. It was not invented. It was not a requirement of the law. It just grew because business people needed it. In the nineteenth century, the Balance Sheet and, later, the profit and loss account were also developed because the business and investment communities needed them. Again, there was no legal or other requirement for the form and content of financial statements, just a need which accountants met by experimenting and discovering new methods.

2.   In the nineteenth century, the need for a balance sheet and profit and loss account to be prepared for shareholders of large companies was recognised and a legal requirement for these financial statements was laid down first in the Companies Act. The law required financial statements but did not lay down the form or content.

3.   In the twentieth century, a series of Companies Acts began to specify the *content* of financial statements and finally the 1981 Companies Act also specified the *form* of financial statements.

4.   In recent years, there has been a great deal of regulation of accounting in the following areas:

   (a)   The form of financial statements.
   (b)   The content of financial statements.
   (c)   The extent of disclosure of financial data.
   (d)   The accounting principles to be followed.

5.   The regulation has come from primarily:

   -   The Companies Acts
   -   The professional accounting bodies in the form of Statements of Standard Accounting Practice (SSAPs)

   and secondarily:

   -   The Stock Exchange
   -   International accounting standards
   -   The European Economic Community

THE NEED FOR REGULATION

6.   The need for some form of financial statements summarising the performance and position of an enterprise has been covered in Chapters 1 and 3 of this manual. In summary this need is to enable actual and potential owners, managers, creditors, tax authorities, employers and other contact groups to make informed judgements on the past performance and actual position of an enterprise and to take decisions based on those judgements.

7.   However, there is a tendency in those reporting (*e.g.* managers to owners, directors to shareholders) to:

   -   present financial statements in a form which they (and not the recipients) find convenient.
   -   give only the minimum information which will be acceptable, or rather less than that.
   -   fail to disclose data they do not wish known (*e.g.* their own remuneration).
   -   use a variety of accounting principles without disclosing which have been used.

8.   As a consequence, various regulatory bodies began to dictate the form, content, extent of disclosure and principles to be used of accounts. This process is fairly well advanced now but will continue for many years.

COMPANIES ACTS REQUIREMENTS

9.   Since the middle of the nineteenth century there has been a steady development in the regulation of accounting by companies in the form of successive Companies Acts. The most recent was very extensive changes in the Companies Act 1981.

10.   This Act is now codified with several others in the Companies Act 1985.

11.   The Companies Acts accounting requirements cover the following ground:

   (a)   Accounting records to be kept.
   (b)   Statutory books to be kept.
   (c)   Annual accounts to be produced.

(d) The use of required formats.
(e) The use of specified accounting principles.
(f) An overriding requirement for the accounts to give a true and fair view.
(g) The giving of particular detailed information about each item in the accounts.

(a) and (b) have been described in the chapters on company accounting. (c) and (d) are outlined below. (e) is discussed in more detail below.

(f) is a very difficult idea which is generally discussed in auditing texts. Briefly, true means Accounts must be simply true. For example, if the Balance Sheet shows Land at Cost £2 million, that must be a true statement. The reality may be more complicated. Should legal charges be included for example? Fair is altogether harder. Does straight line depreciation fairly spread the cost of an asset over the years of its useful life or would reducing balance method do the job more fairly?

12. The *financial statements* required are:

(a) A profit and loss account for each accounting reference period.
(b) A balance sheet as at the date to which any profit and loss accounting is made up.
(c) Notes attached to and forming part of the financial statements.
(d) Where a company does not trade for profit, an income and expenditure account.

Note that a funds flow statement is not required under the Companies Act.

13. The *form* of the financial statements is also prescribed:

(a) The balance sheet must be in one of two formats (*i.e.* vertical or horizontal) shown in schedule 4 of CA 1985.
(b) The profit and loss account should follow one of the four formats (two vertical and two similar horizontal) shown in schedule 4 CA 1985.
(c) Corresponding amounts for the previous year shall also be shown for all items.
(d) Set off is not permitted (*e.g.* bank accounts in credit against overdrafts).
(d) Departure from a Format is only permitted if preservation of the true and fair view requires it.
(e) Once selected, a Format should be used for all subsequent years.

ACCOUNTING PRINCIPLES

14. The following principles should be adopted:

(a) The company shall be presumed to be carrying on business as a *going concern*.

(b) Accounting policies shall be applied *consistently* from one financial year to the next.

(c) The amount of any item shall be determined on a *prudent* basis.

(d) All income and charges relating to the financial year to which the accounts relate shall be taken into account without regard to the date of receipt or payment - the *accruals* convention.

(e) In determining the aggregate amount of any item, the amount of each individual asset or liability that falls to be taken into account shall be determined separately.

- For example, the concept of lower of cost and net realisable value must be applied to individual items of stock and not to stock as a whole.

(f) These rules can be departed from if:

(i) There are good reasons for doing so.
(ii) The reasons and effects are explained in the notes.

An example of departure may be because the company is not a going concern.

Thus the Act prescribes that accounts *must* conform to the going concern convention, the prudence convention, the consistency convention, and the accruals convention.

The required prudence convention specifies:

- Only profits realised at the balance sheet date shall be included in the profit and loss account. This is really the realisation convention.

- all liabilities and losses which have arisen or are likely to arise in respect of the financial year to which the accounts relate or a previous financial year shall be taken into account, including those which only become apparent between the balance sheet date and the date on which the Accounts are signed by the Board of Directors.

This last statement is a very clear exposition of the prudence convention.

Item (e) is a requirement which has no particular name in accounting literature. Shall we call it the individuality convention?

STATEMENTS OF STANDARD ACCOUNTING PRACTICE

15. (a) Accounting measurement and financial reporting have developed over the centuries to meet the needs of businessmen and investors without the guidance of any body of theory. The only regulation has been the Companies Acts but these have tended to regulate the degree of disclosure rather than the principles used.

(b) Such theory as exists in accounting is more an observation of what accountants actually do than a statement of some abstract accounting principles.

(c) Because accounting and reporting developed without any regulation or direction, different principles and methods were found in practice to deal with similar types of transaction (for example, think of depreciation). For this reason, the results and financial position of a company could not be compared with those of another similar company if different accounting principles were used.

(d) In an attempt to impose some uniformity on accounting practice, the professional bodies set up a joint committee – the Accounting Standards Committee and from 1971 onwards the professional bodies have approved a number of Statements of Standard Accounting Practice (SSAPs) prepared by this committee.

(e) Some of the SSAPs are highly technical. Some, however, are relevant to students at Foundation level and the provisions of these have been incorporated into this manual.

SSAPs ISSUED

16. At the time of writing, the following SSAPs are in issue:

1. Accounting for associated companies.
2. Disclosure of accounting policies.
3. Earnings per share.
4. The accounting treatment of government grants.
5. Accounting for value added tax.
6. Extraordinary items and prior year adjustments.
7. Withdrawn.
8. The treatment of taxation under the imputation system in the accounts of companies.
9. Stocks and work-in-progress.
10. Statements of source and application of funds.
11. Withdrawn.
12. Accounting for depreciation.
13. Accounting for research and development.
14. Group accounts.
15. Accounting for deferred taxation.
16. Current cost accounting - withdrawn.
17. Accounting for post balance sheet events.
18. Accounting for contingencies.
19. Accounting for investment properties.
20. Foreign currency translation.
21. Accounting for leases and hire purchase contracts.
22. Accounting for goodwill.
23. Accounting for acquisitions and mergers.
24. Accounting for pension costs.

SSAP 2 – DISCLOSURE OF ACCOUNTING POLICIES

17. The standard distinguishes three ideas:

- Fundamental accounting principles.
- Accounting bases.
- Accounting policies.

18. **Fundamental accounting principles** are defined as the broad basic assumptions which underlie the periodic financial accounts of business enterprises. In this manual we have referred to them as the accounting conventions. SSAP 2 mentions only four:

(a) The "going concern" concept: the enterprise will continue in operational existence for the foreseeable future. This means in particular that the profit and loss account and balance sheet assume no intention or necessity to liquidate or curtail significantly the scale of operation.

(b) The "accruals" concept: revenue and costs are accrued (that is, recognised as they are earned or incurred, not as money is received or paid), matched with one another so far as their relationship can be established or justifiably assumed, and dealt with in the profit and loss account of the period to which they relate; provided that where the accruals concept is inconsistent with he "prudence" concept (paragraph (d) below), the latter prevails. Revenue and profits dealt with in the profit and loss account are matched with associated costs and expenses by including in the same account the costs incurred in earning them (so far as these are material and identifiable).

(c) The "consistency" concept: there is consistency of accounting treatment of like items within each accounting period and from one period to the next.

(d) The concept of "prudence": revenue and profits are not anticipated, but are recognised by inclusion in the profit and loss account only when realised in the form either of cash or of other assets the ultimate cash realisation of which can be assessed with reasonable certainty; provision is made for all known liabilities (expenses and losses) whether the amount of these is known with certainty or is a best estimate in the light of the information available. Note that "accruals" in SSAP 2 covers both the accruals convention and the matching convention discussed in this manual.

19. SSAP 2 makes the point that since the four fundamental accounting principles underlie all financial statements, there is no need to state them specifically in each set of accounts. However, if accounts are prepared under any other, different principles, the facts should be explained.

You may care to contrast these with the Companies Acts list.

20. **Accounting bases** are the methods which have been developed for expressing or applying the fundamental accounting concepts to specific financial transactions and items. There is often more than one recognised accounting basis for dealing with particular items. For example:

Depreciation	– straight line	Stock	– FIFO
	– reducing balance	valuation	– weighted average
	– sum of digits		

21. Accounting policies

Accounting policies are the specific accounting bases judged by business enterprises to be most appropriate to their circumstances and adopted by them for the purpose of preparing their financial accounts. A business has a choice of accounting basis in, for example, stock valuation. It may choose FIFO or AVCO. The actual basis chosen is called its accounting *policy*. For example, if it selects FIFO, FIFO is its accounting policy.

22. SSAP 2 requires that:

The accounting policies followed for dealing with items which are judged material or critical in determining profit or loss for the year and in stating the financial position should be *disclosed* by way of note to the accounts. The explanations should be clear, fair and as brief as possible.

Examples of disclosure of accounting policies, taken from recent published accounts:

"Depreciation of Tangible Fixed Assets
Depreciation is provided by the group in order to write down to estimated residual value (if any), the cost or valuation of fixed assets over their estimated lives by equal annual instalments, mainly on the following bases:

Freehold and long leasehold buildings	Over estimated useful life (24-100 years)
Short leaseholds	Over remaining period of lease
Fixtures and fittings	Over 10 years
Vehicles and equipment	Over 5 years

Depreciation arising on the revaluation surplus of properties is charged to profit and loss account and then transferred to the revaluation reserve."

"Property Development
In the case of certain property development projects the interest on the capital borrowed to finance the project is, where separately identifiable and to the extent that it accrues during the period of development, capitalised as part of the cost of the asset."

"Credit Sales
Profit is taken on goods sold on credit when the sale is effected, except that a deferral is made in respect of the 12 month extended credit sale which are not subject to interest. The service charge on other credit sales is taken to trading profit as it accrues."

"Copyrights. Copyrights are included in the balance sheet at a nominal amount. Acquisitions are written off in the year of purchase."

"Research and development
Expenditure on research and development is written off in the year in which it is incurred."

STATEMENTS OF RECOMMENDED PRACTICE (SORPs)

23. These are a new departure with the first being issued only in May 1986. The first and, at the time of writing, only SORP is on Pension Scheme Accounts. SORPs are to be developed in the public interest and set out current best accounting practice. Unlike Accounting Standards (SSAPs) they are *not* mandatory on members of the accounting bodies and consequently are not always followed.

INTERNATIONAL ACCOUNTING STANDARDS

24. In addition to the SSAPs which apply in the UK, there are also International Accounting Standards which are promulgated by the International Accounting Standards Committee. These IASs have explored much the same ground as the SSAPs (*e.g.* stocks, depreciation etc.) and come to much the same conclusions. In general, compliance with an SSAP will automatically achieve compliance with the corresponding IAS.

THE EUROPEAN ECONOMIC COMMUNITY

25. The UK and the Republic of Ireland are both members of the European Economic Community (EEC). One of the management institutions of the EEC is the *Commission*. The Commission's duties include the harmonisation of company law throughout the EEC and to that end they have issued a number of *Directives*. Each member country is obliged to incorporate the Directives into its own company law. However, there are many optional clauses and while substantial harmonisation in the areas dealt with has been achieved, there are still substantial differences. The principal Directive of interest is the Fourth, that on company accounting. The Companies Act 1981 (now the Companies Act 1985) was the Act which incorporated the Fourth Directive and introduced the Formats and many other features to English law.

Over the next few years many aspects of company law including accounting requirements will be the subject of Directives and eventually incorporated into English law. It is also worth noting that the Accounting Standards (SSAPs) are also influenced by EEC Directives.

THE STOCK EXCHANGE

26. The Stock Exchange has issued some accounting rules which listed (= quoted) companies must follow. These are fewer than the requirements of the SSAP's and the Companies Act and need not be considered at this level.

SUMMARY

27. (a) Bookkeeping and accounting developed in a totally unregulated way until this century.

(b) Regulation is now carried out by:

- the law in the form of the Companies Act and other Acts and regulations.
- the Accounting bodies in the form of the SSAPs and SORPs.
- the Stock Exchange.
- the International Accounting Standards Committee.
- the EEC.

(c) The need for regulation arises out of:

- diversity of accounting practices
- tendencies not to bother with good accounting records
- diversity of form
- tendencies to secrecy
- tendencies to put information in the most favourable light
- tendencies to overstate/understate profits.

(d) Regulation is in the following areas:

Companies Act
- accounting records to be kept
- accounting statements to be produced
- format of accounts
- information to be disclosed
- accounting principles to be followed
- requirement for a true and fair view
- requirements (including time limits) for filing accounts for public ins-pection with the registrar of companies and submission to shareholders.

SSAPs
- accounting statements to be produced (Funds Flow Statements and some others)
- information to be disclosed
- accounting principles to follow
- detailed methods for measuring profit and capital

POINTS TO NOTE

28. (a) It is important to note several ideas:

(i) The prime influence in the *form* of accounts comes from the EEC Directives which are incorporated in UK Company Law. The required formats in the Companies Act 1985 are of European origin and in many ways unsuitable for use in the UK.

(ii) The prime influence on the content and extent of disclosure comes from the Stock Exchange and the Government who are concerned to ensure investors receive adequate information. This desire upon the part of the government to see fair play in financial markets can be seen in the extensive accounting requirement of the Companies Act 1985 together with tight audit requirements.

(iii) The prime influence on the accounting principles to be adopted comes from the accounting bodies. They have been influenced by a number of scandals (*e.g.* GEC AEI in the 1960's) and by a growing sophistication amongst institutional (*e.g.* pension funds, insurance companies, unit trusts) investors that has enabled fund managers to become aware that no comparison can be made of the results of two companies if different principles are used in measuring the results.

(b) The UK company law has for many years required company financial statements to give a "true and fair view" of the results and state of affairs (Profit and Loss Account and Balance Sheet). What exactly a true and fair view is, is very difficult to assess and depends upon the circumstances. This difficult concept is usually discussed in auditing texts.

(c) Regulation in the USA has been much more extensive than in the UK and continental Europe. The reasons for this may include (a) a higher regard for business and hence accounting, (b) more extensive business education with earlier recognition of the faults in traditional accounting, (c) the tendency for US investors who lose money on Stock Exchange deals to sue the auditors of the companies they invested in. Often the cause of action arose from doubt as to the appropriate accounting principles to be used. As with most things, US ideas tend to find their way across the Atlantic in due course.

(d) Before an SSAP is published and approved, an *exposure draft* is published. This is a proposed SSAP and comments and suggestions are asked for from interested parties. The final SSAP takes into account these comments and suggestions. Exposure drafts, unlike SSAPs, are not mandatory on accountants, but they usually set out current best practice.

SELF TESTING QUESTIONS

(a) *How did accounting and bookkeeping come about? (1).*

(b) *Accounting regulation applies in what areas? (4).*

(c) *Where has accounting regulation come from? (5).*

(d) *Why is accounting regulation necessary? (7).*

(e) *List the general Companies Act 1985 accounting regulations. (11).*

(f) *What financial statements are required by the Companies Act? (12).*

(g) *What forms must financial statements take? (13).*

(h) *List the accounting principles to be follows? (14).*

(i) *What are the objectives of the Accounting Standards Committee? (15).*

(j) *What four fundamental accounting principles are found in SSAP 2? (18).*

(k) *Define accounting bases and accounting policies. (20, 21).*

(l) *What is a SORP? (23).*

(m) *What is the relationship between SSAPs and IASs? (24).*

(n) *What was the Fourth Directive? (25).*

(o) *Indicate the Stock Exchange's influence of accounting regulation. (26).*

(p) *Contrast the Companies Act and SSAP regulations. (27).*

(q) *What are the primary influences on form, content, extent of disclosure, accounting principles, accounting method? (28).*

Exercises without answers

1. *Suppose you are on the Board of a public company, the company has had a bad year. What attitudes might the Board take towards the form of, content of, disclosures in, accounting principles used in and the laying and delivering of the annual accounts?*

2. *The price of limited liability is disclosure. Discuss.*

3. *The accounts of a medium sized public company have been prepared, but before they can be published certain notes must be drafted to explain the calculations of some of the figures in the accounts, and to show that the accounts conform to best accounting practice. As an accounting technician, you are a member of the team engaged in writing these notes, with special responsibility for the note on Accounting Policies.*

Required:

(a) *Name the four fundamental accounting concepts which under SSAP2 are presumed to be observed when accounts are prepared, and indicate briefly what is meant by the terms 'Accounting Bases' and 'Accounting Policies'. Explain how the fundamental concepts are related to accounting bases and accounting policies.*

(b) *Give FOUR examples of matter for which different accounting bases may be recognised, including a brief explanation of how each one may have a material effect on the reported results and financial position of the business.*

(AAT)

Appendix I: Answers to practice questions

CHAPTER 1

1. (a) Accounting will affect Penny's business in many ways including:

   (i) **Bookkeeping** – how much is owed to the business by customers, how much is owed by the business to suppliers, a record of receipts and payments, a wages book, etc.

   (ii) **Profit** – she will need to know the profit made each year to enable her to know how well (or badly) she has done and how much tax to pay, to help her plan for the next year and to convince her banker she can repay any loans.

   (iii) **Capital** – she will need to prepare a balance sheet showing her assets and liabilities.

   (b) Many people do keep records of their receipts and payments and of their assets and liabilities and also project these forward in the form of budgets. Perhaps Penny does too.

2. (a) Yes – bookkeeping.
   (b) Yes – bookkeeping but also profit measurement.
   (c) Yes – management accounting.
   (d) Yes – management accounting (or bookkeeping).
   (e) Yes – bookkeeping.
   (f) Yes – profit reporting.

CHAPTER 2

1. (a) Wholesale (sales to retailers), retail (in their own shop), manufacturing (assembling products from components), service (advising others).

   (b) Partnership.

   (c) Sales to retailers will be on credit – so they will have to wait a month (or more) for their money. Sales to the public in the shop will usually result in immediate payment – cash sales.

   (d) Import documentation is rather complex. Buying from British firms will mean receiving invoices and statements of account. They will send out invoices and statements of account to their credit customers.

2. (a) Service; sole trader.
   (b) Retail; partnership.
   (c) Service; association.
   (d) Manufacture, retail, service; company.
   (e) Manufacturing (more strictly extraction); state owned enterprise.
   (f) Manufacturing; company.

All except Sam and Son will trade on credit.

CHAPTER 3

1. (a) The shareholders, the board of directors, the investment community (potential shareholders, advisers, stock exchange professionals etc), suppliers especially the suppliers of new cars and the oil companies, the government especially the tax man and the VAT man, the bank, employees and potential employees.

   (b) This is not easy to spell out as much depends on how powerful some groups are at persuading the directors to give information but probably:

   Shareholders – annual report and accounts.

   Directors – anything they require and can afford to obtain.

Investment Community - annual report and accounts but also other information if they enquire (or "research") into the company.

Government - detailed accounts and inspections can be made of PAYE, NHI and VAT records.

Bank - as much as they require.

Employees - directors tend to be unwilling to supply information to employees but this is changing.

Note that the Annual Report and Accounts is filed at Companies House and can be seen by any member of the public and thus any of the contact groups.

2. (a) Only real limitation is historical. Clearly they would like to know amount of future business and profits for planning purposes.

    (b) Future is also an unknown quantity. Accounting tends to ignore factors like the size of the order book, the quality of the product and the workforce, so outside contacts cannot fully evaluate the business.

    (c) The future again. In general accounting does provide the historical data necessary for Ginger to evaluate his business and the performance of Macbeth.

    (d) Accounting in the past has not sufficiently provided information to enable investors to evaluate the performance or honesty of people like Mr. Smart.

    (e) Main requirement is an agreed measurement process for profits. This accounting provides, but arguments are still possible.

    (f) Main needs are to know future orders, revenues, costs and these, accounting does not provide.

3. Other groups have an interest, eg:

    Customers - is firm solvent and does he properly hand over premiums to the insurers.

    Insurance companies - is Jim solvent and does he pay on time.

    Bank - Jim may have been lent money and the bank will need to monitor his business and his ability to repay.

    Tax man - Jim will have to pay tax on his income and the profit and this is of concern to the tax man.

    Jim's professional body - they will need to ensure Jim's business is properly conducted and that he does not defraud his customers or insurers and that he remains solvent.

CHAPTER 4

1. (a) Advising on or performing bookkeeping; preparing annual accounts; advising on and dealing with tax matters; advising on business matters generally (e.g. on projections of profitability of new shop); advising on, preparing documentation for and negotiating with the bank; advising on computer installation.

    (b) The Chartered Association of Certified Accountants if he wishes to continue with Solange's business. For methods of registering with and studying for the various bodies write to the bodies direct.

2. It has all the attributes in paragraph 13.

CHAPTER 5

1. (a) Bill's business

Balance sheet as at 31st December 19-8 in vertical form

		£	£
Fixed assets			
	Premises		50,000
	Vehicles		11,600
	Fixtures and fittings		5,300
			66,900
Current assets			
	Stock	16,440	
	Trade debtors	12,610	
(i)	Prepayments	1,251	
	Cash at bank	320	
	Cash in hand	35	30,656
			97,556
Less **Current liabilities**			
	Trade creditors	13,920	
(i)	Accruals	270	
(ii)	14% loan	1,000	15,190
			£82,366
(iii)	Capital		£82,366

Note:

(i) *Prepayments and accruals should not be detailed.*
(ii) *This is a current liability as it is payable on 4.3.-9.*
(iii) *Capital = assets - liabilities.*

(b) If working capital were shown, layout would be:

	£	£
Fixed assets		66,900
Current assets	30,656	
Current liabilities	15,190	15,466
		£82,366
Capital		£82,366

(c)   Bill's business
             Balance sheet as at 31st December 19-8

	£	£		£	£
Capital		82,366	**Fixed assets**		
			Premises	50,000	
Current liabilities			Vehicles	11,600	
Trade creditors	13,920		Fixtures and fittings	5,300	
Accruals	270			66,900	
14% loan	1,000	15,190	**Current assets**		
			Stock	16,440	
			Trade debtors	12,610	
			Prepayments	1,251	
			Cash at bank	320	
			Cash in hand	35	30,656
		97,556			97,556

2. | | |
|---|---|
| A contract to supply | - The contract itself had no cost to the business. |
| A caravan at Brighton | - Not a business asset. |
| A pair of scales | - F.A. |
| A life assurance policy paid in advance | - Life assurance is not a business matter. |
| Overdue rent on the shop | - C.L. |
| A bank loan | - C.L. |
| Amounts due to wholesalers | - C.L. |
| An Austin estate car | - F.A. If used for the business |

A fur coat	– A private asset.
Stock of tinned goods	– C.A.
Cost of redecoration	– Not an asset or a liability.
Owing for cash register	– C.L.
The contract	– The contract itself had no cost.
A lease	– The lease itself cost nothing.
Personal computer	– F.A.
Refrigerator	– Does not belong to the business.

3. The entity convention views the *business* as distinct from its owner. From the *business* point of view the capital is a liability to the owner. From the *owner's* point of view, the business is an asset.

4. Abbreviated answer:

(a) **Terry**
Balance sheet as at 30th June 19–8

	£
Fixed assets	32,600
Current assets	24,740
Total assets	57,340
Less **Current liabilities**	22,400
	£34,940
Capital	£34,940

(b)

	£	
Fixed assets		32,600
Working capital:	£	
Current assets	24,740	
Current liabilities	22,400	2,340
		£34,940
Capital		£34,940

(c)

	£		£
Capital	34,940	Fixed assets	32,600
Current liabilities	22,400	Current assets	24,740
	57,340		57,340

5. It does not. It is the *value* of the assets he owned when he died (e.g. home, business, investments, car etc.) less any liabilities (e.g. mortgage on house).

CHAPTER 6

1. Balance sheet – fixed assets £3,100, current assets £5,627, current liabilities £1,000, capital £7,727.

2. Transactions occurring:

	£
(a) Purchase of premises for cash	5,000
(b) Purchase of vehicles for cash	3,000
(c) Payment of expense item in advance	350
(d) Purchase of stock on credit	600
(e) Sale of stock costing £700 on credit (Profit £200 increases capital)	900
(f) Introduction of capital in cash	6,000
(g) Cash transactions 800 + 6,000(f) – 5,000(a) – 3,000(b) – 350(c) = –1,550	

3.

		Note:
Fixed assets	14,820	
Current assets	20,250	(a) Prepayments should be one figure £500
	35,070	
Current liabilities	5,763	(b) Accruals should be one figure £763
	29,307	
Capital	24,307	
Long term liability	5,000	
	29,307	

4. (a) Vehicles should be valued by reference to cost.
    (b) No sub total of fixed assets.
    (c) Stock should appear before debtors.
    (d) Current assets should total £28,380.
    (e) Consequently, total assets should be £65,280.
    (f) Loan should appear under long term liability.
    (g) Capital should equal assets less liabilities £46,870.

CHAPTER 7

1. Paragraph 2 summarises this.

It is necessary to understand bookkeeping and accounts to successfully operate any (even a computerised) accounting system. Changes to the system will be required. New information needs will arise and will need catering for, information needs to be interpreted, planning and forecasting for decision making needs an accountant's input, accountants are trained to do other things, e.g. administration, company matters, credit control, tax matters.

CHAPTER 8

1. Fixed assets £6,900, current assets £4,600, current liabilities £7,600, capital £3,900.

2. Fixed assets £16,800, current assets £4,900, current liabilities £2,600, capital £5,100, long term liability £14,000.

CHAPTER 9

1. Trial balance:

	£		£
Motor car	500	Overdraft	140
Office quipment	3,120	Capital	1,900
Drawings	70	William	1,110
James	100	Philip	640
	3,790		3,790

Fixed assets £3,620, current assets £100, current liabilities £1,890, capital £1,830.

CHAPTER 10

1.

Trading Accounts

	a	b	c	d
	£	£	£	£
Sales	13,400	17,900	19,200	18,000
Opening stock	700	800	3,700	1,200
Purchases	11,000	13,000	14,000	15,800
	11,700	13,800	17,700	17,000
Closing stock	850	1,250	4,800	900
	10,850	12,550	12,900	16,100
Gross profit	2,550	5,350	6,300	1,900
Mark up %	23.5	42.6	48.8	11.8
Gross profit %	19.0	29.9	32.8	10.6

2. (a) 16.67% (100 + 20 = 120 and 20/120 x 100)   (b) 27%.

3. (a) 37%   (b) 51.5%.

4. (i) (a) Yes   (iv) (a), (b) and (c) No.
         (b) and (c) No.

(ii) (a) No
     (b) Yes
     (c) No.

(iii) (a) No
      (b) No
      (c) Yes.

(v) (a) No
    (b) Yes
    (c) No.

6. No, because the charges are for drugs but also for the vet's time. By separating charges into those for drugs and those for time.

7. Time is a matter of opinion or convention.

Profit is calculated on an annual basis. Profit on a contract may go into different years.

8. Closing stock £450; Gross profit £400; Purchases £1,460; Sales £4,000; Closing stock £260.

9. (a) 35.5% (100 + 55 = 155 and 55/155 100 = 35.5%)
    (b) 25.4%.

CHAPTER 11

1. Trial balance:

	£		£
Nutt	167	Oliver	266
Preston	482	Fixed assets (sale)	100
Quint	135	Sales	652
Cash	10		
Purchases	736		

2. (a) No, as purchases are recorded at cost and sales at selling price.
    (b) Yes (to prevent loss and to know what selling price to fix).
    (c) Nutt £167, Preston £482, Quint £135.
    (d) Total cost of antiques purchased £736; total turnover £652.

3. (a) Answers are apparent from (b) to (e).

(b)
Sales		1,015
Opening stock	2,319	
Purchases	755	
	3,074	
Closing stock	2,373	701
Gross profit		314

(c)
	£
Pinkerton	202
Green	246
Gray	233
Scarlet	nil
Black	205
Violet	341
	1,227

(d)
Brown	807
White	140
	947

(e) Bank balance £273.

CHAPTER 12

1.   **Stock account**

31.7.-2	Trading account	<u>23,005</u>	31.7.-3	Trading a/c	<u>23,005</u>
31.7.-3	Trading account	25,987			

Gross profit £26,927

CHAPTER 13

1. Profit and loss account expense inclusions:

		£
Rent	March 19-4 $\frac{1}{4}$	250
	June 19-4 $\frac{1}{4}$	250
	Sept 19-4 $\frac{1}{4}$	250
	Dec 19-4 $\frac{1}{4}$	<u>250</u>
		<u>1,000</u>
Rates	March 19-4 $\frac{1}{4}$	310
	Sept 19-4 $\frac{1}{2}$	662
	Dec 19-4 $\frac{1}{4}$	<u>331</u>
		<u>1,303</u>
Electricity	to 24.4.-4	291
	to 26.7.-4	358
	to 7.11.-4	401
	to 31.12.-4	249
	$\frac{53}{98}$ x 461	
		<u>1,299</u>
Accountancy		<u>850</u>

2. Expense for 19-9 would be: 96 + 40 + 194 + 226 + 140 + 100 + 890 + 1,580 = £3,266

3.

	Henry	Lisa
	£	£
Gross profit	78,717	110,555
Net profit	54,447	69,615
Fixed assets	140,500	119,600
Loan	10,000	
Current assets	26,415	56,240
Current liabilities	14,540	11,860
Capital	162,375	163,980

4. Rent payable 500 + 1,400 + 700 = £2,600
   rent receiveable 500 + 600 + 100 = £1,200

	Accruals	Prepayment
31.12.-7	* 500	500
31.12.-8		** 100

* This item is more properly a payment in advance
** This item is more properly a debtor.

CHAPTER 14

1. Heating and Oil Expense Account

		£			£
1.1.-5	Stock b/f	420	31.12.-5	Stock c/f	1,240
4.3.-5	Evan - Oil	586	31.12.-5	Profit and loss A/c	1,525
3.7.-5	Frank - Oil	269			
5.10.-5	Church - Oil	100			
28.12.-5	Evan - Oil	1,390			
		2,765			2,765
1.1.-6	Stock b/f	1,240			

2. Salaries Expense Account

		£			£
5.4.-5	Cheque - Marvin	3,454	5.4.-5	Profit and loss A/c	5,304
5.4.-5	Cheques C of T	1,280			
5.4.-5	Accruals c/d	570			
		5,304			5,304
			6.4.-5	Accruals b/d	570

Note:

(a) *The accrual is:*

	£
Martin: Salary month ending 5.4.-5	400
Collector: Deductions etc month to 5.3.-5	128
Collector: Employer's NI 5.4.-5	42
	570

(b) *The transfer to profit and loss account is:*

		£
Salary	*12 x 400*	4,800
Employer's N.I.	*12 x 42*	504
		5,304

3. Salaries expense account

	£		£
Cheques	87,643	Profit and loss account	123,072
Cheques	24,310		
c/f	11,119		
	123,072		123,072
		b/f	11,119

4. Advertising revenue account

	£		£
Credit notes	190	Invoices	17,710
c/f	3,145	c/d	400
Profit and loss account	14,775		
	18,110		18,110
b/d	400	b/f	3,145

5. PM Supplies Ltd

	£		£
Credit notes	102	b/f	380
Cash	1,161	Invoices	1,390
c/f	507		
	1,770		1,770
		b/f	507

Packing materials expense account

	£		£
Stock b/f	260	Credit notes	102
Invoices	1,390	Drawings	120
		Profit and loss account	100
		Profit and loss account	1,038
		Stock c/d	290
	1,650		1,650
Stock b/d	290		

CHAPTER 15

1. Note - First two years only have been given.

    (a) **Straight Line**

	Annual Depreciation		Book Value	
	19-4	19-5	19-4	19-5
	£	£	£	£
Item 1	1,560	1,560	6,440	4,880
Item 2	2,750	2,750	13,250	10,500
Item 3	2,500	2,500	5,000	2,500
Item 4	2,300	2,300	12,000	9,700

    (b) **Reducing balance**

Item 1	4,174	1,996	3,826	1,830
Item 2	4,037	3,108	11,963	8,945
Item 3	7,500	0	0	0
Item 4	3,980	2,872	10,320	7,448

    Note: Item 1 - Rate $= 100 \left(1 - \sqrt[5]{\dfrac{200}{8,000}}\right) = 52.18\%$

    (c) **Sum of Digits**

Item 1	2,600	2,080	5,400	3,320
Item 2	4,400	3,300	11,600	8,300
Item 3	3,750	2,500	3,750	1,250
Item 4	3,833	3,067	10,467	7,400

    Note:

    Item 1 - $\dfrac{5}{15} \times (8,000 - 200) = 2,600$

    Item 2 - $\dfrac{4}{10} \times (16,000 - 5,000) = 4,400$

Profit and loss account entries (Item 1)	19-4	1,560 or 4,174 or 2,600
	19-5	1,560 or 1,996 or 2,080
Balance sheet entries (Item 1)	19-4	6,440 or 3,826 or 5,400
	19-5	4,880 or 1,830 or 3,320.

2. **Full year in 19-4**   **half year in 19-4**

(i)	19-7 Gain	£500	19-7 Loss	£500
(ii)	19-7 Loss	£1,400	19-7 Loss	£2,400
(iii)	19-1 Gain	£500	19-1 Loss	£1,000
(iv)	19-7 Loss	£4,000	19-7 Loss	£5,000

3. Vehicle A Loss £1,200   Vehicle B Profit £500
    19-7 charge £28,000 + £500 - £1,200 = £27,300.
    (Assuming no vehicles in the £140,000 are fully depreciated.)

4. (a) No depreciation, it has unlimited life.

    (b) Straight line over 30 years, i.e. £73,500/30 = £2,450 each year. This does assume that the extension has a 30 year life despite the original factory now having only 18 years left. However, these estimates of useful life of buildings are invariably wrong.

    (c) Straight line over 6 years, i.e. £4,340/6 = £723 a year.

    (d) Reducing balance at a rate of approx 19% = £3,040 in the first year. With reducing balance, it is usual to take a full year's depreciation in the first year.

(e) Land value = £2,000 - no depreciation. Mineral rights cost is therefore £60,000. Depreciate on the basis of extraction, i.e. 30/600 x £60,000 = £3,000 in the first year.

Acquires the following assets = incurred capital expenditure.

5.   A fork lift truck - wear and tear; a lease - effluxion of time; a copper mine - exhaustion of mineral or uneconomic costs to extraction; a freehold factory - wear and tear and obsoles-cence; a machine for making electronic devices - wear and tear or obsolescence of machine *or* devices; machinery in a gold mine - wear and tear, obsolescence or uneconomic costs of extrac-tion; a wind turbine - wear and tear, obsoles-cence or uneconomic cost of use; a patent - expiry of patent with time or possible obsoles-cence; copyright - life of author and 50 years after his death, i.e. effluxion of time but obsolescence is also a factor.

CHAPTER 16

1.   Reducing balance method - loss on sale £1,150
     Straight line method   - loss on sale £4,201

2.   (a) £34,052
     (b) Cost £75,120 Depreciation £44,068
     (c) Dodge £6,320 Foden £15,200 Mercedes £12,532
     (d)   Cost   Depreciation
          Dodge   £15,800   £12,480
          Foden   £30,400   £15,200
          Mercedes £28,920   £16,388

CHAPTER 17

1.   William - Total £16,660.25

2.   Nathan   - Total £76,140, Purchases £71,600, Heat and light £2,300, PSA £240, Repairs £2,000

3.   Sales   - £266 + £235 + £209 = £710
     Purchases - £243 + £323 + £216 = £782

CHAPTER 18

1.   Totals   Dr: Discount £34.21 Bank £2,820.42
               Cr: Discount £ 2.34 Bank £767.81   Balance £2,052.61

CHAPTER 19

1.   Informational differences - £100, £1,000.
     Timing differences - £1,566, £234, £540.

Cash Book

	£		£
b/d	2,438	British Gas	100
Wolvborough	1,000	c/f	3,338
	3,438		3,438

Bank Reconciliation Statement at 31 January 19-7

	£
Cash book	3,338
Add unpresented cheques 234 + 540	774
	4,112
Less paid in after date	1,566
Bank Statement	2,546

2. Cash Book £66 - £60 + £439 - £71 = £374
   Bank Reconciliation £374 + £22 - £116 - £72 = £208

3. Cash book £578 + £30 + £9 + £900 + £250 - £1,000 - £100 - £412 = £255
   Bank reconciliation £255 + £621 - £4,988 - £26 = £4,138 overdrawn.

CHAPTER 20

1. Edward   Debtors £25,058   Creditors £14,303
   Jane   Debtors £126,309   Creditors £38,127

2. Alice   Debtrors £2,338   Creditors £9,113
   Kewal   Debtors £53,497   Creditors £56,697

3. Jean   Balance on control account and list total £9,039 and for Akbar £7,354.

4. Total of list and balance of control account should be £12,500.

CHAPTER 21

1. *Petty Cash Book*

				Total	Travel	Post	Staty	Motor	Sundry	Credit Accounts
		£		£						
19.1.-7	b/f	16.44	24.1.-7	3.78					3.78	
20.1.-7	Cash	83.56		2.33	2.33					
				1.37					1.37	
				4.11			4.11			
				5.00				5.00		
				2.44	2.44					
				2.11			2.11			
				5.00					5.00	
				4.10				4.10		
				5.00		5.00				
				3.20		3.20				
				1.50	1.50					
				6.00				6.00		
				12.00						12.00
				57.94	6.27	8.20	6.22	15.10	10.15	12.00
		c/f		42.06						
	100.00			100.00						

2. Totals are: credit account £5.90; Stationery £10.23; Motor £20.29; Travelling £15.20; Loan £5.00; Sundry £3.80; Advertising £3.00. Total expenditure £63.42, balance c/f £36.58.

CHAPTER 22

1. Final trial balances:

	Dick		Doris	(in £')
	Dr	Cr	Dr	Cr
	£	£	£	£
Capital		12,608		23,876
Stock	2,567		3,510	
Purchases/sales	15,863	28,981	40,978	70,432
Expenses	6,080		17,830	
Drawings	5,945		10,322	
Drs/Crs	3,480	2,372	15,726	5,878
Fixed assets	12,250	6,230	10,438	3,428
Bank	4,006		4,810	
	50,191	50,191	103,614	103,614

2. Trial balance:
    Dr + £1,480 + £36 + £17,900 - £18 - £6,800 =   12,598
    Cr - £1,480 - £498 + £6,800 + £4,000 =   <u>8,822</u>
                                                    3,776

3. Trial balance:
    Dr - £487 + £500 - £1,700 + £730 =   - £957
    Cr + £487 + £1,700 + £400 + £100 =   <u>2,687</u>
                                                    3,644

4.   *Suspense A/c*

	£			£
a	576	d		18
h	1,200	e		120
Balance b/f	<u>1,121</u>	i		<u>2,759</u>
	<u>2,897</u>			<u>2,897</u>

Journal entries would be (as an example)

Suspense A/c		576
Sales A/c			576

Net Profit: £12,600 + £576 - £371 + £200 - £120 + £300 + £1,200 - £2,759 + £2,000 = £13,626

CHAPTER 23

1. Net amount of invoice £182.40 - Dr Paul   Cr Sales

2. Two entries:
    (i)   Dr Jim   Cr Sales £600
    (ii)   Dr Cash £570 Dr Discount allowed £30.00 Cr Jim £600

3. The entries to be made are:

(a)	Dr	George	£333	Cr	Sales	£333
(b)	Dr	John	£200	Cr	Sales	£200
(c)	Dr	Purchases	£630	Cr	Dindle	£630
(d)	Dr	Cashbook	£190	Cr	Joan	£190
	Dr	Discount allowed	£10	Cr	Cash	£10
(d)	Dr	Dindle	£585.90	Cr	Cash	£585.90
	Dr	Dindle	£44.10	Cr	Discount received	£44.10

4. Balances will be:
    Rents receivable Cr £517, Rent etc payable Dr £1,509 and Cr £382, Creditors Cr £4,720, Provision for discounts receivable Dr £94.

CHAPTER 24

1. Balances will be:
    Provision for doubtful debts Cr £1,108 Actual £3,624 + Provision £1,108 = £4,732.
    Balance sheet entry will be £156,582.

2. Bad debts in profit and loss £3,858. Provision balance £3,519
    Profit and loss a/c bad debts £3,858 and change in provision £99
    Balance sheet debtors £84,121

3. Profit and loss: Bad debts £7,900 Additional provision £2,349
    Balance sheet: Debtors £412,832.

CHAPTER 25

1.   Sales Cr £53,600, Purchases Dr £35,159, Motor expenses Dr £1,030, HM Customs & Excise Cr Balance £2,696 payable by 31.3.-8.

CHAPTER 26

1.   Financial Statements

Profit and Loss Account

		£
19-8	Profit on sale	230
	HP Interest	300
19-9	HP Interest	450
19-0	HP Interest	132

Balance Sheet

	£		£
HP commitment	3,933	HP interest in advance	600
HP commitment	983		150

He may wish to pay off the item to save administrative time later but also to save interest. Also the existence of borrowing may preclude obtaining further borrowing. In addition the car cannot be sold without repaying the HP loan.

2.

Profit and loss account		
	19-5	19-6
Motor expenses (plus other items)		107
Hire purchase interest	100	500
Depreciation of car		
Balance sheet (liabilities)		
Hire purchase commitment		5,000

CHAPTER 27

1.

Trading and profit and loss account items		
	£	
Sales	5.506	(CR)
Purchases	1,145	
Bad debts	1,063	
Discounting charges	180	
Discount received	40	(CR)

Balance sheet items	
	£
Current assets	
Debtors	150
Bill receivable	150
Cash at bank	3,078
Current liabilities	
Bills payable	220

CHAPTER 28

1. (a) No unless goodwill had been purchased (it would then be included at cost).
   (b) Yes - this is called goodwill.
   (c) No.
   (d) These would be included at *cost* as work in progress.
   (e) Yes - this would be valued at cost £40,000 less depreciation £1,000.
   (f) Yes - value at cost £3,000. Sometimes it may be in at valuation £20,000.
   (g) Yes - value at cost £12,000.
   (h) yes - include at £3,900, £1,950 or £nil.
   (i) Yes - show as a liability £3,274. It is a provision.
   (j) No - include in accounts on actual redundancy.

2. Profit is a measure of endogenous gain in net assets in a period. It is not a physical entity or cash.

A profit implies an increase in net assets. It does not imply an increase in cash although that may be a consequence.

Capital is an asset of the proprietor and a liability of the business.

Other causes of increase in capital my include introductions of Capital.

The two accountants may make different estimates of provisions (see 1(h) above) or may use different policies e.g. on depreciation.

John leaves *assets* less liabilities (including the overdraft) valued at £2 million.

It will be in the aggregate figure of creditors.

Stationery stock will be in the aggregate figure of stocks.

Isaiah's results are quite likely as his increase in sales may be a result of lower prices.

I leave Aunty May to you.

CHAPTER 29

1. Real: Cash, lorries, stock - all Dr.
   Personal: Dr - debtor, drawings. Cr - bank, capital, accrued electricity.
   Valuation: Cr - provision for depreciation.
   Nominal: Dr - wages, rent and rates, deprec-iation expense, purchases, advertising. Cr - sales, discount received.
   Accrued electricity may be considered as nominal if you prefer.

   These classifications are convenient but not conclusive.

2. The stock is at 31.12.-7 and the provision for depreciation is 31.12.-7 also.

3. *Trial balance*

	£ Dr		£ Cr
Car	1,900	Capital	21,900
Drawings	370	Profit on sale	20
Purchases	7,419	Harold	3,969
Rent	500	Sales	7,392
Bank	23,032	Hummel	670
Bonser	510	Downs	690
Wages	140		
Shopfittings	570		
Stationery	40		
Discount	40		
Lewis	120		
	34,641		34,641

CHAPTER 31

1. Capitals are: Hugh £55,900, Heather £193,045, Munro £37,801

2. Hengist Capital £36,590, Horsa Profit £16,189

3. Alan £9,801, Beth £44,363, Claire £98,034

4. Leon £14,290, Mary £4,530, Sue £72,016

5. Geoff: Stock £25,424, Winnie: Sales £253,866, Purchases £179,904,
   Ron: Purchases £94,470, Gross profit ratio 35.8%.

6. Gross profit £6,400, Net profit £2,410, Fixed assets £4,760, Current assets £10,120, Current liabilities £4,350,
   Capital £10,530

Workings

Cash	£		£	Rent	£		£
Recevied from		Banked	15,180	Cash	700	B/f	100
customers	16,380 (i)	Purchases	1,000	C/f	400 (i)	P & L	1,000
		Drawings	200				
	£16,380		£16,380		£1,100		£1,100

Customers	£		£	Fixed assets	Cost £	Depr £	NBV £
B/f	1,500	Cash	16,380	B/f	6,000	2,500	3,500
Sales	17,180 (i)	C/f	2,300	Sold	1,500	1,000	500
	£18,680		£18,680		4,500	1,500	3,000
				Addition	2,600		2,600
				Depreciation		840	(840)
					7,100	2,340	4,760

Suppliers	£		£	
Cash	1,000	B/f	2,300	
Bank	9,730	Purchases	12,380 (i)	Depreciation = 15% x (£7,100 – £1,500)
C/f	3,950			
	£14,680		£14,680	

(i) Balancing figures.

7. Gross profit £55,552, Net profit £17,024, Fixed assets £35,350, Current assets £35,462, Current liabilities £9,268, Capital £61,544.

CHAPTER 32

1. (a) A manual system might be:

- Batch purchase invoices monthly
- Check details with goods inwards notes
- Check details with copy orders
- Enter details in purchase day book ruled as:

Date Supplier Gross VAT Net Purchases Rent Repairs Heat ....

- Post details to supplier's accounts in purchase ledger
- Post day book columns totals to Customs and Excise account and nominal ledger accounts
- Write out remittance advices and cheques

Note that instead of writing out remittance advices, the suppliers "statements of account" could be used. In computer systems, remittance advices are the norm and the system may/should allow for comparison of remittance advices with suppliers' statements of account.

(b) *Computer*   *Manual*

　　Minimal data entry   Laborious writing in

　　Use of master file data (e.g. supplier name and   Laborious writing in
　　address on remittance advice)

　　Accuracy of calculation   Possibility of error

　　Automatic printing   Laborious writing/typing out

　　One-step up date   Consecutive up date

　　Automatic balancing   Need for control account

　　Validity checks   Intelligence of clerks

　　Access required to disc files   Books always available

　　Temporary storage of data on disc (rest of   Books always available
　　data in print outs)

　　Use of unskilled labour   Skilled bookkeeper required

2. (a)

		A	B	C	D	E	F	G
1.	Sales			9,000		9,450		10,017
2.	Op St		1,500		1,800		2,160	
3.	Pchs		5,700		6,219		6,527	
4.			7,200		8,019		8,687	
5.	Cl St		1,800	5,400	2,160	5,859	2,376	6,311
6.	Gr Pr			3,600		3,591		3,706

(b) This spread sheet can be changed to allow different parameters

e.g. (i)   Change turnover growth rate
　　(ii)   Change gross profit rates
　　(iii) Fix purchases and allow stocks to grow
　　(iv)   Relate stock levels to sales

This allows the spread sheet to be a planning tool exploring the consequences of causes of action, e.g. increase turnover will effect stock, debtor and creditor levels and hence borrowing requirements. The accountant is the supplier of this information and thus moves centre stage. Before this easy manipulation of information, this kind of planning tended not to be done. As a side issue, accountants must become much more computerate.

CHAPTER 33

1.

	Terri		Vic		Aled	
		£		£		£
Raw material consumed		661		466		895
Direct labour	336		541		132	
Direct expenses	39		54		21	
		375		595		153
Prime cost		1,036		1,061		1,048
Works overhead		458		674		406
Factory inputs		1,494		1,735		1,454
Work in progress adjust		- 5		- 15		24
Finished goods output		1,489		1,720		1,478
+ 10%						148
Transfer to finished goods						1,626
Purchases, finished goods		103		76		642
Finished goods stock adj		- 21		- 37		- 18
Cost of goods sold		1,571		1,759		2,250
Sales		2,500		2,720		2,800
Gross profit		929		961		550
Admin	221		289		296	
Selling/dist	559		361		316	
Finance	217		63		177	
		997		713		789
Net profit/loss)		(68)		248		(239)

Aled - (a) 10/110 * 178 = 16.2

(b) 16.2 - (10/110 * 160) = 1.6

CHAPTER 34

1. (a) 8,000 - 1,600 + 500 + 405 + 600 = £7,905
   (b) 40 * 32 = 1,280 - 128 - 40 = £1,112
   (c) 4.00 + 2.50 + .50 + 4.20 = £11.20

2.

	A	B	C
FIFO	£1,620	£3,470	£1,400
LIFO	£1,320	£4,220	£1,400
AVCO	£1,540	£3,550	£1,400

3. (a) AVCO
   (b) (i) £5.29
       (ii) £5.50
       (iii) £4.79 (assume order of 120)
       (iv) £5
       (v) £5.20

CHAPTER 35

1. (a) 250 * 20p + 2 * 4 * £3.50 + £6 * 1.6 = £87.60 or 8.76p per tin.
   (b) Direct materials, direct expenses, proportion of production overheads.
   (c) as (a) - overtime premium is an overhead
   (d £87.60 * 1.5 = £131.40

2. £36.00 + £32.00 + £20.80 + 13.79 = £102.59

CHAPTER 36

1. Production - rates, canteen, foremen, oil, royalties, cleaning materials, repairs, paint, nhi, lathe operator, packing materials. (But parts of these eg rates may be non production, royalties if on sales may be a selling cost) much depends on precise circumstances.

Direct - royalties, paint, lathe wages, packing materials.

2.

	Total	Cutting	Joining	Finishing
	£	£	£	£
Rates (area)	28,000	12,000	10,000	6,000
M/c depr (value)	18,000	12,000	4,800	1,200
Power (m/c hours)	38,400	24,000	12,000	2,400
Super (employees)	9,000	4,800	2,400	1,800
	93,400	52,800	29,200	11,400

Machine hour rate - £52,800 / 12,000 = £4.40

3. Materials £62.50 + Labour £76.00 + Overheads £65.50 = £204.00 profit £102,00 so selling price = £306.00.

CHAPTER 37

1.

	A	B	C	D
	£	£	£	£
Materials	200	700.0	500	250
Labour	168	72.0		870
Overheads	468	617.6	760	1,044
Total	836	1,389.6	1,260	2,164

Value at cost except D which value at net realisable value - £2,400 - £2,164 - £290 = £54 expected loss so NRV = £2,164 - £54 = £2,110.

2.

	A	B	C	D	E
	£	£	£	£	£
Turnover	650	300	200	80	500
Costs	450	305	160	74	450
Profit	200	(5)	40	*	50
Work done	650	300	200		500
Cash received	400	230	300		450
Debtors	250	70			50
Provision		14			137

* As contract D has only just commenced and outcomes cannot be foreseen, then value at £74 and set against the excess payment on account of contract C. The balance (£26) should be disclosed as payments on account in creditors.

CHAPTER 38

1. Fire insurance - based on value of assets - fixed but part on stocks may be variable if stocks increase with turnover.

Employer's liability insurance - based on gross wages - thus varies with wages which have both fixed and variable elements.

Depreciation of plant - always treated as fixed although wear and tear is greater with larger activity.

Repairs to building - probably fixed.

Cleaning materials basically fixed but some variable element.

Telephone - difficult, perhaps more production calls when activity is greater, has a fixed core.

Metered water - depends on use - probably variable.

2. | | 19-6 | 19-7 |
    |---|---|---|
    | Profit | | |
    | TAC valuation | 4,010 | 8,820 |
    | MC valuation | 2,710 | 8,620 |

3. | | at £400,000 | at £600,000 |
    |---|---|---|
    | Total costs | | |
    | Labour method | £240,000 | £340,000 |
    | Capital method | £250,000 | £320,000 |

    (a) Use labour method
    (b) Use capital method.

4

	J	K	L
Contribution	24	16	60
Usage	12	10	32
Contribution/usage	2	1.6	1.875
Ranking	1	3	2

Make	20,000	J - usage	240,000
	1,875	L - usage	60,000
			300,000

CHAPTER 39

1. Twood Climbing Club - Accounts year ending 31.12.-7

Bar Trading Account	£		£
Opening stock	780	Sales	4,530
Purchases	3,258		
	4,038		
Closing stock	543		
	3,495		
Gross profit c/d	1,035		
	4,530		4,530
Club house overhead	1,122	Gross profit b/d	1,035
		Net loss on bar	87
	1,122		1,122

Income and Expenditure Account

Expenditure	£	*Income*	£
Bar loss	87	Subscriptions	5,615
Donations	100		
Loss on Annual Dinner	220		
Post and stationery	79		
Depreciation	1,020		
Overheads	3,366		
	4,872		
Surplus	743		
	5,615		5,615

Balance Sheet

	£			£
Accumulated Fund b/f	2,217	**Fixed Assets**		
Surplus for year	743	Cost		4,800
		Depreciation		2,420
	2,960			2,380
Prize Fund		**Current Assets**		
b/f	1,600	Bar stock	543	
Additions	970	Prizes stock	327	
	2,570	Subs in arrear	320	
Prizes	838 1,732	Prepayments	57	
		Bank	2,125	
		Cash	51	3,423
Creditors	1,111			
	5,803			5,803

1. Bar loss and low (23%) gross profit margin indicate low bar prices or low volume.
2. Expenditure is only 87% of income.
3. If increase in expenditure (inflation ?) expected to be 5% then increase in sub is reasonable.
4. Cash reserves are adequate, perhaps should be invested.

2. Bar - Gross profit £2,038, net profit £938.

Income and expenditure deficits - Cricket £7, Hockey £600

Balance sheet - Premises £20,000, Bonds £2,000, Current assets £2,167, Creditors £1,921, Mortgage £13,000, Development fund £5,378.
General funds - Cricket £2,298, Hockey £1,570

CHAPTER 40

1. *Sparks*
Income Statement (= profit and loss account) for the year ending 31.12.-8

	£	£
Fee Income		53,300
less staff costs	28,590	
office occupancy	5,483	
depreciation	2,080	
motor etc	6,300	
	42,453	
WIP adjustment	3,000	39,453
Net profit		13,847

Balance Sheet

	£		Cost £	Depn £	WDV £
Capital b/f	11,433	Equipment	3,900	1,980	1,920
Profit	13,847	Car	8,000	4,400	3,600
Introduced	5,000				5,520
	30,280	Work in progress		12,800	
Drawings	16,211	Debtors		8,800	21,600
	14,069				
Creditors	1,230				
Overdraft	11,821				
	27,120				27,120

Sparks' problems

1. Drawings in excess of profits.

2. Very high work in progress - £12,800 at *cost* compared to fee income at *selling price* of £53,000 (well over 3 months work).

3. Very high staff costs to gross fee income - prices too low?

4. Rising overdraft despite legacy.

Gross Profit - difficulties are:

1. Constituents of work in progress valuation.

2. Fees are for Sparks' own time as well as staff time.

Work in Progress

Cost of staff time + appropriate proportion of office and motor etc overheads.

Should he include his own time? Probably yes.

2. Income can be sectionalised into

Accommodation in farmhouse, gate receipts for day visitors, catering, gear, souvenirs. Catering may be further broken down into: provided for stayers and sold to day visitors.

Expenditure can be sectionalised into:
Food, restaurant costs, accommodation costs, gear, souvenirs. Many costs (e.g. depreciation, rates, some staff) cannot be broken down into sections except arbitrarily. Most sections are inter-dependent.

Depreciation
Depreciation depends on life and salvage values. Much will have indefinite lives if maintained (e.g. roads, lakes, trees).

Some will have limited lives (buildings, equipment).

CHAPTER 41

1. (a)

	Letting £	Sales £
Sales	135,000	264,700
Cost of goods sold		156,900
Gross profit		107,800
Wages	49,650	40,650
Rates	3,000	12,000
Other	31,100	26,500
Depr bdgs	1,168	4,672
Depr caravans	47,880	
	132,798	
Commission		2,180
		86,002
Net profit	2,202	21,798

* I have included the net book value as a cost of sale in caravan sales - other treatments are possible eg loss/profit on sale in lettings account.

(b) Many costs are fixed - rates, other overheads, depreciation of buildings, and these would not be saved. However some alternative use (eg letting) might be made of vacated facilities. Some customers might not use a department if the other department closed down.

(c) Problems are: apportionment of unspecified costs, treatment of let caravan sold, buildings depreciation.

CHAPTER 42

1 and 2. The details of the partnership agreements are a matter for negotiation between the partners but should include clauses as listed in paragraph 3 of the chapter.

CHAPTER 43

1.

		G	A	S	Total
		£	£	£	£
(a)	Profit shares	5,772	6,806	2,062	14,640
(b)	Capitals	8,000	5,000	5,000	18,000
	Current	3,372	4,506	62	7,940
(c)	Profits	6,137	7,152	2,151	15,440
(d)	Profits	956	1,990	(346)	2,600

(e) This would be the same as (a) if drawings were not counted as reducing capital at 31.3.-7 etc. and items reducing interest on capital. It would be illogical to do so as interest is charged on drawings. Capital at the end of the year will be increased by any profit and reduced by drawings thus changing interest on capital in 19-8.

2

		K	S	Total	K	S	Total
(a)	Profits	16,880	9,620	26,500	8,412	15,568	23,980
(b)	Profits	3,380	620	4,000	1,220	4,780	6,000
(c)	Capital partnership 1 - K £25,380 S £13,620						

CHAPTER 44

1. **Realisation account**

	£		£
Fixed assets	16,435	Creditors	12,465
Stock	8,762	Proceeds - fixed assets	15,000
Debtors	12,900	Proceeds - stock	7,500
Creditors paid	12,200	Proceeds - debtors	12,450
		Loss on realisation	
		John	1,441
		Mary	1,441
	£50,297		£50,297

Capital accounts

	John	Mary		John	Mary
	£	£		£	£
Loss on realisation	1,441	1,441	Balance b/f	15,352	11,530
Cash	13,911	10.089			
	£15,352	£11,530		£15,352	£11,530

Cash book

	£		£
B/f	1,250	Creditors	12,200
Proceeds: Fixed assets	15,000	John	13,911
Stock	7,500	Marh	10,089
Debtors	12,450		
	£36,200		£36,200

2. Realisation account

	£		£
Fixed assets	23,875	Creditors	38,970
Stock	24,567	Proceeds: Fixed assets	20,000
Debtors	13,546	Stock	18,000
Creditors settlement	38,965	Debtors	13,000
		Loss on realisation:	
		Harry	5.491
		James	3,661
		Roger	1,831
			10,983
	£100,953		£100,953

Capital accounts

	Harry £	James £	Roger £		Harry £	James £	Roger £
Loss on realisation	5,491	3,661	1,831	Capital b/f	3,000	4,000	1,000
Roger *	99	132		Current b/f	102	860	600
Cash		1,067		Harry *			99
				James *			132
				Cash	2,488		
	£5,590	£4,860	£1,831		£5,590	£4,860	£1,831

*In accordance with Garner v Murray

Cash book

	£		£
Proceeds: Fixed assets	20,000	b/f	13,456
Stock	18,000	Creditors	38,965
Debtors	13,000	James	1,067
Harry	2,488		
	£53,488		£53,488

CHAPTER 45

1.

Capital accounts

	Alec £	Ben £		Alec £	Ben £
Goodwill write off	18,000	12,000	Balance b/d	23,000	22,000
Balance c/f	17,500	22,500	Revaluation of goodwill	12,500	12,500
	35,500	34,500		35,500	34,500
			Balance b/f	17,500	22,500

Goodwill account

	£	£		£
b/f		5,000	Written off:	
Revaluation of goodwill:			Alec	18,000
Alec	12,500		Ben	12,000
Ben	12,500	25,000		
		30,000		30,000

2. (a) *Appropriation Account year ending 31 May 19-8*
        1.6.-8 - 30.11.-8

	F £	G £	£
Shares	6,000	6,000	12,000

1.12.-8 - 31.5.-9

	F £	G £	£
Salary		3,000	3,000
Shares	5,400	3,600	9,000
	14,400	9,600	24,000

(b) *Capital Accounts*

	F £	G £		F £	G £
Goodwill down	12,000	8,000	b/f	35,000	20,000
c/f	33,000	22,000	Goodwill up	10,000	10,000
	45,000	30,000		45,000	30,000

Current Accounts

	F £	G £		F £	G £
Drawings	12,700	9,250	b/f	3,100	820
c/f	4,800	1,170	Share	14,400	9,600
	17,500	10,420		17,500	10,420

(c) Either 58,920 + 24,000 - 12,700 - 9,250 = £60,970

     Or 33,000 + 22,000 + 4,800 + 1,170 = £60,970

3. *Capital Accounts*

    Louise   14,300 + 14,400 - 21,600   = £7,100
    Manuel   6,800 + 14,400   = £21,200   (to Loan A/c)
    Nathan   5,200 + 7,200 - 14,400   = £(2,000)

Appropriation Account

Profit 28,400 less interest 2,955 = 25,445	*Louise*	*Nathan*
Interest on capital	710	(200)
Balance	14,961	9,974
	15,671	9,774

Current Accounts
    Louise   15,671 - 6,200   = £9,471
    Nathan   9,774 - 4,100   = £5,674

Balance Sheet as at 31.10.89

	L	M	N		
Capital	7,100		(2,000)	Net Assets	38,445
Current	9,471		5,674		
Loan		18,200			
	16,571	18,200	3,674		38,445

CHAPTER 47

1. A   Reserves -42 (a debit balance)
    B   Fixed assets 98
    C   Share capital 877
    D   Creditors due in more than 12 months - 600

CHAPTER 48

1. B Taylor Ltd
1983

			Dr £	Cr £
April 1	Applications and allotments account		80,000	
	Share capital £1 ordinary shares			80,000
April 1	Cash		80,000	
	Applications and allotments account			80,000
April 9	Applications and allotments account		100,000	
	Share capital			60,000
	Share premium account			40,000
April 9	Cash		100,000	
	Applications and allotment account			100,000
June 1	First and final call account		60,000	
	Share capital			60,000
June 1	Cash		60,000	
	First and final call account			60,000

2. Applications and allotments account:

Dr: £200,000 + £80,000 + £500,000   Cr: £710,000 + £25,000 + £45,000

Balances: Issued capital £1,600,000; Share premium £400,000,
            Cash Dr £1,480,000 Cr £80,000

3.

	b/f £	a £	b £	c £	d £	e £
Ordinary share capital	60,000	60,000	60,000	120,000	120,000	120,000
Preference shares		40,000	40,000	40,000	20,000	20,000
Share premium		32,000	32,000	32,000	32,000	32,000
Capital redemption reserve					20,000	20,000
Profit and loss account	180,000	180,000	180,000	180,000	160,000	160,000
Property revaluation reserve						30,000
Debenture premium account			2,000	2,000	2,000	2,000
Debentures			40,000	40,000	40,000	40,000
	240,000	312,000	354,000	414,000	394,000	424,000
Net Assets	240,000	312,000	354,000	414,000	394,000	424,000

4. *Jim Boy Limited*

	b/f £	a £	b £	c £	d(i) £	d(ii) £	d £
Share capital ordinary	10,000	12,500	15,000	15,000	15,000	15,000	15,000
Preference shares	8,000	8,000	8,000	8,000	12,000	12,000	8,000
Share premium	2,600	6,100	6,100	6,100	6,100	6,100	6,100
Profit and loss	11,000	11,000	8,500	8,380	8,380	4,380	4,380
Capital redemption reserve						4,000	4,000
Debentures				6,000	6,000	6,000	6,000
	31,600	37,600	37,600	43,480	47,480	47,480	43,480
Net Assets	31,600	37,600	37,600	43,480	47,480	47,480	43,480

CHAPTER 49

1. Bustle Ltd Profit and Loss account year ending 31 December 1986

		£'000
Turnover		290
Cost of sales		190
Gross profit		100
Distribution costs	27	
Administration expenses	30	
		57
Net profit on ordinary activities		43
Tax on profit on ordinary activities		12
Profit on ordinary activities after tax		31
Extraordinary charges		13
Profit for the financial year		18
Dividends: Interim paid	3	
Final proposed	5	
		8
Retained profit for the year		10

CHAPTER 51

1.		*Profit*	*Working capital*
	(a)	-£1,000	+ £1,500
	(b)	0	- £4,000
	(c)	- £16,200	0
	(d)	+ £36	+ £36
	(e)	0	-£2,000
	(f)	- £100	- £100
	(g)	0	+ £25,000
	(h)	0	- £60,000
	(i)	0	0

2		Components	Whole	Profit
	(a)	Crs + £800	- £800	0
	(b)	Drs + £600	+ £600	- £200
	(c)	0	0	- £100
	(d)	Cash + £60,000	+ £60,000	0
	(e)	Drs + £800		
		Stock - £500	+ £300	+ £300
	(f)	Cash - £40,000	- £40,000	0

3   (a)   Generated from operations £19,433. Other sources £1,200. Applications £21,460. Decrease in WC £827.

    (b)   Drawings in excess of profits, new fixed assets of £4,160 with a disposal, reduction in stocks but an increase in debtors, large increase in creditors, overdraft paid off (by not paying creditors on time?)

CHAPTER 52

1. (i) Debtors net of VAT = $\frac{110}{115}$ x £23,000 = £20,000

   Average payment figure = $\frac{20,000}{148,600}$ x 12 = 1.6 months

   (ii) Debtors may be

December	4,800
November	7,400
October	7,800
	20,000

   Therefore average payment period = 2 + $\frac{7,800}{10,100}$ = 2.77 months

2. (i) Creditors net of VAT = $\frac{100}{115}$ x £54,000 = £46,957

   Average payment period = $\frac{46,957}{244,200}$ x 12 = 2.3 months

   (ii) Creditors may be

December	27,400
November	19,557
	46,957

   Therefore average payment period = 1 + $\frac{19,557}{24,200}$ = 1.8 months

3.

		-3	-4	-5
(a)	Debtors/sales	2.9	3.5	4.0
	Creditors/purchases	3.1	4.0	5.0
	Current ratio	1.2	1.4	1.4
	Acid test	0.75	0.75	0.76
	Stock turn	2.1	4.25	4.15

   (b) Stock increasing at a faster rate than turnover. Difficulty in collecting debts (and/or policy to grant longer credit to raise turnover). Creditors are harder to pay despite increase in overdraft.

CHAPTER 53

1. Return on capital employed

	Abel	Ben	Cain	Darren
Return	24 - 15 = 9	26 - 15 = 11	12	18 - 15 = 3
Capital	96	35	126 + 24 = 150	9
ROCE	9%	31%	8%	33%

2. Ratios

	Amanda			Sandra		
	19-6	19-7	19-8	19-6	19-7	19-8
G.P. Ratio %	44	42	37	51	50	51
Net profit/Sales %	10	9	3	11	7	11

Observations:
   (a) Amanda has a consistent decline in GP ratio perhaps to maintain turnover in increasingly competitive times; some attempt to reduce wages costs to match uncontrollable increases in occupancy costs. Little advertising. Net profit declined in 19-8 to reflect lower GP.

   (b) Sandra increasing turnover (by 18% and 15%) whilst maintaining GP ratio. Probably by expensive advertising. Costs are steadily rising hence fall in NP ratio in 19-7 but recovery (higher turnover and GP) in 19-8.

3. (a)   *Shoe*   *Mock*
    ROCE - all suppliers of capital
    Return   53 + 16   115 + 32
                                                                = 69   = 147
    Capital employed   343   980
    ROCE %   20   15

    (b) (i) Return on equity before tax   53/243 x   115/780 x
                                                              100 = 22%   100 = 15%

        (ii) After tax   36/243 x   75/780 x
                                                              100 = 15%   100 = 10%

CHAPTER 54

1. *Capital*   *Boring*   *Risquee*   *Happee*
    Debt   100   (1) 700   800
    Equity   3,100   750   2,100

    (2) *Debt* as a % (Debt and Equity)   3%   48%   28%

    (1) I have included preference shares as a debt. Some commentators would not, but preference shares have many of the characteristics of debt.

    (2) Some commentators calculate the debt equity ratio as debt/equity x 100 i.e. 38% for Happee. It does not matter as long as the basis of the percentage is made clear.

Income

$$\frac{\text{Interest}}{\text{Profit before interest}} \times 100\% \qquad \frac{16}{356} \times 100 \qquad \frac{85}{464} \times 100 \qquad \frac{128}{548} \times 100$$

                                                  = 4.5%   = 18.3%   = 23%

There is no absolute measure of "high", "medium" or "low" gearing. It is a matter of comparing the gearing of a company in a particular industry with the average gearing for that industry. However, Boring is clearly low geared and Risquee relatively high geared. Happee is not high geared in its capital but owing to the relatively low profits, it appears it is high geared on an income measure.

2.   *Randaid*   *Spudfix*
    Return on new assets   20%   24%
    Extra profit (return - int)   £10   £30
    Increase in profit as a %age   20%   12.6%
    Current return on shareholder capital $\frac{60}{400}$ x $\frac{220}{1,100}$ x

                                                            100 = 15%   = 20%
    Return on shareholder capital with new assets $\frac{70}{400}$ x $\frac{250}{1,100}$

                                                            100 = 17.5%   = 23%

CHAPTER 55

1.   *Proton*   *Neutron*   *Positron*
                                                    plc   *plc*   *plc*
    (a) Earnings per share   6p   4p   7.8p
    (b) Price earnings ratio   10   8   12.3p
    (c) Dividend yield   5%   6.25%   5.2%
    (d) Total dividend   £600,000   £300,000   £3,000,000
        Dividend cover   2   2   1.6

No. 60p is the price that a small number of buyers and sellers will buy and sell. To attract a high number of sellers, a higher price has to be offered.

2.   EPS 6.7p; PE ratio 8.25; Dividend yield 4.5%; Dividend cover 2.7; dividend per share 2.5p

3.   (a)   8p;
     (b)   £80,000;
     (c)   £32,000;
     (d)   3.2p.

CHAPTER 56

1.   Watkin
     (a)   Business entity convention. 30% of the rent (and the other motor expenses) are business expenses. But probably the car will appear on the balance sheet at full cost.

     (b)   This can be argued as the money measurement convention (difficult to evaluate orders) or the historical cost convention (order had no cost) or the realisation convention (no profit until sale). Clearly, the *future* prosperity of the business is affected by the extent of unfilled orders but the accounts are *historical*.

     (c)   This has to do with the historical cost convention as assets may be undervalued but also entity convention as creditors can also look to my private assets for payment.

     (d)   Return on capital will look good if property is at a very low valuation, a fault in the historical cost convention. Note that if revalued assets rise, profits will fall because of extra depreciation.

     (e)   This is the going concern convention.

     (f)   At cost because no profit is recognised (under the realisation convention) until a sale has been made.

     (g)   The periodicity convention is to prepare accounts once a year and this is also required by the Inspector of Taxes. However, more frequent preparation is possible at a cost. Stock is the usual problem.

     (h)   If sold the profit on the rods should be included in gross profit - realisation convention. It should include them in stock at cost. The facts must be determined.

     (i)   The accruals convention requires the rent receivable for the whole period to be included even if it has not all been received.

     (j)   The loss on this contract should be provided for under the prudence convention. The loss will be 50 x £5 + £100 = £350.

     (k)   The consistency convention should be followed but a change can be made if there are good reasons and the change is quantified and explained.

     (l)   The materiality convention probably was applied so that cash was included with bank and the loan with debtors.

     (m) This is true as to legal form but the substance of the transaction is that the van is an asset and Carp are creditors. This will be the treatment in the accounts.

     (n)   This *may* be true but again under the substance over form convention the tubing will be treated as stock at cost and a creditor will be included for the amount due. It *may* belong to the supplier but this will be hard to establish against a liquidator or trustee in bankruptcy.

CHAPTER 57

1. *Bangle Limited*
    Forecast Trading and Profit and Loss Account for the year ending 31st December 19-8

	£			£
Administration	39,600	Sales – credit		161,000
Selling and distribution	10,000	Sales – cash		133,000
Depreciation	10,000			294,000
Advertising	11,000	Opening stock	42,000	
Directors' remuneration	22,000	Purchases (2)	178,850	
Net profit (2)	18,350		220,850	
		Closing stock	37,800	183,050
	110,950		(1)	110,950

(1) 40% of 161,000 + 35% x 133,000
(2) Balancing figure.

Forecast Balance Sheet as at 31st December 19-8

	£			£
Share capital	2,000	Fixed Assets		
Reserves	36,350	Cost		50,000
Loan	5,000	Depreciation		34,000
Creditors	30,008			16,000
Overdraft (2)	8,984	Stock	37,800	
Dividend	5,000	Debtors	33,542	71,342
	87,342			87,342

Appendix II: Case studies

CASE STUDY I

1. This case study gives practice in:

   (i) Preparing elementary accounts both as historical events and in forecast form.
   (ii) Elementary ratio analysis.
   (iii) Critically evaluating the amount of profit in relation to capital employed and alternative uses of the proprietor's capital resources.
   (iv) Trading strategies.

   (a) Hamish has been made redundant and has received £6,000 in redundancy compensation which, with his savings of £4,000, he has decided to invest in a greengrocers shop. His first year plans and expectations are:

   - Acquisition of remaining 10 years of the lease on a lock-up for £5,000. (Annual rent £2,000 and rates £1,520.)
   Acquisition of fittings for £2,000 (life 10 years, nil salvage value) and a van £2,000 (life 3 years, salvage value £500).
   - All sales will be at cost, plus 50%.
   - Wages will be paid to an assistant at £90 a week, to include national insurance.
   - Other overheads will be £3,444 a year.
   - Drawings of £100 a week.
   - Stock will average £1,000 at cost.

   Required:

   (i) Assuming that all expectations are met, what *weekly* takings are required to make the venture worthwhile.
   (ii) Draw up a forecast balance sheet at the end of the year. Assume that purchases will be evenly spread through the year and that two months credit is taken from suppliers and that there are no pre-payments or accruals.

   (b) Hamish did take the shop and the actual outcome of events in the first year were:

	£
(i) Sales	61,300
Purchases	40,100
Closing stock	1,400
Creditors at year end	7,300
Wages	5,700
Other overheads	4,100
Drawings	6,380

   The remaining expenses were as expected.

   (ii) Mrs Hamish was required to work part time in the shop and was forced thereby to give up her part-time job losing the wage of £30 a week.

   Required:

   (i) Draw up a trading and profit and loss account for the year and a balance sheet as at the year end.
   (ii) Critically evaluate the accounts in comparison with the forecast.

   (c) After the end of the first year, Hamish has a choice:

   (i) Sell the assets of the shop to Ian for £12,000. In this case Hamish would retain the cash and would pay off the creditors. Hamish could then take a job at £10,000 a year and invest his cash at 10%. Mrs Hamish can resume her part-time job.

   (ii) Retain the business and reduce his prices, in which case, turnover should increase by 30% and gross profit ratio reduce to 33⅓% on cost. Expenses will remain as in the first year.

(iii) Retain the business and increase his prices, in which case turnover should decrease by 10% and gross profit ratio increase to 60% on cost. Expenses will remain as in the first year. In this case, less work will be required and Mrs Hamish can resume her part-time job.

Note that if the business is retained, any cash balance at the end of the first year can be invested at 10%.

Required: Assess the advantages and disadvantages of each proposal and advise Hamish.

CASE STUDY II

The second case study is an extended exercise in bookkeeping containing sections on:
(i)   Books of prime entry.
(ii) Sectional balancing.
(iii) Closing entries.
(iv) Final accounts preparation.

David commenced in business as a wholesaler of lawnmowers on 1 January 19-5. His first month's transactions were:

		£
Jan 2	Purchases on credit: Barbara	800
	Jane	1,524
	Rental invoice from Edna, quarter to 31.3.-4	500
	Rates invoice from Haytown Council quarter to 31.3.-4	360
	Cheque from David's private account paid into bank	6,000
Jan 3	Purchases on credit: Jane	380
	Credit note from Barbara	36
	Insurance invoice from Paula – year to 31.12.-4	168
	Paid Edna by cheque	500
Jan 4	Invoice from Dawn for motor van	3,000
	(price included licence y/e 31.12.-4 – £85; and insurance y/e 31.12.-4 £240)	
	Sales invoice – George	730
Jan 5	Cheque from Jessica – Loan at 12% pa	2,000
	Purchases on credit – Barbara	1,210
	Paid Paul by cheque	168
Jan 8	Sales invoice – Philip	826
	Cheque for cash: Wages	102
	Drawings	100
	Petty cash	20
	Paid Dawn by cheque	3,000
	Petty cash payments: Petrol	5
	Sundries	11
Jan 9	Purchases on credit: Louise	360
Jan 15	Cheque for cash: Wages	104
	Drawings	100
	Petty cash	25
	Sales invoice – Nigel	1,043
Jan 17	Paid Barbara by cheque	764
	Nigel paid (after discount of £26)	1,017
	Petty cash payment: Petrol	7
	Sundries	18
Jun 18	Paid Jane	1,524
Jan 19	Paid Louise (after discount of £18)	342
Jan 20	Purchases on credit – Louise	180
	Sales invoice – Jeff	682
Jan 22	Cheque for cash: Wages	101
	Drawings	100
	Petty cash	30
	Sales invoice – George	2,430
Jan 23	Purchases on credit – Nora	2,450
Jan 24	Petty cash payments: Petrol	6
	Sundries	6
	Drawings	8

Jan 24	Sales invoice – Miles	960
Jan 25	Paid Nora £2,450 less 2% discount	
Jan 26	Sales invoice – Philip	2,812
Jan 27	Purchases on credit – Barbara	1,611
Jan 28	Miles paid £960 less 2½% discount	
	Purchases on credit – Jane	180
Jan 29	Cheque for cash: Wages	103
	Drawings	110
	Petty cash to make up to float of £40	
	Credit note from Jane	141
Jan 30	Invoice for petrol from Matilda	168
	Sales invoice – George	136

Required:

(a) Enter all transactions into appropriate books of prime entry.

(b) Enter all transactions into double entry accounts. You should use three separate ledgers:
- sales ledger
- suppliers ledger
- general ledger.

(c) Balance off accounts where necessary and prepare a trial balance.

(d) Prepare sales ledger and suppliers ledger control accounts.

(e) Prepare a trading and profit and loss account for the month of January and a balance sheet at 31 January, taking into account:
   (i)   Stock at 31 January consisted of:
       16 'A' type mowers which had cost £30 each
       14 'B' type mowers which had cost £43 each
       50 'C' type mowers which had cost £21 each
       6 'D' type mowers which had cost £14 each
   (ii) PAYE and national insurance owing at 31.1.-4 was £207.
   (iii) Depreciation policy is 30% reducing balance.

(f) Enter the transfers to trading and profit and loss account in the general ledger accounts.

(g) Compute the gross and net profit to sales percentages.

(h) Compute the return on capital employed assuming that David's labour is worth £7,200 a year.

CASE STUDY III

The following case study gives practice in:

(i)   Drawing up a partnership agreement.
(ii)   Preparation of partnership accounts.
(iii) Resolving of the problems of partnerships when a partner retires or dies.

Parts (a) and (c) are suitable for role playing with roles for each of the three partners.

(a) Oliver, Phyllis and Quintin intend to set up in business as builders merchants. Details of the partners and the business are:

Oliver: is a wealthy accountant. He is intending to invest £20,000 in the business but work part time only (eight hours a week) mainly in the accounting, systems, commercial areas.

Phyllis: is currently unemployed, having been made redundant from a bankrupt builders merchant firm. She can invest some £2,000 in the business and intends to work full time on the administration, purchasing, stock control and delivering to customers, activities.

Quintin: is a representative for a firm of building material manufacturers. He intends to invest about £5,000 in the business and work part time (about ten hours a week). His main activity will be selling, as he intensive connections in the trade.

The business: The business will be conducted from leased premises. A lease for twenty years on a new property has been obtained at a market rent of £4,000 a year. It is envisaged that profits should be around £25,000 a year.

Required:

(i)   Draw up a list of matters that should be included in the partnership agreement.
(ii) Draw up appropriate specific clauses on the subjects of:
      - profit/loss sharing
      - whether or not to maintain separate partners' capital and current accounts.

(b) At the end of the first year, the trial balance of the partnership was:

		£			£
Fixtures at cost		10,900	Capitals O		20,000
Vehicles at cost		16,380	P		2,000
Drawings O		3,100	Q		5,000
P		8,700	Sales		241,720
Q		4,630	Creditors		38,609
Purchases		204,135	Bank		9,450
Rent		3,000			
Other overheads		25,838			
Debtors		40,096			
		316,779			316,779

Stock was valued at cost at £23,600.
Other overheads included rates in advance of £248 but did not include accruals of £1,200.
The fixtures are expected to have a life of ten years with no salvage value.
The vehicles are expected to have a life of four years with a residual value of £4,000.

Required:

Trading and profit and loss and appropriation account for the first year of the partnership and balance sheet as at the end of the year.

(c) As at the end of year one, Quintin is promoted in his job to another part of the country and wishes to withdraw from the partnership.

Required:

Detail suitable arrangements for the withdrawal of Quintin. The following points may be borne in mind:

(i)   The lease has become worth £5,000.
(ii) The customers introduced by Quintin are likely to continue to buy from the business but a representative will be required. The representative will cost £15,000 a year and will spend one third of his time on existing customers and two thirds on developing new business.
(iii) Bank overdraft facilities of £20,000 have been agreed but future working capital requirements will pre-empt about £15,000 of that.

CASE STUDY IV

The next case study gives practice in:

(i)   Preparing accounts in columnar form to demonstrate the performance of departments or branches.
(ii) Calculating and evaluating performance and liquidity ratios.
(iii) Critically assessing the information contained in accounts but hidden except to the perceptive observer.
(iv) Using accounts to make decisions.

Part (e) is suitable for role playing with parts for Jonas and each of the branch managers.

Jonas owns a business manufacturing light fittings. Sales are handled by three branches, in Manchester, Birmingham and Exeter. Each branch has been open for ten years and each branch manager has been in office since the opening. Each branch is autonomous as to bookkeeping, selling prices, the incurring of overheads and working capital control.

For 19-5, the trial balances of the three branches showed:

	Manchester £'000	Birmingham £'000	Exeter £'000
Sales	1,040	1,530	764
Purchases (from Jonas at fixed prices)	744	1,170	475
Stocks 1.1.-5	256	260	203
Debtors	264	127	223
Creditors	62	97	40
Bank	9	1	6
Fixed assets at cost	164	134	102
Depreciation to 1.1.-5	131	46	50
Wages	114	118	115
Rent	18	44	30
Rates	9	36	13
Repairs	49	3	6
Advertising	36	48	11
Discounts allowed	2	68	–
Other overheads	30	33	31
Head office a/c 1.1.-5	490	392	405
Remittances to head office in 19-5			
Less purchases made	46	23	44
At 31.12.-5:			
Stocks were	270	301	189
Overhead accruals	4	–	7
Rent prepayment	2	–	–
Rates prepayment	–	8	–

Depreciation policy is 25% reducing balance for all branches.

Required:

(a) Prepare trial balances in two column form for each branch as at 31 December 19-5.
(b) Prepare trading and profit and loss accounts and balance sheets for each branch for 19-5.
(c) Compile a schedule showing performances and liquidity ratios for each branch.
(d) List what you can deduce from the accounts and your schedule about:
  (i) Jonas' requirements on supplying goods to his branches.
  (ii) Each branch manager's management strategies and performance.
(e) Jonas is now seeking to open a branch in London. It is his intention to ask one of the existing three branch managers to manage the new branch. Which one of the three should be appointed?

CASE STUDY V

The final case study gives practice in:

(a) Preparing accounting statements for managerial purposes.
(b) Considering appropriate accounting policies and the effect on profit of different policies.
(c) Drawing up financial statements for publication.
(d) Discussing the nature of partnerships and how they differ from private limited companies.

N Ltd was formed to manufacture and market trailers and commenced business on 1 January 19-5.

The following information is available on the activities of the company in the year 19-5.

(a) On 1.1.-5 the company took over the assets of O, P and Co, being:

		£
Plant and machinery		116,000
Stocks	Raw material	36,240
	Work in progress	24,382
	Finished goods	102,485
	Prepayment of rent	2,000

The consideration for the takeover was £350,000 satisfied by the issue of 200,000 ordinary shares of £1 each to the partners of O, P & Co, and £150,000, 15% debentures 19-0/-2 secured by a floating charge on all assets of the company.

(b) The trial balance (excluding item (a) above) at 31 December 19-5 showed:

	£
Sales	2,260,000
Purchases – raw materials	384,000
Purchases – finished goods	471,000
Direct labour	320,500
Carriage inwards	52,000
Royalties payable on production of trailers	6,000
Additional plant	204,620
Rent	40,000
Rates	36,000
Insurances	59,000
General overheads	446,000
Indirect labour	384,905
Proceeds of sale of machine	4,000
Bank overdraft	73,395
Bank interest	10,300
Debtors	493,250
Creditors	106,180
Directors remuneration	96,000
Proceeds of issue – share capital	200,000

(c) Of the expenses, the following analysis can be made (percentages).

	Production	Distribution	Selling	Administration
	£	£	£	£
Depreciation	80	–	10	10
Rent	90	5	2	3
Rates	90	5	2	3
Insurance	70	5	10	25
General	60	10	10	20
Indirect labour	60	10	20	10
Directors remuneration	30	15	20	35

(d) At the year end:

		£
Stocks	– raw materials	51,820
	– work in progress (excluding h and j)	62,709
	– finished goods	181,100
Accruals	– rent	8,000
	– rates	5,300
Prepayments	insurance	1,200

(e) The item proceeds of issue share capital, relates to the sale of 100,000 ordinary shares of £1 each at £1.50 each and 50,000 15% preference shares at par to Q.

(f) The plant and machinery taken over has an estimated further life of 5 years with a salvage value of 10% of its taken over value. The new plant is also expected to last 7 years and have a salvage value of £30,000. The item sold was included in the taken over plant at £15,000.

(g) During the year there was a burglary when stock costing £90,100 was stolen. It has not been recovered and the loss is not insured.

(h) The company constructed three very large trailers early in the year for use as transporters to carry the company's products to customers. The cost of manufacture included materials £30,000 and direct labour £27,000.

(i) Directors remuneration was:

	£
O (Chairman)	25,000
P	36,000
Q	14,000
R	13,000
S	8,000

(j) In February 19-5, a contract was signed for Z Ltd, for the manufacture of a special giant trailer. The contract price was agreed at £200,000 with completion in March 19-7. At 31.12.-5; work done to date had cost £86,000, the estimated costs to completion are £93,000 and £60,000 had been received on account and had been included in sales.

(k) Of the debtors £16,000 are considered definitely bad and £34,000 are doubtful.

(l) The company have commissioned a computerised budgeting system at a cost of £155,000 included in general overheads. This has been used in the business and four copies have been sold to other companies at £20,000 each. Firm orders for three more have been received and other sales are in prospect.

(m) The company proposed to pay the preference dividend and an ordinary dividend of 10p a share.

(n) Ignore taxation.

Required:

(i) Prepare two column trial balance incorporating item (a).

(ii) Prepare manufacturing, trading and profit and loss account for the year 19-5 for internal purposes. You should devise suitable accounting policies. The directors are particularly anxious to maximise the measure of profit.

(iii) Prepare a balance sheet as at 31.12.-5 in Format 1.

(iv) Prepare a profit and loss account in Format 1 suitable for publication and complying (as far as the data is available) with the minimum requirements of the Companies Acts.

(v) Draw up a 'statement of accounting policies'.

(vi) The company is in effect a partnership between O and P who were in business together before joining with Q in N Ltd. O and P work full time in the business, but Q only attends the weekly board meetings. R and S are employee directors with no shareholdings. Q is dissatisfied with the fees paid to him and the company's trading policy which is to expand by importing trailers from Italy.

Write a report, advising Q on possible remedies for his dissatisfaction and contrasting the rights of O, P and Q in the company with the rights they would have had if the venture had been a partnership under the Partnership Act 1890.

Appendix III: Glossary of Accounting Terms

Absorption the sharing out of the costs of a cost centre among the products which use the cost centre.

Account a record in a double entry bookkeeping system that is kept for each (or each class) of asset, liability, revenue and expense.

Accountant a person who practices accountancy.

Accounting a set of theories, concepts and techniques by which financial data are processed into information for reporting, planning, controlling and decision making purposes, or the process of recording, classifying, reporting and interpreting the financial data of an organisation.

Accounting equation an expression of the equivalence, in total, of assets = liabilities + owners equity.

Accounting period that time period, typically one year, to which financial statements are related.

Accounting policies the specific accounting bases selected and consistently followed by a business enterprise as being, in the opinion of the management, appropriate to its circumstances and best suited to present fairly its results and financial position.

Accounts payable amounts owed to suppliers for the purchase of goods and services: commonly called creditors.

Accounts receivable amounts that customers owe an organisation for goods and services supplied: commonly called debtors.

Accruals (that which has accrued, accumulated, grown) expenses which have been consumed or enjoyed but which have not been paid for at the accounting date.

Accruals convention the convention whereby revenue and costs are accrued (that is, recognised as they are earned or incurred, not as money is paid or received), matched with one another so far as their relationship can be established or justifiably assumed, and dealt with in the profit and loss account of the period to which they relate.

Accumulated depreciation the part of the original cost of a fixed asset which has been regarded as a depreciation expense in successive profit and loss accounts: cost less accumulated depreciation = net book value.

Acid test ratio the ratio of current assets (excluding stock) to current liabilities.

Activity ratios ratios used to analyse a firm's effectiveness in using specific resources: examples include stock or work in progress turnover ratios.

Allocation the charging of discrete, identifiable items of cost to cost centres or cost units. A cost is allocated when the cost is unique to a particular cost centre.

Amortisation an equivalent word to depreciation: commonly used for writing off, as an expense to profit and loss account, of the capital cost of acquiring leasehold property.

Annual return a return required to be made each calendar year to the Registrar of Companies by all companies. The return contains sections on shareholdings, directors, indebtedness and other matters and must include the annual accounts.

Annuity a fixed sum payable each year for a number of years. Annuities can be purchased from insurance companies for a fixed capital sum. The annuity method is a complicated and archaic method of depreciation.

Apportionment the division of costs among two or more cost centres in proportion to the estimated benefit on some sensible basis. Apportionment is for shared costs.

Appropriation account an account following the profit and loss account of partnerships and companies which accounts for the appropriation or division of the profit amongst the parties entitled. In the case of partnerships the persons entitled are the partners and partners' salaries, interest on capital, residual share and other entitlements should be included. In the case of companies the division is between dividends, provisions for taxation, transfer to reserve, bonus issues and retentions.

Articles of association the internal regulations for the running of a company. All companies must have Articles. Many adopt table A (a model set in the Companies Act) with modifications.

A.S.C. (the Accounting Standards Committee) a committee of the C.C.A.B which produces SSAPs (statement of standard accounting practice). The procedure is for the A.S.C. to produce an Exposure Draft for public comment, to amend the draft where required after public comment and to issue the SSAP. The several bodies of accountants then accept the SSAP and it becomes mandatory on the members of the accounting bodies.

Assets the economic resources of an enterprise that are expected to benefit future time periods and that can usefully be expressed in money terms.

Asset value a term which expresses the money amount of assets less liabilities of a company attributable to one ordinary share.

Associated company a company which is not a subsidiary of an investing company but one in which the investing company has a long term interest and has substantial influence over its affairs. Usually the investing company must have between 20% and 50% of the equity capital of a company for that company to be an associated company.

Attributable profit that part of the total profit currently estimated to arise over the duration of a contract which fairly reflects the profit attributable to that part of the work performed by the accounting date.

Auditing the independent examination of, and expression of opinion on, the financial statements of an enterprise by an appointed auditor in persuance of that appointment and in compliance with any relevant statutory obligation.

Authorised capital the amount of capital stated in the Memorandum of Association. The company cannot issue more than the authorised capital but the amount can be increased providing the prescribed procedures are followed. Authorised capital is usually divided into shares of a specific monetary value and possibly into preference and ordinary classes.

AVCO (average cost) a method of valuing fungible assets (notably stock) at average (simple or weighted) input prices.

Bad debts debts known to be irrecoverable and therefore treated as losses by inclusion in the profit and loss account as an expense.

Balance sheet a financial statement showing the financial position of an enterprise in terms of assets, liabilities and owner's equity at a specified date.

Bank reconciliation statement a statement which explains the difference in the balance shown by a cash book from that shown by a bank statement. The differences are caused by differences in the timing of issuing cheques and their presentation to the bank and similar timing differences.

Bankruptcy a legal status imposed upon a person by a court, either on his own petition or on the petition of his creditors. Usually a trustee is appointed to receive and realise the assets of the bankrupt and to distribute the proceeds to his creditors in accordance with the law.

Bases (accounting bases) the methods which have been developed for expressing or applying fundamental accounting concepts to financial transactions and items. There may be more than one basis for dealing with any particular item. For example there are several methods of depreciation. The particular accounting basis chosen by an enterprise for a particular item is known as an accounting policy.

Base stock a method of valuing individual stock items which assumes that there is always an irreducible minimum quantity in stock. That quantity is valued at the price which prevailed when the line was first stocked, possibly many years earlier. The balance is valued on LIFO or other method. SSAP9 disapproves of the base stock method.

Benefits in kind things or services provided by a company to directors and others in addition to cash remuneration. The best known are the provision of free use of a motor car. The value of benefits in kind are usually taxable.

Bill of exchange a piece of paper involving several parties: the drawer who prepares the bill: the drawee who on accepting the bill becomes liable to pay the amount of the bill at some date specified in the bill to the holder of the bill at that time; the holder of the bill who may be the drawer or some other person who has purchased the bill from the drawer or subsequent holder. Bills are negotiable (transferable) and a common transfer is from the drawer to his bank. This is called discounting as the bank normally gives less for the bill than the face value. A bill of exchange has been likened to a post-dated cheque.

Bond a formal written document that provides evidence of long-term indebtedness. Bond has mainly American usage; the British equivalent is debenture.

Bonus issue an issue of new shares to existing shareholders made possibly by the capitalisation of reserves. No payment is made for the shares. Other words for this rather pointless procedure are scrip issue, capitalisation issue and (in US) stock dividend.

Bookkeeping the art of recording an enterprise's transactions in the books of account of the enterprise. Bookkeeping is ideally carried out using the formal system known as double entry bookkeeping.

Book value the amount at which an asset is carried in the accounting records. The value is usually original cost less accumulated depreciation. Alternative phrases are net book value and written down value. Book value rarely corresponds to subjective values such as saleable value.

Budget a formal quantitative expression of management expectations generated for any area that management deems critical. Examples are the sales budget, purchases budget, cash budget and capital expenditure budget.

Called-up capital when shares are issued the sums due may be payable by instalments either at fixed dates or when the directors so determine. A request for payment is known as a call and that part of the share capital which has been repaid or requested is known as the called up capital. If a shareholder has not paid a call the amount due is known as calls in arrear.

Capital an imprecise term meaning the whole quantity of assets less liabilities owned by a person or business. The capital account of sole proprietor is equal to the assets less liabilities of the business. The capital accounts of partners measure the sums due to the partners by the partnership and sum to the total assets less liabilities of the partnership.

Capital allowances reductions in the measurement of profit used by a business in assessing its tax liability to recognise capital expenditure. In effect capital allowances are a formal system of depreciation allowances to replace the accounting methods of depreciation. In recent years accelerated capital allowances have permitted businesses to write off much capital expenditure in the year of purchase. Currently capital allowances more nearly conform to commercial depreciation.

Capital expenditure expenditure that provides long term benefits. Most capital expenditure is on fixed assets.

Capital redemption reserve a capital reserve created by a transfer from revenue reserves on the occasion of redemption of redeemable share capital.

Capital reserve a liability to shareholders that cannot be paid either because the law prohibits it or because the directors or the Articles so determine. Capital reserves are represented by some of the assets on the other side of the balance sheet; they are not themselves assets!

Cash strictly coin of the realm and banknotes but in accounting use includes bank accounts.

Cash book the double entry account used to record cash transactions and also transactions with the bank. The term is universally used even if the record is actually in another form than a book, eg on magnetic disk.

Cash discount the granting of a reduction in the amount payable by a debtor to induce prompt payment (= settlement discount).

Cash flow a very imprecise term. A cash flow statement is a statement that shows the sources and uses of cash over a period.

Cash point withdrawals a facility whereby a bank customer can withdraw cash from a machine situated outside or inside his bank.

CCAB the consultative committee of the accounting bodies - the vehicle through which the accounting bodies cooperate.

Chart of accounts a listing of the titles and numbers of all accounts found in a double entry system.

Cheque a bill of exchange drawn on a banker and payable on demand.

Clock card cards used in a factory to record the time worked by a worker. The card is stamped automatically by a clock at the entrance to the factory. Modern clocks can interface with computer systems.

Common stock the US equivalent of ordinary shares.

Company a body corporate whose affairs are regulated by the Companies Act.

Compensating error a bookkeeping term for two separate errors whose separate effects are cancelled out. Thus the errors do not give rise to a difference in the trial balance.

Conservatism an accounting convention whereby revenue and profits are not anticipated, but provision is made for all known liabilities (expenses and losses) whether the amount of these is known with certainty or is a best estimate in the light of the information available.

Consideration in accounting usage, the amount to be paid for the acquisition of a business. The consideration may be in cash or other assets or securities.

Consignment generally the sending of goods. In a restricted sense the sending of goods to an agent for him to sell; the ownership of the goods being retained by the consignor until the goods have been sold by the consignee.

Consistency an accounting convention whereby there is consistency of accounting treatment of like items within each accounting period and from one period to the next.

Consolidated accounts the financial statements of groups of companies whereby the separate financial statements of the individual companies are combined in accordance with a set of established principles.

Contingent liabilities a potential obligation or liability the eventualisation of which depends on some future event beyond the control of the firm.

Continuous inventory the process of recording the amount of stock of each category on a continuous basis so that the amount of stock held of any category can be instantly discovered without recourse to a physical inspection in the warehouse.

Contra (against) a bookkeeping entry by which a liability to a supplier is reduced by (is set against) a sum due by the supplier who is also a customer.

Control account a memorandum (not part of the double entry system) account, the balance of which reflects the aggregate balances of many related subsidiary accounts which are part of the double entry system. Control accounts can be kept for customers (sales ledger) accounts and suppliers (bought ledger) accounts.

Convertible loan stocks a loan stock incorporating the right of the holder to convert the loan stock into equity shares under certain conditions in accordance with prescribed terms.

Conversion cost part of the cost of stock comprising: costs which are specifically attributable to units of production, ie direct labour, direct expenses and sub-contract work: production overheads: other overheads, if any, attributable in the particular circumstances of the business to bringing the product or service to its present location and condition.

Copyright an intangible asset that gives its owners or heirs the exclusive right to produce and sell an artistic, musical or published work for a stipulated period of time.

Corporation tax a tax payable on the income and profits of companies and certain other entities including clubs and societies.

Cost accounting an area of accounting that deals with the collection, analysis, control and evaluation of costs.

Cost behaviour the change in a cost when the level of output changes.

Cost centre a location, function or item of equipment in respect of which costs may be ascertained and related to cost units.

Cost convention an accounting convention whereby the acquisition of goods, services and other resources is entered in the accounting records at cost.

Credit the right hand side of a double entry account.

Credit control a generic term for all those measures and procedures instituted by a firm that trades on credit to ensure that customers pay their accounts. Procedures include evaluation of a customer's credit worthiness and comprehensive collection procedures.

Creditors those to whom a firm owes money. In a balance sheet the term describes the aggregate sum owed to its creditors.

Creditors settlement period a liquidity ratio which may indicate the ability of an enterprise to pay its debts as they fall due. Calculated by (creditors/goods supplied on credit in the year) x 12 if expressed in months.

Cumulative preference shares preference shares where the rights to dividends omitted in a given year accumulate. These dividends must be paid before any subsequent dividends are distributed to ordinary shareholders.

Current accounts in a partnership the sums due to partners which have arisen due to undrawn profits shares.

Current assets those assets which the management intend to convert into cash or consume in the normal course of business within one year or the operating cycle, whichever is longer.

Current cost accounting a system of accounting which recognises the fluctuating value of money by measuring current value by applying specific indeces and other devices to historical costs. CCA is the system required by SSAP16.

Current liabilities debts or obligations that will be paid within one year of the accounting date. The Companies Act 1985 prefers the expression Creditors - amounts falling due within one year.

Current ratio an accounting ratio purporting to measure liquidity. It is calculated as current assets total divided by current liabilities total. It has been suggested, with little justification, that a healthy business should have a current ratio greater than or equal to two.

Cut-off the difficulties encountered by accountants in ensuring that all items of income and expense are corrected ascribed to the appropriate accounting periods.

Cycle the activities involved and the time taken for a firm to complete a typical transaction from, for example, acquisition of goods to the receipt of the sums due by the customer who buys them.

Data facts and figures (Latin = given).

Day book a book of prime entry. The sales day book is a listing of sales invoices. The purchase daybook is a listing of purchase invoices. From the daybooks postings are made to the double entry system.

Debenture a document which creates or acknowledges a debt. Commonly used for the debt itself. Debenture deeds issued by companies usually contain details of the loan and have clauses concerning payment of interest, repayment of capital, security etc.

Debit note a document sent to a person, usually a supplier, whose account it is intended to be debited. Usually it reports a short delivery or overcharge and seeks a credit note as a response. Only the credit note is entered in the books.

Debt a sum due by a debtor to his creditor. A generic term for a company's borrowings.

Debtors those who owe money. Used in a balance sheet to describe the total sum due to the business by its debtors.

Debtors payment period a calculation of the average time taken by credit customers to pay their debts. It is usually calculated by (debtors/credit sales for a year) x 12 to give a result in months.

Deferred liabilities liabilities that exist but where payment has been postponed to some unknown future date. Used particularly for taxation which has been postponed by accelerated capital allowances, stock relief or some other cause.

Delivery note a note sent by a supplier to accompany the goods. Often it is in duplicate and the carrier retains a copy signed by the recipient to act as evidence of good delivery. Similar to an advice note.

Depletion method a method of depreciation applicable to wasting assets such as mines or quarries. The amount of depreciation in a year is a function of the quantity extracted in the year compared to the total resource.

Deposit account an account with a bank, building society or other financial institution carrying interest.

Depreciation is a measure of the wearing out, consumption or other loss of value of a fixed asset whether arising from use, effluxion of time or obsolescence through technology and market changes. Depreciation should be allocated to accounting periods so as to charge a fair proportion to each accounting period during the expected useful life of the asset. Depreciation includes amortisation of fixed assets whose useful life is pre-determined (eg leases) and depletion of wasting assets (eg mines).

Diminishing balance (= reducing instalment) a method of depreciation whereby the cost or agreed value of the asset is written off over its expected life by the application of a percentage to the written down value.

Direct costs those costs comprising direct materials, direct labour and direct expenses which can be directly identified with specific jobs, products or services.

Direct debit a facility given by banks by which (by prior agreement) a creditor can extract money directly from his debtor's bank account.

Directors persons elected by the shareholders of a company to manage the company. Collectively the directors form the Board of directors. Most boards have a chairman and one director is often designated as managing director or chief executive.

Disclosure a principle holding that an entity must provide a complete recording of all facts important enough to influence the judgement of an informed user of financial statements.

Discount a monetary deduction or reduction. Settlement discount is given for early payment of a sum due. Debentures can be issued or redeemed at a discount. Trade discount is a simple reduction in price given to favoured customers for reasons such as status or bulk purchase. Bills of exchange can be discounted (sold) to a bank at less than face value. The discount recompenses the bank for deprival of funds from the date of sale to the maturity date of the bill.

Dishonour to fail to pay or be unable to pay a Bill of Exchange or a cheque.

Dissolution the break up of a partnership.

Dividend a distribution of its earnings to its shareholders by a company. A distribution of part of the sum due to creditors in bankruptcy or liquidation.

Dividend cover a measure of the extent to which the dividend paid by a company is covered by its earnings (profits).

Dividend yield a measure of the revenue earning capacity of an ordinary share to its holder. It is calculated by dividend per share as a percentage of the market or quoted price of the share.

Double entry bookkeeping a method of record keeping developed in Renaissance Italy which now has universal acceptance.

Doubtful debts a reduction in profits (by a charge to profit and loss account) to recognise the probable loss to be suffered because a debt is likely to prove uncollectable. The debts remain in the books (unlike actual bad debts) but are contra'd by an account with a credit balance called a provision for doubtful debts.

Drawings cash or goods withdrawn from a business by a proprietor for his own use.

Dual aspect a principle that implies that all transactions have two aspects and thus affect two double entry accounts. For example a credit sale involves a debit to the customer's account and a credit to the sales account.

Earnings another word for profit, used particularly for company profits.

Earnings per share a performance measure used by investment analysts. The measure is calculated by total profits divided by total number of ordinary shares and is stated in the profit and loss accounts of quoted companies. Its calculation can be complicated and is covered in SSAP3.

Earnings yield an indicator of interest to investors. Calculated by earnings per share as a percentage of the quoted share price.

EDP – Electronic Data Processing the keeping of records including double entry records by computers.

Entity convention a convention that a business can be viewed as a unit that is separate and apart from its owners and from other firms.

Equity the ordinary shares or risk capital of an enterprise. Also a system of law and a trade union for actors.

Exceptional items items which are of abnormal size or incidence but are not extraordinary items because they derive from the ordinary activities of the company. They might include abnormal charges for bad debts, write offs of stocks and work in progress, abnormal provisions for losses on long term contracts, most adjustments of prior year tax provisions. Exceptional items should be separately disclosed.

Expense a cost which will be debited in a profit and loss account as a period cost.

Exposure draft a document issued on a specific accounting topic by the Accounting Standards Committee for discussion. After representations, discussions and amendments it may become a SSAP.

Extraordinary items those items which derive from events or transactions outside the ordinary activities of the business and which are both material and expected not to recur frequently or regularly. They may include profits or losses arising from discontinuance of a significant part of a business, the sale of an investment not held for sale. Extraordinary items are shown separately after the results derived from ordinary activities have been computed.

Factoring the sale of debtors to a factoring company to improve cash flow. Factoring is a method of obtaining finance but some factoring companies also offer services such as credit worthiness checks, sales ledger maintenance and collection of debts.

Fictitious assets items which appear on the assets side of a balance sheet not because they have value but because they are debit balances. Examples are formation expenses, discount on issue of debentures or a debit balance on profit and loss account. Modern accounting practice and the vertical presentation of balance sheets has largely eliminated fictitious assets.

FIFO first in, first out; a method of valuing fungible assets, especially stocks, which values the items at most recent input prices.

F.I.I. franked investment income; dividends from UK companies received by other UK companies. These dividends have been paid from profits which have already suffered corporation tax and do not have to suffer additional corporation tax.

Financial statements balance sheets, profit and loss accounts, income and expenditure accounts, funds flow statements and other documents which formally convey information of a financial nature to interested parties concerning an enterprise. In companies, the financial statements are subject to audit opinion whereas other statements such as the chairman's report are not.

Fiscal year the government's year, ending on 5 April.

Fixed assets business assets which have a useful life extending over more than one accounting period. Examples are land, buildings, plant, machinery, vehicles.

Fixed cost a cost which in the short term remains the same at different levels of activity.

Floating charge an arrangement whereby a lender to a company has a floating charge over the assets generally of the company gives the lender priority of repayment from the proceeds of sale of the assets in the event of insolvency. Banks frequently take a floating charge when lending.

Folio a page in a ledger or daybook on which an entry can be made. From the latin for leaf.

Format a specific layout for a financial statement. Several alternative formats are prescribed by the Companies Act 1985.

Franchise an arrangement whereby small businesses are licensed to supply some good or service, rights to which are held by the originator of the good or service. Franchising is a fast growing sector of business.

Freehold the best possible or absolute title to land.

Fundamental accounting concepts the broad basic assumptions which underlie the periodic financial accounts of business enterprises. The term appears in SSAP2. In this work I have used the word convention in preference.

Fungible assets assets which are indistinguishable one from another. In the case of a stock line which is fungible it is not possible to determine which consignment it came in and consequently what its input cost was. Therefore assumptions such as FIFO or LIFO have to be made.

Futures contracts for the sale and purchase of commodities at an agreed price and for delivery and settlement at an agreed future date. Trading in futures, often by professional speculators tends to stabilise prices.

Gearing (leverage in US) the relationship between fixed interest and equity securities in the financing structure of a company. A company which is heavily reliant on borrowing is said to be high geared and a company which is largely equity financed is said to be low geared.

General ledger the collection of accounts of a double entry system. Often used for real and nominal accounts only. Customers and suppliers accounts being held separately.

Generally accepted accounting principles the set of assumptions, concepts and procedures that provides a foundation for measuring and disclosing the results of business transactions and events. Includes both conventions, bases and presentation practices.

Gilt-edged securities securities and investments with negligible risk of default in interest or capital. Principally government securities.

Going concern an accounting convention which assumes that the enterprise will continue in operational existence for the foreseeable future. This means in particular that the profit and loss account and balance sheet assume no intention or necessity to liquidate or curtail significantly the scale of operation.

Goodwill an intangible asset representing the value of the whole business in excess of the tangible assets which compose it. On a balance sheet goodwill should appear only if it had an input cost to the business. Goodwill valuation arises as a problem on changes in partnership profit sharing or personnel.

Gross profit the excess of sales price over the cost of the product sold.

Gross profit ratio gross profit as a percentage of sales.

Ground rent rent paid for land as opposed to rent paid for buildings. Ground rents usually apply when land is let on very long leases, eg 99 years.

Group a set of interrelated companies usually consisting of a holding company and its subsidiary and sub-subsidiary companies.

Group accounts the financial statements of a group wherein the separate financial statements of the member companies are combined into consolidated financial statements. A subject of great difficulty to advanced accounting students.

Hire purchase a method of financing the acquisition of assets whereby the purchaser pays by instalments. In law the ownership of the goods does not pass to the buyer until the last instalment has been paid.

HIFO highest in, first out, a pricing policy where costs are collected for a job on the basis that the cost of materials is the highest input price.

Historical cost the accounting convention whereby goods, resources and services are recorded at cost. Cost is defined as the exchange or transaction price.

Imprest a fixed amount of money used to meet petty cash (or other) expenditures for a period. At the end of the period the imprest is made up again to its original figure.

Income and expenditure accounts financial statements which measure and report the income and expenditure of a period of a non-trading body such as a club, society, charity or professional body.

Incomplete records that branch of accounting which deals with the production of financial statements of enterprises which do not have full double entry bookkeeping. Sometimes called single entry.

Income statement any financial statement which measures and reports the revenues, expenses and net income of an enterprise. Examples are profit and loss accounts and income and expenditure accounts.

Income tax a tax imposed on the income of individuals and partnerships. The tax is collected from employed persons by means of the PAYE (pay as you earn) system.

Indirect cost labour, material and expense costs which cannot be identified with particular products. Collectively known as overhead.

Information meaningful data that is used in reporting, planning, control and decision-making activities.

Insolvency the state of being unable to pay debts as they fall due. Also used to describe the activities of practitioners in the fields of bankruptcy, receivership and liquidation.

Intangible assets assets which have long term value but which have no physical existence. Examples are goodwill, copyright, patents and trademarks.

Interest the amount paid by a borrower to a lender for the use of the money lent.

Interim dividend many companies pay a dividend in respect of a financial year in two instalments. The final dividend is paid after the year end when the results are known. The interim dividend is paid during the year usually after the results for the first half of the year are known.

Inventory a detailed list of articles of any kind. Used by accountants as another word for stock.

Investments a class of asset consisting of shares or loan stocks of companies, financial institutions or the government.

Invoice a document issued by a vendor to a buyer giving details of the transaction.

Issued capital that part of the authorised capital of a company which has actually been issued to shareholders.

Journal a chronological record which serves as an entry point for transactions into a business's accounting system. From the data in a journal the entries in the double entry system are made. There may be a main journal and subsidiary journals such as a sales journal. Day book has the same meaning.

Kind things rather than cash. Drawings can be in cash or kind.

Labour hour rate a method of absorption where the costs of a cost centre are shared out among the products using the centre in proportion to the number of hours of direct labour in the centre used on each product.

Leasehold land rented from the owner of the freehold. Leases can be for any period. Leases with less than 50 years to run are called short leases and other leases are called long leases. It is possible to buy a leasehold interest in the property and when this has occurred the cost appears on the balance sheet. It is then amortized (depreciated) over the period of the lease.

Leasing a contractual arrangement whereby the use of a good is enjoyed by one party (the lessee) while ownership remains with another party (the lessor).

Ledger the book or computer file in which the double entry accounts are kept. The ledger may be divided into sections containing particular types of account eg customers accounts in the sales ledger, suppliers accounts in the bought ledger, all other accounts in a nominal ledger (also called private or general) ledger.

Leverage an american word for gearing.

Liabilities present obligations resulting from past transactions or events that require the enterprise to pay money, provide goods, or perform services in the future.

LIFO, last in first out, a method of valuing fungible assets whereby an asset is valued at very old input prices.

Limited companies companies registered under the Companies Acts in which the liability of the members is limited to the amount unpaid on the share capital or to a specific amount in the case of companies limited by guarantee.

Limiting or key factor a factor of production which is in limited supply and which thus constrains output.

Liquidation the procedure whereby a company is wound up, its assets realised and the proceeds distributed to the persons entitled.

Liquidity the ease with which funds can be raised by the sale of assets.

Liquidity ratios ratios that purport to indicate the ability of a business to meet current debts as they fall due. Examples are the creditors settlement ratio, the current ratio and the acid test ratio.

Listed companies companies whose shares are quoted on a recognised stock exchange or (paradoxically) on the unlisted securities market.

Long term contracts contracts entered into for manufacture or building of a single substantial entity or the provision of a service where the time taken to manufacture, build, or provide is such that a substantial proportion of all such contract work will extend for a period exceeding one year.

Long term liabilities obligations expected to be paid after one year. Called in the Companies Act: creditors - amounts falling due after more than one year.

Machine hour rate a method of absorption where the costs of a cost centre are shared out among the products which use the centre in proportion to the number of machine hours in the centre used on each product.

Management accounting the provision and interpretation of information which assists management in planning, controlling, decision making and appraising performance.

Manufacturing accounts financial statements which demonstrate the total costs of production in a period and in some cases derives a factory profit.

Marginal costing a system of cost analysis which distinguishes fixed costs from variable costs.

Marginal cost the additional cost incurred by the production of one extra unit.

Market value the amount that an asset would realise if sold on a completely open market. Market values are influenced by whether the asset would be sold by forced sale or in the normal course of business and by whether the value takes into account existing use or possible alternative uses.

Mark up percentage (or average mark up) gross profit expressed as a percentage of cost of goods sold.

Matching convention an accounting convention whereby revenue and costs are accrued, matched with one another so far as their relationship can be established or justifiably assumed, and dealt with in the profit and loss account of the period to which they relate.

Materiality a convention dictating that an accountant must judge the impact and importance of each transaction (or event) to determine its proper handling in the accounting records. Materiality influences the degree of aggregation in financial statements and the extent of disclosure of particular items.

Memorandum of association a document which outlines a company's constitution and defines the scope of a company's powers. All companies have one.

Minority interests the interests in the assets of a group relating to shares in group companies not held by the holding company or other members of the group.

Modified accounts financial statements which are shortened versions of full financial statements. The Companies Acts permit small and medium sized companies to file modified accounts instead of full accounts. Full accounts must however be produced for shareholders.

Money measurement the accounting convention that requires that assets, liabilities, revenues and expenses shall be expressed in money terms.

Mortgage a transaction in which an asset (usually land) is given as security for a loan. The effect is that the mortgagor (borrower) cannot dispose of the asset without first repaying the loan and that the mortgagee has, in the case of default, priority of payment from the proceeds of sale of the asset.

Negotiable instruments a document of title that can be freely negotiated (transferred) by delivery or delivery with endorsement. Examples are bills of exchange and promissory notes.

Net book value the balance sheet or carrying value of an asset; cost or valuation less accumulated depreciation.

Net realisable value the actual or estimated selling price of an asset (net of trade but before settlement discounts) less all further costs to completion and all costs to be incurred in marketing, selling and distribution.

Net worth the difference between total assets and total external liabilities of an enterprise: equivalent to the capital of the proprietor.

NIFO next in first out, a pricing policy where costs are collected on the basis that the cost of materials is the cost of the next delivery.

Nominal ledger a division of the ledger which contains the nominal accounts and usually also real accounts and the capital account.

Nominal value the face value of a share or debenture as stated in the memorandum. Will not always be the same as issue price which may be at a premium and will almost never correspond to market value.

Notes attached to and forming part of the accounts, additional information which amplifies or explains the data found in financial statements.

Objectivity a principle requiring that accounting information be free from bias and verifiable by an independent party. It is for objectivity reasons that accountants have adopted the cost convention.

Obsolescence the ending of an assets useful life for reasons other than deterioration. Obsolescence is caused by new technology and market changes and is an increasing problem.

Operating cycle the period of time it takes a firm to buy inputs, make or market a product and collect the cash from a customer.

Opportunity cost the cost of a foregone alternative.

Ordinary shares the equity capital of a company. The holders of these shares are entitled to the balance of the distributed profit and in a winding up to the balance of the assets after all other claims have been met.

Overdraft facility an arrangement with a bank whereby the account holder can borrow up to an agreed amount.

Overtime premium the actual hourly rate less the normal hourly rate paid to workers who do overtime, that is, work more than normal hours.

Overtrading a paradoxical situation in which a business is successful and does so much business that stocks and debtors rise leading to working capital and liquidity difficulties.

Owners equity the interest of the proprietor(s) in the net assets of an enterprise; the capital of a business.

Paid up capital that part of a company's share capital which has been both called up and paid up.

Partnership the relationship which subsists between persons carrying on a business in common with a view to profit.

Par value an amount specified in the memorandum of association for each share and imprinted on the face of each share certificate. It is the figure which appears on the balance sheet for share capital. As a value it has no significance.

Patent an intangible asset permitting its owner to have exclusive rights to use, manufacture and sell a product or process.

Periodicity an accounting convention that assumes that for reporting purposes the life of an enterprise can be divided into discrete time periods such as years.

Perpetual inventory a method of maintaining records of stock held, on a continuous basis.

Personal accounts double entry accounts which tell a story about the dealings of the enterprise with a person or institution. Example are debtors, creditors and loans. Share capital and reserves are also personal accounts.

Petty cash a fund used to make small cash payments, usually kept on the imprest system.

Piece work a system where workers are remunerated at so much an item produced or job performed.

Post balance sheet events those events both favourable and unfavourable that occur between the balance sheet date and the date at which the financial statements are approved by the board of directors. They can be adjusting or non-adjusting events.

Posting the process of entering up double entry accounts from the data in books of prime entry.

Preference shares a class of share capital in which shareholders are entitled to a fixed rate of dividend in priority to ordinary shareholders and to priority in a winding up over other classes of shareholders.

Premium an amount paid in excess of par or nominal value. Premiums can arise on issues and redemptions of shares and debentures.

Prepayments an amount on a balance sheet representing the cost of future benefits which have already been paid for.

Price earnings ratio a ratio of interest to investment analysts. The stock exchange quoted price of a share divided by the earnings per share. The ratio is quoted for every share daily in the Financial Times.

Prime cost the total of direct costs.

Prime entry books of, a bookkeeping term for the books or computer files containing the first recording of transactions. From the books of prime entry the double entry accounts are posted.

Prior year adjustments material adjustments applicable to earlier years arising from changes in accounting policies and from the correction of fundamental errors.

Private company any company that is not a public company.

Private ledger a division of the ledger in which nominal and real accounts are maintained.

Profitability ratios ratios that purport to examine an enterprise's success (or lack of it) during an accounting period. An example is the return on capital employed.

Pro forma a preliminary invoice giving the usual details of the sale. On payment the goods are despatched.

Promissory note a negotiable instrument containing a promise to pay the holder a sum of money at a specified date.

Pro rata in proportion to.

Prospectus a document offering shares or debentures to the public or a section of the public. Prospectuses must conform to the requirements of the Companies Acts and the Stock Exchange.

Proprietorship the assets less liabilities of a business; the capital of the business.

Provision provisions for liabilities or charges are defined in the Companies Act 1985 as any amount retained as reasonably necessary for the purpose of providing for any liability or loss which is either likely to be incurred, or certain to be incurred but uncertain as to amount or as to the date on which it will arise. Retained in this context means treated as an expense in the profit and loss account.

Public company a public company is a company which states in its memorandum that it is a public company, ends its name with the designation 'public limited company' or plc or its Welsh equivalent and has a minimum share capital of £50,000.

Quick ratio (= acid test ratio) a ratio that purports to indicate liquidity. The ratio is current assets less stocks over current liabilities.

Quoted company a company whose shares are traded on the Stock Exchange or the unlisted securities market. The price of the company's shares is quoted in the Stock Exchange daily official list and in the serious newspapers.

Ratio analysis the use of mathematical relationships to study a firm's liquidity, activity, profitability, and coverage of obligations. Ratios can be compared with those of previous years, expectations, other businesses and trends can be established.

Real accounts double entry accounts for assets with actual physical existence, eg stocks, fixed assets.

Realisable value the amount that an asset can be sold for.

Realisation account a double entry account used to measure the profits or losses on assets and liabilities on an event such as a change in a partnership which involves revaluations of assets including goodwill.

Realisation convention an accounting convention that postulates that a profit should not be counted as accruing in connection with an asset until that asset has been sold and turned into cash or into a legally enforceable debt.

Receivership the appointment of receiver to take over an asset which is the subject of a charge given to a lender. A receiver can be appointed by a court or by the lender when the terms of the loan deed allow.

Redemption the repayment of shares or debentures.

Reducing balance a method of depreciation whereby the cost is expensed over its useful life by the application of a percentage to the written down value.

Registrar of Companies a civil service department located in Cardiff which maintains a file for each registered company. Companies have a legal obligation to file numerous documents with the registrar. Company files are open to the inspection of members of the public.

Reporting the process whereby a company or other institution informs interested parties (eg shareholders) of the results and position of the company by means of financial statements.

Reserves a company has reserves if its assets exceed its specific liabilities. Reserves are thus liabilities to shareholders, arising primarily from undistributed profits.

Replacement cost the cost at which an identical asset could be purchased or manufactured. SSAP9 dictates that replacement cost should not be used for stock valuation.

Retentions that part of a company's profits which are not distributed as dividends.

Return on capital employed a profitability ratio being income expressed as a percentage of the capital which produced the income. A difficult idea to use because of the problems of defining income and capital.

Returns profits or gains flowing from the ownership of assets (eg return on capital employed); damaged, undelivered or unwanted goods sent back to vendor; a document or report required to be submitted to some authority (eg the annual return of a company).

Revenue amounts charged to customers for goods sold or services rendered.

Revenue expenditure an expenditure that benefits only the current accounting period.

Rights issue an invitation to existing shareholders to subscribe for new shares in the company.

Sales journal (= sales day book) a book of prime entry in which the details of sales invoices are entered chronologically. From the sales journal, entries are posted to the customers' accounts and in total to the sales account.

Sales ledger a division of the ledger in which an account is kept for each credit customer.

Salvage value (= residual value) the amount that a business expects to receive upon disposal of an asset at the end of the asset's useful life.

Scrip issue (= bonus issue) an issue of shares to existing shareholders involving no payment of money. A book entry crediting share capital and debiting reserves is made.

SEC Securities and Exchange Commission, an agency of the US government that oversees the securities market and prescribes accounting principles and reporting practices for quoted companies.

Secret reserves a now prescribed practice whereby companies concealed the extent of their profits and capital by understating the value of assets or overstatement of liabilities.

Sectional balancing the division of a double entry system into sections so that each section can be balanced separately. See also control accounts.

Secured liabilities obligations where the probability of payment is enhanced by the creditor taking a charge over an asset (a fixed charge) or assets generally (a floating charge).

Securities financial assets such as shares, debentures and loan stocks.

Segmental reporting the practice of breaking down profits and capital employed into sections to show the separate results of distinct products, geographical areas or classes of customer.

Settlement discount a reduction in the amount payable offered to a debtor to induce rapid payment.

Shares a division of a company's ownership into numerous equal parts. A shareholder may have one or more shares.

Single entry a bookkeeping system which falls short of orthodox double entry. Also used as synonym for incomplete records.

Sinking fund a largely obsolete practice where an enterprise puts sums aside on a regular basis to ensure that money will be available to meet an obligation or to replace an asset.

SORP statements of recommended practice, a statement of accounting practice produced by the ASC and approved by the accounting bodies.

Spreadsheet a computer program which enables accountants and others to draw up financial statements and analyses in matrix form and to manipulate figures.

SSAP statement of standard accounting practice, statements of accounting practice are mandatory on members of the accounting bodies.

Standard cost periodically predetermined costs calculated from management's estimates of expected levels of costs and of operations and operational efficiency and the related expenditure. Standard costs can be compared with actual costs and the variances analysed.

Standing order an instruction to a bank to make specific payments at specified intervals, eg mortgage repayments or subscriptions.

Statement of account a document sent by creditor to his debtor setting out the transactions of a period between them and finally showing how much is owed.

Statement of affairs a listing, with values, of assets and liabilities. A balance sheet is a formal statement of affairs.

Statutory books the books that a company is required to keep by law. They include the register of members, register of directors and secretaries, and others.

Stewardship an arrangement where the property of one party (eg the shareholders of a company) is entrusted to and managed by another party (eg the directors). Stewardship reporting is the accounting by means of financial statements by the management to the owners.

Straight line a method of depreciation that allocates the cost of a depreciable asset, less salvage value over the estimated useful life in equal instalments.

Subsidiary company a company of which more than half of the equity capital is owned by another company.

Substance over form an accounting convention whereby a transaction is accounted for in accordance with its substance or commercial reality rather than its legal form

Sum of digits a depreciation method that allocates the cost less salvage value of a depreciable asset over its useful life in steadily diminishing instalments.

Surrogate something which can stand for something else.

Suspense account an account which has as its balance the difference on the trial balance which was caused by bookkeeping errors.

T account a form of presentation of a double entry account named for its shape - debit on the left, credit on the right and title at the top.

Tax credit the tax inputed to a dividend payment. No further tax is payable on the dividend unless the recipient is liable to higher rates.

Till roll a roll of paper or some electronically recorded record of sales made and cash (or cheques etc) processed through a till or cash register. The primary record of cash sales.

Total absorption cost a system of costing where all costs (or just production costs) are ascribed to products. Thus the total absorption cost of a product includes its direct cost and a fair share of both fixed and variable overhead costs.

Trade discount reductions in sales price given to favoured customers, special classes of customer or for bulk purchase. Accounting is always on the net amount of the invoice.

Trademarks an intangible asset consisting of the right to exclusive use of a particular mark or motif.

Trading account a financial statement which measures and demonstrates the gross profit of a period.

Transaction any event or activity of a firm requiring an entry in the double entry system.

Transposition errors posting errors in which digits are transposed, eg 69 entered as 96.

Trend analysis an approach to financial statement evaluation involving comparison of the same item or ratio over two or more years.

Trial balance a listing in two columns (debit balances and credit balances) of all the balances in a double entry system.

True and fair view the Companies Act requires that the balance sheet and profit and loss account of a company must give a true and fair view. The phrase is discussed in auditing texts.

Turnover another term for the total sales in a period.

Unquoted investments investments in shares or debentures which are not quoted or traded on a stock exchange.

Unsecured creditors those creditors who do not have the benefit of a charge over any asset.

Valuation accounts double entry accounts with credit balances which counter balance an asset with a debit balance. Examples are provision for doubtful debts and provision for depreciation.

Variable cost a cost which in the short term tends to vary in magnitude following the level of activity.

VAT or Value Added Tax a tax levied on most sales in the EEC including the UK and the Irish Republic.

Voucher any document supporting entries in a journal or ledger.

Warranty a promise made by a seller or manufacturer to remedy defects in product quality and performance. Warranties may imply a contingent liability.

Wasting assets assets which are used up in producing goods. Can be applied to all fixed assets but usually confined to mines, quarries and mineral rights.

Weighted average any average calculation which involves giving differing weights to the several elements of the set, particularly used in the valuation of stock on the average cost method.

Winding up the liquidation of a company, when its assets are realised and the proceeds distributed to the parties entitled.

Window dressing the manipulation of the items in financial statements to show the results or position in the most favourable light to attract investors etc.

Working capital the excess of current assets over current liabilities.

Work in progress (=work in progress) the inventory of goods started but not completed during the period.

Write-off to write something off is to debit it to profit and loss account. If something has continuing value (eg a fixed asset) then the whole cost is not written off but only a part of the cost (by the depreciation process).

Written down value the cost of an asset less accumulated depreciation. Also known as net book value and carrying value.

Yield the return on an investment usually expressed as a percentage.

INDEX